The Knights of Bahá'u'lláh

This book is dedicated to

the Knights of Bahá'u'lláh

for their sacrifice of going where no Bahá'í had gone before and opening up the far-flung and commonly isolated goals

of Shoghi Effendi's Ten Year Crusade

The Knights of Bahá'u'lláh

Earl Redman

GEORGE RONALD
OXFORD

George Ronald, Publisher
Oxford
www.grbooks.com

A catalogue record for this book is available from the British Library

ISBN 978–0–85398–605–8

Cover design: Steiner Graphics

CONTENTS

ACKNOWLEDGEMENTS

After obvious sources such as *The Bahá'í World*, *The American Bahá'í*, various books and a variety of Internet sources had been checked, finding stories on the Knights of Bahá'u'lláh proved to be difficult. Unlike my previous books, these stories required the help of many Bahá'ís from around the world before they could be written. It turned into a grand treasure hunt with leads appearing in some of the most unlikely places. This book was written mostly by relying on help from the Divine Concourse. Word spread, sometimes through my own actions and sometimes through the actions of others. The result was that suggestions of sources came from so many unexpected places that the book ended up including stories of all 257 Knights. One example is when I met Jason Wiley at the Bahá'í Summer School in Poland. Jason lived on the island of Hawaii and knew one of my missing Knights. He connected me with the Knight's daughter, who connected me with the Knight. In the end, people in 26 countries contributed to this book.

Because of the many people involved, I am compelled to thank them all. Many of the stories of the Knights would not have been discovered had they not graciously shared their own stories or the stories of their mother, father, grandmother or grandfather. With the help of those named below, this book is able to share the stories of the 257 Knights of Bahá'u'lláh.

Knights of Bahá'u'lláh Dwight and Carole Allen, Ted Anderson, Nosrat Ardekani, Gerrold Bagley, Sheila Banani, Geertrui Ankersmit Bates, Jenabe Caldwell, Charles Duncan, John Fozdar, Ben Guhrke, Sean Hinton, Florence Ullrich Kelley, Roshan Aftábí Knox, Húshmand Manúchehrí, Sohrab Payman, Lionel Peraji, 'Abbás Rafí'í, Fred Schechter, David Schreiber, Jean Sevin, Helmut Winkelbach, Elinor Wolff and Hormoz Zendeh all readily shared their stories. Ted Anderson's son, Chris, shared a copy of his father's book about the years in the Yukon.

David Schreiber's daughter, Rosalie, initially provided me with information about her father, then was able to put me into contact with him. Rafi 'Abbas sent me his wonderful remembrances of his father, Kámil 'Abbás. Suzy Cardell assisted with her father's story.

An interview with Laurel Baumgartner, daughter of Knight Elinore Putney, filled in the story of their lives in Unalaska. Ben Guhrke's wife, Marvel, graciously copied out the parts of his biography pertinent to this book. Jim Schechter worked with his father, Fred, to help with his story. Layli Nottingham, the daughter of Jenabe and Elaine Caldwell, kindly shared family photos of Unalaska, while their son, Mark Caldwell, shared his mother's story. Kalim Chandler connected me with Sheila Banani. Shirin Fozdar-Foroudi connected me with her father, John Fozdar, and Barry True improved the story of his parents. Foad Katirai provided some basic information about his parents and Fulya Vekiloglu contributed the story of her parents, the Vekils, on Cyprus.

Connecting with Nosrat Ardekani was a multistep affair. First, Ann O'Sullivan suggested that I write to her daughter-in-law, Bahié Mary Hamilton, who lived in Tunisia. Bahié and her mother, Chahine Rassekh, put me in touch with Bahié's aunt, Shahnaz Ardekani in Senegal, who arranged for me to have a 45-minute Skype interview with her mother, Nosrat Ardekani, Knight of Bahá'u'lláh for Morocco who also lives in Senegal. Chahine and Shahnaz also helped with editing their mother's story. Bahié put me in contact with her uncle, Knight of Bahá'u'lláh 'Abbás Raff'í, in Luxembourg, and Rowshan Mustapha, son of the Knight for Spanish Sahara, Muhammad Mustafa Soliman, in Tunis. 'Abbás contributed the story of how he and his parents pioneered to Morocco and also greatly expanded the story of Muhammad-Alí Jalali, another pioneer to Morocco.

Rowshan Mustapha helped not only by contributing the story of his father, but also with stories of Knights Labib Esfahani, Amin Battah, Enoch Olinga, Fawzi and Bahia Zein (Zaynu'l-Ábidín) and Shoghi-Riaz Rouhani. He also read through the manuscript and offered many good suggestions to improve it.

Roshan Aftábí Knox, Knight of Bahá'u'lláh for Goa, and her husband, Dermod, allowed me to visit them and record their stories, Roshan for her pioneering and Dermod for his pilgrimage. Geertrui Ankersmit Bates, in New Zealand, edited, corrected and added to her story about pioneering to the Dutch Frisian Islands, while Gisela von Brunn wrote the story of her mother, Ursula, pioneering to the German portion of those islands. James Holmlund improved the story of Marie Ciocca and helpfully put me in contact with Gerrold Bagley and Sohrab Payman. Gerrold wrote the story of his family of five Knights on Sicily and also improved the story of fellow Sicilian Knight Emma Rice. Guilda Navidi-Walker and Vidá Navidi sent me emails full of wonderful stories about their parents, Monaco Knights Shamsí and ʻAzízuʼlláh Navídí. Deborah McKinley, the widow of Knight Hugh McKinley, spent a huge amount of time going through the diaries and papers of Hugh and his mother, Violet, in order to contribute the story of their efforts on Cyprus. Olive McKinley also added her remembrances of Hugh and Violet. Masroor K. Bhargava, son of Knight of Baháʼuʼlláh Shyam Beharilal Bhargava, very graciously put together the story of his fatherʼs life. S. Maureen Dailey shared her research into the lives of Elise Schreiber and Dunduzu Chisiza. Rosanne Groger, the granddaughter of Knight Louise Groger, very helpfully put together the story of her grandmotherʼs life and contributed it to the book.

Thelma Batchelorʼs many contacts and her own library helped uncover many stories. She was truly my source of sources. After she posted my missing Knights on discussion sites in the United States, offers of help flooded in. Susan Gammage also posted my request on her website, resulting in still more offers of help.

Enoch Tanyi, son of Knight of Baháʼuʼlláh David Tanyi and author of the book *David and Esther Tanyi: Adam and Eve of the Baháʼí Faith in Cameroon* (George Ronald, 2016), graciously sent me biographies of Knights Benedict Eballa, Martin Manga, Edward Tabe and Samuel Njiki, as well as improving the story of his father. P. K. Premarajan, treasurer of the National Spiritual Assembly of India, provided the story for Khodarahm Mojgani and Rowhani Qudratullah, who were named as Knights for pioneering to Mahé.

Several authors shared information from their books and research. Marlene Macke, who published *Take My Love to the Friends: The Story of Laura R. Davis* (Chestnut Park Press, 2011), provided information on several of the Canadian Knights. J. A. McLean, who was writing a book about Cliff and Catherine Huxtable called *A Love That Could Not Wait* (One Voice Press, 2015), very kindly provided information on their pioneering efforts to the Gulf Islands in Canada. Gamal Hassan, author of *Moths Turned Eagles* (National Spiritual Assembly of the Bahá'ís of Ethiopia, 2008), reviewed the story of Sabrí and Fahíma (Raissa) Elias and offered suggestions that improved their story. He also shared his knowledge of Fawzi and Bahia Zein and Shoghi-Riaz Rouhani. Don Brown very kindly improved the story of Jameson and Gale Bond, using material from his book, *Sole Desire Serve Cause: An Odyssey of Bahá'í Service* (George Ronald, 2017).

The story of Mehraban Sohaili, Knight of Bahá'u'lláh for the Comoros Islands, came from his son, Isfandiar. To find the story about Elizabeth Bevan, the Knight for Rhodes, I first followed a suggestion from Thelma Batchelor and contacted Muna Linkova. Muna connected me with Elizabeth's daughter, Haleh Golmohammadi, who added her mother's story to the book. Lua Rohani-Sarvestani shared a biography of Kamálí Sarvistání written by his wife, Rezvanieh, with the aid of her son. I greatly appreciate the family's help. Zarangiz Misra sent me the story of her mother, Gulnar Aftábí, one of the Knights for Diu Island in India, and Sitarih Ala'i, daughter of Knight Lilian Wyss, helped improve the stories of her mother and her uncle, Frank Wyss.

Bharat Koirala was helpful in providing information about Udaya Narayan Singh, Knight of Bahá'u'lláh for both Sikkim and Tibet, and Penny Walker, with help from Larry Robertson and Dirgha Shah, was a great help in filling out that story. Gavin Reed, Secretary of the Alaska National Spiritual Assembly, searched their archives and provided interesting material about the Knights for Baranof Island, Helen Robinson and Grace Bahovec. Anneliese Haug was able to give me some information about Knight Geraldine Craney and her brother Rolf Haug, Knight for Crete. Anneliese also put me in contact with Guenther Haug, Rolf's brother, who completed Rolf's story. Susan Gammage shared information on her web blog about Bruce Matthew. Jennifer Dewar provided information about Malcolm King, while Patricia Paccassi shared stories about Esther Evans. Alex Boysen put me in touch with Dr Hooshang Rafat who was able to fill in some of the blanks in the lives of Lofoten Knights Loyce Lawrence and Mildred Clark. Gregory Dahl also helped improve both Loyce's and Mildred's stories. In addition, Greg, as a member of the National Spiritual Assembly of Bulgaria, contributed correspondence between Annemarie Krüger-Brauns and the Universal House of Justice, thus improving the accuracy of that story.

Crispin Pemberton-Pigott contributed stories about Dick Stanton and Edythe MacArthur. Helen Gardner also contributed to Edythe's story by requesting information from the National Canadian Archives which added significantly to it. Dorothy Frye and her daughter, Karen Stanley, researched Ethel and Arthur Crane both online and at the US National Bahá'í Archives, greatly improving their stories. Joel Nizin, of the Teaneck, New Jersey, Local Assembly, and Florence Kelley were also able to add bits about the Cranes. Rayyan Sabet-Parry offered a nice story about 'Abbás Katirai. Mariam Rowhani, the daughter of the first Somalian Bahá'í, shared the story of how her father became a Bahá'í through the efforts of Mihdi and Ursula Samandari.

The story of Knights Kenneth and Roberta Christian was greatly improved by the remembrances of Sylvia Benatar. Rochan Mavaddat and Chowghi Rouhani were very helpful with the story of Shoghi-Riaz Rouhani. Rochan also sent my stories to Knights Ezzat Zahra'i and Jean Sevin for their corrections, and to the families of Shamsí and 'Azízu'lláh Navídí and Fereydoun Khazrá'í for improvements. Arcela Khazrá'í, Fereydoun's wife, also contributed to his story. Violetta Zein contributed several interviews she had conducted, which improved the stories of five Knights. Suzanne Locke-Nyrenda shared her research and memories of several Knights. Suzanne, along with S. Maureen Dailey, did a prodigious amount of research to unearth the story of Dunduzu Chisiza, and Stephen Licata provided extra details about Gertrude Eisenberg. Chris Cholas very helpfully shared Shirley Warde's memoirs.

Barbara Geno shared an interesting story about Gail Avery, and Nina Walters contributed her memories of being a child in Morocco with her parents, Evelyn and Richard Walters. Jyoti Munsiff, daughter of Meherangiz Munsiff, shared the obituary she wrote. Tom Roberts sent notes he had taken from a talk by Knight Patrick Robarts, while Richard Battrick wrote about his experiences in the Loyalty Islands after Knight Daniel Haumont left. Will C. van den Hoonaard added his remembrances of Kay Zinky, and Bahiyyih Nakhjavani and Mary Victoria helped with the story of Paul Adams. Claire Greenberg served for a while with Eskil Ljungberg and contributed her memories, while Eleanor Dawson and Adam Thorne provided background for Geraldine Craney's story. The story of Elizabeth Stamp benefited from the help of Jagdish Saminaden and Barbara George.

As they had done for my previous books, Lewis Walker of the US National Bahá'í Archives, and Duane Troxel of the Heritage Project of the National Spiritual Assembly of the United States were of considerable help in my search for elusive Knights. Lewis also reviewed the manuscript, making many helpful suggestions and then researching some of the Knights with weak stories.

I wrote to a number of National Spiritual Assemblies who helped locate those people who knew the stories the book needed. I would like to thank the National Spiritual Assemblies of the Mariana Islands, Germany, Belarus, India, Japan, Romania and Sri Lanka for their assistance in connecting me with sources. The researchers at the Bahá'í World Archives at the World Centre helped also fill in stories of a few Knights for whom I could find little information. Suzanne Mahon, of the National Spiritual Assembly of New Zealand, also assisted the research.

Although every effort has been made to include photographs of every Knight of Bahá'u'lláh, it proved impossible to find all of them; just over 20 are not shown in the illustrations. In the last weeks before going to print a worldwide search took place in which the following people gave generously of their time: Sitarih Ala'i, Irma Allen, Thelma Batchelor (whose efforts in coordinating part of the search earns her the title of detective-in-chief), Brigitte Beales, Arthur Lyon Dahl, Gregory Dahl, Roger Dahl of the US Bahá'í Archives, Jennifer Dewar, Ralph Dexter, Anita Graves, David Hassall, Graham Hassall, Anneliese Haug, Jean Jaklevick, Foad Katirai, Jena Khadem Khodadad, Shabnam Koirala Azad, Joo Jong Kung of the Canadian Bahá'í Archives, Lois Lambert, Keith McDonald, David Merrick, Lindsay John Moffat, Clare Mortimore, Godfrey Nix, Pat Paccassi, Lua Siegel, Margo-Amee Smallwood, Duane Troxel, Paddy Vickers, John Walker, Lewis Walker, Michael Walker and Scott Wolff.

Larry Staudt carefully combed the text for typos and confusing bits, distinctly improving its readability. As he has for my previous books, Maurice Sabour-Pickett also chased down my typos and grammatical bumbles with his piercing accountant's eyes.

Not everything I received was in English, so I had to tap into the skills of Carmel Irandoust to translate French into English, and Mitra Rahmani to translate the ten-page story of Kamálí Sarvístání, which was written in Persian. Mitra's daughter, Sahar, typed up her mother's handiwork. Foad Kazemzadeh translated Sohrab Payman's story from Persian to English.

May Hofman, as she had done in my three previous books, suffered through my piles of prose, checked endless endnotes and made this into a book. My appreciation knows no bounds.

And penultimately, I would like to acknowledge, at his own request, that Cyrous Heydarian contributed nothing to this book, but he did offer me a mandarin orange.

And I can't forget my wife, Sharon O'Toole, who steadfastly supported my seemingly endless search for information, proofread many of the stories, offered helpful suggestions and usually put up with the great piles of books that threatened to avalanche across the office.

INTRODUCTION

Who were the Knights of Bahá'u'lláh?

The Revelation of Bahá'u'lláh set in motion forces designed to create an 'ever-advancing civilization'[1] based on the unity of God, the unity of His Messengers and unity of all the peoples of the world. These forces were the initial impetus for the creation of what will be a Golden Age of peace and prosperity. With the coming of the Golden Age, Shoghi Effendi, the designated Guardian of the Faith of Bahá'u'lláh and great-grandson of Bahá'u'lláh, wrote that 'the banner of the Most Great Peace, promised by its Author, will have been unfurled, the World Bahá'í Commonwealth will have emerged in the plenitude of its power and splendor, and the birth and efflorescence of a world civilization, the child of that Peace, will have conferred its inestimable blessings upon all mankind.'[2] This Golden Age was 'destined to witness the emergence of a world-embracing Order enshrining the ultimate fruit of God's latest Revelation to mankind, a fruit whose maturity must signalize the establishment of a world civilization and the formal inauguration of the Kingdom of the Father upon earth as promised by Jesus Christ Himself'.[3]

Before that could happen, however, the teachings inherent in the Revelation of Bahá'u'lláh had to plant themselves in the hearts of the peoples all around the world. Bahá'u'lláh appointed His Son, 'Abdu'l-Bahá, as His Successor and the Centre of His Covenant and charged Him with the task of guiding the world toward the Golden Age. With this mandate, in 1916 and 1917, 'Abdu'l-Bahá wrote a series of fourteen letters collectively called the *Tablets of the Divine Plan* and sent them to the North American Bahá'í communities.

Set forth in those fourteen Tablets, Shoghi Effendi explains, is 'the mightiest Plan ever generated through the creative power of the Most Great Name'. It is 'impelled by forces beyond our power to

predict or appraise' and 'claims as the theatre for its operation territories spread over five continents and the islands of the seven seas'.
Within it are held 'the seeds of the world's spiritual revival and ultimate redemption'.[4]

These Tablets contained a Plan for the spiritual conquest of the entire
planet. It was this Plan that Shoghi Effendi was implementing when he
created the Ten Year Crusade, a global endeavour to illumine all parts
of the world with the Teachings of Bahá'u'lláh.

At Riḍván 1953, Bahá'ís lived in 2,500 localities in 129 countries
around the world and had managed to form a dozen Bahá'í National
Spiritual Assemblies. When Shoghi Effendi announced that the Ten
Year Crusade would start that Riḍván, his goal was to spread the Faith
of Bahá'u'lláh across the whole earth through pioneers, Bahá'ís who
would arise and move to these far-flung sites. This task of proclaiming
the Revelation of Bahá'u'lláh to every corner of the globe fell to a group
of men and women who arose and accepted the challenge to go to the
many isolated goals the Guardian had selected. These people were given
the title of Knight of Bahá'u'lláh for going where no Bahá'í had gone
before. Because of their efforts, and the efforts of many other international and home-front pioneers during those ten years, the initial 12
National Spiritual Assemblies grew to 56 by 1963. The amazing success
of this great venture of spiritual illumination resulted in the Bahá'í Faith
becoming established in 11,210 localities in 259 different countries,
dependencies and principalities during that single decade. The Knights
of Bahá'u'lláh played the leading part in this spiritual drama.

Starting in early 1953, a flood of pioneers began to flow out across
the world to fill Shoghi Effendi's goals for the Ten Year Crusade. The first
to reach his post, and subsequently be named as a Knight of Bahá'u'lláh,
was Suhayl Samandarí, who arrived in Mogadishu, Somalia, then part of
Italian Somaliland, on 19 March 1953. The last of the Guardian's goal
areas wasn't filled until 'Abbás and Rezvánieh Katirai reached Russia's
Sakhalin Island 37 years later, in March 1990. A total of 255 people earned
the title of Knight of Bahá'u'lláh. Two of them, Elise Schreiber and Udaya
Narayan Singh, earned double titles for pioneering to two goal areas each.
Most lists, therefore, will show 257 Knights of Bahá'u'lláh. One Knight,
Enoch Olinga, inspired five others to arise and fulfil Shoghi Effendi's
goals, each subsequently becoming a Knight of Bahá'u'lláh themselves.

By June 1953, pioneers were spreading over the world in ever-increasing numbers. Some of the goals were opened easily and a few Knights had immediate success in raising up followers of Bahá'u'lláh, but most places proved to be difficult. Some of the goal areas were hard to find and get to, others were difficult to remain at, and in many, it was tough to try to teach the Bahá'í Faith in the face of strong opposition. Thirty-five of the Knights, almost 15 per cent, were refused longer-term visas and forced to leave their posts. Fourteen pioneers were only able to stay at their posts for four months or less, each one forced to leave by the authorities. John Chang could not spend more than 14 days on Hainan Island, China. Jeanne Frankel and Margaret Bates were allowed only a brief 16 days on the Nicobar Islands, while Frank Wyss was forced to leave the privately-held Cocos Islands after just 17 days spent confined to the airport. Most of those souls who arose to do the Guardian's bidding devoted a period of months or years to their goal area, but then moved on. Twenty-seven, however, remained at their posts for the rest of their lives.

Forty per cent of those who became Knights left from the shores of Canada and the United States. The nationalities of the Knights of Bahá'u'lláh, however, showed the global nature of the Faith even at that time. They came from over two dozen countries scattered around the globe representing every continent. It also showed the advancement of the principle of the equality of men and women: 131 Knights were men and 126 were women. Fifty-one couples, twelve of whom were newly married, and families filled the Guardian's goals. Sixty-nine women opened goal areas, mostly singly, but 22 went out in pairs. Contrastingly, 66 single men fulfilled goal areas, but only eight went out in pairs. Interestingly, of the 17 goal areas set out by the Guardian in the Pacific region, 12 were opened by women. Half of the European goals and 6 of 14 goal areas in North America were filled solely by women. Nine native black African Bahá'ís arose to become Knights of Bahá'u'lláh, six within six months of their accepting the Faith. Twenty-four of the Knights had become Knights within two years of accepting the Faith.

The oldest Knight was Nellie French, who pioneered to Monaco at the age of 85, while the youngest were Edward Tabe, a youth from Cameroon no older than 14 (who within a year raised up a Local Spiritual Assembly) and Carol Bagley, who pioneered with her parents to Sicily at the same age. Thirteen Knights were teenagers and eleven were over 70. One Knight, Catherine Huxtable, was wheelchair-bound, while another, Jean Deleuran, was partially paralysed from polio.

What was a Knight of Bahá'u'lláh?

Shoghi Effendi didn't immediately call the pioneers who filled his goals Knights of Bahá'u'lláh. On 28 May 1953, he wrote that he would be 'making periodic announcements of the names of the valiant knights upon their arrival at their posts'.[5] On 8 June, a letter written on behalf of the Guardian to the National Spiritual Assembly of India stated that 'an illuminated "Roll of Honour" on which will be inscribed the names of the "Knights of Baha'u'llah" who first enter these 131 virgin areas' would be placed 'inside the entrance door of The Inner Sanctuary of the Tomb of Baha'u'llah.'[6] This was the first time the title 'Knight of Bahá'u'lláh' was used.

Amatu'l-Bahá Rúḥíyyih Khánum, Shoghi Effendi's wife and a Hand of the Cause, explained where the term 'Knight' of Bahá'u'lláh came from:

> Shoghi Effendi said that posterity would be proud of these souls who were the spiritual conquerors, his own term, of the entire globe. And on whom he conferred the unique title of Knights of Bahá'u'lláh. I remember when he devised this title, how astonished I was that he should go back to the middle ages . . . (When) you received your knighthood, you had certain oaths of allegiance and service to take. It's not a light term, knighthood. Shoghi Effendi attached tremendous importance to the Knights of Bahá'u'lláh.[7]

The Guardian in *The World Order of Bahá'u'lláh* quoted 'Abdu'l-Bahá when He used the word 'knight' when referring to the 'knights of the Lord' who would arise in dark times:

> In the darkest moments of His life, under 'Abdu'l-Ḥamíd's regime, when He stood ready to be deported to the most inhospitable regions of Northern Africa, and at a time when the auspicious light of the Bahá'í Revelation had only begun to break upon the West, He, in His parting message to the cousin of the Báb, uttered these prophetic and ominous words: 'How great, how very great is the

Cause! How very fierce the onslaught of all the peoples and kindreds of the earth. Ere long shall the clamor of the multitude throughout Africa, throughout America, the cry of the European and of the Turk, the groaning of India and China, be heard from far and near. One and all, they shall arise with all their power to resist His Cause. Then shall the knights of the Lord, assisted by His grace from on high, strengthened by faith, aided by the power of understanding, and reinforced by the legions of the Covenant, arise and make manifest the truth of the verse: "Behold the confusion that hath befallen the tribes of the defeated!"[8]

He also quoted the same passage in *God Passes By* and *Messages to the Bahá'í World 1950–1957*. At the end of the first year of the Ten Year Crusade, Shoghi Effendi again used the Master's phrase:

On the eve of this Riḍván Festival marking the opening of the second decade of the second Bahá'í century, and coinciding with the termination of the first year of the World Spiritual Crusade, I hail with feelings of joy and wonder the superb feats of the heroic company of the Knights of the Lord of Hosts in pursuance of their sublime mission for the spiritual conquest of the planet. The first twelve months of this decade-long enterprise unexampled in its scope, significance and potentialities in the world's spiritual history and launched simultaneously, amidst the climax of the world-wide festivities of a memorable Holy Year, in the American, the European, the African, the Asiatic and the Australian continents, have witnessed the hoisting of the banner of the Faith of Bahá'u'lláh in no less than a hundred virgin territories of the globe . . . The northern frontiers of a divinely guided, rapidly marching, majestically expanding Faith have been pushed, in consequence of the phenomenal success recently achieved by the vanguard of Bahá'u'lláh's crusaders, beyond the Arctic Circle as far as Arctic Bay, Franklin, 73 degrees latitude. Its southern limits have now reached the Falkland Islands in the neighborhood of Magallanes, the world's southernmost city. Other outlying outposts have been established in places as far apart as Sikkim at the foot of the Himalayas, the Lofoten Islands in the heart of the European Northland, Fezzan on the northern fringe of the Sahara Desert, the Andaman Islands and the Seychelles, the penal colonies in the Indian Ocean, the three Guianas and the leper colonies on the Atlantic Coast, the Faroe and Shetland Islands, the wind-swept and inhospitable archipelagos of the North Sea, Hadhramaut on the sun-baked shores of the Arabian Peninsula, St. Helena isolated in the midst of the South Atlantic Ocean and the Gilbert Islands, the war-devastated, sparsely populated Atolls situated in the heart of the Pacific Ocean.[9]

The Knights were motivated by many things, but few wrote about how they understood the significance of what they were doing. Ben Guhrke, a Knight to Kodiak Island, Alaska, wrote in 1954 about the Ten Year Crusade, saying that this was

the first time in the history of man that such a thing has taken place on such a scale. Since the beginning, men have migrated from one place to another but motive makes the difference. In the past, brave hearts have ventured out into the world to find new homes but they have done so mainly because they were economically forced to, because they sought escape from tyranny and slavery, or just because they were dissatisfied on general principles . . . But who ever heard of a people dispersing to every story book land on earth, or every different city within a land, in disregard of danger and material comforts to firstly demonstrate, for their fellow men, a new way of life, and secondly to teach a frustrated humanity how it can be achieved. The purity of motive, speaking relatively and generally, makes this World Crusade unparalleled in the history of benevolent undertakings. In the eyes of the world we have sacrificed everything which they have put a value on, including home, economic security, friends and relations; this is our greatest teaching medium for it is the proof of our sincerity under their standard of values . . .

At first I had always viewed the Crusade as a group of objectives aimed at culminating at some unknown future date in the actual reality of the new world order. Though this is true, I often found myself thinking about how far off that was or how much had to be done and this left me a little dejected. Then the realization came that this great endeavor was above all a fulfillment. When evaluated in the light of the tremendous burden placed on the shoulders of the American Bahá'ís this becomes even more apparent. Everything in our past history points to this nation being prepared for some great spiritual mission. We, more than any other country, have been able to cast aside the shackles of natural law and political subjugation, thus freeing us to assume a role in the drama of coming events into which no nation has ever been cast before, that of being a prime instrument in bringing about the spiritual, physical and political unification of the entire globe. A poor and humble nation has no alternative, it must be submissive in order to survive but when a nation is blessed with greatness in practically all fields of human endeavor, it is blessed in a much greater sense; it has the right to make a choice! It can choose the path that leads to power and vainglory which will sow the seeds of its own eventual destruction as the past has shown us in so many instances, or it may choose the, as yet, untrodden path of humility and service. The Crusade years may well find this country making this crucial decision. Great steps have been taken in both directions but as yet the scales do not seem tipped to any definite side. In the struggle between constructive and destructive forces, which isn't really a struggle as both are necessary, the Bahá'í Crusade remains the greatest positive step taken by any group and certainly the most optimistic. Even if America should go a long way down the wrong road, it will only prove to be a stern lesson which in itself, will guide us back to fulfilling that for which we were granted such a unique birthright. This Crusade is a living example of what America, as a nation, must do and the policy she must put forth, sooner or later. Not only is it a fulfillment in that God's kingdom on earth is being built, but it is a harbinger of things to come. How we, the Bahá'ís of the world, think today, is the way tomorrow's total humanity will think. What we, the Bahá'ís of the world, do today will speed up the conscious awareness of God's will in the minds of the people. . . . God's Plan is the time table and Bahá'u'lláh's plan is the train that has to maintain a schedule; the Guardian is the engineer speeding us along; we must do everything in our power to make his task the easier. The pioneers must integrate themselves into their new surroundings firm in the conviction that remaining is the least of what is expected of them. An ever constant flow of funds must lubricate the new machinery we have set into motion to insure smooth operation without undue, and time consuming, delays.[10]

Those designated as Knights of Bahá'u'lláh by Shoghi Effendi were supposed to be the first pioneers to open his virgin territories. It is obvious from examining the Roll of Honour that some goal areas had multiple pioneers who arrived at different times, all of whom received the accolade of Knight of Bahá'u'lláh. The Morocco International Zone had thirteen pioneers who arrived in seven groups between 30 September 1953 and 12 April 1954. All were named Knights of Bahá'u'lláh. There are a number of explanations for this:

- If more than one person or group arose independently to pioneer to the same goal, they all became Knights.

- If a Knight was only able to stay at his or her post a very short time, or died after being at his or her post just a short while, those who replaced them were given the title.

The Guardian also set a deadline for receiving the title of Knight of Bahá'u'lláh. In a cablegram dated 4 May 1954, he wrote:

> The Roll of Honor, after the lapse of one year since the launching of the World Crusade, is now closed, with the exception of pioneers who have already left for their destination, as well as those first arriving in the few remaining virgin territories inside and outside Soviet Republics and satellites.[11]

This ruling affected some couples and teams where one went first to open the goal while the other had to finish up various tasks before being able to follow.

Examples of this include brothers Habíb and Labíb Esfahani, in French West Africa (now Senegal), and Elinore and George Putney, in the Aleutian Islands. Labíb reached the goal of French West Africa in November 1953 and was followed by Habíb in April of 1954. Since Labíb arrived before the Guardian's deadline, both received the title of Knight of Bahá'u'lláh. Elinore Putney arrived in the Aleutian Islands on 2 May 1954 and even though the Caldwell family had been there since 10 August 1953, she arrived just in time to be given the title. Her husband, George, who arrived a short time later, was not given the title. David Tanyi arrived in French Togoland in 1954 but his young wife

Esther, pregnant with their first child, was not able to join him until six months later, after the deadline, and was not given the title, although she was subsequently just as much a pioneer as he was!

The boundary of May 1954, however, was not always applied in a consistent manner. Adíb and Vahídih Baghdádí, husband and wife, arrived at their goal in Hadhramaut in December 1953 and early 1955, respectively. Both received the title. Conversely, Cynthia Olson reached Guam in April 1954 and became a Knight of Bahá'u'lláh. Her husband, Edgar, who arrived in 1955, did not. In the end, it was Shoghi Effendi, the Guardian, who put the names of those he considered to be Knights of Bahá'u'lláh on the Roll of Honour.

The Knights of Bahá'u'lláh whose stories are included in this book are only those shown on the Roll of Honour created by Shoghi Effendi and included in *The Bahá'í World*, volume XX, in 1992. Many lists of Knights are available in various locations, notably the Internet, that were formed from the names listed in Shoghi Effendi's letters. Not all of these, however, are listed on the scroll because a number were included by error. For example, Joan Powis is not uncommonly listed as a Knight of Bahá'u'lláh for Southern Rhodesia because she was included in the list of Knights in *The Bahá'í World*, volume XIII[12] and in two messages from the Guardian in *Messages to the Bahá'í World*.[13] She was not included on the Roll of Honour published in *The Bahá'í World*, volume XX, however. The Research Department at the Bahá'í World Centre has clarified her position by writing that Joan

> moved to Southern Rhodesia from Nairobi, Kenya, in February 1954, shortly after declaring as a Bahá'í, in order to get married. Her arrival in Salisbury was reported to the Guardian by Kenneth Christian, and on the basis of the report she was named as a Knight of Bahá'u'lláh. Subsequently, through the Hand of the Cause of God Musa Banání, Joan Powis explained to the Guardian that she had made the decision to move to Southern Rhodesia prior to becoming a Bahá'í, and that she did not feel deserving of any special honour. The Guardian accepted her explanation that she was not in fact a pioneer, and removed her name from the Roll of Honour.[14]

Another person occasionally named as a Knight of Bahá'u'lláh was Peter Lugayula, who was thought to have pioneered to the Ashanti

Protectorate in Africa.[15] In a reply to a letter written by Enoch Tanyi in 2004, the Research Department at the World Centre wrote:

> Mr Lugayula was one of a group of three youths from Kampala who went to Akropong, Gold Coast, having been accepted as students at Livingstone College. Although he was listed as a Knight of Bahá'u'lláh for Ashanti Protectorate in a cablegram dated 21 March 1954, subsequent explanations provided by the Local Spiritual Assembly of Kampala revealed that he had not gone to that country.[16]

Shoghi Effendi initially selected 131 places around the globe as his goals during the Crusade. When Anticosti Island, Canada, proved very difficult to open, he allowed the Canadian National Assembly to name an alternate goal.[17] They added the Gulf Islands in British Columbia, Canada. Because Mary Zabolotny did manage to fill the Anticosti goal, there ended up being a total of 132 new areas to be opened to the Bahá'í Faith. In 1969, the Universal House of Justice awarded Cliff and Catherine Huxtable, who pioneered to the Gulf Islands, the title of Knight of Bahá'u'lláh.

Of the Guardian's goal areas, ten proved to have already been opened to the Bahá'í Faith by travel teachers. Interestingly, 68 of the 122 remaining goals were islands and a further 21 were in Africa. In a letter he wrote to John Leonard, Knight of Bahá'u'lláh in the Falkland Islands in the South Atlantic, Jameson Bond, a Knight to the Franklin District in the Canadian far north, wrote:

> There is a lot I would like to share with you about the spiritual significance of islands in the global development of the Faith . . . Over half the 131 virgin goal areas of the Crusade were islands! And this represents a main part of the spiritual conquest of the planet in the name of Bahá'u'lláh. Blessed are ye![18]

A total of 65 Knights earned their titles by pioneering to Africa, while 48 more became Knights in Europe. There were 43 Knights of Bahá'u'lláh in the Pacific Ocean area, including those in Indonesia and Malaysia. Another 28 people became Knights in North America and 27 others earned the title in the Caribbean. In the Indian subcontinent, including India, Sikkim and Tibet, there were 18 Knights. Thirteen people gained the title by opening up areas in the Indian Ocean while another 14 did the same by going to islands in the Atlantic Ocean. Then there was one Knight to Mongolia.[19]

During the first year of the Ten Year Crusade, 189 pioneers opened up 90 of Shoghi Effendi's goal areas. In 1954, another 48 more pioneers filled 16 more goal areas. That filled all but 16 of the Guardian's chosen places. In 1955, four more places were opened by five pioneers. Two places, Spitsbergen and the Chagos Islands, were opened in 1956 by solitary pioneers. Two more areas were opened in 1957 and one more in 1958. Two final goal areas were opened in 1959 and were the last to be filled during the Crusade. They were followed by a nine-year gap before the goal areas in the Communist-dominated areas began to be filled. In 1968, Romania was opened, followed by Moldova. Interestingly, Moldova was opened by Annemarie Krüger-Brauns who made three short travel teaching trips there between 1974 and 1984. When the first Moldovan declared his faith, the Universal House of Justice awarded her the title of Knight. White Russia, now Belarus, had its Knight in 1978, while the Mongolian goal was filled in 1988. The Guardian's last goal area, Sakhalin Island off the far eastern coast of Russia, was finally filled in 1990.

Marching orders

On 7 December 1953, Leroy Ioas, as a member of the International Bahá'í Council in Haifa, sent a letter to the pioneers with what amounted to their marching orders:

> You are now the representative of the Faith in your area, and the beloved Guardian feels assured that you will arise to the great opportunity that has come to you, to become the one to quicken the souls in your virgin territory and become the spiritual conqueror of that new land. The Guardian realises you will have many problems and difficulties, but he urges you to persevere under all circumstances, not to become disheartened in any way, but relying solely upon Bahá'u'lláh and His quickening Spirits, arise at once to carry forward the teaching work.
>
> The Guardian makes the following suggestion with regard to teaching in virgin areas at this critical time:

1. No publicity should be secured
2. No articles should be placed in newspapers or magazines
3. Do not contact Authorities or Political Leaders
4. Do not discuss Government policies in any way
5. No effort should be made toward a public proclamation of the Faith
6. Proceed with great caution
7. Be very wise in the manner in which the Teachings of the Faith are presented.
8. Make friends, and when these friends gain confidence in you and you in them, gradually confirm them in the Faith.
9. What is needed is a complete reliance upon Bahá'u'lláh; pure consecration to the Faith, and then energetic but wise presentation of the Divine Teachings. Such selfless, sacrificial devotion will attract the divine confirmations, and gradually you will confirm souls who will join you as strong supporters of the Faith in your area.[20]

Sacrifices

Why would a legal counsel with the rank of brigadier-general in the Department of Defence go to a desolate island with just a few score inhabitants? Where it was so hot that he cooked his fish on rocks on the beach and so isolated that the arrival of an eggplant on the tide was the cause of celebration? That is what Munír Vakíl did on a tiny island off Oman. When Bertha and Joe Dobbins consulted about whether they could arise and answer the Guardian's call, they realized that both could not go. Joe, therefore, stayed home and supported his wife as she garnered the title of Knight of Bahá'u'lláh. For the next 16 years, until he passed away, he continued to support her, a couple living apart for the sake of the Cause. Pouva Murday spent six days living with 40 others in a cargo hold only 20 feet square in order to peel 650 coconuts a day in abysmal conditions in the Chagos Islands so that he could fill one of the Guardian's goals. Raḥmatu'lláh Muhájir gave up a potential job that included a nice house, servants, car and driver and a good salary for a job paying just US$25 a month in a place where the toilet was two boards placed over a stream full of water snakes.

The sacrifices made by those who answered the Guardian's call are obvious in the stories in this book. All the Knights of Bahá'u'lláh had to sacrifice to earn their title, some much more than others. John Robarts couldn't even get off the ship that took him to Africa before he was being offered jobs. Many others, however, were never able to find work and thus were forced to leave their hard-won goals.

But there were bounties that came with rising to the challenge. Most were excited to be able to fill a goal set by the Guardian. Beyond the title, whenever a Knight of Bahá'u'lláh arrived in Haifa on pilgrimage, Shoghi Effendi would joyfully bring out his Roll of Honour and show them their names inscribed thereon. Other pilgrims didn't have that bounty. At Riḍván 1957, he wrote of the Knights of Bahá'u'lláh:

> A special tribute, I feel, should be paid in this survey of worldwide Bahá'í achievements, to the heroic band of pioneers, and particularly to the company of the Knights of Bahá'u'lláh, who, as a result of their indomitable spirit, courage, steadfastness, and self-abnegation, have achieved in the course of four brief years, in so many of the virgin territories newly opened to His Faith, a measure of success far exceeding the most sanguine expectations. Such a success, reflected in both the numerical strength of these territories and the range and solidity of the achievements of the Bahá'í crusaders responsible for their opening and development, has surpassed to an unbelievable extent the goals set for them under the Ten-Year Plan.[21]

Arrangement of the stories

Initially, most suggestions as to how the stories should be presented were to arrange them alphabetically by country, alphabetically by Knight or chronologically by when the Knights arrived at their goal. Each of these ideas made it difficult to see the relationships between the pioneers and their movements. In this book, the Knights are grouped so that their interactions can be seen. The grouping of the stories is by geographic area. Within a goal area, the stories are presented from north to south and in chronological order within a specific goal area. An example of the interaction of pioneers is that all the pioneers for Spanish Sahara, Rio de Oro and Spanish Morocco passed through or ended up in Tangier, in Shoghi Effendi's goal known as the Morocco International Zone, where there were other Knights. By grouping the Knights for North Africa, this interaction becomes clear. Similarly, this method is able to illustrate how Enoch Olinga's pioneering to Cameroon resulted in five other Knights arising from Cameroon and going to neighbouring countries.

The stories begin in Africa because Shoghi Effendi was very interested in that continent. From there, the sequence is an around-the-world tour, as though the reader is visiting all the Knights.

Many of the goals set by the Guardian in 1953 now have new names. To help the reader, the Knights are listed in two appendices, both of which include modern place names in addition to the original name used by Shoghi Effendi. Appendix I lists the Knights alphabetically by goal area and Appendix II lists them alphabetically by name.

Names of the Knights

The names of many of the Knights with Persian or Arabic origins created difficulties when I was searching for information. Shoghi Effendi used his standard transliteration to convert them from Persian to Western script and these are the names he inscribed on the Roll of Honour. Unfortunately, the spellings of some of the names vary greatly across the range of sources, both published and unpublished. This is particularly obvious in the *Bahá'í World* volumes from 1953 to 1963, where the use of diacritical marks – the accented letters – is very common. In later volumes, particularly in the obituary sections, the most common change is the elimination of diacritical marks. In the cases where I had reports or memoirs from the Knights themselves, their children or their grandchildren or relatives, I used the spellings they used, even when they differed from Shoghi Effendi's. The next standard for name spelling came from books written about the Knights and the obituary sections of the *Bahá'í World* volumes, followed by Shoghi Effendi's own spelling on the Roll of Honour. In cases where the modern names vary notably from those on Shoghi Effendi's scroll, his names are included in parenthesis.

NORTH AFRICA

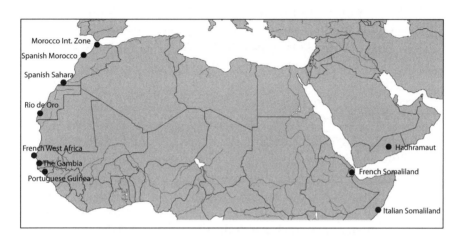

MOROCCO, INTERNATIONAL ZONE
Manouchehr Hezari and Hormoz Zendeh

The first Bahá'ís to answer Shoghi Effendi's call for pioneers to Morocco were Manouchehr Hezari (1922–2010) and his 19-year-old nephew, Hormoz Zendeh (b. 1934). Hormoz's parents went on pilgrimage and came back inspired to pioneer. Hormoz had just finished school in Iran and was eager to pioneer, but learned that it was almost impossible for him to get a passport and exit documents without having completed a period of military service. 'Through divine assistance', however, the needed documents were acquired and he and Manouchehr flew from Iran to Rome and then to Madrid. Since they already had Spanish visas, the Spanish authorities said they did not need anything else, so on 29 September 1953, they drove to Algeciras and took the ferry to Tangier. While on the crossing, an elderly gentleman asked if they were Bahá'ís. When they admitted that they were, the man introduced himself as Muhammad Mustafa, formerly the secretary of the National Spiritual Assembly of Egypt and now on his way to Rio de Oro (now Western Sahara) to fulfil another of the Guardian's goals. The two younger pioneers felt 'very encouraged and enriched by him'. Arriving in Tangier on 30 September 1953, Manouchehr and Hormoz immediately cabled Shoghi Effendi.[1]

But the excitement of having arrived at their goal was tempered just three weeks later, on 21 October, when the local authorities ordered them to leave within 48 hours. Apparently, though the Spanish believed that Tangier was under their jurisdiction, the French disagreed – and they had more political say. In order to stay, Manouchehr and Hormoz needed French visas, so they returned to Madrid. With the aid of the Spanish Bahá'ís and many prayers, they were able to acquire the needed visas at the French embassy in Barcelona. On 20 November, the two pioneers were back in Tangier, this time with all of the necessary documents to allow them to stay. By the time Manouchehr and Hormoz returned to Tangier, a sizable group of other Bahá'í pioneers were there, including Muhammad Mustafa, who had been expelled from his pioneering goal of Rio de Oro, Hussein and Nosrat Ardekani, 'Alí-Akbar, Sháyistih and 'Abbás Rafí'í, Elsie Austin and Muhammad-Ali Jalali. With so many Iranians arriving so suddenly, the Government was suspicious of their motives and it took the efforts of a lawyer and the National Spiritual Assemblies of France and Iran to reassure them sufficiently for the group to acquire resident visas.

Initially, Manouchehr rented a small shop and repaired electronic equipment. He and Hormoz held prayer meetings and shared information about the Bahá'í Faith.[2] By the beginning of 1954, the teaching efforts of the Bahá'ís began to pay off. Hussein Ardekani hired a woman named Rosa as a shop assistant and she subsequently became a Bahá'í. A Mr Hamri also declared his Faith and, by Riḍván, American pioneers Richard and Mary Suhm had arrived to add their support. All of these Bahá'ís allowed the first Local Spiritual Assembly of Tangier to be formed.

Shortly after the election of the first Local Spiritual Assembly of Tangier at Riḍván 1954, Manouchehr's wife, Hovieh, his daughter, Roya, and his parents, Rachid and Laal Hezari, joined them. Hormoz was responsible for integrating the new pioneers into the community. He helped them find housing and acted as their interpreter. He also joined a sports club, which allowed him to introduce the Faith to young people of many different nations.

By early 1955, the Tangier Bahá'í community was firmly established with the addition of American pioneers Evelyn and Richard Walters and Shoghi-Riaz Rouhani, from Egypt. When the Bahá'ís in the Canary Islands asked for help in forming their first Local Spiritual Assembly, Riaz and Hormoz flew to the island. They discovered that the local community had eight members, so Riaz returned to Tangier and Hormoz had the privilege of being on that first Local Assembly. By the end of July, a new declaration allowed Hormoz to return to Tangier, where he discovered that his mother, Homayun, and younger brothers Sohail and Sepehr had arrived. In the autumn, his father, Zabihu'lláh, and his oldest brother, Farhang, joined the rest of the family. Hormoz helped his father set up a small business and then, because there were so many pioneers in Tangier, he moved to Tetuán to help form that Assembly. In August 1957, Hormoz moved to Germany to complete his studies. After finishing his training, he married and moved to Baden-Württemberg.

Hormoz's uncle, Manouchehr, later worked for the Voice of America and his family stayed in Morocco until 1982 when they moved to Austin, Texas, for their daughter's education.[3]

Muhammad-Ali Jalali

Muhammad-Ali Jalali (early 1900s–2006) arrived in Tangier on 6 October. He had been a famous Islamic cleric with a large following in Iran, and had actively tried to protect the Muslims by attending Bahá'í teaching events to keep his followers from being 'misled'. Mr Jalali had once criticized the Bahá'í Faith in one of his sermons. A Bahá'í who heard the sermon invited him to his home and gave him a book of Bahá'u'lláh's Writings. Being a pure-hearted soul, he had a dream of 'Abdu'l-Bahá, after which he started a serious investigation of the Bahá'í Faith, soon becoming a well-known Islamic scholar and Bahá'í teacher.[4] Soon, he became a Bahá'í and arose to travel teach in India, Pakistan and Bangladesh. When the goals of the Ten Year Crusade were announced, Mr Jalali pioneered to Morocco, being one of the first to arrive.[5]

A few weeks after his arrival as a Knight of Bahá'u'lláh in Tangier, the National Spiritual Assembly of Egypt, which had administrative jurisdiction over Morocco, wrote and asked if he knew where Elsie Austin, another pioneer from the United States, was staying. He did not, but he then had a dream in which he saw a certain hotel. The next day, he went out and found the hotel from his dream and learned that there was an American lady there. The hotel clerk called the woman, who was indeed Elsie, and told her that a 'Mr. Bahá'í' was there to see her. When she came down from her room, she found Mr Jalali, but since they had no language in common, all they could do was say some prayers together. The next day, Mr Jalali brought Hussein Ardekani and 'Abbás Rafí'í, both Knights of Bahá'u'lláh, to the hotel. Since Hussein spoke some French and 'Abbás some English, the four Knights were able to converse.[6]

Mr Jalali spoke Arabic and had a good knowledge of the Qur'án, which allowed him to teach the Arabic-speaking population. These talents allowed him to attract an artist of Berber origin, by the name of Hamdi, into the Faith. He also taught the 17-year-old 'Abbás Rafí'í classical Arabic and helped him and many new Bahá'ís deepen in the Writings of the Faith.[7]

Mr Jalali later pioneered to Algeria and the Canary Islands before settling in Spain. Travel teaching was his passion, however, and he travelled widely in Africa. When Eastern Europe opened up, even though he was quite elderly, he travelled to Tajikistan and Uzbekistan.[8]

Hussein and Nosrat Ardekani

Nosrat (b. 1931) and Hussein Rouhani Ardekani (1922–2007) and their four-year-old daughter, Shahlá, arrived in Tangier on 1 November 1953, followed three days later by her parents, 'Alí-Akbar Rafí'í and Sháyistih Rafí'í and her 16-year-old brother, 'Abbás.[9]

Nosrat had desperately wanted to pioneer, but her husband was very occupied with his business. After discussing the possibility of pioneering, they decided that they would have to send someone else in their place. Even after sending a pioneer, Nosrat prayed fervently for her husband to change his mind about pioneering. Then Hussein went on pilgrimage. As a member of the Persian National Teaching Committee, he asked the Guardian to pray for the success of the teaching and pioneer efforts of home-front pioneers within Iran. The Guardian replied, 'Yes, yes, they will have success, and you, also, will be successful in your pioneering.' This was a baffling answer for a man who wasn't planning to pioneer. Upon returning home, he one night shared his pilgrim notes with a group of friends. When he mentioned this statement of Shoghi Effendi, one of those listening exclaimed, 'Hai! You are Rouhani Ardekani. And what did the beloved Guardian say to you? He said you have to be successful in your pioneer post. Why do you sit here and you don't go?' After a thoughtful moment, Rouhani turned to his wife and said, 'Nosrat, now we are also pioneers. We have to go and pioneer.'

Though it was very difficult to arrange all of their affairs, they proceeded. In order to overcome the pleas of some of his family not to go, the Ardekanis sent their carpets, silverware and other things to Tangier. This allowed them to tell their families that they had to go since their things were already on the way. Finally, they departed Iran, going first to Switzerland so that Hussein could see a doctor. He was completely exhausted by all the stress of the preparations. The doctor told him that he must not work for two years; he needed the rest. From Switzerland, the family flew to Madrid then on to Tangier, arriving in November. They quickly obtained a two-month visa to look into business opportunities. When Nosrat's parents arrived three days later, they were only able to obtain one-week visas, but her father hired two lawyers and after two months managed to assure the local authorities about the intentions of the Bahá'ís and to acquire the needed visas.[10] When they met the other Bahá'ís, the Ardekanis found the man they had sent as a pioneer in their place, possibly Mr Jalali, and they served together for a while.

After a few months, the carpets and other things that the Ardekanis had sent from Iran arrived. Officials said that such carpets couldn't just be for a home and that Hussein must be planning to sell them, so charged him US$1,000 in duties, which was an enormous sum. Hussein opened a shop in which he hoped to sell the carpets and silver to recover the money, but ultimately he ended up selling almost none of them. To help him in the shop, Hussein hired a young Spanish woman, Rosa (mentioned in the story above). She became the first resident of Tangier to become a Bahá'í. In the end, Hussein traded the shop and its contents for a house in Tangier.

The Ardekanis thought that they should study Spanish and French in order to teach, but Shoghi Effendi told them that they should, instead, learn Arabic so they could teach the native Berber people. In April 1954, the first Local Spiritual Assembly of Tangier was formed.

With the Tangier Assembly formed and since there were enough Bahá'ís, the Ardekanis went to Casablanca and joined Mr Masrour, who had pioneered there before the Ten Year Crusade. It required divine assistance for the pioneers to get to Casablanca to form that first Local Assembly. Normally, it was very difficult to get visas for that area, but the Ardekanis' passports were somehow mixed into a pile of other passports which had already been approved for visas. Thus they received their visas. They were joined by American pioneers Evelyn and Richard Walters, who were also divinely assisted in staying in Casablanca (see their story below). The group was able to form the Local Spiritual Assembly of Casablanca later in 1954. When the Ardekanis returned to Tangier to collect their belongings and then tried to re-enter Casablanca, they were refused new visas and told it was almost impossible that they had been allowed to go the first time.

Looking for new opportunities, in 1955 Hussein and Nosrat pioneered to the Canary Islands along with her sister and her sister's husband to help form the first Local Spiritual Assembly of Tenerife that Riḍván. They weren't allowed to stay very long in Tenerife because their teaching activities had attracted the attention of the police. Returning to Morocco, they went to Larache in Spanish Morocco. Nosrat's parents had been there for the formation of the first Local Spiritual Assembly of Larache in 1956. After an exciting time of teaching, the Ardekanis moved to Meknes, where they were involved in the formation of that first Local Spiritual Assembly in 1959. Some time later, the Rafí'ís also moved there and it was where Mr Rafí'í passed away. Meknes proved to be a very active Bahá'í area with many people coming into the Bahá'í Faith there.[11]

In 1956, the first Regional Spiritual Assembly of North West Africa was formed and some time after that, Hussein Ardekani was elected to that body. A few years later, he went to Senegal as a representative of the Assembly to assess that country. Finding no Bahá'ís, he determined that, since there were many Bahá'ís and pioneers in Morocco, the family should pioneer to Senegal, which they did in January 1962. The authorities would not allow them to stay, however, so after six months they returned to Morocco. In 1966, they tried again to pioneer to Senegal. The only way they could stay in the country, however, was on student visas, so Hussein began studying medicine and Nosrat took up French. After seven years, the police became suspicious as to why they never seemed to finish their studies and threatened to expel them, again. They wrote to the Universal House of Justice asking for prayers so they could stay in Senegal. The prayers of the House of Justice were successful because the family was still there in 2013. When Amatu'l-Bahá Rúḥíyyih Khánum passed through Senegal in 1971, Hussein Ardekani was serving as a Counsellor.[12]

'Alí-Akbar, Sháyistih and 'Abbás Rafí'í

'Alí-Akbar (1882–1965), Sháyistih (1907–1992) and 'Abbás Rafí'í (b. 1937) pioneered to Morocco, arriving on 4 November 1953. Their road to Morocco began in Rafsanjan in south-eastern Iran where 'Alí-Akbar was a successful pistachio farmer. The Bahá'ís in Rafsanjan were strongly persecuted and in 1951, during Ramadan, a mob attacked and burned the local Bahá'í Centre and threatened the Rafí'í home. The mob, however, passed the house and attacked the Bahá'í cemetery instead. 'Alí-Akbar stood steadfast before this violence and refused to leave.

When Shoghi Effendi announced the Ten Year Crusade, the Rafí'ís decided to attend all four Intercontinental Teaching Conferences. At the Stockholm Conference in July, Hand of the Cause Ugo Giachery read the message from the Guardian and called for pioneers. 'Abbás remembered that

> There was an electric atmosphere, infused with the utmost feeling of spirituality. I was sitting next to my parents. I heard my mother suggesting to my father to also go on the stage and volunteer. My father seemed shocked initially; he turned to her and said, 'Do you know what you are suggesting? Do you know how much debt I have?' Then my mother looked at him and replied, 'Bahá'u'lláh Himself will sort things out'. After one or two minutes of reflection, my father took her hand and said, 'Let us go!' So the three of us got on stage and registered.[13]

'Alí-Akbar was 71 years old at that time, suffered from chronic bronchitis and was extremely weak. When they asked Mr Giachery where they should go, he asked 'You know English?' 'No'. 'French?' 'No'. 'Arabic?' 'No'. So it was suggested that they go to Tangier in Morocco.[14]

The family returned to Iran, then attended the Intercontinental Conference in New Delhi in October. While they were there, it was announced that the first pioneers to Morocco, Manouchehr Hezari and Hormoz Zendeh, had reached their post. Their telegram was sent from the Hotel Carlton. This news elated the Rafí'ís because it meant that there would be other Persian pioneers there.

The family began their journey on 23 October, stopping over in Bombay where some of their luggage was stolen. They continued through Beirut, Cairo, Rome and Madrid before arriving in Tangier on 5 November 1953. Then their problems really began:

At the airport they checked our passports and realized that we did not have an entry visa. Then a tedious and long conversation started. Of course, the most difficult part being my poor English skills coupled with their French accent. The police asked me what the aim of our trip to Tangier was. I replied very proudly, 'We have come pioneering.' They asked what pioneering was. So I answered, 'We are Bahá'ís and have come to teach people about the Bahá'í Faith.'

From then on the mood changed and we were denied entry . . . I then translated my father's statement that this was an international zone and we did not need a visa. But the officer explained that it would only be the case had we come as tourists for a short time, if we intended to stay, however, we had to have a visa. Then he asked where we were going to stay. I told him in the Carlton Hotel. When he heard Carlton Hotel his mood became even worse and we were wondering why. The whole conversation took over an hour. The whole time my mother was reciting the Tablet of Aḥmad and my father was lighting one cigarette after another while I struggled to translate . . . the policeman told us that he would only give us a visa for 48 hours during which time we had to report to the main police station. It was in fact a very painful experience, but fortunately we were able to pass the control.

We hired a taxi to go to the city. When I mentioned Hotel Carlton the driver was amazed and could not believe it, but said OK and agreed to take us. In fact we had thought that Hotel Carlton was part of the Ritz Carlton hotel chain but it turned out that we were mistaken.

French cities normally had three sections, a European one which was very modern and similar to other French cities, an Arab section which consisted of an old style town with very narrow streets or alleys and quite dirty, and the Jewish section which aesthetically was between the other two. The taxi stopped in the middle of the Arab section and told us to get out. I asked him where Hotel Carlton was. He explained that due to the narrow streets he could not advance and we had to walk the rest of the way to get there. Of course this revelation was catastrophic for us because my father had a hard time walking. We tried to make him understand that with all the luggage and my father's poor health we could not possibly walk. He then called a few Arab boys who were playing close by and told them to carry the luggage, but we still had to walk. My father who was quite fragile and weak would walk about 50 to 100 metres, sit down, light a cigarette, smoke it and then start walking again until we finally arrived at a very old and small building which was supposed to be the hotel. With astonishment I told one of the boys that this was not a hotel. He then pointed to a hand-written inscription on one of the walls, which said: Hotel Carlton. When I asked about the reception, he motioned upstairs. This again was a challenge for my father who now had to climb up the stairs . . . Our main goal was to meet Messieurs Hezari and Zendeh. So we proceeded up a very narrow stairway. At the reception there was a Spanish-speaking lady whom I asked about the two gentlemen. She made a hand gesture implying that they were gone and said 'POLICIA'. After our experience at the airport and upon seeing hand gesture we understood too well what had happened. Upon seeing our expression, she realized our great disappointment and tried to explain that there was another gentleman from Iran.

. . . Finally we rented a room and prepared tea. We always carried the necessary 'equipment' because my father was a heavy tea drinker besides being a heavy smoker. Over the next few hours I went at least three to four times to inquire after the gentleman we expected so badly. Finally she came and informed us that he had arrived. It was such a great relief to meet him. It was in fact no other than Mr Mohammad Ali Djalali [Muhammad-Ali Jalali] who had arrived after Mr Hezari and Mr Zendeh. He confirmed that the police had sent the two gentlemen out of the country and said that he would most probably have to leave as well. Nonetheless he said, 'I have good news for you. Mr and Mrs Rohani Ardekani have arrived!' Of course we were most happy and eager to meet them. He told us to have some rest, as it was already late, and assured us that he would take us to them the following morning.[15]

The family found a more reputable hotel the next day and Mansour Masrour, a pioneer in Casablanca, was called for consultations. He quickly brought in a Tunisian lawyer, a Mr Ayoub, who had married the daughter of a Bahá'í. Mr Masrour and Mr Ayoub went to the police station the next day, but their entreaties were for nought. At that point, a French lawyer joined the fray, but the police were adamant that no visa could be issued. Finally, after consultations with the two lawyers and the police chief, the clearest path seemed to be to contact the French Ambassador in Tehran, explain to him the non-political nature of the Bahá'í Faith and request a letter from him to the authorities in Tangier clarifying this principle. The National Spiritual Assembly of Iran sent Dr Mesbah and his French wife to the Ambassador and the letter was duly written and delivered. All of this took two months, but the Rafí'ís finally had their visas.[16]

During the following months, a number of local people became Bahá'ís and were deepened by Muhammad-Ali Jalali. Then on 26 March 1954, the group received a letter from the Guardian calling for the election of the Local Spiritual Assembly at Riḍván, less than a month away. After an 'enthusiastic and feverish effort', there were enough Bahá'ís both to form that first Local Spiritual Assembly of Tangier and also for the Ardekanis and the Suhms to go to Casablanca and form that Assembly.[17]

In July 1954, 'Alí-Akbar and 'Abbas Rafí'í returned to Iran for two months. They visited the House of the Báb in Shiraz, then continued to Rafsanjan, where they encouraged the friends to pioneer. Several accepted the challenge. From Rafsanjan they travelled to Tehran, where they visited the house where Bahá'u'lláh had been born, then departed for Cairo. While there, Hand of the Cause Músá Banání arranged for Mr Rafí'í to go to Tunis to participate in the dedication of the second Bahá'í Centre in Africa and give the Bahá'ís a special donation for the Centre from the beloved Guardian.[18]

After forming the Tangier Local Assembly, the Rafí'ís moved to

Rabat and Larache, helping to form local assemblies in both communities. In May 1955, 'Abbás moved to Hamburg, Germany, to continue his education, which he had been unable to do while in Tangier. He stayed with a German family and earned his diploma in March 1958.[19] His parents moved to Meknes, where 'Alí-Akbar passed away in 1965.[20] His wife Sháyistih remained in Morocco until her death in 1992.[21]

'Abbas went to a German-speaking university in Leoben, Austria in October 1958 to study steel engineering. In 1963 he married Joubine, and their first child, Neda, was born the following year. While in Austria, he served as a member of the Austrian National Teaching Committee and the Austrian National Spiritual Assembly. 'Abbas moved to Luxembourg in 1967 and was elected to their National Assembly the next year, serving on that body until 1993. He was also the representative for Ḥuqúqu'lláh.[22] He is presently living in Indonesia.

Elsie Austin

Elsie Austin (1908–2004), an African-American lawyer and a member of the National Spiritual Assembly of the United States, arrived in Tangier on 24 October 1953. Elsie promoted racial unity from her earliest days. In Cincinnati, Ohio, she was one of only two African-American children in her school. When her class used a book that denigrated Africans, she pointed out the errors and educated her classmates on the contributions of Africa. She was the first African-American woman to graduate from the University of Cincinnati Law School in 1930 and also the first to serve as assistant Attorney-General of Ohio. Elsie became a Bahá'í in 1934. In 1946, she was elected to the National Spiritual Assembly of the United States until she arose to pioneer in 1953.[23]

When Shoghi Effendi announced the Ten Year Crusade, Elsie and four other members resigned from the National Assembly to accept his challenge. Elsie had read the Guardian's appeals for pioneers, then went on pilgrimage in February 1953. Afterwards, she wrote:

> When I came back home, I just sat down and thought about it: 'You know you are always talking about how much you love the Faith. Well, this is the time to show it.' And it really was a sacrifice for me to go at that time, but I made up my mind that I would go. So I went in and asked my General Counsel if I could have a year's leave

of absence and he said yes. I told him I wanted to give a year of my life to the Faith . . .[24]

On the way to Tangier, Elsie's ship had a short stop in Casablanca, where she knew a Bahá'í lived, though she didn't know where. She said, 'I got off the boat for just a few minutes and I thought if only I knew where that Bahá'í was. So, I walked up the street saying the Greatest Name and turned the corner and bumped into Mr Masrour. I had seen him once before. We stood there with a long hug.' As she sailed on to Tangier, she didn't know that on the same ship were five other pioneers heading for Spanish Morocco: John and Earleta Fleming, Alyce Janssen and Luella McKay and her young son.

Elsie arrived in Tangier on 24 October 1953, believing that she was the only Bahá'í there.

> It was then Tangier International Zone. I chose it because it was an international city, governed by an international council and had an international police force and court, managed by a 13-member international committee. I thought that this was an interesting thing, an international city and perhaps I could get legal work, as law is my profession. When I got to Tangier, I discovered that the official language[s were] Arabic, French and Spanish and while I knew some French and Spanish, I was certainly not fluent enough to do any legal work. And I didn't know Arabic at all.[25]

The National Spiritual Assembly of Egypt had written to the other pioneers that she would be arriving, but didn't say where she would be staying, so the local Bahá'ís didn't know how to find her. Then Muhammad-Ali Jalali had his dream about a hotel and went out and found it.[26] Elsie wrote:

> And the second night that I was in Tangier I was in a little hotel and my phone rang and the lady said there is a person down here to see you. Well, I didn't know anybody in Tangier. I said, 'What person?' She said, 'Mr Bahá'í.' And here was this perfectly dear believer from Iran, a Mr Jalali, who spoke no English, mostly Persian and nothing else. And we just stood there and said, 'Alláh'u'Abhá' to each other. And I guess everybody wondered what was wrong with us. He was

26

trying to tell me something. He said, 'Police, police' every now and then. So, I sat down and began to say the Remover of Difficulties. And then when I had finished, he said, 'Tomorrow, tomorrow.' I gathered that he meant that he was coming back.[27]

Mr Jalali hurried over to the home of Hussein and Nosrat Ardekani and told them about finding Elsie.[28] Elsie wrote that

The next day he came back and he brought Mr Ardekani, who spoke some French and Persian. He explained to me that Mr Jalali had been into Tangier, but that the police hadn't permitted him to stay. They were very difficult with the Persian believers and that was what he was trying to tell me. He had been there and he was trying to tell me also that Mr Mustafa and 'Amin Battah from Egypt had also been into Tangier . . . [but] had been made to leave.[29]

One of the first things Elsie did was to contact the social and educational services, then she went to the American School:

I went to the principal's office and introduced myself. He said, 'I know you.' And my eyes widened. He said, 'Yes, were you not connected with the Delta Sigma Theta Sorority?' I said yes. I was at one time their national president. He said, 'Well, you set up a chapter at a University in Louisiana when I was president there and I wrote you. I remember your name.' And then with the utmost grace, he called in several of his teachers, introduced me to them and told them to show me around . . . They became very dear friends. This was unheard of because I knew nobody in Morocco.[30]

In December, Muhammad Mustafa was in Tangier, having been expelled from Spanish Sahara. Elsie wrote, 'He is a wonderful soul and inspired and cheered us all during those dark days when it seemed as if the Persian friends would not receive their residence permits.' She also noted that they were able to get together now and then with Alyce Janssen and John and Earleta Fleming, pioneers to Spanish Morocco, because they did their banking in Tangier.[31]

For the first year in Tangier, Elsie couldn't find work and lived off her savings. She had two meals a day then made up a bouillon cube thickened with oatmeal in the evening. At the end of her first year, she was offered a job at the American School. But that meant extending her leave-of-absence. Elsie returned to America and asked for another year's extension, realizing that she had been very immature when she initially decided to pioneer:

> I thought I would go and pioneer a year. Then I went out and stayed in Morocco, I had to go back at the end of that year and ask for more time. They told me that I couldn't have another extension, but, as my General Counsel put it, 'Go ahead and resign and get it out of your system and when you come back, we'll hire you back.' I think he thought it would be a year longer and I thought it might be a year longer, but I didn't have an idea it would stretch out as long as it did.[32]

She went back and joined the faculty of the American School and stayed on that staff until she left Morocco in 1957.

Soon, there were two Moroccan believers, but

> Teaching the faith in that area of the world was extremely difficult because the country . . . had a state religion – Islam. It tolerated the Christians and tolerated the Jews but the Bahá'ís [were a different issue] . . . We proceeded mainly by building up friendly contacts around the city . . . We had a great many picnics and teas in which we would entertain. We would go to the homes of people that we met and be entertained . . . And in that way a family of Moroccans joined the faith and became very devoted Bahá'ís.[33]

Not everyone was happy to have a group of Bahá'ís in their midst, and Elsie wrote:

> When our Bahá'í activities extended into other areas than Tangier, we met serious pressure . . . In fact, one of the great tragedies of the Faith occurred in Morocco, when Bahá'ís who were mainly Moroc-cans were put into prison [1962]. And there had to be much effort on the part of the Bahá'í communities outside of Morocco and around the world through the United Nations . . . to do something about that. And after about a year or so, they were released but many of them forfeited their jobs and their pension rights. For instance,

one of the Moroccan believers lost her husband. And the government said because he was a Bahá'í they didn't owe him anything [as
a pension] . . . So there were grave tests for them and for us too.[34]

When Elsie left in 1957, there were Local Spiritual Assemblies in
Casablanca, Tetuán, Larache and Tangier. Elsie returned to Africa in
December 1959, pioneering to Lagos, Nigeria to work with the US
Foreign Service. She was there long enough to help form the first Local
Spiritual Assembly of Lagos. In 1965, her job was transferred to go to
Kenya.[35] While in Africa, she served on the Auxiliary Board for four
years.[36] She returned to America in 1969 and settled in Silver Spring,
Maryland where she worked as a consultant in human relations and
law.[37]

Richard and Mary Suhm

Richard Suhm (1925–1996) and Mary Kelsey (1925–2002) were
married in October 1952 and shortly thereafter pioneered to Whitefish
Bay, Wisconsin, in order to form a Local Spiritual Assembly. After the
Intercontinental Teaching Conference in Wilmette, the young couple
began to plan a move to Africa. Mary's parents, Curtis and Harriet
Kelsey, left on pilgrimage on 1 December 1953, one day before the birth
of Richard and Mary's first child, Gregg. The new parents telephoned
the grandparents, who asked if they would like to ask Shoghi Effendi
anything. 'Yes, please ask him where he would like us to pioneer' was
the response. A month later, Richard and Mary received a postcard
saying that Shoghi Effendi said they could go to Tangier, Morocco, in
the International Zone where they didn't need visas.

Finding a ship to Tangier was difficult, but the family, with three-
month-old Gregg, finally managed and boarded their ship in New York.
Unfortunately, there was a dock strike and no porters to help load the
car they were bringing. They arrived on 12 April 1954. Richard found
work with an American investment bank and a daughter, Wendy, was
born there. Then Mary fell ill with polio and Shoghi Effendi advised
them to return to America for treatment, so in 1956 they left Tangier.[38]

Evelyn and Richard Walters

Evelyn (b.1920) and Richard Walters (1913–1999) arrived in the International Zone in April 1954. Richard had begun attending firesides in the 1930s. When he began bringing home Bahá'í literature, his mother became antagonistic. One night she had a dream in which Jesus was holding Richard in His arms, which she interpreted as meaning that the Bahá'í Faith was the path to Hell. Consequently, she gave Richard an ultimatum: either the Bahá'í literature had to leave or he had to leave. Richard left and became a Bahá'í.[39]

Evelyn first heard about the Bahá'í Faith in 1936. By the autumn of the next year, at the age of seventeen, she was convinced of the truth of Bahá'u'lláh's Revelation and eager to become a Bahá'í. The older Bahá'ís told her that first she had to attend classes, so that she would know what she was joining. After attending three classes a week, she became a Bahá'í two years later in New York. Shortly afterwards, Evelyn went to Green Acre where she met Richard. The two were married in 1941 in Teaneck, New Jersey.[40]

In September 1942 they pioneered to Albuquerque, New Mexico, for the first Seven Year Plan, arriving with just $15.[41] Evelyn served on the first Local Spiritual Assembly there. On one occasion, the daughter of President Woodrow Wilson visited the community and when asked if her father had gotten his fourteen points for world peace from 'Abdu'l-Bahá's teachings, she confirmed that he had. In 1947, Richard and Evelyn, with their two children, Nina and Richard Jr, pioneered to Tucson, Arizona, to re-establish that Local Assembly.[42]

Evelyn and Richard were at the Intercontinental Teaching Conference when the Ten Year Crusade was announced and decided to pioneer. Richard worked three jobs in order to save enough money to go. Finally, the time came to sail, but there was a dock strike and there were no porters to help with the luggage, including Richard's carpentry tools. When they finally boarded their ship to Morocco, they were surprised to find Richard and Mary Suhm on board, also heading to Morocco. With everyone on board with their luggage, there was a long, unexplained delay before the ship actually sailed. It wasn't until they arrived in Tangier that they learned that there had been a bomb threat to their ship. Evelyn wrote, 'there were a few men searching around the ship's deck as if looking for some-one or some thing. Naturally they didn't tell us of the threat. We all would have wanted to jump off the ship.'[43]

When they finally arrived in Tangier, the Rafí'í family gave up their bedroom to the Walters until they found a place of their own. Before pioneering, Richard had worked 16-hour days for six months to finance their move to Tangier, but they needed a stable income.[44] Richard needed a job to allow him to stay. Evelyn wrote:

> When we were about to rent an apartment, we went to the bank to exchange our money and we were told of the hopeless conditions for finding employment in construction. We were told to try Casablanca at the American air base in French Morocco. In the meantime, a cable came from the Guardian asking if there were more than enough for the LSA in Tangiers, could they move to Casablanca and perhaps create another LSA. My husband made a mad dash for the American Air Base at Noeuaseur south of Casablanca.[45]

This last effort, to an American air base on the day of Riḍván and the last chance to form the Local Spiritual Assembly that year, initially resulted in nothing. Richard missed the bus back to Casablanca so he decided to sit there in the sun and pray until the next bus departed an hour later.[46] As he sat there, an American approached and demanded to know who he was and asked, 'What are you doing here? This is the area of the American military base and nobody is allowed to be here.' Richard explained that he had come to look for a job, but had found none. The man asked what he could do and when Richard answered that he was a carpenter, the man excitedly said that he had been looking for someone with his qualifications.[47]

Evelyn continued:

> It was so interesting to see God's hand at work. The day my husband arrived at the Base, the employment office had just sent a cable to their office in New York requesting to have two carpenters sent ASAP. They said, if the carpenters had not left yet [he] would have a job. And of course God arranged that the carpenters hadn't left so my husband dashed back and we moved to Casablanca. He had become employed the very next day.
>
> We still needed one more Bahá'í to form the LSA. Mr Masrour

phoned Rabat and told a French Bahá'í to come tomorrow so we can form the LSA. She came on Saturday and the LSA was formed, a photograph was taken and a copy sent to the Guardian.[48]

Evelyn described their living conditions:

By then we had just enough money to pay our hotel bill. We moved out to the American Air Base 30 miles south of Casablanca, where we were given a family unit living quarters, which consisted of two Quonset huts. It was furnished with Army cots and a small wooden table with metal folding chairs. There was no kitchen, no refrigerator or bathroom facilities. We had to use a common latrine along with 15 other families. Ice was delivered daily. We cooked on two one-burner stoves.

Life was very difficult for the children. Six months later we moved into the city of Casablanca, into a brand new apartment building, which was the only one with steam heat. We found this apartment through an American Bahá'í who had been living in Casablanca for many years, but who had been inactive. My husband came across him on the Base where he was working. His name was Rama Gibson, brother of Amoz Gibson. Later a tragedy occurred to him. He was killed by an Army truck accident. We contacted his wife who was a French lady and not a Bahá'í. We asked her if she would like us to conduct a Bahá'í Funeral. She said yes and was very grateful.[49]

Rama's wife later became a Bahá'í.

Richard wrote to the American National Assembly about their teaching efforts:

The friends in the States should realize how easy a time they have in teaching. One language will do fine there but in Casablanca it is necessary to teach in French, Spanish, English and Arabic depending upon which group your contact falls into . . . Which means that to find contacts one has to attract them. This makes you realize more than ever that actions are your only instrument for teaching, since in not speaking their language you can't stir their attention by a well turned word or present a clear explanation from the teachings in answer to questions of the spirit. You must strive patiently to win friends before you can teach. And then you may have to turn him over to another Bahá'í for the study work. This is known as detachment.[50]

Teaching was difficult and the French authorities were worried about these newcomers. Evelyn continued her description of life in Casablanca:

> Casablanca in French Morocco was in a state of rebellion by the Arabs against the French rule. A curfew was declared during the night, and it made it difficult for the Bahá'ís to hold meetings, especially at night.
>
> We later learned that the local Authorities sent a spy to our firesides. We were later told by a local spy that if we had mentioned the slightest thing against Muhammad or Islam they would not have hesitated to kill us with a sword concealed in a cane.
>
> Gradually two Arab Moroccans, who worked in my husband's unit, declared themselves Bahá'ís. This was a dangerous thing for them to do. The Moroccan men working in my husband's unit on Base became very friendly and felt free to visit our home. especially on their Moroccan holidays. They would bring Moroccan delicacies from their meager sources.
>
> When one Moroccan worker lost his little girl, he came to our home and poured out his grief to us as he would to any other Moroccan. This was the extent of their trust in us. They didn't do this with other Americans. They called my husband their (true brother).[51]

It took two years of discreet teaching efforts before the first native Casablancan became a Bahá'í. It was a dangerous time to be in Casablanca. The Arabs assumed that the Walters were French; there were two attempts to assassinate Richard and one attempt to kidnap Nina.[52]

In December 1960, Richard was told that all the American bases in Morocco were being closed down and that his job would be over. The Walters planned to move back to America until the European Teaching Committee asked if they would consider going to a European goal city. When they said yes, the Committee sent them to Portugal, where they lived 'in a little town . . . outside the town of Almada, called Larangeiro' (near Lisbon). Evelyn reported that apparently 'no foreigner had ever lived there, and we were the object of great curiosity and ridicule because of our cultural customs'.[53]

Their tests in Almada weren't limited to the people. When they arrived, their belongings had mistakenly been earmarked for shipment to America instead of Portugal, so they had no furniture and ended up initially sleeping on the floor. When their landlord saw that, he gave them some straw mattresses. Finally, after two and a half months, their things arrived, just in time for a Naw-Rúz celebration. But the early conditions resulted in their son falling ill. Since they spoke no Portuguese and the local doctor spoke no English, it was very difficult:

> Our son was rushed to the hospital, supposedly for appendicitis. He was taken to a hospital used for poor people. Their rules prohibited seeing the patients for three days after an operation. This was very painful for us and our son, who suffered even more because he could not speak the language, and he was ridiculed by the nurses. When we brought him home he was still in pain. One of the English Bahá'ís told us about a British Hospital and we brought him there and they immediately took an X-ray which they didn't do in the Portuguese Hospital. We then learned he had been misdiagnosed. They performed another operation immediately. He survived the operation, but he died the next day. He ascended to The Abhá Kingdom on May 9, 1961 at the age of nineteen.[54]

These struggles affected their marriage and the Walters divorced. Evelyn pioneered to Madeira Island for a year, then returned to Albuquerque, New Mexico, where she enrolled herself in a Business College at the age of 47. In 1972, she moved to Santa Fe, New Mexico, to help re-establish their assembly and three years later, went to Lahaina, Maui, in the Hawaiian Islands, to help the youth.[55]

In 1992, Evelyn was invited to the gathering of the Knights of Bahá'u'lláh in Haifa. Not having enough money to go, she put the problem into God's hands. The problem was quickly solved when the Local Spiritual Assembly of Albuquerque put out a call for contributions to help her go. In Haifa, Evelyn shared a hotel room with Mary Suhm, with whom she had sailed to Morocco so many years before.[56]

Shortly after receiving her invitation to Haifa, Richard contacted her after a 27-year silence. He had cancer, but they quickly decided to remarry. Evelyn was a 73-year-old bride. Never ones to retire from service to the Faith, the remarried couple pioneered to Texarkana, Arkansas.[57] When Richard died in 1999, Evelyn moved back to Albuquerque.

Spanish Morocco

Fawzi and Bahia Zein

Fawzi (1911–1975) and Bahia Zein (1926–2013) (also spelled Fawzí and Bahíyyih Zaynu'l-'Ábidin) arrived in Tetuán from Egypt on 11 October 1953. Fawzi's parents had moved to Egypt from Iran to escape the persecution of the Bahá'ís and had the bounty of being with 'Abdu'l-Bahá when He was in Egypt. Bahia's father grew up in Palestine and met 'Abdu'l-Bahá at the age of 18. Fawzi met Bahia in Egypt and they were married in 1946.[58]

When Shoghi Effendi launched the Ten Year Crusade, several Hands of the Cause went to Egypt to encourage the Bahá'ís to pioneer. At one of these meetings, Fawzi and Bahia stepped out into the hall for a few minutes and quickly decided to go:

> The following weeks witnessed packing and giving away of their meagre property, in order to depart as fast as possible. Selection of North Morocco as their pioneering destination was made by Bahia, when she apparently pointed her finger haphazardly to a spot on a globe that was presented to her. It was not easy at that time for civil servants in Egypt, such as Fawzi, to get permission to leave the country, but he was still with his Iranian passport and thus the family got their exit visas without any problem.[59]

They arrived in Tetuán with only a 15-day visa, no knowledge of the area, not speaking the local languages and no jobs. Their material means were limited and they had two young sons, Kamal and Sharrif. Fawzi displayed artistic talent from a young age and he was teaching in one of the Art Schools in Egypt when he decided to pioneer. This experience he put to use in Tetuán. A Spanish security chief recognized his talent and put him to work making drawings for a publication the chief was planning. His talent later gained him a job on the faculty of the Fine Arts School there. His ability at the school and exhibitions of his work locally enabled the family to acquire permanent resident visas. Bahia spoke French and English besides Arabic, and with that ability, she found a job in tourism.[60]

Both collaborated to have the door of their simple residence open for the young seekers. Teaching the Faith had to be discreet, but they were able to send Shoghi Effendi a 'family' photograph with the first two believers in Tetuán.[61] One of the new believers was a secretary to that Spanish security chief and was the first among the Berber race to embrace the Faith. In 1955, they were able to form a Local Spiritual Assembly composed entirely of Moroccan Bahá'ís, keeping themselves in the background.[62]

Then in 1961, some of the Moroccan Bahá'ís in Tetuán and neighbouring localities such as Nador were arrested and put to trial for 'heresy and apostasy'. They were imprisoned for their beliefs and Fawzi was picked out as a source of the problem and immediately fired from his job. The family was blacklisted and could not meet with Bahá'ís, even to the extent that they had to change sidewalks if a Bahá'í was approaching them anywhere in town:

> This persecution was a blessing in disguise. It showed the sublime fortitude of the nascent Moroccan Bahá'í community to both their compatriots and the entire world beyond. The prisoners felt themselves quite special for being singled out for the ultimate sacrifice of martyrdom, since many of them received death sentences. Even, and as a token of gratitude to those who ushered them into the Faith, some of them sent Fawzi and Bahia a rosary that was tenaciously made of olive pits. However, the shock waves that were generated by such harsh sentences prompted a retrial. After more than a year of imprisonment, the Bahá'í prisoners were acquitted. Additionally, the perpetrators fell from power into disgrace and exile. The Constitution of Morocco was, in subsequent years, amended to covertly recognize the presence of Bahá'ís among the populace.[63]

Fawzi and Bahia were forced to leave the country soon after the first arrests. After consultation with Bahá'í institutions, they went to Tunis where they served until 1966. Fawzi went first to prepare things for the family. That left Bahia alone with the two children. It was a perilous time for her: at one point, she 'was attacked by the parents of one of the Bahá'í prisoners, almost strangling her'. After six months' isolation, she was able to join Fawzi in Tunis. Her sacrifices resulted in her being able to attend the World Congress in London at the end of the Crusade.[64]

Later in 1963, Fawzi visited Egypt for the first time in a decade when his brother died. Getting permanent residence in Tunis proved to be very difficult and in 1966 they looked at other pioneering possibilities. They considered Limoges, France, because Fawzi loved to work with ceramics, which the city is known for, but ultimately chose to move to California, where his cousin and her husband, Bahia and Robert Gulick, lived.[65] Fawzi served on several Local Spiritual Assemblies before his passing in 1975.[66]

In 1976, Bahia married Dennis Garden and continued to serve the Faith until her passing in Oregon in 2013.

Luella McKay, John and Earleta Fleming, and Alyce Janssen

On 24 October 1953, two weeks after the Zeins arrived, Luella McKay (1918–1995), John (1928–2007) and Earleta Fleming (b. 1922) and Alyce Barbara May Janssen (1900–1964) arrived in Spanish Morocco.[67]

Luella was from Oregon, United States, but her family moved to San Francisco when she was young. In 1937, her mother encountered Rose Shaw who brought her into the Bahá'í Faith. Luella became the first black Bahá'í youth in the city. In 1945, she married Jasper McKay. The Faith was the centre of her life.

Californian John Fleming became a Bahá'í in October 1953 and just a month later submitted his application to pioneer in the Crusade, stating: 'It is my duty as a Bahá'í to help spread Bahá'u'lláh's teaching. Shoghi Effendi considers Africa as a key goal country during the Ten Year Crusade.' Shortly before submitting his application form in October 1953, he married Earleta Cranshaw, who had been a Bahá'í since 1944 and served for a year on the San Francisco Local Assembly.

Luella had attended the Intercontinental Teaching Conference in Wilmette and afterward wrote to volunteer to pioneer to Madeira Island or Africa, offering herself, her sister Earleta, Earleta's husband, John, and her friend Alyce. Since she, Earleta and John were black and Alyce was white, she requested a post where mixed race groups were accepted. The Committee sent them to Spanish Morocco.[68]

Luella recalled

with profound tenderness the feeling of oneness, the mutual sharing of resources both tangible and intangible, that marked every step of what might otherwise have been a harrowing and distressing experience: the bedsprings without mattresses, the leaks in the ceilings, the unwanted lice, the bugs in the flour. These physical inconveniences intensified our fervor and increased our dedication to the goal we had set out to accomplish.[69]

Since they were the only Americans in the area, the presence of Luella, John, Earleta and Alyce was quickly known. Though not able to teach directly due to language and governmental reasons, they attracted people by their character. John had medical and hospital experience and quickly became an unofficial village medic, with people bringing their injured to him for help.[70] By early 1955, their quiet teaching efforts had resulted in declarations of faith by two Spanish Moroccans and two Spaniards in Cueta.[71]

In the summer of 1954, Shoghi Effendi asked if any of Luella's group would be able to pioneer to Spanish Guinea. Though it was extremely difficult for a single woman to be granted a visa, Luella was given a one-month visa and in March 1955 sailed to Fernando Pó (now called Bioko). Her visa was extended to six months so she could study the native music and languages. Soon thereafter, however, another pioneer arrived who did not teach with wisdom. The new pioneer 'acted very unwisely and without authority in teaching his creed. He became carried away with his enthusiasm and so was misunderstood and jailed.' The result was that Luella was forced to return to Spanish Guinea, leaving behind one Bahá'í, Titus Appan Uwak. Titus was instrumental in saving all of Luella's books by smuggling them out of her hotel under his clothes.[72]

Earleta, John and Alyce all returned to America in August 1956.[73] John had accepted to return and help his ailing uncle with his business.[74] Earleta and John later returned to Spanish Morocco in September 1958 and stayed until 1961, when their daughter, Kimberly, became very ill and the local doctors were unable to diagnose the cause.[75]

Luella remained at her post until May 1959 when the Local Spiritual Assembly of Cueta was formed. Returning to America, Luella organized the first certified school of cosmetology for the inmates of a Detroit prison. She hosted many firesides and deepenings, gave lectures and served on the Goals Committee for Michigan. In 1981, she wrote a book that called African-Americans to a 'spiritual awakening of the noble role they must play in the building of the Kingdom of God and the new world order'. She died in 1995.[76]

Alyce continued to pioneer, going to Switzerland, Italy and the Canary Islands, before settling one last time in Santa Rosa, California.[77]

RIO DE ORO (NOW SPANISH SAHARA)

Amin Battah

Amin Battah (1926–2010) was born into a Bahá'í family in Cairo, Egypt. When Shoghi Effendi announced the goals of the Ten Year Crusade, Amin immediately arose and, in spite of having a good job with the Government, chose one of the two most desolate goals that the Guardian had given to the National Spiritual Assembly of Egypt: Rio de Oro on the northwest coast of Africa. His goal was a desert colony of Spain and also a military zone. Amin travelled overland to Tripoli where he managed to obtain a visa. When he arrived in the town of Villa Cisneros in the Spanish Sahara in early October 1953, the Spanish military authorities were not happy to have him there and kept him away from the local population. On 28 October, after just a few weeks, Amin, along with another Knight of Bahá'u'lláh, Muhammad Mustafa Soliman (see next story), was forced to leave. The two Knights were flown to Tetuán in Morocco. Amin then went to Tangier in the International Zone of Morocco. Unfortunately, in neither place was he able to acquire a visa that would allow him to stay. Amin later learned that after he and Muhammad Mustafa were given their visas for Spanish Sahara, the Spanish Government prohibited any further visas to the area.[78]

The Guardian told him to go to Benghazi in Libya. Amin stayed in that post for a year. He arrived with virtually no money and had a difficult time finding work. Finally, he was able to get a job as a teacher in a place called Farzougha, 70 kilometres east of Benghazi. When, two months after his departure for his teaching post, the Bahá'ís in Benghazi had heard nothing from Amin, they went to check up on him. When they arrived, they found

A road sign reading Farzougha. . . . on the roadside, but besides an old farmhouse well off the road there was nothing. Out of the farmhouse came Amin with hair and beard slightly less than a cave man's. The nomad parents of the children in school had kept him alive. They brought him bread and food and milk.[79]

In August 1954, the Egyptian Bahá'ís in Benghazi were forced to leave and Amin returned to Egypt. For the next two decades, he suffered intermittent imprisonment, including beatings and the bastinado. In spite of his ill treatment, Amin remained an active member of the Egyptian national Bahá'í community until his passing in 2010.[80]

Muhammad Mustafa Soliman

Muhammad Mustafa Soliman (1898–1981) was 16 when he first heard of 'Abdu'l-Bahá. One day he visited a friend who worked at the telegraph office and saw a copy of the book, *Ten Days in the Light of Acca*, on the desk. When a third person came by, picked up the book and commented unfavourably on 'Abdu'l-Bahá, Mr Mustafa retorted, 'A Person with such principles and so many followers cannot be but True. I am one of His Followers!', which was news to his friend. Muhammad Mustafa later served for many years as the secretary or chairman of the Egyptian National Spiritual Assembly and was the first Bahá'í to have an exclusively Bahá'í marriage when he wed Farida Naimi, and the first to register his children as Bahá'ís.[81]

When the Guardian announced the Ten Year Crusade, Mr Mustafa had been a Bahá'í for almost 40 years, had made several pilgrimages where he met the Guardian, and was the chairman of the Egyptian National Assembly. During these visits, he had translated a number of important documents at the request of Shoghi Effendi. When the Ten Year Crusade was announced, he immediately arose and chose Spanish Sahara as his goal to fulfil. Leaving Cairo, he travelled to Benghazi, where his son, Rowshan, lived, arriving on 24 August 1953. Rowshan writes:

> All the money he had left in his pocket when he got here, literally would not have bought him a simple meal, and here he was telling me that he intends to go to Spanish Sahara, some 6000 Kms. away. I called Yusuf Jarrah who was a pioneer with his wife and two children, and we consulted. Yusuf knew a bank manager. We went to

see him together. I obtained a loan on my salary and Yusuf added his guarantee. None of us had any savings really. With the loan and a contribution from Yusuf and his wife Hayat, father was on his way.[82]

From Benghazi, Muhammad Mustafa travelled by bus to Tripoli, where he obtained visas for Tunisia, Algeria, Spain, Morocco and Spanish Sahara. From Tripoli, he flew to Tunisia, rode a train to Algeria, then sailed to Alicante, Spain. On 30 September, he sailed to Tangier. While on board the ship

> he noticed a couple of young men sitting on some sort of bench. He could hear them speak in Persian together. He sat next to them and picked up a conversation in English. They did not seem in a mood to speak with a stranger. He asked them where were they going and they said to Tangier. Then he asked why they were going to Tangier. They looked to one another and seemed very uneasy and replied 'For business'. Mr. Mustafa pressed further with his questions: 'Which business? Pioneering?' The two strangers looked surprisingly at each other, and were more surprised to hear their questioner say: 'Alláh'u'Abhá !', and responded by hugging him and introduced themselves: They were Manúchihr Hizari and Hormoz Zandeh from Iran, who became Knights of Bahá'u'lláh to Morocco International Zone (Tangier).[83]

On 4 October 1953, Muhammad Mustafa arrived at Cabo Juby in Spanish Sahara. He was treated 'very generously' by the government officials and was able to visit a school. Six days later, he was allowed to continue to the capital town of the territory, Al 'Aioun. The officials were so helpful that they allowed him to fly there on a military plane. In a letter to his son, Rowshan, he wrote that upon his arrival,

> Two officers met me . . . and took me to the government house where I was given a beautiful large room with bath and nice furniture. The inhabitants presented their respect to me every day and they said they were in a feast. On Tuesday I was received by the Governor to whom I expressed my gratitude to the Spanish government consuls and personnel, both civil and military for their kindness. I said that I came to this country because of a deep desire to know its

inhabitants, my Faith and belief is harmony amongst the peoples of all the nations, to the extent that to me the interests of Spain are as dear as those of Egypt and the Sahara. For this reason I am not concerned with politics because I consider it the cause of separation between peoples. My other reason for coming to this country is to learn the Hassaniya language and study the old scripts that were left by Sheikh Ma el-'Ainin. He repeated that I was welcome and asked how long I intended to stay. I answered that that depended on two matters: the first being your approval, for if you do not approve, I shall leave immediately this very moment. The second reason was my waiting for news from Egypt, if all be well I shall stay for some time, otherwise I shall leave regretfully. He asked what sort of news? I answered that these were family news, the health and education of my children and such matters. I added that I do not need any material assistance, I had what was necessary, all I need is moral assistance. The Governor said that I may stay as long as I wished.[84]

For three weeks, Mr Mustafa was allowed to visit anyone he wished and he went many times to visit the local people in their tents, shops and, sometimes, their homes. On 28 October, however, he and Amin Battah were loaded onto a plane and flown to Tetuán in Morocco. Muhammad Mustafa's efforts, however, resulted in two new Bahá'ís in Al 'Aioun.

Shoghi Effendi suggested that he go to Benghazi and he worked there from December 1953 until July of the next year. He then moved to Tunisia and Egypt. In 1954, he was appointed an Auxiliary Board member and spent the next two years back in Tunisia where he helped prepare for the election of the first Regional Spiritual Assembly of North West Africa.[85]

After Shoghi Effendi passed away, Muhammad Mustafa vociferously told everyone to turn to the Custodians. In 1958, he returned to Egypt when the Government disbanded all Bahá'í assemblies and, as an Auxiliary Board member, rallied the Egyptian Bahá'ís. He was jailed in 1965 and again in 1972, this time at the age of 75 along with 92 other Bahá'ís, including women and children. They were accused of treason and espionage. Fortunately, they were released after 40 days.[86] Mr Mustafa served on the Continental Board of Counsellors for the last six years of his life. He passed on in Cairo in 1981 at the age of 84.[87]

FRENCH WEST AFRICA
(INCLUDES PARTS OF WHAT ARE NOW CÔTE D'IVOIRE, NIGER, MALI, BURKINA FASO, SENEGAL, MAURITANIA)
Labíb and Habíb Esfahani

In 1952, Labíb Esfahani (1923–2013) was a successful Egyptian banker from Port Said, who spoke Arabic, French, English, Italian, Greek and Persian. He was quite comfortable working at his bank, but the Guardian's call the next year changed his life. To fulfil one of the Guardian's goals, he left his job, found another with a bank in Dakar in French West Africa (in the part that is now called Senegal) and moved there on 5 November 1953.[88] When he arrived at the airport, the Customs officer

> asked him for the object of his visit. Labíb said he came to work in Dakar. The Officer refused him entry and Labíb went out of the airport not knowing what to do. Suddenly the Officer sent after him and asked him whether he knew English. Labíb answered he did. The Officer asked him to help him translate letters in English for him, and Labíb did that. Then the Officer asked him if he would translate his answers to the letters in English and type them for him. That Labíb also did. Then the Officer told him that he will let him in.[89]

In 1955, Labíb moved to Abidjan, a part of French West Africa that became the Ivory Coast (now Côte d'Ivoire).[90] Three years later, Labíb met Lucienne Arakélian and the couple wished to have a Bahá'í marriage. Since there was no Local or National Assembly in French West Africa at that time, Labíb had to write to the Regional Spiritual Assembly of North West Africa, based in Tunis, 4,000 kilometres away, to find out how to do so.[91]

Between 1964 and 1983, Labíb worked for the same bank in Dakar where he had previously been employed. He was soon sent to Koalack, about 150 kilometres southeast of Dakar, as a branch manager. While there, he made trips into The Gambia with Hussein Ardekani since they were both on the National Teaching Committee. Hussein would drive his car from Dakar to Koalack, then they would take Labíb's car into The Gambia. On one trip, they met a Gambian Bahá'í who said that his daughter lived in Koalack with her husband. When they returned to Koalack, they looked up the couple and discovered that the husband had four wives and many children. Labíb taught them about the Faith and the whole family became Bahá'ís.[92]

Later, Labíb worked in a branch of his bank in Nigeria. During his stay in Nigeria, he was one of the organizers of an International Bahá'í Conference and helped with the teaching work in Lagos, Port Harcourt, Aba and Kano. In 1983, the family was obliged to leave Africa and move to France. He died in Versailles in 2013. Mohsen Enayat, one of the young Egyptian Bahá'ís who pioneered during the Crusade, wrote:

> Since our childhood Labíb was a hero in our eyes for his games on the beach of Port Said. Later as a youth he again was a hero in our eyes for his decision to pioneer with his elder brother Habíb to West Africa at a time we knew little about the Senegal. They opened our eyes to a service that up to that point was not familiar to Egyptians: leaving the safe life of Egypt and venturing into the jungles of black Africa. Their example was a door opening that allowed a number of youth to participate in the Ten Year Plan in response to the Beloved Guardian's call. After accomplishing his duty, Labíb can now proudly wing his way to the Abhá Kingdom.[93]

In April 1954, Labíb was followed by his brother Habíb (1922–2001), who also pioneered to Dakar. Before pioneering, Habíb had worked as an accountant in Port Said and served on the Local Spiritual Assembly there. He stayed in Dakar until being forced leave in 1960, going to Côte d'Ivoire. He remained in Côte d'Ivoire until his death.[94]

THE GAMBIA

Fariburz Rúzbihyán

Fariburz Rúzbihyán (Feriborz Roozebehyan) (about 1892–?) arrived in Bathurst (now called Banjul), The Gambia, from Iran on 19 February 1954. He was born in Bombay, India, into a Bahá'í family. His father, Kaykhusraw Rúzbihyán, had been a member of the Bombay Local Assembly in 1905 when American Sydney Sprague was in Lahore,

*Fawzi and Bahia Zein,
Knights of Bahá'u'lláh to
Spanish Morocco, with their
children Kamal* (standing)
and Cherif, 1960

*Alyce Janssen, Knight of Bahá'u'lláh
to Spanish Morocco*

Knights of Bahá'u'lláh to Spanish Morocco, on the day they left to pioneer. Left to right:
Alyce Janssen, John Fleming, Earleta Fleming, Luella McKay, with Luella's son Nicholas

Knights of Bahá'u'lláh to Morocco, International Zone. Left to right, back row: *Abbas Rafí'í, Muhammad-Ali Jalali, Hormoz Zendeh, Manuchehr Hezari, Hussein Ardekani;* front row: *Elsie Austin, Sháyistih Rafí'í, child, 'Alí-Akbar Rafí'í, Nosrat Ardekani*

Evelyn and Richard Walters, Knights of Bahá'u'lláh to Morocco International Zone, with Dorothy Baker

Mary and Richard Suhm, Knights of Bahá'u'lláh to Morocco International Zone, with Ellen Sims (right), *pioneer to French Cameroon, at their leaving party in West Englewood, New Jersey, 1954*

First Spiritual Assembly of the Bahá'ís of Casablanca, Morocco, 1954

*Amín Battah, Knight of Bahá'u'lláh
to Río de Oro (Spanish Sahara)*

*Muhammad Mustafa Soliman,
Knight of Bahá'u'lláh to Río de Oro
(Spanish Sahara)*

*Habíb Esfahaní, Knight of
Bahá'u'lláh to French West Africa.
His brother Labib (not shown) was
also named a Knight*

Fariburz Rúzbihyán (left), *Knight of Bahá'u'lláh to The Gambia, with Mavis Nymon, Knight of Bahá'u'lláh to Togo, and Nelson Ethan Thomas, the first Gambian Bahá'í*

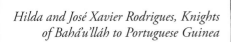

Hilda and José Xavier Rodrigues, Knights of Bahá'u'lláh to Portuguese Guinea

Adib Radi Baghdadi. Knight of Bahá'u'lláh to Hadhramaut. His wife Vahidih (not shown) was also named a Knight

Husayn Halabi, Knight of Bahá'u'lláh to Hadhramaut

Suhayl Samandarí, Knight of Bahá'u'lláh to Italian Somaliland

Mihdi and Ursula Samandari, Knights of Bahá'u'lláh to Italian Somaliland, with Hand of the Cause George Townshend

Knights of Bahá'u'lláh on board the African Sun*: Fred Schechter, Knight of Bahá'u'lláh to French Somaliland* (second from left) *with his parents; Frederick and Elizabeth Laws, Knights of Bahá'u'lláh to Basutoland, on the right*

Sabrí and Fahíma (Raissa) Elias, Knights of Bahá'u'lláh to French Somaliland (Djibouti)

Pakistan. When Sprague fell seriously ill, Kaykhusraw volunteered to care for him and when things were the grimmest, Kaykhusraw prayed and offered his life, that of a teashop owner, for that of the man who 'had left his native land and travelled far, in an alien land, under trying conditions, to serve the Cause of God'. Sydney Sprague survived, but Kaykhusraw did not.[95]

Fariburz Rúzbihyán attended St Xavier College in 1907, but was forced to leave due to illness. When he was advised to leave India for his health, he moved to Iran.[96] He went on pilgrimage in 1909 and met Dr Susan Moody, who was on her way to open a medical clinic for women in Iran at the request of 'Abdu'l-Bahá. The Master told Mr Rúzbihyán that Susan was his mother and he must go with her and assist her, which he did until she passed away in 1934.[97] With the announcement of the Ten Year Crusade, Fariburz Rúzbihyán, who was in his mid-60s, arose and at first tried to go to Bhutan. Unable to obtain a visa, he changed his goal to The Gambia.[98]

Mr Rúzbihyán suffered from asthma and fever and these soon put him in the hospital in Bathurst. During his first six months in the country, he was hospitalized four times for ten to fifteen days each.[99] But instead of being detrimental to his efforts to teach the Faith, it introduced him to Nelson Ethan Thomas, who quickly became a Bahá'í:

Up to six or seven months, however I tried, I only was able to confirm one Christian Syrian and was so fed up with illness and lack of success that I wrote a petition to our most beloved Guardian asking for his fervent prayers in the Holy Shrines for my success and health. As soon as the petition reached Haifa my health improved and I was able to confirm one more Christian in the Hospital in the same ward where I was. There also I got an inspiration to try to collect some of the prophecies in the Qur'án regarding this Holy Faith, for the benefit of the Muslim population who have a majority here. As soon as I was out of the hospital I collected these prophecies and began to teach the Cause to an influential Muslim and in a short time he was convinced and confirmed. Then the mercies of the Most Merciful God began to pour on me and in a short time I was able to get a large number of the pure souls confirmed in this Holy Faith, and this was only due to the fervent prayers of our most beloved Guardian. During the Riḍván of this year [1955] four

Local Spiritual Assemblies were formed in four towns of Bathurst, Serekunda, Lamin and Birkama and a group was formed in the town of Bakau. Now there are several hundred Baha'is in Gambia and daily this number is increasing.[100]

At one point in 1955, Fariburz Rúzbihyán went to the town of Birkama, about 25 miles away. The town had about 15,000 inhabitants and he went there to see a friend he had met at football games in Bathurst. The friend had not expressed any particular interest in the Bahá'í Faith, so Mr Rúzbihyán was very surprised when he arrived in Birkama:

There I met an acquaintance whom I had met in Bathurst . . . told him that I had come to Birkama to speak to some few people about the Bahá'í Faith. When I told him this, he advised me to go to the Muslim Mosque and await him, because he was going to bring a large number of his friends. After waiting for about half an hour all at once I saw a large number of people coming towards the Mosque and at first I was taken aback because I thought that they may be coming to punish me for defiling their Mosque with my footsteps, but later I found that all saluted me in Islamic fashion and sur- rounded me. My friend also came towards me and stood beside me to translate my words to those who could not understand. At first I was too dazed be able to speak but later I mentioned the Greatest Name and asked Bahá'u'lláh to help me. Receiving strength I began first by giving them the prophecies from Qur'án for this Faith regarding the appearance of Mahdi (the Báb) and Masaya (Bahá'u'lláh) and then I gave a short history of Faith and at the end the principles of this Holy Faith. On conclusion I asked them whether any person wished to ask any question and only one person asked that whether in this Faith a black man will have the same status as a white man and I replied that this Faith abolishes all sorts of prejudices especially for colour, and whether white, black, yellow or red everyone is to be considered as human and all should love each other and this reply satisfied him so much that he at once came forward and asked me to enlist him as a Baha'i.[101]

Fariburz Rúzbihyán was only able to stay in The Gambia for two years, leaving in April 1956 because of his health, but during that time,

300 people accepted the Faith of Bahá'u'lláh and six Local Spiritual Assemblies were formed. He returned in 1957 at the request of Shoghi Effendi and bought a house in the town of Serekunda to serve as a Bahá'í Centre.[102]

PORTUGUESE GUINEA (NOW GUINEA-BISSAU)

José Xavier Rodrigues and Hilda Summers

José Rodrigues (1931–1985) and Hilda Summers (1916–2004), from Portugal, pioneered to Portuguese Guinea. José, known as Xavier, first encountered the Bahá'í Faith at the age of nineteen when he attended a meeting at the home of American pioneers Valeria Nichols and Charlotte Stirratt. He quickly became a Bahá'í.[103] Hilda became a Bahá'í in 1948 and was on the first Local Spiritual Assembly of Lisbon the next year. She married Xavier in 1951 when he was 20 and she was 37.[104]

Two years later, in September 1953, after attending the Stockholm Intercontinental Teaching Conference, the couple heeded the Guardian's call and pioneered to Bissau, the capital of Portuguese Guinea (today known as Guinea-Bissau) on 19 September 1953. Xavier and Hilda were only able to stay until March 1955 when their application for residence was refused. Immediately after the rejection, they received a police summons ordering them to leave on the next boat. Their efforts were not without results, though it wasn't until after they left that they bore fruit. They had been able to teach the Faith to Duarte Vieira who later became a Bahá'í in Portugal. Having committed themselves as pioneers, Xavier and Hilda were back in Africa in June 1956 as pioneers in Luanda, Angola, where they stayed until just before violence broke out in 1960.[105] Returning to Portugal, Hilda was elected to the Local Spiritual Assembly of Amador and then, in 1962, to the first National Spiritual Assembly of Portugal.[106]

The family remained in Portugal until 1973 when Xavier pioneered to Dili in Portuguese Timor. He only stayed for ten months, but was under constant police surveillance. Returning to Portugal, his health deteriorated and forced him to leave his job as a miner. He spent the remaining years of his life 'making beautiful translations of Tablets and prayers of the Central figures, and messages, letters and compilations received from the Universal House of Justice. He had a natural gift for translation and took great pleasure in this service.'[107] Hilda continued her service to the Faith, being elected to the Local Assemblies of Viana do Castelo and Lisbon.[108]

ITALIAN SOMALILAND (NOW PART OF SOMALIA)

Suhayl Samandarí, Ursula and Mihdi Samandarí

Suhayl Samandarí became a Knight of Bahá'u'lláh when he pioneered to Italian Somaliland in March of 1953, one of the first to arise and fill one of Shoghi Effendi's goals. He arrived in Mogadishu with only a two-month tourist visa, but he managed to set up a display of his own paintings and Persian handicrafts at a commercial fair soon after his arrival. He noted that the result was 'rather satisfactory. Because when I applied for extension of my visa, it was granted for 18 months.' That allowed him to obtain a licence to open a shop where he sold handicrafts from Persia. In November, he was joined by his aunt and uncle, Dr Mihdi (?–2008) and Ursula Samandarí (1909–2003).[109]

Ursula Newman was born in Surrey to a Church of England family. In 1936, she learned of the Bahá'í Faith from Richard St Barbe Baker, Hasan Balyuzi and Dorothy Ferraby and became a Bahá'í two years later. She noted that 'Although I believed in Jesus Christ I was no longer a believer in Church teachings. I first attended Bahá'í meetings out of impersonal interest and a desire to meet Persians. I read and studied and attended meetings for two years. *Gleanings* (a book of Writings by Bahá'u'lláh) was the strongest influence.'[110]

Ursula first pioneered in 1945, going to St Ives in the United Kingdom. Along with Kathleen Brown and Jessica Young, she was the first to pioneer in the British Isles in the Six Year Plan.[111] Ursula served on the Local Spiritual Assembly of London and in 1948, moved to Dublin, Ireland, where she was a member of its first Local Spiritual Assembly and served as secretary to George Townshend (later named a Hand of the Cause). Olive McKinley remembered that Ursula was a 'magnificent teacher of the Faith' and said that 'she had a wonderful sense of humour and everything seemed a joy and hilarious occasion to her – no wonder David Hofman (Mr Townshend's biographer) wrote that George Townshend missed his secretary so much when she had gone from Dublin.' The next year, Ursula moved to Belfast where she met Mihdi Samandarí. Ursula was a member of the National Spiritual Assembly of the British Isles from 1945 until 1951.[112]

Ursula and Mihdi married in 1951 and pioneered to Nairobi, Kenya two years later. Answering Shoghi Effendi's call for pioneers to virgin areas, the Samandarís moved to Mogadishu in Italian Somaliland in November 1953.[113] Mihdi, as a doctor, found work at the Ministry of Health. Not speaking the local language, he needed an interpreter/language teacher and Abdullahi Abdi was offered the position. Every morning for two months Abdullahi spent three to four hours in the Samandarí home teaching them the language.[114]

Abdullahi was very impressed with Mihdi and Ursula. He wrote, 'They were so open-hearted and extremely kind to me especially when I would visit their home. They were such happy people always smiling. I understood from the beginning that they were quite different from other people . . .' He continued: 'The foremost thing that attracted me to the glorious Bahá'í Faith before even reading any Bahá'í books was the character, love and attitude that I saw in the Samandaris.' One of Mihdi's patients was General Daud Abdulla, the chief commander of the Somali armed forces. The General was very taken with the Samandaris and soon became an undeclared Bahá'í. One day General Abdulla asked Abdullahi: 'Have you become a Bahá'í?' Abdullahi replied, 'Why not? The Bahá'í Faith is the solution to all the problems of the world'.[115]

Then in February 1955, Aziz Yazdi came to Somalia on his way to pioneer in Kenya. Mihdi asked if he could introduce Abdullahi as a Bahá'í when Aziz arrived. Abdullahi replied:

'Yes, why not?' He jumped and embraced me. And then he ran to and called his wife Ursula, who also embraced me so heartily as soon as she was told. We went to the airport together. He asked me if I knew the Bahá'í greeting. Yes, I told him as I learned it from the great Bahá'í book – 'Bahá'u'lláh and the New Era' and it is 'Alláh'u'Abhá' and I was ready to say it to Mr. Aziz Yazdi. Dr. Samandarí and his wife Ursula went to the airport and brought Mr. Yazdi home. I told Mr. Yazdi, 'Alláh'u'Abhá' as soon as I met him and he embraced me so hard with penetrating love and smile. He was a great man full of Bahá'í love like his friends the Samandaris. I will never forget his spiritually shining face.[116]

Abdullahi immediately began teaching his friends about the Bahá'í Faith and bringing them to the Samandaris. By 21 April 1955, his friends, Mohammed Elmi, Abdullahi Egal, Hassan Jama, Mohamed Sugulle and Ali Said had also become Bahá'ís and they were able to form the first Local Spiritual Assembly of Mogadishu. Within a year, several Muslim clerics, including a famous leader educated in Egypt, began to attack the Faith in their mosques, saying that the misguided Bahá'ís were misleading the country's young people and 'we have to stop it before it is too late'. Abdullahi's father, who was unhappy that his son had accepted the Faith, insisted that the Samandaris would soon be deported and that Abdullahi would probably be killed. The son quoted the Qur'anic verse 'Welcome death, if you are true believers'. His father didn't question him again.[117]

Ursula Samandarí served on the Regional Spiritual Assembly of North East Africa from 1961 until 1970. At the request of the Universal House of Justice, the Samandarís pioneered to Cameroon in 1971 and Ursula was quickly elected to the Cameroonian National Assembly, serving from 1972 to 1974 and 1974 to 1986. Mihdi served as a Counsellor in the 1970s.[118] Ursula passed away at her pioneer post in 2003.[119]

FRENCH SOMALILAND (NOW DJIBOUTI)

Fred Schechter

Fred Schechter (1927–2017) became a Bahá'í in New York in 1949. His first memorable encounter with the Bahá'í Faith was in 1947 while taking a required course on comparative religion taught by Dr Raymond Frank Piper. The reading included five pages of the Bahá'í Writings. Piper had given a talk at the Centenary Program in Chicago in 1944[120] and later had the privilege of an interview with Shoghi Effendi. In 1949, Fred noticed an advertisement for a Bahá'í meeting in the Syracuse University newspaper. He remembered the Faith from his philosophy course and decided to attend. Lowell Johnson hosted the meeting in his home and Fred was the first to show up for the meeting. While waiting, Lowell asked if he would like to read something from the Founder of the Faith. When given a copy of *Gleanings from the Writings of Bahá'u'lláh*, he read the first page and thought, 'if there is a true religion, this is it'. Fred attended meetings for about nine months.[121]

Fred's relationship with his parents was important to him and he asked their acceptance in his life-changing decisions, like joining the armed forces and becoming a Bahá'í. Fred said:

> My parents live in New York. On Spring Break I went home to talk to my parents about the step I'm about to take in enrolling as a Bahá'í. We came from a Jewish background so my mother took me to the Synagogue to the Friday night service as the Rabbi was meant to inspire people. In the middle of the service my mother looked at me with the look of 'ok, you can enroll as a Bahá'í'. My father was relatively indifferent.[122]

Years later Fred discovered a pamphlet on the Bahá'í Faith he had collected at the 1939 New York World's Fair. He had actually first heard of the Bahá'í Faith when he was 12 years old.

In early 1950, the University librarian, William Miller, asked Fred about his future plans and if he would like to pursue a degree in Library Science. William also pointed out that with this degree it would be possible to find jobs in any country. With another year of education, Fred acquired a degree in something that would prove useful in his future. He graduated with an AB degree in American Studies in 1951 and received a Master of Science degree in Library Science in June 1952.[123]

In January 1951, Shoghi Effendi wrote a letter about the Africa Two Year Plan that started Fred thinking about that continent. With Bill and Marguerite Sears at Green Acre that summer, he mentioned going to Africa. The immediate response was, 'Someone get paper and pencil.' 'Someone get an envelope.' 'Someone get a stamp.' They weren't going to let this offer get away![124] Fred wanted to pioneer indefinitely, but told his parents that it was a British two-year plan, insinuating that he would only be gone for two years. They didn't see any problem with that. His mother had read some of the messages of the Guardian, and when the objectives were explained to her, she said, 'If Shoghi Effendi said it's alright then it's alright.'[125]

The path to Africa was convoluted. In March 1952, he was approved to go to Somaliland. Four months later, he was to be partnered with Ted Weiss and they would be supported by the National Fund for six months. In August, the Africa Committee of the American National Assembly wrote Fred, saying that the 'work situation there is hopeless' and suggesting that they go to Kenya instead. While waiting for his future to be worked out, Fred had applied for work in the United States – and received seven job offers. His goal was to pioneer so he took the only one, at the Queensboro Public Library in New York, that would accept him on a short-term basis. He began work in early August. But in October, the British Africa Committee asked if he would consider going to Northern Rhodesia, to which he responded, 'I am completely at your disposal.'[126]

By February 1953, he and the Africa Committee had settled on Kenya and he planned to join Frederick and Elizabeth Laws in New York to sail aboard the *African Sun*. Fred received his visa for Kenya later in February and was disappointed to find it was only valid for six months. The day before he sailed, Fred discovered that he couldn't leave the country without permission from the American Draft Board. He set up a quick meeting with the Board and received his permission. Fred and the Laws sailed on 10 March and had a leisurely seven-week cruise around Africa, stopping at Walvis Bay, Cape Town, Port Elizabeth, Durban, Lorenço Marques and finally Mombasa.[127]

Fred and the Laws arrived in Nairobi on 1 May and were met by Ted Cardell. Fred noted that the Bahá'í community there consisted of seven Africans, three Persians, three English pioneers and three Americans.[128] They included Aziz Yazdi, who later served as a Counsellor member at the International Teaching Centre, and Claire Gung, who became a Knight of Bahá'u'lláh for Southern Rhodesia. Fred was very impressed with the Bahá'í community, writing:

> My personal impressions of Bahá'í Community life in Nairobi are that it's quite wonderful. We've got people from four continents, with all their differences, living together, helping each other grow and mature . . .
>
> We have found that our new Bahá'ís declare themselves more from what may be termed spiritual reasons. They accept the same provisions as all Bahá'ís, but the details of Administration and the various ordinances are understood slowly . . . At our public meetings and firesides, the new Bahá'ís take turns as speakers and chairmen. Some of their talks have been excellent . . .
>
> When our beloved Guardian's cable reached us calling for pioneers, four of six Africans volunteered . . . Actually it is the African who gets the contacts, interests his friends, and generally spreads the

news around. The pioneer is there to prove the Faith by his life and words and to guide the new community.[129]

By June, pioneers were on the move to fill the Guardian's Ten Year Crusade goals. On 17 June, Bessie Barnham, secretary of the American Africa Committee, wrote Fred that the American National Assembly wanted him to pioneer to French Somaliland.

Fred received a three-month visa for French Somaliland on 12 June and on 24 July sailed for Djibouti. With a stop in Mogadishu, where he was met by Suhayl Samandari, he arrived in Djibouti on 2 August. Over the next month, Fred wrote about his impressions:

> It is Hot! It wasn't bad enough to find such heat, but the French authorities toyed with me all day, decided whether or not they should let me off the ship. This was from 9 in the morning until 5 in the afternoon when the ship sailed. After deciding I wasn't dangerous and getting a $300 bond, they let me ashore. I had supper and went to sleep. I haven't stopped perspiring since I arrived . . .
>
> Djibouti is a pleasant enough city, but the heat is terrible. Yesterday I wandered around through the streets just looking around and saying Ya Bahá'u'l-Abhá. I'm the only American at all in French Somaliland . . . Very few people understand English and my French is a little crude, but so far I've been able to get along. [4 August 53]
>
> Djibouti is one city the National Geographic will overlook, and I think the French would like me to overlook it too. They already think that I'm a newspaper man or a writer of some sort, and are not too happy with the prospects of my staying around . . . As most towns, Djibouti is divided into various sections. There's what may be termed the European residential area; the business part, divided into Greek owned shops, Indian and Arab shops, and the big shipping agencies; then there's the Arab quarter; and finally the huge shack-town where the vast majority of the Somalis live.
>
> With this divers population, the languages used are also divers. The population can't exceed 25,000, and the languages are Arabic, Somali, French, Greek, Gujerati, Italian, and combinations of all of them. Arabic could be considered the lingua franca . . .
>
> Almost the entire population of French Somaliland lives in Djibouti. There are a few thousand nomadic shepherds tending their

flocks in the hills around the Ethiopian border . . . Most of the country is lava rock with not a thing growing on it. From talking with some Somalis, I've learned that before World War II, there wasn't a green thing in Djibouti . . . but during the war . . . the British blockaded the port and the French had nothing to do so they imported some trees from Ethiopia . . .

At certain of the street corners are water pipes where the Somali women and Arabs gather with their water cans to get the day's supply of fresh water . . .

Since nothing grows here, everything is imported. The only local industries are the port and a salt mill . . .

Djibouti is the other extreme from a tourist resort, and I've been blessed with a security officer following me around . . .[130]

Fred became friendly with the Chief of the Sureté and let him know why he was there: 'We'd go lawn bowling together and talk about everything.'

Finding work was Fred's first concern. On 26 September, he wrote, 'I had a job and then I didn't have one.' One place wanted an American, but when the Englishman in charge was replaced by a non-English-speaking Frenchman, the job disappeared.[131] To fill in his time, he began giving English lessons. In mid-October, General Charles de Gaulle visited Djibouti and the locals organized a parade. Fred noted, 'I think the army was left over from Waterloo. One of the tanks broke down in the middle of the square and all the cranking barking dogs couldn't move it. Finally, they had to drag it away.'[132]

Teaching the Bahá'í Faith was restricted by the Guardian's admonition not to teach openly and by Fred's limited French. In September, however, he went to an office looking for work and met a Somali man who spoke English. They began to get together after work and talked about many things, including the Faith. The man was Catholic and had represented French Somaliland during the Holy Year 1950, which had included an audience with the Pope. The man and his wife read one of Fred's pamphlets about the Bahá'í Faith.[133]

By late October, it was becoming obvious that jobs were essentially non-existent and renewing his visa a big problem. Fred noted, 'Unofficially, I've been told to stop talking with the non-French population if I hope to renew my visa.' The unofficial word came from his friend, the

Chief of the Sureté, who 'reminded me of the French motto "Liberté, égalité, fraternité" (Liberty, Equality, Fraternity) in Paris" but then added ". . . not in Djibouti."'[134] That severely limited his time with his Somali contact. On 5 November, his visa extension was refused. Two days later, he was on the train to Addis Ababa with a 15-day visa. Arriving there after 38 hours, he noted, 'This is a very beautiful country after Somaliland and I'm freezing.' He began with what he thought was a two-month visa,[135] though his goal was to return to Djibouti.[136]

Initially, job opportunities in Addis Ababa looked promising at the National Library, but something always delayed it. In December, the US Africa Committee asked if he would consider pioneering to the Fezzan in Libya. 'Abdu'l-Bahá had been threatened with exile in the inhospitable desert of that area and the Guardian wanted Bahá'ís to pioneer there. Fred's response was:

> Am ready to leave for Fezzan on the next camel. I can imagine what it's like if God didn't permit 'Abdu'l-Bahá to go there. But if someone's gotta go, I can claim to have been vaccinated against anything in Djibouti – and anyway it's cold in Addis . . . I'd like to know whether there's something I can do there besides bathe camels . . .
>
> Just went to the U.S.I.S. library to see what I could find on Fezzan. It's an oasis in the desert! I doubt whether there's any non-Arab or local tribesmen there. So if all concerned think a rather unmoslem looking American can pass as a shaykh, I'd be happy to go to the mosque five times a day.[137]

Two weeks later, the Committee recommended that he remain in Addis Ababa.

By mid-January 1954, Fred was facing another visa expiration date. He was trying to get the job at the National Library, so decided to request a 30-day extension to his current visa. When he applied for the extension, he was told that his old visa was already a month expired. It turned out that he had applied for a two-month visa, but had been granted only a visa for one month. Since the visa was entirely in Amharic, which he couldn't read, and no one had informed him of the reduction, he had blissfully overstayed his time. The official was very accommodating: he went so far as to go through all the documentation for the old visa and changed the dates to make it a two-month one.[138]

By daily visits to the National Library and the Immigration Office, he was finally granted a six-month visa. While waiting, Fred taught English at an adult higher education centre to a mixed group of Ethiopians, Arabs, Indians, Armenians and Greeks. But with his new visa, which allowed him to work, nobody would hire him. In late February, he was offered a job in Cape Town, South Africa, as a librarian. Asking for advice, the Africa Committee cabled back, 'Advise go Capetown'.[139]

The weeks passed and no visa was received. Finally, Fred was given a job with a commercial firm working for an Armenian gentlemen who owned a retail store. The Armenian didn't speak English, so his son, who spoke English, usually handled the correspondence. Fred did the correspondence while the son went on vacation to Europe. The office faced the street and Fred recalled seeing members of the royal family stop and step out of their limousines, and people bowing down to them.

During this time, Fred was in touch with Lowell and Edith Johnson in Cape Town. Edith was working at the University of Cape Town Library and knew Fred was a librarian. The librarian at the University was interested in US-trained librarians, so without an in-person interview, Fred was hired and the Head Librarian arranged a South African visa. But then, Hand of the Cause Músá Banání wrote and suggested Fred return to Nairobi. Fred was a bit conflicted: stay in Addis Ababa, go to Cape Town or return to Nairobi. Finally, after three months, his visa for Cape Town arrived and by August, he was there. It was a dramatic change from Djibouti and Addis Ababa. He wrote that for pioneers coming from America, 'the change was about as much as between Norfolk and Newport News on the ferry', meaning very little different from America.[140]

Bill Sears, then an Auxiliary Board member under Hand of the Cause Músá Banání, came to Cape Town in 1956. Bill wanted Fred to help with the teaching work and the preparations for the election of the Regional Assembly for South and West Africa. Fred said,

> I told him I would have to give notice . . . He said 'You're having too good a time here, we need help on the farm in planning for the election of the Regional Assembly.' I told him I couldn't since I had a job. After much back and forth I told him I would have to give 3 months notice but still hadn't committed to going . . . He said it was important to come to the farm. I hadn't told him, but the next

day I put in my resignation at the library. A couple of weeks later, I received a letter from Mr Banani, praising me for my decision to go to work in the Johannesburg area. I knew this was done as to reinforce the fact that I should go to Johannesburg. The next time I saw Bill Sears, I told him 'That was a low blow', having the Hand of the Cause send me a letter when I hadn't fully committed that I would come to Johannesburg . . . You had absolutely no confidence in me,' 'Just wanted to make sure,' he said.[141]

One of the preparations for the Regional Spiritual Assembly election was to build a dormitory on the Sears farm for the African delegates – because of apartheid, they could not stay with the other delegates. The entrance to the farm had a long driveway and arrangements were made so that Michael Sears would be working on the gate at the entrance to the road and about halfway up the driveway Reginald Turvey, whom the Guardian had called the 'Spiritual father of the Bahá'ís of South Africa', would be sitting and painting. Michael was to signal to Reg if any potential disturbances might happen so the meeting could be immediately disbanded.[142]

By 1958, Africa's goals had been achieved, but there was still work to do in South America. Fred said that 'I was off again.' He travelled to Uruguay with Bill Sears Jr., arriving in 1959. They participated in a campaign to raise up the second Local Spiritual Assembly in the country along with Julia Bulling, a pioneer from Chile. In 1960, Fred and Julia were married. Under the direction of the US Foreign Goals Committee, the newlyweds went to the Dominican Republic in preparation for the election of the first National Assembly there. But, when Julia was eight months pregnant, the Hands of the Cause and the US Committee requested that they go to Ecuador prior to the first elections in that country because Covenant issues had arisen. Their first son, therefore, was Ecuadorian. A few months later, the Hands of the Cause requested that they move to Uruguay, where they both served on the National Spiritual Assembly. Their second son was born there. In 1965, economic conditions caused them to move to the United States, where their daughter was born.[143]

After they returned to the United States, Fred served on the Auxiliary Board and the Continental Board of Counsellors and from 1993 to 1998 was a Counsellor at the International Teaching Centre at the Bahá'í World Centre.[144]

Sabrí and Fahíma (Raissa) Elias

Sabrí Elias (1906–1995) became a Bahá'í in about 1921 in Egypt and when Shoghi Effendi asked the National Spiritual Assembly to send a pioneer to Abyssinia (Ethiopia) in 1933, Sabrí Elias volunteered. He arrived in Addis Ababa near the end of that year and raised up the first Local Spiritual Assembly, which was elected in 1934. When the Italians invaded the country in 1935, he was forced to return to Egypt. After a dangerous and exhausting trip back to Egypt, he immediately set off from Port Said to see Shoghi Effendi, taking with him 18 copies each of *Bahá'u'lláh and the New Era* and *The Bahá'í Principles* pamphlet, which he had had translated into the Amharic language at Shoghi Effendi's request. Arriving in Haifa, Shoghi Effendi greeted him with 'You have returned victorious and triumphant – because you were the cause of linking the north of Africa to the south!'[145]

Mr Elias had brought a goriza (a rare black and white monkey of Ethiopia) skin as a personal gift to the Guardian, but the Guardian accepted it as a gift from Ethiopia to the Bahá'í World Centre and had Sabri himself place it in the Archives at the back of the Shrine of the Báb in the presence of the other pilgrims and resident Bahá'ís. It was, he said, the fulfilment of a prophecy in Isaiah that stated: 'In that time shall the present be brought unto the LORD of hosts of a people scattered and peeled, and from a people terrible from their beginning hitherto; a nation meted out and trodden under foot, whose land the rivers have spoiled, to the place of the name of the Lord of hosts, the mount Zion.'[146] Since Mr Elias was sick from this arduous journey, Shoghi Effendi sent him to the Bahá'í village of Al-Adasiyya, where he recovered.

In 1941, Sabrí Elias married Fahíma (later called Raissa, b. 1920), and in 1944, after the British pushed the Italians out of Ethiopia, the couple with their two young children went back to Addis Ababa, remaining there until 1954. During that time, they were able to acquaint Emperor Haile Selassie I with the Bahá'í Faith through Mr Gila Bahta, a gifted young Ethiopian lawyer who accepted the Faith soon after their return to Ethiopia.[147] He later served on the Continental Board of Counsellors.

In early 1954, Shoghi Effendi sent a letter to the Bahá'ís of Addis Ababa asking them to send a family to fill the goal of French Somaliland (now called Djibouti), left vacant when Fred Schechter was not able to gain residency. When it became apparent that no others were willing to go, Sabrí and Raissa volunteered. Their first problem was their two oldest children, Hussein and Safa, who attended schools where the local Amharic language and English were spoken but where no one spoke French, the language of French Somaliland. They finally managed to enrol the children in a boarding school. Then their strong ties to Addis Ababa made it difficult to break away. This wasn't made easier by the local Bahá'í community which did not want to lose them. Finally, after they had sold everything possible, they were ready to leave, but they were warned that the Government in Djibouti, the capital of French Somaliland, did not like Egyptians and would not allow them to stay. One night, Raissa had a dream in which someone took her to meet the Báb. When she came into His presence, she begged to know if they were doing the right thing. The Báb's reply was, 'Rest assured! Do not grieve! You will pioneer and settle. You will obtain the residence permit within one month – thirty days to be exact'. With the reassurance of the dream, Sabrí and Raissa left with their two youngest children, Carmel, four years old, and Malakout, who was two. The family arrived in Djibouti on 6 May 1954 during a time of intense heat. Raissa put ice on her daughters' bodies to cool them down, but even so, Malakout said, 'I am about to go to God.' Her older sister responded saying, 'Alright! Please give Him my regards.'[148]

The family had very little money and as the days passed, their worry increased. After 29 days, they still had no visa or a permanent place to live. But at 10 a.m. on the thirtieth day, there was a knock on the door and they were told to go to the Department of the Interior. Upon their arrival, they joyously received their resident visas. Their next problem was a place to live, but they had no money, just a house in Alexandria, Egypt, which they couldn't sell because the Egyptian Government had banned any money being transferred out of the country. At noon on the same day, there was another knock on their door. This time it was a stranger who said that some Egyptians wanted to meet them. When the hotel manager assured them that they were good people, Sabrí and Raissa went with him and met an Egyptian family who lived in Djibouti, but who were about to move to Alexandria. They needed a house there. 'With lightning-speed', they made out a sale contract. The family then offered to furnish Sabrí and Raissa's house with furniture, fans and a refrigerator that they could not take with them.[149]

Their first two years in Djibouti were very difficult and their first new Bahá'í only made things worse. He was so enthusiastic about teaching his new faith that opposition quickly arose. People on the streets hurled both insults and stones at the Bahá'ís and mobs harassed them. Then in 1955, Shoghi Effendi sent a telegram asking that all spiritual assemblies in the area send protest cables to the Shah of Iran about the persecution of the Bahá'ís in that country. The cable included the Local Spiritual Assembly of Djibouti, which didn't exist, but Sabrí obediently wrote a cable and took it to the post office. The Post Master wondered at this man sending a cable to the Shah of Iran and Sabrí was soon called before the Town Clerk, who wanted to know about this Bahá'í Faith. The Clerk requested some literature to study. A month later, the man called Sabrí back and told him, 'Your religion is immaculate because Bahá'ís absolutely do not interfere in political matters.' It was the opening of the door to teaching.[150]

In February 1956, Shoghi Effendi wrote asking them to form the first Local Spiritual Assembly of Djibouti at Riḍván. At that time, there were seven Bahá'ís in the community and the continuous persecution made teaching difficult. Raissa then had to make a train journey to Addis Ababa and on the return was examining the other passengers, wondering how she could find a receptive soul. Suddenly, Raissa found herself speaking to the others in her car: 'My brothers! Have you heard about the new Message that has been brought by God's Messenger for today, Bahá'u'lláh – the Message that calls for the unity of mankind, universal love and peace, and that considers the Earth as one country and mankind its citizens?' Surprised but blank stares met her outburst – from all but one man who asked, 'What is the name of this Messenger?' By the time the train reached Djibouti, the man was a Bahá'í.[151]

On 19 April, the Djibouti Bahá'ís still numbered only eight. Raissa had a Bahá'í niece who had expressed interest in joining them, but had not done so. Then at two o'clock in the morning on 20 April, there was a knock at the door. When they opened it, they found her niece, Fawziyya, there. The Assembly was formed.

In late 1955, Raissa recounted the story of a contact's pilgrimage to Hejaz. The man, Mr Mahmúd Harbí, was a popular young leader in the area and had been given the message of Bahá'u'lláh. When Mahmúd went on pilgrimage, the Eliases gave him a Tablet of Bahá'u'lláh for protection. When he returned, he recounted this story:

Something very strange happened to me in Híjáz. One day I lost my wallet. I was very sad, not because of the wallet, but because with it I had lost the prayer you gave me. I walked the streets deep in sorrow and thought. My eyes were attracted by something glittering in the sun. It was a golden ring, and on its stone was carved something exactly similar to the one you have on your ring stone. I was amazed. How can this happen when I was sure there were no Bahá'ís in Híjáz?[152]

When Mahmúd showed the Eliases the ring, it had the Greatest Name engraved on it. They were all amazed that Mahmúd, who was very attracted to the Faith, should, of all the thousands of people in Híjáz, find the ring. When Sabrí related this story by letter to his family in Alexandria, a reply came that the ring had been lost by an Iranian pioneer to Arabia, who happened to be on a visit to Alexandria when the letter was read.[153]

Sabrí and Raissa remained in Djibouti until 1959 when they moved back to Egypt in order to advance the education of their children.[154] In 1960, the Egyptian Government began harassing the Faith, ordering the dissolution of all administrative bodies. In 1968, the Eliases moved to Libya where they stayed for three years before returning to Alexandria. Raissa went to a Bahá'í Continental Conference in Nairobi in 1976 and asked where they could pioneer. She was willing to go anywhere, but Sabrí said he would go anywhere but Djibouti. At the Conference, Raissa met Omar Dúrání, an old friend to whom they had taught the Faith and who had come from Djibouti specifically to ask Raissa and Sabrí to return there. When Enoch Olinga joined the conversation and said that no one else was capable of serving in Djibouti, Raissa accepted. Once home with the news, Sabrí was not happy. But when a few days later, a visitor arrived, he changed his mind. The visitor carried a letter from the Universal House of Justice blessing their return to Djibouti. In May 1977, Sabrí and Raissa were back in Djibouti. For the next 11 years, they continued the work they had started in 1954. When Sabrí was 82 years old, they returned to Alexandria[155] where they lived until Sabrí's passing on 22 October 1995. Afterwards, Raissa lived for some time in Morocco and Syria, all along engaged in vigorous teaching of the Bahá'í Faith. After breaking a hip, she had to return to Egypt, living in Cairo with her daughter Carmel, until her passing on 28 June 2014.

HADHRAMAUT (NOW PART OF YEMEN)

Adíb and Vahídih Baghdádí, and Husayn Halabi

Adíb Radí Baghdádí (1905–1988) pioneered to Hadhramaut from Iraq in early 1955. Adíb came from a family with a Bahá'í history beginning with his grandfather, who was the first Arab to become a Bábí. Adíb was a long-time teacher and pioneer in Mosul and Sulaymaniyyih in Iraq and served on the National Spiritual Assembly. When the Intercontinental Teaching Conference was held in New Delhi in 1953, he really wanted to go and when he was refused leave from work to do so, he quit his job of 32 years. Before the Conference began, Adíb dreamed that Shoghi Effendi called for pioneers to virgin territories so, when the dream came true at the Conference, he chose the most inhospitable goal he could find, then immediately went there in December 1953. His goal was Hadhramaut, in what is now known as Yemen.

Hadhramaut is in the interior of the country in a desolate area and Adíb couldn't find any sort of work for the first year. Finally, in early 1955, he managed to find a way to support himself, so he sent for his wife, Vahídih. There were no schools there so the three oldest Baghdádí children had to stay at the New Era School in India and their parents didn't see them for four years. Adíb and Vahídih remained in Hadhramaut for six years before returning to Iraq, where they pioneered in the north of the country. Five years later, they pioneered to Kuwait and later went to Lebanon. They were forced to leave Lebanon when the Iraqi Government refused to renew their passports. The family then moved to Canada.[156]

Husayn Halabi (1921–1980) arrived in Hadhramaut near the beginning of 1955, about the same time as Vahídih. Shortly after his arrival, Kamálí Sarvistání visited him, passing through on his way to his own Knight's post in the Socotra Islands A short time after Mr Sarvistání's arrival, Husayn fell extremely ill and the visitor spent the next several months caring for the ill Knight. After several months, Husayn's father arrived to take care of him, but after just three days, the father died of a heart attack. In May 1955, Husayn's brother-in-law came and collected him for treatment elsewhere, freeing Mr Sarvistání to continue to his own pioneering post.[157]

SOUTHERN AFRICA

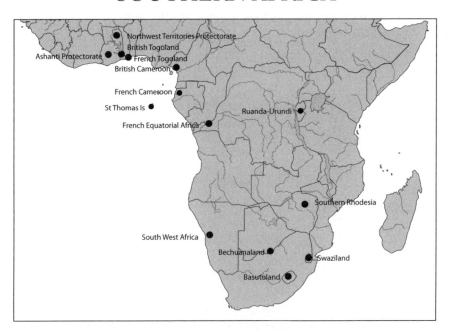

BRITISH CAMEROON (NOW PART OF CAMEROON)

Enoch Olinga

Enoch Olinga (1926–1979) first learned about the Bahá'í Faith in 1951 in Uganda. At that time, he had been a translator working for the government, but was disillusioned and his heavy drinking led to his dismissal. 'Alí and Violette Nakhjavání moved to Kampala and one day, 'Alí was driving to work with one of the first two Ugandan Bahá'ís, Crispin Kajubi. Crispin had become a Bahá'í in December 1951, along with Fred Bigabwa. On the way, they encountered Enoch, who was walking. Mr Nakhjavání said:

Crispin told me, 'Stop the car! Stop the car!' I did and he rolled the window down and he called Enoch . . . He called him and said, 'This is the man I told you about.' He had spoken to him about the Faith and about me, so he asked me if he could invite Mr Olinga to sit in the car and join us that particular morning to our house [to study the Writings]. I said, 'Of course.' So, that was when I met Enoch for the first time.

From that time onwards, he would come to our house . . . I found out that his home was not very far from our home, so it was easy for him just to walk over . . . Luganda was not his native language, but he was so proficient in English that he was able to help Crispin, who was a member of the Luganda tribe . . . not Enoch Olinga's tribe, which was the Teso, in translating prayers from English into Luganda . . . He became very involved in service even before he had become a Bahá'í.[1]

Mr Na<u>kh</u>javání described how Enoch became a Bahá'í:

He became a Bahá'í as the result of a pilgrimage undertaken by Mr and Mrs Banání . . . Those of us who were in Kampala, including the Banánís themselves, we thought that it would be a good idea for the Banánís to carry a letter from the Bahá'í group in Kampala requesting Shoghi Effendi to pray for a public meeting we were planning to have during the pilgrimage of the Banánís in Haifa . . . So, we wrote such a letter and the Banánís carried the letter and submitted the letter to Shoghi Effendi. Shoghi Effendi said yes, that he would pray on that particular day.

We had the meeting in our home and we invited all the contacts we had at that time. The room was full, even people were sitting on the carpet . . . We were expecting, really, mass conversion to happen right there in this room because we were aware that Shoghi Effendi was praying. But actually, nothing happened, so we were very disappointed. And everybody left. We were sitting in the room – there was Violette, there was Mr Hainsworth, who was a Bahá'í pioneer from the British Isles, and myself.

It was about . . . 7 or 7:30 in the evening and we heard a knock at the door. We opened the door and we saw this young man. It was Enoch. He said, 'May I come in. I have a few questions I was wondering about.' We said, 'Of course, you can come in.' He came in and he sat and most of his questions were based on Biblical passages and prophecy. He wanted to see what the Bahá'í point of view would be on such passages in the New Testament. We tried our best and we offered some answers to him and he seemed to be quite satisfied. Then there was a moment of silence. And then he said, 'I have yet another question. How does one become a Bahá'í?'

I will never forget that moment when he asked this question. I looked at Violette; I looked at Philip Hainsworth, and I looked at myself. All three of us had tears in our eyes because this was the culmination. This was the climax of the events of the day . . . In those days, it was not easy to become a Bahá'í in Uganda. We didn't have declaration cards, we didn't have any assembly. Everything had to be referred to the British National Spiritual Assembly. We explained to him that he had to write a letter to the British National Assembly expressing his feelings about the Faith and then the National Assembly will decide. It was not an easy thing for an Ugandan to accept that even in the Bahá'í Faith, everything had to be referred to London, because Uganda at that time was a British protectorate and everything had to go to London. So, here the Bahá'ís are coming with a world religion and, again, a letter has to go to London. But it was not a real test and he was able to pass it. He said he understood. That's how he left us that evening.

Of course, we were delighted when we were alone and discussing this whole thing. Well, very early the next morning, before he went to his work, there was a knock at the door and there was Enoch with his letter. He delivered his letter then went to his work. We were delighted. We immediately, of course, sent the letter to the National Spiritual Assembly in London. Very soon we received a reply saying that he was welcomed into the Bahá'í community and his declaration of Faith was accepted and approved. That was the beginning.[2]

Enoch stopped drinking immediately and his change in attitude attracted considerable attention. This newly dynamic young man of 26 took the Faith to his Teso tribesmen and within two months had succeeded in forming the first Local Spiritual Assembly of Kampala.[3]

Enoch then went to his home village of Tilling and soon there were 17 Bahá'ís there. The people were so impressed with Enoch that they wanted to meet the 'white man' who had converted him. When Enoch came back the next month with 'Alí Nakhjavání, 90 more Tilling villagers, including Enoch's father, became Bahá'ís. Shoghi Effendi was thrilled with his success and shared it with the world:

> Rejoice to share . . . thrilling reports of feats achieved by the heroic band of Bahá'í pioneers . . . particularly in Uganda, in the heart of the continent, reminiscent alike of episodes related in the Book of Acts and the rapid, dramatic propagation of the Faith through the instrumentality of the dawn-breakers in the Heroic Age of the Bahá'í Dispensation . . . The goal of the seven-month plan, initiated by the Kampala Assembly, aiming at doubling the twelve enrolled believers, has been outstripped. The number of Africans converted in the course of the last fifteen months, residing in Kampala and outlying districts, with Protestant, Catholic and pagan backgrounds, lettered and unlettered, of both sexes, representative of no less than sixteen tribes, has passed the two hundred mark.[4]

When Enoch heard the Guardian's Ten Year Crusade call to open new territories, he quickly responded, becoming, eighteen months after his declaration, a Knight of Bahá'u'lláh to British Cameroon. When asked why he chose British Cameroon, he said that it was because it was the farthest away from Uganda.[5] In August 1953, with Samson Mungono, Max Kanyerezi and the Nakhjavánís in a Peugeot station wagon, they drove to British Cameroon 3,000 kilometres away, dropping Samson in the Belgian Congo, and Max in French Equatorial Africa, which made Max a Knight of Bahá'u'lláh. The last stage of their journey was tough. At one point, their car broke down 80 kilometres from the nearest town. Enoch volunteered to go get help. Enoch was not a jungle man; he lived in the city, so he was quite worried about snakes, strange tribes and dangerous animals. After walking for 56 kilometres, during which he was afflicted by a severe storm and had to avoid elephants, Enoch was exhausted, covered with mud, worried about the Nakhjavánís and scared.[6] He stopped and cried out, 'Why have I come here? I have left my family in Uganda. I've come here in the jungles of Cameroon and different countries. Why am I here?' He fell asleep from exhaustion and had a dream of Shoghi Effendi. In the dream, 'Shoghi Effendi held his hands and pulled him out of this mud and sat him next to him . . .

and he said, "I am so pleased with you."' It was a different Enoch who awoke.[7]

Meanwhile, the Na<u>kh</u>javánís had repaired the car and chased after Enoch. When they found him, he was so ill that he had to be hospitalized for two days and could not travel for a week. On 15 October, however, they entered British Cameroon. Shoghi Effendi had called for the goals to be opened before the end of the Holy Year and Enoch did that. Arriving at the first town in British Cameroon, Mamfe, Enoch rushed to the post office to cable the Guardian. It was 4 p.m. and the office was closing, but Enoch begged the postmaster to send his cable, which he did. Shoghi Effendi named Enoch a Knight of Bahá'u'lláh.[8]

The next day, they reached Victoria, now called Limbé. Enoch found lodging through a young couple named David and Esther Tanyi.[9] David became the second Bahá'í and Esther the first woman to enter the Faith in Cameroon. From his arrival in October 1953 to April 1954, Enoch brought Samuel Njiki, Edward Tabe, Albert Buapiah, Martin Manga, Ben Eballa and several others into the Faith. At the beginning of April, a Message from the Guardian calling on African Bahá'ís to arise and fill the goals of the Ten Year Crusade, inspired the new Bahá'ís.

> Urgent entry African believer virgin territories British French Togolands Ashanti Protectorate Northern Territories Protectorate before Ridván will ensure victory. Shoghi[10]

So inspired were the Cameroonian Bahá'ís that all nine wanted to pioneer. Since only five were needed, the group had an election and consequently Samuel Njiki pioneered to Douala in French Cameroon, David Tanyi went to French Togoland, Edward Tabe to British Togoland, Benedict Eballa to the Ashanti Protectorate and Martin Manga to the Northern Territories Protectorate. This was a unique event in the history of the Ten Year Crusade where a single Knight of Bahá'u'lláh raised up five more Knights. In addition to creating more Knights of Bahá'u'lláh, Enoch also raised up the first Local Spiritual Assembly by Ridván 1954. In addition to Limbé, 12 other areas were also opened to the Bahá'í Faith.[11]

Not everyone was happy with Enoch's teaching activities. A 'jealous European' at one of the places Enoch worked accused him of 'political intrigue' and managed to get the police to investigate. Not only did the subsequent report exonerate Enoch, but the investigating detective became a Bahá'í.[12]

When the first Regional Spiritual Assembly of North West Africa was formed in 1956, Enoch was elected to serve on that body. In October 1957, just five years after becoming a Bahá'í and at the age of 31, Enoch was appointed a Hand of the Cause by Shoghi Effendi. The cable announcing his appointment was sent to Mr Banání, who asked Enoch to come to his home. When the young man arrived and was given the cable, he 'read it and then prostrated himself flat on the floor, a mark in Africa of deep submission to one's Liege.'[13] For the next 22 years, Enoch travelled throughout Africa and then the world in service to the Faith he so loved. He was chosen by his fellow Hands to be the opening speaker at the World Congress in 1963, and later met the Dalai Lama in India. Enoch also represented the Universal House of Justice at the elections of many first National Spiritual Assemblies across the globe. When the Faith was banned in Uganda in September 1977, Enoch's first reaction was to instantly obey and then to write to the Government explaining the nature and status of the Bahá'í Faith, though to no avail. Enoch and the secretary of the National Assembly moved the invaluable archive materials to a safe place and closed up the National Headquarters. Because of his prominence, Enoch's name was placed on a list for elimination, but he refused to leave the country, saying, 'What do I have to fear? Did the Báb run away? Did Bahá'u'lláh run away? Did 'Abdu'l-Bahá run away?' Tragically, on 16 September 1979, with the Faith finally free of its two-year ban in Uganda, five unknown armed men came into his home and murdered him, his wife, Elizabeth, and three of his children, Tahirih, Lennie and Badi.[14]

FRENCH EQUATORIAL AFRICA (NOW CONGO)

Max Kanyerezi

Ugandan Max Kanyerezi (1918–1991) was spiritually inclined from a young age. In 1934, at the age of 16, he twice had the same dream in one night. In the dream,

A large figure stretches up and starts to roll up the earth, as one would roll up a newspaper. People are running in panic. Three officials sit on a hill where people are to register in the Book of Life. Young Max approaches the table where they are inscribing the names. The eldest tells him, 'Go and learn to register your friends, thereafter you will also be registered.'[15]

This propelled Max to become a minister, like his father, and then a farmer, but he failed at both. In 1952, a co-worker told him about a new religion. By chance, Max met one of his relatives, Crispin Kajubi, who had joined this new religion. Crispin guided him to 'Alí Nakhjavání. Finally, during a meeting which lasted from 9 one morning to 3 a.m. the next morning, all Max's questions were answered and he became a Bahá'í. Max worried what his father, the Christian minister, would say. But his father solved that by having a dream in which Christ announced that He had returned in Uganda. Max was able to explain what the dream meant and, though his father never became a declared Bahá'í, he became a Bahá'í in his heart.[16]

Max and his wife, Florence, attended the International Teaching Conference in Kampala and he made the decision to take the Faith to Brazzaville in French Equatorial Africa (later to become the capital of Congo). On 30 August 1953, Max climbed into the Nakhjávánís' car along with Enoch Olinga and headed south. Max was dropped in Brazzaville while the others continued to the Cameroons. In his new post, Max found that his lack of French or the local languages did not stop people from understanding the Message he had brought and soon a Local Spiritual Assembly was formed.

Max returned to Uganda in 1955 and began lengthy travel-teaching trips throughout East Africa. He was later elected to the first National Spiritual Assembly for Central and East Africa and then appointed as one of the first group of Auxiliary Board members.[17]

FRENCH TOGOLAND (NOW TOGO)

David Tanyi

David Tanyi (1928–2000) was a devout Protestant in October 1953 when a muddy car pulled up in front of the shop where he worked in British Cameroon. A white man came in and asked for film, then left. Then he returned and asked if David had malaria medicine. David said no, but he knew where to get it, so the man waited until he was off work. Driving David back after picking up the medicine, the man asked if he could help find inexpensive housing for some African friends of his. The next day, an Ugandan walked up and introduced himself as Enoch Olinga. From him, they learned that the white man and his wife were 'Alí and Violette Nakhjavání. Soon Enoch was telling them about the Bahá'í Faith. Then one day Enoch asked:

> Suppose as we live here in this town, a cry is sounded warning the citizens of the drifting of the sea into the town and of a wild beast roaring into the town, then immediately each and every one started building a wall around their house to protect themselves, family and property, but one other person raised a call that all must come together and construct one strong wall around the whole town in order to protect everything and everyone, which of these two instructions should be followed and why?[18]

Esther said the one building the wall around the whole town was wiser, because he was protecting even the poor and the orphans. Enoch said that was the Bahá'í message. David and Esther became Bahá'ís. One day in April 1954, only six months after Cameroon had been opened to the Bahá'í Faith, Enoch brought a cable from the Guardian that called for five new areas to be opened:

> Urgent entry African believer virgin territories British French Togolands Ashanti Protectorate Northern Territories Protectorate before Ridván will ensure victory. Shoghi[19]

David wrote that 'While we contemplated holding a meeting regarding the contents of this cable, two days or so later, 'Alí Nakhjavání arrived . . . A meeting was convened. At this time our community numbered nine and we were sure of forming a Local Spiritual Assembly on April 20, 1954.'[20] When the cable was read, the new believers 'surged forward with zeal to respond to this specific call of the Guardian'. Enoch hadn't expected these newly declared Bahá'ís who knew very little about the Bahá'í teachings to arise so spontaneously. Enoch remembered:

> As soon as the news reached their attentive and sensitive ears the

believers reacted in such a manner that a spectator could take them for drunkards . . . Pioneering offers poured in like locusts and clear signs of obedience to move the next minute were made manifest, forgetting their property and loving relatives and families.[21]

Since there were only five destinations and nine Bahá'ís, an election was held and five were chosen to settle in the virgin territories: David Tanyi, a clerk-bookkeeper, to French Togoland; Edward Tabe, an office messenger, to British Togoland; Samuel Njiki, a clerk, to French Cameroon; Benedict Eballa, a salesman, to the Ashanti Protectorate; Martin Manga, an apprentice auto-mechanic, to the Northern Territories Protectorate. All resigned their jobs to become pioneers.

At the end of this phenomenal meeting, 'Alí Nakhjavání was in tears and overcome with emotion. The Cameroonians were surprised and worried by this reaction, because they feared that the Bahá'ís would take them away and enslave them. 'Alí Nakhjavání explained

> that in their Persian culture, one could weep for both joy and sorrow, that he wept for sorrow for his countrymen who denied Bahá'u'lláh and are still persecuting the Bahá'ís, and for joy for us for accepting the Faith and at the point of sacrificing our families and friends to go to foreign countries in order to teach the Faith.[22]

Thus reassured, the new pioneers made their preparations. Just a few days after receiving the cable, on 10 April 1954, and with a deadline of 21 April – only eleven days later! – set by the Guardian, the group set off, with David leaving behind his pregnant wife, Esther. The Guardian was

> deeply moved by . . . the manner in which the friends received his call to pioneer in the virgin areas. He feels that people who have been Bahá'ís for only a short period, have arisen to carry the Glad Tidings to people of new lands. The manner in which the Faith has spread in Africa is truly remarkable, and overshadows the manner it has spread in other parts of the world. It indicates how glorious will be the future of the Faith in that great continent.[23]

On 10 April, 'Alí and four of the new pioneers flew to Lagos. David, who suffered from a disability in one leg, wrote:

71

At about 2 p.m. we departed and arrived in Lagos a few hours later. We checked in at Palace Hotel, Broad Street . . .

On Monday, 12 April 1954, we went to get our West African passports. We did not need any travelling documents to travel from Tiko to Lagos because British Cameroon, in which Tiko was located, was part of Nigeria. Because 'Alí had arrived earlier and made arrangements we only had to present our photographs and sign for our passports. On Tuesday 13 April . . . We got a vehicle (Tarzan Transport) and set off for Lomé, Togo. The vehicle was a truck with two compartments; a front and back compartment. The back compartment had more comfortable non-wooden seats. 'Alí and I sat in front beside the driver. Since it was slightly difficult for me to keep my legs down, 'Alí placed his bag down for me to keep my legs on. But when I hesitated he told me that he really had nothing precious in the bag, and that I was more precious to him than the bag.

After a long drive, we arrived in Lomé on the night of Tuesday, 13 April. 'Alí lodged at the Hotel du Golf while we lodged at Tarzan Transport transit quarters.[24]

'Alí continued with Martin, Edward and Benedict while David went to a hostel and met a young man from East Africa. This was Herbert Sikombe, who just happened to be a Bahá'í there trying to get a visa to study (see also Dunduzu Kaluli Chisiza, below pp. 92–7). The next day, David cabled the Guardian of his arrival. On 2 May, Vivian Wesson and Mavis Nymon arrived in Lomé from America (see following story). David and Herbert greatly enjoyed learning from the knowledge and experiences of their new companions. Unfortunately, the two women were not able to extend their four-month visa and were forced to leave.[25]

When the Americans left, the newly married David became very lonely in Lomé. After a while, he wrote to Enoch Olinga and Hand of the Cause Músá Banání asking to be allowed to go home, which he expected them to agree to. Instead, Enoch wrote, 'I hope you will resign yourself to teaching the Message of Bahá'u'lláh', and Mr Banání wrote, 'Physical weakness does not appear in the picture'.

I was only six months old in the Faith, and the first time of ever leaving my homeland and my beloved newly married wife. The

French, I could not speak. The local dialects too I could not speak. How to meet and to introduce the Faith to people was a problem. . . . I was constantly at the sea shore, where I spent most of my time. I would spend long hours there, meditating and praying for God to give me a friend who was bilingual in both French and English . . . One day while I was sitting at the sea shore as usual, a tall ebony black boy came up to me and greeted me in French, and started to address me in French. When I told him in English that I could not understand French, he started talking in English.[26]

This was Emmanuel Ocloo. He had seen David frequenting the shore and was drawn to introduce himself. He soon became a Bahá'í.

David was finally joined by Esther in December after their son, Enoch, was born. At Riḍván 1955, the group elected their first Local Spiritual Assembly and a year later, they had 22 believers, with 7 children. Another 16 had also become Bahá'ís, but had moved to other areas before Riḍván.[27] David and Herbert Sikombe extended their teaching efforts into Benin where three people accepted the Faith.[28]

In 1957, the Tanyis were asked to go to Ghana. They arrived in Tamale on 3 March and the Tanyi home became a centre of Bahá'í activity. David served on the District Teaching Committee for Ghana. In 1970, he was elected to the first National Spiritual Assembly of Ghana. He served on the body for several years, usually as the Treasurer, but also as Chairman. In December 1989, the Tanyis returned to Cameroon.[29]

Vivian Wesson and Mavis Nymon[30]

On 2 May 1954, American pioneers Vivian Wesson (1895–1994) and Mavis Nymon (1921–2013) arrived in Victoria and joined David Tanyi and Herbert Sikombe in their efforts to teach the Bahá'í Faith. Vivian Wesson was the daughter of a Baptist minister in Texas. In 1919, she married Henry Wesson and two years later, she learned of the Faith when she was Corinne True's maid in 1921. She said, 'The first year of my Bahá'í life was spent in her home as a maid. I was ill with stomach (peptic) ulcers and of very little use to them. I think she kept me on just to teach me the Bahá'í way of life. I'm sure no maid ever had the care and privileges which were give me by the whole family.' After her husband died in 1951, Vivian wanted to pioneer to Africa so in 1953 she applied to the United States Africa Teaching Committee.

The Committee partnered the 59-year-old African-American Vivian, from the deep south, with a 33-year-old white woman named Mavis Nymon from Fargo, North Dakota, and sent them to French Togoland. The two didn't meet until they boarded the ship in Boston, but they developed an immediate and permanent friendship. Mavis grew up in North Dakota and had to relearn how to walk after having polio at the age of three. She had wanted to proclaim the Cause of God in Africa since she was a youth, but couldn't find a religion in accord with her beliefs. She first heard of the Bahá'í Faith in 1950, then began to investigate it two years later. After taking a class at the Louhelen Bahá'í School in Michigan, she declared her faith and was promptly elected to the Local Spiritual Assembly of St Paul, Minnesota, where she was an instructor at the University of Minnesota.

Obstacles quickly popped up to their plans. Initially, they couldn't get visas for French Togoland. They overcame this by getting visas to go to Liberia, in hopes of getting the Togoland visas from there. On 27 April 1954, Vivian and Mavis landed at Monrovia, Liberia, just in time to rush from the ship to the Bahá'í Feast. The next day, William Foster and Valerie Wilson took them to various embassies and, at the end of the day, they had their visas. But time was running out if they were to be in Togoland by the end of the Riḍván period, 2 May. Miracles continued to happen. Their ship from Liberia to Accra, Ghana, arrived in Ghana five days early, on the evening of 1 May. The next day going through Customs, Vivian and Mavis asked about getting a taxi to Lomé in Togoland. The man informed them that it was Sunday and there was no way to travel. But the two women needed to be in Lomé by that night so they began to pray. Soon a man called Carl Allotey asked if he could help them. Vivian and Mavis explained their predicament so Carl took them to his house where they met Venance Ayivor, a teacher in Accra but also a member of one of the most prominent families in Lomé.

Carl soon had a car lined up and he, Venance, Vivian and Mavis departed Accra at 3:00 p.m., reaching their destination at 9:30 that night. Vivian and Mavis had achieved their goal and became Knights of Bahá'u'lláh, but they were Knights with no place to stay. All the hotels were full. Finally, Carl found them a place to stay with his cousin at

1:30 a.m. The next day, the cousin's brother gave them a room. Carl was so affected by his black and white visitors that he became a Bahá'í in June.

But then, for Vivian and Mavis, the problem of visas came up again. They only had a four-month visa. The French bureaucracy offered many verbal assurances, but even after repeated visits to the Chef de Sureté, the police, they could not get any of the official documents signed. There were suggestions that the authorities were worried that the two Bahá'í women would 'contribute to the general unrest and were encouraging people to agitate for independence'. With no visas, Vivian and Mavis, Knights of Bahá'u'lláh for French Togoland in spite of such a brief stay, turned to Liberia, where they were welcomed.[31]

Vivian had always wanted to teach literacy and she and Mavis soon had the Bahá'í Literacy School up and running in the Bomi Hills, a mining region forty miles from Monrovia. Hand of the Cause Enoch Olinga appointed Mavis to the Auxiliary Board in 1957. In the middle of 1958, Mavis had to return to America and went back to school, successfully completing her Masters and PhD in nutrition and public health. From 1960 to 1983, she taught at North Dakota State University. She also did travel-teaching in Norway, Germany, Greece, Hong Kong, Iceland, Lebanon, Nigeria, Panama, Uganda, Turkey and the United Kingdom. She passed away in 2013.[32]

Vivian continued with the school, but the work load was too much for her. She was appointed to the Regional Teaching Committee and made a gruelling 2,700-mile travel teaching trip with Valerie Wilson. In 1970, at the age of 75, Vivian moved to Sierra Leone. After seven years serving there, she returned to the United States in a wheelchair, settling in Palo Alto, California, where she died in 1994.

French Cameroon (now part of Cameroon)

Samuel Njiki Njenji and Meherangiz Munsiff

Samuel Njiki (1935-1983) and Meherangiz Munsiff (1923-1999) arrived in French Cameroon on 9 and 16 April 1954, respectively. Samuel worked as a typist between 1950 and 1954. He first heard of the Bahá'í Faith in the spring of 1954 at the age of 19 from Enoch Olinga. He had only been a Bahá'í for a few weeks when Enoch Olinga read the cable from the Guardian to a group of Cameroonian Bahá'ís calling for the remaining unopened territories to be opened by Africans. Samuel was one of those elected to go, and left for Douala in French Cameroon aged just 19 (see David Tanyi, pp. 70–71 above for details of the amazing story of this event). Samuel later noted how 'he and the other believers were convinced of the true implications and deep significance of the Guardian's call'.[33]

Meherangiz Munsiff arrived a week after Samuel in Douala, coming from Madagascar, where she had pioneered in April 1953. Born in India, her name, which meant Giver of Love, had been given to her by Bahíyyih Khánum, the Greatest Holy Leaf. She became a Bahá'í very young and against her father's wishes (though decades later he, too, accepted the Faith). She was still a teenager when she began teaching about Bahá'u'lláh. During one of her talks, she met 16-year-old Eruch Munsiff and five years later, they were married. During her first pilgrimage, she became enamoured with Shoghi Effendi and tried to share that love during her travel-teaching trips. When the Ten Year Crusade began, Meherangiz and Eruch decided that she should pioneer first to Madagascar and then French Cameroon. Eruch, who was then an attaché at the Indian Embassy in London, stayed home with their daughter, Jyoti.[34]

Meherangiz had arrived in Tamatave in Madagascar on 21 April 1953 and moved a few days later to the town of Antananarivo. Since she was the wife of the attaché of the Indian Embassy in London, an Indian couple offered her a place to stay. In July, Gilbert Robert, a Frenchman living on the island, came to see her. He was 'traumatized by the two years he served in Vietnam' and 'was determinedly searching, in all the books . . . for a Teaching capable of eradicating the calamity of War. Those same fratricides of the time were the end of his faith in justice and the love of God.' When he heard about Meherangiz and her teaching, he wanted to find out what she had:

When Meherangiz appeared, I was stupefied by her elegance and beauty. Her face was radiating with spirituality and her eyes were full of laughter and a keen intelligence. I was so impressed that I nearly forgot all the trick questions that I had prepared for her. I asked them. Her answers were pertinent and clearly expressed. As she answered, I felt increasingly disarmed by her knowledge and her smiling modesty.[35]

Meherangiz moved into a hotel and the expense rapidly reduced her funds. She also fell ill, so Gilbert and his wife, Daisy, offered her a room in their home. While she lived with the Roberts, two police officers stood guard outside of the door. Meherangiz would go out and invite them in for tea. This started a rumour: 'Beware of the Bahá'ís: they go and offer you some tea and before you know it, you are a Bahá'í.'[36]

Over the next three months, she brought Gilbert and Daisy into the Faith. They declared on 27 December 1953. Two others also became Bahá'ís over the next two weeks – all were French. This made Meherangiz both happy and sad. The sadness came because she felt her mission was to teach the local Malagasy people. Then, one night about midnight,

> someone knocked at our door. I opened it and found a young Malagasy man who was asking to see Mrs Munsiff. I refused, telling him that she was very tired and asking him to come back during the day. He refused to move. I finally woke our friend up. The visitor returned to her a Bahá'í book that she had lent him and was silent for a while. I then asked him to leave; he still did not move. Finally he asked, trembling with hesitation what it was he needed to do to become a Bahá'í.[37]

The next day Daniel Randrianarivo became the first Malagasy Bahá'í. Meherangiz left Madagascar on 20 January 1954. By the following Riḍván, Gilbert and Daisy had helped bring in nine more people into the Faith, including six more Malagasy. They were able to form their first Local Spiritual Assembly.[38]

Samuel Njiki and Meherangiz did not know each other, so arranged to meet on the steps of the post office in Yaoundé, French Cameroon, in April. Arriving first, Samuel sat holding his Bahá'í prayer book so she could easily recognize him. Initially, Samuel fell ill, but recovered. Meherangiz also became ill and was forced to leave after a year. In August 1954, a letter written on behalf of the Guardian to Samuel stated that

> The Guardian becomes very happy when he contemplates the fact that so many of the new African Bahá'ís have arisen to pioneer for the Faith. He feels those of you who are doing this are laying the foundation for great spiritual service in the Cause of God, that you are rendering historic service, and that you are becoming the honour

and glory of the African people. The full extent of your deeds and services will be greatly valued and appreciated.[39]

Because of their efforts, however, they were able to form a Local Spiritual Assembly at Riḍván 1955. Samuel stayed until 1960, when he returned to Limbé, Cameroon, where he served on the Local Spiritual Assembly until he passed away in 1983.[40]

The pioneering years were very difficult for Meherangiz; she was away from her family with little money and with scant knowledge of the languages of the people she met. After her year with Samuel in French Cameroon, she returned to Britain so weak with malnutrition that she was hospitalized for three months. In the late 1950s, because of her husband Eruch's diplomatic position, the family moved to America where she made a 32-state teaching trip by bus, often accompanied by her daughter Jyoti. She visited the Hopi, Navajo and Zuni Indian tribes, staying with them and teaching them the Faith. Unschooled, 'with no formal education',[41] her knowledge came from the Bahá'í Writings and her efforts resulted in many awards. When the Guardian wrote that Eruch's work as a diplomat could have political implications, he gave up his job and the family returned to Britain where Meherangiz worked with the BBC, broadcasting in both English and Hindi. For four decades, she travelled the world to teach the Bahá'í Faith, visiting some 170 countries on every continent while Eruch stayed home to support her. Her teaching in Japan was particularly successful. During her last twenty years, her mission was to share a course on how to pray regularly and with the correct attitude. Meherangiz sincerely wished to 'die with her boots on', but also to be buried near the Guardian. In April 1999, she collapsed with cancer in Italy, but was still able to return to London before passing away in June.[42] She and Eruch are buried within a few feet of the Guardian's resting-place.

BRITISH TOGOLAND (NOW PART OF GHANA)

Edward Tabe and Albert Buapiah

Edward Tabe (b. 1940) was the youngest Knight of Bahá'u'lláh, a station he shared with Carol Bagley on Sicily, and, unlike most others of comparable age who pioneered with their parents, Edward pioneered alone.

As a junior youth of about 12 or 13, he found a job as a messenger in a hospital in Limbé, Cameroon. He made the acquaintance of David Tanyi and, since they were from the same tribe, Edward spent most of his time in David's home. When Enoch Olinga brought David and his wife, Esther, into the Bahá'í Faith, Edward also became a Bahá'í. At the beginning of April 1954, Edward was one of the Cameroonian Bahá'ís elected to fill one of the Guardian's goal areas (see David Tanyi, pp. 70–71 above for details).[43]

Edward was born sometime in 1940 so, technically, he was probably only 13 or 14 when he became a Bahá'í and a Knight of Bahá'u'lláh. Enoch Tanyi believes that Edward may have added a year to his age in order to become a Bahá'í because one had to be 15 to declare as a Bahá'í. And since he was away from his parents and there was no way to verify his claim to be 15 because of a lack of any official documents, it was accepted.

The group of young pioneers chosen along with Edward flew to Lagos, Nigeria, then travelled by truck to Lomé, French Togoland. Edward then continued to nearby Ho, in British Togoland, arriving there, and becoming a Knight of Bahá'u'lláh, on 14 April 1954. He quickly found a job in the Education Office. Since Ho was just a few kilometres from Lomé, where David Tanyi was pioneering, the two pioneers sometimes visited each other. Young as he was, Edward could teach the Faith and by Riḍván 1955 he was able to form the first Local Spiritual Assembly of Ho. Between 1957 and 1959, he was a member of the West Africa Regional Teaching Committee and his activities with the committee helped him open up many other areas to the Faith. In 1960, Edward moved abroad, returning from time to time. In 1971, he spent a week travelling with Amatu'l-Bahá Rúhíyyih Khánum.[44] He again went abroad in 1975 and, except for a brief visit in 1981, remained away. It is not known what happened to him after 1981.

Albert Buapiah was a native-born man from British Togoland (now part of Ghana) who became a Bahá'í in October 1953 through the efforts of pioneers Major and Zara Dunne. Albert was followed into the Faith by his wife, Grace, and by November 1953, there were ten Bahá'ís. Albert pioneered to British Togoland in April 1954 and helped form the first Local Assembly of Osenase, Ghana.[45]

ASHANTI PROTECTORATE (NOW PART OF GHANA)

Benedict Eballa[46]

Benedict Eballa (1938–2006) was the second youngest Knight of Bahá'u'lláh, pioneering to the Ashanti Protectorate at the age of 16. His goal later became the Gold Coast and is now part of Ghana. In 1949, he met Martin Manga and the two became close friends. Ben's mother was a staunch Catholic and encouraged him to become the same, but he was revolted by the actions of the priests. He became so disenchanted with what he saw of religion around him that he changed his name from the Christian name of Benedict to his father's name, Yalla. Because of this, his mother asked the missionary school not to give him his certificate of completion. Leaving home, he and Martin were living in a compound behind the Tanyi home. When David Tanyi learned of the Bahá'í Faith from Enoch Olinga in October 1953, the two youths quickly became aware of the new teachings and both became Bahá'ís. Ben loved to read and devoured books on the Faith sent from England and the World Centre.

On 10 April 1954, after having been a Bahá'í for just a short time, Ben was one of the group that included Martin Manga, David Tanyi and Edward Tabe who, escorted by 'Alí Nakhjávání, departed on their pioneering adventure (see David Tanyi, pp. 70–71 above, for details). They first flew from Cameroon to Lagos, Nigeria, then travelled by bus to Accra, British Togoland. On the way, Edward Tabe stopped at his pioneering post in Ho, David Tanyi stayed in French Togoland, while Ben and Martin continued on an air force plane to Kumasi in the Ashanti Protectorate. Martin continued on the plane to his post in Tamale in the Northern Territories Protectorate.

Ben arrived in Kumasi on 16 April. He spent the first week in a hotel and began talking with those he met. In exploring his new home, he met a Nigerian who prepared and sold tea and bread. His selling spot was a gathering place and Ben asked about Cameroonians. He was introduced to a fellow Cameroonian, Peter Baker, who took him in and treated him as his son. Ben continued to expand his circle of contacts by going to the YMCA for tea and discussions on many topics, including the Faith. Fairly quickly, some of his contacts became Bahá'ís, including Boateng Solomon. Ben soon began helping a woman who ran a kindergarten, teaching some of the children. When the woman died, Ben was put in charge of the school.

During his time in Kumasi, Ben sent regular reports of his activities to Auxiliary Board member Valerie Wilson. At Riḍván 1955, Ben was able to help form the first Local Spiritual Assembly of Kumasi, even though he was not old enough to serve on it. Later in that year, both his mother and brother died and he was compelled to return to Cameroon.

Ben returned to Ghana in 1961 and was then awarded a scholarship in Germany to study Anthropology. By 1972, he had earned his PhD and in 1980 was made head of the Department of Social Anthropology at Cameroon's University of Yaoundé. He became well known and several times was approached about entering party politics. He flatly refused. Ben ascended to the Abhá Kingdom in 2006.

Northwest Territories Protectorate
(now part of Ghana)

Julius Edwards

Julius Edwards (1902–1985) pioneered from Jamaica to the Northwest Territories Protectorate, arriving on 29 September 1953 to earn the title of Knight of Baháʼuʼlláh.[47] In Jamaica, Julius was very active in promoting the welfare of the black people. He founded the Jamaica Economic-Socio Society, served as chairman of the Universal Negro Improvement Association and was an advisor to two Prime Ministers of Jamaica. After becoming a Baháʼí, he accompanied Dorothy Baker to a regional teaching conference in El Salvador, at which he also served as chairman.

Julius was able to spend just three months in the town of Tamale, but even so was able to confirm three souls and form a group.[48] Government restrictions forced him to leave. After leaving Tamale, he continued to Liberia, where he settled and began teaching. His services there were recognized by the President of Liberia, William Tubman, who awarded Julius a special citation. Julius's influence on Tubman also resulted in the President making a visit to the Baháʼí World Centre during an official visit to Israel in 1962.[49]

In 1957, Vera Douglas arrived in Liberia on an excursion with her aunt, who knew Julius. Within a few months, both Vera and her aunt had accepted the Bahá'í Faith and were elected to serve on the first Local Spiritual Assembly of Monrovia at Riḍván 1958.[50] Vera and Julius were married in 1960. Vera later became an Auxiliary Board member and was very active in Liberia and all the nearby countries. The couple remained in Liberia until 1979. Moving to Grenada in December 1980, they continued teaching the Faith until Vera's death a year later.[51] Julius remained until his passing in 1985.

Martin Manga[52]

Martin Manga (b.1934) arrived in the Northwest Territories Protectorate on 16 April 1954. During his childhood, after attending primary school, Martin, along with two siblings, began working for an uncle as a blacksmith and then a mechanic. When the uncle decided that the number of people he was caring for was too large, he evicted Martin and his siblings, who then went to live with their aunt and uncle, Esther and David Tanyi. Here, they roomed with Ben Eballa and learned of the Bahá'í Faith through Enoch Olinga.

Martin became a Bahá'í along with several others. The newly formed group received a message from Shoghi Effendi calling for pioneers to be sent to various places (see David Tanyi, pp. 70–71 above for details). Nineteen-year-old Martin promptly quit his auto-mechanic apprenticeship and departed on 10 April with David Tanyi, Ben Eballa, Edward Tabe and 'Alí Nakhjavání. Martin arrived in Tamale in the Northwest Territories Protectorate (now part of Ghana) on the afternoon of 16 April. As he passed through the airport, an official wondered at such a young man travelling alone. Martin was only five feet five inches tall and looked young for his 19 years. Upon being questioned, Martin replied that he was there to 'acquire life experience', which made the official ask, 'At this age?' A health official took Martin into the town and left him in the market square. Not knowing what to do, Martin sat under a tree with his single piece of luggage:

After a long wait, not knowing where to go to, he tried unsuccessfully to talk to passers-by, with the aim of finding where to lodge. Their responses were often unfriendly, derisive, noncommittal or aloof. Their remarks in the Hausa language were on the lines of: 'I don't understand English'. Those who were rude told him:

'Ga'fara!'– when used derisively, this means, 'Clear off!' or 'Leave me in peace!'

Martin did not know what to do next. He sat under a tree, from which he saw a brewer of tea start to kindle a fire to brew and sell his tea. He went up to him and asked him if he knew of any Cameroonian in town. His response was negative. Then he saw a barber working under a tree and getting ready to close for the day. Martin approached him and asked him if he knew of any Nigerian or Cameroonian in town. The barber took a careful look at him and asked where he was coming from and what he had come to do this far from his home land.

'I come from Cameroon and I have come to acquire some experience in life,' replied Martin Manga.

Stunned, the barber paused for a while before querying: 'At this age?'

However, he was more helpful, and asked a small child to show Martin a certain woman called 'Mammy Yaoundé', who earned her living by brewing and selling 'pito', an alcoholic beverage made from millet or guinea corn. This lady was able to offer Martin accommodation. By this time, he had only £14 remaining, out of which he contributed £1 per day for his living expenses.

Job hunting was difficult, but he met a man who was able to get him a job as a mechanic – but for a fee. Martin couldn't pay the whole amount, so paid part and promised the rest from his first pay check. That left him with only five shillings, which quickly dwindled to two shillings with still a week left to go before payday. Those two shillings bought him six large cups of gari (roasted cassava dough), two of which he gave to a friend. To stretch those four remaining cups, each day he soaked half a cup of gari in water then spiced it with pepper.

When the end of the month arrived, Martin was paid about £20, so he went to a restaurant for a proper meal. But,

He was so famished that he could not even eat well. The proprietor noticed Martin Manga's inability to eat and walked up to him. 'Son, why aren't you eating? Don't you like the food?' he enquired.

'No,' replied Martin. 'I have been so hungry these past days that I have lost appetite for food.'

Noticing Martin's foreign English accent, the proprietor pressed on with another question.

'But, son, where do you come from?'

'Cameroon,' Martin Manga replied.

'Hmm?! What have you come to do in this part of the world?' asked the proprietor.

For the third time, Martin Manga replied: 'To acquire experience in life.'

And, for the third time, he received the curious query: 'At this age?'

Julius Edwards was also a Knight of Bahá'u'lláh for the Northwest Territories Protectorate, having arrived in late September 1953. He had only been allowed to stay for about three months, but he had brought three people into the Faith. Martin met two of them, Mr R.A. Som and Martin Asumang, and with them he began building a Bahá'í community. His teaching time was very limited because he worked from 6 a.m. to 6 p.m. Monday through Friday, 6 a.m. to 2 p.m. on Saturday and 6 a.m. to noon on Sunday. Notwithstanding the difficulties, Martin was able to bring enough people into the Faith to elect the first Local Spiritual Assembly in the Northwest Territories at Riḍván 1955. In April 1957, Martin had to return to Cameroon to care for his ailing mother. He continues to share the Faith to the present day.

St Thomas Island (now Democratic Republic of São Tomé and Príncipe) and Spanish Guinea (now Equatorial Guinea)

Elise Schreiber[53]

Elise Schreiber (1925–2012), a young schoolteacher and journalist from America, has the distinction of being a Knight of Bahá'u'lláh for two areas – St Thomas Island (known in Portuguese as São Tomé), off the coast of Gabon, and Spanish Guinea (now known as Equatorial Guinea). Elise, whose mother had become a Bahá'í during the time of 'Abdu'l-Bahá, was born in Chicago in 1925. Elise loved to tell stories about Bahá'u'lláh and 'Abdu'l-Bahá to her younger brothers – David, who became a Knight of Bahá'u'lláh to the Leeward Islands, and Eugene, who pioneered to Japan and Korea. Like most young Bahá'ís of her generation, Shoghi Effendi's guidance would forever shape her life. To be near the House of Worship in Wilmette and to continue deepening in the Faith, Elise attended the National Teachers College (now National Louis University) in Evanston, Illinois and earned a degree in education. After graduating in 1947, Elise pioneered to San Diego, California, where she taught elementary school and sang in the San Diego Civic Opera. She also helped form the first Spiritual Assembly of the Bahá'ís there.

Like most young Bahá'ís of her generation, Elise felt a deeply personal connection to Shoghi Effendi:

In 1951, Elise pioneered to Colombia, South America, where she joined . . . long-time American pioneer Gayle Woolson in Bogotá. It was a time of great turmoil in Colombia. A violent and bloody revolution had taken place just two years before, and there was still an undeclared civil war. The government was extremely repressive, and the Bahá'í work progressed but slowly.

Elise taught English as a second language, and served on the Spiritual Assembly of Bogotá. She later moved to Medellín, where she dedicated herself to helping raise that small, loyal group to an Assembly. Building upon her excellent reputation as a teacher of English, she founded her own school in Medellín, serving as its Director. Her Academia y Club de Nueve Idiomas (Academy and Club of Nine Languages) employed a dozen language teachers, had over four hundred students, and became a cultural center of the city.

As a foreigner in a police state, Elise had to be wise and discreet when teaching the Faith. There were few seekers, and it was a slow and laborious process to bring in new believers. She had prayed constantly and shed many tears over the teaching work there. Yet she persevered, her soul sustained by the words the Guardian himself had written to her in Medellín: 'Indeed, the more difficult the conditions may be, the more meritorious the task becomes.'

Elise wrote an article about the approaching Dedication of the Bahá'í House of Worship in Wilmette, Illinois . . . Entitled *Templo Universal de Luz* (Universal Temple of Light). It was published in the 20 December 1952 issue of *Mire!* magazine – just five months before the Dedication. It was so well received that the magazine bestowed its Credentials of Journalism on Elise, which would later prove indispensable. But most meaningful to her was the letter she received from the Guardian, saying that he was 'pleased to see such a representative article on the Faith in Spanish'.

Elise attended the dedication of the House of Worship in Wilmette in May 1953 and heard Amatu'l-Bahá Rúḥíyyih Khánum announce the Guardian's goals for the North American Bahá'í Community. When Rúḥíyyih Khánum came to Spanish Guinea, 'Elise felt them [those two words] enter her being with such power that "it was as if a thunderbolt had issued them"'. She knew instantly that she would arise to go there. Being torn between staying in Colombia and fulfilling one of the Guardian's goals, she wrote him to ask which should take precedence. She did not receive a reply in time for her departure for Africa, but through fervent prayer she felt guided to go.

She sailed first to the Canary Islands where she received a cable from the National Spiritual Assembly of the United States asking her to also try for entry to São Tomé e Príncipe (St Thomas Island), another of Shoghi Effendi's goals. At that time, São Tomé was a Portuguese colony while Spanish Guinea was controlled by Spain. To acquire her visa for her first goal of Spanish Guinea, she went to Spain where she was told that 'Spanish Guinea was a military and penal colony, and no place for her to go. She was persistent, explaining that as a journalist, she needed to pass through there for a book she wanted to write about Africa. The credentials she had received from *Mire!* magazine, which she still carried, had suddenly become invaluable.'

With her Spanish Guinea visa in hand, Elise went to Portugal to do the same for São Tomé. The authorities again tried to dissuade her, saying that the 'country was "a place of revolts", and no foreigners were allowed in. It was known as the Chocolate Island, and was closely guarded, as it was where the Portuguese Empire, still using slave labour, grew much of the world's chocolate. Just a few months before, there had been a bloody revolt in São Tomé, and there remained a great distrust of foreigners bringing new ideas.' Constant prayer, though, overcame the obstacles and her second visa was granted.

On 27 February 1954, after five 'long and torturous months' of waiting and a final journey as the only woman on a 1,000-ton freighter, Elise arrived at the island of São Tomé. The Feast of 'Alá was held on 2 March and as she prepared for the Nineteen-Day Fast, Elise prayed, asking Bahá'u'lláh to send a thirsty and trustworthy soul to her. Two days later, Carlos da Silva, a Portuguese poet and journalist, came to interview her for the local newspaper. After determining his interests and sincerity for a few days, Elise gave him the Teachings. He became enraptured with the beautiful words of Bahá'u'lláh – saying they were 'as the melodies of Mendelssohn' to his ears – and declared his Faith. One by one, Carlos brought her several other like-minded seekers.

In secrecy, Elise taught them, keeping no declaration cards or lists because of the danger. Every night and day she poured the Teachings into them without ceasing, as their souls were so thirsty. She was able to bring seven waiting souls into the Faith in São Tomé. They were Carlos da Silva (the first Bahá'í of São Tomé) and his wife, Antónia; Henrique Côrte-Real (the Economic Minister of the island) and his wife, Maria; and Henrique Teixeira, Sr. Carvalho, and Mel Cardoza – all originally from Portugal.

Day by day, as the new believers deepened in the Faith, and grew stronger in the Covenant, they became very dear to each other. Their clandestine meetings, as well as their being the first souls in their country to recognize the new Messenger of God, evoked in them a strong sense of spiritual kinship with the earliest Christians. They studied most every night in the da Silva home, and sometimes in the jungle, which they named their 'jungle catacombs'.

One night, through Bahá'í consultation on teaching, it was determined that Elise should take the Faith to two educated brothers, who were known to be leaders among the free blacks of São Tomé. One of the Bahá'ís who knew the brothers arranged a midnight meeting, and Elise went, under cover of night, to carry the Faith to them. One brother was absent, but the other received her graciously, though he was quite ill with malaria. He listened with interest, and was impressed with the Teachings. Though he did not accept the Faith then, he promised to inform his people of her message, and Elise returned in darkness. Through this deed, Elise was able to take the Faith to the black population of the island, as well as the white.

The Commandant of São Tomé, a ruthless man who had been summoned there to quell revolts, was suspicious of Elise and took her in for questioning several times. During these interrogations, she would silently pray the Greatest Name over and over again. One such time, she told this powerful man, 'I have protection.' When he asked if she had a gun, she declared, 'I have something much more powerful than that. I have the power and protection of God, and He is protecting me from you right now!' Elise later said she did not know whence such audacious words had come, but the Commandant left her alone for a time after that.

The faithful little community was frequently harassed by the Commandant's police. Strange occurrences led Elise to realize that her life was threatened more than once. Through all of it, she felt God's protection surrounding them. She had no thought for her own safety, but proceeded cautiously for the sake of the new Bahá'ís, who would remain there after she left the island. Once, in anguish because of these troubles, she asked if they were sorry that she had brought them the Faith. Maria Côrte-Real assured her, 'Before you came our eyes were closed, but you opened them, Elise! All I want is to be a good Bahá'í.'

When some time later, da Silva and Teixeira were imprisoned for being Bahá'ís, Carlos wrote, 'my suffering is a cause of acquiring spiritual qualities and for obtaining Divine attributes. I have hope that through the help of 'Abdu'l-Bahá, Who every night comes to speak with me, I am turning into a good Bahá'í for the Victory of God . . . God knows the whole truth and has all the power in the world.'

On 19 April, after less than two months, the Commandant deported Elise on a small plane to Port-Gentil in French Equatorial Africa (now Gabon), just south of Spanish Guinea. 'Before she boarded the plane, the Commandant told her, "Your friends will suffer," and his words struck through her heart like a knife.'

The French authorities in French Equatorial Africa were not very happy to receive the deportee and only allowed her into the country 'because they assumed she was a missionary, come to see Dr Schweitzer at Lambaréné. When they found she was not, they wanted to deport her to the United States.' Luckily, she was able to convince them to deport her, instead, to Spanish Guinea. Thus they inadvertently helped her to fulfil her original intention and incidentally, make her a double Knight.

The Governor of Spanish Guinea in Santa Isabel (the capital now known as Malabo) had been warned about Elise by the Commandant of São Tomé. But she flew on a private plane to Bata on the mainland, 'right under the nose of the police, who were preoccupied with some important military exercises' on 17 May. For the next two months, she spread the Faith of Bahá'u'lláh:

Elise was able to confirm one soul, Sr. José Ramos Espinosa, a 'most highminded' Spanish writer and young businessman. José was very interested in African tribal cultures and had written a book about the abundant life of the jungle. He told Elise about the King of the peaceable Benga tribe, on the island of Corisco, and she longed to take the Faith to this King. In June of 1954, José arranged for Elise, as a journalist, to accompany an expedition of Spanish engineers, who were surveying the islands of Spanish Guinea for future lighthouses.

Elise set out with them to the island of Corisco. It was a rigorous trip, taking a total of six days of travel by small boat to each outlying island, and hours of hiking through dense jungle. In Corisco, some of their guides were of the Benga tribe and spoke to her of their King. This was the opportunity she had prayed for, and she slipped away from the expedition and hiked through the jungle with them for three hours to meet their King.

The King of Corisco, Santiago Uganda Mdelo, was very dignified at ninety-five years of age. He said he had been expecting her, then asked her to speak to him in English, which greatly surprised her. King Uganda told Elise that he had had a dream that someone was coming to him with a message 'precious as pearls'. She discovered there was also an old Benga prophecy that a 'fair-skinned girl' would bring to them – the Protestant remnant of the Bengas – word of the returned Christ, and would make their people very happy! Both the King and his nephew, George E. Robinson, eighty-five, 'radiantly accepted Bahá'u'lláh'. Enraptured, they gave thanks to God many times for her coming. Before leaving, she gave two prayers in English to the King: the Remover of Difficulties, by the Báb, and the Prayer for All Nations, by 'Abdu'l-Bahá, and promised to send other Bahá'ís to them in the future. Then the guides took her back through the jungle.

When she returned, it was nightfall. The engineers were very angry, as she had been gone eight hours! But she calmed them down, and returned to Bata with them in the morning. There she stayed and continued to deepen José in the Teachings, so that he would be able to carry on the work of the Faith in Spanish Guinea after she left.

Elise revealed that, 'José Ramos, the first Bahá'í of Spanish Guinea, proved to be brilliant, staunch, daring and faithful – the kind of believer that could win my heart.' When he proposed marriage to Elise, she accepted. At that time, however, they were unable to have a Bahá'í wedding in that part of Africa, or in any other country nearby. So they planned that after her return to Colombia, he would follow her, and they would be married there, or in the United States.

On 29 June, when her visa expired, the Governor deported her on a ship to Barcelona, saying 'he didn't know how she came to be in their country in the first place'. It was a sad leaving because José had to stay behind.

Though she wanted to return to Colombia and marry José, the US National Spiritual Assembly asked her to go to either Florida or Montgomery, Alabama, a city with no Bahá'ís. She chose the latter, arriving in November 1954 and quickly finding work in an elementary school. She found that teaching among the black people in Montgomery was easier than what she had experienced elsewhere. She visited their churches and spoke to their ministers, including Reverend Robert Abernathy and Dr Martin Luther King Jr. King invited her to speak at his church, saying 'he was interested in all spiritual teachings that advocated unity, peace, and racial equality'. But then racial turmoil began anew when the US Supreme Court declared school segregation unconstitutional, and Elise, who had been energetically teaching African-Americans, found herself in the middle of it. At that time, it was illegal for a white person to enter a black neighbourhood unless they were on business, so she became an 'Avon Lady', selling cosmetics door to door. While in Montgomery, Elise received a delayed letter from the Guardian, affirming that her decision to go to Africa had been the right one.

Elise and José, still in Spanish Guinea, maintained their connection through letters until the summer of 1955 when the US National Spiritual Assembly told her to stop all her correspondence with the believers in Africa as it would jeopardize the Bahá'í work in South Africa. Her obedience 'brought a crushing grief into her young life' because she never again heard from or saw José. She remained unmarried for the rest of her life.

From Montgomery Elise wrote the Guardian of her deportations and the suffering Bahá'ís in São Tomé. Later, Hand of the Cause Leroy Ioas told her that he had been with the Guardian when this news reached him, and that 'the Guardian had bowed his head and sat a long while in sadness. But then he had slowly raised his head, and spoken resolutely, "No, it is to their glory!"' He later wrote to assure her of his loving prayers for them.

Elise moved to New York in 1956, taught school and studied at Columbia University. Following the death of her father, she joined her mother in Nevada City, California. She spent the following years getting a Master of Arts degree in Speech and Drama from California State University at Sacramento, giving many public talks, presentations, firesides, and deepening classes. As a singer, Elise also released an album called *Songs of the New Age* with the Writings set to music by Bahá'í composers.

In 1991, Elise, as a Knight of Bahá'u'lláh, received an invitation from the Universal House of Justice for the Centenary Commemoration of the Ascension of Bahá'u'lláh at Bahjí. Before going to Haifa, she returned to São Tomé and, worried about getting a visa, she legally changed her name to Elise Lynelle to avoid problems. She spent two months travel teaching on the island, but was unable to find any of the small and steadfast group she had raised up.

In 2004, Elise returned to Equatorial (Spanish) Guinea to join the over 1,000 Bahá'ís in celebrating their Golden Jubilee. While there, she learned that her beloved José had passed away many years earlier. Elise joined him on 26 February 2012, after a long illness, in Grass Valley, California. At her burial, former House of Justice member Hooper Dunbar placed on her simple casket a bouquet of yellow roses – a loving gift from the National Spiritual Assembly of Equatorial Guinea.

RUANDA-URUNDI (NOW RWANDA AND BURUNDI)

Mary and Rex Collison

Rex (1884–1983) and Mary Collison (1892–1970) married in 1920 and became Bahá'ís in 1925. Their conversion began in the autumn of 1924, when they began studying a book Howard Colby Ives had left in Geneva, New York. The Collisons met Howard and Mabel Ives in January and quickly came into the Faith through their loving guidance.[54]

Mary was appointed to the first Outline Committee by the National Spiritual Assembly to prepare deepening study outlines. The first of these, 'Science and the Bahá'í Faith', was written by Rex. In 1928, they made a 17,000-mile travel-teaching trip from coast to coast and back. Mary also served on the National Teaching Committee, as a teacher at Bahá'í summer schools, and as a travel teacher between 1945 and 1952.[55]

Mary and Rex were involved with the construction of the North American House of Worship, then in 1952, at the ages of 60 and 68 respectively, they pioneered to Kampala, Uganda, from California. With the launching of the Ten Year Crusade, Mary and Rex were the first Americans to arise and on 1 May 1953, with Dunduzu Chisiza (1930–1962) as their translator, pioneered to Ruanda-Urundi.[56]

In spite of their visa, the trio were only able to stay for 18 months because of governmental policies, but by the time they left, there were 20 Bahá'ís.[57] Back in Uganda, the Collisons were involved with the construction of the Mother Temple of Africa and then became its custodians.[58] The couple returned to California in 1966, settling in Geyserville. Mary passed away in 1970, but Rex continued teaching the Faith as best he could. He lived until the age of 99, still doing his own cooking and household chores.[59]

Dunduzu Kaluli Chisiza

Dunduzu was the son of a village headman in Nyasaland (Malawi), the youngest of 11 children. When Dunduzu finished primary school, in order to further his education, he and his best friend, Herbert Sikombe (see David Tanyi, p. 72 above), went to the Livingstonia Boarding School run by Presbyterian missionaries. Highly intelligent, Dunduzu passed his tests with the highest marks, even though he commonly did not attend classes. From this dichotomy, he learned about racism. One of his teachers, in particular, was outraged that the mischievous Dunduzu could do so well with so little effort. Dunduzu didn't help his cause because he was 'just too clever and fearless for his own good'. And when she thought he was misbehaving, the teacher, in an overt display of racism, would call him a 'monkey'. The teacher finally conspired with others at the school to fail Dunduzu, even though he normally had the highest grades in the class. That failure taught Dunduzu about racism and strongly affected his future.[60]

Herbert Sikombe's father had gone to Tanganyika (now Tanzania) and become the head of the Police Department in Iringa in the far south of the country. Dunduzu, at 19, was able to get a job as a clerk in the Police Records Office there. But both Dunduzu and Herbert wanted to further their education and when they learned about the Aggrey College in Kampala, Uganda, they were able to be accepted. One of their teachers, Frobisher Kagwa, first introduced them to the Bahá'í Faith:

> Dunduzu was highly skeptical. He had witnessed the hypocrisy of the white Europeans he knew, who professed their religion but did not practice it. According to Herbert, Dunduzu carried a deep distrust of all white people. While his father had surely influenced him, Du had had enough of his own experiences with the racists at the Livingstonia School, who had (nearly) sabotaged his future when they could not bend him to their will, to steer clear of whites.
>
> Nevertheless, he and Herbert attended this talk, and heard an introductory presentation on the Bahá'í Faith by Mr. 'Alí Nakhjaváni, who was pioneering in Uganda at that time. Du was at first unconvinced, but was soon won over. Not only by Mr. Nakhjaváni's sincerity, but also his assertions of the equality of all religions and of all men, and by the logic of his elucidation of Biblical prophesies and proofs of Christ's return in Bahá'u'lláh.[61]

In his own words, Dunduzu wrote about his acceptance of the Faith:

> So it was that I who was made to detest white men with the religion they brought, was now challenged by another white man to accept another religion; I who cherished the Teachings of Christ but who strongly doubted that Christ was the Son of God, was now being challenged to acknowledge His Return; I who believed in the expulsion of the white man from Africa, was now ironically being made to consider him as a brother. It was a frightful insomnia that I had

that night. A deadly war was going on within my divided self. Its end seemed to be continually put off by a warning a student had yelled directly after we came out from the lecture. He said, 'Don't forget for a minute that white men brought their religion and took our land. This fellow is bringing a new technique of keeping you quiet while his friends snatch our land and domineer over us.' I confess that I could not prove the contrary, yet some invisible force seemed to push me to a decision.

The following day witnessed the end of my war. I had turned things over for nine and a half hours of the previous night. The result was that I had trampled down every bit of a doubt within me.[62]

Dunduzu already had strong political leanings and this was another huge challenge for him to overcome. He wrote:

Later in the evening a teacher asked me, 'Do you really understand what you have done? I understand Bahá'ís have nothing to do with politics. Is that what you are going to comply with?' 'Yes . . .' I started to speak, but he interrupted. 'What a loss to Nyasaland . . . Just why have you believed in the Bahá'í Faith?'.

'I believe in the Bahá'í Faith because it's the only solution to political problems. And if I have a solution to our political problems I don't think it is useful to fiddle with politics. Let me add, sir, that the only thing that an African can do to regain his freedom is to expel Europeans from Africa. But this is impracticable in view of the fact that Europeans have hydrogen bombs while we have only spears. The alternative to the above solution is to compromise our claims. But why take only half of what we want while the Bahá'ís give us the whole? They give us full equality. Mr Kagwa who has been with the Bahá'ís for a considerable time will bear this out. Equality, which every African wants today, is what the Bahá'í Faith gives us and that is why I identify myself with it.[63]

Herbert also accepted the Faith. When Dunduzu left for Butare, it was the last time the two devoted friends would see each other.

When the Ten Year Crusade began and the Intercontinental Teaching Conference was announced for February 1953, both Dunduzu and

Herbert attended and were galvanised by the talks of the Hands of the Cause and others. When the Collisons asked Dunduzu to join them in Ruanda-Urundi as their interpreter, he eagerly accepted. On 1 May, the trio arrived in Butare, shared a home together for the next eighteen months and taught the Faith. Less than a year later, on 11 March 1954, the Collisons wrote:

> Our passports have been renewed for another 2 years. We seem to have reached the limit of English-speaking contacts here. Of these we think two will probably become Bahá'ís in time but we have found it very difficult for various reasons to find time when they are able and willing to meet with us either in their own homes or here.
>
> We are not at all discouraged as to the eventual progress of the Faith in R.-U. Although education is conspicuously lacking, many people here are thinking for themselves. Many are eager to talk with us directly. Teaching through a translator is most difficult for all concerned. He [Dunduzu] indeed is a rare interpreter who doesn't take most of the spirit out of anything in transmitting it.[64]

After Dunduzu and the Collisons were forced to leave their post, Dunduzu returned to Nyasaland for a short while, then in 1955 moved to Southern Rhodesia where he found work as a clerk interpreter for the Indian High Commission and also served on the first Local Spiritual Assembly of Salisbury. During this time, Dunduzu's old political urges re-emerged and he joined the African National Congress, a political party. This resulted in consternation in the Bahá'í community:

> When the LSA discovered this, they had to take action. This was very distressing for the Bahá'ís, who earnestly tried to dissuade him, for they knew and dearly loved this exceptional African believer.
>
> In due course, Dunduzu received several warnings from the LSA and the Auxiliary Board member, even from the Guardian himself. Still, he could not be dissuaded from participation in the ANC. It has been noted that he was mistakenly convinced that he could somehow help his fellow Africans better (or sooner) by joining the ANC than by adherence to the Bahá'í Faith alone.
>
> Consequently, in 1956 the inevitable happened and Dunduzu lost his administrative rights. The Auxiliary Board member who

had handled the situation told me that this action had caused the beloved Guardian much sadness, for he dearly loved Dunduzu.[65]

In 1957, Dunduzu went to Birmingham, England, to study Development Economics at Fircroft College. While he was there, the Guardian died in London. Dunduzu attended the funeral and was 'as inconsolable in his grief as every Bahá'í present . . . Dunduzu was exceptionally heartbroken by the Guardian's passing, that at his funeral he cried a lot . . . sobbing intensely, and saying that he was so sorry for his actions.'[66]

In 1958, Dunduzu returned to Nyasaland and married Towela Humbo Myamtawali. In March of the next year, Dunduzu's political activities resulted in his being imprisoned until September of the following year, whereupon he resumed his position as the Secretary General of the Malawi Congress Party (MCP). He was elected to the Legislative Council in 1961 and became the parliamentary secretary to the Minister of Finance. Later in the same year, he travelled to India and published a book titled *Africa: What Lies Ahead*. The book shows a strong influence by the teachings of the Bahá'í Faith. Dunduzu organized a symposium on economic development for Nyasaland in 1962.[67]

By 1962, Dunduzu was becoming disillusioned with the Congress Party because of all the disunity affecting it and began to think of forming a new political party. But before he did so, he went to visit the new Mashriqu'l-Adhkár in Kampala – and a transformation occurred. Two Bahá'í Counsellors from Uganda, Oloro Epyeru and Kolonario Oule, told what happened:

> Bahá'í friends in Uganda called . . . to have one last heart-to-heart talk with him. They had poured out their hearts . . ., again pointing out the great spiritual danger should he remain on his current path. They had brought out quotations from 'Abdu'l-Bahá and the Guardian, and had implored him with all the sincerity of their love for him. He was so special to all of them, and they urgently wanted to reach him.
>
> . . . On that very day, Dunduzu changed. Somehow he had the longed-for epiphany, and realized the error of his former actions. They said that Dunduzu vowed to them that day that he would return to Nyasaland and immediately resign from the MCP. They felt that Dunduzu was finally willing to sacrifice it all for the sake of Bahá'u'lláh, and this had brought great joy to their hearts.[68]

Back in Nyasaland, Dunduzu was driving late at night in September 1962 when, somehow, the car left the road and Dunduzu was killed. The circumstances were very nebulous and political intrigue was suspected. It is thought, however, that he was going to meet members of the Malawi Congress Party to resign and renounce politics for the Faith.

SOUTHERN RHODESIA (NOW ZIMBABWE)

Ezzatu'llah Zahra'i[69]

Ezzatu'llah Zahra'i (b. 1926), called Ezzat, came from a Bahá'í family living in Qazvin. He was a young Bahá'í who had pioneered to Tabriz in 1947 during the 45-Month Plan of the National Spiritual Assembly of Iran. His path to Africa began with a proposed trip to Mexico in 1951. At that time, the Guardian had requested that Persian Bahá'ís not travel to the United States and Ezzat's trip to Mexico required a stopover there. Consequently, he wrote to the National Spiritual Assembly and asked permission for the stopover. The Assembly forwarded the request to Shoghi Effendi. Writing for the Guardian, Lotfullah Hakím replied that the request was not allowed, but that 'Shoghi Effendi urges him to go to Africa for teaching work'. Baffled at the reply and about what he should do, he consulted with his mother, who convinced him that he had to do what Shoghi Effendi asked.

Ezzat began his journey by travelling to Tanganyika (now Tanzania), where he was granted a one-month visa upon his arrival in November 1952. When that visa expired, he was able to get another visa for Kenya. While in Nairobi, he met Aziz Yazdi and several other pioneers, as well as Richard St Barbe Baker, a Bahá'í who had first gone to Kenya in 1920 as a Conservator of Forests. St Barbe, as he was known, had become well known for his tree-planting programmes and as the founder of a group called Men of the Trees, which advocated planting and conserving trees. In 1929, he was invited to Palestine by the High Commissioner of Palestine to apply his forestation programme to the arid country. Having become a Bahá'í, St Barbe went to meet Shoghi Effendi. When a Palestinian chapter of Men of the Trees was formed, the Guardian became the first life member.[70]

St Barbe offered to take Ezzat in his Humber station wagon to the Intercontinental Teaching Conference in Kampala in February 1953.

After the Conference, Ezzat and other would-be pioneers gathered around Shoghi Effendi's map of goals. He and another Persian youth, Enayat Sohaili, chose Mozambique. Acquiring a one-month visa, Ezzat went to the town of Lorenço Marques in that country and moved in to the Polana Hotel. On 14 April, Ezzat met three Bahá'ís who were passing through by ship: Fred Schechter, already a Knight of Bahá'u'lláh for Djibouti, and Fred and Elizabeth Laws, who would soon be Knights of Bahá'u'lláh for Basutoland. A few days later Ezzat was arrested and interviewed by the secret police, who confiscated all his books and letters. For the next month, Ezzat was in and out of the secret police offices and also spent a short time in jail. Finally, he was expelled on 29 May 1953.

Before being expelled, Ezzat had managed to get a visa for Northern Rhodesia with a 24-hour transit visa for Southern Rhodesia. When he landed in Bulawayo, Southern Rhodesia (now Zimbabwe), he apprehensively approached the Police Formalities officer at the very end of a long queue. When he finally reached the British official, the man looked at Ezzat's passport, then exclaimed that he had lived in Iran and was delighted to meet an Iranian. It turned out that the man had banked in the same place that Ezzat had worked. When the official asked why he was in Southern Rhodesia, Ezzat said he was there for a visit. When the man asked how long he was staying, Ezzat blurted out 'twenty days'. He suddenly had a 20-day visa.

Ezzat continued on to Salisbury (now Harare), then immediately sent a cablegram to Shoghi Effendi announcing that he was at his post, not realizing that he was the first pioneer to reach that country. A Rhodesian businessman he had met in Mozambique had arranged a room for him and was ready to give him a job at his import-export firm. He put Ezzat in contact with a local law firm to apply for his residence permit.

Ezzat couldn't teach openly because of the unwritten apartheid policies of the country, so he would go to the park each evening and pray that the people in Salisbury would discover the Bahá'í Faith. The law firm managed to renew his 20-day visa, but then Ezzat was informed that he would have to leave the country before a resident permit could be issued. He was advised to go to Elizabethville (now Lubumbashi) in the Belgian Congo.

Ezzat spent July and August 1953 in the Belgian Congo waiting for his resident permit, but on 18 August, he was informed that it had been denied. He had spent only 40 days in Salisbury, but it was enough to gain him the title of Knight of Bahá'u'lláh. After working for a short while in Elizabethville, he moved back to Kenya and settled in Mombasa, where he stayed until his pilgrimage in May 1957.

During the pilgrimage, Shoghi Effendi asked him to go to Egypt. The Suez war had cut off communication between the Egyptian Bahá'ís and the Holy Land and the Guardian wanted them to know that he had not forgotten them. Ezzat quickly agreed without thinking. Then he began thinking of the problems he faced. Shoghi Effendi suddenly stopped and looked at him, saying, 'Yes, you will have to be very careful.' Ezzat went to Istanbul to get a new passport, one without an Israeli stamp. He was told that it would be impossible, but Shoghi Effendi had given him the task. He asked the Persian consul in Istanbul for the new passport, explaining that he had been in Israel and couldn't enter Egypt with his current one. 'Why the hell did you have to go to Palestine?' the consul asked. Ezzat said he was a Bahá'í and had gone on pilgrimage. He needed the new passport to do some important business in Egypt. Ezzat then said that he could have lied and said he had lost his passport, but lying was not possible. The consul noted Ezzat's travels through Mozambique, Rhodesia, Congo, Kenya and Tanganyika and began asking questions about the countries. Finally, the consul said he had been to Palestine and had visited the Persian Gardens in Haifa. He then gave him a new passport. Ezzat spent two weeks in Egypt travelling from city to city, telling the Bahá'ís news from the Ten Year Crusade, assuring them of Shoghi Effendi's prayers for them, and collecting statistics which he later sent to Haifa.

After completing the Guardian's request, Ezzat travelled through Europe visiting the Bahá'ís, and finally settling in Paris. He married Annette Riis in 1961. In 1984, he decided to retire and asked the Universal House of Justice where they should pioneer. The House responded that it preferred that they stay anywhere in France, so they remained in Paris.

'Aynu'd-Dín and Tahireh 'Alá'í

The next pioneers to Southern Rhodesia, Iranians 'Aynu'd-Dín (?–1982) and Tahireh 'Alá'í (1906–1992), were more successful in remaining there. Tahireh came from a Baháʾí family in Tehran and had attended the Tarbíyat School for Girls. In 1932, she married ʿAynuʾd-Dín ʿAláʾí, who worked in the Iranian Ministry of Finance.

In 1952 Tahireh was on pilgrimage from Iran and heard of the Guardian's desire for pioneers to Africa. She and her husband attended the Intercontinental Teaching Conference in Kampala the next year, where they decided to stay in Africa. Initially they lived in Kenya, but then acquired visas for Mozambique. The visas, however, quickly expired so they decided to move to Southern Rhodesia.[71]

ʿAynuʾd-Dín and Tahireh ʿAláʾí arrived in Salisbury, Southern Rhodesia (now Harare, Zimbabwe), on 4 December 1953 and joined Claire Gung, whom they had known in Kenya. They were only allowed to stay until August 1954 when their visa could not be extended. They returned to Kenya.[72] Back in Nairobi, Azíz Yazdi helped them to obtain resident visas and they were soon elected to the first National Spiritual Assembly of Kenya. After eighteen years in Africa, the ʿAláʾís returned to Tehran in 1972. Seven years later, they pioneered to Le Cannet on the French Riviera where they were able to help form the first Local Assembly. ʿAynuʾd-Dín was struck and killed by a car in 1982. Tahireh made one final trip to the Baháʾí World Centre in 1986.[73]

Claire Gung

Claire Gung (1904–1985) was born in Germany in 1904 and arrived in England in 1930. Claire became a Baháʾí in 1939 after caring for a terminally ill Baháʾí who said many prayers aloud. The prayers attracted her. In 1941, she pioneered for the first time, to Northampton, then, seven years later, to Cardiff. There followed pioneering efforts in Brighton and Belfast.[74]

When Shoghi Effendi tasked England with opening Africa in 1950, Claire was one of the first to respond. She was initially discouraged, being told that 'as a woman alone you can not do in Africa what you have done in England'. Unfazed, she found a job as a matron in a boy's school in Lushoto, Tanganyika (Tanzania). Selling many of her possessions in order to buy passage, she went to buy a ticket on the steam ship *Warwick Castle*, which sailed the next day. The clerk, however, said that there were none available. Not knowing what else to do, Claire stood where she could see the booking office and began praying. Soon, a man arrived, went to the office and said that he wanted to cancel his booking. Claire quickly bought the ticket.[75]

Claire sailed to her post on 3 January 1951 and was seasick the whole way. Then, having left a wintry Britain, she found herself a month later in the roasting heat of Africa. Before leaving England, Claire had had many doubts and had emptied her heart in a letter to Shoghi Effendi. Arriving at the school and finding his reply awaiting her, she was uplifted:

> You have voiced the same suffering, the sign of the same mystery, as has been voiced by almost all those who have been called upon to serve God. Even the Prophets of God, we know, suffered agony when the Spirit of God descended on them and Commanded them to arise and preach. Look at Moses saying 'I am a stutterer!' Look at Muhammad rolled in His rug in agony! The Guardian himself suffered terribly when he learned he was the one who had been made Guardian.
>
> So you see your sense of inadequacy, your realisation of your own unworthiness, is not unique at all. Many, from the Highest to the humblest, have had it. Now the wisdom of it is this: it is such seemingly weak instruments that demonstrate that God is the Power achieving the victories and not men. If you were a wealthy, prominent, strong individual who knew all about Africa and looked upon going out there as fun, any services you render, and victories you have, would be laid to your personality, not to the Cause of God! But because the reverse is true, your services will be a witness to the Power of Bahá'u'lláh and the Truth of His Faith.
>
> Rest assured, dear sister, you will ever increasingly be sustained, and you will find joy and strength given to you, and God will reward you. You will pass through these dark hours triumphant. The first Bahá'í going on such an historic mission could not but suffer – but the compensation will be great![76]

Claire spent two years as the sole Bahá'í in her part of Tanganyika. It was a difficult time because of the apartheid policies. One night after a particularly notable example of racism, she told the staff at the dining table: 'I refuse to eat with anyone who treats another human being like that. What sort of family do you come from? You have no manners at all.' In early 1953, Claire moved to Nairobi.[77]

In February, Claire attended the Intercontinental Teaching Conference in Kampala and was inspired to pioneer to one of the Guardian's goal areas for the Ten Year Crusade, Southern Rhodesia, arriving on 6 October 1953 in Salisbury. Her arrival in Salisbury was inauspicious. There was a celebration going on and no hotel rooms were available. One hotel finally give her a room for one night. The next night was spent in a 'sleazy hotel' where she was accosted by a drunk. When she went to the Post Office to cable the Guardian of her arrival, she waited in line for a long time before she realized that she was in the wrong line, the one for blacks. The whites had their own, much faster, line. Claire soon found a job as a housekeeper and governess with the Gemill family on a 20-acre estate outside the capital. When they went to get her residence permit, they discovered that she had none of the necessary documentation. But since it was the last day of the Holy Year, Claire predicted a miracle and that was what happened. At first, the Immigration official declared that nothing could be done, but Mrs Gemill insisted that she needed Claire. When the official asked for her birth certificate, she had none, but replied, 'You know I have been born or else I would not be here.' She left with papers to be signed and Mrs Gemill took her to her lawyer, arriving without an appointment, but leaving with all the needed signatures.[78]

In January 1955, Claire went on pilgrimage and met the Guardian. When she told him that she worried at her lack of teaching success, 'he countered by stating that, on the contrary, she was the "Mother of Africa".'[79] Then on 20 March 1955, Moses Makwaya and Berard Toni declared their belief in Bahá'u'lláh and at Riḍván a month later, the first Local Spiritual Assembly was formed.[80]

Claire stayed in Southern Rhodesia until April 1956, when she moved her pioneer post to Nyasaland (now Malawi).[81] She joined Enayat Sohaili, who had pioneered there three years previously. It was a very difficult time. There were no good jobs and decent housing was almost non-existent. Claire worked at several hotels, including the Shire Highlands, which is now close to the present National Bahá'í Centre. She also found work in a hospital, at an accounting firm and in several homes.[82] After Enayat was forced to leave in early 1957, Claire carried on alone until July of that year, when she moved to Kampala, Uganda.[83]

In Kampala, Claire found work in the Aga Khan Nursery School. After three years, she opened her own kindergarten, financed by her own money. Not having sufficient funds for much more than the basics, she asked the Bahá'ís to collect soda bottle caps, match boxes and match sticks, which she turned into toy furniture and used to help the children to learn the numbers and the alphabet. The school was located in the King's domain and soon some of the royal children were her students. By 1962, Claire's kindergarten was well known. She was interviewed on TV twice and there were articles about the school in the local papers. In March 1963, she was able to incorporate the school as Auntie Claire's Kindergarten Ltd.[84]

Eventually, there were almost 200 children in the school, including those of the King, government ministers, diplomats and other important people. In 1968, Claire built a new and larger school, again with her own funds. She trained a staff of ten Ugandans and made many of the toys for the children herself.[85]

In 1979, Claire had a dream in which Hand of the Cause Enoch Olinga was in great danger. Soon afterwards, he and some of his family were murdered in Kampala. After the murder, Claire was the only pioneer remaining in Kampala and was in a life-threatening situation, but she refused to leave her school.[86] She remained in Africa until her death in 1985. Her final resting place is near the grave of Hand of the Cause Enoch Olinga.[87]

Kenneth and Roberta Christian

Kenneth (1913–1959) and Roberta Christian (1913–1971) pioneered to Southern Rhodesia in December 1953. Roberta grew up in New York State and married Kenneth, a college professor, lecturer and writer. Both were very active in the Faith. Roberta edited the *Bahá'í News* for three years and wrote two popular children's books. Kenneth served on the National Spiritual Assembly of the United States and was one of the five members who resigned to pioneer.

The Christians were excited about pioneering as part of the Ten Year Crusade and Kenneth wrote to the Guardian for advice. Receiving their answer, the couple, along with their 12-year-old son, Roger, headed for Southern Rhodesia by ship on 10 December, and throughout the 19-day journey, Kenneth 'talked, prayed and planned'. They reached their pioneering post on 1 January 1954.

That same month, the Christians visited a furniture shop owned by a Jewish couple, Sue and Sylvia Benatar. It began a life-transforming adventure for the Benatars:

> They had explained that they were not buying furniture just yet but as they intended settling in Salisbury they wanted to find out what was available so that when they moved into a house of their own they would have some idea what to buy. 'Sue' told me that they knew no one in the town so he had invited them to come for dinner. He was quite excited about meeting them as they seemed very nice people!
>
> When they came for dinner I was immediately attracted to them – warm, kind, interesting people! And we had never met Americans before! Kenneth told us he had been a professor of English Literature at the University in Michigan. We were very surprised that they had left America to come to live in Rhodesia and asked them why they had done so. They said that they were not happy with the education system where their son went to school as it was too liberal. The children did not have to learn to read or write unless they wanted to etc. Another reason was that Roberta, because of her health, needed to live in a drier climate. We accepted their reasons but wondered why they could not find solutions to these problems in other parts of America! We saw them very often and we all became very fond of each other.[88]

Southern Rhodesia at that time had no laws segregating the races, though they were segregated in reality. Sylvia noted, 'There was no law against Africans mixing socially with the white people but they could not own property in the white areas although they could live in houses built for them on white-owned property. At that time most of the black people were uneducated and were simply employed in the white areas. Their families lived in "Reserves" much as they had always lived, in round mud huts.'[89]

Sue Benatar had been born and raised in Salisbury and tried to use his contacts to help Kenneth find a job, but without success. Sylvia wrote:

> Roberta and I had even thought of taking over an ice cream business which was for sale and supplying frozen foods which at that time nobody had ever heard of! We had become very close friends and

saw each other frequently. One day they came to ask if we could lend them some blankets for a friend who was passing through as they had none to spare. We agreed but they told us that they would like us to meet him beforehand as he was an Egyptian and rather dark-skinned. 'Sue' replied that this was not a problem and that his mother was also born in Egypt! Anyway, their friend arrived and presented himself at our house. Again, we felt this warmth and became friends immediately. It happened to be Hassan Sabri! Hassan and 'Sue', both being great jokers, later enjoyed a lifetime joke by calling each other names such as 'You Arab, You!' and 'You Jew, You!' whenever they saw each other in different parts of the world![90]

Then Sue contacted the authorities charged with employing staff for the future University of the Federation of the Rhodesias and Nyasaland. They said they would definitely have a position for Kenneth – but unfortunately not for another eighteen months. This was a difficult time for the Christians, who were rapidly running out of money. Then Dwight Allen, a Knight for Greece who had a position at the University of Athens, wrote and told Kenneth that he had to leave and that Kenneth could have the position if he was willing to move to Athens.[91] Finally, the Christians asked Shoghi Effendi if they could go to Athens and be pioneers there. The Guardian approved and Kenneth and Roberta went to Greece where he took over Dwight's job.

When the Christians left Salisbury, they had not spoken of the Faith to Sue and Sylvia. Sylvia noted that 'As their name was Christian and we were Jewish we never broached the subject of religion, assuming that they were Christians.' It wasn't until six months later, when Larry and Carol Hautz arrived, that they learned about the Bahá'í Faith. The Guardian had warned the pioneers not to teach openly and to concentrate on the native population and the Christians had followed his request. Larry had been given the Benatars' names and he immediately began teaching them the Faith. Both became Bahá'ís in April 1955, just in time so that the first Local Spiritual Assembly of Salisbury could be formed.[92]

Teaching in Greece was very difficult because of a law that made it illegal to have 'people come to a home for the purpose of promulgating any religion other than the religion of the country'. The Christians spent three years in Greece before returning to America in 1957.[93]

Kenneth's next job took him to Jakarta where he was one of only two non-Persians on the Local Spiritual Assembly. He quickly came to love and be loved by the Indonesian people. Kenneth died in 1959; after his death, Roberta moved to California and then, in 1967, went to Alaska to help complete the goals of the Nine Year Plan.[94]

SOUTH WEST AFRICA (NOW NAMIBIA)

Edward Cardell

Englishman Edward (Ted) Cardell (1918–1999) became a Bahá'í in 1949 in Canada. When he returned to the United Kingdom, he began to photograph Bahá'í events, sending copies of the photos to the Guardian. With the beginning of Britain's Africa plan in 1950, Ted wanted to pioneer, but he had little money and needed a job. The Africa Committee

> suggested to me that I get a return ticket and just go and look for a job. So, I did, but with only a couple hundred dollars in my pocket and thinking that if I couldn't get a job in a couple of weeks, I may as well get the return ticket home.
>
> Well, there were about four or five photographic firms in Nairobi and a newspaper. I went out there, tried all these and totally failed to get a job and ended up with nothing in my pocket and living in a hotel two or three thousand miles from home. It was a rich experience and I think everybody needs this! So, now I thought this is about the time to start praying. What else could you do? So, I prayed for a bit then fell asleep. And when I woke up, I got the idea to go down to the newspaper office again, which I did and they gave me a job instantly at double the salary I had been getting in London. They suddenly realised the Queen was coming out to Kenya and they didn't have a full-time photographer.[95]

Three months after Ted arrived in Nairobi, Aziz Yazdi joined him and for six months they tried to teach the Bahá'í Faith, but with no results. Finally, a few people accepted Bahá'u'lláh's message. In 1952, Ted went on pilgrimage and met Shoghi Effendi. He was the only pilgrim and at the dinner table at night was surrounded with Hands of the Cause and International Bahá'í Council members, in addition to the Guardian and Rúḥíyyih <u>Kh</u>ánum. It was a humbling experience for someone who had only been a Baháʼí for a year and a half.

Even though Ted was already a pioneer in Kenya, the Guardian had fired him up. At the beginning of the Ten Year Crusade, Shoghi Effendi sent a map to the Baháʼís in Kenya, where there were nine pioneers and nine native Baháʼís. Ted said:

> We laid it out on the floor and we all started looking at it. There were only twelve national assemblies in those days. Each had a great big coloured dot with lines of that colour running to the territories to be conquered by that country. England only had about twelve lines overseas. We were only a small community in those days, maybe about three or four hundred and only half of those are active. Where we would find people to conquer these countries, God only knew. Fred Schechter and Fred and Beth Laws had just arrived before the map came. They were joking with us, saying that they had stopped off at Walvis Bay, a territory on the southwest coast of Africa [South West Africa, now Namibia], and it was desert for a thousand miles along the coast and 300 miles inland. And they said, 'You know, some poor devil will one day have to go and pioneer that place.' We were having a good old chuckle about it.
>
> Well, the Guardian sent a message by the pilgrims that nine pioneers in Kenya was too many, so five of us walked and went to all parts in the Ten Year Plan. The Guardian had said to me, nobody deserves to make a pilgrimage, but you go there to get your batteries charged and your soul uplifted so you can go out and do extraordinary things. So when we laid this map on the floor, Aziz Yazdi saw one blue line going from England down to Southwest Africa and he said, 'Oh, look Ted!' And I said, 'I am not going!' Well, of course I did, because what can you do when the Guardian says so. That was the way the Guardian had his effect on you. I was the only single Baháʼí who'd had Africa experience.[96]

Ted arrived in Windhoek, South West Africa, on 13 October 1953. Ted was a photographer, but arrived in Windhoek not knowing German or any of the local languages and with only US$400. His first two jobs, in a photography shop and as a packer in a warehouse, only lasted three weeks each. Because he treated everyone in the same friendly way, he was then given a job as an insurance salesman. The insurance job lasted for two years before Ted was fired for being late returning from a holiday. Luckily, Knight of Bahá'u'lláh and future Hand of the Cause John Robarts was able to get him a job with Prudential Insurance.[97]

Teaching the Faith in a country that proscribed interactions between blacks and whites was very difficult and it was two years before he could actually teach. The door to teaching the native people came when Shoghi Effendi chose Kuanyama as the language of South West Africa. Initially, Ted could find no one who could adequately speak the language. Visiting the Methodist Church and acquiring a Bible in Kuanyama, he used his own English Bible to write a one-page explanation of the Bahá'í Faith in Kuanyama. When he heard that the gardener at the Methodist Church, Joseph, was Kuanyama, he gave him the explanation to check:

Joseph . . . laughed very heartily. He said, 'It is terrible!' So, I said, 'Do you know a translator?' He said, 'Yes! I have a great friend who is a very good translator. He works for the police.' I said, 'No, no, no.' The Guardian had warned us to stay away from clergymen and police at all costs.

Anyway, the next night I went along and there was [his] friend, Hilifa, the police interpreter, destined to become the first Bahá'í. And he was such a sweet man and he was so understanding. He was a kind of go-between between the whites and the blacks. He was able to smooth many an upset between the blacks and the whites in the Government and that was splendid. He was a treasured man to both sides. And here he was – fell into my lap just like that. So, I showed him the translation and we had to start afresh.[98]

Ted and the translator, Hilifa Andreas Nekundi, worked on the pamphlet for several weeks. The meetings had to be very clandestine in the country; at night and working under a shielded torch, Hilifa translated a several-page pamphlet about the Faith, becoming interested himself.

In order to teach Hilifa, Ted and a friend hired a cottage in the seaside resort Swakopmund. Ted and Hilifa would find the most isolated beaches where they studied *Bahá'u'lláh and the New Era* undetected. Ted told Hilifa that he could become a Bahá'í by writing to Shoghi Effendi. Hilifa sat on the beach and wrote to the Guardian. When the letter was finished, Ted embraced Hilifa and welcomed him into the Faith of

The Baháʼí community in Nairobi, c. 1953. From this community came several Knights of Baháʼu'lláh to other parts of Africa

arly pioneers in Nairobi: Aziz Yazdi, Claire Gung, 'Mother of Africa', and Edward (Ted) Cardell. Claire became a Knight of Baháʼu'lláh for Southern Rhodesia, and Ted for South West Africa

Contributed by Adrienne Morgan

Enoch Olinga, Knight of Bahá'u'lláh to British Cameroon, and 'Alí Na<u>kh</u>javání (seated) with *(left to right, standing): Benedict Eballa, David Tanyi and Samuel Njiki Njenji, Knights of Bahá'u'lláh to Ashanti Protectorate, French Togoland and French Cameroon*

Vivian Wesson, Knight of Bahá'u'lláh to French Togoland, with David and Esther Tanyi and their children Mbu and Enoch, 1955

Mavis Nymon, Knight of Bahá'u'lláh to French Togoland, 1956

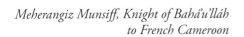

Meherangiz Munsiff, Knight of Bahá'u'lláh to French Cameroon

Edward Tabe, Knight of Bahá'u'lláh to British Togoland

Left to right, standing: *Hassan Sabri, Philip Hainsworth, Aziz Yazdi, Jalál Nakhjávání.* Seated: *Max Kanyerenzi, Knight of Bahá'u'lláh to French Equatorial Africa, Tito Wanantutzi, Oloro Epyeru and Sylvester Okurut*

Julius Edwards Knight of Bahá'u'lláh to Northwest Territories Protectorate

Martin Manga Knight of Bahá'u'lláh to Northwest Territories Protectorate

Knights of Bahá'u'lláh to Ruanda-Urundi: Dunduzu Chisiza with Mary and Rex Collison

Elise Schreiber, Knight of Baha'u'llah for Spanish Guinea (Equatorial Guinea), 1954

The first Bahá'í of Burundi, Selemani Bin Kimbulu (standing left), *with other Bahá'ís including Mary Collison* (front, left) *and Reginald (Rex) Collison* (front, right)

Ezzatu'lláh Zahra'i (standing, left), *Knight of Bahá'u'lláh to Southern Rhodesia, with Ursula and Mihdi Samandari, Knights of Bahá'u'lláh to Italian Somaliland; the people sitting are unidentified*

'Aynu'd-Dín and Tahireh 'Alá'i, Knights of Bahá'u'lláh to Southern Rhodesia

Roberta and Kenneth Christian, Knights of Bahá'u'lláh to Southern Rhodesia, with their son Roger

Knights of Bahá'u'lláh to Bechuanaland (Botswana): Patrick, Audrey and John Robarts, with daughter Nina, too young to be named a Knight

Knights of Bahá'u'lláh to Swaziland John and Valera Allen (sitting) *and* (at rear) *their son Dale and his wife Irma*

Frederick Laws, Knight of Bahá'u'lláh to Basutoland (Lesotho)

Knight of Bahá'u'lláh Elizabeth Laws, known as 'Malerato' (Mother of Love), in Lesotho

Bula Mott Stewart, Knight of Bahá'u'lláh to Swaziland

Bahá'u'lláh. Then Ted said that they should go swimming. Hilifa didn't know how to swim and when a big wave washed them over, Hilifa disappeared beneath the water. For a couple of minutes, Ted was panicked, thinking that he had just drowned the first South West African believer. Luckily, Ted managed to pull Hilifa to safety.[99]

Because of local censorship, Ted took Hilifa's letter to London to mail. While Ted was in England, Hilifa sent a second letter emphatically declaring himself a Bahá'í. Shoghi Effendi quickly responded, calling Hilifa the first South West African Bahá'í and expressing the hope that Hilifa could become 'the means of teaching many of your people the Faith, and of helping Mr. Cardell to establish a Spiritual Assembly in Windhoek . . .' Hilifa fulfilled the Guardian's wish.[100]

Michael Sears joined Ted in Windhoek in April 1957. In March 1958, Ted left in order to find a wife, a task in which he succeeded when he married Alicia Ward,[101] whom he met at the American House of Worship. Ted and Alicia returned to Africa and settled in Kenya for several years then moved to Britain, where Ted served on the National Spiritual Assembly and Alicia was deeply involved in children's education.[102]

Ted was replaced in 1959 by Gerda and Martin Aiff and their six young children. Like Ted, they faced the challenges of apartheid where the black and white Bahá'ís were unable to meet together or teach outside their race. They came up with an innovative way to keep the Faith alive and growing. In order to teach the native Africans, the white women would gather conspicuously in the front of the house while the men and the African seekers secretly met in the back. To keep communication open between the two races, Martin Onesmus, an African Bahá'í employed by the Aiffs and living with them, was able to act as a courier between the black and white Bahá'ís. When the first Local Spiritual Assembly was elected in Windhoek in 1965, Mr Onesmus was one of its members.[103]

BECHUANALAND (NOW BOTSWANA)

John, Audrey and Patrick Robarts

The Canadian Robarts family, including parents John (1901–1991) and Audrey (1904–2000) and children Patrick (1934– 2013) and Nina (b. 1940), pioneered to Bechuanaland in October 1953. Audrey's

great-great-great grandmother was a Cree Indian from British Columbia. Audrey studied piano in Paris and became fluent in French.[104] John
and Audrey were married in 1928 and became Bahá'ís in 1937. John
was instrumental in developing the Bahá'í communities in Hamilton
and Ottawa, served on the Ontario Regional Teaching Committee
and was the chairman of the National Spiritual Assembly of Canada
between 1949 and 1953. In 1949, John visited seven of America's ten
European goal countries for the second Seven Year Plan. The next year,
he visited the British Isles and Ireland.[105]

When Hand of the Cause Fred Schopflocher died shortly before
the New Delhi Intercontinental Teaching Conference, John offered to
attend the conference in his stead; Shoghi Effendi quickly accepted.
While there, John and his wife, Audrey, became enthused with pioneering and cabled the Guardian offering their services, suggesting Iceland,
Labrador, or the Yukon.[106] On 22 October 1953, Shoghi Effendi
cabled back 'Bechuanaland highly meritorious'.[107] Upon receiving the
cable, John 'phoned Audrey and asked her where Bechuanaland was.
She didn't know. He said, "Well, we'd better find out – because that's
where we're going!"' Audrey 'read from an encyclopedia about this small
British protectorate in South Africa, it sounded awful – snakes, extreme
heat, malaria.'[108]

Initially, since he was in university, 19-year-old Patrick was not
included in the pioneering efforts. Patrick cabled the Guardian and
Shoghi Effendi replied that he could go to a university in South Africa.[109]

In spite of never having heard of the country before, the Robarts
immediately began preparations. Just after Christmas, John and Audrey,
along with son Patrick, aged 19, and daughter Nina, 13, boarded a ship
for the three-week trip to Cape Town, South Africa. Surprisingly, John
was offered jobs by two insurance companies before he was even off the
boat. He accepted one as a district manager with Prudential Assurance
Company of South Africa.[110]

In February 1953, just 16 weeks after receiving Shoghi Effendi's
cable, the Robarts family crossed the border into Bechuanaland. When
the family went on pilgrimage two years later, Shoghi Effendi asked
who was driving the car when they crossed into their goal country.
Patrick said that he was, whereupon the Guardian said that he was the
first pioneer into Bechuanaland. Patrick later said that that meant he
became a Knight of Bahá'u'lláh before his illustrious father, who was

riding in the back seat. Shoghi Effendi used this story to explain that the pioneers should remain in the background and the Africans should be in front. He explained what he meant by saying that when the family first crossed into Bechuanaland, the young and inexperienced Patrick was driving the car, but his older, wiser father was in the back seat. The pioneers should similarly let the young, inexperienced African believers drive the car of the Faith. The pioneers should be in the back seat ready to offer guidance whenever it was needed.[111]

Within a few days they had purchased a house and moved in. Almost immediately, visitors began to arrive, including Bill and Marguerite Sears. John was also soon appointed to the Auxiliary Board by Hand of the Cause Músá Banání. Before 1954 was over, the Robarts had their first native believer, Dr Modiri Molema. Before becoming a Bahá'í, Dr Molema had been politically active in a banned party, so he had to keep his declaration secret for a while. When Dr Molema began to have firesides in his home, Audrey made 125 yards of curtains to cover his windows. The doctor also gave the Robarts letters of introduction to six of the chiefs in the region, which opened many doors.[112]

In 1956, John was elected to the Regional National Spiritual Assembly of South and West Africa. In February 1957, the first Local Spiritual Assembly in Bechuanaland was formed in Mafeking. With that accomplished, the Robarts moved to open Bulawayo, Southern Rhodesia (now Zimbabwe) and the next year were able to form the first Local Spiritual Assembly there. With John gone so much as a Regional Assembly member and an Auxiliary Board member, Audrey became adept at driving the corrugated unpaved roads, sometimes alone. Then John was appointed a Hand of the Cause in October 1957, which, with the passing of the Guardian a month later, increased his work load. The Robarts moved back to Canada in 1966 and settled in Rawdon, Quebec.[113] John continued his world-wide travels until 1987. When he passed into the Abhá Kingdom in 1991, Audrey continued. In 1992, she travelled alone through four countries in southern Africa. Visiting the area of her early exploits, she was hailed by the National Assembly as the 'Beloved Mother of our country'.[114]

SWAZILAND

Bula Mott Stewart, John and Valera Allen

Bula Mott Stewart (later known as Heather Harmon) (1908–2007) was the first Bahá'í to reach Swaziland during the Ten Year Crusade, arriving on 11 April 1954. Bula became a Bahá'í in the 1940s and became known for her firesides and public speaking. In 1952, she was appointed to the Regional Teaching Committee of Eastern Pennsylvania. When the Ten Year Crusade was announced, and thinking that her knowledge of parasitology would make it possible to find work, she chose Swaziland and, for a time, ran a medical laboratory for Albert Schweitzer. In 1955, however, Shoghi Effendi asked her to move to South Africa where she successfully taught the Faith in spite of the racist laws. She later served in Hong Kong and the Pacific.[115]

John Allen (1907–1980) learned about the Bahá'í Faith when he married Valera (1902–1993) in 1925. In 1954, they decided to fill one of Shoghi Effendi's goals in Africa. They were worried at first about their children, since the youngest two were still at university. The Guardian replied that their pioneering would be an inspiration to their children. Shoghi Effendi's comment proved correct because all three of their sons became pioneers: Dwight and his wife Carole were Knights of Bahá'u'lláh to Greece and also pioneered in Africa; Dale and his wife Irma pioneered to Swaziland; and Kenton with his wife Mary were the first Bahá'ís to settle in Savannah, Georgia, United States, and also pioneered to Africa.[116]

The Allens arrived in Swaziland on 19 April 1954 in a Volkswagen Beetle they got in Mozambique that was loaded with camping equipment because they did not know what to expect. They initially stayed at the Swazi Inn, then rented a house for a year while they built their own home next to the Inn. Valera's mother, Maude Fisher, who was 82 years old, had planned to go with John and Valera, but was delayed by her health, thus did not gain the title of Knight of Bahá'u'lláh. Maude arrived in late summer with two of the Allens' sons, Dale and Kenton. The two lads attended the University of Witwatersrand in Johannesburg for about six months before returning to the United States to complete their education. Maude's age and poor health didn't slow her down. She made travel teaching trips to Mozambique, Southern and

Northern Rhodesia and South Africa and she was soon known as a grandmother to many. She died at her post in 1957, the first pioneer to do so in Swaziland.[117]

The Allens immediately began teaching and their efforts were soon quite successful. Isaiah Phala and his wife, Jemima, were among the first local people to accept the Bahá'í Faith. Several members of the royal family also became Bahá'ís. In 1955 it was possible to form the first Local Spiritual Assembly of Mbabane.[118]

Roads in those days were mostly dirt and rough, and John wore out two trucks building local centres in Hlatikulu and Pigg's Peak. He was appointed an Auxiliary Board member by Hand of the Cause Músá Bánáni with responsibility over Northern and Southern Rhodesia (now Zimbabwe), Nyasaland (now Malawi) and Mozambique, an area over 1.3 million square kilometres. John travelled extensively, usually with a full set of spare tyres on the roof of his car.[119] John also used his knowledge of cars to get around the restrictions on interactions between whites and blacks, by helping whoever was having car problems. One day he stopped to help a man who, unknowingly, had simply run out of petrol. Pulling out a container of fuel he always carried, he became friends with the man, who turned out to be Prince Manzini, the son of King Sobhuza II. This chance encounter led to the Allens giving slide shows at the Prince's school, an introduction to the King, the enrolment of several members of the royal family into the Faith and the official recognition of the Faith by the Government.[120]

In addition to raising up a Bahá'í community, the Allens were very active in promoting economic activities:

John was a first class entrepreneur. He owned a successful new car business when he left California, and always encouraged people to start businesses . . . John had the attitude that pioneers should make things that would help the indigenous friends to become independent. He asked his sons, Dale and Kenton, to help revive the pineapple canning business in Swaziland. In 1960 Dale arrived with [his wife] Irma and started planting many pineapples. Six months later, Kenton arrived with [his wife] Mary and their son Andy. Kenton helped remodel the cannery processing equipment and was able to stay four years. Dale and John sold the cannery in 1968. John liked the project because it created hundreds of jobs.

Later John worked with the Swaziland government to have Swazis get land cleared and plant pineapples.[121]

John later served as chairman of the National Spiritual Assembly of Swaziland when it formed in 1971. The Allens helped many pioneers settle into Africa and built, and largely financed, schools and local centres.[122] They initially opened a Bahá'í pre-school and then added a grade school and high school at the Bahá'í temple site on Malagwane Hill.[123] John passed away in 1980 and Valera remained at her pioneer post until her passing in 1993.[124]

BASUTOLAND (NOW LESOTHO)

Elizabeth and Frederick Laws

Frederick Laws (1913–1987) embraced the Bahá'í Faith in May 1936. Eleven weeks later, he brought Elizabeth (1888–1978) into the Faith and in 1939, they were married. They tried to pioneer to Chile in 1940, but were refused visas, so pioneered to San Diego, California, instead.[125]

When Shoghi Effendi called for pioneers in 1952, Elizabeth and Frederick Laws arose and left America on 23 January 1953 for Nairobi, Kenya, including a car and trailer in their luggage. Arriving in Nairobi to find a thriving Bahá'í community, they looked elsewhere to settle. Shoghi Effendi, in a cable of 28 May, said that all Bahá'í communities with more than 15 Bahá'ís should disperse, and offered those who arose and went to virgin areas the title of Knight of Bahá'u'lláh. The Laws built a 'little house' on their trailer chassis, then drove 4,000 kilometres to Basutoland, arriving on 13 October 1953.[126] On the way, their car broke down four times.

During the first nine months living in hotels, they accomplished little, but then they decided to do something different. One day in 1954, Elizabeth and Frederick drove down a dirt road pulling their little house trailer and stopped in front of the 'tree-shaded' home of Mary and Chadwich Mohapi. It was a momentous event for the Mohapis:

One day in the afternoon . . . my wife and I were sitting outside in the sun when we saw a strange car . . . people of European descent came from the car. We then sent our first son, Selai, to find out where they came from: he came to us with them . . . they asked us if they could be permitted to have the use of one wall over which they could put a canvas for the day (for shelter). We asked them who they were, where they had come from . . . we wanted to know their intentions. They told us they had come from a far-off land, that they were looking for people to whom they could teach the Word of God. Clowningly, I said 'You can come and live with us in this rondoval (round hut) over here!' They said they would be grateful to do that. We asked them, 'How are you going to live with black people? Don't you know that we do not love white people? We have never stayed with white people before.' They said that did not matter to them, they could live with us. I said to my wife, 'Let us try this out and see whether these people are genuine . . . We were puzzled because we had been joking and they had, in innocence, taken us seriously. We were now surprised and also frightened,' Mr Mohapi recalled.

That very evening they invited us to dinner in the rondoval with them. We were afraid of going in there with them, but we saw what beautiful faces they had . . . they served us with meals instead of us serving them with meals. The following morning they invited us for breakfast and through the great love they showed they made friends with our young children by the end of the second day. We still asked ourselves what these Europeans wanted living amongst us. The eve of the third day they invited us not for a meal, but for prayers. We were greatly surprised. It appeared to us that we had come by a bone that had a very nice marrow in it. Then they stayed and they became our real friends. We gave them new names – the man, Lerato (Love), and the lady, Malerato (Mother of Love).[127]

Only after making friends of the Mohapis did Elizabeth and Frederick begin to teach Mary and Chadwick the Faith. Then one day both Mary and Chadwick fell ill. The Laws took the children into their own rondoval and cared for their parents. Over time, the actions and the words of the Laws made a deep impression on their hosts. Other Africans began to come to see white people and black people living together and soon the Mohapi home became a centre from which the Faith spread to other parts of the country.[128] By April 1955, there were about 70 Bahá'ís in Basutoland and the Laws were adopted as honorary Basutos.[129]

After two and a half years, with the Bahá'í Faith growing well in

Basutoland, the Laws went south and spent six weeks with pioneers Bill and Marguerite Sears near Johannesburg, then after consultation with Hands of the Cause Músá Banání and Paul Haney, they pioneered on to The Gambia and Liberia where they stayed until 1957, when they returned to the United States. In 1976, they pioneered for eight months in Tanzania and on their return pioneered to Wapato, Washington, on the Yakima Indian Reservation. It was there in 1978 that Elizabeth passed away.[130]

INDIAN OCEAN

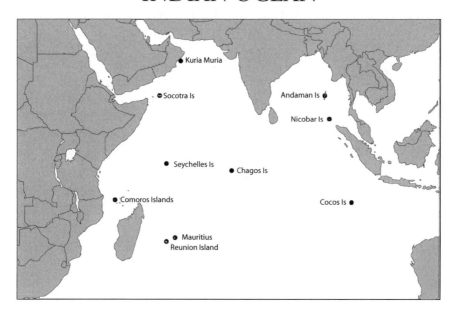

KURIA MURIA (OMAN)

Munír Vakíl

Munír Vakíl (1900–1976) was born in a house adjacent to the House of Bahá'u'lláh in Baghdad and was a very active Bahá'í in Iraq. During the turbulence over the House of Bahá'u'lláh in Baghdad, Mr Vakíl was its caretaker. He later served on the National Spiritual Assembly of Iraq and also held a very high position in the Ministry of Defence as a legal counsellor to the Ministry and, consequently, held the rank of Brigadier.[1]

After the Intercontinental Teaching Conference in New Delhi, Mr Vakíl asked Hand of the Cause Dhikru'lláh Khádem where he should go in response to the Guardian's call. Mr Khádem told him that he could go any place, just to close his eyes and put his finger randomly on the list of goals. When Munír Vakíl did so, he found his finger on a place he had never heard of before: Kuria Muria. After a few months, he still hadn't found the island, but finally his persistence paid off and he located the five small, rocky islands off the coast of Oman. In January 1954, he jubilantly wrote to Mr Khádem saying, 'I found it! I am on an isolated and desolate island in the Indian Ocean with very few inhabitants.'[2]

Mr Vakíl had gone first to Hadhramaut where he spent a long time trying to get permission from the British, who oversaw the islands. When permission was finally received, there just happened to be a specially chartered boat going to the island.[3] Finally arriving at his goal in January, he wrote, 'There is no sign of civilization here. There are no houses, huts, or facilities of any sort. Our food is fish from the ocean. We catch the fish and bake them on hot rocks in the sun.' There were only 59 people on the island.[4]

One day, an eggplant washed ashore and Mr Vakíl was very excited. He cooked the great discovery and shared it with the others on the island. The natives, seeing his reaction to the eggplant, asked him why, if he was so used to such unusual foods, had he ever come to Kuria Muria? His reply was that he came because he loved them. In a letter to Mr Khádem, he said that he'd lost a lot of weight and was not well, but was not going to leave his post. He built himself a small hut for shelter from the rain, which he shared with some domesticated animals, and lived like the natives did, something that baffled them.[5]

Munír Vakíl's arrival was at first marked with great suspicion by the Arab inhabitants, who interviewed him and then secretly sent a report of his arrival to the Sultan of Muscat, who owned the islands. The Sultan then contacted the Britain Resident, who oversaw the islands. The Resident, in turn, was very concerned to find that there was an Iraqi general living there, so the Resident made a special trip to find out what he was up to.[6] The Governor's visit resulted in him being very impressed with Mr Vakíl's 'selfless devotion and perseverance'. He also passed word about him to his family, the only report they received while he was there.[7]

Mr Vakíl proclaimed the Bahá'í Faith to the islanders, but his health continued to degrade until, several months after his arrival, Shoghi Effendi encouraged him to leave and return to Iraq. Dhikru'lláh Khádem was in Baghdad when he returned, and wrote:

He was frail, exhausted, and very ill. The friends asked him about his pioneering experiences at a meeting one night. Munír described his search for the island and the condition of life there. After he finished, one of the friends got up and said, 'Munír did not know where he was going. Now I know where Kuria Muria is and what it is like. I am prepared to replace him. We cannot leave a pioneering post vacant.[8]

When Munír Vakíl returned to Baghdad, he was put under intense pressure to resume his old job at the Ministry of Defence and take a promotion, but he instead pioneered to the Seychelles, where his family joined him in 1955. They stayed in the Seychelles until 1962, when a Local Spiritual Assembly was functioning.[9]

Socotra Islands

Kamálí Sarvistání[10]

In March 1955, one of the remaining pioneering goals of the Ten Year Crusade was achieved when Kamálí Sarvistání (1924–1983) finally reached the Socotra Islands, one of the most difficult posts to fill. This group of four islands lie 240 kilometres east of the Horn of Africa at the mouth of the Gulf of Aden.

Kamálí Sarvistání left home in Iran at the age of 16 and worked for an oil company for several years until his father visited him. His father told him that he had two options: to get married or to go pioneering. He chose the latter and went to Dubai. When the Ten Year Crusade was announced, he wanted to fill the goal to the Socotra Islands, but the pioneering committee was not enthusiastic. However, when Hand of the Cause Mr Samandarí visited him and heard of his desire to pioneer, he strongly approved and in 1954, Mr Sarvistání was on his way.

With a friend named Mr Vasaelie, Kamálí Sarvistání sailed to Muscat and then to Sohar, both in Oman, where their adventures began. The men left the boat in Sohar for a bath and some shopping and so missed the ship when it sailed. They immediately set out on foot to catch the ship at its next port of call, but again missed it. They finally managed to board a fishing boat and set off to chase down their ship, which they were finally enabled to do. Continuing with their original ship, they sailed to the town of Aden in Yemen.

Upon our arrival in Aden we were prevented from disembarking the boat by officials who told us that we would need a guarantor in order to be allowed to disembark. We spoke no Arabic and were utter strangers in that land. We tried to tell the officials that we knew Mr Molavi and that we wanted to visit him. After a lot of hassle and many questions, an English person took pity on us and agreed to act as a guarantor by vouching that we would visit our friend and return to the boat.

We got off the boat and after asking for directions found Mr Molavi's shop. Mr Molavi did not know us personally but we had in our possession a letter from Mr Samandarí. After reading the letter, Mr Molavi realized that we were trying to reach our pioneering post and directed us as to the best way to reach Socotra via Mokala [Hadhramaut in Yemen]. He gave us a letter and after a few hours we left for Mokala on board the ship.

With the letter of introduction, the expectant pioneers sailed to Mokala, where they contacted the Knight of Bahá'u'lláh Husayn Halabi. They both began working for Husayn, but very soon Mr Vasaelie had to return to Dubai. After about a month, Husayn fell ill and Kamálí Sarvistání spent the next several months caring for him. Husayn's father arrived to take charge of him, but after just three days had a heart attack and died. Finally, Husayn's brother-in-law came and took the ill Knight away for treatment. Released from his caring task, Kamálí Sarvistání continued to Socotra.

He arrived at his long-desired post in May 1955 and sent a message to Shoghi Effendi via the ship that brought him to the island. He was only at his pioneering post for three months when a letter arrived from Hand of the Cause Mr Banání and his wife urging him to go home and get married and then return to Socotra with a wife and another pioneer. Obediently, Mr Sarvistání returned to Bahrain and then Kuwait. Fairly quickly, he found and married Rezvanieh Zoljalali on 25 September 1955. After the marriage, the couple were joined by Mr Tavakoli and began the voyage back to Socotra. They sailed to Dubai and then on to Muscat, where they missed their boat. Nineteen days later, they sailed on the next boat for their destination, but this boat broke down, forcing a delay of 12 days. When repairs were completed, the ship again sailed, but again broke down, this time in the open ocean:

It took three days before another boat was able to reach us. Eventually we were able to transfer ourselves to the new boat which was more akin to an open plank of wood that slowly drifted towards Socotra. It was almost morning when we heard a lot of commotion from the workers only to realize that they were praying aloud. We realized that the boat had almost sunk but thankfully we had been spared as the sea was calm. As we neared Socotra it became impossible for the boat to continue on any further. Two small fishing boats collected us and the three of us stepped onto the soil of our pioneering post after a journey that had spanned forty long days.

The couple and Mr Tavakoli settled into their pioneering post. Rezvanieh wrote that

we were greeted by a merchant who was a friend of Mr Kamálí and who looked after us. We found the people of Socotra to be very kind and we arrived at our house later that evening. It was an old room and very primitive and basic. After a month we moved to a slightly better home and this was where I met a lifelong friend named Noor. Socotra has a stormy season that lasts around four months during which the sea becomes impassable and even fishing halts. Most people grew their own vegetables such as onions, beans, sweet potatoes and courgettes, as well as many palm trees. However, it was still necessary to import dates due to their high level of consumption. Mr Kamálí and Mr Tavakoli would buy and sell goods, while Mr Kamálí would also assist people with health issues and import medications, especially malaria tablets, to the island and even administered injections when required, making him a very useful member of the community. [I] started sewing by hand for people and after around a year was able to afford to buy a sewing machine.

The Kamálí Sarvistánís' first son was born about the time of the passing of the Guardian. The family remained on the island for 11 years, until it was necessary to find education for their children. With the permission of the Universal House of Justice, they then moved to Dubai.

SEYCHELLES

Kámil 'Abbás[11]

Kámil 'Abbás (1911–1980) was the first Bahá'í to land in the Seychelles, arriving on 8 November 1953. His father, 'Abbás, accepted the Bahá'í Faith six years after the passing of Bahá'u'lláh. He became an eloquent speaker in spite of being illiterate, but his new faith so antagonized his family that they tried to kill him. He escaped by running across the flat rooftops of his neighbourhood. Because of his father, Kámil grew up in a Bahá'í family. As a youth in Baghdad, he studied and made himself fluent in Persian, English and German. He also taught himself short-hand and typing, using all his skills to translate Bahá'í documents from one language to another. At the age of 17, Kámil wrote to the Guardian expressing his desire to 'sacrifice everything for the Faith'. Shoghi Effendi replied, 'May God assist you to spread the message.'

Kámil was elected to the Local Spiritual Assembly of Baghdad and then, in 1935, to the National Assembly of Iraq, on which he served as secretary. He also served on the Bahá'í Youth Committee in Baghdad. In 1951, he was sent as a Bahá'í delegate to a United Nations conference of non-governmental organizations (NGOs) in Turkey. Afterwards, the delegate report noted:

> Of historic significance is the fact that the Bahá'í delegation was officially received at the reception given by the Governor of Istanbul for the assembled delegates. Also, that the Conference should have been held at the Palace of Sultan 'Abdu'l-Hamíd, the arch-enemy of the Faith; and the Faith mentioned so frequently at the Palace![12]

Upon his return, Kámil was questioned by the secret police about why he had gone to Turkey.

When the goals of the Ten Year Crusade were announced, Kámil and his family chose the Seychelles. Their plan was that Kámil would go first and his family would follow when he was settled. Kámil attended the Intercontinental Teaching Conference in New Delhi, India, and immediately afterwards left for the Seychelles.

Kámil's stay in the Seychelles was short. Unfortunately, he was forced to depart after just five weeks, on 21 December, because he was not able to obtain a resident visa and for health reasons. During that time, however, he taught the Faith to Marshall Delcy, a local Anglican teacher. Kámil had barely gone when Abdu'l Rahman Zarqani, who had originally planned to go to the Chagos Archipelago, came to the island in January 1954 from India, where he had been the secretary of the National Spiritual Assembly.[13]

Back in Iraq, Kámil went to a number of Arab States at the request of the Guardian. In 1957, he was appointed to the Auxiliary Board for protection, travelling to India, Pakistan and Iran. During the same year, he was involved in the successful search to find the remains of Mírzá Buzurg, Bahá'u'lláh's father.

Kámil participated in the election of the first Universal House of Justice in 1963 as a member of the Iraqi National Spiritual Assembly and also attended the World Congress in London. In the early 1970s, he and three other Bahá'ís documented the House of Bahá'u'lláh in Baghdad.

In 1973, Kámil was arrested and sentenced to life imprisonment: 'He was so firm and steadfast in the Cause of the Blessed Beauty that the prison authorities watched [him] carefully. At times they oppressed him and at times tried to persuade him to recant, but without avail.' He was released from prison in September 1979. In June of the following year, Kámil died in the hospital that had been built on the site of the Riḍván Garden in Baghdad, where Bahá'u'lláh had declared His station. His final words were: 'I am coming to you, Bahá'u'lláh.'

'Abdu'l Rahman Zarqani

'Abdu'l Rahman Zarqani (1923–1994) pioneered to the Seychelles on 15 January 1954, arriving three weeks after Kámil 'Abbás departed. He was born in India of Muslim parents and at the age of about 25 attended his first Bahá'í talk where his interest was immediately aroused. He became a Bahá'í in 1948, whereupon he was forced out of his parent's home at knifepoint by his father. Undeterred, he actively served the Bahá'í Faith. In 1952, at the age of 29, he became the youngest secretary of the Indian National Spiritual Assembly. 'Abdu'l Rahman was deeply involved with the organization of the New Delhi Intercontinental Teaching Conference in 1953, but when it was over, he wrote to Shoghi Effendi expressing his dilemma of wishing to pioneer, but also of having a huge work load as the secretary of the National Assembly.

Shoghi Effendi replied, 'Approve pioneering'. Just a week later, on 8 January 1954, he sailed to the Seychelles on his way to the Chagos Archipelago, leaving his wife, who was about to have their second child, in India to join him later.[14]

Arriving in the Seychelles, 'Abdu'l Rahman found that it was impossible to go to the Chagos Archipelago because he could not get a job there, a requirement for the privately-owned island. The Chagos goal remained unfulfilled until 1956 when a pioneer from Mauritius, Pouva Murday, achieved the goal. 'Abdu'l Rahman settled into the Hotel Continental in Victoria, on Mahé Island, Seychelles, hoping to find a way to the Chagos, and began teaching the Faith. In February, he contacted Marshall Delcy, Kámil 'Abbas's contact, and in June Marshall became the first person to accept the Faith in the Seychelles. Also in June, 'Abdu'l Rahman found work as a shipping clerk and was joined by Manuchehr Ma'ni (Ma'ani), who pioneered from Iran. Joseph Samuel Rioux became the second native believer when he accepted the Faith in August.[15]

In March, 'Abdu'l Rahman wrote to the Guardian asking if he should return to India since it appeared impossible to reach his goal of the Chagos Islands. The Guardian's reply read, 'Rahman must remain Seychelles if unable proceed Chagos – Shoghi.' Leroy Ioas added that 'if you find it utterly impossible to enter the Chagos Archipelago, then the Guardian would appreciate your remaining permanently in the Seychelles Islands'.[16] Obediently, 'Abdu'l Rahman stayed in the Seychelles.

Successful teaching efforts brought three more native believers into the Faith and, when Munír Vakíl, the Knight of Bahá'u'lláh for Kuria Muria, arrived in January 1955 from Iraq, they were able to form the first Local Spiritual Assembly at Riḍván with four pioneers and five local Bahá'ís. 'Abdu'l Rahman's wife, Munirih, and daughters arrived shortly afterwards.[17] By March 1957, there were 18 local Bahá'ís and eight pioneers in the islands.[18]

During the next two years, the Faith expanded to Praslin and La Digue Islands. In 1957, a Bill of Incorporation was submitted to the island's Legislative Council by the Local Spiritual Assembly of Victoria and, after a hot and intense debate, was accepted. 'Abdu'l Rahman approached the radio station in 1966 about airing a Bahá'í programme and in 1969 the Seychelles Bahá'í Community was the first Bahá'í community in the Indian Ocean with a radio programme. 'Abdu'l Rahman remained in the Seychelles until his passing in 1994.[19]

Comoros Islands

Mehraban Sohaili[20]

Mehraban Sohaili (b. 1922) came from a Bahá'í family who had pioneered to Quetta, Pakistan, both he and his father serving on the first Local Spiritual Assembly there. Mehraban attended the New Delhi Intercontinental Conference in 1953 and there volunteered to fulfil one of the Guardian's goals in order to 'bring happiness to the heart of our beloved Guardian'. Initially, he was asked to pioneer to the Mentawai Islands, but Raḥmatu'lláh Muhájir managed to get the necessary visas first, so the Goals Committee for Asia asked Mehraban to go to the Mariana Islands in the Pacific. The Marianas, however, were only open to American citizens, so his visa request was denied. Then the committee gave him the goal of the Comoros Islands, between Mozambique and the island of Madagascar. After six months, he acquired the necessary visa.

Mehraban left Karachi on 12 August 1954 and after 16 days, arrived in Dzaoudzi, the capital of the Comoros Islands, on Mayotte Island. He immediately sent a telegram to Shoghi Effendi and received the reply, 'Assure fervent prayers – Shoghi'. Initially, Mehraban was supported, both materially and spiritually, by Mr and Mrs Isfantiar Bakhtiari of Karachi.

The Comoros Islands consist of four islands, none of which had running water – all water was from the collection of rain. Since there were no hotels, he initially stayed with an Indian merchant. Because of his teaching activities, some of the people began to agitate against him and his host turned against him. After two months in Dzaoudzi, Mehraban moved to the larger town of Moroni on Grand Comoros Island, where he found an abandoned house with broken windows near the shore. For the next several months, he travelled the four islands on foot and bicycle. He had to be very cautious in his teaching because of the many fanatic Muslims, but after a time several people of Malagasy origin became Bahá'ís and a group was formed. His teaching caused one of the islanders to decide to kill him. But when the man arrived and saw a Qur'án on the table, he began to ask questions. The man soon realized that he had been misled by other people into believing that Mehraban was against Islam. The man left, Mehraban wrote, with a smile.

At the end of his first six months, he was able to renew his visa for an additional six months. During this time, Jalál Nakhjavání visited Mehraban and helped him enrol more people into the Faith. Mr Rakoto-Andriambalo and his family were introduced to the Bahá'í Faith on one of Jalál's visits. After only fifteen days, Mr Rakoto-Andriambalo accepted Bahá'u'lláh and was soon followed by his wife.[21]

After his second six-month visa, Mehraban requested another extension, but this time it was denied. The police claimed that some community leaders objected to his being there. His arguments to no avail, Mehraban left the Comoros on 10 September 1955 and went to Madagascar. Hand of the Cause Músá Banání said he should stay as close as possible to the Comoros so that he would be ready when it was possible to return. Unfortunately, he could not get a visa for Madagascar so he sailed to Dar es Salaam in Tanganyika, where he was met by Jalál Nakhjavání.

Mehraban was only able to stay in Dar es Salaam for a year before his visa renewal was rejected so, in consultation with Hand of the Cause Mr Banání, he decided to go to Somalia. For the next four years, Mehraban stayed in Somalia, extending his visa every six months. When he applied for a permanent visa, it was rejected. Aziz Yazdi suggested that he might be able to settle in Kenya, and within two months Mehraban had a visa and work permit. He arrived in Nairobi on 19 September 1959.

Mehraban worked for Aziz for the next four years as a salesman and travelled extensively through Kenya, Tanganyika and Uganda and was able to visit many Bahá'í communities. He worked closely with Hand of the Cause Mr Banání and 'Alí Nakhjavání. In April 1963, he went to London and travelled in Europe before returning to India. In August, he married Rezwan Najmi and a week later, the couple went to Nairobi. Though deeply involved in the work in Kenya, Mehraban kept trying to return to the Comoros Islands, applying unsuccessfully for permanent visas in 1956 and 1961. In 1977, the International Teaching Centre suggested he try to visit the islands for short periods. Consequently, he was able to return to the Comoros on 2 March 1977 for two weeks. During this visit, he was able to confirm 18 people in the Faith.

In 1985 when the Comoros Islands became an extension goal for Kenya, he returned with his 17-year-old son, Isfandiar, for a two-week teaching trip from 7 to 20 March. They were not able to find many of Mehraban's 1953 contacts, but there were two islanders who had become Bahá'ís in Africa and had moved back to the Comoros Islands. Each afternoon, the father and son visited people who were all Muslim but who were very friendly and open to the Faith. In addition to the capital, Moroni, where they stayed, they also visited a farming village on a mountain top and a fishing village. During their visit, 60 people became Bahá'ís and Local Spiritual Assemblies were formed in Moroni, the mountain village and the fishing village. A few days before the end of their visit, the police, acting on a complaint, found them in the fishing village and took them and all of their literature back to the capital for questioning. Their passports were confiscated and they were told not to contact any of the local people. A couple of days later, they were put on a plane out of the country. Unfortunately, the Assemblies did not long survive the opposition of the clergy and the government.[22]

MAURITIUS

Ottilie Rhein

Ottilie Rhein (1903–1979) chose Mauritius as her goal. Ottilie was born in Germany, but moved to the United States at a young age to seek adventure, settling in Chicago, where she managed a boarding house. One of her tenants, Betty Powers, was a Bahá'í, but Ottilie's interest was barely aroused. In 1941, she was drawn to the House of Worship in Wilmette and attended meetings about the Bahá'í Faith, becoming a Bahá'í soon afterwards. Immediately, Ottilie pioneered to Arizona to fulfil a goal of the Seven Year Plan and then moved on to San Mateo, California.[23]

Ottilie Rhein enthusiastically embraced the goals of the Ten Year Crusade. At first, she thought of joining Rex and Mary Collison in Uganda, but the emphasis on virgin areas moved her to choose Mauritius instead. A search for information on the island was futile so she simply packed up and went. When she finally arrived, it was in a pouring rain on 11 November 1953, and she had little idea what to expect.[24]

Initially, Ottilie lived in a 'posh' hotel next door to the Bishop of Mauritius, which didn't give her much contact with the local population. Probably after her six-month visa had expired, she returned briefly to Africa and then with a new visa came back to Mauritius and moved into an apartment. Her neighbour, Roland Lutchmaya, said:

> Her way of establishing contacts at the very beginning was to go to

the shop to buy her necessary supplies. One day she met a young Chinese student who was studying for his O Levels, he was eighteen. He was curious about this stranger and so they started talking. She would keep giving him books and would invite him for tea. After a while, the young man, named Yim Lim, converted to the Bahá'í Faith and thus became the first Bahá'í of Mauritius.[25]

Yim Lim became a Bahá'í on 20 February 1955.[26]

Ottilie was able to extend her visa for three additional years. In a letter printed in *Bahá'í News* in July 1954, Ottilie wrote:

> Mauritius has no native population so to speak. One is either descended from the 'Master or his slaves'. People in government service rarely ever stay any longer than 3–5 years. Most everyone is glad to get away again and you can't blame them after you know what man did to Mauritius since his arrival and settlement on this island. Several years ago they swamped the place with electric stoves and all sorts of appliances far too heavy for the generators. As a result electricity is very much curtailed, which means spoiled meat and food poisoning.[27]

In August 1955, Aziz Shayani came and joined her for three months. Within that three months, 16 more islanders became Bahá'ís.[28] In a letter written in November 1955, Ottilie wrote:

> Am swamped with requests for books; how wonderful to see them even copying the prayers and other writings. I am amazed, the change that has taken place in so short a time. Once you find a few ready ones, they are, so to speak, the eyes and ears of their country. Have from seven to 20 people every afternoon. It's hard on my little bank account, even with serving only tea and cookies, but a joy for the soul. Can you imagine people spending 50 cents carfare daily for several weeks to come and learn the glad tidings? . . .
>
> Was told this P.M. that we can expect several new believers tomorrow, when we shall commemorate the birth of Bahá'u'lláh.[29]

By Riḍván 1956, there were 50 Bahá'ís and they were able to elect four Local Spiritual Assemblies. Two more Assemblies were formed in 1958.[30]

Ottilie's visa expired in the spring of 1956, so she moved to Kampala, Uganda. She was able to go on pilgrimage in late 1959 and soon afterward pioneered to Chile for three years. In 1963, she returned to California. The National Spiritual Assembly of Mauritius wrote to her in December 1978, addressing her as the 'Spiritual Mother of Mauritius':

> It is highly significant that God's Message for this day was planted in this island by a lady. We turn our hearts in thankfulness to Bahá'u'lláh that you were chosen for this and we pray to Him that He bring you eternal joy and happiness. Present generations may not be aware of the import of such a feat by you, but your name will forever be associated with the Faith in Mauritius and future generations will befittingly mark the event of your first coming to Mauritius. It may not be without meaning that when you landed in Mauritius on that morning of Sunday, the 11th November 1953, it was raining heavily – the happy presage of a bountiful harvest . . .[31]

She passed away in California eight months later.

REUNION ISLAND

Opal and Leland Jensen

Opal (1912–1990) and Leland Jensen (1914–1996) opened Reunion Island, southeast of Madagascar, to the Bahá'í Faith in November 1953. Leland was a third-generation Bahá'í and both he and Opal had attended the School for Drugless Physicians,[32] which trained them as chiropractors.

When Opal arrived on Reunion Island on 1 November 1953 she spoke no French, the main language, and was without her husband, Leland, who didn't arrive until May 1954. The Jensens were not allowed to practise as chiropractors, but they were financially supported by the National Spiritual Assembly of the United States. In spite of the challenges of teaching in a strongly Catholic country, the Jensens were able to help form a Local Spiritual Assembly in the capital of St Pierre at Riḍván 1955. This success, however, came with a price and the Jensens were forced to leave Reunion the following December.[33]

They moved to Mauritius for six months and continued their teaching efforts.[34] Eddy and Roland Lutchmaya were very impressed with Leland:

> [Eddy] Leland was a good teacher. He went through all the topics of the Faith with great constancy and was very thorough in his teaching method. He helped us to really see the similarity and the Unity in the teachings of the Faith. He was a man of calibre. He was a doctor, specialized in homeopathy, and this was very impressive at the time, yet he was very approachable. The way he taught was to give all the details, never holding anything back, answering all the questions you had in a clear and simple manner, very logically.
>
> [Roland] I was truly impressed by the fact that here were two doctors, him and his wife, two Americans, who were living here in Mauritius, sleeping practically on the ground, with strictly the bare necessities for their life and they were not even allowed to practice medicine . . . This, what I considered a true sacrifice, touched me.[35]

Unfortunately, when Mason Remey declared himself to be the second Guardian in 1960, Leland Jensen followed him and became a Covenant-breaker. He was imprisoned for sexual misconduct in 1969. Between 1979 and 1995, Leland and another man made twenty predictions about disasters of one sort or another. These predictions included a nuclear holocaust in 1980, during which he led his followers into fallout shelters, and a collision of Halley's Comet with the earth in 1986. Not one of the predictions came to pass.[36]

CHAGOS ISLANDS

Pouva Murday[37]

Pouva Murday filled one of the toughest of the Guardian's goals, the Chagos Islands, in early 1957. The privately-owned Chagos Islands, whose only town is Diego Garcia, are 500 kilometres south of the Maldive Islands and 700 kilometres south of India.

Pouva's grandfather had no education and had been brought to Mauritius to work in the sugar cane fields. He was known as Kuli 78, because that had been his number in the cane company's log book. Pouva's father was better educated and was able to find a better job.

Pouva, though, wanted a real education and dreamt of becoming a schoolteacher. He went to school and qualified to teach, but his first job was with the Customs department. It was a good job and paid well, but he wasn't a teacher.

As he walked through the streets of Port Louis, he had long wondered why, if there was only one God, there were so many different churches, mosques and places of worship and why everyone was divided by religion. One day in January 1956, a friend raced up to his house, banged on the door and insisted that he come with him. Pouva asked,

'What's the matter?' [Paul] said, 'Never mind, just come with me.' So, Paul and Pouva, they came running up these streets. Pouva was chasing Paul and Paul went down one alley and up another one and finally he came to this house and he said to Pouva, 'Come on in.' And they came in and Pouva looks around and he sees a conglomeration of races. Somebody is talking at the other end of the room. It was a fireside meeting. A Bahá'í fireside.

Pouva sat down next to Paul and he listened. He heard this Bahá'í teacher tell them about the oneness of humanity, 'We are all the leaves of one tree, the drops of one ocean and there is only one God. Well God, if there is only one religion in the world, and to this one religion there were these different speakers; there was Abraham, Moses, the Christ, and today we have Bahá'u'lláh, who is going to unite all the religions of the world into one faith, one God, one family' – Pouva is falling off his chair. He is listening to this and when the speaker finished, Pouva stood up and asked, 'What do you call the religion that you are speaking about? What do you call people who believe in that?' And the speaker said, 'Bahá'í. [Pouva] said, 'I am a Bahá'í.'

The speaker said, 'Wait a minute, you just came in the door about 20 minutes ago.' Pouva said, 'What difference does it make? Is it going to change? Is it going to change if I go outside?' He said, 'I believe this in my heart and soul. Well they gave him some books, and like the early Dawn-breakers, he went home and was up all night, studying, studying, studying the words.

The house was the home of Ottilie Rhein, the Knight of Bahá'u'lláh for the island, it was 19 January 1956 and the speaker was Leland Jensen, who came to Mauritius after being forced to leave Reunion Island. At the next Riḍván, Pouva was elected to the Local Spiritual Assembly and then elected secretary. He wanted to know how to do his job and thought that the best way would be to read the messages from the National Spiritual Assembly and Shoghi Effendi. One day, he brought in a letter from the Guardian and asked:

'What's the matter? What happened? Why isn't there anybody on the island of Chagos?' And they looked at Pouva like he was mad. And they said, 'Pouva, you understand that the island of Chagos is owned by a private company? You can't just go to that island. They have the worst people in the world to work on that island; it's worse than Devil's Island. They get one pound a month, which is $2.80. All they get is some rice each morning. They have to catch their own fish. If they die, they bury them on it. They don't bring them back to Mauritius. And you sign a 3-year contract. Now, who would want to go there?' But Pouva says, 'There is a letter from the beloved Guardian, Shoghi Effendi, and it says he is praying for someone to go to Chagos. Why hasn't somebody gone?' They said, 'Pouva, don't you understand? It is impossible.' Pouva said, 'The beloved Guardian is asking for a volunteer.'

Not satisfied with the Assembly's response, Pouva wrote to the Guardian, asking him to pray that he would have the strength to fulfil the goal of pioneering to the Chagos Islands. The Guardian responded quickly, saying that he would be praying for Pouva in the Shrine of Bahá'u'lláh. Pouva went back to the Local Assembly and said, 'I'm going to Chagos.' They repeated that it was impossible. Pouva countered, saying, 'Well, I'm going to go there. The Guardian is praying at the Shrines and I know that it will come to pass.'

Every three months a small boat made the voyage between Mauritius and the Chagos Islands and it was due in just three days after Pouva had made his decision. First he had to get a photo of himself for the job application form.

[He] had a friend of his who was a Chinese photographer and he asked him to take his picture to put on his form when he applied. The Chinese gentleman refused to do it. He said, 'Pouva, you're crazy. I won't take your picture.' Pouva pleaded with him. He had such faith and such fire and such devotion that the fellow said 'I'll do it for you.' Another fellow, a policeman, wanted to arrest Pouva and put him in jail until the boat went out to protect him so that he wouldn't go to the island. Pouva talked him out of it, saying he must go . . .

Well, he got the paper somehow and he applied and he went in and had to see the Magistrate. The Magistrate looked at his record and looked at his background, his education, then he looked up at Pouva and he said, 'Why?' And the Bahá'ís, by the way, were all down the hall there, praying . . . And Pouva just looked at the man with the Greatest Name in his heart and said, 'If I don't leave this island, I'll die.'

The night before Pouva was to leave, Auxiliary Board member William Sears and Robert Quigley were on Mauritius and they all prayed throughout the night. In the morning, a letter arrived. In the letter was Pouva's appointment as a schoolteacher. Suddenly, there was a dilemma. The other Bahá'ís asked, 'Pouva, what are you going to do? All your life you've dreamt of this moment to be a schoolteacher. Now you have the paper that says you are. You're on the list. You made it! What are you going to do?' Pouva simply said, 'I'm going to be a teacher. I'm going to be teaching the Faith of Bahá'u'lláh.'

Forty men boarded the small tramp steamer; Pouva was the only one who boarded with 'radiance'. Bill Sears was there to see him off. Pouva repeated 'Alláh-u-Abhá' and the Remover of Difficulties prayer over and over as the ship pulled away. He was also given some of Bahá'u'lláh's dried blood to 'protect him at the post'. After six days living in a cargo hold only 20 feet square packed with the 40 men, they arrived at the Chagos Islands.

Pouva was the only Bahá'í on the island, but the Mauritius Bahá'ís were very resourceful:

A friend of one of the Bahá'ís was a telegrapher on the ship and they made a whole [plan] with him. They would send him a little note and he would slip it to Pouva Murday when he got to this island every three months. And they worked out a whole code . . . 'The game' meant that there was a Bahá'í meeting and when they said 'attempt a goal', that would mean contacts, good contacts. And 'goals' would be declared Bahá'ís. 'Momma' would be the National Spiritual Assembly of South and Southwest Africa and 'Papa' would be our beloved Guardian.

Needless to say, the letters went back and forth about all the games and the attempted goals and all the goals because the Faith started spreading and [went] on fire because of his sacrifice. His sacrifice at that moment started the island of Mauritius on fire.

Life was extremely difficult on the islands. The work, however, was hard physical labour at slave wages. The company which owned the island hired men to peel 650 coconuts each day, separating the tough husks from the usable centres. Pouva said that the workers were often whipped and some were 'fed to the sharks' (thrown into shark-infested waters).[38] Pouva was beaten many times and his health was ruined. Shoghi Effendi had told him to only teach the Faith quietly and that he did, enrolling a few others into the Faith. The nascent group could never meet together because of the watchful eyes of the managers. After nine months, he came back emaciated. When Pouva's story was sent to the Guardian, Rúḥíyyih Khánum said that Shoghi Effendi's eyes filled with tears and he called Pouva 'My hero'.

Pouva returned to Mauritius where he remained an active Bahá'í. He was able to attend the London World Congress in 1963. There he met Rúḥíyyih Khánum and she passed on a message which the Guardian had verbally given to her for him before he passed away.[39]

Pouva married Shanta Appa in 1958, having the first Bahá'í wedding on Mauritius.[40] In 1966, Pouva and Shanta moved to Antananarivo on Madagascar at the request of the Indian National Spiritual Assembly. He found work, first in a supermarket and then with the US National Aeronautics and Space Administration (NASA). While he worked, Shanta visited the villages near the town. In May, the teaching efforts bore fruit when Loulou Rajaonarivo accepted the Faith on her 15th birthday.[41] Loulou's parents also became Bahá'ís through the patient efforts of the Murdays. Since Pouva worked for the Americans, he was suspected of actually working for the CIA and after two years, the Malagasy Government asked him to leave.[42]

Pouva later moved to America and was involved in teaching campaigns in various places, including mass teaching in the American

South in the early 1970s and in the Caribbean. He was also appointed an Auxiliary Board member. Pouva later lived in the Hawaiian Islands and California, where he managed several hotels. With the hotels, he was able to host large Bahá'í events. He also hosted teams of youth on travel-teaching trips. In 1994, he hosted a large reception for the Brazilian media who were covering their country's soccer team in the United States. To each member of the media, he gave Bahá'í literature. Pouva currently lives in California.[43]

ANDAMAN ISLANDS

Khodadad M. Fozdar

Dr Khodadad Fozdar (1898–1958) was the first Indian Parsi to accept the Bahá'í Faith, having been taught by his wife, Shirin, in 1925. Though his acceptance of the Bahá'í Faith antagonized his mother and other relatives, Khodadad Fozdar was not deterred. His position with the State Railways allowed him to send Shirin all around India to teach the Faith. In 1935, Dr Fozdar's visit to the Holy Land strengthened his faith and, in 1950, during the Indian National Spiritual Assembly's Seven Year Plan, he and Shirin pioneered to Singapore, where they started a school for underprivileged women. The Fozdars were able to help elect the first Local Spiritual Assembly of Singapore in 1952.[44]

When Dr Fozdar heard the Guardian's call at the Intercontinental Teaching Conference in New Delhi in 1953, he quickly volunteered to go to the Andaman Islands, east of India, arriving there on 24 November 1953. The authorities in Port Blair, however, did not like having a Bahá'í on the island and after only four months, he was forced to leave. But during that short period, four people accepted the Faith.[45] The National Spiritual Assembly of the Andaman and Nicobar Islands was formed in 1984.[46]

Dr Fozdar returned to Malaysia, settling in a virgin area. They were able to establish three Local Assemblies before he died in 1958.[47]

NICOBAR ISLANDS

Jeanne Frankel and Margaret Bates[48]

Most pioneers spent some time at their posts teaching the Bahá'í Faith either directly or indirectly. Few spent as little time as the mother/daughter team that chose the Nicobar Islands. For them, the journey to their post was almost as significant as what they did when they got there. Jeanne Frankel (1931–2012) discovered the Faith on a ship bound for the Netherlands and quickly became a Bahá'í. She immediately pioneered to Nice, France, with her mother, Margaret Bates (1897–1997), who was not a Bahá'í at that time, but who quickly accepted the Faith.

Jeanne Frankel had only become a Bahá'í the year before, but in May 1956, she and her mother were looking at the few remaining pioneering goals for the Ten Year Crusade. They were excited about the chance to become Knights of Bahá'u'lláh, but it seemed to come down to Spitsbergen or Nicobar. One was cold and one was hot. Both were really isolated. Then a telegram came from Shoghi Effendi recommending the hot one.

They needed a reason other than being a pioneer for the Bahá'í Faith in order to get their visas from India, which controlled Nicobar. A *New Yorker* magazine article connected them with Dr John Pallister, Curator at the Museum of Natural History in New York. His first impression of the women, aged 26 and 59, was not optimistic, but after hearing the true reason why they just had to go, he agreed to train them as field researchers in entomology – insects. They departed New York on 14 December 1956, loaded with boxes of 'killing jars' and cyanide in addition to everything else they thought they would need on what they assumed was a primitive island. Plus their little dog, Muñeca. They didn't, however, know much of anything about Nicobar.

Their first stop was Genoa, Italy, and they arrived to find the Suez Canal closed because of Egypt's nationalization of the vital waterway. The result was that Jeanne and Margaret had to go the long way around to India via the tip of Africa. When they reached Mogadishu, Somalia on 23 January 1957, they were surprised to be met at the dock by a crowd of Bahá'ís, including Mr Samandarí (probably Suhayl Samandarí, the Knight of Bahá'u'lláh who pioneered there in 1953). On 27 January they arrived in Bombay, India, where the ship's captain worriedly told the ladies that the Health Office had come aboard to see them. When they met the Officer, the first thing he said was, 'Alláh-u-Abhá!' The next day, Jeanne and Margaret went to the American Express travel office to book their passage to Nicobar. The clerk, however, could find no mention in any of his books of any sort of transportation to the island. After some delay, he did find a boat, but it would not leave until late February, four weeks away. Later that day, they went back to American Express, but instead of being given tickets, they were given the information that they did not have the necessary permits to go to Nicobar. For those, they would have to go to New Delhi.

When they arrived in New Delhi, they were met by the chairman of the National Spiritual Assembly, Mehdi Samimi, in whose home they were to stay. The next day they went to the Home Ministry where they were bluntly told that the islands were closed to all foreigners. The only suggestion was to write a letter explaining why they wanted to go there. They duly wrote the letter and delivered it on 13 February. Four days later, the strange Bahá'í coincidences began. They went for lunch at the edge of a polo field where they met the Minister of Production (and birth control, an apparently similar field) and General Thimayya, well-known in India for his peace-keeping work in Korea. At half time, Prime Minister Jawaharlal Nehru drove up. Jeanne and Margaret were among those he greeted. He promptly invited them to have tea at Government House with him and his daughter, Indira Gandhi.

A few days later, General Thimayya invited the as yet unknighted pioneers to his home for a benefit evening. They talked about Nicobar with the General and, as the gala ended, he promised to fly them down. But not until he returned from a month-long trip to Europe. On 3 April, Jeanne and Margaret went to Government House for tea with the Prime Minister and his daughter. Indira Gandhi met them at the door and gave them tea cakes she had made herself. After briefly meeting Nehru again, they were left in the care of Indira Gandhi. She quickly figured out that they were Bahá'ís, but thought it was a sect of Islam. When her visitors explained that it was actually a world religion, Ms Gandhi asked for books on the Bahá'í Faith.

Jeanne and Margaret next met with Joint Secretary Pudget Singh on 24 April, who told them that India was neutral and if he allowed an American to go to Nicobar, he would then have to allow a Russian. He stated that as no foreigners had ever been to the island, he wasn't about to break that tradition with two women. He said that there was no precedent for a foreigner visiting the island. Grasping at straws, the women asked if he would reconsider if they could prove that a foreigner had been on Nicobar. The Joint Secretary said yes.

A Bahá'í had, however, managed to visit the island. Sheriar Noo-reyzdan had been able to acquire a one-week tourist visa and had gone to Nicobar some time between Riḍván 1956 and Riḍván 1957. Returning home to Bombay, he applied for permission to move to the islands, but had not been able to do so before Jeanne and Margaret arrived.[49]

Jeanne and Margaret were still in New Delhi on 10 May and feeling very desperate. Finally, Jeanne decided that the only thing left to do was pray, so she went to the roof and began saying the Remover of Difficulties prayer over and over. After several hours of praying, Jeanne was exhausted and fell asleep. She dreamed that she and Shoghi Effendi were walking up Mount Carmel and that the Guardian was bent over because of the work he had to do. She dreamed that maybe she could help him just a little so she put a finger against his back and began to push. He immediately stopped and looked at her, then broke out laughing. He then grabbed her finger, spun around and pulled her to the top of the mountain. Shoghi Effendi then said, 'You thought that you would help me, but I have pulled you to the top of the mountain.' With that, Jeanne woke up and realized that she wasn't helping Shoghi Effendi accomplish the goal; he was helping her.

Nine days later, they attended a dinner at the American Embassy. During dinner, they overheard a pilot mention Nicobar and they quickly asked him about the island. He had recently landed there when his plane had run out of fuel. When he told her that he had been there with his commanding officer for three hours, Jeanne asked if they would write a letter about their visit. The fliers did and the two women raced to the office of Pandit Pant. Mr Pant recognized the precedent and said he would authorize their visit. But then he noticed that Jeanne's passport would expire on 28 July. At that point, he said the only way he would okay the visit was if they would promise to return by 28 July and further promise never to go back. Reluctantly, they agreed.

Jeanne and Margaret finally sailed from Calcutta on 19 June on their way to Nicobar. They first stopped at Port Blair in the Andaman Islands. There the Commissioner took a fancy to Jeanne, and things began to unravel. She didn't drink or didn't gamble and she definitely did not like the Commissioner's company. He took offence very quickly and threw roadblocks in their way, extorting money in a variety of fashions. There were two Bahá'ís in the Port Blair area and Jeanne and Margaret spent some joyous time with them. They were hungry for Bahá'í books so the women gave them several. Soon thereafter, the Commissioner called the women into his office to complain about their lack of attention to him. When they arrived, they saw the books they had given the Bahá'ís on the desk and quickly realized that the two Bahá'ís had been imprisoned. The only way he would let them out, he said, was if they would promise not to try to convert the people on Nicobar. They did promise not to try, but they did not promise not to do. The Commissioner obviously did not like Bahá'ís and made some very critical remarks about Dr Khodadad Fozdar, the Knight of Bahá'u'lláh for the Andaman Islands.

On 2 July 1957, with the nine-day delay at Port Blair, they arrived at Nicobar. After six months of worry and trouble, they had arrived. Everyone was happy to see them, from the Indian Air Force commander to the people, including, surprisingly, the local bishop. Bishop Richardson attended a meeting at the home of a businessman at which Jeanne and Margaret gave a slide show and talk about churches of the world. The pictures included photos of the Shrine of the Báb and Bahá'í Houses of Worship. Jeanne and Margaret worried about what the Bishop might think, but he disarmed them saying that he had visited the Shrines in Haifa and had been very taken with them.

The two women were taken to an unkempt house. There was no electricity or running water. As they struggled to light a gas lamp and camp stove, a man named Harram Das arrived. He got the lamp lit and the stove going and procured water from the well. Harram left them with a supply of coconuts – in their almost impregnable husks. The next day, Harram brought a man named Nicolas Loa who quickly became their helper and guide. Life was rather idyllic. They went out with Nicolas and their jars collecting interesting insects to take back to Dr Pallister. Then on the fourth night, their little dog Muñeca began barking and Jeanne found a snake coiled on her bed. She moved her hand and the snake struck, but the small dog met the snake in midair. Jeanne grabbed a hatchet she kept under her pillow and chopped the snake into several pieces. The snake, however, had bitten the dog. The snake was very venomous, but the small dog survived, though it was flown to Singapore for treatment, unbeknownst to them, by the Air Force commander. The next day, they found another snake on their porch.

On their seventh day on the island, Nicolas asked them if they sang and prayed. Saying that they did, he asked them about which church was right. That led to the first mention of Bahá'u'lláh on Nicobar. The next day, they told Nicolas that they couldn't go out into the jungle to collect insects because it was a Holy Day. They told him about the Báb being killed by people who were afraid of him. On July 9, Nicolas came to their commemoration of the Martyrdom of the Báb, very curious to know the story of the Báb.

Jeanne and Margaret only had 16 days on Nicobar, but those who assisted them all learned about the Bahá'í Faith, though they had to ask to know about it at first. When the pioneers left on 19 July, they left some Bahá'í books. Twenty-seven years later, in 1984, Nicobar, along with the Andaman Islands, formed their National Spiritual Assembly with 19 Local Spiritual Assemblies. There was one final bounty gained from their trials. Before his death, General Thimayya, who had helped them in New Delhi, asked the military authorities to change his records to show that he was a Bahá'í.

After leaving the Nicobar Islands, mother and daughter moved to Penang for a year, then travelled through Hong Kong, Japan and South Korea, before returning to America. In 1959, Jeanne and Margaret were able to settle in the Cocos Islands, replacing the expelled Frank Wyss who had originally pioneered there in 1955, but had not been allowed out of the airport (see following story). They quickly raised up a Bahá'í group.[50] In 1965, the two women pioneered to Spain for two years and then returned again to the United States. Jeanne was back in Malaysia for six months in 1968 and both she and her mother pioneered to Costa Rica in the early 1970s.[51]

COCOS ISLANDS

Frank Wyss

Frank Wyss (1927–2007) filled one of the Guardian's last goals in June 1955 when he succeeded in getting to the Cocos Islands, a small atoll no more than two metres above the Indian Ocean at its highest point. Frank's parents were both Swiss, but they met and married in Sydney,

Munir Vakil, Knight of Bahá'u'lláh to Kuria Muria

Dr Khodadad M. Fozdar, Knight of Bahá'u'lláh to the Andaman Islands

Kamálí Sarvístání, Knight of Bahá'u'lláh to Socotra Islands, with his wife Rezvanieh and their children

Kámil 'Abbás, Knight of Bahá'u'lláh to the Seychelles, with his family

'Abdu'l Rahman Zarqani,
Knight of Bahá'u'lláh to the Seychelles

Pouva Murday,
Knight of Bahá'u'lláh to the Chagos Islands

Ottilie Rhein,
Knight of Bahá'u'lláh to Mauritius

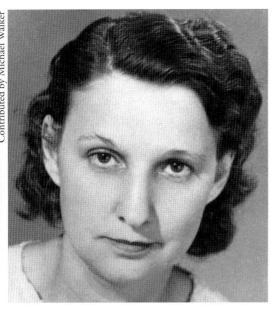

Opal and Leland Jensen
Knights of Bahá'u'lláh to Reunion Island

Margaret Bates and Jeanne Frankel,
Knights of Baháʼuʼlláh to the Nicobar Islands

Frank Wyss,
Knight of Baháʼuʼlláh to the Cocos Islands

Mehraban Sohaili,
Knight of Baháʼuʼlláh to the Comoros Islands

Australia, and had two children, Frank and Lilian, both destined to become Knights of Bahá'u'lláh.[52] Frank and his sister, Lilian, had accepted the Bahá'í Faith at the Yerrinbool School in Australia in 1944. The Guardian commented in a letter expressing his happiness that 'such enlightened youth as Lilian and Frank Wyss had expressed their intention of joining the Faith'.[53]

Early in the Ten Year Crusade, Frank and another Bahá'í had planned to take a worldwide trip which was to include a pilgrimage to Haifa. But Shoghi Effendi sent him a message to 'postpone pilgrimage', so Frank checked with the Australian Foreign Affairs Department and learned that he did not need permission or a visa to go to the Cocos Islands, one of the Guardian's goals. The only thing he knew about the islands was that it was a stop on the air route between Australia and South Africa.[54]

He flew to the island on 4 June 1955. Since he knew there was no accommodation on the island, he took a tent and food and planned to camp. James Heggie wrote, 'I fear he will find it very quiet.'[55]

Arriving on the island, the owner, Clunies Ross, would not allow him to stay and Frank was put on the next flight off the island, which left on 22 June. According to Rodney Hancock, a pioneer to Papua New Guinea, 'since this episode the island has been sold to the Australian Government for $2.6 million, the money was invested in a shipping line and consequently the owner went into bankruptcy, and lives in exile in Western Australia. See what happens when one goes against the plan of God!!!'[56]

Frank was kept in confinement at the airport during his 18 days on the island, consequently he was 'not very happy at being named a Knight of Bahá'u'lláh as he could not stay at his post'. Later in 1955, Frank went on pilgrimage and met the Guardian and expressed his concern. Shoghi Effendi said 'that he had gone to his post, and would have stayed if he could. He also mentioned how wonderful it was to have a brother and sister (Lilian to Samoa) inscribed on the Roll of Honour as Knights of Bahá'u'lláh.'[57] The Guardian continued speaking about the Knights, saying, 'It is a spiritual station. They have accepted the honour of being a Knight of Bahá'u'lláh, they must also accept the responsibility.'[58]

Frank later served on the National Spiritual Assembly of Australia before pioneering to Papua New Guinea in 1958 to assist Rodney Hancock, who had been the solitary Bahá'í there since 1954. Rodney remembered that

Frank arrived in Rabaul in July 1958 with no money, nowhere to live and no job! At that time, I also had just left my job and wanted to start my own business to be able to serve the Faith better. Frank went from company to company finding work but was several months before finding work in a cocoa buying company. Although he had no experience in business (he was brought up on a farm, and did a course in chiropractic in the US) he excelled after a very short time, and learnt the intricate art of buying and selling cacao beans on the world market. Whilst Frank was trying to get a job I was able to give him a meal once a week to supplement his diet of copra, which was all he could afford at that time.

The Asian Teaching Committee from Adelaide was our support in the first few years and we formed a Committee known as BANG (Bismarck Archipelago and New Guinea Teaching Committee) which in those days was responsible for the furtherance of the Faith in Papua New Guinea. Frank was an excellent member and travelled to different villages in PNG and overseas teaching. On a visit to Fiji he met a friend of Irene Jackson (10-year crusade pioneer to Fiji), Luise Dorendorf, who later came to Rabaul to work as a shipping clerk. They met up again and were married in the first Bahá'í marriage in Papua New Guinea. The Bahá'í marriage ceremony was conducted by Frank's mother who came from Australia especially for the wedding. Mrs Wyss also made the wedding cake from a Swiss recipe, which was magnificent. Luise did not become a Bahá'í but was always supportive of the Faith.[59]

For medical reasons Luise and Frank moved to Canberra, Australia in 1970 where Frank resumed his practice as a chiropractor again. He also served as an Auxiliary Board member and remained in Canberra until the time of his passing in 2007.

INDIA AND THE HIMALAYAS

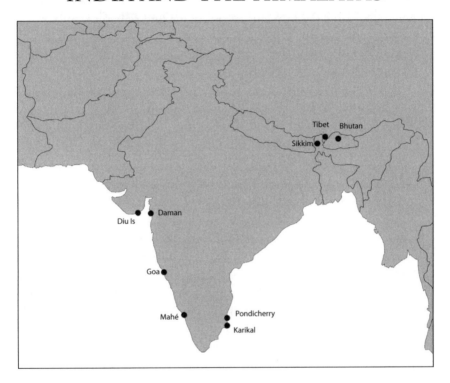

Diu Island

Gulnar Aftábí, Kaykhusraw Dahamobedi and Bahíyyih Rawhání

Gulnar Aftábí (1927–2008), a cousin of Roshan Aftábí, the Knight of Bahá'u'lláh for Goa,[1] Kaykhusraw Dahamobedi (1932–2005) and Bahíyyih Rawhání arrived on Diu Island, an old Portuguese trading post off the coast of northwest India, on 24 December 1953.[2]

Gulnar's awareness of the Bahá'í Faith was enhanced when her father, who was a Bahá'í, unknowingly enrolled her in a school for

Zoroastrians only in Bombay (now Mumbai). For being a Bahá'í, she was expelled. In 1939, Martha Root had visited Pakistan and Gulnar Aftábí and her father attended her talks. Gulnar was very inspired by Martha's talks and vowed to devote her life to service. But in 1943, she married and spent the next ten years raising her children. Gulnar became a Bahá'í in 1945, at the age of 18, in Bombay. In early 1953, an Australian couple visited Bombay on the way to their pilgrimage, and Gulnar asked them to take a message to Shoghi Effendi asking about pioneering. The couple refused to take the message, but while on pilgrimage, the Guardian spoke to the couple about the Bahá'ís of India, then surprised them by adding, 'Tell Mrs Gulnar Aftábí to go pioneering and she will find happiness.' The couple passed through Bombay on their return and relayed Shoghi Effendi's message to her.

When Gulnar attended the Intercontinental Teaching Conference in New Delhi she was inspired to volunteer to pioneer to Diu. Before she could go, however, she had to arrange for her son and daughter to attend the Bahá'í New Era School, not realizing that, because of a conflict between India and Portugal, it would be four years before she could see them again.[3] Two of her friends, Bahíyyih Rawhání, whose father was the chairman of the Local Spiritual Assembly, and Kaykhusraw Dahamobedi, who was 22 at the time,[4] decided to join her in opening up Diu.[5]

The trio left Bombay by ship on 14 November 1953 and arrived at their post on 24 December. Diu at that time was a remote and isolated place. There was no electricity and no public water supply. There were a few wells, but most had salty water. In order to get clean water, people had to walk a few miles to the border where there were two wells with sweet water. For the first 15 days, the three women stayed in the Circuit House, but then found other accommodation; Gulnar found a house close to a girls' school. In May 1954, the Portuguese began to restrict the movement of people between India and Diu. This meant that Gulnar, Bahíyyih and Kaykhusraw were confined to the country, because if they left, they would not be able to return. Bahíyyih did leave after a few months.[6]

The initial reaction of the local population was that the women must be fugitives because those were the only people who went to Diu, escaping from India, or smugglers. Living next to the girls' school gave Gulnar the opportunity to try to make friends with the schoolgirls. At first, they avoided her, but gradually they began to stop by and visit. When the girls learned that Gulnar could do embroidery work, they requested that she come to the school and teach them the skill. Though she didn't know much Portuguese, she agreed. The very next day, the Governor sent a car to collect her and take her to his palace. Learning that Gulnar spoke English, the Governor's wife wanted Gulnar to teach her that language. Two months later, when the Governor's two daughters returned from Portugal for vacation, they also wanted to learn English. The Governor then asked Gulnar to move into the palace to make it easier to teach. Gulnar did not want to do that because she wanted to live among the people in order to teach the Bahá'í Faith. She asked to be able to think over the offer for a while. Gulnar decided to write to the Indian National Assembly about her dilemma, but before she could send it, the Portuguese authorities closed the borders to all Indian citizens.[7]

Gulnar was soon teaching English classes at the palace, visiting the girls' school with the Governor's wife twice a week, and teaching English to youth and elders. And since few of the Portuguese officials knew English, she also began classes at the Officer's Club for army officials and the Police Commissioner. Because of all of these activities involving the Portuguese authorities, she was easily able to renew her residential visa each year. In 1958, there were enough Bahá'ís to form the first Local Spiritual Assembly of Diu.[8]

With that goal successfully achieved, Kaykhusraw left Diu and moved to the United Kingdom where he served on the Local Assembly of Havering.[9] In 1960, the National Spiritual Assembly of India asked Gulnar to move to Goa to replace her cousin, Roshan Aftábí, who had had to leave. She reached the border of Diu in July and was immediately arrested and interrogated by the Diu Police Commissioner, who suspected that she was an Indian spy. Gulnar was put in a prison cell on Saturday and informed that she would have to stay there until the Court convened the following Monday. That night, as she sat in her dark cell, praying to Bahá'u'lláh for protection, a police officer came in and shone his torch on her. He immediately recognized her because she had taught him English. He asked why she was in the prison, and when Gulnar told him her story, he apologized several times for the way she had been treated and made arrangements for her to stay in a hotel in Margoa. After her release, she continued to Goa and gave public lectures in Margoa and in Panjim (the capital). She lived with a doctor's family in the basement of his family hospital until March 1963, when she returned to Mumbai.

In 1968, Gulnar's daughter Zarangiz went to Goa for medical studies. She stayed there for five years and was able to help form Local Spiritual Assemblies in Panjim and Margoa, the two largest cities in Goa.[10]

Firoozeh Yeganegi, who had pioneered to Goa with Gulnar's cousin, Roshan Aftábí, visited the Guardian a few years after leaving her pioneer post. He showed her a photograph of a group of pioneers and, pointing to Gulnar, said, 'she is a real pioneer'.[11]

DAMAN

Ghulám-'Alí Karlawala

Ghulám-'Alí Karlawala (1896–1978) heard about the Bahá'í Faith in India in 1926. At first, he strongly resisted, arguing that all revelation had ended with the Prophet Muhammad. But his teacher, Dr M. E. Luqmání, persisted until he realized the truth of the Faith. Being barely literate, he used the few Bahá'í books that were available to teach himself to read. In 1942, he pioneered to Bhopal and was so successful that the Muslim clergy rose up against him. Calling a Bahá'í scholar well acquainted with Islam, the two men met for a month with the Muslim priests, but the only result was that Ghulám-'Alí was expelled. Unperturbed, he simply went and taught the Faith elsewhere.[12]

Hearing Shoghi Effendi's call for the Ten Year Crusade, Ghulám-'Alí went to Daman, a Portuguese colony on the west coast of India, arriving on 21 June 1953. He found that teaching the Faith was very difficult because a prohibition on alcohol was in place in India. It seemed that because of the prohibition, most people in Daman brewed liquor to sell to the Indians. Consequently, most people drank heavily. When asked why he kept trying, Ghulám-'Alí replied, 'Two things prompted me to make ceaseless efforts in giving the Message, the need of the people to be brought from the path of negativity to the path of God, and my desire to please our beloved Guardian.'[13]

Ghulám-'Alí taught avidly and soon came to the attention of the mullahs. Afraid to confront him themselves, they called for Muslim divines from Bombay to come. Ghulám-'Alí met with them, but refused to discuss his own beliefs, instead preferring to talk about the Day of Judgement and the revival of Islam. Then the butchers of Daman, who were all Muslim, complained about Ghulám-'Alí's 'anti-Islamic' activities to the Government. The police investigated the claims, but after meeting Ghulám-'Alí, they decided that he was only advocating peace and good will. The result was that stricter measures were introduced that protected Ghulám-'Alí.[14]

At one time a Shí'ih priest began attacking the Faith in his sermons. He advertised these sermons for Muharram, the first month of the Muslim calendar and the second holiest month after Ramadan and the month of mourning. Ghulám-'Alí attended one of the sermons where the priest, after giving a

brief reference to the historical events which had taken place in Muharram, and a few words about the greatness of the Shí'ih Imáms, started attacking the Bahá'í Faith. When he finished, he invited questions. Ghulám-'Alí got up and said, 'I had come to learn about the history of the sacred month of Muharram, but you brushed those events aside with a few words and spent your time abusing the Bahá'ís. What have you to say about the advent of the promised Qá'im which has been repeatedly referred to by the Imáms? Don't you know that the most important mission of the Imáms was to prepare the Muslims to receive the Qá'im? How can you prove that the Báb was not the One they had referred to?'

No sooner had he said this than there was an uproar in the mosque and Ghulám-'Alí was attacked by the fanatical mob. His clothes were torn, his pockets picked, his shoes stolen and his spectacles broken.[15]

The police at first thought that Ghulám-'Alí was drunk, but that was quickly debunked. Though he had been beaten for asking his question, it also brought an abrupt halt to the priest's attacks on the Faith.

Toward the end of his stay in Daman, Ghulám-'Alí became very ill. Two Bahá'ís were sent by the National Spiritual Assembly of India to check on him and they spent several days taking care of him. After two years, he was able to leave with a Local Spiritual Assembly in place. During the last three years of his life, Ghulám-'Alí's eyesight failed and though he could no longer work as a plumber, he still opened his shop every day to teach the Faith. He died in 1978, still teaching.[16]

GOA

Roshan Aftábí and Firoozeh Yeganegi

Roshan Aftábí (Knox) (1932–2016) and Firoozeh Yeganegi (1923?–2008) arrived in Goa in late June 1953. Goa at the time of the Ten Year Crusade was a Portuguese colony on the west coast of India, but is now the smallest Indian state. Roshan's father was a Bahá'í who had visited 'Abdu'l-Bahá in Alexandria and Roshan was the first of his children to accept the Bahá'í Faith. She was a very active Bahá'í youth in Bombay (Mumbai), where her father had a restaurant. In 1952, at the age of 20, she decided she wanted to pioneer to Madagascar. Her father, however, vetoed the idea because her goal was too far away and she was too young.[17] Undeterred, Roshan wrote to the Guardian about her dilemma. The reply, written on his behalf, read:

> Perhaps you will not only be able to secure your parents' consent, but be able to find some older person who also desires to go there as a pioneer and then you will no longer be alone, and they would not have cause to worry over you. He urges you to serve the Cause actively and devotedly in Bombay pending the time when you can arise and go forth in foreign fields, and assures you of his loving prayers for your success.[18]

When Shoghi Effendi launched the Ten Year Crusade at Riḍván 1953, Roshan was ready with a companion, Firoozeh Yeganegi, a young widow of about 30, to take up his challenge. The two women, with permission of Roshan's parents, chose Goa for their goal. Goa at that time was a very poor area where access was constrained. There were no trains that connected India with Goa, so the train carriage with passengers for Goa was decoupled and left sitting in an isolated area overnight, waiting for a train from Goa. The only two passengers aboard the abandoned carriage that night were Roshan and Firoozeh and they had an anxious night.[19]

The two pioneers arrived in Goa near the end of June and moved into a hotel. After four months, Roshan and Firoozeh went to the Intercontinental Teaching Conference in New Delhi. At the conference, Shirin Fozdar ran up to Roshan and gave her a big hug: 'Oh, you've done a wonderful thing!' Roshan wondered, 'What have I done now?' and Shirin said, 'Now, the Guardian has named you a Knight of Bahá'u'lláh.'[20] Roshan didn't know that the title came with her opening Shoghi Effendi's goal area.

Roshan found a job as a secretary, but being fairly poor, she had to walk the three miles to work each day, repeating the trek in the evening. She credited dawn prayers with achieving her goal to pioneer, so she and Firoozeh got up at daybreak each morning for prayers. The authorities noticed this early morning activity with some suspicion. After about a year, when the women went to get their residential permits, the official said, 'We've been watching you. We thought you were sending messages to India at dawn.' Roshan explained exactly why they were there and that they avoided any sort of political activity, after which the official exclaimed, "My God! I wish all our citizens were like you two!' Roshan then asked, 'Could we have our residential permit?' and the man said, 'We would be only too happy to give it to you.'[21]

Roshan and Firoozeh quietly tried to teach their Faith. Some, including the priests, were suspicious of two young single women, but most people were very friendly. Roshan started taking Portuguese language lessons and found her teacher and her family open to spiritual conversations. No one, unfortunately, became a Bahá'í while they were in Goa.[22]

After two years of poor food and missed meals due to a lack of money, the long walks to and from work, and poor sanitation, Roshan became ill and had to return to India for an operation. Two days after arriving, her father died and, as the oldest child, it became her duty to arrange everything. After a month, she was ready to return to Goa, but the Indian authorities refused to allow her to re-enter because of the increased tensions between the Indian and Portuguese Governments. After much fruitless effort to return to Goa, one of Roshan's friends who lived in Cardiff, Wales, invited her to pioneer there in order to reform the Local Spiritual Assembly. Since Goa appeared to be closed, Roshan went to Cardiff. One day, after the Local Assembly had been formed and when there were sufficient Bahá'ís in Cardiff, Marion Hofman (who was pioneering there with her family) pointedly said, 'I wonder who will pioneer to Scotland?' Taking the hint, Roshan went to Edinburgh and helped reform that Assembly.[23]

In 2003, Roshan returned to Goa and was amazed to find that there were almost 600 Bahá'ís there.[24] Roshan lived in Honiton, Devon, in the United Kingdom and passed away in 2016.

Firoozeh later moved to Australia from which she made 23 travel-teaching trips to Fiji. She died in 2008 and is buried near the House of Worship in Sydney.[25]

MAHÉ

Lionel Peraji

Lionel Peraji (b.?) attended the New Delhi Intercontinental Conference in 1953 and offered to go to Mahé, at that time a French colony on India's southwest coast. At the end of the Conference, all the volunteers met with the treasurer of the National Spiritual Assembly. Lionel was offered funds to help him get settled, but was also told that the Fund could not support him for long.[26]

On 20 October 1953, Lionel Peraji arrived in Mahé.[27] He found a room in a moderately-priced hotel and immediately began teaching the Faith by making the Cause known to the proprietor. Lionel wrote that

> the following day, I met a few other people and announced the Cause of God and while discussing I observed one friend by the name, Mr Nair, indicating interest to know more about the Cause of Bahá'u'lláh. I met him frequently and had several discussions and finally he embraced the Cause of God, signing the Enrolment Card which I mailed to the National Office, New Delhi.[28]

At the beginning of the following month, when he received his stipend from the National Assembly, Lionel was reminded of the limited resources of the National Fund, so he spent much of his time unsuccessfully trying to find work. At the end of his second month, deeply regretting his inability to find work, but not wishing to be a burden on the National Fund, he returned home.[29]

Qudratullah Rowhani and Khodarahm Mojgani

In March 1954, Lionel Peraji was replaced by two young pioneers, Khodarahm Mojgani and Qudratullah Rowhani (1922–2001). Khodarahm had wanted to pioneer from an early age, but had worried about the problems and finances. In October 1953, he attended the Intercontinental Teaching Conference in New Delhi and heard Artemus Lamb, a pioneer to Costa Rica, talk about the challenges he had faced and overcome in his efforts to pioneer:

> En route to his post, his boat caught fire in the Panama Canal and all his belongings were lost except for the clothes he was wearing, his passport and about $25 which he had in his pocket. The insurance company refused to reimburse his loss and as a result, he was left in a foreign land without anything . . . His family asked him to return home but he decided to continue with his journey. On arrival in Costa Rica, much to his surprise, he found the Beloved Guardian's cable assuring him of ardent prayers for his success. Although he faced a number of hurdles and difficulties, he was able to establish himself as a pioneer in his post . . . Mr. Lamb explained that from the moment we decide to go pioneering, difficulties are bound to arise, but with prayers, reliance on Him and patience, all will work out.[30]

Inspired by Mr Lamb's talk, Khodarahm returned to Bombay, where he met Alvin and Gertrude Blum, who were on their way home after pilgrimage and who would soon become Knights of Bahá'u'lláh for the Solomon Islands. They said that the Guardian had talked about the Chagos Islands in the Indian Ocean, so Khodarahm tried to pioneer there, but after months of effort, he was unable to get permission to go to the privately-owned islands. Khodarahm then contacted the National Spiritual Assembly of India and they suggested Mahé, a small territory on the coast in southwest India administered by the French. Lionel Peraji had only been able to stay for a short time and the Guardian had said that any vacant pioneering post should be quickly filled. Khodarahm and Qudratullah Rowhani, also from Bombay, offered to go. The two men were able to obtain three-month visas. As they collected their visas at the French Consulate, the Secretary said that he was from Mahé and predicted that they would leave their goal within the first week.

Khodarahm and Qudratullah left Bombay by train on 2 March 1954 and arrived in Mahé three days later. They were greatly encouraged when, upon their arrival, they received a loving message from Shoghi Effendi assuring them of his prayers. Mahé was a small fishing village on the coast surrounded by India on the land side. It consisted of about one square mile of territory. Most of the inhabitants were fishermen, but there were also a few schoolteachers and civil servants. The primary language was Malayalam, though a few spoke a little French and English. Khodarahm wrote:

> The Hindus were in the majority followed by Muslims and a sprinkling of Catholics. The basic food of the people was boiled rice, fish, coconut, chilli powder, tapioca, yam and plantain. The weather . . . was extremely hot for four to five months of the year, and there were monsoon rains for another five months. It would rain day and night, often non-stop for one or two weeks continuously. The remaining two months of the years the weather was moderate.
>
> We also discovered that there were no essential services such as electricity or tap water or medical facility. Drinking water was drawn from very shallow wells and had to be boiled to avoid various tropical diseases . . .
>
> There were no hotels, only two tea shops. Each tea shop had one or two very small rooms on the second floor which could be rented for a night or two. I can never forget the first night of our arrival in Mahé: we rented one of these little rooms for the night. There were two narrow wooden cots with a thin straw mat which served as the bedding. We had brought our own bedding which we spread on these cots. Soon after laying down, we both felt our bodies scratching. As there was no electricity, we lit the little kerosene lamp by our side and saw that there were hundreds of large bedbugs all over us. Although we removed our bedding and lay down elsewhere to avoid the bedbugs, they followed us. Finally, we got a bucket of water mixed with some kerosene and we had to catch the bedbugs and throwing them into the bucket. We could not sleep until morning.[31]

It was obvious that life in Mahé wasn't going to be easy, but soon after their arrival, things got worse. The Indian Government, which didn't like a French colony in their midst, placed an embargo on supplies to Mahé, including many basic things such as cooking fuel, bread, sugar, tea, coffee, salt, vegetables, eggs and cooking oil. Luckily, the embargo only lasted a few months.

Shoghi Effendi told Khodarahm and Qudratullah to be very tactful about teaching the Bahá'í Faith in order to allay the suspicions of the Government and the people. Even so, the local people suspected them of being either smugglers or criminals who had run away from the law in India. In order both to establish themselves and to overcome these suspicions, Khodarahm and Qudratullah pooled their resources, which amounted to about $500, and opened a small variety shop they named the Maxwell Store. Khodarahm said that they sold

> very basic items such as biscuits/cookies, sweets/candies and every-day items like soap, parts for kerosene lamps, needles, thread, etc. We also sold fountain pen ink: families could not afford to pay for a whole bottle of ink and instead would buy only enough ink for only one day and return the next day for another 15 drops of ink. This meant that often there was as much ink on the floor and my clothes as I had sold.
>
> We would purchase these items from the nearby cities on the mainland and re-sold it at our store for a very small profit margin . . . we had to accept credit and we were paid only once the resident had received remittance payment from a relative abroad or by govern-ment salary.[32]

The store allowed Khodarahm and Qudratullah to expand their circle of friends, especially among the schoolteachers and civil servants. Though many expressed interest in the Faith, none accepted it, so they wrote to the Guardian. He replied that they needed to be patient and persevere in pioneering. Khodarahm wrote that they knew then that they 'were there for the long haul; we prayed, waited and waited for Divine assistance'.

In October 1957, Khodarahm attended the South India Teaching Conference where he met a long-time pioneer who asked how their teaching efforts were going. Khodarahm admitted that they had many sympathizers, but no declarants. The pioneer told him that he needed to get married. 'As long as you are unmarried, people will not be able to have enough trust and confidence in you to accept what they are told about this new Faith and to declare their Faith in Bahá'u'lláh.' Khodarahm replied that he was too young and financially unstable, but the pioneer simply told him about the daughter of a pioneer in Belgaum, Mona Sarooshi. Khodarahm took his advice and proposed to Mona Sarooshi that same evening. We were engaged the next morning at 7:30 a.m. with the blessing of her parents. At 9:30 a.m. I left Belgaum for my pioneering post. Two months later we got married on December 30, 1957 at the Winter School in Poona . . .[33]

A few months later Qudratullah married Firoozeh Bahram and the two couples continued running the Maxwell store while living in a two-bedroom apartment. The marriage advice turned out to be true because Mona was able to connect with the women and share the message of Bahá'u'lláh, particularly after the birth of their son, Foad. Finally, after five years, the first two residents of Mahé accepted the Faith. On 21 March 1959, Captain A. C. B. Nambiar, a retired army officer, and Mr E. K. Vijayram, a schoolteacher, became Bahá'ís. By the next Riḍván, in 1960, there were 17 Bahá'ís and they formed the first Local Spiritual Assembly of Mahé. Unfortunately, Qudratullah and Firoozeh had to leave Mahé shortly before the Assembly was elected because Firoozeh's father became ill and passed away.

After 12 years in Mahé, the damp and the heat had badly affected the health of both Khodarahm and Mona. Since there were no English-language schools in Mahé, Foad was sent to the New Era boarding school in Panchgani. But when their daughter began having the same health difficulties as her parents, they decided that it was time to leave. They did, however, leave a community of thirteen Bahá'ís and a Local Spiritual Assembly. In 1966, the family returned to India; then, in 1967, went to Iran to visit his family there. In 1975, moved by a Message of the Universal House of Justice, Khodarahm and Mona pioneered to Port Coquitlam, British Columbia, Canada, and then to Richmond Hill, near Toronto.[34]

PONDICHERRY

Sa'íd and Shawkat Nahví

Sa'íd Nahví (1910–1987) arrived in Pondicherry on 21 July 1953 and Shyam Beharilal, a 'youthful pioneer',[35] joined him in August 1953. Sa'íd's wife, Shawkat, followed him the following November with their two children Susan and As'ad, who were three and eight years old, respectively.

Sa'íd was born to Muslim parents in Iran in 1910 and went to school at the Tarbíyat Bahá'í School in Tehran. In 1925, he moved to France to further his education and became associated with the Bahá'í students there. He went on pilgrimage in 1935 and met Shoghi Effendi, an event that strongly affected him. In 1943, he married Shawkat 'Alá'í, sister of Shu'á'u'lláh 'Alá'í, who was later appointed a Hand of the Cause. Sa'íd studied law and provided translation services for the Iranian Government.[36]

Sa'íd was a member of the National Teaching Committee when the Ten Year Crusade was announced. He and Shawkat went to Bombay and asked the National Spiritual Assembly of India where they should go. Since Sa'íd spoke French, they were sent to Pondicherry, a French colony on the southeast Indian coast. Both Sa'íd and Shawkat found work at a school called Sri Aurobino Ashram, where she taught kindergarten and he taught mathematics and chemistry. The head teacher at the school was Madame Richard, who had met 'Abdu'l-Bahá at the home of Laura Dreyfus Barney in Paris. Because of that, Shawkat remembered that their life in Pondicherry was fairly easy.[37]

While in Pondicherry, the Nahvís were able to share the Bahá'í Faith with the Governor and the French Consul. They stayed in Pondicherry for seven years until the National Spiritual Assembly of Iran asked them to go to Sri Lanka, where they were the first pioneers to Kandy.[38]

In 1964, Sa'íd and Shawkat returned to Iran, where he served on the Local Spiritual Assembly of Tehran. In 1979, the family moved to California, United States, from which Sa'íd made travel-teaching trips to French Guiana, American and Western Samoa, the Cook Islands, Fiji, Loyalty Islands, New Caledonia, New Zealand, Tahiti, Tonga and Vanuatu. Sa'íd served on the Local Assembly of Dana Point from 1979 until 1986. The next year, he passed away.[39]

Shyam Beharilal Bhargava

Shyam Beharilal Bhargava (1924–1993) pioneered to Pondicherry in August 1953. There is considerable confusion about his name. On Shoghi Effendi's map, the name is spelled 'S. Beharilal' while on the Roll of Honour published in the 1992 volume of *The Bahá'í World*, it is given as 'Shyam Bihari Lal'. In Poostchi's recently published book *Dawn of the Sun of Truth, Tamil Nadu, India* (2015), the name is spelled

'Shyam Beharilal'. Shoghi Effendi's cablegram of 20 September 1953 used the spelling 'Shyan Behrarilal'.[40] Shyam's son notes that

> Bhargava is basically a caste name as well as a surname. In those days it was not uncommon to disregard surnames, for people were used to the system of being referred to by their given names along with their father's given names, as was the practice from the times of Mogul rule in India. My father began using his surname later on when we, his children, had to be admitted in schools and he had to register his business.[41]

Shyam's father was a Bahá'í and had visited 'Abdu'l-Bahá in 1920 before travelling to England, where he spent considerable time with Shoghi Effendi. Consequently, the young Shyam, who was born in Jaipur, Rajasthan, India, grew up hearing stories of the Master and the Guardian. After finishing university, he moved to his father's sugar factory in Siwan and was able to help raise up a Local Spiritual Assembly. He later moved to Calcutta and married Ms Danish in what the Guardian called the 'historic performance' of the first marriage of Bahá'ís from both Hindu and Muslim backgrounds.[42]

When the Ten Year Crusade was announced, Shyam consulted with his father and, leaving his wife and 18-month-old daughter, moved to Pondicherry:

> At that time the most famous place in Pondicherry (now called Pudducherry) was the 'Ashram', the affairs of which were run by a French-born lady who was deeply respected and addressed as 'The Mother'. It was to this place that young Shyam gravitated, where he initially found shelter and commenced his teaching work. Despite language difficulties, since he spoke neither French nor Tamil, he managed to make friends and slowly set about expounding and explaining the principles of the Faith and the life of Bahá'u'lláh in one to one conversations. At first the Mother took him to be a benign young man, but as time wore on it became evident that a number of the inmates of the Ashram were coming under the influence of the teachings of the new age and daring to question the traditions and values of former dispensations. As a result, the Mother began discouraging and dissuading those under the

influence of the 'Ashram' from discussions with this young man with radical ideas.

So it was, then, that Shyam had to shift his focus from being Ashram-centric to teaching those who had no connection with it. He moved his living quarters to very modest lodgings elsewhere and started wandering around the city spreading the Word among anyone and anybody who would care to listen. As always, in view of his limited personal resources, the focus was on direct teaching to individuals or small groups at a time. His reports to the National Bahá'í Office were often printed in the *Bahá'í News* as news from our 'Youthful Pioneer' – and this name stuck.

The biggest problem which he now faced was the lack of suitable employment for a man of his qualifications in this purely trading port. Whatever he could manage was not enough to sustain him, nor to bring his family whom he had left behind at Calcutta. His resources were now fast depleting and the time had arrived to take a final decision. Realizing that he could not continue indefinitely at Pondicherry, he returned to Calcutta after about one year in his pioneering post. He hoped that he would be able to change his circumstances and then return some time in the future.[43]

Back in Calcutta, Shyam was able to find work and his income was sufficient to enable him to finance his travel-teaching work in the area. After several years, his financial resources grew enough so that he was able to also fund many other travel-teachers. Shyam still desired to return to Pondicherry, but 'Hand of the Cause, Tarázu'lláh Samandarí, advised him to remain at Calcutta which he felt was the place that he was needed and would be most effective in his services'. This he did. He divided his time

> between his business and his service to the Faith. Five days a week were meant for his business with evenings divided between firesides and visits to the other members of the Community. Saturdays would see his office converted into a Bahá'í office when only Bahá'í administrative work would be done; and on Sundays he would travel with his wife to various villages in the countryside to teach the Faith. His increasingly important position in the wider community also allowed him to share the Faith with the Governor of West Bengal,

successive Chief Ministers, the Speaker of the Legislative Assembly and the Chief Justice of the High Court.[44]

The election of a Communist government in Calcutta induced him to move to New Delhi, but he was forced to return to Calcutta by the failure of his plans. In later life, he suffered a stroke and was confined to a wheelchair. When he attended the gathering of the Knights of Bahá'u'lláh in Haifa in 1992 in his wheelchair, he 'was taken to the Shrine of Bahá'u'lláh for prayers. It is reported by those present that on reaching there he amazed everyone, as if with an unseen force he arose from the wheelchair and walked into the Shrine taking hold of the door and exclaimed aloud, "O Bahá'u'lláh, I stand here to serve thee!"'[45] Shyam died the next year.

KARIKAL

Shírín Núrání and Salisa Kirmání

Shírín Núrání (1918–1984) and Salisa Kirmání (?–2006), both from India, opened up Karikal, another French colony not far from Pondicherry, arriving on 30 August 1953. Shírín's father was an outstanding teacher of the Faith, so she was born into a Bahá'í family in Bombay. She was a nurse by training.[46] At the age of 22, she served on the Local Spiritual Assembly of Bombay.[47] She married and had two children, but her husband died after just three years. She later moved to Hyderabad and completed her nursing and midwife course.[48]

Salisa Kirmání also came from a Bahá'í family. Her grandfather, Mihrabán Bulbulán, had become a Bahá'í from Zoroastrian background.[49] Salisa was instrumental in establishing what became the Bahá'í New Era School in Panchgani. In 1945, along with Mrs Mobedzadeh and Mrs Manavi, she moved to Panchgani and opened a Bahá'í hostel with 16 children. The three women began classes and within a short time had 40 students enrolled. Salisa was called to return to her home within a year or so.[50]

Salisa and her husband went on pilgrimage for 19 days in 1952, so when the Guardian announced the Ten Year Crusade, Salisa was ready. During the Feast of Kamál on 1 August 1953, the subject of two unfilled goals came up. Salisa wrote:

I . . . requested the secretary of the Local Spiritual Assembly of Pune, who was speaking about it, to give us information about the weather and schools in Karaikal and Mahé. The secretary asked me 'Why are you asking this question? Do you intend to go and settle there?' I felt as if the beloved Guardian had asked me the question. I replied 'Yes'. All the friends were surprised and happy. My husband, Mr Kermani, was in Hyderabad for his business tour. I informed him about my intention. He wrote back saying that he would find a a companion for me and that was Shirin Nourani.[51]

Shírín and Salisa left for Karikal on 27 August, arriving there three days later:

There, we came to know that their language was Tamil and educated people knew French. To our surprise they did not know either Hindi or English. We also found out that Karaikal was a small town surrounded by paddy fields, and that we could not stay at a guest house or a hotel. We met the mayor at his residence and he arranged accommodation in a new house for us . . . We had informed the mayor about our intention to settle in Karaikal as pioneers to teach the Bahá'í Faith forever . . . The mayor was very kind to us and sent us furniture and a lady servant. Our early days in Karaikal were a little funny. As we were unable to speak the Tamil language, shopkeepers usually showed us the amount we could pay them . . .[52]

In October, the two women went to New Delhi for the Intercontinental Teaching Conference and learned that they had each been awarded the title of Knight of Bahá'u'lláh. Returning to Karikal, a press correspondent visited them and asked many questions about the Bahá'í Faith and what they were doing in Karikal. The next day, 'it was printed in the papers that two Bahá'í sisters had come down to Karaikal to teach the Bahá'í Faith'.[53]

Shírín was unable to find work in Karikal. Initially, her offer to work as a volunteer was turned down, so she concentrated on raising up a Bahá'í community. She later served as a part-time volunteer at the government hospital. Shírín also did beautiful embroidery works of the Greatest Name, which she donated for fund raising. She also gave free sewing lessons. To spread the Faith, Shírín would 'set out from her home every Sunday morning with her handbag. In that bag would be a prayer book, some biscuit packets and sweets. She would go and visit the nearby villages, mostly on foot, and teach children's classes.'[54]

The first person to accept the Faith was Vijayaraghava Iyyangar, a journalist for *The Hindu* newspaper. They were able to form the first Local Spiritual Assembly of Karikal at Riḍván 1957.[55]

After 12 years, Salisa's husband's health began to deteriorate and, after consultations with Hand of the Cause Jalál Kházeh, she left Karikal to care for him. Though he was never able to join her, he did offer to build a Bahá'í Centre there, which, with Salisa going back to Karikal to oversee the work, was built in spite of the 'shrewd and cunning' contractor.[56] Salisa was appointed to the Auxiliary Board in the 1950s by Shoghi Effendi and later served on the Continental Board of Counsellors from the early 1970s until 1980.[57]

With Salisa gone, Shírín's parents joined her in Karikal. Unfortunately, they were unable to remain, so the National Spiritual Assembly sent Bahá'ís to help her. In about 1970, her father and one son died. The National Assembly then asked Shírín's mother to join her, which she did, though she too passed away in 1977 and was buried in the newly acquired Karikal Bahá'í cemetery. Shírín's brother, Mr Shahpour Ardeshir Khojestegan, moved to Karikal in 1983 and bought a house for them to live in. A few days after the purchase, however, he too passed away and was laid to rest alongside Shírín's mother in the Bahá'í cemetery. In 1984, a State Teaching Conference was held in Karikal at Shírín's request. On the final day, while serving tea to the participants, she passed into the Abhá Kingdom.[58]

SIKKIM AND TIBET

Udaya Narayan Singh

Udaya Narayan Singh (1929–2009), in answer to the Guardian's call, left his home in Bombay and arrived in Gangtok, Sikkim, on 3 August 1953. He first came in contact with Bahá'ís in Bombay a few years before the Ten Year Crusade. He and his brothers had a machine workshop and did auto repairs, but he lived to teach and was very knowledgeable about the Bahá'í teachings and their relationship to Hinduism.[59]

Upon arriving in Sikkim, Udaya Narayan immediately cabled the

National Spiritual Assembly of India that he had arrived. His first problem was a place to live:

> There was no hotel in Gangtok; there were only a few sweet shops and tea stalls. My immediate problem was where to stay. Some friends said, 'There is the Thakureswari temple where you can stay.' I went to the temple and met Ramchandra Tiwari, the priest, and asked if I could stay there. He was from the village of Chhapra in Bihar, India. At that time 99% of the Indian population in Sikkim was engaged in business. I settled down in the premises of the temple and started to look for a proper residence. First I went to see the Indian Ambassador Mr Kapoor. I presented to him some Bahá'í books and informed him of my purpose in coming to Sikkim. He knew about the Bahá'ís because he had been the Indian Ambassador in Iran before being assigned to Sri Lanka and now Sikkim. He said, 'I would like to welcome you to Sikkim. You do what you have come to do. If you face any difficulty let me know, I will try to help you'. I thanked him and said, 'If I continue to enjoy your goodwill, I should have no problem.' I left and continued my search for some suitable accommodation. A businessman from Bihar who owned a sweet shop gave me a room above his shop and immediately I started living there. The interesting thing about Sikkim at that time was that it was very small and everyone knew everyone else.[60]

Initially, Udaya Narayan was able to freely tell people about the Bahá'í Faith, but then he began to notice that the same people began to avoid him.

> I found out afterwards that the secret police had been shadowing me all the time, and people had become aware of this. At that point I became very sad. One night I sat down to pray and asked Bahá'u'lláh 'What should I do? What is your wish?' Just at this time a close friend in Delhi wrote me, 'Do not be disheartened. Bahá'u'lláh will assist you with His blessings, and you are protected by his troops on high.' I went to sleep at 2 in the morning, and when I got up, I decided to see the Indian Ambassador and inform him of the situation. As I started climbing the hill towards the Ambassador's residence, it was a happy coincidence that he was coming down the

hill. The moment I said, 'Namaste' he asked me how things were and whether I was successful in my mission. I said, 'It has become very difficult for me to stay here. Sikkim's intelligence agents have been constantly following me, so it has become hard to contact anybody. When I talk to people, they do not tell me directly what the problem is. I am tired and discouraged. It feels as if people treat me like someone who carries a contagious disease.'

He said, 'Come with me.' He called the Superintendent of Police and said, 'Don't you know that there is an Indian citizen that has come to Gangtok? He does not belong to any political party. He is an Indian and a Bahá'í. His being here can only be beneficial to the country; no harm will come through him.' Whenever I visited him he was kind and courteous. He knew quite a lot about the Bahá'í Faith and was sympathetic towards it. When I left him and was heading back to my room, I saw a police inspector coming towards me. He greeted me with a salute and asked how I was. I knew the Ambassador's telephone call had worked![61]

Udaya Narayan spent two years in the independent kingdom, learned the Nepali language, and succeeded in raising up a small Bahá'í community.[62] The first person to accept the Faith of Bahá'u'lláh in Sikkim was Kedar Nath Pradhan, who later was the first pioneer to settle in Nepal in 1956. Udaya Narayan said, 'I suffered a lot in Sikkim in the beginning, but in the end it proved to be a fruitful territory for the Faith.'

Udaya Narayan then heard that another of the Guardian's goals for the Ten Year Crusade was Tibet:

I became prepared to undertake that mission. Baijanath [Singh] arrived from India and I right away introduced him to everyone in Gangtok and travelled to other areas with him before I left for Tibet. The good news was that everyone had a positive attitude towards the Bahá'ís. The Judge of Sikkim High Court called me one day and said, 'I have a lot of regard for you and the Bahá'ís, but I myself cannot be a Bahá'í. I would like to invite you to my home and discuss the Bahá'í Faith.' The Magistrate, Mr Mahendra Pradhan, who later also became the Secretary (govt.) of Sikkim, became a Bahá'í.[63]

In the middle of 1956, Udaya Narayan left Sikkim and went on foot to Tibet, crossing the border at Yatung.

> I went there as a businessman but my only desire was to proclaim Bahá'u'lláh's mission. I knew teaching the Faith would be difficult. Many young boys from Tibet went to schools in the Indian border towns of Kalimpong, Gangtok and Kurseong. I established contact with these young students; most of them were from well-to-do families . . . There was a village close to Yatung where a young man, Chiten Tashi, became the first Bahá'í in Tibet. At that time the only teaching material I had was a small pamphlet in Tibetan. Many understood Nepali so I used to speak in Nepali. Because of the pamphlet in Tibetan, I was arrested and imprisoned for seven days. People used to ask me questions in an indirect way, and if they had specific questions about the Faith, they would come see me only at night.
>
> The authorities were afraid that I was trying to create feelings against the government. I told them that I had not aroused any ill feelings towards the government nor had I anything against the country. While I was in prison, my friends in the business community brought me food. When the Indian and Nepalese businessmen appealed to the government on my behalf, they released me from prison.[64]

In 1958, Udaya Narayan left and went to Fari, leaving five Bahá'ís in Yatung. He lived in Fari for 11 months and noted that the society at that time was completely dominated by the Buddhists and steeped in superstitions.[65]

While living in Tibet, Udaya Narayan returned to Sikkim every six months. It wasn't an easy trip. He could travel for ten miles by jeep, but the rest of the journey had to be by mule. He was helped on his way back and forth because he had two Bahá'í friends, Hari Shankar Verma and Munni Lal Yadav, at the Indian border checkpoint.[66] Udaya Narayan's efforts in Sikkim and Tibet won him the honour of being a double Knight of Bahá'u'lláh.

By 1961, Udaya Narayan, along with all the other Indians living in Tibet, had returned to India and was an active teacher of the Faith in the Bombay area. In connection with the goals of the global Seven Year

Plan that extended from 1979 to 1986, the National Spiritual Assembly of India asked him to pioneer to Nepal. Again, he responded to the call of the institution, and in 1981 he settled in Biratnagar, a city in south-eastern Nepal with few Bahá'ís. Udaya Narayan travelled extensively from village to village and was greatly loved by the people. He was able to raise up many new Bahá'í communities, particularly in Morang and Sunsari Districts and helped to form a number of Local Spiritual Assemblies in the area. The National Spiritual Assembly of Nepal, which had to be dissolved in 1975 because of restrictions on religious organizations at that time, was reformed in 1982 and Udaya Narayan was elected to that body.

JoAnne Pach Koirala remembered Udaya Narayan:

In those early days of the 1980s Mr Singh, Bharat Koirala, and David Walker walked through the dusty roads to the Tharu villages one after another. This was done to help the local Bahá'ís with their delegate elections and in forming Local Spiritual Assemblies during the Riḍván period. Mr Singh lived in Biratnagar at the Regional Bahá'í Centre and from there he walked so frequently visiting Bahá'í friends and communities that the soles of his shoes always wore thin. Years later I remember looking at his worn dusty shoes and I thought, 'these shoes are signs of his labour of love for Bahá'u'lláh'.

At the time of the 1988 Bahá'í International Convention in Haifa, Israel, Udaya Narayan Singh, Ramachandran Raja, Larry and Shyama Robertson, and I were delegates for Nepal's National Spiritual Assembly . . . One unforgettable moment from these sacred days in Haifa was a time when we went to the Shrine to pray. I was seated in the Shrine of the Báb and when I opened my eyes I saw the radiantly peaceful face of dear Mr. Singh facing me . . . I thought it was a vision at first, but then I realized this devoted follower of Bahá'u'lláh was at peace in prayer at the Shrines.[67]

Udaya Narayan served on the National Spiritual Assembly until 2000, when he was incapacitated by a heart attack. Penny Walker noted that when he travelled around Nepal, 'he would be greeted warmly by both adults and children in the villages with "Namaste, Uncle"!', a sign of respect and affection. He also 'had very few clothes or other possessions, and the one room he lived in was spartan in furnishings – a bed, small desk, a bookcase, and two plain wooden chairs . . . I saw how the spirit he exemplified in the Ten Year Crusade carried over to his pioneering in Nepal – he longed for nothing in life except the chance to share the Message of Bahá'u'lláh.'[68]

In about 2004, he returned to India to be near his brother's family in Varanasi. He passed away in 2009.[69]

BHUTAN

Shapoor Aspandiar Rowhani and Ardishir Furúdí

Shapoor Aspandiar Rowhani (1931–1985) and Ardishir Furúdí, both young men in their early 20s, heard the call for pioneers in Bombay in 1953 and decided to open the Kingdom of Bhutan to the Faith. Their first problem was that they didn't know where Bhutan was and had to go home and find it in an atlas. In early 1954, the two men set out and managed to reach Bhutan in June, but were denied entry into the country. By a strange chance, while at the border they met Bhutan's Prime Minister, Jigme Dorji, who happened to be a brother of the Queen, and he was intrigued by what the two youths had travelled so far to share. After hearing about the Bahá'í Faith, the Prime Minister not only allowed them into Bhutan, but he also provided them with a pack train of mules and supplies.

After a terrifying trek through dense forests encountering snakes and leeches for the first time, they arrived in Bhutan in June. Barely had they arrived when Ardishir received an emergency communication asking him to return to Bombay, so Shapoor was left alone to face the ingrained traditions and superstitions of the age-old Buddhists, while knowing almost nothing of the language. Shapoor had great difficulty publicly teaching the Bahá'í Faith, but soon the villagers began to 'surreptitiously visit his wooden hut at night to hear more of the Message he had come to convey and to read laboriously the Bahá'í books in Hindi'. Shapoor even managed to present the Faith to the Bhutanese royal family.

But then the Prime Minister, who had become a good friend, quietly said it was time to leave. Apparently, the Queen's European doctor had been trying to bring in a Christian missionary for a long time, but had always been refused, and the Prime Minister was afraid that the doctor would hear that he had allowed a Bahá'í into the country. That would cause many problems. So Shapoor left, losing all his belongings and food in a dangerous river crossing, but eventually reaching Calcutta.

Upon reaching Bombay, Shapoor joined his father in business and was soon elected to the Local Spiritual Assembly until his death in 1985, serving as chairman for 27 years.[70]

CHINA, INDONESIA AND MALAYSIA

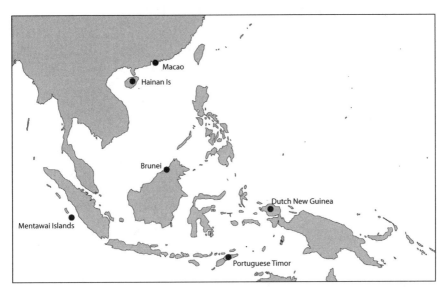

MACAO

Frances Heller

Californian Frances Heller (1909–1990), from Louisiana, was a devout Catholic who read the Bible and discovered things that didn't fit with the Catholic Church. At the age of 16, she began a search of the world's religions, looking for the true one. One day Frances went to visit friends in Wilmette, but when they weren't home, she went to see what 'mysteries' she could find in the Bahá'í House of Worship. Discovering the bookstore in Foundation Hall, Frances bought two of everything. When the clerk asked her why, Frances replied, 'If this is as good as it sounds, then someone else needs to know about this.' Frances married Sydney Heller in 1948 and soon afterward attended her first fireside in the home of Mamie Seto in San Francisco. What she learned created turmoil, making her ask why the Catholics had not recognized Bahá'u'lláh. So, she decided to visit Rome and ask the Pope three questions: 1) Do you know about Bahá'u'lláh and His claims? 2) If so, do you believe they are true? and 3) If not, why not? and if so, why aren't you a Bahá'í? She received an audience with Pope Pius XII in the fall of 1951, but as she was dressing in her robes, she suddenly realized why the Pope hadn't recognized Bahá'u'lláh, and fled. When she returned to San Francisco, she immediately declared her Faith.[1]

She decided to go to the Intercontinental Teaching Conference in New Delhi in October 1953. On her way, she stopped for a few days in Hong Kong and made a one-day trip to Macao. Macao at that time was a Portuguese colony and Frances learned that she could get a visa to stay there. Immediately after the Conference, she returned to Macao, arriving on 20 October 1953.[2] When she arrived in Hong Kong, she had an unusual experience:

> Yesterday afternoon I took the ferry to the Kowloon side of Hong Kong. I was strolling around the shops when (being a woman) a Chinese brocade dress attracted my eye. A man came out and invited me in to look at it. I really cared not to go in, but I let him talk me right into it. It finally turned out that he was the only Bahá'í in Hong Kong! . . . Of course we all know that only God could get Bahá'ís together in this way. For this I am more than grateful.[3]

In Macao, Frances rented a house at No 9 Ave Dr Rodrigo Rodrigues and began taking classes in dance and Chinese brush painting. Soon after she moved in, a Chinese woman, Mary Shia, asked if she would teach her son English. Frances also taught Mary about the Bahá'í Faith and she became the first native Bahá'í in Macao.[4]

One day in August 1954, Frances went fishing and met Manuel Ferreira, a Portuguese man who asked if she would teach him English. The textbook Frances used was *Bahá'u'lláh and the New Era*. As they studied English, Manuel learned about the Bahá'ís and on 25 October, declared his Faith in Bahá'u'lláh. Soon, others of her neighbours were reading *Bahá'u'lláh and the New Era*:

> My friendly neighbours are reading the *New Era*. Everyone has been wonderful. I do not feel like a stranger here . . . Sunday there were

four boys here and they enjoyed so much reading from the *Hidden Words*, and *The Bahá'í Pattern of Life*. They are now reading the *New Era*.[5]

One day in November, Frances received a letter from Carl and Loretta Scherer, who were soon to join her as pioneers in Macao, informing her that Hand of the Cause Mr Khádem would be visiting. Frances couldn't go meet him because there was a typhoon warning, so she sat at home praying that he would phone her. Then at 6:30 p.m., she said, 'my door began to rattle. I went from my bed to answer the call, and who should be there but Mr Khádem. We went about Macao, met the neighbours, and had lunch with one.'[6]

On 9 December, Frances was joined by pioneers Carl and Loretta Scherer, who also became Knights of Bahá'u'lláh, and in 1954 by Mr and Mrs Ishmat'u'lláh 'Azzízí. Near the end of 1954, the Guardian wrote to Frances and told her that there were too many Bahá'ís in Macao and that she could leave, which she did in November. But once a pioneer, always a pioneer, and in March she was at a new post in Mexico. In the spring of 1956, she received a message from Shoghi Effendi asking her to go to the Gilbert Islands to replace Roy and Elena Fernie, who had been forced to leave. To reach the Gilbert Islands required Frances to first go to Fiji. She arrived there in late 1956 and, while waiting for her visa, taught the Faith. One day she met three Fijian girls. One of the girls, Tinai, whose uncle later became the King of Fiji, was interested in the Faith and Frances took her to the Bahá'í centre where she met pioneer Donald Hancock from New Zealand. Tinai and Donald later married and Tinai later was appointed to the Continental Board of Counsellors. Finally, in the spring of 1957, Frances sailed to the Gilbert Islands where she lived in a thatched hut and taught her neighbours English and the Bahá'í Faith.[7]

Due to deteriorating health, Frances returned to the United States on 4 November 1958,[8] staying a few months in Hawaii to teach the Faith. She went to London in the fall of 1962 to help prepare for the World Congress. Following the Congress, she travelled with Rúhíyyih Khánum on a teaching trip through Norway and Scotland. Sydney and Frances moved to California in 1978 and then to Louisiana in 1980. Frances passed away the next year.[9]

Carl and Loretta Scherer

Carl (1900–1982) and Loretta (1907–1980) Scherer arrived in Macao on 8 December 1953 from Wisconsin. The Scherers were married in 1925 and Carl had a job in China from 1931 to 1936. Returning to Wisconsin, the couple discovered the Faith and became Bahá'ís in 1949. When the Ten Year Crusade was announced, the Scherers decided to go to Macao.

Initially, they were only given a visa for seven days, but a week after their arrival their visa was extended for two to four years. In January, they wrote:

> Sunday we had seven attending our fireside which was held at Frances' home. The friends are most anxious to hear about the Faith. The session lasted three and a half hours. Not having an oven I made a batch of doughnuts and they went over big – something you cannot buy here.[10]

Carl was appointed an Auxiliary Board member, initially for Southeast Asia and then for Japan, Korea and the Northern Pacific.[11] While he travelled, Loretta worked in Macao. The Scherers attended the Teaching Conference in Nikko, Japan, in 1955.[12]

One of their early contacts was Yim Pui Foung, a prosperous merchant who exported jade, antiques and embroidery. Loretta went into his shop one day looking for a wooden statue and soon he was studying the Bahá'í Faith. On 15 July 1954, he became a Bahá'í.[13] On 19 April 1957, the Scherers had an interview with the Governor of Macao, Pedro Correia de Barros, who mentioned that he had heard of the Faith in Mozambique.[14]

The fledgling Macao Bahá'í community decided to hold their first public meeting on 8 December 1958 in a room in the local high school. There was some initial opposition:

> On December 8, 1957 the community held their first public meeting. According to an account written by Mr Scherer, they had difficulties from the beginning. They reserved a room in a local high school. But the Presbyterian Church brought pressure to bear and permission was cancelled. Then a primary school gave them permission to use one of the rooms. Another Protestant church applied pressure on the principal so that the primary school would withdraw

permission. However, due to the intervention of Mr Chang, permission was once more granted. The advertisement in the newspaper had to be altered suddenly but the meeting resulted in the largest non-Bahá'í audience ever; fifteen people. There was a total of twenty-two people including the Bahá'ís. Mr and Mrs Datwani and Mr Sherwani came from Hong Kong to attend this first public meeting. Those three Bahá'ís held Indian passports. Some time after that Macau was closed to possessors of Indian passports and the three were unable to make more trips to Macau for a time.[15]

By Riḍván 1958, there were enough Bahá'ís in Macao for the first Local Spiritual Assembly to be formed. The Scherers stayed in Macao until after the Spiritual Assembly was functioning and then moved back to Wisconsin, but they were soon on their way to another pioneering post, this time in Portugal where Carl served on the National Spiritual Assembly. They returned to Wisconsin in 1963, participating in the World Congress on the way. In 1970, the Scherers were off to another pioneering post, this time in Madeira, where they stayed until 1973, when they pioneered again to Macao. Loretta's poor health and their slim finances made them make one final trip back to Wisconsin after just three months.[16]

HAINAN ISLAND

John Chang

John Chang became a Bahá'í in Macao in May 1955. The next year, he translated 22 prayers from an American prayer book into Chinese; it was the first Chinese-language prayer book. John was a member of the first Local Spiritual Assembly of Macao, elected at Riḍván 1958. On 19 August 1959, John arrived on Hainan Island, off the coast of China, thus becoming a Knight of Bahá'u'lláh. He managed to spend two weeks travelling there with his wife and child. He thought that a family would attract less attention from the Communist authorities then a single man. At that time, only Chinese were permitted to visit the island. When John returned and reported to the National Spiritual Assembly of North East Asia, he noted that some people 'showed interest in the Faith', but added that 'they would not dare join a religion at that time'.[17]

BRUNEI

Charles Duncan and Harry Clark

Charles Duncan (b.1924) and Harry Clark arrived in Brunei, a small country on the island of Borneo surrounded by the Sarawak state of Malaysia, on 19 February 1954.[18]

Charles, an African-American, was a talented musician and composer. He first heard of the Bahá'í Faith in 1939, when he was only 15, and went to the summer school in Geyserville, California, as a guest of Florence Keemer. As they drove in the evening from Sacramento to Geyserville, Florence and John Eichenauer explained to Charles what the Bahá'í Faith was. He accepted Bahá'u'lláh immediately, but was a bit confused by the three Persian names Bahá'u'lláh, 'Abdu'l-Bahá and Shoghi Effendi. Charles told his friends in Sacramento about the Faith, but they were not interested. After the night ride, he attended youth classes in the Faith. He also attended a talk given by Marzieh Carpenter (later Gail) about Muhammad and Islam. Charles was very taken with it and wrote, 'She explained so many things that I had heard from Christians who knew nothing about Islam . . . That talk helped to sinch me to the Cause, but Mrs Keemer kept me studying and explained the Faith to me . . . She had me study *Gleanings* with Mr and Mrs Kuphal afterwards in Sacramento. So when I finally signed the card in 1950 I felt grateful to Mrs Keemer.'[19]

Harry Clark, who was white, came into the Faith through Charles. All the Bahá'ís that he met in Geyserville and Sacramento were white, including Marzieh Carpenter, Kathryn Frankland, George Latimer and Willard Hatch, among others. This had an effect on his future as a pioneer to a foreign country. Charles wrote:

> We did not choose our goal area, it chose us. When we were in Chicago at the launching of the Ten Year Crusade Harry and I tried to go to Africa but it turned out that the committee was on the East Coast while we were on the West Coast where the Oriental teaching committee was. We didn't mind that. We knew that the goals were for the Dutch East Indies, Macau and another place that we could not go to. Persia was supposed to do Brunei, but they did not have anyone they could send from their country, so they wrote to the NSA of America and asked if the U.S. could help them out.[20]

Kaykhusraw Dahamobedi, Gulnar Aftábí and Bahíyyih Rawhání, Knights of Bahá'u'lláh to Diu Island

Roshan Aftábí,
Knight of Bahá'u'lláh to Goa

Firoozeh Yeganegi (left),
Knight of Bahá'u'lláh to Goa

Ghulám-'Alí Karlawala,
Knight of Bahá'u'lláh for Daman

Shawkat and Sa'íd Nahví, Knights of Bahá'u'lláh to Pondicherry, with their children As'ad (eight years old) and Susan (three years old) who pioneered with them; the passport photograph from 1953

Shyam Beharilal Bhargava,
Knight of Bahá'u'lláh to Pondicherry

Salisa Kirmání and Shírín Núrání, Knights of Bahá'u'lláh to Karikal, with believers in Karikal, 1960

Shapoor Aspandiar Rowhani, Knight of Bahá'u'lláh to Bhutan

Udaya Narayan Singh, twice Knight of Bahá'u'lláh, to Sikkim and Tibet, in later years in Haifa

The visit of Hand of the Cause Shu'á'u'lláh 'Alá'í to Macao, 1960, with members of the Spititual Assembly and other Bahá'ís. John Chang, Knight of Bahá'u'lláh to Hainan Island, is standing at the far left.

John Chang, Knight of Bahá'u'lláh to Hainan Island, with Mrs Chang, 1957. Mr Chang (Cheong Sui Choi) was headmaster of the Leng Nam Middle School in Macao and known as a community leader.

Knights of Bahá'u'lláh to Macao Carl Scherer, Loretta Scherer
(left) *and Frances Heller,* (right)*, 1954*

*Knights of Bahá'u'lláh John Chang
(Hainan) and Carl and Loretta Scherer
(Macao) with the Macao Bahá'í community.*
Left to right, seated: *Mr Ferreira, Mary
Shia, Louie Shia, Loretta Scherer and Paul
Kao;* standing: *Paul Shia, John Chang, Carl
Scherer, Mr Yim and William Yang*

*Loretta Scherer with Lt. Col. Yuan Mien-hsien
and Hand of the Cause Zikrullah Khadem
November 17, 1953 when the Scherers stopped
at Taiwan on their way to their pioneer post of
Macao*

John Fozdar,
Knight of Bahá'u'lláh to Brunei

Charles Duncan,
Knight of Bahá'u'lláh to Brunei

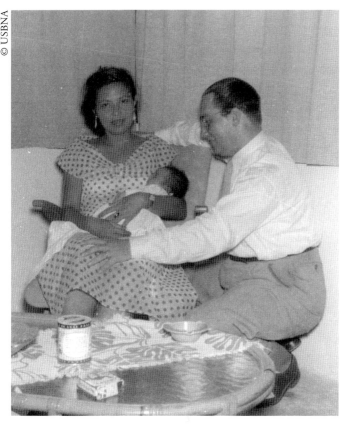

Lex Meerburg and Elly Becking Meerburg, Knights of Bahá'u'lláh to Dutch New Guinea, with their daughter Monica Alexandra, 1956

Írán and Raḥmatu'lláh Muhájir, Knights of Bahá'u'lláh to the Mentawai Islands

The first Spiritual Assembly of Dili, Portuguese Timor, 1958, with Knights of Bahá'u'lláh José Marques (left) *and Harold and Florence Fitzner* (standing fourth from left, and seated second from left respectively)

Knights of Bahá'u'lláh Harold and Florence Fitzner in Portuguese Timor, photographs from the 1960s: with the Bahá'í community and Greta Lake (seated left), *visiting from Sydney; and picking fruit in the market*

Charles and Harry visited North Borneo for several weeks on their way 'to make things look natural and to get a visa into Brunei'. They were very taken with how friendly and curious everyone was about them. Very much encouraged by the friendliness they found in Borneo, the two pioneers sailed by ferry to Brunei.[21]

Harry remained in Brunei for only six months because he couldn't accustom himself to a culture radically different from what he was used to. Returning to America, he was ultimately unable to remain in the Faith.

By October, Charles was living in a house in a section of the town that was built over the river – Brunei was known as the Venice of the East – and approachable only by boat or a 'maze of rather rickety bridges'. He was the only non-Chinese living there. His room had a good view of the river in several directions, including down:

I can see the river flowing under my room through the cracks between the floor boards. This house . . . has walls made of unpainted boards, the roof is thatched with palm leaves and the whole house is built on stilts which sink down into the mud. When the tide is low, it is possible for a person in a boat to pass underneath; but when the tide is high, the water is only about four feet below the floor . . . the houses have practically no furniture in them, the people ordinarily sit on the floor, eat on the floor, and sleep on the floor. They spread mats on the floor, use a pillow and a blanket. Sometimes it gets quite cold and you feel as if you were going to freeze to death.

They speak only Chinese and Malay although two of the younger fellows know a smattering of English. In spite of the language barrier, they are extremely warm, friendly, lovable people. They all know that I am a Bahá'í but I haven't been able to tell them more than that. They see the picture of 'Abdu'l-Bahá that I have on my desk and ask whether it is my father. My Malay vocabulary is not extensive enough to say that He is the Center of the Covenant.

. . . we expect to enroll our first Bahá'í next week at the 19-Day Feast. She is an Indian and was born a caste Hindu, but the family later accepted Christianity and she was educated as a Christian. She married a Muslim and to pacify the family of her husband became a Muslim.[22]

Charles didn't have trouble meeting people because the Malays were eager to learn English:

> A few weeks ago I stepped into one of the coffee shops for coffee and a young man waved to me to join him. I did. He said he wanted to study English. I told him I would teach him English in exchange for lessons in Brunei Malay . . . A few days later a few of his friends met me and wanted to study, too. That made a total of four, but when the first class convened there were six. The next class had about nine and the one after that had twelve . . . The Malay lessons have not been so good because the boys are not systematic in teaching and I have had no time to study . . . As a stratagem, I recently changed from eating in the Chinese restaurant to the Malay restaurant and the desired effect was achieved.[23]

Language was the biggest barrier, but there was an unexpected problem. Since Charles was African-American, most people in Brunei thought the Bahá'í Faith was a 'Negro religion (just like Islam was a Malay religion to them)'. And since Charles was nice to everyone, people were coming to believe that all black people were 'nice'. Charles summed up his teaching experience in Brunei saying: 'I am not discouraged – just perplexed. If I sit and wait for an opportunity to come, I feel I am being lax; and if I keep bringing up the subject, I feel I am forcing things.'[24]

Charles left Brunei for Thailand in 1956. Eight years later, he pioneered to Taiwan, where he was an Auxiliary Board member,[25] and then to Korea.[26] He also went to Hong Kong and Macao. Following this, Charles pioneered to Japan for 17 years and then moved to China, where he encountered an English lady named Hilary, whom he married. After 11 years in China, Charles and Hilary moved to Italy to be with their granddaughter. They are still there, living in Rome.[27]

John Fozdar

On 9 April 1954, John Fozdar (b. 1928) arrived in Brunei, at that time a British Protectorate. John was the son of Dr Khodadad M. Fozdar, Knight of Bahá'u'lláh for the Andaman Islands, and Mrs Shirin Fozdar, a tireless campaigner to raise the status of women.

John had worked in Singapore as a doctor and had attended the

Intercontinental Teaching Conference in New Delhi the year before where he learned that Iran had been given the goal of sending pioneers to Brunei. Because of politics, it was very difficult for an Iranian to get permission from the British, so John, who had an Indian passport, offered to go. His offer accepted, John applied for a job as a doctor. He also requested that a family servant, Ratilal Tribhuvan, come with him. The Brunei authorities accepted the servant because 'they thought that I was some religious freak who had to have special cooking'. 'When my launch reached the jetty', John wrote of his arrival in Brunei, 'I walked along the wharf and saw a white man and a black man there. I went up to them and said: "You must be Harry Clark and Charles Duncan" . . . I did not think that in that small place there would be another pair of a white and dark man walking so harmoniously.' The two earlier Knights of Bahá'u'lláh had not known that John was coming so it was a great surprise.[28]

John quickly found himself doing all the surgical work at the General Hospital Brunei and this enabled him to meet with many well-connected people. One of these was a businessman who had heard John was coming. Cheok Chin Hong contacted John and soon became the first resident Bahá'í in Brunei. One of his two sons also became a Bahá'í. Two others became Bahá'ís through Charles Duncan. His friend, John Woods, who worked in the Public Works Department, became interested in the Bahá'í Faith. His wife was Indian and had an adult daughter, Daphne. Both Woods and Daphne became Bahá'ís after firesides in John Fozdar's home.[29]

Late in 1954, John paid a surprise visit to his parents. When he was asked to accompany an ill patient to Singapore, he asked for a couple of days off to visit his parents. Though his boss wasn't happy, John managed to make a quick visit to his parent's home in Malacca. The visit was so hastily arranged that John had no time to inform them. His mother happened to look out of the window and called to her husband, 'Come, come, see how much that man looks like John.' When John's father looked, he said, 'That is John.' They had a wonderful visit.[30]

In August 1955, the Government officially heard the name of the Faith when Shoghi Effendi asked all Bahá'í localities to send a message to the Shah of Iran asking for justice following the partial demolition of the dome of the Ḥaẓíratu'l-Quds in Tehran. John promptly did so. Two days later, while playing tennis with the Minister of Posts, the Minister said that he knew about the cable to the Shah. When a surprised John asked how he knew about it, the Minister said he had to vet the message since it was being sent to a Head of State. He had consulted with the British authorities, received clearance and the message had been sent off.

John wanted to get out of Brunei city and visit the people in the countryside and tell them about the Faith. The Medical Department of Brunei did clinical work outside the city, but doctors did not go along. John was the first doctor to visit the villages. He described one of his visits:

> We got a boat and I travelled with the medical team of hospital assistants and nurses. During the evening, after work and before retiring, the village would gather around me and listen to me while I explained my background and beliefs. This may have been the first time that they heard the name Bahá'í in that part of Brunei . . .
>
> On one visit to a longhouse, perhaps in 1955 or 1956, when my assistant was Suleiman – a hospital assistant – after listening to their medical problems, I talked to them on various subjects, including Bahá'í. After some time, Suleiman told me that I should go to sleep as the Ibans [the village people] would be happy to talk all night. I followed his advice. The next morning, while we were getting ready and packing, the chief came and told me that during the night they had consulted about what I had said about Bahá'í Faith and they would all like to become Bahá'ís.[31]

After Charles Duncan left Brunei for Thailand in 1956, John's brother Minoo Fozdar, and Mangubhai Patel, came to Brunei, so the small group began holding Feasts. Mr Seah Teck Heng, an ethnic Chinese Bahá'í from Kuching, Sarawak, also arrived in Brunei that year. With his arrival, a number of Chinese contacts who had been hesitant about becoming Bahá'ís became emboldened to do so and the Brunei Bahá'í community continued to expand.

Brunei was not a large place and it was easy to get to know everyone. Since John had good relations with the British authorities, when his parents came to visit it was easy to arrange a meeting with the Sultan, Sir Omar Ali Saifuddin, and his wife. During the meeting, the Sultan was told of the Bahá'í teachings. John later had other opportunities to meet the Sultan and continued to tell him of the Bahá'í Faith.

In 1956, John decided that, with his work contract coming to an end, it was time to go to the United Kingdom and finish his surgical studies.

This decision had repercussions all the way up to the Sultan, and soon the Prime Minister, after consultations with the Sultan and British authorities, offered to send John to study in the United Kingdom on a government scholarship if he would return and serve for five more years. John wrote: 'I remember my feelings that everywhere else, pioneers are struggling so hard to remain at their posts with the fear of being expelled. And here, I was being invited by a Muslim government to go back by special invitation.' He accepted, learning later that he was the first non-Brunei citizen to receive such a scholarship. He left in the spring and spent two years in his studies, returning in November 1958, accompanied by his new wife, Margarethe (Grete) and his infant daughter, Shirin.[32] In his absence, the first Local Spiritual Assembly was elected in 1957.[33]

Back in Brunei, John found conditions to be very different. On the good side, there was a functioning Local Spiritual Assembly, but the politics of the country were changing. In September 1959, a new constitution put Brunei in charge of all internal administration, with the British only responsible for defence. By 1960, with the British gone, their positions were being occupied by Muslim Malays and this led to the intense promotion of Islam. John's boss was replaced by a new man who joined the concerted effort across the country to replace all non-Muslim doctors in government service. John's boss was so antagonistic that he urged John's own patients to sue him. By November, John himself was a patient in the hospital with a bleeding ulcer from all the pressure. In 1961, he sorrowfully decided that to stay was impossible, but he had a bond to pay for the early cancellation of his contract. Though he managed to negotiate a reduction for the time he had already served, it was still more money than he had. John's mother sold her own house in Singapore to pay the debt. Released, John, Margarethe and Shirin moved to British North Borneo.[34] The Bahá'í Faith was later banned in Brunei by the Government. Despite this ban, government statistics show that there were about 10,000 Bahá'ís fairly recently.[35]

DUTCH NEW GUINEA (NOW PART OF INDONESIA)

Elly Becking and Lex Meerburg

Elly Becking (1918–2005) learned of the Bahá'í Faith from Eleanor Hollibaugh, an American pioneer to the Netherlands, and became a

Bahá'í in that country in June 1951. She was elected to the first Local Spiritual Assembly of The Hague the next year.

When she attended the Intercontinental Teaching Conference in Stockholm in July 1953, she had no plans to pioneer anywhere. Elly was Dutch, but having grown up in Dutch New Guinea (now part of Indonesia), she and her fiancé, Lex Meerburg (1925–1996), were planning to move back there. But Lex was not a Bahá'í and Elly 'thought that [she] knew too little of the faith'. Surprisingly, she found herself volunteering to go as a pioneer. Shoghi Effendi was delighted and wrote to her expressing his hopes 'that, in the near future, your future husband will decide to join the ranks of the followers of Bahá'u'lláh, and will lend his reinforcement to your teaching activities'.[36]

Elly acquired a three-year contract to work for the Ministry of Agriculture, Fishing and Food Supply in Dutch New Guinea and departed with an engagement ring from Lex, arriving in October 1953. They were married by proxy a year later and Lex found his own three-year contract and joined her. The early teaching was difficult and Shoghi Effendi encouraged her. He

> urged her to persevere in her task and never to become disheartened, as this is a most meritorious work, and those who pioneer in virgin territories are receiving special bounties from God in this historic period . . . He attaches the greatest possible importance to your presence in that virgin country and he urges you under no circumstances to abandon your post, but to persevere and with tact and patience gradually build up contacts with the local people, so that you can seek out those souls who are waiting to hear the Message of Bahá'u'lláh, and will prove the most receptive.
>
> The most important thing for the pioneers to do in these countries into which it is difficult to gain entry, is to be very careful not to antagonise the officials, the missionaries or the local people, as this might cause them to be deprived of their possibilities of gaining a livelihood or to be driven out of the country . . .[37]

Unfortunately, Elly and Lex had to leave in 1959 because of political unrest. They returned to the Netherlands, where Elly was elected to the Amsterdam Spiritual Assembly. In April 1960, they opened the Dutch town of Diemen to the Faith.[38]

MENTAWAI ISLANDS (PART OF INDONESIA)

Raḥmatu'lláh and Írán Muhájir

Raḥmatu'lláh Muhájir (1923–1979) was born into a distinguished Baha'i family. He was very active in the Faith as a youth and pioneered for the first time after graduating from high school, going to Azerbaijan for two years. He then went to medical school. In 1951, he married Írán (b.1933), daughter of 'Alí-Akbar Furútan, who was appointed a Hand of the Cause of God just two months after their wedding.

Raḥmatu'lláh returned from pilgrimage in 1953 on fire with the desire to pioneer, so he and his 19-year-old bride wrote to the Continental Pioneering Committee, volunteering to go anywhere they were needed. Collis Featherstone, then a member of the National Spiritual Assembly of Australia and New Zealand, proposed a goal swap with Iran: they would fill a Persian goal if Iran could send a pioneer to the Mentawai Islands in Indonesia. The Pioneering Committee passed this goal to the Muhájirs. The couple had never heard of the islands before and didn't even know what country they belonged to, but knowing that it was a goal from Shoghi Effendi, they determined to go. Raḥmatu'lláh promptly wrote to Khodarahm Payman, who lived in Jakarta, and asking nothing about the conditions of the island informed him that they were going to go pioneering there.[39]

The Muhájirs went to the Intercontinental Teaching Conference in New Delhi in October where their offer to pioneer to the Mentawai Islands was accepted. But when Írán met with the International Goals Committee in Tehran, that Committee disagreed, saying that they were too young and just married. When she informed Raḥmatu'lláh, he was 'absolutely livid' and couldn't believe that a group mandated by Shoghi Effendi to promote pioneering would reject volunteers. They took the rejection to the National Spiritual Assembly, which had two Hands of the Cause and two future Hands of the Cause serving on it. The Assembly approved of the Muhájirs going to the Mentawai Islands.[40]

Wasting no time, the Muhájirs left Tehran in January 1954 for Jakarta, where they connected with Khodarahm Payman. The morning after their arrival, Raḥmatu'lláh went directly to the Ministry of Health to look for a job, ignoring the Khodarahms' objections that they should first learn some Indonesian and get acquainted with the local health system. That night, Raḥmatu'lláh was radiant and Khodarahm amazed. When Raḥmatu'lláh had said that he was a doctor, he had been immediately taken to see the Deputy Minister who offered him a plum position in the city of Bukittinggi with a good salary, a house, a car with a driver and servants. Raḥmatu'lláh turned him down and instead insisted on going to the Mentawai Islands, a place the Deputy Minister himself had never even heard of until that moment. In disbelief, the Deputy Minister found himself giving the man before him a three-year contract that paid $25 a month on an island he hadn't known existed.[41]

Their introduction to the Mentawai Islands began when their ship arrived offshore on 4 February. Írán wrote:

Nothing in our life had prepared us for the Mentawai Islands . . .

The boat had to drop anchor a long way from shore, and we were told to climb down a rope ladder, hanging at the side of the boat. Then we had to board a rowing boat, crewed by two men who appeared to be completely naked. My first thought was to run back to the cabin and hide . . . However, my hand was held firmly by Raḥmatu'lláh, who was quietly chanting the Tablet of Aḥmad. . .

Mixed with the mainland residents greeting us were a few native men and women clad only in very narrow loincloths, their bodies covered from forehead to ankle in tattoos of the most ornate and fascinating designs. Everyone was wading through the mud, covering their head with . . . banana leaves.

A narrow plank was thrown over the lake of mud for our benefit. Raḥmatu'lláh just waded into the mud while holding my hand and helping me manoeuvre down the slippery, wobbly plank. My patent-leather high heels were not designed for this sort of thing and, after a few steps, I was flat on my back struggling with the mounds of wet slippery leaves, which were mixed in with the black smelly mud.[42]

Írán's fall into the mud and her subsequent flood of tears broke the ice and she was quickly taken in hand by several women. The 'Mayor' of the village offered them the use of a house, and soon everyone in the village was following the Mayor and the new arrivals to the house. It proved to be in really bad condition:

The roof had gaping holes, the walls were rotten and termites were feasting on the remaining wood. A few goats had occupied the door-less rooms, and chickens were nesting in the corners . . .

. . . Chamat [the Mayor] assured us that the water snakes, which . . . were now slithering around us were completely harmless . . . Huge rats were running about, some sitting on their hind legs and observing us with curiosity.[43]

The local schoolteacher offered them the temporary use of the school since school was not in session. The toilet facilities turned out to be two slippery wooden planks over a stream filled with water snakes. Supplies were basically non-existent and took most of a year to order and receive. One lady decided to teach Írán to cook over firewood, not realizing that this newly married 19-year-old didn't know how to cook at all. The Muhájirs quickly came down with malaria.[44]

Shoghi Effendi told the Muhájirs that 'the spread of the Cause, while difficult, would lead to such wide acceptance by the Mentawai people as to eclipse even the victories in Africa. But to achieve this, great sacrifices were needed.'[45] Raḥmatu'lláh very soon began his trips to the various villages, travelling by foot or by canoe for 10 to 40 days at a time. While he was meeting and treating the villagers, Írán stayed home and learned Indonesian and before long could hold her own in the language. Time quickly lost all meaning because their only time-piece, Írán's watch, broke quite soon after their arrival. When the Fast came around, they guessed at the starting date and ended up fasting for 22 days before they realized it.[46]

The first declaration of faith came after a year, when Levi Tambuan became a Bahá'í. He was soon followed by four others.[47] Then, in mid-1954, Raḥmatu'lláh visited the village of Si Pai Pajet for the first time. One of his rowers was Amata Sinanga and Raḥmatu'lláh told him about Bahá'u'lláh. Amata replied that the people only accepted things collectively so when they arrived in the village, Raḥmatu'lláh found himself facing the 25 elders of the village and telling them about the Bahá'í Faith. When he finished, the elders began consulting about what they had heard and a few hours later came back and announced that what they had heard was good and that they had all decided to become Bahá'ís.[48] Two other villages shortly thereafter went through the same process and soon there were 200 Bahá'ís. At Riḍván 1956,

Local Spiritual Assemblies were elected in each of the three villages.[49] Dempsey Morgan remembered Raḥmatu'lláh recounting how one day when canoeing up a river, he heard people in another canoe on the other side of the river. One voice asked, 'Who is the Báb?' and another would answer, 'The Báb is the Forerunner.' The first voice then asked, 'Who is Bahá'u'lláh?' and the second responded with 'He is the Prophet for today.'[50] After four years, there were 7,000 Bahá'ís and five Bahá'í schools. The Muhájirs left the islands in September 1957, after Raḥmatu'lláh was appointed a Hand of the Cause.[51]

As a Hand, Raḥmatu'lláh travelled the world, visiting over 140 countries. In 1961, he spent nine months in India during their mass teaching efforts in the small villages and countryside. The result was thousands of new Bahá'ís. His efforts in South America were also prodigious. On his final trip, he arrived in Quito, Ecuador on 26 December 1979, greatly fatigued. For three days, he worked to raise the Bahá'í community to greater heights, but then suffered a sudden heart attack and died. He is buried in Quito.

PORTUGUESE TIMOR (NOW EAST TIMOR)

Harold and Florence Fitzner and José Marques (Moucho)

Australians Harold (1893–1969) and Florence (1906–1980) Fitzner were Knights for Portuguese Timor. Harold and his future wife, Florence Parry, first heard of the Bahá'í Faith at a meeting in 1927 with Hyde Dunn. Four years later, Harold and Florence were married;[52] both served on the Local Spiritual Assembly of Adelaide and were involved in the Bahá'í magazine *Herald of the South*. Harold was also a member, and for many years chairman, of the National Spiritual Assembly of Australia and New Zealand.[53]

Harold and Florence attended the Intercontinental Teaching Conference in New Delhi in October 1953 and were inspired to offer to go to Portuguese Timor. Before leaving the conference, they began the process of obtaining their visas but soon discovered that only Portuguese citizens were allowed to go to their chosen destination.[54] Their determination aroused some curiosity and they were interviewed by Australian security officers who wanted 'to know why an Australian couple nearing retirement were so desperately attempting to gain entry to a poor, remote, neglected and all-but-forgotten Portuguese-speaking colony'.[55] Shoghi Effendi even offered them alternative posts. Then, surprisingly, when the Australian Department of External Affairs wrote directly to the Governor of Timor, permission was granted. Harold retired early in order to go.

On 9 April 1954, Harold sailed from Perth to Jakarta, where he was met by Khodarahm Payman. He then flew to the port of Dili in Portuguese Timor, arriving on 30 June 1954. Another pioneer, José Marques (1907–1998; listed as José Moucho in *The Bahá'í World*, 1998–1999) arrived from Portugal on 28 July and Florence joined them on 5 October. All three became Knights of Bahá'u'lláh.[56]

Their new home, Dili, consisted of two long streets and few possibilities of obtaining work. Most of the inhabitants were Portuguese and Chinese, with the Timorese people living in small villages scattered across the island. After Harold's first venture into the interior of the island, he reported that he felt 'like jelly' because of the rough roads. There were few English-speakers so communication was difficult. The Catholic Church dominated life in Dili so much that the Bishop was a member of the ruling cabinet. Officials viewed the three new people with 'distrust and opposition'. When the police asked their religion and were told Bahá'í, they had never heard of it and wrote down 'Protestant-Bahá'í'. José was unable to find work in Dili and finally requested financial support from the National Spiritual Assembly of Australia, which had jurisdiction over the area. But having an unemployed Portuguese citizen receiving money from Australia created great suspicion about the new arrivals and, in November, José and Harold were jailed briefly.[57]

When Florence arrived in Dili, being a teacher by profession, she opened a school to teach English and, coincidentally, introduce the students to the Faith. Harold built an 11-room school a few years later to handle more students.[58]

In August 1955, José cabled Shoghi Effendi, asking for advice, but the authorities intercepted the cable, whereupon they searched José's apartment, confiscated all his Bahá'í books and interrogated both José and Harold for hours. When the Fiztners' application for permanent residence was refused the next month, all three pioneers expected to be deported. Amazingly, they were allowed to stay because of the intervention of the Bishop of Timor, Jaime Guolard. The Bishop's help came, however, with strings attached: they could not contact the native Timorese people.

With the Fitzners' English classes and other contacts, the people of Dili began to learn of the Faith. In March 1955, Irene Nobae De Melo, a 24-year-old Portuguese nurse, became the first to accept it. She was followed by Nevis, a solicitor and director of the Economic Department, in April 1957, and by February 1958 the Dili Bahá'í community had eleven Bahá'ís and was able to elect its first Local Spiritual Assembly. With a functioning Bahá'í community, the Fitzners wanted a Ḥaẓíratu'l-Quds. Since no funds were available, they mortgaged their own home to make it possible.[59]

In 1962, the Fitzners were able to leave their one-room apartment and move into a house built for their needs with a 'lounge and dining rooms, three bedrooms and three bathrooms and a "schoolroom" in place of a garage'.[60] When a member of the Australian National Spiritual Assembly visited the Fitzners in 1966, he wrote about the 'procession of teachers, doctors, administrators, professionals and even soldiers who passed through Harold and Florence's house'. He went on to note that

> The secretary of the Indonesian consulate and his wife revealed to me the similarity of the principles of Bahá'u'lláh to Indonesia's official five principles . . . The Governor expressed appreciation for the English teaching services rendered by Mr and Mrs Fitzner . . . the wife of one of the directors of the public service upon study of English with the Fitzners eventually obtained a Cambridge certificate, enabling her to teach at Mozambique High School in Africa.[61]

Harold's health began to deteriorate as early as 1957. He was bedridden for the last six months of his life with cancer and passed away at his post in April 1969. Florence remained at her post until 1975. She left Timor only planning to visit Adelaide, but while she was there, Portuguese Timor was annexed by Indonesia and she was not allowed to return.[62]

José married Maria Olga Menezer in 1957 and moved to the town of Turascai, about 100 miles from Dili the next year. José stayed in the country for nineteen years, founding his own coffee plantation and serving on the Local Spiritual Assembly of Dili.[63] In 1972, the couple moved to South Australia.[64]

THE PACIFIC ISLANDS

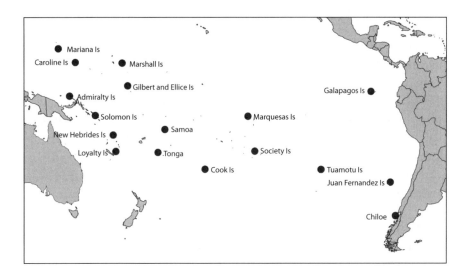

MARIANA ISLANDS

Robert Powers and Cynthia Olson

Robert Powers (b. 1934) and Cynthia Olson (1903–1988) arrived separately in Guam, one of the Mariana Islands, part of Micronesia, in May 1954. Robert was a young Bahá'í sailor from Arizona who was lucky enough to find himself posted to the naval air station on the island. He was the son of a prominent California Bahá'í who promoted good race relations and the equality of men and women within the police forces around that state.[1]

Cynthia Olson went to work for the *Miami Herald* in 1925 and then moved on to another job in Washington DC. Going on vacation to a resort run by Orcella Rexford, a long-time American Bahá'í, Cynthia was introduced to the Bahá'í Faith and became a Bahá'í in 1939.[2] Hearing the Guardian's call for Bahá'ís to get out of the cities, she moved to Wilmington, Delaware, where she met Edgar (Olie) Olson, who ran a small grocery store. Cynthia taught Olie the Faith and he accepted in 1944, enabling the Wilmington community to have its first Local Spiritual Assembly. A year later, they were married.[3]

Cynthia and Olie attended the Intercontinental Teaching Conference in Chicago in May 1953 and decided to go to one of the Guardian's goals:

> They studied maps, consulted atlases and visited libraries searching for information about the places specified by the Guardian to be 'opened' to the Faith of Bahá'u'lláh.
>
> Serving on the Bahá'í National News Service at the time, [Cynthia] had occasion to travel frequently . . . to Chicago to meet with the other members – Nina Matthisen and Al Reed . . .
>
> During spare hours after the committee sessions, Nina and Cynthia together would pore over maps – for the Matthisens also were thinking of going out as pioneers. With the surface of the earth dotted with possibilities, it seemed there were no limits – the world was now wide open for their choice![4]

The Olsons wrote to the Guardian, listing the 'nice, warm' places they were considering, including Cyprus. The reply, written by Shoghi Effendi's secretary, approved their list of possibilities. Shoghi Effendi added a handwritten note at the end of the letter and, in the same ink, crossed out Cyprus, thus deleting it as a possibility. The Olsons learned that a man they knew had been the former Governor of Guam. When they wrote to him, he enthusiastically endorsed the island and its business opportunities. Cynthia and Olie wrote to the Asia Teaching Committee of the US National Assembly offering to go to Guam, but were informed that several other families were already planning to go to the Marianas. The Olsons wrote to several other possible places, receiving either negative answers or no response. They began to get worried because the end of the first year of the Crusade was fast approaching and the Guardian wanted pioneers at their posts by that date.

In 1954, Guam was controlled by the United States Navy and visitors needed special security clearance. Ultimately, none of the other prospective pioneers was able to get the clearance. Olie applied to the US Navy Command and on 24 April, the Olsons were surprised to receive their clearances. Cynthia wrote:

Consternation! Apprehension! Now they were committed! They considered. Which one should go? Cynthia was timid about both prospects – setting out alone or staying and running their business, or selling it. One way or another, funds would be needed to enable one, and eventually both, to go. The decision . . . was that 'Olie' should stay and carry on at home. Cynthia should proceed alone.

On 27 April, Cynthia and Olie left home headed in different directions, she to Guam and he to the National Convention in Chicago. Cynthia arrived on Guam in the early hours of 2 May. Immigration officials initially denied her entrance because she had no vaccinations, having been told that none were needed. Virtually all others arriving on Guam were military personnel, all of whom had had vaccinations. Cynthia stood her ground and after studying their regulation books, they allowed her to enter. She rushed to the telegraph office to let Shoghi Effendi know that she had arrived, but found it closed, so she waited all night to cable the Guardian. The next morning, she phoned Olie at the Convention and informed him of her arrival.[5]

Cynthia spent her first week staying with Frances Pangelinan, a young woman who was in charge of the American Red Cross office on Guam. Frances had met Charlotte Linfoot, a long-time Bahá'í, at an American Red Cross conference a few years before and, when Cynthia left for the island, Charlotte had cabled Frances asking her to meet the new pioneer. Guam had no hotels or apartments for rent and few houses. After a week, though, she rented a small house on Route 10 in Barrigada.

When Cynthia first went into the house, she saw a few cockroaches in the bathroom. Later, when they went back with groceries:

A horrible sight greeted her: roaches of all sizes crawling out of the hidden machinery and along the refrigerator walls. The owners had just reconnected it and the heat of the motor and the cold it generated had disturbed the pests in their nests. 'Well,' she said to herself, 'I'll put some cereal and bread in the oven; that should be tight.' It wasn't. The next morning there were roaches in everything . . . For two days she lived on canned soup which she opened and consumed out of the can.

. . . That first evening and the next day she had some serious talks with Bahá'u'lláh. Never had she been so dismayed at a situation, and never had she prayed any harder. She was overwhelmed. The problem appeared insurmountable . . . Stuck in a house running over with bugs, with no transportation and no place to go. 'Please God, help me!'

For a lady used to clean, comfortable American living, it was a big test. Soon, however, she had bug spray and proceeded to evict her unwanted tenants.

On 5 June, just a month after her arrival, Cynthia and Robert Powers held their first Feast together on the beach near the village of Inarajan. They picked the site because it was 'an inviting grassy spot by the water'. They later learned that the name Inarajan meant 'spiritual light' in the local language. Cynthia and Robert held public Holy Days, placed weekly advertisements in the local paper and contributed Bahá'í books to the two island libraries.[6]

Cynthia hadn't driven a car for 18 years, but the widely scattered nature of Guam's businesses required one. She noted that 'she was afraid to take the wheel because it had been so long since she had driven. One of her most earnest prayers to Bahá'u'lláh was that she might not injure anyone by her driving.'

Cynthia's first job on Guam was working for radio station KUAM. When she was auditioned for the job, she had to read a commercial for 'Libby's Little Brown Beans'. Having forgotten her reading glasses, she was forced to read slowly 'to give sufficient time to make out the next' word. She was given the job, but her first assignment was to write 20 commercials for San Miguel Beer. Cynthia also edited the news. Before long, however, she was given a programme of her own called 'Woman's World', a live, daily show featuring 'home-making tips, recipes, new tid-bits, human interest stories, and arranging interviews' of interest to both the native Guamian women and the military wives. The show became quite popular and soon Cynthia was known across the island. The programme also allowed her to mention the Bahá'í Faith on occasion. The first time was Riḍván 1955 when she broadcast a programme on calendars of the world, during which she was able to mention both the Báb and Bahá'u'lláh. Later, she became a journalist for the United States Trust Territory of the Pacific, a position that allowed her much more contact with the Micronesians.[7]

Mildred Mottahedeh gave the first Bahá'í fireside on Guam in July

1954. She was the representative of the Bahá'í International Community to the United Nations and the Guardian had asked her to visit all the Bahá'í pioneers in the central and south Pacific. The next visitor was Virginia Breaks, Knight of Bahá'u'lláh to the Caroline Islands. Virginia became a regular visitor. In October, DeWitt and Louanna Haywood, with their children Carl, Joy and Ann Marie, arrived as Bahá'í pioneers from Illinois. People were initially suspicious of the family because no one came to Guam looking for a job – they all had contracts. Robert Powers had been transferred away by this time, so Cynthia had been on her own and she was overjoyed to have new Bahá'í companionship.

The first person to become a Bahá'í on Guam was Charles Mackey:

Cynthia received a letter from Jessie and Ethel Revell whom she had known when they were living in neighboring cities in the US East Coast. The Revell sisters were assisting the Guardian in Haifa, but they were alert to every opportunity for teaching the Faith. They wrote of a man, Charles Mackey, who had attended firesides in their mother's home in Philadelphia many years before and who was now living in Guam. This they had learned from their brother who had kept up a correspondence with Mr Mackey and who thought the latter's interest in the Faith persisted. The Revells also wrote to Mr Mackey.

[Cynthia] and he met and discussed the Faith. After the Haywoods' arrival, he began attending the firesides regularly. He took books home to read. Hearing some mention of a Nineteen Day Feast, Charles Mackey was intrigued, and eager to attend. In as kindly a way as possible, the others explained that the Feasts were occasions when Bahá'ís gathered together; they prayed and talked about matters of interest to the Faith worldwide; the Feasts were very special occasions for the Bahá'ís. This incited his interest more. Quite soon after that – on 4 March 1955 – he wrote a letter to the Bahá'í group asking to be a Bahá'í.

In late 1954, Cynthia bought a 'desirable quonset hut' on a cliff in Maite and moved into her new home. She notes that it met a condition of the Guardian that a Bahá'í home should be 'easily accessible' and also was large enough for Bahá'í events. The first Bahá'í event was the Feast of Sharaf on 30 December and included Virginia Breaks.

By March 1955, Olie had decided 'enough'. He had not been able to sell his business so he decided to liquidate the stock. Since his store, Olsons' Foods, was well known for carrying 'imported delicacies, fancy cheeses, teas, spices and all manner of food gift items', customers flooded in as soon as the announcement was made and emptied the shelves in just a few days. Thus liberated, he arrived on Guam on 6 April 1955. With his arrival, the Bahá'ís formed a group and began to function as a proto Local Assembly. Olie became a popular TV executive and owner of what became a famous pancake house. Olie noted that his Swedish pancakes were so renowned that he worried that he would be remembered more for his pancakes than his services to the Faith.[8]

The following November, Ellis Adkins, who had heard of the Bahá'í Faith in America prior to coming to Guam, embraced the Faith. One of his co-workers, Antonio Alfonso, became a Bahá'í in March 1956. With the return of Robert Powers for a short time, the Bahá'í group now had eight members. They only needed one more to form their Local Spiritual Assembly. Then one day, Cynthia noticed a young man from Palau walking to the high school. This was Joe Erie Ilengelkei and she offered him a lift. This began a friendship. Joe moved away after school, but then returned. Cynthia met him

> by chance on a downtown street some time later, they stopped to talk. Cynthia and 'Olie' learned that Joe had found a job – but the very day he was to start work, he noticed that he was coughing up blood and had gone to a doctor; he was being admitted to Guam Memorial Hospital's tuberculosis ward the day following this chance meeting.
>
> Tucked in with books and magazines the Olsons took to Joe at the hospital was a copy of *Bahá'u'lláh and the New Era*. On their next visit, he was filled with excitement. 'I read that book,' he said. 'It is like my old religion. I want to be a Bahá'í. How can I be a Bahá'í?'
>
> They explained and discussed the Faith together. Joe asked for more literature, and they brought it to him. They then called for a nurse and asked that the identity card at the foot of his bed be changed to read 'Bahá'í Faith' which he said was his true religion.

His declaration, on 7 April 1956, was the first from a native Micronesian and it allowed them to elect the first Local Spiritual Assembly of

Guam two weeks later. Knowing the importance that Shoghi Effendi put on incorporating Assemblies, they immediately began that process, working with the National Spiritual Assembly of India, Pakistan and Burma. Success was achieved on 8 April 1957.

Olie travelled extensively for the Faith. In 1969, he made a six-month teaching trip through many islands in the South Pacific. In addition to serving on the Local Spiritual Assembly, he was also instrumental in acquiring property for both the Temple site and the National Ḥaẓíratu'l-Quds.[9]

In 1972, the National Spiritual Assembly of the Bahá'ís of the North West Pacific was elected, with Cynthia as a member. When the first National Spiritual Assembly of the Mariana Islands was formed in 1978, Cynthia was elected to that body for two years. In May 1988, Cynthia, still at her post, passed into the Abhá Kingdom.[10]

Olie continued his work for the Faith, visiting the other islands. In 1988, he made a final trip to Palau and Yap before going to Canada for a vacation. In September 1989, while visiting friends in Nova Scotia, he passed away.[11]

CAROLINE ISLANDS

Virginia Breaks

Virginia Breaks (1906–1993) arrived on the island of Moen, Truk (now known as the Chu'uk Islands) in the Caroline Islands on 16 November 1953.[12] Virginia initially lived in Indiana, but moved to Hawaii in 1941 to further her education. After earning a Master's Degree in statistics, she moved to San Francisco, where she learned of the Bahá'í Faith. She became a Bahá'í in August 1947.

Before becoming a Knight of Bahá'u'lláh, Virginia had attended the Intercontinental Teaching Conference in Wilmette where she heard the list of goals:

> Looking back it seems to me that events in my life were preparing me to come to the Caroline Islands, even before I accepted the Faith of Bahá'u'lláh. It was there [at the Conference] that the Caroline Islands were mentioned as one of the 131 places where there were no Bahá'ís. That name went right to my heart.[13]

Virginia learned of a job with the Department of Public Health in the Caroline Islands and, since a job was a requirement for being allowed to settle there, applied for it. At first, her application was refused because they wanted a man with experience. Virginia wrote to the Director of the Department of Public Health asking to be considered if they could not find a man. She was given the job.[14] When she arrived, her new employer was not there to meet her since he also worked as a stevedore at the ship dock. Virginia found living conditions rustic.[15] There were no hotels and the only accommodation available was in Quonset huts left by the US Army.[16]

Teaching was slow at first: 'Maybe it would be a good thing if every one on the home front could be in a virgin area for a while – a virgin area where they couldn't talk freely about the Faith. Maybe then they would begin to appreciate what it means being at home where you are so free.'[17] Virginia connected with Stem Salle, a new believer who had heard of the Faith from Mary Hill, head of the Trust Territory School of Nursing in Koror.[18] It wasn't until 1960 that the first Caroline Islander accepted the Faith.[19]

The people of the Caroline Islands, as well as the Marshall and Mariana Islands, were Micronesian and the Guardian had chosen Micronesian Kusaiean as the language into which the Bahá'í Writings were to be translated. Virginia was involved in the accomplishing of this goal.[20]

Virginia was able to teach people from beyond Truk, and one of the most notable was Betra Majmeto, the first Marshallese Bahá'í who later became an Auxiliary Board member and then a Continental Counsellor. Virginia also introduced the Faith to Rose Mackwelung, from the island of Kosrae in the Gilbert Island group. Rose became a Bahá'í when another Knight of Bahá'u'lláh, Cynthia Olson, read her the book *Thief in the Night*. She became a member of the first National Spiritual Assembly of the North West Pacific.[21] Virginia also lived and taught the Faith on Saipan in the Mariana Islands and in the Gilbert and Ellice Islands, settling in 1970 on the island of Pohnpei.[22]

To keep up her spiritual strength and maintain a wider perspective, Virginia attended the North East Asia Conference in Japan in 1955, the Second International Teaching Conference in Kampala in 1958, and the All-Philippine Teaching Conference in Manila in 1959. She also went on pilgrimage in 1962 and attended the World Congress in

1963.[23] When Amatu'l-Bahá Rúḥíyyih Khánum visited the Pacific area in 1984, Virginia was living on Pohnpei and escorted her and Violette Nakhjavani around Pohnpei and Chu'uk.[24] During the World Congress after the Ten Year Crusade, the Guardian had expressed the hope that the pioneers would remain at their posts even though the Crusade had been successfully completed. Virginia took that to heart and lived in the Caroline Islands, passing away on Yap in 1993.[25]

ADMIRALTY ISLANDS

Violet Hoehnke

Violet Hoehnke (1916–2004) pioneered from Australia to Manus Island, in the Admiralty Islands near Papua New Guinea, in July 1954. Born of English/German parents, she became a Bahá'í in 1939;[26] she served as a nurse during World War II and was greatly traumatized by the experience. This caused her to turn to prayer in order to find a reason to live. Violet arose in 1948 to teach her new Faith, pioneering first to Melbourne and then to Balarat. After attending the Intercontinental Teaching Conference in India in 1953, she decided to pioneer to the Admiralty Islands.[27]

Resigning her nursing position at the hospital in Balarat, Violet went to Lorengau on Manus Island, Papua New Guinea, where she found work as a nurse with the Health Service. Unlike most people of European or American background, Violet invited the local Melanesian people into her home and also visited them in their homes. Racial segregation was strong in the islands and her mixing with the non-whites quickly antagonized the Australian authorities and offended her boss, who transferred her to a hospital on Raboul on the island of New Britain.

The move did nothing to stop her teaching efforts, which were enhanced when she teamed up with Rodney Hancock, a 21-year-old New Zealander, who had arrived in Raboul at about the same time. Teaching was particularly difficult because permission had to be obtained from the authorities before they could visit the villages. Prejudice was always a problem and Rodney was beaten on one occasion by drunken Europeans[28] while Violet was robbed and harassed several times in her own home.[29] New Britain was a rugged island and visiting the people required them to climb steep mountains, drive along tortuous roads, and sail through sometimes stormy seas, but in 1956 a teacher in the village of Munawai, Apelis Mazakmat, met Violet and became a Bahá'í: [30]

> Of mixed Catholic/Methodist parentage, he clashed with a Catholic priest in 1949 who refused to wed him to a Methodist woman. He became a Bahá'í early in 1956, after learning more about it from Rodney Hancock in Rabaul. Mazakmat took Hancock to some New Ireland villages, and introduced him to friends he thought would be interested in the Bahá'í teachings. Of the several villages Hancock spoke in, the response in Madina was the most immediate, and several people joined. [31]

A Local Spiritual Assembly was elected in Madina in 1957.

In 1965, Violet was appointed to the Auxiliary Board and was elected to the National Spiritual Assembly in 1969. Between 1973 and 1979, she was a member of the Continental Board of Counsellors for Australasia. [32] Violet stayed at her pioneering post for 50 years.

SOLOMON ISLANDS

Gertrude and Alvin Blum

Gertrude (1909–1993) and Alvin Blum (1912–1968) pioneered to the Solomon Islands, arriving on 1 March 1954. Gertrude Blum came from a Russian Jewish background in New York. Her first encounter with the Bahá'í Faith took place when she was invited to talks given by Orcella Rexford and Keith Ransom-Kehler in 1929. After Keith finished her talks, she asked if anyone wanted to join the Faith. Gertrude said 'yes' in January 1930. In 1939, Gertrude tried to pioneer to South America, but was unable to get a visa. She was then asked to pioneer to Vermont, but could not find any place to live. She ended up pioneering to Birmingham, Alabama, and confronting its embedded racism. In 1941, she met Alvin. [33]

Alvin also came from a Russian Jewish background and grew up in New Jersey. By 1936, he wanted nothing to do with religion until a friend invited him to a Bahá'í meeting. Three weeks later, Alvin became a Bahá'í. He was deepened by Howard Colby Ives. Meeting Gertrude in 1941, they decided to get married, but the Second World War began and delayed the marriage until 1945. The young couple moved to Little Rock, Arkansas, for two years. Alvin had been in New Zealand during the war and in July 1947, they moved there and bought a clothes manu-facturing business. In 1949, the Bahá'ís had the opportunity to buy land for a Bahá'í summer school, but did not have the money. Gertrude solved the problem by trading a diamond ring her mother had given her for the land. In 1951, Gertrude and their five-year-old daughter, Keithie, made a travel-teaching trip to Fiji.

When the Ten Year Crusade was announced, Alvin cabled the Guard-ian asking which was more important: going to Wellington to form an Assembly or going to a virgin area. Shoghi Effendi cabled back, 'Advise virgin areas Pacific'. At the Intercontinental Teaching Conference in New Delhi, Alvin learned that the Solomon Islands were difficult to enter, so he chose them as his pioneering goal.[34]

Alvin, Gertrude and seven-year-old Keithie sailed to the Solomon Islands and arrived in Honiara on 1 March with just a two-month tourist visa. To reach the shore required rowing in a small dinghy. Once on the beach, the three new pioneers found themselves alone on the sand with their luggage and no taxis until a passing priest offered them a lift to the only hotel in a town consisting of a garage with a Shell sign and several corrugated iron Quonset huts left by the American army. As they settled into their single room, young Keithie looked out the window and saw her first Solomon Islander: 'a very dark woman working outside . . . She has enormous fuzzy hair as well as big hoopy rings through her ears and through her nose. A skinny smoking pipe sticks out of her mouth. Most amazing to me is that she is wearing no top.'

Alvin spent his first two weeks on the island looking for any kind of work. When the manager of the hotel abruptly quit, the owner hired Alvin to take his place. At the same time, the Blums found themselves before the British Chief of Police, who had a thick folder on his desk with their name on it. After several hours of their trying to explain both their intentions and the Faith, he reluctantly allowed them to stay to manage the hotel and extended their visas. Shoghi Effendi had told Alvin to set up a business, which he did, starting with a taxi business for hotel customers. The Chief of Police managed to get Alvin fired as hotel manager in July and then demanded a £500 bond in order to be allowed to stay without a job. Alvin was forced to cable Horace Holley in America with a request for the money and the National Spiritual Assembly of Persia, who oversaw the islands, supplied the funds. Difficulties with the authorities persisted until Hugh Blundell, of New Zealand, contacted the District Commissioner of Guadalcanal. The Commissioner had initially been less than friendly, but Hugh was good friends with the Commissioner's father, who also knew Alvin, and a letter quickly improved relations with the authorities. The Blums had been renting a house which the owner tried to force them to buy. When the now-friendly Commissioner heard of this, he said that the Government was taking over the property for non-payment of taxes and offered the Blums a 99-year lease/purchase of 2.5 acres. Alvin started many businesses, including a bakery, an ice cream shop, a laundry and dry cleaning business, a general store, and a hotel.

By early 1955, Bill Gina, a local teacher at the agricultural college, and John Mills, a newly arrived Australian, were the first two people to accept the Faith in Honiara. Bill, dark of skin, was intrigued when Alvin shook his hand on their first meeting, then invited him to their home, something no other white person in town had done before.

With two new Bahá'ís in town, the local clergy and the police became concerned. The Superintendent of Police attended a fireside, then sent an officer to other meetings until he was convinced that the Bahá'ís presented no threat to public order. The clergy, however, publicly denounced the Bahá'ís. Then one night, Hamuel Hoahania, the chief of an area, came to the Blums' home. He had heard about the Bahá'í Faith from two workers in the Blums' bakery and he wanted to know about it. He was impressed that the Blums invited him into their home for dinner, something few other white people did at that time. After accepting the Faith, Hamuel carried it to hundreds of islanders and was the key to large-scale enrolment.[35] His enrolment resulted in the election of the first Local Spiritual Assembly at Riḍván 1957.[36] In 1978, Hamuel was elected to the National Spiritual Assembly of the Solomon Islands and was present at an election of the Universal House of Justice. Alvin Blum died in 1968, still at his pioneering post. Gertrude was honoured by Queen Elizabeth II in 1989 as a Member of the Order of the British Empire (MBE)[37] and passed away in Honiara in 1993.

New Hebrides

Bertha Dobbins

New Zealander Bertha Dobbins (1895–1986) arrived in the New Hebrides on 17 October 1953. She was a caring person and a teacher. In 1923, she decided to become a Church of England missionary to India, but first took a teaching job in Australia and began investigating religion. In 1929, Joe Dobbins, a fellow seeker after truth, invited her to a fireside with Hyde and Clara Dunn. Both quickly recognized the truth of the Revelation and became Bahá'ís. Four years later, in 1933, Joe and Bertha married. Bertha served on both Local and National Spiritual Assemblies and edited *Herald of the South*, the Bahá'í magazine of New Zealand and Australia.[38]

In September 1953, they felt the urge to arise and fill one of Shoghi Effendi's goals, but they couldn't both go. After family consultation 'around a winter fire', Bertha left for the New Hebrides, now Vanuatu, and Joe stayed home to support her and take care of their two children, aged 17 and 19. Initially, she was only supposed to stay on Vanuatu for three months.[39]

Bertha sailed on the *Caledonia* along with Gladys Parke and Gretta Lamprill, who were going to fulfil the goal for Tahiti.[40] Bertha wrote:

I arrived in Port Vila on the 17th of October, 1953, and said the Greatest Name as my feet touched New Hebridean soil. Miss Gladys Parke and Miss Gretta Lamprill . . . accompanied me to the Hotel Rossi, Port Vila, where I stayed until 28th March 1954 . . . On the 29th March . . . I moved into the hut owned by Chung Yueng brothers, Chinese . . . and although living facilities were practically nil, I was glad to have a home. Later, this hut acquired an atmosphere of its own. A never-ending line of visitors, mostly native, came to hear 'the Story', so I called the place Núr Cottage, and it was here, on 9th August 1954, that the Bahá'í school began.[41]

And so the seed-sowing goes on! The trading vessels which travel between the islands, mostly carrying copra, do not cater to passenger travel, and the boats which do occasionally call and are capable of taking passengers are frightfully expensive. In spite of these obstacles the Message has spread from the little cottage on the hill to all the islands . . . As I pen these lines a hurricane is sweeping down . . . I dare not open the door . . . But my mind lifts to the future. One cannot but feel that some day the . . . South Pacific will become ablaze with the glory of God.[42]

Bertha's arrival did not go unnoticed. Peter Kaltoli Napakaurana, one of the first to accept the Message she brought, wrote:

During 1953 there were many stories circulating in Port Vila, on Efate Island, and subsequently all over the New Hebrides, about the arrival of a woman missionary who had brought new teachings from God. This person was Mrs Bertha Dobbins. In 1954, I heard this news inside the Chief's nakamal [traditional meeting place]. . . and decided that I should go and find out for myself the new Message. So one Sunday morning, I went to visit this woman missionary. She explained some of the sacred verses in the Bible, and I heard the name Bahá'u'lláh for the first time. I was very interested in her explanations. Some time later, I went back to Mrs Dobbins and told her that I wished to join the Bahá'í Faith.[43]

When Bertha's three months were up, the Guardian asked her to stay for an additional three months, which she happily did. But six months away from her family was just the beginning. At the request of Shoghi Effendi, she remained at her post with the goal of establishing the first National Spiritual Assembly of the New Hebrides.

In February 1954, Alvin, Gertrude and Keithie Blum passed through on their way to their own pioneering post in the Solomon Islands. For the three days the Blum's boat was anchored, Bertha stayed aboard and told of her troubles finding food and of some of the 'frightening encounters with rebel gangs'.[44]

In 1958, a prefab building was sent by the National Spiritual Assembly of Australia so that Bertha could continue her school. Eleven years later, in 1969, after 16 years of separation in the service of God, Joe passed away in New Zealand. Bertha continued with her Bahá'í school until 1971, when it was closed at the direction of the Universal House of Justice because of the expense of upkeep. Bertha then turned the building into the local Bahá'í centre. Her steadfast efforts finally resulted in success in October 1971 when the first National Spiritual Assembly of the New Hebrides was formed. Bertha had the bounty in 1973, at the age of 84, of going on pilgrimage with Hand of the Cause Collis Featherstone and his wife Madge. Bertha finally returned to New Zealand in 1977.[45]

LOYALTY ISLANDS

Daniel Haumont

Daniel Haumont (1925–1993) moved from France to Tahiti in 1954 and went on to the Marquesas Islands the next year. It was there that he discovered the Bahá'í Faith and became a Bahá'í. The Loyalty Islands were part of France's territorial possessions and they refused to allow any but French citizens to settle there.[46] Being French opened the door to Daniel and he moved to Maré Island in the Loyalty group on 11 October 1954. He only stayed there for two weeks before deciding that he could not 'make his life there' and returning to Tahiti.[47] Daniel spent the next 17 years living in Tahiti and New Caledonia before moving back to France in 1989.[48]

In 1971, the Loyalty Islands were visited by Richard Battrick and three members of the National Spiritual Assembly of the South West Pacific Ocean, George Wayenece and André Trabé, both Melanesian, and Jeannette Outhey. The Catholic Church was not happy with their visit, Jeannette was questioned by the police and Richard was jailed for four days because he did not have his passport. Ultimately, Richard was able to travel from island to island for two months teaching the Faith.[49]

MARSHALL ISLANDS

Marcia Stewart

Marcia Stewart (1904–1966) grew up in California in a wealthy family, 'in an atmosphere of glamour, ease and culture'. She lived in Paris during the 1920s. Marcia was taught the Bahá'í Faith by Valeria Nichols and became a Bahá'í in 1938. She pioneered to Chile in 1940, then to Costa Rica in 1946 and Honduras in 1950. In Chile, her post was at the very southern tip of the South American continent in Punta Arenas.

One of the people she brought into the Faith quoted Marcia as saying: 'Bahá'u'lláh wants me to have an LSA, and I will have one.'[50]

So, in 1954, at the age of about 50, she decided to fill Shoghi Effendi's goal to the Marshall Islands, in the middle of the Pacific Ocean. At that time, she was a member of the Regional Spiritual Assembly of Central America and operated a school.

The Marshall Islands were part of the United States Trust Territory and the site of some of America's early atomic bomb tests; consequently, it wasn't easy to get there. Luckily, Marcia had good connections in Washington DC and was able to get a three-month visa, which she was later able to renew using the same contacts. Shoghi Effendi sent her a cable requesting that she be in the islands between 1 April and 2 May 1954. Unfortunately, she did not receive the cable until 16 April. Hurrying off from California for Hawaii and then the Marshalls, she missed another cable telling her that the islands were not possible to enter and that she should not try. She was already on her way and wrote: 'The strange hold-up of that cable so impressed everyone concerned that I am now practically assured of early entry, almost as a matter of obligation.' It did take her a few days to sort out the problem, but on 9 May she wrote Horace Holley, Secretary of the US National Spiritual Assembly, that she had permission to enter the islands and was only waiting for her Navy security clearance. Finally, in July she left Hawaii for Japan, from where she sailed to Majuro in the Marshall Islands, arriving on 7 August 1954.[51]

Ultimately, Marcia was only able to stay for six months, until March 1955, but she took full advantage of her time, travelling to the various atolls. She wrote: 'I have been busy doing what everybody does, making friends, etc. I went on a field trip of a week, visiting various other atolls, and especially like Jaliut. I am planning to go there within the next 10 days to spend a couple months.' In another letter, she noted: 'I am here as a writer, but also I never hesitate to talk about the Faith and I find quite a lot of interest in spiritual and religious matters. Most of my very good friends here are Catholic or Jesuit priests! This is probably natural, since I lived in a Latin American Catholic environment for so many years.'[52]

During her last two months, she became very ill and for years afterwards suffered a painful skin ailment. Forced to leave when her second visa expired, she returned to Central America.[53]

Marcia pioneered to El Salvador for a time, but returned to Honduras and a home she called 'Karbala'. The following years, with her wealth gone and health worsening, were difficult. In 1960 she was bedridden and too ill to travel for a year, and stayed in a hotel in the town of San Pedro Sula. When she was strong enough, she pioneered to El Salvador, but was back in her 'Karbala' home in Honduras by March 1966. She died there in August of that year.[54]

In 1967, the first Local Spiritual Assembly of Majuro, the first anywhere in the Trust Territory of Micronesia, was formed.[55]

GILBERT AND ELLICE ISLANDS (NOW KIRIBATI)

Roy and Elena Fernie

American Roy Fernie (1922–1964) grew up in the Panama Canal Zone and learned about the Bahá'í Faith there, in good part from the woman who became his wife, Elena Marsella (1913–2002), who was the secretary of the National Spiritual Assembly of Central America and the Antilles at that time. Elena had been born in Rhode Island and attended a Catholic school in New Hampshire. Rejecting the religious teaching she was given there, she was open when her aunt mentioned the Faith to her for the first time in June 1939 and became a Bahá'í that same year. She had pioneered to the Dominican Republic in 1945[56] and was elected to the National Spiritual Assembly in 1950.[57] Elena was also a concert pianist and worked for the US Foreign Service.[58]

Roy became a Bahá'í in March 1953, and to his surprise, his father, who couldn't understand why Roy would give up a 'new job that was worth more than a million dollars', disinherited him. In spite of that, two months later, he married Elena and three months after that, the couple began to prepare to pioneer to the Gilbert and Ellice Islands.[59] Their efforts were slowed because they didn't know where the islands were, and no one in Panama was able to help them.

When they finally did find and make their way to the islands, there were no hotels and initially the authorities tried to keep them out because there was no accommodation for them. A Gilbertese trader named Schultz unexpectedly offered to allow the Fernies to stay in his home on Tarawa until they could build their own. The Fernies arrived on Abaiang Island, in the Gilbert group, now called Kiribati, on board Schultz's trading ship on 4 March 1954.[60]

[A]fter a five hour trip we landed in the lagoon at Abaiang and I don't know how it was done, the Gilbertese there were ready to greet us and they came out waving and it seems their custom was to take imitangs (white people) off the ship and carry them on their back.

[T]here we were with our feet on the shore and some more Gilbertese appeared on the shore line. One was an oldish man – his name was Abram – which is Gilbertese for Abraham. He had a little boy with him who was related to him in some way and the little boy came on up to me with an egg. I was considerably surprised at receiving an egg but anyway I smiled at him and I took the egg. I no sooner had the egg in my hand when Roy snatched it out of my hand – he was an amateur magician and he could do all kinds of tricks so he snatched this egg out of my hand, pretended to crush it on the little boy's head and then it supposedly dropped out of this little boy's nose. Well this absolutely sent these Gilbertese into shrieks of laughter. They couldn't stop laughing. They laughed for about half an hour and Abaiang was all doubled over with laughter and all the other Gilbertese were just beside themselves they were practically falling on the ground and rolling over and over with laughter.

[W]hen it got dark we suddenly began to hear crackling and outside Gilbertese houses they are all swept clean or else around the houses is nice crunchy gravel . . . and we thought 'what on earth is going on?' . . . finally when we looked out we saw faces and faces began to appear about 3 feet up and four feet up – everywhere they could see through the grill, tall ones standing in front, we looked around the three sides and we were absolutely surrounded, there seemed like hundreds of Gilbertese and they were silently without a word, walking all on the gravel peering in at us . . .

Well we looked at each other and we looked all around at all the sea of faces, brown faces, and we thought 'good heavens, what are they doing, and what will we do?' . . . Finally we decided we would greet them. So we said 'konemoui' [Ko na Mauri] (a Gilbertese greeting meaning 'may you be blessed') . . . and they just stood there and looked at us . . . Finally Roy said 'music is an international language', so we had a short wave radio and we turned the radio on and music started playing and Roy went 'ah, ah' a big pause and delighted sighs all around three sides of the room and we saw that that pleased them very much. So the music played . . . nothing else was said all dead silence outside still. I don't know how long this went on but it seemed to us an absolute eternity . . . Finally there was a stir outside and a sense of excitement. All of a sudden a voice said in very clipped English 'they would like to see an exhibition of the magic arts'. We said 'who's that?' He said 'my name is Peter Koru Kanare' . . . Were we ever glad to hear someone speaking English . . . It turns out that Abram and this little boy had been so pleased with the trick that Roy had performed that the news had gone up and down the island post-haste. Every Gilbertese on the island knew that Roy could do some magic. . . .[61]

Shoghi Effendi specifically told them not to teach the Faith, but simply to make friends and attract them with love. When the Government proposed to build a school on the island, the Fernies offered financial and other help. They soon had a non-denominational school on land leased by the Fernies where the pioneers taught English and the principles of the Faith through their actions.[62] Roy also put on magic shows, played the piano and sang, all of which attracted attention.

The missionaries, always suspicious of outsiders, quickly guessed that Roy and Elena were there to do more than study the flora and fauna, and they were soon spreading rumours that Roy and Elena were 'dangerous' and were being investigated by both the FBI and Scotland Yard. The local authorities accepted the accusations without question and the persecution began. One day a Catholic priest saw the word 'Bahá'í' on correspondence to the Fernies and did some research on the Faith. He then wrote a series of 'scathing' articles in the *Star of the Gilberts* magazine.[63] The priest also attacked the Faith in the Catholic newsletter, which, contrary to his expectations, actually led to the spreading of the Faith.[64]

The priest's vitriol didn't stop Peter Kanare Koru, who had formerly been a Catholic seminarian and mission teacher, from accepting the Faith in June 1954. Peter had initially been attracted by Roy's magic and music and had become his interpreter.[65] A voracious reader of English, Peter devoured every book the Fernies had, though the Guardian cautioned him to follow the example of Roy and Elena and not openly teach. Following Peter's declaration, both the Catholics and the Government began to publicly harass the Bahá'ís and were able to force them out of their building and into an unfinished one.[66] Peter was charged with influencing people with magic.[67]

The Catholic bishop in Tarawa asked the Government to expel the Fernies and exile Peter back to his home island. The Government required a religious organization to have at least a hundred members to be registered and have missionaries. They used this to get rid of the troublesome Bahá'ís.[68] In June 1955, Peter was exiled from the island with only 24 hours notice. But, as 'Abdu'l-Bahá always insisted, persecution could only result in a tremendous victory for both Peter and the Bahá'í Faith:

> Peter bore his persecution with such fortitude and returned so much good for evil that over half the village threw off (their) Faith, and came en masse to our house one morning at 3:00 a.m., asking for teaching in the Baha'i Faith.
>
> The next day about 90 people appeared, and since it was Peter's last day on Abaiang, he taught his people the Baha'i Faith directly for the first time. That was a day full of tremendous emotion. Peter was so happy to achieve his heart's desire – freedom to teach his beloved Faith. The people were already pledging themselves to be loyal to their new religion, and listened raptly to Peter's teaching. At the same time, the hearts of everyone were grieved, for Peter's only crime was to behave so like a Bahá'í that the veils . . . were stripped from the people's eyes, and they saw with perfect clarity that the new religion, Bahá'í not only talked about love, but practiced it constantly.
>
> Since we are I Matanga (white people), we could not be banished like Peter. All that they (the missionaries) could do was to request the Resident Commissioner to ask us to leave . . . We went to Tarawa to be interviewed by him, and after breaking down all the false accusations, the Commissioner's only reason for desiring to deport us was that he can't imagine the effect our presence has on the people.
>
> Before we left for Tarawa, over 100 Gilbertese had declared their intention to be Bahá'ís. We had helped them to elect three practice Assemblies. During our absence the rumor was spread that we would never return, but the only result was that nearly 100 more decided to become Bahá'ís. Also, while we were gone, a district officer, with one of the Bahá'ís, went from village to village up and down Abaiang, taking the names of those who desired to be Bahá'ís. The total figure: 225![69]

First Spiritual Assembly of the Bahá'ís of Guam, 1956: Robert Powers (standing left), *Edgar and Cynthia Olson* (standing 3rd and 2nd from right), *Knights of Bahá'u'lláh to the Mariana Islands*

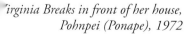

Friends gathered to say 'Bon voyage' to Virginia Breaks (centre), *Knight of Bahá'u'lláh to the Caroline Islands, 1953.* Left to right: *Tony Seto, Mildred Nichols, unidentified, Virginia Breaks, Mamie Seto, Joyce Dahl*

Virginia Breaks in front of her house, Pohnpei (Ponape), 1972

First Local Spiritual Assembly of Honiara, Solomon Islands, 1957, with Knights of Bahá'u'lláh Gertrude and Alvin Blum. Back row: *Geoff Dennis, Shebual Mauala, Alvin Blum, Bethuel Bama, John Mills;* front row: *Harry Chandra, Gertrude Blum, George Kwota, Ruhi Mills*

Violet Hoehnke, Knight of Bahá'u'lláh for the Admiralty Islands (Papua New Guinea), and Rodney Hancock in Rabaul, Bismarck Archipelago, Territory of New Guinea, 1955

Daniel Haumont, Knight of Bahá'u'lláh to the Loyalty Islands

Roy Fernie, Knight of Bahá'u'lláh to the Gilbert and Ellis Islands (Kiribati)

Bertha Dobbins (centre), *Knight of Bahá'u'lláh for the New Hebrides Islands, with Bahá'ís on Vanuatu*

First National Spiritual Assembly of Central America, Mexico and the Antilles, 1951: Front row, third from left, *Elena Marsella, Knight of Bahá'u'lláh to the Gilbert and Ellis Islands*

National Spiritual Assembly of the Bahá'ís of Australia and New Zealand, 1953, with five Knights of Bahá'u'lláh. Left to right, standing: *James Heggie, Lilian Wyss, Knight of Bahá'u'lláh to Samoa, Dulcie Dive, Knight of Bahá'u'lláh to the Cook Islands, Alvin Blum and Gertrude Blum, Knights of Bahá'u'lláh to the Solomon Islands, H. Collis Featherstone;* front row: *Gretta Lamprill, Knight of Bahá'u'lláh to the Society Islands, Stanley P. Bolton, Knight of Bahá'u'lláh to Tonga, Ethel Dawe*

Lilian Wyss, Knight of Bahá'u'lláh to Samoa, and years later, dancing

Elsa and Dudley Blakely, Knights of Bahá'u'lláh to Tonga

Edith Danielsen (right), *Knight of Bahá'u'lláh to the Cook Islands, with Rima Nicolas and Tuaine Karotaua (Peter Titi), 1955*

Marcia Stewart, Knight of Bahá'u'lláh to the Marshall Islands, with Estaban Canales (left) *and Artemus Lamb* (right), *about 1945*

National Spiritual Assembly of the South West Pacific, 1975: Left to right, standing: *Kalman Kiri, Owen Battrick, Jean Sevin, Knight of Bahá'u'lláh to the Tuamoto Archipelago, André Trabé;* middle row: *Martine Caillard Dahl, George Wayenece, Jeanette Battrick;* front row: *Charles Pierce, Robert Chaffers*

Gretta Jankko, Knight of Bahá'u'lláh to the Marquesas Islands, a photo from 1972

Gladys Parke, Knight of Bahá'u'lláh to the Society Islands

Haik Kevorkian, Knight of Bahá'u'lláh to the Galapagos Islands

First National Spiritual Assembly of Ecuador, 1961. Left to right: *Gayle Woolson, Knight of Bahá'u'lláh to the Galapagos Islands, Juan Luis Aguirre, Guillermo Sotomayor, Raúl Pavón Mejía, Dorothy Campbell, David Beckett, Khalílu'lláh Bihjati, Fereydoun Monadjem, and Patricia Conger*

First Spiritual Assembly of Buenos Aires, 1940, with Salvador (standing, centre) *and Adele Tormo* (seated 2nd from right), *Knights of Bahá'u'lláh to the Juan Fernandez Islands, Chile*

Louise Groger, Knight of Bahá'u'lláh to Chiloe Island, Chile

Being exiled from Abaiang Island didn't cool Peter's zeal for his new Faith. Back on his home island, he soon brought a Protestant minister into the Faith and the two of them spread the Word of Bahá'u'lláh across that island.[70]

In September, after the Bahá'ís showed neither hatred nor retaliation for the persecution, 325 Gilbertese signed a document expressing sympathy for the Faith. Roy was deported in November 1955 for being a 'divisive influence'.[71] When the Resident Commissioner informed them of the order, he asked "Shall I reserve passage for one person, or two?' Elena remembered that 'For one, brief, pregnant moment Roy and I looked at each other, then Roy said, "one".'[72]

Since only Roy's name was on the deportation order, Elena remained at her post. The problem of not being a registered religion was quickly solved by the great influx of new Bahá'ís and on 24 September 1955, the Faith became officially recognized.[73] The Churches' objections had backfired.

Through Elena's solitary efforts, by Riḍván 1956 there were four Local Assemblies and five groups.[74] Later that year, there were 200 Bahá'ís in the islands in ten villages with three Local Spiritual Assemblies.[75] Elena served alone until 8 February 1957 when Frances Heller, a Knight for Macao, joined her.[76] By October 1958, both Roy and Elena were on Truk Island with Virginia Breaks.[77] Roy tried every way to return, but was ultimately stopped by his death in 1964. Elena continued to be very active in the Faith, serving on the National Assemblies of Central America and Hawaii. Later, she moved to Asia and was a Counsellor for Northeast Asia from 1973 to 1980.[78] Elena lived the final years of her life in Hawaii, passing away in 2002.

SAMOA

Lilian Wyss

Australian Lilian Wyss (b.1929) became a Knight of Bahá'u'lláh on 14 January 1954 when she arrived in Apia, Samoa (formerly known as Western Samoa). Lilian became a Bahá'í at the Yerrinbool Winter School, New South Wales, on 5 June 1944, a month before her 15th birthday. Her brother, Frank, also became a Bahá'í at the same time and pioneered to the Cocos Islands, giving the title of Knight of Bahá'u'lláh to both sister and brother. Three years after the summer school she moved to Switzerland, as her parents wanted her to meet her relatives. In 1950, she pioneered to Oslo, Norway. After six months, at the request of the European Teaching Committee, she returned to Zurich, Switzerland, where the friends were working towards the formation of the Local Spiritual Assembly. In 1952, Lilian wrote to the Guardian, offering to pioneer to Africa. In a letter written to her on the Guardian's behalf, dated 4 June 1952, she was asked to 'Return to Australia, and render pioneer service there, in order to enable your own country not to fail in its Plan.' In December 1952, Lilian arrived in Australia, and as requested by the National Spiritual Assembly of Australia and New Zealand, visited Bahá'í communities in four states to assist with the teaching work. At Riḍván 1953, Lilian was elected to the National Spiritual Assembly.[79]

Following the Intercontinental Teaching Conference in New Delhi later that year, six members of the Australia and New Zealand National Spiritual Assembly resigned and pioneered, including Lilian.[80] Lilian hadn't gone to the Conference, but Gretta Lamprill, secretary of the National Spiritual Assembly, telephoned her and read the Guardian's announcement. Gretta asked, 'Have you anything to say to the Guardian?' 'Yes, I will go', replied the 23-year-old Lilian.[81]

However, like most people at that time, Lilian had no idea where all the islands Shoghi Effendi listed were. Speaking at the 50th Anniversary celebration of the Faith's arrival in Samoa, Lilian said:

> In Australia and New Zealand when we learned of the goals in the Pacific Islands we were rather stunned. At that time, dear friends, the Pacific was like a vast unknown black space. We had no idea how one got to any of the islands. We found out there was a boat once a month from Australia to Tahiti and one from USA to Australia and another one or two from New Zealand to some islands. Margaret Rowling and I were given the job of putting a manual together covering the islands of the Pacific that were mentioned. It was to contain information on how to get there, climate, currency, something about the country, how to enter, etc. etc. We went to Thomas Cook, a famous travel agent, but they had little knowledge. So we went to the library and to the offices of a magazine that covered several of the islands.[82]

Initially, she found a contract to work in the Solomon Islands and so set that as her goal. But a 'sensationalized' newspaper story caused her prospective employer to back out of the deal. Before the newspaper interview, Lilian had talked with Alvin Blum, who had urged her to go. He said that if anything went wrong, he and his wife, Gertrude, would take the goal instead. So the Blums went to the Solomon Islands and Lilian simply changed her goal to Samoa.[83]

Lilian flew in a seaplane from Sydney to Auckland, New Zealand and attended a Bahá'í summer school, where she met Suhayl Ala'i. She then sailed to Suva, Fiji, where she met the small Bahá'í community and Roy and Elena Fernie, who were headed for their pioneering post in the Gilbert and Ellice Islands. Her ship continued on to Tonga and she finally arrived on 14 January 1954.[84]

Samoa was another world for Lilian. She said:

When you arrived by ship in Apia you were rowed ashore. Wherever you went in Samoa there were paopaos or outrigger canoes lined up on the shoreline. There was a partially sealed road that lead to Apia and at night people often sat on the road and played their ukuleles and sang. The few import/export businesses in Apia had trading stores in some of the villages. There was very little electricity, mainly in Apia. Most of the homes were Samoan fales. And there were two cargo/passenger vessels each month. The main income was from copra and cocoa. When Suhayl and I married we lived on top of the only bank. There were some cracks in the wood of the floor so you could see something of what went on below. One day the bank manager sent one of the staff up to ask me to stop washing the floor as the water was dripping onto the bank notes![85]

She was soon enthralled by the people who lived there:

You should see how these people have become ablaze. Before they heard of the beloved teachings they were as dead and now they are blazing beacons suddenly sprung alight . . . How pure in heart they are and yet some of their questions indicate such depth that one is awed. It truly is an example of how even the comparatively uneducated are already educated spiritually by God.[86]

The day after her arrival, Lilian found a job as a private secretary for Ted Annandale, head of one of the largest trading companies. But all was not perfect. She was bitten by a centipede which caused her leg to swell up horribly. Then, about six months after arriving, she was in the hospital, unconscious with double pneumonia. And while in the hospital, she developed hepatitis and turned bright yellow. Mr and Mrs Annandale took great care of her and even took her to their plantation to recover.[87]

In November 1954, Lilian married Suhayl Ala'i in Suva, Fiji, the closest place with a Local Spiritual Assembly. The Local Spiritual Assembly was supposed to arrange the wedding:

> Fiji at that time was a colony of Great Britain and it was segregated – the Fijians, Indians, Chinese, Europeans, etc. all lived in their own areas. I asked the Local Assembly to make the marriage arrangements, but when I arrived with my Samoan bridesmaid, I found that nothing had been done! Suhayl was on a ship on his way to Fiji and we were supposed to be married in the next couple of days then catch the ship back to Samoa. I went to the Government Office and spoke to the Registrar who was an Englishman who was happy to arrange the legal marriage until he found out that neither of us lived in Fiji and we were just passing through, so to speak. He said it could not be done. Then he started asking me questions. Why did we want to marry in Suva? So I explained a little of the Faith and then gave him the consent letters from Suhayl's parents, duly authorized by the NSA of Persia and translated by the British Consulate in Tehran, and the letter of consent from my parents also authorized by the NSA of Australia and New Zealand. He read them with some astonishment and then remarked that we had really planned things. After talking a little longer he told me that he had the authority to grant a special marriage licence and he would do so on one condition. He said that he wished to attend the marriage. I then had to explain that it would be in the Indian part of town and there would be only few Europeans present. He said that he would come and he would perform the civil ceremony there. He came and had a good time.
>
> Several years later, after the National Assembly was formed in Fiji, they applied for legal registration of the Faith. This same man was still in office and he granted it immediately.[88]

Lilian described the wedding for the *Round Robin*, a newsletter distributed by the Canadian New Territories Committee (Samoa was a Canadian goal):

> You will want to know about this wedding. It was a cosmopolitan assemblage! A Persian groom, Australian bride, Swiss parents, Samoan bridesmaid, Indian, Fijian, German, New Zealand, English and Australian audience, about 40 guests. Music was played as everyone was anointed with attar of roses. A legal ceremony was performed, then the Bahá'í marriage, the marriage lines and the Tablet, the Sermon on the Mount, the Báb's address to the Letters of the Living. Suhayl ended the ceremony by chanting a prayer in Persian. Pineapple juice, savouries, sandwiches, cakes, fruit and ice cream, and then the cutting of the cake, with a big saw!
>
> Suhayl and I are paying a short one day visit to American Samoa next week and you may be sure that we shall say the Greatest Name there. The people living in Western Samoa can't get to American Samoa without permits (US Territory) but to save us the bother, our boss has signed us [on] one of the company's vessels as members of the crew. Personally, I think we'll be hanging over the rail feeding the fishes all the way! Pity the Captain![89]

In March 1955, Lotoa Lefiti married Emmanuel Rock, who had become a Bahá'í before the Ten Year Crusade. In February of the next year, Lotoa signed her declaration card and became the first native believer. Later in 1956, Mr Sa'ialala Tamasese, from a prominent family in Samoa, declared his belief in Bahá'u'lláh. In the *Round Robin*, Lilian described his search for the Bahá'í Faith:

> A girl told us that her father was interested in learning something of the Ala'is' religion, and as a result he has been visiting several times to hear more and more of the Faith. During his visits he eagerly listened to the Teachings and the Bahá'í explanations of Bible prophecy, etc. One day he told us that his village chief wanted to know about our religion and to visit us. We decided that it would be more courteous if we paid a visit to the Chief's home. The meeting I had with the Chief proved to be extremely friendly and it seemed that he was very much taken with the Bahá'í teachings. He has extended to the

Group an open invitation to visit him whenever we wish, and has also expressed the desire to learn more of the Faith. We invited our contact to attend our Sunday afternoon class and when he came last Sunday night he also brought another friend informing us that this was another person who wished to follow his path. We had a wonderful Sunday class . . . we are thankful that the way is opening up somehow, at last, but we are very cautious at the same time, not to arouse any antagonism from the churches. Our contact has invited all the Group to his daughter's wedding next Saturday afternoon.

It is indeed with joyous and thankful hearts that we are writing this letter and are enclosing the card of the newest declared believer in Western Samoa, Mr Sa'ialala Tamesese. You will no doubt recall that in a recent letter we mentioned that one of the people here was studying the Teachings. Sa'ialala joined us officially at the last Nineteen Day Feast and it was a wonderful occasion for us all. Through Sa'ialala's efforts we now have another person interested, and we all pray that he too may understand a little of Bahá'u'lláh's Revelation.[90]

He was the first indigenous believer to openly and continuously teach the Faith and remain steadfast in the Cause until his passing. He passed away in September 1965, and his Bahá'í funeral service in Samoa was a significant public proclamation for the Faith, attended by politicians, chiefs, clergy and members of the Royal Tamasese family.[91]

On another occasion, Niuoleava Tuataga walked into Suhayl's office with a Bible under his arm, demanding to know about this new religion. Suhayl asked him to return after work, which he did. They talked for many hours that night and many more the night following, making his family very upset. Niuoleava had been training to become a minister, but ended up becoming a Bahá'í. He went on to translate the first prayer book, the *Hidden Words, Gleanings* and the *Seven Valleys and the Four Valleys*.[92]

The first Local Spiritual Assembly was formed at Riḍván 1957.[93] Both Lilian and Suhayl were on that first Assembly of Apia, Western Samoa. The friends were active in teaching, children's classes, literature translation, and working towards the acquisition of a Bahá'í Centre. In December 1958, the Local Assembly of Apia arranged the first summer school in Samoa.[94] In 1959, Enoch Olinga became the first Hand of the Cause to visit Samoa. That same year, the first Ḥaẓíratu'l-Quds in

Apia was built and a Bahá'í burial ground of six plots was purchased. In addition, the first Samoan Teaching Conference was held on 4 October 1959, with participants from Western and American Samoa.[95]

Also in 1959, Lilian and Suhayl, with their two children Badi and Sitarih, moved to American Samoa to keep it open to the Faith. Their third child, Riaz, was born in American Samoa in 1960. Lilian and Suhayl both served on Local Spiritual Assemblies in Pago Pago (the first Local Spiritual Assembly in American Samoa) and Fagaitua. They both also served on the South Pacific Regional Spiritual Assembly when it was established in 1959. In 1968, Suhayl was appointed as a member of the newly created Continental Board of Counsellors for Australasia.[96]

Lilian was a member of the National Spiritual Assembly of Samoa from its formation in 1970 until 1989, and served many years as its Treasurer. She also served on the Local Spiritual Assembly of Ili'ili. She was a member of a National Committee that was responsible for radio and television programmes produced in American Samoa, and was active in literature development work. For a number of years, she served on the editorial board of *Herald of the South* magazine, was also one of the three Deputy Trustees of Ḥuqúqu'lláh serving on the Board for the Northeast Pacific, served on the Institute Board of American Samoa, and was an active tutor of study circles.[97]

The crowning distinction of the Samoan Bahá'í community was the declaration of the first reigning monarch to accept the Message of Bahá'u'lláh, His Highness Susuga Malietoa Tanumafili II, who accepted Bahá'u'lláh in 1968, though it wasn't until 1973 that he was able to publicly declare his faith.[98] His Highness passed away on 11 May 2007. Samoa also became the home of the Mother Temple of the Pacific Islands. In January 1979 His Highness laid the cornerstone of the House of Worship, and in September 1984 participated in its dedication ceremony.

Lilian's beloved husband, Suhayl, passed away in Samoa in 1995, and is buried near the House of Worship. On 10 December 2010, at the age of 81, Lilian returned to live in Australia with her family. She had pioneered in the Samoan Islands for nearly 57 years. Much to her surprise and delight, on arrival in Australia she was welcomed at the airport by a group of Samoan Bahá'ís and former pioneers to Samoa, all now residing in Southeast Queensland. Since that time, Lilian has been an active participant in a triannual Pacific Group gathering, where

Pacific Island Bahá'ís and their friends residing in Southeast Queensland gather to pray for the advancement of the Faith in the Pacific and elsewhere, and to share a picnic and singing, as well as news and stories of service to the Five Year Plan. These gatherings bring great joy to Lilian's heart; especially as Pacific Island youth and adults are serving local communities on periods of service and homefront pioneering in the land of her birth. Since March 2011, Lilian has resided in the Gold Coast City Bahá'í community and at the age of 87 continues to serve as a study circle tutor.[99]

Tonga

Stanley Bolton

Australian Stanley P. Bolton (1929–2015) arrived on Tonga on 25 January 1954 and was followed six months later by Dudley and Elsa Blakely. Stanley's parents, Stanley W. and Mariette, were very active early Australian Bahá'ís who built a home at Yerrinbool that became the first Australian Bahá'í summer school. Stanley Jr had polio when he was two years old, making a 'miraculous' recovery. In 1948, at the age of 19, he earned a Doctor of Chiropractic degree, followed in 1959 with a Philosopher of Chiropractic degree. At the age of 22, in 1951, he was elected to the National Spiritual Assembly of Australia and New Zealand. He went on pilgrimage in October 1953 and was powerfully impressed by the Guardian. Shoghi Effendi told him that his parents 'had pioneered and built institutions in Australia' and said that the son should do the same in the Pacific, stressing the importance of the 'spiritual axis' between Australia and Japan. The Guardian said that 'the young people of Australia should pioneer in the Pacific, "particularly the young men". He nodded with his head to emphasize the point. Then he said, "Particularly the unmarried young men," opening his eyes wide and emphatically.'[100]

Stanley Jr was one of the six members of the National Assembly of Australia and New Zealand to resign and pioneer. He noted that he was advised that 'accommodation could not be guaranteed. There were no banks. Shipping was only once a month and planes less frequent.' Undeterred, he cabled the Minister of Police and happily received a six-month visa within a few days.[101]

Landing on Tonga, Stanley walked up the main street where he was approached by a 'brown-eyed, stocky Polynesian'.

'Cigarettes?' he asked.
'No thank you', I replied.
'Whiskey?'
'No, thank you.'
'You want a woman?' he whispered.
'No', I said firmly.
'What religion are you? Mormon? Seven Day?' he said, surprised that I was not interested in his merchandise.
'No', I said as I walked on. 'I am a Bahá'í.'
Within five minutes of setting foot on this South Sea island para-dise, mention of the Faith had been made! This was a significant prelude to my nine months pioneering in Tonga.[102]

Stanley's first job was a surprise. A few weeks after his arrival, he was offered the position of 'temporary assistant master at the Tonga High School' at the behest of the Cabinet. He had some qualifications for science and maths, but had no teaching experience or teaching qualifications.[103]

I was approached quite out of the blue to take on the job and even when they were told that I had no teaching experience they still insisted that I should take it. They are desperate for teachers and anyone who can help out is considered an angel.

The other day a group of about a dozen youngsters, girls and boys, came up to me after science and I could see there was some-thing on their mind. One of the prefects acted as spokesman, and, pointing to my ring, asked what the sign meant. I was surprised they should take the trouble to ask me but, of course, pleased as punch. I thought to myself that here is just an example of the inquiring child mind, I was happy to tell them the story; what it was, what it meant and a little about the Baha'i Faith. When I finished there was an awkward but meaningful silence. Then the prefect who was the spokesman said, 'Yes, we know. We read about it in Pix (magazine) in the library and saw your picture.' I was astonished and tickled pink. It seemed surprising that they should see that small picture in a Pix over a year old and connect it with me. The fact was, they were checking to make sure it was I. Of course it went around the school like wild-fire, and in a day or two even the headmaster was talking to me about it. So now the whole school knows I am a Baha'i and Pix has taught them silently without a word from me.[104]

He held the job for five months and his availability may have helped keep the school open until the permanent staff arrived.[105]

Having arrived in January 1954, Stanley was instrumental in forming the first Local Spiritual Assembly of Nuku'alofa the following Riḍván, just three months later. Nuku'alofa means 'land of love' in Tongan and Stanley found that to be true. In September 1954 he married Judy, whom he met there. Shortly after their marriage, the couple moved to Australia. Stanley served on the National Spiritual Assembly for 21 years, starting in 1965, serving variously as chairman, vice-chairman and treasurer. Stanley returned to Tonga in 2004 for the 50th Anniversary of the arrival of the Faith there.[106]

Dudley and Elsa (Judy) Blakely

Americans Dudley (1902–1982) and Elsa (Judy) Blakely (1895–1988) arrived on Tonga on 12 July 1954. Dudley Blakely was a nephew of Lua Getsinger. Dudley and his wife, Elsa, taught the Faith in British Guiana in South America in the 1930s.[107] They arrived in the Tongan capital of Nuku'alofa and were met by Stanley Bolton, who draped them with 'beautiful leis of frangipani'. Within a month, they had experienced a tropical storm and an earthquake.[108]

Dudley was an artist, an architectural and industrial designer and a boat builder. He soon found work with the Tongan Government, designing several buildings as well as stamps and coins. The Blakelys started a class for young Tongan men in September to help them learn English[109] and Elsa became friends with Queen Salote and was a frequent visitor to the palace. She also became involved with promoting women's rights and worked with the Queen on an institute for women. They travelled to remote villages to share the Message of Bahá'u'lláh.

In September, the Blakelys wrote:

Our eight months here, despite the material difficulties that almost overwhelmed us at times, have been the happiest of our lives. Patience, unending patience, is the characteristic we have most to cultivate, for things move very slowly in Polynesia. But the love of these wonderful people, the realization of their qualities, makes the waiting no trial, for we know that in their own time they will become jewels of great worth in the diadem of the Bahá'í world community.[110]

In August 1955, the first Tongan accepted the Faith of Bahá'u'lláh. This was Harry Terepo.[111]

In 1957, Lisiata Maka, a lawyer and advisor to the Supreme Court, accepted the Bahá'í Faith and became very active. He translated the Writings into the Tongan language, obtained legal incorporation for the Local and National Spiritual Assemblies and also served on the Regional Spiritual Assembly and as a Counsellor.[112]

In spite of early opposition, the three pioneers were able to form the first Local Spiritual Assembly, in Nuku'alofa in 1958 and another in M'ua in 1960. The Faith grew rapidly, and today its members form about 6 per cent of the population.[113] The Blakelys left Tonga in 1963 and moved to Hawaii. In 1977, the couple pioneered to the Bahamas for a year before settling finally in Georgia in the American South.[114]

COOK ISLANDS

Edith Danielsen

When American Edith Danielsen (1909–1984) learned of the goals of the Ten Year Crusade, she ran her finger over a map until it found the Cook Islands and decided that was where she would go. Edith reached the Islands on 14 October 1953. Edith grew up in Washington state, married Ted Danielsen in 1933 and first heard of the Bahá'í Faith from Janet Stout in Alaska. The Faith struck no obvious chord with Edith until years later when she met another Bahá'í in Washington state. She promptly wrote Janet Stout asking her to 'Send me everything you have about the Faith.' Janet sent her books which she devoured in her excitement. She became a Bahá'í in February 1949. Her husband accepted the Faith two years later, just a few months before he was killed in a plane crash.[115]

With the loss of her husband, Edith offered to fill one of the Guardian's goals. Arriving on Rarotonga in the Cook Islands via Fiji and Samoa, Edith described her new home by saying that 'the road around the island is only twenty-one miles long, yet out of the center of the ten-mile width rise jagged green-swathed peaks, scraping the clouds at two thousand feet'.[116] Her outgoing personality and musical skills quickly allowed her to tell people about Bahá'u'lláh.

Edith described her first months on the island:

When I first came here I said nothing about the Faith. However, news travels like lightning here and the two wires I sent aroused a lot of curiosity, especially as there was some discussion about the one to Haifa, as they didn't know how to send it or how much to charge. Several days went by and I still offered no explanations. Finally the time was ripe and someone asked me and I got to talk at length about the Faith. Yesterday afternoon I was most pleased in having the chance to go into considerable detail to Tui and Barry – the first Maori I have had an opportunity to mention the Faith to . . .

The people are sweet and kind. One is being constantly delighted. The other day Tui and I were walking along the village road up town and caught up with four or five Maori women, They all began chatting away in Maori. Of course, I couldn't understand a word, but I looked at them and smiled . . . Tui is the perfectly beautiful Maori wife of one of the men stationed here. She is the kind they use in their publicity photos. Whenever she comes out to board 'mama' (a two-seated station wagon made of spare parts left by the US army, and wood and canvas) she has a flower behind each ear. The one on the left she takes out and gives me to wear.

Rarotonga, November 21, 1953. I have been meeting some of the local women. One here in the hotel has eagerly read every Bahá'í book I have with me at the moment and discusses it with me frequently . . . Because of her interest I have had the opportunity of mentioning the Faith in front of quite a few of the people living at the hotel, and some knowledge is apparently traveling around the back roads in the village.

Rarotonga, January 27, 1954. It's been wonderful to have a Bahá'í [Dulcie Dive, who arrived on 18 January] here as you can all guess. It has given me that 'good' feeling and a refreshed outlook. I again feel like I could go out and conquer a few little old worlds! It is an unnamable something . . . the advantages of two Bahá'ís instead of one. I don't know how to express it but it is very real.[117]

Edith spent her first year at the Hotel Rarotonga, but was then able to move to the Maori village of Muri. Setting up her home on the beach in the village opened the door to many teaching opportunities. Edith had brought a Hammond electric organ and a generator to power it. When she began to play, people crowded in to listen:

> The next few nights brought droves of people – thirty-five in the house, twenty outside the lattice. and ten hanging over the windowsill back of the organ . . . So many young men were here every night that the Kekau shack soon became known as the YMBC (Young Men's Bahá'í Club)! One young man, who, it seems, stood on the road and directed the others down here, was nicknamed 'the prophet'.
>
> Out of this number came the few who were sincerely interested in the Faith. They asked for weekly firesides – which started immediately. Some of these were not going fast enough and they asked for private study classes. Out of this there was one who still wasn't going fast enough so we had daily lessons. March 8th he became the first Cook Islander Bahá'í.
>
> The big groups coming every night took their toll in fatigue, as those who wished to discuss the Faith remained after the others left which was often at midnight. Finally it was decided that Wednesday night should be for Bahá'í discussion only – no music or colored slides. The following night became 'community night' when everyone could come and it would be for entertainment – but Bahá'í discussion inevitably follows at the end of that night also.[118]

A young girl named Rima Nicolas White moved in with Edith to help her and, in 1955, she accepted the Faith.[119] Edith left the islands in 1958 after contracting filariasis, a tropical parasitic disease, and returned to America for treatment.[120] She revisited the Cook Islands briefly, but later in 1958 pioneered to Taiwan. After working for nine years to help establish that Bahá'í community, she moved to New Zealand, where she served on the National Assembly, and then settled in Kirkland, Washington. She remained there until her passing in 1984.[121]

Dulcie Dive

New Zealander Dulcie Dive (1919–1962) arrived in the Cook Islands on 18 January 1954. Dulcie was part Maori and became a Bahá'í in 1938. She married Jeffrey Dive in 1943, but he died not long afterwards. Initially, she served the Faith in her home country, but then moved to Australia. She served on the National Spiritual Assembly of Australia and New Zealand from 1944 to 1948 and again from 1951 to 1954.[122] She was an active teacher of the Bahá'í Faith; she was one of the members of the National Assembly who resigned to answer the Guardian's call for pioneers and joined Edith Danielsen in Rarotonga.[123]

Dulcie found work as a shop manager for A.B. Donald, the largest trading company on the island, and lived in a home that she renovated at the opposite end of the Rarotonga Island from Edith. Not having much money, Dulcie learned how to ride a bicycle. Edith noted that for one Feast, 'She biked all the way out here in the dark to have the Feast with us as it was Rima's first Feast . . . then had to bike back late in the dark. Seven miles each way over bad roads.'[124]

During her first year in the islands, they worked to translate the *Hidden Words* into the local version of Maori:

> The second volume of Hidden Words (Arabic) has gone to press. This is in Rarotongan Maori . . . I asked a Maori who had heard nothing of the Bahá'í Faith to read back to me in English the section we had finished so that I might see what kind of sense it made to him. The shock was terrible; I was sick and discouraged, but as he went on I began to suspect what was later verified, namely, that his command of English was too limited to properly translate the Maori words. However, he became interested enough to ask permission to attend the next translating session.
>
> The task of translating into Maori is extremely difficult . . . because the Maoris had no written language prior to the arrival of the missionaries and they are still not well advanced in their own language. It is a very meager language, with one word often meaning many different things. It is . . . impossible to get the finer shadings of thought across . . .
>
> One of the chiefs of the same tribe . . . finally kept an appointment to come and talk with me about the Faith. We discussed it for

an hour and a half and he took home with him the sheet on Basic Facts of the Baháʼí Faith. He is fully in agreement with everything he has been told so far . . .

Last Friday I stopped by home in the middle of a progressive dinner party and found two unknown women talking on our private verandah. They were two pioneers on their way home. [This would have been Gladys Parke and Gretta Lamprill, who were pioneering in Tahiti]. Their visas had expired and they could not renew them without leaving the island for at least four months . . .[125]

In March 1955 another Cook Islander, Tuaine Karotaua, became a Baháʼí and in 1956 they were able to form their first Local Spiritual Assembly. Before Riḍván, since there were nine Baháʼís in the village of Muri, the pioneers began having 'practice' assembly meetings:

A 'practice Assembly' elects new officers every six weeks in order that all may gain experience in Baháʼí administration. One of the most difficult of the institutions to explain and understand is the Baháʼí Fund. It took a long time . . . for the idea of voluntary contributions to take root in their hearts. We had to appoint an assistant treasurer to help with the reports because the treasurer could not even read and write his own language . . . When we had accumulated 19 shillings, they were very proud, and when it was put to a vote whether we should withdraw part of it to buy a present for a non-Baháʼí who had done a big translation job for us or all chip in, they wouldn't hear of touching the money in the treasury! Even though slightly out of order to discuss the amount we might each give, I let them do it as it stirred up interest and helped no end to overcome the old attitude. I had originally offered to make up the difference so that we could buy a really good shirt . . . I was so relieved that some of them felt that though it was nice of me they should be responsible for the full amount.[126]

One night in August 1958, Dulcie knelt down to say her prayers with her dog, Snowy, beside her. Suddenly, Snowy

growled, which is the first time I've heard him growl. I looked up from my knees and saw a dark masked figure standing in the bedroom door . . . In a split second I was on my toes crying, 'Help, help." I pushed past the youth grabbing what he had in his hand (not realizing it was a knife until I felt the sharp cuts) . . . so he could not strike me.

In a short time, Koringo, his wife Pere, another neighbour Macro, and others came to my aid. They soon had me in the hospital where they stitched three cuts to the right hand . . . and then next morning operated on the left hand to tie a tendon.

I am lucky to be alive . . . While the doctor was sewing me up I was thinking of the knights of old as they went forth and returned from battle with their scars. Well, here is a Knight of Bahá'u'lláh who'll carry the scars of pioneering in her hand. I also thought of the blood of the 'martyrs' – well, there's plenty of my blood on the soil of Rarotonga.[127]

Dulcie was elected to the first Regional Spiritual Assembly of the South Pacific in 1959 and served until 1962. In that year, her health declined rapidly and she went to Auckland for an operation. She passed away in September.[128]

SOCIETY ISLANDS

Gretta Stevens Lamprill and Gladys Parke

Australians Gretta Stevens Lamprill (1890–1972) and Gladys Parke (1896?–1969), both over 60 years old, arose and filled the goal for the Society Islands by pioneering to Tahiti on 29 October 1953.

Gretta was born in Hobart, Tasmania, in 1890 and first heard of the Bahá'í Faith sometime between 1908 and 1912 when her mother showed her a newspaper story about Bahá'u'lláh. After listening to travel teachers Hyde and Clara Dunn and Effie Baker, Gretta accepted the Faith in 1924 to become the first Tasmanian Bahá'í and later became known as the 'Mother of Tasmania'. She raised up the first Local Spiritual Assembly of Hobart in 1944.[129] From 1948 until 1953, she served on the National Assembly.[130] In 1953, when the Ten Year Crusade was announced, Gretta, the Assembly secretary, was one of six members of the National Assembly to answer the Guardian's call to pioneer.[131]

Gladys was from Balarat, Australia, but moved to Launceston,

Tasmania, as a child. She trained as a nurse, as had Gretta, and learned of the Faith from Gretta. The two women became known as the Bahá'í Twins, because they were inseparable. In 1953, Gladys was asked to serve as the hostess at the Ḥaẓiratu'l-Quds in Sydney. With the call of the Crusade, Gladys and Gretta joined forces and pioneered.[132]

The two women arose and travelled to Tahiti. Since their visas only allowed them to stay for three months at a time, they had to leave and return three times. Their model behaviour softened the hearts of the authorities and they were allowed to stay for six months on their fourth visa. They were successful enough to see the first Local Spiritual Assembly elected before their final departure.

Gretta and Gladys moved to Launceston, Tasmania. In 1963, the two women answered the call to fill one of the last of Australia's homefront pioneering goals by going to Devonport, where they were able to form the first Local Spiritual Assembly. Gladys passed to the Abhá Kingdom in 1969. Gretta followed her three years later.[133]

TUAMOTU ARCHIPELAGO

Jean Sevin

Jean Sevin (b.1927), a Frenchman from Paris, arrived in the Tuamotu Archipelago on 17 January 1954, settling on Makemo Island.[134] He accepted the Bahá'í Faith in Lyon in 1944, much to the dismay of his mother, who kept asking when he was going to return to the 'true religion of my fathers'. When Shoghi Effendi made his appeal for pioneers at the beginning of the Ten Year Crusade, Edith Sanderson decreed that he could not leave because he was her reader.[135] Jean's father, when he heard of his son's isolated, mid-Pacific goal, at first thought it was humorous, but not understanding the power of faith then became angry when he realized just where his son was planning to go.[136] The Guardian, however, supported Jean's desire to fill the goal to the Tuamotu Archipelago and said that 'the work he could accomplish in France could not compare with what he would be doing for the Cause by pioneering in a virgin territory'. The Guardian even wrote to the Local Spiritual Assembly of Paris saying that Jean's pioneering would prove to be a bounty for France. This would prove to be true when Jean made teaching trips back to France.[137]

The Tuamotu Archipelago, part of French Polynesia, consists of about 400 islands on 130 low-lying atolls in an area the size of Europe. Since there were no hotels on the island, Jean had to have a host for a while. In all of the islands, there were only about 3,000 inhabitants and travel between the islands was difficult. The only way to visit other islands was by using the rare supply schooners. Jean was impressed by the hard-working and courageous Catholic priests, and moved to an island where the priest was 'sympathetic'. Unfortunately, he proved spiritually unreceptive to the Bahá'í message.[138] Jean was, however, able to help a radio operator accept the Revelation of Bahá'u'lláh.

Work was scarce and the only job Jean was able to find was as a rat exterminator. The primary resources of the islands were mother-of-pearl and copra, dried coconut meat that the rats loved to eat. Because the copra was valuable, Jean was able to spend his five years on the island exterminating the rats.[139]

Jean, along with three native believers, was able to spread the Faith to a hundred of the 400 islands in the group.[140] In 1958, Jean's father joined him and they went to Tahiti. His father left after a year.[141] On a travel-teaching trip to France in 1959, Jean said: 'If I had remained in France, I might have given the message to a dozen persons in the last five years, but because I went pioneering I have been able to give the message to more than 3,000 in a few months.'[142] Jean was able to stay for a few years in Tuamotu, but then he moved among the New Hebrides, French Polynesia, the Tuamotu Archipelago and New Caledonia. In 1962, Jean married Liliane Michelle in Papeete. Michelle was the daughter of Madame Ariane Vermeesch Drollet who had been taught the Faith by John and Louise Bosch when they visited Tahiti in the 1920s. In 1968, Jean moved to Noumea on New Caledonia at the request of the Universal House of Justice.[143]

MARQUESAS ISLANDS

Gretta Jankko

Gretta Jankko (1902–1973) was originally from Finland, but emigrated to Canada in the 1930s. She returned to Finland on a visit and was trapped there by the outbreak of the Second World War. When the war was over, she moved to the United States and married, but her husband died just months later. Gretta became a Baha'í in 1951 through Gertrude Eisenberg.

Gretta was living in Vancouver, Canada, at the beginning of the Ten Year Crusade and initially thought that because she was translating the Writings into Finnish for Shoghi Effendi, the call for pioneers didn't concern her. But after prayer and meditation, she realized that she could do her translations anywhere in the world so she chose to go to the Marquesas Islands. The Marquesas are in the middle of the South Pacific, very isolated and were the 'least known virgin goal assigned to the Canadian Community'. The islands were administered by France so she began her journey by going to Tahiti. The authorities were not very cooperative, but her persistence finally paid off and, 'amid warnings and exhortations', she was given an eight-month visa. Sailing on a small supply ship, Gretta arrived at her destination in March 1954. Her lack of French inhibited her teaching efforts, but she spoke of Bahá'u'lláh to whom she could.

Gretta lived in a small, primitively furnished room, eating mostly bananas and breadfruit with rare treats of meat, butter, eggs and milk. She wrote:

> All the time on those islands I was very happy. I loved the people and we were very close to each other; they asked me many times not to go away from the islands. My typewriter was a miracle to them; they would sit on the floor silently for long hours as I typed the translations. An old seaman, who knew some English, was the interpreter, but how much he understood of what I was saying, I never knew. We would talk about the great happenings of this Day of God. They had their Bibles, and I tried to show them important prophecies which were fulfilled. The older generation could not read or write; they would nod their heads and were eager to listen. They felt something, I am sure, but how much they grasped I cannot say. They used to stand in awe before the Greatest Name, and the small children almost every morning brought fresh flowers 'for the Prophet', placing them before the picture of 'Abdu'l-Bahá. I told them every time that it was the great Son of the Prophet, the Master; but each morning they would repeat, 'for the Prophet'.[144]

When her visa was about to expire, she had to return to Tahiti and again to plead her case. Again she was successful, but with the stipulation that when it expired, she had to leave. Then one night sometime after her return to the islands, someone broke into her room and almost strangled her to death. After an inquiry, the Chief of Police told her she must leave immediately because he could not be responsible for her safety. Gretta reluctantly left the island in 1955, but continued her service to the Faith in Finland.[145]

GALAPAGOS ISLANDS

Gayle Woolson and Haik Kevorkian

Gayle Woolson (1913–2011), an American of Syrian ancestry, became a Knight of Bahá'u'lláh when she pioneered to the Galapagos Islands in 1954. Growing up in an Arabic-speaking Muslim family in Minnesota, Gayle became a Bahá'í in 1932, learning of the Bahá'í Faith from Clement Woolson, whom she married three years later. Though Clement sadly died just a few months after the wedding, she and her family, many of whom had become Bahá'ís, served the Faith in North Dakota, Wyoming and Arkansas. In answer to the First Seven Year Plan, she pioneered to Costa Rica in 1940 where she was one of the founders of the Bahá'í community there and helped form the first Local Spiritual Assembly in 1941. She moved to Central America in 1945. The next year, she was sent to Colombia by the Inter-American Committee to resolve a problem of Covenant-breaking by the first Bahá'í pioneer to the country, whose attacks on the Faith ultimately required police protection for some Bahá'ís there. Ultimately, the former pioneer took legal action against the Faith, making 'gross misrepresentations of [the] objectives and of the incorporation of the Local Spiritual Assembly of Bogota'. Gayle was appointed to represent the Faith in the court case, which after a difficult and lengthy effort was ultimately resolved in favour of the the Faith.[146] Gayle was elected to the first Spiritual Assembly of South America in 1951. In 1953, she moved to Ecuador to strengthen the community.

On 9 April 1954, along with a companion, she arose again and went to the Galapagos Islands. She arrived just a few weeks before Haik Kevorkian (1916–1970) came from Argentina. Gayle's stay was short, but she quickly became acquainted with her neighbours and shared her message.[147] After less than two months, she was appointed as one of the first Auxiliary Board members for the Western Hemisphere, which required her to return to the mainland. She served on the Auxiliary Board for 14 years in Ecuador and in 1961 was elected to the National Spiritual Assembly of Ecuador. Moving to El Salvador in 1968, she also served on the National Assembly of that country. She served at the Bahá'í World Centre for five years from 1970, where she did translation work. Gayle returned to the United States in 1975 and was an active travel teacher nationally and internationally.[148]

Haik Kevorkian's family had come to Argentina from Syria in 1937. When May Maxwell made her journey to Buenos Aires in 1940, Haik contacted her by phone just before her fatal heart attack. After her passing, he devoted himself to caring for her grave. When the Ten Year Crusade was announced, Haik pioneered to the Galapagos in May 1954. He managed to stay on the Galapagos for two years, living in 'a small hut without sweet water or lights, unaccustomed to the limited diet of the island which offered no vegetables and only rarely meat'. By pioneering, Haik also had to leave his fiancé, Aurora de Eyto, behind in Argentina. They were married when he returned to Argentina.[149] The first Local Spiritual Assembly of the Galapagos was formed in 1977.[150]

JUAN FERNANDEZ ISLANDS, CHILE

Adela and Salvador Tormo

Salvador (?–1960) and Adela Tormo pioneered to Robinson Crusoe Island in the Juan Fernandez Islands on 7 November 1953. The Tormos were the first Argentines to become Bahá'ís, having been taught the Bahá'í Faith by Francis Stewart in 1939. At Riḍván 1940, Salvador was elected chairman of the Local Spiritual Assembly of Buenos Aires. In a letter to Shoghi Effendi in May 1941, he reported that the police in Buenos Aires had been 'interrupting' Bahá'í meetings, but that after the Faith was explained to them, the Bahá'ís were given an official permit to hold meetings.[151]

Salvador attended the All-American Convention in May 1944, representing his home country. He again represented Argentina at the first South American Bahá'í Congress held in Buenos Aires in November 1956.[152] By November 1954, Salvador had translated the *Kitáb-i-Íqán* into Spanish.[153]

When the goals of the Ten Year Crusade were announced, Salvador and Adela pioneered to Robinson Crusoe Island, where they very quickly raised up a Local Spiritual Assembly.[154] The Tormos left the islands in 1955 and were replaced by Frances Stewart from the United States.[155]

In 1957, Salvador was elected to the Regional Spiritual Assembly of Argentina, Bolivia, Chile and Paraguay and at Riḍván 1960 was elected secretary of the National Spiritual Assembly. He also translated many of the Bahá'í Writings into Spanish and served as manager of the Bahá'í Publishing Trust in Buenos Aires. Salvador was killed in a plane crash in late 1960 in Uruguay, as always in service to the Cause.[156] In 1961, Adela was elected to the first National Spiritual Assembly of Argentina.[157]

CHILOE ISLAND, CHILE

Zunilda Gonzales Jara de Palacios and Louise Groger

Zunilda Gonzales Jara de Palacios and her daughter pioneered to Chiloe Island, in southern Chile, arriving on 18 October 1953.[158] Unfortunately, attempts to find further information about them have been unsuccessful. Louise Groger (1907–1999) joined them in Castro, the largest town on the island, on 13 June 1954. Louise bought a house in which the three Bahá'ís lived.[159]

The following information about Louise Groger has been contributed by her granddaughter, Rosanne Groger.[160]

> Louise was born in 1907 in San Francisco, where she grew up, married, and started a family. As a young teen, she was extremely concerned with such things as the meaning and purpose of life and contemplated the big questions of existence and mortality. One such question that rambled around her young mind and rattled her soul was: Would she have been one of those sanctified beings in the early days of Christ to have recognized His station as the Son of God and the Luminous Mirror of the Sun of Reality? Would she have had the eyes to see, the ears to hear and the courage to follow? Louise even prayed that she might have been one of those early believers in the days of Christ. In her own words in a later diary she wrote that
>
> From about the time I was 13, I was very much concerned with

such things as the reason and meaning and purpose of life, especially my own religious beliefs. I remember coming to the conclusion, quite possibly helped to it by extensive and voracious but hardly intelligently directed reading, that the only answer as far as reason and purpose were concerned must be service and that, since God stood in no need of service, it must mean service to other human beings.

Louise was an avid reader and one of her goals as a young girl was to read all the books in the San Francisco Public Library. It was this thirst and appetite for knowledge that compelled her to search for the answers to her questions throughout her youth and young adulthood as a wife and mother of three children:

> . . . the idea suddenly came to me that if Christ's teachings had once been an effective basis for men's living, but just couldn't be imagined to solve the world's problems today just by being practiced by individuals, there must be a new message that would show us how to solve them and that I would know about it sooner or later and could rest in peace in the meanwhile.

It would be another six years before Louise would find deliverance. It was decided in 1935 that she should go and visit her parents in Chicago where her father, a clerk in the US army, was stationed . . .

Her parents decided that they would all journey to Wilmette, a suburb of Chicago, to visit a mysterious temple. Louise's mother Pearl, a devout Catholic, had already written to Louise about this temple describing it as having been built by an 'Eastern sect of sun worshippers' that now sat incomplete and abandoned except for a caretaker . . . Louise initially felt disappointed after visiting the Bahá'í Temple, but upon leaving the site she felt an undeniable compulsion to return . . .

Louise's life took a dramatic turn when she declared herself a Bahá'í in San Francisco on 12 October 1936 at the age of 29. This decision came with consequences – for a period of time her mother would not talk with her and the weekend gatherings with extended family members became less frequent as Louise observed the daily practice of being a Bahá'í. The leisure Sundays with family activities, which might have included light beer drinking and a card game of Pinochle, Canasta, or Bridge, began to be replaced with Local Spiritual Assembly meetings, Sunday public meetings, devotions, and a host of other Bahá'í community life activities . . .

Louise's children, Theresa, Beatrice and Richard (Dick), who had all been attending catechism classes, were now also attending Bahá'í children classes and in due time decided that they too were Bahá'ís. The priest of their neighbourhood church was very understanding with the family's decision and wrote a gracious letter accepting their decision. Ted, Louise's husband, became a Bahá'í in 1941, followed by his mother.

Between 1936 and 1949, Louise and her family became regular participants at Geyserville, the Bahá'í School in Northern California established by John and Louise Bosch. The first time they went, the great excitement for the children was to find the 'Big Tree' where the Bahá'í friends gathered for their meetings. Initially, there was confusion as to where this 'Big Tree' was located, but there at the end of a rambling stretch of green lawn majestically stood the 100-foot tall 'Big Tree' with three branches extending out from the trunk said to be representative of the three central figures of the Bahá'í Faith. The family's Bahá'í identity was forged and strengthened by the relationship with John and Louise Bosch and the annual gatherings at Geyserville. Louise and her husband Ted served on the School Committee with Mrs Amelia Collins, Mrs Marguerite Sears, Florence Mayberry, members of Leroy Ioas's family and John Bosch between the years 1941 and 1948. Ted was a member of the building and maintenance crew.

Louise was elected to the Local Spiritual Assembly of the Bahá'ís of San Francisco from 1938 to 1949 and served as the secretary for most of those years. In 1937, when the first Seven Year Plan was launched, the first teaching project based on 'Abdu'l-Bahá's Tablets of the Divine Plan, Louise felt a 'call' in her heart for the request for pioneers to South America:

When the first call came for Latin American pioneers, the urge to go was considerable. Obviously, of course, it was impossible. That didn't make it any easier for me to tell myself so each time the need was brought up again. It taught me a lot that I hadn't learned before and left me with a finite impression, actually a picture which I felt would be fulfilled, of being a Bahá'í pioneer in Central America one day. I felt it might be far in the future but would surely come. Since becoming a Bahá'í, I have been able so often to look back and see plan and pattern developing in my life with such regularity and such purpose that I have even learned to expect certain types of feelings to have premonitory meanings for me.

In 1949 a knock at Louise's door on Agua Way in San Francisco changed her life forever. News had arrived that her husband Ted had been in a tragic accident that claimed his life. Grieving for the loss of her husband and the children's father. Louise, a widow at the age of 42, was now contemplating what she would do for the rest of her life. As a California delegate to the National Bahá'í Convention in 1948 and 1950, she revisited her past desires and hopes about pioneering. It was not until the call came from the National Bahá'í Convention in 1950 that she again thought about South America: 'Although I did think of South America in the year that followed, I had no feeling for it at all. Then came the reports of the Convention and the urgent call for anyone who could to offer. And suddenly it seemed that I could do what just before I equally thought I couldn't do. When Millie [Collins] suggested Punta Arenas it seemed perfect, my feeling for it, I mean.'

Louise, a practical woman, considered the financial cost of pioneering with the basic necessity of proper clothing and knew that her current wardrobe would be suitable in Punta Arenas, where the fog and overcast skies were similar to the weather patterns in San Francisco. In 1950 Louise packed her bags and went to South America, to the very tip of the continent, Punta Arenas, where she served as a pioneer for several years. She wrote that 'I was under the impression that it was a great deal worse than it has been so far. Puerto Rico or Haiti though, so much nearer home, warm, probably in every way more attractive, didn't have the slightest attraction for me.'

Louise experienced another loss while there, the passing of her mother Pearl. After completing a two-year pioneering commitment in Punta Arenas, Louise went to Santiago where she decided that she would return to the United States and make arrangements to go back to South America for a longer and more permanent period of time. While in the States Louise attended the dedication in 1953 of the Mother Temple of the West in Wilmette, the magical place where it all began 18 years earlier, and witnessed the official launching of the Ten Year Crusade.

Upon her return to Santiago, Louise found that her hopes and plans for a new life that included the promise of a new romance had been dashed upon the rocks of destiny. She met this test with firm resolve and obedience and instead of returning home, Louise now turned for guidance as to where she would best be used as a pioneer. Instructions came that she should go to the virgin territory of Chiloe, an island off the coast of Chile, where the Guardian wanted a Bahá'í. Obediently she consented and went, not knowing that she was to be titled a Knight of Bahá'u'lláh. There she nursed a broken heart through service and teaching the local population about Bahá'u'lláh. Louise was fluent in Spanish and was able to open the territory with the beginnings of a Bahá'í community. She saw the bounty of God in her new and final pioneering post in Castro, Chiloe.

Teaching was slow, but in March 1955, the first resident of Chiloe accepted the Faith, though he soon left to move to Santiago. In 1957, another person became a Bahá'í. In 1958, Zunilda and her daughter moved to Santiago, leaving Louise on her own as the sole pioneer.[161] In early 1959, Salvador Tormo visited Louise and spoke about the Bahá'í Faith to nine of her contacts. The next day, one woman and her daughter returned to learn more, then promised to return again with some of her neighbours.[162]

Louise lived on the island for 16 years and supported herself through gardening, by selling her fruits, vegetables and flowers as well as taking in female boarders. It was a quiet and simple life that suited her.

In 1968, Louise returned to America and settled in northern California where she worked in the Grogers' family business, The New York Dry Goods Store. The business was situated in a historic state park of the old gold rush town of Columbia, where Louise would dress as a pioneer woman of the 1860s as part of the tourist attraction. In this new environment, Louise once again grew her beautiful garden. She was a woman ahead of her times, as she practised recycling before it was a word in our common vernacular. Louise's lifestyle was underscored with 'waste nothing'. She often would recycle her bath water in her garden, compost her leftovers, and burn paper products. Louise was already pioneering the path of independence, as she was a lone Bahá'í in Tuolumne County for much of her homefront pioneering days in northern California from 1968 to 1994.

In December of 1993, at the age of 86, Louise journeyed back to her pioneering posts – Punta Arenas and Chiloe – with her daughter, Beatrice Link-Groger, and granddaughter, Rosanne Groger. There they witnessed a vibrant town square in Castro where a beautiful church was located, named Iglesias de San Francisco. All over the island were beautiful roses said to be the descendants of Louise's garden. Myth or reality... This rose, so symbolic of Louise's love for Bahá'u'lláh and obedience to His Will, now perpetually blooms all over Castro. One of those special 'roses' that bloomed as a result of Louise's garden was an 11-year-old neighbour who used to peer over the fence watching Louise lovingly cultivate the soil in order to grow beautiful and fragrant flowers. This sweet child, Mirna, was now a grown woman with children of her own living in Santiago. During this trip there was a happy reunion between Louise and Mirna. Many tears of joy were shed and it became especially emotional upon learning that Mirna had become a Bahá'í. These seeds of love that Louise had planted while in her pioneering post were now bearing fruit.

Louise's life was a treasury of soul-stirring questions, investigations, and explorations which played out on the 'canvas of her life' like the strokes of an artist's paintbrush, a writer's pen or a gardener's green thumb, with purpose and pattern. She saw life and opportunities framed by windows and doors that held limitless possibilities, and with 'a little bit' of imagination and 'a lot' of faith and trust, Louise opened these 'doors and windows' by following the promptings of her heart, thus providing the spiritual leadership and lasting legacy that created the beginnings of an early American Bahá'í family of the 20th century.

In Louise's final days, she was surrounded by children, grandchildren, and great-grandchildren as well as members of the Bahá'í community. Enveloped by love, she was very aware of everyone in her presence while carrying on a coherent conversation. She often kept everyone laughing with her impatient humour as she remarked, 'How much longer do I need to be kept around?' 'Let's get on with it!' She was ready to close her eyes forever only to open them again to see everyone looking at her which caused her to say, 'Oh darn, I'm still here.' On March 22, the 2nd day of the Bahá'í year 155 (1999), on the eve of the closing of what 'Abdu'l-Bahá called 'this radiant century', 'this century of light', 'the like of which mankind will never again witness', Louise Elizabeth Atwell Groger, Knight of Bahá'u'lláh, took her spiritual flight to the Rose Garden of her Best Beloved.

ALASKA AND CANADA

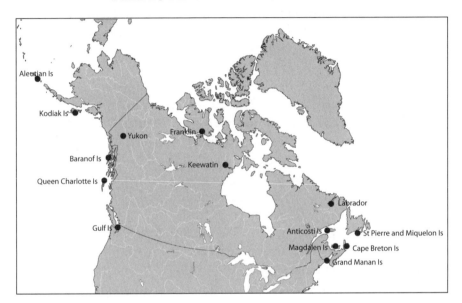

ALASKA

KODIAK ISLAND

Jack Huffman and Rose Perkal

Jack Huffman, son of Alaska pioneers Vern and Evelyn Huffman, was in the Navy when he was transferred to a base on Kodiak Island, Alaska. He arrived there on 1 June 1953, not knowing that it was one of Shoghi Effendi's 'virgin territories' or that Rose Perkal would arrive just over a month later specifically to fill that goal.[1] Jack's posting lasted probably less then a year. Shoghi Effendi magnanimously gave both the title of Knight of Bahá'u'lláh.

Rose Perkal (1904–2001) was a diminutive woman, less than five feet tall, from New York. Describing her reaction when she heard about the goals of the Ten Year Crusade, she said, 'I would like to go pioneering but I would like to go to a warm place and I ended up in Alaska!'[2] She arrived at Kodiak on 8 July 1953.[3] Soon after arriving, she wrote:

> God is good to me and I am grateful for having the opportunity of being able to serve the Cause as such. At first one may be a little dismayed as I was when I first came in, but then as one looks around with the eyes of a Bahá'í, he sees a wonderful future for this lovely island.[4]

In mid-1955, Rose wrote that one of her contacts, Kenneth Yarno, had become very interested in the Bahá'í Faith. It wasn't too long before Kenneth became a Bahá'í. Shortly thereafter, Kenneth asked Rose to marry him, which she did in August. Rose remained on Kodiak for a month after her marriage, then the couple moved to Fairbanks, where she worked for the Territorial Police, manning the radio telephone.[5] In 1960 Rose pioneered to Switzerland. She didn't speak French or German but found that she could get by in Yiddish. After a brief sojourn in the Dominican Republic, in 1966 she pioneered to South Africa. As a member of the South African National Spiritual Assembly in 1978, she attended the International Convention in Haifa. At one point, another delegate said: 'A group of African believers started singing lustily in the Eastern Pilgrim House and there was Rosie, right in the midst of them, singing her lungs out. Long after I, and other younger celebrants, had gotten worn out and left, Rosie remained with the last die-hards, belting out songs with the best of them.'[6] In 1986, while in her 80s, Rose decided to pioneer again, but this time to be closer to her sons in California. She continued to serve the Faith until she passed into the Abhá Kingdom in 2001.[7]

Ben Guhrke

Ben Guhrke (1924–2015) arrived on Kodiak Island on 1 February 1954. The son of a German immigrant to the United States, Ben had spent time in the Merchant Marine before training as a chiropractor at the Palmer School in Davenport, Iowa. The brother of a fellow student, Les Marcus, had introduced Les to the Bahá'í Faith and Les convinced

Ben to attend a fireside. Ben was hesitant at first, but when told that he might meet some women there, he went. He forgot all about the women at that first fireside as the speaker, Ali Kuli Khan spoke:

> . . . as he spoke I was gripped to attention. Where did this come from? . . . Words came like pearls cast on black velvet and I in their glow. Apprehension gave way to excitement. So much of what he said, the rational garbed in good spirit touched the ethos of my nature. True! . . . It was just a beginning! Later that night, back at home, I dipped into some Bahá'í literature . . .[8]

Ben and Les attended firesides with speakers such as Curtis Kelsey, Juliet Thompson, Saffa Kinney, Genevieve Coy, Stanwood Cobb and William Sears. One meeting at Juliet's home was particularly interesting because Hand of the Cause Mr Samandarí was going to speak, with Fred Sudhop, a well-known Bahá'í speaker, participating:

> . . . the attendees were many and the seats were few, resulting in a sea of squatters. As a dignitary, Mr Samandarí was provided with a chair facing everyone. Mr Sudhop, too late for a proper seat, plopped to the floor as part of the audience. Now! He was a big man, over six feet tall and as such looked like a mountain rooted among hills. It wasn't too long before he began to squirm in seeming anguish. Meanwhile, Mr Samandarí, a small, lean and aged person, speaking no English, perched decorously on his chair, perceived Fred's discomfort. Instinctively he swooped down on the hapless fellow and like a David and Goliath, practically wrestled a bemused Fred into the vacated chair and retreated to sit in Fred's vacated place on the floor.

Ben declared his belief in Bahá'u'lláh in September 1952. In May of the next year, Ben and Les attended the Intercontinental Teaching Conference in Wilmette and both were inspired to volunteer to pioneer. Initially, the Pioneer Committee suggested Ben go to St Helena Island in the middle of the Atlantic. Ben agreed, but a few weeks later when Elizabeth Stamp reached the island, the Committee asked if he would go to the Canary Islands instead. Again, he agreed, but after six more weeks, the Committee informed him that Gertrude Eisenberg had filled that post. Finally, they asked if Ben would go to Kodiak Island in Alaska to replace one of the two original Knights, Rose Perkal, who had had to leave. Again, he agreed and on New Year Day, 1954, 26-year-old Ben was on his way.

In Seattle, Ben contacted Doug and Betty Harris, well-known for their hospitality. They got Ben together with George and Elinor Putney and their three children, themselves on their way to Alaska and their post on Unalaska. Arriving in Juneau, Ben went looking for Gladys Steward, who had pioneered to the Alaskan capital in September 1953:

> Going ashore, I managed to dig up some kind of address, and bundled up against the elements, leaning into the gale with a flashlight in hand, I went to find her . . . I found her lodgings and knocked on the door. The weak and afflicted voice that bade me to come in came from a bruised and bandaged lady of sixty, propped up in her bed – and so, Gay Stewart related how, that day, on a steep and icy pavement a belligerent gust had cast her down. Battered, but not beaten, she hosted my visit from her casual perch. I returned to the ship with a light step pushed by the persistent wind.

From Juneau, Ben continued to Seward, where he took the train to Anchorage. Arriving in subzero (F) cold, he was astounded to hear someone say, 'Are you Ben?' Verne Stout and Vern and Evelyn Huffman, having heard through the 'grapevine' that he was coming, were there to meet him. The Huffmans were the parents of Kodiak Knight of Bahá'u'lláh Jack Huffman.

On 1 February, Ben boarded a DC-3 bound for Kodiak:

> Faced with my first time in an aircraft . . . the take-off was tense, the turbulence scary and the anxious landing on a runway wedged between the water's edge and a mountain, sobering. With a lift into town my journey came to an end at the humble Kodiak Hotel. Travel weary and feeling very alone, I wrapped up in the 'Remover of Difficulties' and found sleep. The next morning I awoke to the excitement of engaging my new surroundings, starting with some food. . . Crossing Main Street, with a café in sight, I froze; at my feet lay the silver half-dollar that paid for my breakfast, which was taken as a good omen. Emerging sated into sunlight and temperature in

the 40s, I took a turn around this fishing village dressed as a town but that called itself a city. Main Street, about four blocks long . . .

My meandering gave occasion to ask three kids walking by for some directions. On hearing that I was someone new to Kodiak . . . they were all excited to be telling me all they knew about everything. They happened to be off on the ritual adventure of carrying a rock to the top of Pillar Mountain to be stacked on the cairn being erected to the glory of all the kids in town. Would I join them? If so, I had to carry a rock too. The boys were between 10 and 12 years old [and] we chatted our way up the half mile road to the top. The view was spectacular! On three sides irregular coastlines pushed against a blue and shining sea while behind us crowded many-shaded mountains crowned in snow. We deposited our rocks and turned to the foreground of our vista. Far below lay the town, poised to be inundated by waves of islands that created channels for seaplanes to land on, boats to sail through, whales to transit and halibut to be caught in . . . So it went until they told me we were taking the shortcut back to town. This meant going right down the face of the mountain, squatting on our heels and backside to slide down steep patches of snow. What a ride! . . .

The need to get a job was urgent. Chiropractic, still in its infancy as a system of health care, was not legally recognized in Alaska . . . I went first to the bank, close to my hotel where I was interviewed by the owner himself. From pinched features and a shrewd eye, Marshall Crutcher lashed me with questions wondering, no doubt, who comes from New York City to get a job in Kodiak, Alaska? The exact questions are long forgotten but my answers must have been artful enough to get me the job . . .

I quickly made rental arrangements, hardly believing that within a week of my arrival I was settled and only had to cross the street to get to work on time.

My new career began behind a Burroughs posting machine of which there were two tucked in a cozy corner of the floor plan. Next to me, poking away at the other machine sat an elderly man with a great white beard that looked like it might have been cropped to keep it from flowing over the keyboard. My compatriot turned out to be Father Sturmer, the Russian Orthodox priest for Kodiak who felt the need to augment his clerical stipend with a bank salary.

Given the 'Good News' of a new revelation, he, in his own way honored the message – what great discussions charged our lunch breaks!

Ben began to get acquainted with the people of Kodiak. Initially, to meet people, he went to the Elks Club where liquor flowed freely. The regulars at the club thought of him as 'a Bahá'í migrant from Knudsen's soda fountain'. Then he was told about a Bahá'í contact who worked at the Kodiak Naval Air Base, Charley Lee. Ben and Charley quickly became friends, though Charley soon moved to Anchorage to marry a Bahá'í lady named Lois. Through her, Charley quickly became a Bahá'í and, in 1957, the treasurer of the first Alaskan National Spiritual Assembly. Ben also found Jack Huffman. He too, coming to the end of his deployment with the Navy, left the island.

After five months on Kodiak, Ben wrote in June 1954 that a

surprising number of religious groups are represented here. Once a week we even have a pathetic group of Evangelists singing and preaching on one of the street corners while most of the townspeople pass them by with a deaf ear figuring them some kind of freaks and dismissing the matter abruptly. The Baptists, for years, have been sinking money into their missionary endeavor amongst the natives in the small villages around the island trying to woo them away from rituals of Russian Orthodoxy with no success. There is a Catholic and a Baptist church in town and the Christian Scientists meet every Sunday in the bank; they are a small group but represent some of the most substantial citizens including the bank president.

Ben had long been looking for a wife and, 15 months after arriving on Kodiak, a lady suddenly caught his attention. It started when he wanted a boat he couldn't afford:

One Saturday . . . I was lusting over a particular skiff and outboard motor which I couldn't hope to buy. Mr Acherson, an owner of the business, perceiving my frustration, offered to let me pay for the rig in instalments. For the first time in my life, I bought something I couldn't pay for outright. A few Saturdays later, I was happily putt-putting along the town's Near Island Channel shoreline when, in passing a house situated high on the left bank, I recognized the petite Japanese lady that worked as a loan assistant in the bank. She was hanging out washing. It struck me that it would be fun to invite her for an excursion among the islands. I knew she lived alone, so I beached the skiff and scrambled up to the house. She was stunned in surprise by whom, and what for the sea had cast me to her shore; but she came along for the ride. Harriet and I were married about eight months later – what a ride!

The path to our engagement had not been a lighthearted stroll in the park. Harriet [was] born in Hawaii of Japanese immigrant parents in 1918, she was nine years my senior . . . [she had] married a Caucasian serviceman whose parents' ethnic bias against the union had left a wound to sear the soul . . . The couple was relocated to the Naval Base on Kodiak where . . . they were divorced; he returned to his home . . . and she pleased to remain in Kodiak. Now, there she was, under the shadow of a great hurt, facing a decision that could reawaken the demon just put to rest. Into the breach, like a Moses on Mt Sinai, stepped Bahá'u'lláh with the law of parental consent for marriage. Harriet's father, Seiji Komesu, who lived as a widower in Hawaii, quickly gave his approval. With my Pop such things were never simple. He would analyze, cogitate and then ruminate well into time; so it was; and when the word came some months later, the approval came as a benediction.

I know that in many ways, Harriet was quite overwhelmed by the whole Bahá'í marriage experience. It had meant flying to Anchorage for the ceremony which had to be officiated by Alaska's only Spiritual Assembly. Instead of being conducted, witnessed and honored in the bosom of friends and acquaintances, she found herself in the midst of strangers and none of the familiar trappings of her Christian Faith . . . The marriage and reception took place in the home of Verne and Janet Stout . . . The friendly love lavished on Harriet did much to allay any misgivings she might have had. For cockeyed reasons that could only be generated in Alaska, we had to spend our first night in the Anchorage Community's recently acquired log cabin destined to become Alaska's first Ḥaẓíratu'l-Quds. The building was not yet fully equipped for occupancy but we had no choice; resulting in the memory of taking sponge baths standing in a dish pan of warm water in a none too warm kitchen.

Back on Kodiak, the newlyweds moved into Harriet's little apartment, bought an old 'clunker' car to get around in, and settled down.

In July 1956, Ben was working at the bank at a teller's window when one of his customers greeted him with 'Alláh-u-Abhá!' With that shock, Ben met two new pioneers to the island, Bob and Karin Leonard. Recently married, they wanted to pioneer and Bob, who was in the Navy, had managed to acquire an assignment to the Kodiak Naval Air Station. Ben was overjoyed to have Bahá'í companionship. With the arrival of the Leonards, a fireside was started and its first successes were Dean Booker, another Navy man, and a young cannery worker, Gilbert Munro.

News of the passing of the Guardian in November 1957 was a long time getting to the Bahá'ís in Kodiak. Bob Leonard saw the news in a 'maliciously biased article' in *Time* magazine. It was a few weeks more before they received confirmation. The Leonards, unfortunately, moved back to the United States in early 1958 and were gone for a year and a half before returning.

When Dean Booker left Kodiak in 1958 to marry a Bahá'í in Anchorage, there were four Bahá'ís on the island. But when 1962 arrived, the Bahá'í community expanded rapidly. Harriet and Gilbert's wife, Shirley, both declared, then Bob Roys professed his faith. Alethe Hogberg, Karin Leonard's mother, moved from her pioneering post in Sweden when her husband died. At Riḍván, they had a community of eight Bahá'ís. It was then that Elinore and George Putney and their children moved from Unalaska to Kodiak. On 7 September 1962, Kodiak formed its first Local Spiritual Assembly.

Interestingly, though Kodiak was part of Alaska, it was not a part of the Alaska Bahá'í Community until Riḍván 1964. Before that time, Kodiak was administered by the American Western Hemisphere Teaching Committee under the jurisdiction of the US National Spiritual Assembly. Soon after Kodiak came under the Alaska National Spiritual Assembly, Ben was elected to that body in a by-election.[9]

Ben and Harriet were in Kodiak during the 1964 Alaska earthquake, during which the town dropped until half of it was inundated at high tide. To acquire fill for rebuilding the town, the Navy used the cannons on its ships to blast the mountains.[10]

By 1965 Kodiak had a strong Assembly, so the Guhrkes pioneered to Naknek on Bristol Bay. Ben was hired as the Borough Manager and impressed everyone with his integrity. Local canneries, which had managed to pay lower taxes by bribing Borough officials, found Ben uncooperative and their taxes helped build the Borough's first high school.[11]

In 1970, the Guhrkes were called to the Bahá'í World Centre where Ben worked in the Finance and Personnel Departments. He was also able to put his chiropractic skills to use with the World Centre staff and learned how to play golf. In 1986, Harriet died and was buried in the Bahá'í cemetery at the foot of Mt Carmel. Ben's golfing led to an encounter with Marvel Gray, who also worked at the World Centre and in 1988, they were married. Marvel had been a pioneer in Africa and Brazil between 1966 and 1981 before she went to serve in Haifa. In Brazil, Marvel was the secretary to Hand of the Cause Jalál Kházeh. The Guhrkes were in Haifa during the first Gulf war and Marvel noted that everyone was required to have a 'safe room'. Ben complained that 'the Iraqis waited until he got into the bath to send out their rockets', so he made the bathroom their safe room.[12]

Ben and Marvel left the World Centre in 1994 and moved to Rio Rancho, New Mexico, near Albuquerque.[13] They travelled through all 50 states and parts of Canada on travel-teaching and golfing trips. Ben passed to the Abhá Kingdom in February 2015.[14]

ALEUTIAN ISLANDS

Jenabe and Elaine Caldwell

Though Jenabe (1926–2016) and Elaine Caldwell (1928–2014) initially decided to pioneer to a warm place, they ended up in a cold one. Jenabe came from a Bahá'í family. His mother had learned of the Faith when a friend suggested they attend a talk by Martha Root as she passed through their small Montana town.[15] Jenabe acquired his name when Jenabe Fádil-i-Mazindaraní made a teaching trip to Montana. The soon-to-be parents asked Jenabe Fádil to name their son, preferably with his own name. The ever-modest visitor offered Jenabe Esslemont, which the parents accepted, not knowing that Jenabe was a title and not part of his name. The young Jenabe drifted away from the Faith until the passing of his father, when his interest was rekindled. When he married Elaine and they were living in Washington state, they began to study the Faith on their own and in 1950 decided to become Bahá'ís. The local Bahá'í community was quite surprised to have someone named Jenabe wanting to become a Bahá'í.[16]

Jenabe and Elaine Caldwell went to the All-American Teaching Conference in 1953 and there volunteered to be pioneers. Their first choices were all nice, warm places and they decided on Tonga. But the very day they finished filling in all the forms for visas and other things, they received a call from Dorothy Baker. Dorothy said that Shoghi Effendi had requested that three specific goal areas be filled. Two were easy and one was hard. Dorothy asked the Caldwells if they would go to the hard one, the Aleutian Islands in Alaska. So they exchanged nice and warm for cold and windy.[17]

The journey to Alaska was long and difficult, and included sliding off a rain-slickened road into a ditch, getting stuck in the sand and being faced with washed-out bridges.[18] Reality began to hit home when they arrived in Anchorage, Alaska, on 28 July 1953 and found that there were no jobs on the islands and that most of the people lived on government relief. The only ways to get to the islands, some 600 miles from Anchorage, were by plane or boat. The pilot told them bluntly, 'Leave those people alone; they have their religion,' and refused to fly them. When they contacted the ship captain, he asked why a young man with a wife and three very young children would want to go to the Aleutians. When told, he replied that 'I like your spirit, young man, and I'll tell you what I am going to do. I am going to take you, your family and all your luggage out to Unalaska for $120, and next month I'm going to bring you all back for nothing.' It was a ten-day journey across the open ocean and they were all very sick.[19] The ship visited Seldovia, Port Graham and Kodiak, where the Caldwells visited with Knight of Bahá'u'lláh Rose Perkal. From Kodiak, they stopped at several isolated communities and passed the active Sishalden volcano. Eight years later, the ship's captain stopped by the Bahá'í Centre in Unalaska and asked for information on the Bahá'í Faith.[20]

On 10 August, Jenabe and Elaine, with Daniel, David and six-week-old Mark, arrived on Unalaska Island. Word had spread of their coming and they were met at the dock by the local missionary who asked, 'Are you a Christian gentleman?' Jenabe replied, 'Oh yes, and a Muhammadan and Buddhist gentleman also.' The missionary went away and told everyone that the new arrivals were not Christian and had come to take Christ away. Later, when Jenabe tried to pray in the missionary's church, he was told that he was not welcome.[21] The first thing the Caldwells tried to do was send a cable to Shoghi Effendi telling him of their arrival. The only telegraph was run by the army and they had never sent an international cable before. It took them two days to figure out how to do it. Then, when the Guardian's reply arrived, it created more of a stir because the station had never received an international cable, either.[22]

The Caldwells found a 'well ventilated' two-bedroom furnished house and moved in. Jenabe found work as a bouncer and garbage collector, but when the missionary accused him of taking a job from a native, he quit. They spent the remainder of the summer picking a 'bathtub' full of blueberries and canning salmon. One day, Elaine remembered,

> Jenabe came home . . . and threw a LARGE salmon into the sink. I had never done any fishing before and did not know what to do with this fish that moved every time I tried to touch it, but since the sink was unusable until the fish was cleaned, I soon had to come to grips with the situation and get it cleaned and out of there.[23]

To survive, Jenabe built himself a boat from scrap materials and fished while Elaine chopped firewood and did the laundry by hand. The first winter was brutal and Elaine wrote that

> drifting snow covered much of the house. For three long months the storm raged and the wind continued unabated. One day it was so windy, I was going to the store (about 5 blocks away), couldn't stand up and got blown back. I decided that we didn't need whatever I was going to buy at the time. In the unheated living room of our house, Jenabe was re-doing an old fish net which he was able to get. He would periodically come into the kitchen to warm up and then go back to work on the net again after he thawed out . . .
>
> I baked 8 loaves [of bread] per week when the children were small and this increased to 16 loaves a week later on.[24]

They opened a small radio repair shop and ended up with more work then they could handle, since almost every ship that visited Unalaska had some sort of radio problem. This also gave them a chance to teach the Faith since the 'people on the boats had nothing else to do but listen . . .'[25]

During the summer of 1954, the Caldwells bought two old army buildings for $2.50 apiece plus a lot for $150 and began to build a home/Bahá'í Centre. Since they had to scrounge building materials from the abandoned army buildings, the project took a long time and they weren't able to move in until 10 November.[26]

Shoghi Effendi, who could always read between the lines of Jenabe's letters, told them to ask for financial help from the National Spiritual Assembly of the United States, but the Caldwells couldn't bring themselves to do it. Then, just as the money ran out, a man came to their door. He was the superintendent of Standard Oil Company and he needed an electrical engineer, which was what Jenabe was, though his area was electronics. Jenabe didn't lack for work after that.[27]

Finally, the day came when the Caldwells decided it was time to proclaim the Bahá'í Faith to the 50 families on Unalaska, but just as they prepared to do so, a cable came from the Guardian which read, 'Do not openly proclaim the message of God in this place, when you have confidence in them and they have confidence in you, then slowly confirm them in the Cause of God.' Over the years, 'the hate gave way to tolerance, the tolerance gave way to acceptance and finally all gave way to mutual love and respect.'[28]

In 1954, Elinore Putney and her three children arrived in Unalaska and Jenabe started up a small fish cannery. He went to Anchorage and sold shares in the cannery to the Bahá'ís, then came back and bought a piece of land for the building. Elaine wrote that at the new cannery,

> Jenabe and I were the only employees. Our days were long, about 16 to 18 hours, in which he would catch the fish, load them in the skiff, and then return to the cannery. In the meantime, I was busy getting breakfast, cleaning the cabin, taking care of necessary duties for the children, gathering wood on the beach for the stove, washing diapers and doing other laundry in water that I hauled from the river. After breakfast, Jenabe would begin cleaning the fish while I washed dishes. We would send the boys to pick coal in a field near the cannery. The army had bulldozed the coal into the ground so that the children had to pick it out. It would take them nearly all day . . .
>
> Now that the children were settled, Jenabe and I would cut the fish, put them in cans, and cook them. This entailed using an exhaust box, hand seamer and pressure cooker. The older children

assisted us in making the cans that first year, which arrived flat. We then had to round them out with a machine, seal one end and after the fish was cooked and in the cans, turn them 20 times on the sealer. We managed to can 43 large cases of salmon that year . . .[29]

The next year, 1955, they canned 500 cases of fish and held children's classes for the Caldwell children, Putney children and any other children who showed up.

In March 1956, Elaine gave birth to a daughter, Layli Roshan. The baby was born at home with the help of an Aleut midwife. This greatly increased their standing in the eyes of the native people. Also during the year, they completed the translation of 'Blessed is the Spot' into Aleut with the help of Vassa Lekanoff. The Caldwells and the Putneys held Bahá'í study classes for three women, one of whom was Vassa, who became the first Aleut believer.[30]

The local missionary who had constantly opposed them drowned in 1957. The Russian Orthodox priest, who was friendly, was not above using the Bahá'ís to inspire his congregation. When needed work was not done by his parishioners, he threatened to have Jenabe do it. Invariably, this inspired the congregation to arise and do the work themselves.

In 1957, Elaine left Unalaska for the first time to attend the first Alaska National Convention. The next year, two people became Bahá'ís in the town, but neither was local and consequently both left. The Putneys left in 1962 for Kodiak, leaving the Caldwells and Vassa as the only Bahá'ís until the autumn of the next year when Gordon and Ruth Craig, their four children and Addie Nordstrom pioneered to Unalaska. The Caldwell family took a much needed holiday in 1963 and attended the World Jubilee in London, travel-teaching on the way.[31]

The cannery had expanded considerably and was employing several local workers and had switched to king crab. By 1963, their success was so great that the big canning companies conspired with the bankers in Seattle to force them out of business. Then came the great Alaskan earthquake of 1964 that destroyed most of the other canneries, but left Jenabe's Unalaska cannery unharmed.[32] When the earthquake happened the community expected a tidal wave, so Elaine loaded up the company bus and drove as many townspeople as possible to higher ground. It was very cold and snowy as they waited, and finally Elaine decided that

I would rather drown then freeze, so went home. As it turned out, the tide was only two feet, when normally it got up to five feet. Several canneries in Alaska (which had been trying to eliminate us) were destroyed in the quake and tidal wave and we were able to lease the plant to another company very quickly. The earthquake had answered all of our problems in a matter of three minutes.[33]

Shortly after the earthquake, the Caldwells moved to Edmonds, Washington, near Seattle, for a year. They also pioneered to Mexico. In the 1970s, Jenabe and Elaine returned to Unalaska for a year, living at the cannery. By that time, the cannery was one of the largest in Alaska. During this time, they instituted the Bahá'í Work Force project, which employed 40 Bahá'ís who all contributed either a portion or all of their paycheck to the Bahá'í fund. At the end of the year, they sold the cannery and were able to return considerably more funds then they had been given when they first opened the operation.[34] In one case, the disbursement after the sale allowed Betty Becker, an Alaskan pioneer to Chile, to purchase a Bahá'í Centre in Punta Arenas. The first Local Spiritual Assembly was formed in Unalaska during the 1970s.

Jenabe was appointed an Auxiliary Board member and when the Alaskan Bahá'í community began what they called 'Massive Encounter' for the spiritual conquest of Alaska, he was the one put in charge of operations.[35] By the mid 1970s, the Alaska Bahá'í community soared from 400 to 4,000 declared believers. Jenabe later pioneered to Japan and Hawaii.

Elaine remained in Alaska and worked at the National Bahá'í Office for many years, with a few years out to serve at the Bahá'í World Centre.

Elinore Putney

Elinore Putney (1933–2009), with her children Laurel, Kathleen and Georgia, arrived on Unalaska in the Aleutian Islands from San Francisco on 2 May 1954.[36] Elinore had met George Putney when they were both attending firesides in San Francisco in 1953. Elinore was just out of high school and 19 years old. George had been widowed the year before and had two children, Laurel and Kathleen. Elinore and George both became Bahá'ís and were married. The Ten Year Crusade excited them and, since George had been to Guam on a ship, they decided to go there. The family moved to Seattle in preparation for Guam, but had to pause while baby Georgia was born. While in Seattle, the Western Hemisphere Teaching Committee asked them to consider going to the Aleutian Islands instead, which were very remote and isolated, to join the Caldwells. George had also been to Unalaska so the Putneys changed destinations.[37]

When the family arrived in Anchorage, they spent a few days with Verne and Janet Stout before boarding a plane to Unalaska. George was working on a tugboat at the time, so it was only 21-year-old Elinore, 5-year-old Laurel, 4-year-old Kathleen and 4-month-old Georgia who stepped off that plane. Elinore, being a city girl and not having a clear idea of where she was going, arrived wearing stylish clothes and high heels. The airport, however, was on the separate island of Dutch Harbour and the new arrivals had to cross the bay in a skiff to reach their new home. Luckily, the weather was good.[38]

At first, Elinore and the children lived with Jenabe and Elaine Caldwell, but Elinore soon found them a place of their own. Laurel noted that

> We didn't know our own mom . . . She knew she was going to be by herself although . . . she also knew that the Caldwells were there, although she didn't know them. She had nice visits with Janet Stout and I know they corresponded for years while she was out there by herself while my dad would be gone working on a boat somewhere. My mom, I'm sure she had a lot of challenges. We moved out of the Caldwells' house into a little teeny – like a little shed. It was just tiny. It had a kitchen and I'm sure there was a bathroom in there somewhere.[39]

The challenges of living in a very isolated fishing village were immediately evident. The town of Unalaska had about a hundred inhabitants and occupied a sandy spit between a creek and the head of Iliuliuk Bay. All of the residents were Aleut except for the Caldwells, the Putneys, a couple of communications men, the schoolteachers and the store manager. Access to and from the airport was by small skiff until the 1970s when a bridge was finally built (and officially named 'The Bridge to the Other Side' following a contest won by Bahá'í Ray Hudson). Elinore found a two-bedroom, two-storey house after a short time and the family moved into more comfortable quarters. Laurel remembered that we ate a lot of fish. My mom learned how to cook from Elaine [Caldwell]. Elaine showed her how to do things: how to clean a fish – she'd never done anything like that. She made fish soup, fish spaghetti, fish patties, fish burgers. You name it, we ate it that way. Lots of fish. We rarely seriously had anything else to eat. She made some mashed potatoes once and was looking at us two girls – the baby wasn't eating yet – trying to make it nice so she said, 'I'm going to make some gravy.' Remember, she was 21. She made blue gravy. We never forgot it. We loved our blue gravy. Sky blue. We picked berries and she always made sure that we had something to eat, we had good clothes . . .

She learned how to put in a year grocery order and have the whole thing come out on the boat. She learned to sew with an old treadle sewing machine and our house became a little beehive of activity.

. . . My mom used to get us a box every month from the Alaska State Library in Juneau. It had art prints you could hang up. I think you were allowed to keep them for three months. It would have music, records (long-play records), books, all kinds of books. That box would come and we all would sit down and abandon everything else to read and listen to everything. I grew up listening to opera, like Rigoletto, and classical music. That's what we would listen to. We didn't think anything of it. My dad would bring in some of the folk songs, Johnny Cash, Marty Robbins. Once in a while we'd get that radio tuned in and catch KFQD. In December on a cold night we could pick it up. We just didn't have much. Didn't have any refrigeration. We finally got an old fridge that Mom turned up high and kinda used it for a freezer. We did have running water, though. We also had an oil cook stove . . .

We had children's classes – Elaine was usually our children's class teacher, but the parents commonly took turns. We mostly had Feast at the Caldwell's house because that was the official Bahá'í Center after it was built. Before that we would just trade back and forth. Mom's letters from Janet Stout were always very welcome. There wasn't much money. Lots of lean times and you had to depend on what you could catch out there in the creek or out in the ocean. People shared. Everybody took care of everybody . . .

Because we didn't have refrigeration, we learned how to can

food. We had a pressure cooker and every couple of months we'd get an old mutton sent in from the sheep ranch at the end of the island at Chernofski. The mail boat would come around and make one pass by there and pick up any freight and bring it in to Unalaska. The first couple of nights we'd all have lamb chops and ribs, and the good stuff, but then after that it was all from a jar. And of course the kidneys and things have to be mixed in there. Mom would make us what she called kidney pie and we'd be 'O boy, O boy, O boy!' We'd be eating it very carefully, because all of a sudden you'd get a piece of kidney and (sour face).

She sewed all the clothes for us. I remember one time she got some fabric from somewhere. I'm sure she ordered it. A paisley print and she made us all nice blouses. Elaine did the buttonholes because she was really good with buttonholes. My mom made skirts and little boleros (short jackets) for us . . .

There were no land animals in Unalaska except maybe foxes and squirrels and stuff like that, but no bears or moose or big stuff. We used to go out quite a bit, us and her and the neighbour kids and have good times together. We'd pick berries, dig clams . . . We'd get up early in the morning when it was low tide out in the skiff with a garden rake and scoop Dungeness crab up. Get some water boiling, cook crabs and eat them right there on the beach.

My mom had two babies out there with just a midwife. Elaine, too gave birth to Layli. It's what you did.[40]

When asked what people did in such an isolated place, Elinore replied:

We visited, we read, we played cards, we played Charades, we went on picnics. There was a white man in town with a flatbed truck. He'd load up half the town and drive out somewhere it'd take hours to get to if you walked, and we'd eat and watch the kids play, and visit. That's what people did in Unalaska in those years – visit, read and play cards. Henry Swanson, an old man who lived near us, came over every day. Never missed a day. He told us stories of when he was a kid in Unalaska, and of his years trapping before the bottom fell out of the market for fox. He reminisced about World War I; he was a treasure. He was like a grandfather to the girls. He'd take them in his dory over to an island where they'd have 'campfire tea' and pilot bread.[41]

During the summer of 1955, Janet Smith began visiting Unalaska on the *MS Hygiene*, a Territorial Department of Health ship that delivered medical services to isolated areas.[42] Janet initially wasn't supposed to be on the ship, but when someone became unavailable, Janet was asked to go, with life-changing consequences. She was soon asking questions about the Faith. Each time the ship came into port, she asked more questions.[43] The *MS Hygiene* was not a very seaworthy ship and consequently had a high crew turnover. One day when the ship was in Unalaska, its First Mate suddenly quit. The only person with the proper credentials to replace him turned out to be George Putney. When he came aboard, his duffle bag was full of Bahá'í books and he and Janet had many discussions about the Faith.[44] By the next year, Janet had become a Bahá'í, the first person to declare in Unalaska.

One of the first people Elinore met was Vassa Lekanoff, a young neighbour who had a little girl about the same age as Georgia, and they became inseparable. Though Janet Smith was the first person to become a Bahá'í in Unalaska, Vassa became the first Aleut Bahá'í.[45] Vassa visited Elinore later in Kodiak after the family had moved there from Unalaska. Just before Vassa passed away in Anchorage in 2003, she sent a message asking Elinore to come see her, which she did, and the two friends had their last visit. Teaching the Faith was slow because of the influence of the Russian Orthodox Church, but was always on their minds. Henry Swanson, one of their dearest friends, was very attracted to the Faith, but would never sign a card. Just before the family left Unalaska, the Putney kids 'sat him down and looked him in the eye and said, "Are you a Bahá'í?" To which he replied, "Yes!"'[46]

One of the exciting events was the wonderful visit of Auxiliary Board member Florence Mayberry in 1958:

> The unpredictable Aleutian weather behaved perfectly for Florence's quick trip to Unalaska where the Caldwells and Putneys have been pioneering for several years. The first night Florence met with these two Bahá'í families to tell them of her pilgrimage and bring them news from the Hands. The next afternoon she showed her slides to all the school children. That night, the first public Bahá'í meeting was held in Unalaska in the beautiful new Ḥazíra . . . According to Florence, there is no more beautiful Ḥazíra any place than this one far out in the Aleutians. The main meeting room seats 80 people,

has wonderful lighting facilities, and large windows overlooking the Bay and Bering Sea . . . the local group was gratified that one quarter of the town came to the meeting – 27 adults, including 23 contacts. After the meeting, there were refreshments, and 6 contacts stayed till midnight for further discussion, including two local people.

The Unalaska Bahá'ís have started weekly classes on Friday nights at the Center and they write that a recent session lasted till 5:00 a.m. Six or seven contacts have been coming. They closed their report by saying: 'We had a marvelous time while Florence was here; words cannot describe the spiritual uplift we received from our first Bahá'í speaker and visitor!'[47]

In 1962, the Putneys left Unalaska because Laurel was ready to start high school and there was no high school in Unalaska. They moved to Kodiak where three more children were added to the family. Elinore hosted weekly firesides during the 15 years they lived there. George would find the contacts and light the fire while Elinore would nurture and sustain them. In 1977, Elinore and the children moved to Anchorage; unfortunately, she and George had separated by that time. Elinore was very active in the community, serving on the Local Spiritual Assembly, writing the *Anchorage Bahá'í Lights* newsletter and even going back to school and earning a degree, cum laude, in anthropology. She remained in Anchorage until shortly before her passing on 1 December 2009.[48] George remarried and pioneered to Easter Island for a time.

BARANOF ISLAND

Helen Robinson

Helen Robinson (b.1909) first pioneered to Alaska in 1944 with her husband, Rob, and children Donna and Robbie. Helen had discovered the Bahá'í Faith through the teaching efforts of Lorol Jackson.[49] Her advancement in the Faith was full of great tests. Her husband threatened to divorce her when she became a Bahá'í, but her steadfastness ultimately won him over.

The Robinsons moved to Anchorage where, in 1945, Donna became the first youth in Alaska to declare her faith in Bahá'u'lláh. The family moved to Idaho about 1950.[50] When the Ten Year Crusade was announced, Helen returned to Alaska to fulfil the goal for Baranof Island. She arrived in Sitka, on the island, on 29 September 1953. She wrote:

> To explain about the spiritual beauty, the breathtaking loveliness of the islands is impossible . . . Sitka is an Indian Village and we are the 'Outsiders'. They are very friendly and a joy to work with . . . The native and Eskimo come here from 124 villages in Alaska . . . They come to you from all over the territory and will return remembering you were a Bahá'í if nothing more . . . my first 'contact' was a young man dying from leukemia . . . The friendship with this young man and the change of outlook and attitude affected many people. We talked about the 'open door' and he read many pamphlets and saw the slides of the Shrines and Gardens, etc. People of course saw this transformation and knew it was the Bahá'í Teachings . . .
>
> I learned so much on this trip all alone . . . the greatest being that one never 'walks alone' when serving the Lord. I'll never fear again. Doors opened for me all the way, all I had to do was walk through. Mrs A. lost her son in Korea and was a very sad lady when we met. She said, 'Why I never saw the great beauty of this lovely island until you came here and brought me these wonderful Teachings. I am grateful.'
>
> Dear Friends when I started to write you I told myself it must be brief as you are all so busy. I am afraid I get carried away with joy, remembering the great beauty of these people and their country. It is a grand and glorious experience and I wish all the Friends would pioneer alone without fear.[51]

Unfortunately, she was forced to return to Idaho in March of 1954.[52] Helen made teaching trips to Alaska in 1959 and two years later pioneered to Sweden with her husband, Rob. They visited Alaska again in 1963.[53]

Grace Bahovec

Grace Bahovec was born in Haiti in 1897 as Grace Mayfield. She was adopted by an American family in Butte, Montana[54] and then, in 1912, began touring as a singer, dancer and waitress in the American

Northwest. In about 1922 she moved to Alaska looking for 'work and romance'. In 1925, after three years of work in Petersburg, but no romance, she decided to take one last trip before heading south. To travel to Baranof Warm Springs, she had to charter a fishing boat owned by Fred Bahovec. He supplied the romance and they were married. For 11 years, they raised fox and mink for their furs, but then switched to making jewellery from precious stones they found around Baranof. Their work was soon well known and Grace was featured in *Ebony* magazine in 1948. In a small place such as Baranof, population 10, the residents had multiple jobs. Besides making jewellery, hunting and canning things they grew or collected, Grace assisted her postmaster husband, was a weather recorder for the US Weather Service and an election judge.[55]

Some time before the end of 1946, Grace had gone to Anchorage looking for jade for her husband, who carved stones into rings and other jewellery. While there, she heard a radio talk on the Bahá'í Faith and visited Honor Kempton and Dagmar Dole, both pioneers to Alaska at that time, at Honor's business, the Book Cache. Dagmar told her where to find jade and both women told her about the Faith. Grace attended many meetings with the Bahá'ís and asked many questions. Finally, at a dinner with the Bahá'ís before returning to Baranof Warm Springs, Grace declared 'I am one of Bahá'u'lláh's jewels and He has found me. I came for jade but I have found a priceless jewel.'[56] Grace remained in Baranof until 1959.[57]

Unusually, Grace was not named in any of the Guardian's cables and letters as being a Knight of Bahá'u'lláh, but her name, without a date, was placed in the *Bahá'í World* volume that covered the Ten Year Crusade, published in 1970.[58] It was also included on the Scroll of the Knights of Bahá'u'lláh included in the *Bahá'í World* in 1992.[59] When the Research Department at the Bahá'í World Centre was queried about Grace, they replied that no additional information about her was found in their records.[60]

Gail Avery

Gail Avery (1903–1995) grew up in Montana and learned about the Bahá'í Faith from her sister. She quickly realized that Bahá'u'lláh was the Promised One and became a Bahá'í in 1948 at the age of 45.[61] At the age of 30 her first marriage ended, so Gail returned to school to learn medical technology. She went on to become an X-ray technician. Becoming a Bahá'í and a grandmother, Gail returned to school again and studied nursing in order to be able to serve the Faith in China. She never made it to China, but she did make teaching trips for the Faith to Peru and Mexico.⁶² When she attended the National Bahá'í Convention in Chicago in 1953 and heard Rúḥíyyih Khánum tell people not to write to Shoghi Effendi for advice on where to pioneer, but to just do it, she decided to do just that. Gail finished her nursing studies in Montana, and pioneered to Sitka on Baranof Island in Alaska, arriving in February 1954.⁶³

Gail found the life of a Knight of Bahá'u'lláh to be much easier than she expected. Her job in the Public Health Service Hospital at Mount Edgecumbe was good and the hospital was actually better than the one she had left.⁶⁴ After two years, she took a job as an X-ray technician in the Sitka Community Hospital. Gail later worked at the Sitka Pioneer's Home until she retired in 1970.⁶⁵

Shortly after arriving in Sitka, Gail homesteaded on Dove Island, a short distance west of Sitka.⁶⁶ She would row daily to Sitka, no matter what the weather. Gail was a tough lady. On one occasion when Gail and her daughter, Alice Machesney, were rowing home with their groceries, the boat overturned in the rough seas and the women and their supplies were dumped into the cold water. After being rescued and rewarmed, Gail went back and recovered all the groceries by diving to the bottom of the sea.⁶⁷

In 1957, Gail met and married Albert Davis, a full Tlingit Indian who later became the leader of the Native Coho Clan. It was difficult being a white person married to a Tlingit and she had to struggle at first to blend the two cultures. She and Albert split their time, living part of the year on Dove Island and part of the year in Albert's clan house. She was later adopted into the tribe and given the honour of receiving a Tlingit name.⁶⁸

Baranof Island and Sitka were administered by the Canadian National Spiritual Assembly. In 1958, the Hands of the Cause in the Holy Land decided that only Baranof Island would continue to be under the Canadians and that all other islands in the area were to be under the jurisdiction of the new National Spiritual Assembly of the Bahá'ís of Alaska. This meant that when Gail was living on Dove Island, a quarter mile offshore from Baranof Island, she was under the care of Alaska, but when she and Albert moved into his clan house, she was under the jurisdiction of the Canadians.[69]

In her retirement years, Gail wrote cryptograms and a column called, 'It is remembered' for the *Daily Sitka Sentinel* and published a book of poetry called *More Than a Touch of Madness*.

Albert and Gail remained in Sitka for the rest of their lives. Albert passed away in September 1995, followed six weeks later by Gail in November.

CANADA

YUKON

Joan and Ted Anderson

Joan (1928–2000) and Ted Anderson (b.1924) reached the town of Whitehorse, Yukon, Canada, on 23 September 1953. Ted was the son of a Lutheran minister. His interest in religion took him to the Union Theological Seminary where his doctoral research led to his discovery of the Bahá'í Faith. The discovery, however, was made at the Minneapolis Public Library when he came across a book about the Faith written by Dr Albert Watson, an early Canadian Bahá'í.[70] What he found intrigued him enough so that he wrote his thesis on the Bahá'í Faith. Though his thesis was accepted and all his course work completed, he was denied his PhD because the university worried that 'a member of a non-mainstream religion could not be an objective scholar of theology'. Ted, however, considered himself to be a Bahá'í by December 1948, before he had even met a member of the Faith.[71]

Soon after declaring, Ted met another new Bahá'í, Canadian nurse Joan, who joined the Faith in 1950. Ted was asked to give her a tour of the House of Worship in Wilmette and they ended up spending the rest of the day together. Ted had been praying for six months to find a wife, so when he returned to his apartment, he immediately wrote Joan a letter and proposed marriage. They were married in June 1952.

A year after they were married, Joan and Ted went to the All-American Intercontinental Teaching Conference in Chicago in May 1953. When the call was made for pioneers, Ted nudged Joan and said, 'Let's go!' She agreed. After attending the Bahá'í summer school in Ontario, they were asked 'How would you like to go to the Yukon?' The young couple walked into the woods, consulted and then agreed. Three months later, they sailed on the last passenger steamer of the year to Skagway, Alaska and boarded the White Pass and Yukon train headed for Whitehorse, with no jobs or a place to stay. They arrived in the town on the banks of the Yukon River at 4 p.m. on 23 September.

Their first impression of Whitehorse, Yukon, home of 5,500 people, was

> one of distinct shock. There were many tar-papered shacks along the railroad tracks. 'Main Street' and all of the other streets were unpaved and dusty. The leaves had already fallen from the little aspen trees, and we knew that winter would probably be coming soon. A fellow passenger on the train, who knew of our plans to settle there, exclaimed, 'If I were you-all, I'd get right back on board this train and head south!' We were tempted to agree with him, but didn't admit it.
>
> We carried some of our baggage a block down Main Street to the Whitehorse Inn – which we were told had changed hands during a poker game. For $7.50 a night we got a room without bath – and, as Joanie noted in her diary, 'PRAYED LIKE MAD!'

They quickly discovered that there was no place for rent; several houses were, however, for sale. They 'looked at several houses for sale, and learned some "unpleasant facts regarding the Yukon". Ted jokingly suggested that if we couldn't find a house we could always live in a nearby abandoned stern-wheeler river boat. Joanie didn't appreciate the joke, and cried.' But then a small house inside a railroad turnaround was discovered, and was purchased on 25 September. The family selling the house was so happy to be rid of it and be able to leave the Yukon that they threw a party for the new owners. At the party, Ted met the accountant for the US Army Pipelines office in Whitehorse and the next day was given a job. By the end of October, Joan had found at job at the Whitehorse General Hospital.

By November, the Arctic winter had closed in and their well went dry. They had to buy '11 pails of water' to be delivered by truck. A week later, that water was gone and they were forced to melt snow. Temperatures were down to −40° C/F by the new year and the water pipes in the kitchen and bathroom kept freezing. One day, Ted 'tried to beat the cold on the long walk to catch the pipelines bus – by wearing a plastic raincoat over his overcoat. When he sat down in the bus the plastic shattered! – much to his embarrassment, and to the amusement of all aboard the bus!'

Ted and Joan survived their first Arctic winter. The next June, they received a letter from the Guardian stating:

> He urges you to concentrate on the native population, as it is for that reason that we have opened new countries to the Faith. May you be confirmed in this teaching effort among the natives. The great goal would be an assembly in Whitehorse, made up of Native Bahá'ís, or at least the majority Natives.

On 17 September, Rex King spent two months in the Whitehorse area on his way to his pioneering post in Alaska. On 1 October, Auxiliary Board member Florence Mayberry arrived for a one-day visit. The teaching activity finally bore fruit when Robin Fowler accepted the Faith on 1 November. Rex also taught the Bahá'í Faith to Dr Donald Kidd, a geologist and 'a deaf mute of great capacity', by typing, lip reading and sign language. Dr Kidd accepted the Faith a year later.

February 1955 was a big month. On the 23rd, Roy and Joan Ziegler arrived as pioneers and, five days later, Christopher Anderson was born. Then in April, the fledgling Bahá'í community faced its first attack when the Anglican Bishop spoke about 'Baha'ism' in his Easter letter, writing that 'Many questions have been asked about the latest cult to arrive in the Yukon largely through the instrumentality of "Uncle Rex" [King]. Space is limited and one can only give a few thoughts gleaned from *The Chaos of the Cults* . . .' Ted initially wrote a rebuttal, but then it was decided to simply begin advertising the Faith in the newspaper. In May, Frances Wells arrived in Whitehorse with a fresh salmon for the Andersons in her suitcase. Frances was on her way to pioneer to Barrow, Alaska.

Another new believer, Lorne Murphy, accepted the Faith in 1956 and Florence Mayberry returned for her second visit in October. The next year, three more people became Bahá'ís and a second son, Mark, was born to the Andersons. In January 1959, the small Bahá'í community set itself a Two Year Plan that called for nine new Bahá'ís by Riḍván 1959, 18 by Riḍván 1960 and 36 by Riḍván 1961, including at least one Native believer. Little did they know what was coming. 1958 was also the inaugural year for the Yukon Bahá'í Conference at Jackson Lake; 28 people attended.

Things began to change in 1959. The first Local Spiritual Assembly of Whitehorse was elected at Riḍván. In July, Ellsworth Blackwell, who had been a member of the US National Spiritual Assembly, came to Whitehorse. Ted invited a member of the Tlingit tribe named Sally Jackson to hear Ellsworth speak. At first she wasn't particularly interested – until she heard that he was black. After that first meeting, she noted:

> The meeting was altogether different from what I imagined. My idea of gatherings of this sort was that it would be solemn and sad, but I was pleasantly surprised. There was laughter and happiness at this fireside and as Ellsworth spoke on about Christ and Bahá'u'lláh and other Prophets gone by, of love and God, I had a feeling that here was something I had been searching for a long, long time. This feeling became stronger as I attended more firesides. The true friendliness and love shown towards me by the Bahá'ís (God bless them) particularly attracted me.[72]

That September, Sally attended the Yukon Bahá'í summer school where she became the first Tlingit to accept the Faith in the Yukon. She was the beginning of a flood. Within the next few decades, almost a hundred members of the Johns family, of which Sally was a part, became Bahá'ís. In 1960, the Whitehorse Bahá'ís were 'praying, united and fervently' for 12 new declarations. Eleven people had come into the Faith, but they were disappointed that they couldn't find the twelfth. Then on 9 September, Chief Albert Isaac arrived at the Andersons' door and related a remarkable story, as recorded here by Ted:

> Within a few minutes Chief Isaac was telling us of a remarkable experience of six days ago . . . He was hungry and fishing was poor and he and his wife prayed to God for help. At the age of 78 . . . he finds it difficult to hunt far from camp. Suddenly he saw something move, discovered by use of glasses that it was a caribou, waited until it moved within range and killed it . . . and thanked God for the answer to his prayer.
>
> The Chief then went on to tell the story of a stirring spiritual

experience he had three years ago . . . he was in the hospital and close to death. As he described it . . . he considered himself dead for two days and walking down the broad highway that forked to heaven and hell. Beyond the fork – on the way to heaven – a Man with a long flowing beard stopped him . . . He reverently described this Man as 'God' and told of being asked, 'What do you drink?' And his honest answer 'liquor'! The Man replied, 'Is not the water I created good enough for you?' He then showed him a small object of unusual shape and design and told the Chief he was sending him back home. Chief Isaac then went on to relate how he seemed to miraculously and quickly visit New York and California, suddenly found himself in the hospital bed again feeling well – returned from the dead . . .

'God answered your prayer and sent you that caribou,' I felt moved to emphatically comment, and added, 'and God brought you and I together here'. I brought out a large photograph of 'Abdu'l-Bahá and showed it to him. He was obviously deeply moved and said 'That's the Man Who talked to me!' . . . I . . .told him the essentials of Bahá'í history and belief . . . After I had shown him where 'Abdu'l-Bahá had travelled . . . he excitedly asked to be shown again where New York and California were . . . the places of his spiritual travels when he was near death three years ago. When I brought him over to the Temple model, I was quite oblivious of the Bahá'í ring hanging from one of the pylons . . . Chief Isaac quickly noticed the ring and identified it with the object of his spiritual experience . . .

Four days later, another person declared, helping them exceed their goal.

In January 1961, the excitement began. Jim Walton, a new young Tlingit Bahá'í, began teaching and at one point

suggested it was time we had a Bahá'í 'fireside' meeting in our home – and that night brought NINE NATIVE FRIENDS (Chief Billy Smith, Mrs Frank Sidney, Fanny Smith, Drury and John McGundy, Scurvy Shorty, Gerald Scarff, Jim and Gladys Smith). Sally Jackson read a little from an Alaskan teaching book – giving the basic principles of the Faith – and Jim Walton translated and explained further in the Tlingit language.

The meeting was wonderful, and when they were finished CHIEF BILLY SMITH . . . said: 'The troubles have been falling on my people like rain, but now God seems to be gathering them all under His tree. I am glad you have told us this.'

Then Jim went around our living room, shook each person's hand, and told us that all nine of them wanted to be Bahá'ís!!! Ted took Jim aside and expressed surprise that they had all accepted the Faith so quickly. Jim said that he had already talked to them before tonight – but agreed to go back and very carefully explain to each one what it meant to be a Bahá'í.

The amazing thing about these new Native Bahá'ís was that they immediately arose and began teaching their families and friends. During the month of January, about three dozen people, mostly Natives, became Bahá'ís. In June, Ted went to the village of Champagne. He recalled that he

was introduced to Chief Johnny Fraser and Bobby Kane. The Chief, to my surprise, said everyone was in the house waiting to hear what I had come to tell them. As we entered the house, I whispered to Dave Jackson to suggest that he give a little talk first. He quickly responded and said words to the effect that the Indian people have been lost long enough, and that the Bahá'í Faith is what they have been waiting and looking for – that unlike the churches we weren't there to ask for money or to run down their native religion or way of life. I vividly recall that he said, 'We have come here for one pure and simple reason, and that is to tell you that Christ has returned. Now Ted Anderson here will tell you more about it.'

I . . . responded with a simple talk about the essentials of the Bahá'í Faith, and pointed out some of the things in the native religion and way of life that Bahá'ís also believed in – such things as honesty, cleanliness, avoiding drinks that destroy the mind, care for orphans, respect for parents and elders, and practical as well as spiritual education for all . . .

. . . Dave Jackson . . . asked Jennie Williams and Katie Ralston to speak in the Indian language of that area and to explain things further. This they did simultaneously in different corners of the Chief's large house.

Then I had an impulse to call on little Peter Johnny to add to this. He jumped up, walked across the room to where about ten people were sitting, and spoke to them in their language in a very animated way. I was told he had said, 'God has gathered us all together under the "Tree of Life" and we are all one big family.'

I sat back and watched the amazing process of every one of these new native believers ardently teaching. Dave Jackson and Frank Williams were deep in conversation with Bobby and Bessie Kane. Jennie Williams and Peter Johnny were talking to the ladies across the room. Katie Ralston was talking with Jessie Allen – and soon afterwards enthusiastically tapped Ted on the shoulder and said, 'My cousin . . . she believe! She Bahá'í!'

After a few minutes, Frank Williams said we have a new brother in our family – Bobby Kane. Dave (Jackson) told me that Bobby had heard of the Bahá'í Faith from Chief Albert Isaac, believed in it, and has been praying that Bahá'ís would come to Champagne! Although he doesn't read much, he is most anxious to learn as much as possible – so he can explain it better to the rest of his people. He fully expects that many more will accept the Faith.

While returning to our car for the drive back to Whitehorse, Dave again surprised me by pulling out of his pocket six signed enrolment cards.

Hand of the Cause <u>Dh</u>ikru'lláh <u>Kh</u>ádem spent a week in Whitehorse in July helping with the amazing teaching campaign.

Entry of Native believers into the Faith continued in 1962. Dora Wedge, who had had a vivid dream about a special man who took her to a 'very beautiful building where people from all over the world were gathered', became a Bahá'í. Years later, when she went on pilgrimage, she recognized the building of her dream as the Shrine of the Báb. In December, Peter Simple, an Athabaskan Indian from Fork Yukon, Alaska, attended a Winter Worship in Whitehorse to give a class on the *Hidden Words*. Before he spoke, Ted gave a talk using copious notes he kept in a big briefcase. Then Peter

> got up and started his little course on *The Hidden Words* of Bahá'u'lláh. With a big twinkle in his eye – and a broad grin on his face – Pete looked at Ted and his big briefcase and said, 'I'm no Ted

Anderson. I don't carry my brains around in a suitcase!' Pete then pulled out from his hip pocket a single piece of paper, unfolded it, and explained that when he was asked to give this course he thought about it, prayed about it . . . and decided that 'God made us perfect, and that's the way he wants us back!'

At Riḍván 1963, three Local Spiritual Assemblies were formed: White-horse, Whitehorse Flats and Carcross. There were 112 Bahá'ís in the Yukon. Florence Mayberry was back again for the Yukon Bahá'í Con-ference in August. In May 1964, the Universal House of Justice gave Canada its goals for the Nine Year Plan. The Whitehorse community was stunned to see that their goal was to form 'at least ten Assemblies in the Yukon'. Luckily, Ugo and Angeline Giachery arrived in June to help. At Jackson Lake, Dr Giachery helped start the first building on the Yukon Bahá'í summer school site: 'Dr. Giachery wielded an axe to start trimming it for further building. Most of the men and many of the women then took a turn with the axe – representing at least four Indian tribes (Yukon, Tlingit, Athabaskan, and Mohawk), Eskimos, Blacks, Jews, Italians (Dr Giachery).'

On 15 January 1965, Ted received a telegram announcing that he had been appointed to the Auxiliary Board for proclamation. A month later, the Whitehorse area Bahá'ís held their first Yukon Bahá'í Conven-tion where they elected six delegates to the National Convention. Three of the delegates were Native. The Andersons attended the Convention, after which Ted made the first tour of 'his' area as an Auxiliary Board member. His travels took him to Ohio, Michigan, Wisconsin, Iowa, Nebraska, Kansas, Oklahoma, Texas, New Mexico, Arizona, California (where they visited the Giacherys), Oregon, Washington and British Columbia before returning to the Yukon.

At the Yukon Bahá'í Convention in January 1968, Johnny Johns, who was not a Bahá'í, brought two of his relatives who were. Ted didn't feel that they could ask Johnny to leave when the Convention started, so Ted asked if he would like to say a prayer. Johnny accepted and recited 'O God! Refresh and gladden my spirit . . .' He was visibly moved by the prayer. Ted then passed out ballots to elect the Convention chair-man. Coming to Johnny, Ted explained that only Bahá'ís could vote. Then he asked if Johnny wanted to vote. Johnny's immediate answer was 'Yes', whereupon he signed a declaration card.

During 1967 and 1970, the Whitehorse Bahá'í community had the bounty of visits by Hands of the Cause Ṭarazu'lláh Samandari and John Robarts, as well as Curtis and Harriet Kelsey, Elena Marsella, Knight of Bahá'u'lláh for the Gilbert and Ellice Islands, Sheila Rice-Wray, Rowena Currington, pioneer to Alaska's Pribloff Islands, and Counsellor Florence Mayberry.

In September 1970, Auxiliary Board member Jenabe Caldwell arrived to begin an ambitious two-month outreach project in order to help reach the House of Justice goal of 10 Local Spiritual Assemblies by Riḍván 1972. Hand of the Cause Enoch Olinga and Counsellor Florence Mayberry provided more inspiration. Three teams were organized: the pre-team to deliver invitations in each community; the main team, which presented the programme; and the follow-up team, who met all new believers and deepened them. In Carmacks ten people enrolled, while in Pelly Crossing, 80 people attended a meeting. At Mayo, Native Louise Profeit was warned that the Bahá'ís were devils. Louise, who later served on the Canadian National Spiritual Assembly, went just to see what devils looked like – and became one herself. In Dawson, 30 people became Bahá'ís. Everywhere, the teaching work was producing incredible results. By the time Enoch Olinga arrived in mid-October, there were 229 new Bahá'ís in the Yukon.

At Riḍván 1971, a year before the end of the Plan, 11 Local Spiritual Assemblies were elected in the Yukon: Whitehorse, Carcross, Carmacks, Pelly Crossing, Dawson, Teslin, Watson Lake, Upper Liard, Whitehorse Flats, Porter Creek and Elsa. The goal had been achieved.

With all of that done, Joan and Ted were given permission to leave Whitehorse. In April 1972, after 19 years in Whitehorse, they moved to Red Deer, Alberta, and started again. They left 400 Bahá'ís in the Yukon and a solid Administrative Order. Many of the Bahá'ís, if not most, were Native, just as Shoghi Effendi had called for.

KEEWATIN

Dick Stanton

In September 1953, Dick Stanton pioneered to the town of Baker Lake in the Keewatin region of far north of Canada. Baker Lake was a tiny Inuit village near the northwest end of Hudson Bay. At that time, Baker

Lake, which began as a trading post for the Hudson's Bay Company, had less than a hundred people. One of his first efforts was to place a copy of *Bahá'u'lláh and the New Era* in the library of the Hudson Bay vessel that visited the village.[73] Dick was forced to leave and in November 1958, Mary and Ken McCulloch were going to Baker Lake to hold the post. In the early 1960s, Dick pioneered to China, where he stayed for five years. He then returned to Canada where he taught at Dunbarton High School in Pickering Township, Ontario.[74]

FRANKLIN

Jameson and Gale Bond

Jameson (Jamie) (1917–2007) and Gale Bond (1919–2009), pioneered to the District of Franklin above the Arctic Circle in July 1953.

In 1945, while serving in the Navy, Jamie met Lloyd Gardner, one of only two Bahá'ís of the 100,000 people in the Canadian Navy. He began attending discussion groups and later that year he met John Robarts, who was visiting Halifax to give a public talk on the Bahá'í Faith. After the war, Jamie moved to Toronto and continued attending Bahá'í meetings and having personal discussions with John Robarts. In April 1947, Jamie went to John Robarts' office and declared his belief in Bahá'u'lláh. He attended the formation of the first National Spiritual Assembly of the Bahá'ís of Canada, in 1948.[75]

Gale Keass, originally from Hungary, immigrated with her family to Alberta, Canada when she was 9 years old. At the age of 20 she moved to Vancouver and in 1942 attended her first fireside. For the next seven years, she continued her search until she accepted Bahá'u'lláh in November 1949. Two months later, she moved to Toronto and in late December 1950, she met Jamie Bond, who was attending university. In 1951, Gale pioneered to Jamaica and Jamie to Coral Harbour in the District of Keewatin, Northwest Territories. During this separation, the two began to correspond.

On 14 July 1953, Jamie and Gale were married in the Maxwell House in Montreal and the next day they boarded an icebreaker and headed for their pioneering post at Arctic Bay at the north end of Baffin Island. The nautical trek took two months and on their way they stopped briefly at Buchanan Bay on Ellesmere Island. While the ship transferred materials for a new police post to shore, the Bonds went ashore then hiked about a mile inland and stopped by a small glacial stream. A few days later, Jamie wrote to Rúḥíyyih Khánum that 'my wife and I were privileged to celebrate the Feast of Names at Buchanan Bay, Ellesmere Island, District of Franklin (Latitude 79° North)'. They included some Arctic poppies picked at the location. Shoghi Effendi cabled the news to the Fourth Intercontinental Teaching Conference in New Delhi, India, included the following: 'Feast Names celebrated last August two stalwart crusaders weather station Buchanan Bay desolate Ellesmere Island latitude seventy-nine degrees less than seven hundred miles from North Pole.'

Jamie began his job at the weather station and Gale cooked for the small crew. Gale had little experience in cooking, but a friend in Toronto had given her a cookbook and the advice to place her trust in Bahá'u'lláh. Their house was heated by a coal stove and a space heater. They had running water from their water barrel that was filled by carrying water from a nearby lake in the warmer months and chunks of ice during the winter.

As their first winter deepened, the sun disappeared and life without the sun became difficult for the small crew. Tensions became intense between the three crew members and Gale and Jamie. The small group were so isolated that resupply was done by parachute. On 17 December 1953, a plane dropped 21 hampers of food and supplies and 17 bags of mail. Life in such an isolated spot was very difficult:

> The bitter cold, the dark months from November to February and the isolation were oppressive. The four men posted at the station took weather readings twice each day and radioed them back to Head Office in Toronto. This took a total of about 5 hours per day for each person. But for Gale, the cook, the work was much harder and longer preparing three meals and afternoon snacks for everyone and managing the many other household duties with the assistance of an Eskimo helper and his daughter.
>
> Worst of all, living in isolation with three strangers who lived by very different values and attitudes from Gale and Jamie led to very stressful relations among them. As relations soured, meals were eaten in tense silence and whenever Gale and Jamie attempted to start a conversation the other men would stamp their feet until Gale

and Jamie would stop talking. Jamie was threatened with physical violence and at one point one of the men became emotionally unstable, threatened Gale's life and had to be evacuated by plane.

Throughout this period and throughout all their time in the Arctic, Gale and Jamie persevered through praying together, reading the Writings and attempting to live their daily lives in accordance with the teachings of the Faith. They held Nineteen-Day Feasts and celebrated the Holy Days. They recorded minutes from their Feasts including the readings that were recited, and the results of their consultation, their teaching plans, problems to be resolved and actions to be taken.[76]

There were no visitors until the following summer. In April 1954, an airdrop of mail brought an unexpected invitation to apply for one of six positions as 'Resident Field Officer – Canadian Arctic'. Only one of the positions was in the District of Franklin, in Frobisher Bay, below the Arctic Circle – the Guardian's goal was the virgin territory of the District of Franklin beyond the Arctic Circle. Gale and Jamie were unsure if Jamie should apply and face the possible loss of their pioneering post. Finally, they decided to fill in the application and see what happened next, knowing that there was no way to mail it. A few days later, a man with a dog sled came through and agreed to carry the letter the 200 miles to the south, from where an aircraft took it on a 'mercy flight' to the Canadian south. Jamie was one of six successful candidates out of 350 applicants.

The Bonds spent two years at Arctic Bay, until August 1955. After leaving Arctic Bay, Jamie met with the Head of the Department of Northern Affairs, and learned that the Anglican and Roman Catholic Bishops, who were members of the territorial council advising the Federal Government on policy, had complained that Gale and Jamie were Bahá'í missionaries and would use his position to promote the Bahá'í Faith. As a result, a condition of his employment was that they were not allowed to teach the Bahá'í Faith to Eskimos (Inuit).

After a series of telegrams to the Guardian, approval was given to proceed with the position in spite of this restriction. The new job began with a six-month orientation in Great Whale River in Northern Quebec. Jamie was then able to return to the District of Franklin in 1956 with a transfer to a new post at Cambridge Bay, above the Arctic

Circle. Gale joined him a short while later when their house was ready.

In 1957 they were invited by the Guardian to go on pilgrimage. To their sorrow, they arrived in London two days after the Guardian passed away. They attended the funeral and brought a large bouquet of roses on behalf of the Knights of Bahá'u'lláh around the world. Pilgrimage was cancelled and Gale and Jamie were about to cancel the rest of their plan, but were encouraged to continue with their trip, so they visited France, Switzerland, Germany, Italy, the islands of Crete and Rhodes as well as Turkey. On the islands of Crete and Rhodes they learned that the Bahá'ís could not openly teach the Faith and were more restricted than Gale and Jamie were in the Canadian Arctic.

Back in Cambridge Bay, they rededicated themselves to serving the Faith. They could not teach the Inuit people but nothing was said about not teaching the non-native residents. Although Jamie had to be more careful because of his position, Gale used every opportunity to mention the Faith whenever they had visitors or opportune moments with non-native members of the community.

The Bonds lived in Cambridge Bay until 1962. During this time, they adopted an 11-month-old baby girl they named Susan and then, three years later, a 16-month-old boy they named David.

In September 1961, the local Anglican Minister's stove blew up. The Minister, Reverend Bill Evans, went to Jamie for a new stove and then Gale began a conversation with him about the Bahá'í Faith. She lent him *The Heart of the Gospel* by George Townshend. A few days later he came back asking for another book, and she gave him *Gleanings from the Writings of Bahá'u'lláh* and *Kitáb-i-Íqán: The Book of Certitude*. She told Bill that these books were the Sacred Writings of Bahá'u'lláh, the Prophet-Founder of the Bahá'í Faith and the Messenger of God for this age.

What followed were months of clandestine meetings involving Gale, Jamie, Bill, and his wife Muriel. Bill declared his belief in Bahá'u'lláh to the Bonds on 6 December 1961. Four days later, Bill finished the service in his church, removed his robes and announced to the congregation that he had become a Bahá'í. Not long after this, the Bonds were moved to Frobisher Bay and then to Pond Inlet, all still within the District of Franklin.

The Bonds stayed in the District of Franklin to the end of the Ten Year Crusade, when Jamie's declining health forced them to leave. Jamie was instrumental in arranging for a replacement pioneer, Tom

Garraway, so that the goal was not lost. Jamie was elected to the Canadian National Spiritual Assembly in 1967 and served there until April 1982. In a later letter to John Leonard in the Falkland Islands, he wrote:

> In 1982, I was released from many years service on the Canadian NSA so Gale and I responded to the wonderful statement of the Guardian and the House about the 'water (southern) hemisphere', about the spiritual significance of the islands of the Pacific and about the spiritual axis with Australia and Japan as the pole!
>
> So we spent 8 months as travelling teachers in Oceania and the following year returned to New Zealand as pioneers.[77]

The Bonds settled in New Zealand in 1985. Jamie served on the National Spiritual Assembly from 1986 to 1988. In 1988, they moved to Vancouver Island, Canada. During these years, Gale made 11 teaching trips to Hungary between 1974 and 1992 and represented the Canadian National Spiritual Assembly at the election of the first National Spiritual Assembly of the Bahá'ís of Hungary. Gale returned to Hungary in 1993 for the celebration of the 80th anniversary of 'Abdu'l-Bahá's visit to that country. She visited once more in 1998.

Over their six decades of dedicated service to the Faith, Gale and Jamie Bond made numerous travel-teaching trips to more than 50 countries in five continents, from the Arctic Archipelago to the South Pacific to Eastern Europe. They participated in various historic events throughout their years of service marking a unique period in the development of the Cause of Bahá'u'lláh across the planet.

LABRADOR

Howard Gilliland and Bruce Matthew

Howard Gilliland (1920–1962), an Air Force captain, reached Labrador through the military in early 1954 as the communication officer.[78] Howard became a Bahá'í in November 1948 in Great Falls, Montana. At Goose Bay, he had great difficulty finding somewhere to live because of a policy that gave high-ranking officers priority. Twice he was offered a house only to have the offers rescinded. In May 1954, his wife, Sue, was planning to join him with their children because housing was

Rose Perkal, Knight of Bahá'u'lláh to Kodiak Island, Alaska,
a photo taken on arrival, August 1953

Ben Guhrke, Knight of Bahá'u'lláh to Kodiak Island, Alaska,
with (left to right) *Helen Gregg, Mary Jane Mikoria and*
Carole Kelsey

very low*Contributed by the National Spiritual Assembly of the Bahá'ís of Alaska*

Helen Robinson, Knight of Bahá'u'lláh to Baranof Island, with her family Donna, Rob and Robbie, 1945

Gail Avery Davis, Knight of Bahá'u'lláh to Baranof Island, on Sitka, 1979, with (left to right) Carol Simpson, Carolyn Ramsey, Bart Southwick, Alice Machesny and Evert Simpson

© Ebony magazine

Grace Bahovec, Knight of Bahá'u'lláh to Baranof Island, mountaineering with her husband Fred, 1948, and in her jewellery workshop

Knights of Bahá'u'lláh to the Aleutian Islands: Elinore Putney, Knight of Bahá'u'lláh, with her husband George Putney (left), Elaine and Jenabe Caldwell (right), Knights of Bahá'u'lláh, with Vassa Lekanoff

Joan and Ted Anderson, Knights of Baha'u'llah to Yukon, with sons Chris and Mark, in Whitehorse, 1958

Dick (Richard) Stanton, Knight of Bahá'u'lláh to Keewatin

Jameson and Gale Bond, Knights of Bahá'u'lláh to Franklin, stopping at Craig Harbour, Ellesme[re] Island on the way to their pioneer post

Bruce Matthew, Knight of Bahá'u'lláh to Labrador

Edythe MacArthur, Knight of Bahá'u'lláh to Queen Charlotte Islands

Catherine and Cliff Huxtable, Knights of Bahá'u'lláh to the Gulf Islands, on Salt Spring Island, 1959

Doris Richardson, Knight of Bahá'u'lláh to Grand Manan Island

Kathleen Weston, Knight of Bahá'u'lláh to the Magdalen Islands

©USBNA

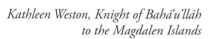

©USBNA

Kay Zinky, Knight of Bahá'u'lláh to the Magdalen Islands

Irving and Grace Geary, Knights of Bahá'u'lláh to Cape Breton Island

Jeanne Allen, Knight of Bahá'u'lláh to Cape Breton Island. Her husband Frederick (not shown) was also named a Knight

Ola Pawlowska, Knight of Bahá'u'lláh to St Pierre and Miquelon Islands, with Roland Lettuenen, later to become professor of French at York University, Toronto

Mary Zabolotny McCulloch, Knight of Bahá'u'lláh to Anticosti Island, with her husband Ken McCulloch in 1964

supposed to be available. Unfortunately, the house offer was revoked and she never was able to go to Labrador. Teaching the Bahá'í Faith at an Air Force base was difficult in that most people were transient, only there for a short while. Howard left in February 1955 and was killed in a car accident in 1962.[79]

Bruce Matthew (?–2007) was born in Scotland, but in 1949 was living in Hertfordshire, England. Bruce had decided that a world government was the key to creating world peace, so he began searching for an organization promoting such an idea. After moving to Canada in September of 1953, he saw a small advertisement in the *Toronto Star* newspaper about a public meeting at the Bahá'í Centre. After listening to Laura Davis speak at the meeting,

> he went over to a group of the ladies and asked, 'Do you believe in world government?' They replied, 'Oh yes, see here this poster which lists the principles of the Bahá'í Faith.' Bruce exclaimed, 'Oh good, I'd like to become a Bahá'í!' They replied, 'Oh no, first you have to attend firesides so that you know what you are accepting'. . . Bruce got Laura's address and went to her home most Saturday nights for the rest of the year. 'I could have and would have declared at any moment, but it wasn't until December that Laura remarked to me that she thought I was ready, and so I "declared" then'.[80]

Three months later, in March 1954, Bruce volunteered to pioneer. He was interviewed by the Goals Committee who asked him to go to Goose Bay, Labrador. Goose Bay had an important airfield run cooperatively by the American and Canadian Air Forces and the only way to get there was to secure a job with a company called Drake-Merritt in Moncton, New Brunswick. He flew to Moncton on 20 April and an interview was arranged:

> It was a day of brilliant sunshine which, coming through the windows of the bus, left me feeling uncomfortably hot. The second part of the trip, about two miles, was completed on foot. I removed my coat – a rash move in light of what happened later, as a cool wind was blowing – to enjoy the walk.
> When I met the personnel officer he said . . . I wouldn't be interested in the only position they had to offer, because of my teaching

qualifications. So I asked him what the position was and he said, a medical secretary in the hospital. They had a small hospital on the base. I said, 'I'll take it.' He looked at me, and I repeated, 'I'll take it.' So he agreed . . . I accepted at once and was told to return on Wednesday, April 21, at 9:00 a.m., to embark by air for Goose Bay. This date happened to be the deadline the Guardian had given for all pioneers to reach their new goals. I was jubilant.

But later in the afternoon I started sneezing. I was privileged to attend the election of the Moncton Assembly that evening, the 20th, but by this time my eyes were streaming and my head was so clogged up I felt quite ill. After the election was completed . . . I made arrangements for a taxi . . . returned to my hotel and tumbled into bed.

In the small hours, a most strange thing happened. I had been fast asleep when, with startling suddenness, I sat bolt upright in bed. Instantly I was wide awake . . . My first feeling was that of bewilderment . . . then my mind focused clearly and the reason became apparent. My face was flushed and my body burning with fever. I was very ill indeed. Immediately I was plunged into gloom, and could have wept, for I knew I was quite unfit to go to Goose Bay in four or five hours.

I knew I must take action at once – but what? If I called a doctor, he might pack me off to hospital. That was quite unthinkable. What other solution was there? Perhaps I can be forgiven for not thinking of it sooner, but my head throbbed painfully and my heart was heavy with melancholy at the thought that after all I might not get to Goose Bay in time. In resignation I had stretched out my hand to pick up the phone to call a doctor when the thought occurred to me: healing prayers!

I . . . hastily turned the pages of the red prayer book to the first healing prayer. I could barely say the words, which in my state were meaningless, I was too ill to concentrate. As I was nearing the end of the second healing prayer I suffered what I can only describe as a seizure. The blood drained from my body, starting at the scalp and passing downward in an ice-cold wave, leaving gelid prickles in its wake. My breathing became painfully constricted. I had to force out the words of the third healing prayer in slow gasps. I truly thought I was going to die . . .

Again, with the most astonishing abruptness, the blood returned to my body and the fever lifted . . . It seemed I was cured . . . I sat on the edge of the bed waiting for the fever to strike again. Eventually . . . I was convinced. Except for a sniffle, I was quite well.[81]

When Bruce arrived at Goose Bay the next day, he was surprised to find that he was sharing an open barracks room with 20 other men in bunk beds. Beyond the lack of privacy, his bed was near the door and consequently had a constant stream of men passing by, all too often in states of inebriation.

Bruce and Howard met when they could, but Howard's work schedule required him to work from very early to very late. They did commonly manage to meet for lunch on Sunday. At one point, Howard's roommate was away and he invited Bruce to use the empty bed for a break from the barracks. That night, after Bruce had said his prayers aloud, he noted that Howard said his prayers silently and thought that was a little strange. The next morning, Howard left early and Bruce got up and began saying his prayers aloud. Almost immediately, a loud voice began complaining from the next room and Bruce learned why Howard prayed silently – the rooms had paper-thin walls.[82]

By October, Bruce had become an Air Force Court Reporter, but was a civilian working amongst military people. Teaching was very difficult though he tried his best, passing out a considerable quantity of pamphlets.[83] Bruce lamented, 'Perhaps the Guardian will some day tell us why it is that people always wait until they have one foot on a train, boat or plane before they casually turn and ask, 'By the way, what is this Bahá'í Faith?'[84] One man, searching for a Qur'án, was introduced to the Faith and soon said that he was considering becoming a Bahá'í. Three months later, however, he went to England for his education.[85]

In 1956, after 20 months, Bruce's job was phased out and he moved to St Johns on Newfoundland Island. There he met Bill Howells, the first pioneer there, and the two taught the Faith. Bruce ran a short-lived secretarial school, then worked as a secretarial teacher at the Sanatorium and in a vocational school. He left St Johns in 1965 and moved to a town near Windsor, Ontario, and later to Alliston, Ontario, north of Toronto.[86]

QUEEN CHARLOTTE ISLANDS, BRITISH COLUMBIA

Edythe MacArthur

Canadian Edythe MacArthur (1906–1994) and her sister, Doris Richardson, both wanted to become Knights of Bahá'u'lláh and both achieved their goals, albeit on opposite coasts of Canada: Edythe pioneered to the Queen Charlotte Islands off the western coast of British Columbia in August 1953 and Doris to Grand Manan Island on the Atlantic side of the continent.

Edythe was born into an evangelical Christian family and it was at a Revival meeting that she 'thought that there just had to be a bigger, better and broader way to be of service to the whole wide world than to stand up and be "saved"'. She became a Bahá'í in a Toronto suburb in 1936.[87] In 1948, she pioneered for the first time. It was not a successful adventure. After a time, she was overcome with loneliness and one night she abruptly left and went home. Arriving there, she learned that her father had passed away the night before. She said she was never sure whether she had failed the pioneering test or answered divine guidance.[88]

Edythe's next pioneering post, Calgary, was more successful and she was on 'cloud nine'. Then John Robarts asked if she would pioneer to Kingston, Newfoundland. Spending a year and a half there, Edythe said that it was 'one of the most compatible Bahá'í communities' and was a 'peek into a heaven'.[89] In 1953, Edythe attended the Intercontinental Bahá'í Conference in Chicago. She wrote that some went 'never to return the same as they had arrived . . . My Spiritual Mother (my sister Doris Richardson) signed immediately – she to Grand Manan Island, East Coast of Canada, and I to the Queen Charlotte Islands, West Coast of Canada. John Robarts, with whom we registered, coined a phrase, "we had covered the water fronts".'[90]

Edythe's pioneering post in the Queen Charlotte Islands was isolated and four miles from her nearest neighbour: 'I learned isolation. My daily visitors were mostly black bears, coons, chicken hawks and herds of deer.' But when Edythe discovered the island's native people, she wrote: 'This Queen Charlotte Island was not only special, but especially special. On its land there is one of the greatest and most widely known Canadian Indian tribes – the Haida.' Edythe was joined by other pioneers and a group was soon formed.[91]

In 1954, she asked Shoghi Effendi for permission to pioneer to Africa, which was granted.[92] For two years, she was the nurse for the Canadian Hadden family, who had pioneered to South Africa. When the Haddens returned to Canada, Edythe moved to Southern Rhodesia and managed a small hotel for several years. Of those years, she wrote:

> The garment of words couldn't possibly contain what passion I feel for this land, Africa, and its people. The love, the tragedies one experiences on that part of the earth's surface, is engraved for all time within the habitation of the heart. We formed the first LSA in Capetown. I pioneered to Windhoek, S.W. Africa. There, I was on the 'treason list' as a possible suspect as one believing in the 'brother-hood of man'. I was a Bahá'í-sitter (as John R. [Robarts] named me) in Zululand for a year and a half. It was here I learned the African is closer to knowing God, and is prepared, listening and waiting for the 'return of a Redeemer'. It was a bit startling to realize that here on this Continent [North America] we are still to be convinced [of] there being a God. Our noonday prayer is a constant reminder. With the African, it is a reality. My heart bled when I left Africa.[93]

After two years in Africa, Edythe returned to Canada and pioneered to the Queen Charlotte Islands, again, and then to several communities in Ontario, to Yellowknife, Northwest Territories, Labrador and Nova Scotia. Her last pioneering post was Bowmanville, Ontario,[94] where she spent the rest of her life.[95]

GULF ISLANDS, BRITISH COLUMBIA

Catherine and Cliff Huxtable

Catherine (1932–1967) and Cliff Huxtable (b.1932) pioneered to the Gulf Islands, a group of islands off the coast of Vancouver Island, Canada, on 13 October 1959. The Gulf Islands were not on the Guard-ian's original list of pioneering goals, but in January 1956, after several years of futile efforts to fill the goal to Anticosti Island (see below), the Guardian gave the Canadian National Spiritual Assembly permission to choose another goal. They chose to replace Anticosti Island in the Atlantic with the Gulf Islands in the Pacific:

He has decided that, in view of the fact that Anticosti is so extremely difficult to get into, the Canadian Assembly can choose some other goal as substitute for Anticosti. In other words, a territory or an island in the vicinity of Canada, which has never been opened to the Faith, may be opened in the place of Anticosti, and thus the goals of the Ten Year Plan will not be decreased. On the other hand, Anticosti should be maintained as an objective; and every effort be made to get a Bahá'í in there.[96]

Interestingly, within a few months, Mary Zabolotny did manage to fill the Anticosti goal, but the Gulf Islands goal remained.

Catherine's life was beset with health problems. At the age of ten, she was diagnosed with a rare type of muscular dystrophy and given only a decade to live. At the age of 15, she was confined to a wheelchair. Cliff and Catherine met at a dance at the University of Toronto in 1950 that Catherine attended as a spectator, and two years later both had embraced the Faith. Cliff first learned about the Bahá'í Faith from his brother, Wes Huxtable, who became a Bahá'í in the late 1940s. Cliff and Catherine married in May 1955.[97]

When Shoghi Effendi told the Toronto Bahá'ís to disperse in 1956, the Huxtables, accompanied by Eileen White Collins, sister of poet Roger White and not a Bahá'í at that time, pioneered to Regina, Saskatchewan, arriving at the end of 1957. They helped reform the Local Spiritual Assembly, then in 1959, intrigued by the view of the distant Gulf Islands during a visit to West Vancouver, the Huxtables decided to pioneer there.

This time Cliff and Catherine were accompanied by Bernice Boulding who, like Eileen, was not a Bahá'í. The trio arrived on Salt Spring Island on 13 October 1959. The next year, Bernice became the first person to declare her faith in Bahá'u'lláh in the Gulf Islands. Cliff, with an Honours degree in Arts and Sciences, began working as a self-employed manual labourer, digging ditches, clearing brush, doing form and concrete work, and rough carpentry. With the benevolent assistance of the island 'baron' Gavin Mouat, Cliff found a job as a deckhand on the British Columbia ferries. In the winter of 1960, Mr Mouat convinced Cliff to accept the position of principal of a small elementary school on Saturna Island for the remainder of the school year. The Huxtables returned to Salt Spring Island during the summer vacation. A highlight of this time was meeting with Rúḥíyyih Khánum in West Vancouver in 1960. Rúḥíyyih Khánum and Catherine continued to correspond following their meeting.

When Catherine became pregnant, her doctor advised abortion because of her weakened state, but following a normal pregnancy and delivery, their healthy son, Gavin Clifford Huxtable, was born on 27 June 1962. Because of Catherine's radiant, winsome personality and wheelchair status, the Huxtables' friendly hospitality, and Cliff's position as teacher and later vice-principal, the couple became well-liked, familiar figures on the island of some 1,500 souls. Although they proceeded cautiously at first, the Huxtables began to hold firesides within a few months of their arrival. Cliff wrote:

> Catherine had a warm and sincere interest in everyone she met. Their home was open to all comers even to the sacrifice of her precarious health which required an ordered, settled and tranquil existence. Her dynamic contentment afforded encouragement to others burdened with difficulties. Her illness was turned into a blessing, and her overcoming its limitations, an instrument of attraction.[98]

About 1960, a local doctor and Oxford don, British mountaineer Dr Robert Bourdillon, introduced the Huxtables to Fletcher and Elinor Bennett at a child-rearing group. By 1963, the Bennetts had become Bahá'ís. Fletcher went on to be appointed an Auxiliary Board member and flew his personal plane all over the west of Canada and Alaska. Following the arrival of pioneer Kate Saunders and three other new enrolments, the first Local Spiritual Assembly of the Gulf Islands was formed on 21 April 1964, with Catherine elected chairman.

By 1962, Cliff had become joint vice-principal of the newly built consolidated high school in the main town of Ganges. With the added domestic responsibilities that came after the birth of Gavin, Catherine's declining health, and the stress of dealing with students' discipline problems, in addition to finding and employing new helpers for Catherine, Cliff's health began to fail. Doctors recommended two years of bed rest for acute exhaustion. The proverbial last straw that finally induced them to leave the island was nine months of ongoing harassment from a mentally deranged neighbour over a minor property dispute the man instigated. The neighbour intermittently threatened Cliff with a rifle during this period. For their own well-being and survival, the Huxtables began to make plans to leave the Gulf Islands.

The way out came at the May 1965 Canadian National Bahá'í Convention in Winnipeg, Saskatchewan, which Cliff attended as one of the newly elected regional delegates. Following a stirring appeal for pioneers by Hand of the Cause Dhikru'lláh Khádem, and after an all-night prayer vigil with friends, Cliff was moved again to pioneer – this time to St Helena Island in the South Atlantic, a goal that the Canadian National Spiritual Assembly had recently acquired. When Cliff phoned Catherine the next morning to inform her of his decision, she readily agreed. 'I have been praying for a miracle,' she said. 'Let's go.' After making a cross-Canada travel-teaching trip from October 1965 to May 1966, the Huxtables made their way, via Dublin and London, to mountainous St Helena Island where they arrived on 9 April 1966.

St Helena is a small island 2,000 kilometres west of the African continent in the middle of the Atlantic Ocean. In the insular atmosphere of the 16-kilometre-long island, teaching the Bahá'í Faith was a slow, cautious process. Against all odds, Cliff succeeded in finding employment as principal of the Secondary Selective School, a job that included a house. Over the next 16 months, Catherine's health declined rapidly. She died in Cliff's arms in the early morning of 25 October 1967, beating the doctors' diagnosis by 15 years. Catherine was buried high in the centre of the island overlooking the majestic scenery of St Helena to the South Atlantic beyond. Two years later, upon the recommendation of the Hands of the Cause, the Universal House of Justice named the Huxtables as Knights of Bahá'u'lláh for the Gulf Islands. That same year, 1969, Cliff married a local St Helenian, Delia Duncan, who later became a Bahá'í. They had two children, Jane and Robert. Cliff and Delia Duncan Huxtable remain today on St Helena Island.

GRAND MANAN ISLAND, NEW BRUNSWICK

Doris Richardson

Doris Richardson (1901–1976) was born in Ontario, Canada and became a Bahá'í in 1939. She married American Mr Richardson when she was just sixteen. Mr Richardson's mother was a strong Catholic and pressured Doris to raise her own son in that faith. Doris, however, stood fast in her beliefs. Her search for the truth led her to Mary Baker Eddy and Christian Science, but some of the teachings such as racial intolerance pushed her away, so when Howard and Mabel Ives introduced the Richardsons to the Faith, Doris accepted the message. Doris's daughter, Helen Charters, remembered that Mr Richardson loved playing the 'devil's advocate' at his wife's firesides and though he never became a Bahá'í he 'deeply respected the Bahá'í Faith and what it meant to Mother'.[99]

Doris's Sunday firesides attracted many university students. She also conducted a children's class.[100] She was elected to the first National Spiritual Assembly of Canada in 1948[101] and spent her Bahá'í life as a pioneer, first to Scarborough, Ontario, then to the Maritime region in 1951, answering a call of the Guardian. With Shoghi Effendi's call for pioneers in the Ten Year Crusade, Doris arose and went to Grand Manan Island on 2 September 1953, where she lived until 1974, supporting herself by managing a summer hotel, the Marathon Inn, and acting as a matron at a girls' school. She also travelled around the islands in the area selling biscuits.[102] In 1958, Doris excitedly announced the first Bahá'í declaration on the island:

How wonderful to be able to share with you my supreme joy! After four years . . . to have someone say they wanted to be a Bahá'í, and begin to read and search is perhaps an experience that is indescribable. It has been my feeling for some time that Edward Somers was a believer, and recognized Bahá'u'lláh; nevertheless he had not really done any studying for himself until this summer.

Then, when Arno Chesley was here recently on her vacation, he declared his belief in the Bahá'í Faith to her . . . Bless him, for he little realizes what it means to be the first believer on Grand Manan.[103]

In 1958, Doris submitted an article to the Grand Manan newspaper and was surprised and delighted to see that it was printed just as she had written it. It was the first time the Faith had been mentioned in the paper and a sign that both she and the Faith had been accepted.[104]

Doris remained on Grand Manan until the formation of the first Local Spiritual Assembly. She passed away, still at her post, in 1976.

MAGDALEN ISLANDS, NEW BRUNSWICK

Kathleen Weston

The Magdalen Islands are at the mouth of the St Lawrence River in Canada. Kathy Weston was the first pioneer to reach the islands when she landed in Charlottetown on Prince Edward Island on 22 September 1953. Her husband Ernest followed her and was able to find a job, but by mid-January 1954, he had lost the job and they were finding that teaching the Bahá'í Faith was very difficult. The result, however, was that they began to learn about the importance of prayer:

> . . . we have been tested . . . Ernest lost his job and I took sick . . . and working very hard under difficulties. I was becoming terribly concerned and impatient feeling that we had not been doing enough – there just was no one to tell about the Faith. I felt I myself had not been really an instrument in Bahá'u'lláh's hands . . . because of all this – Ernest and I are really learning dependence on prayer. Ernest had never felt he knew how to use prayer. I was beginning to feel I was not worthy to pray – We borrowed [a] little prayer book . . . and we read and studied and we prayed.[105]

Through sincere prayer, they soon began finding people interested in spiritual matters. A girl attending university elsewhere came home for Christmas and connected with the Westons. Then a man came to them asking about the Faith. They held a fireside and ten seekers showed up. Kathleen wrote that 'Ernest spoke on servitude – we discussed till 1 a.m. The boys were deeply interested and several of the girls intensely interested. Oh dear Ruth [Moffett] how thrilled we were – our prayers were being answered – Ernest knows the importance of prayer.' In January 1954, they held a public meeting for World Religion Day.[106]

Kay Zinky

On 15 April 1954, Kay Zinky (1903–2000) landed on Grindstone Island, northeast of Prince Edward Island. Kay was a teacher, opera singer and inventor before she became a Knight of Bahá'u'lláh. In 1938, she sang with the Pueblo (Colorado) Symphony. She also sang at the

Hollywood Bowl and at a World's Fair. She learned of the Bahá'í Faith
from Loulie Mathews and enrolled in 1947.[107] Kay's grandson described
her as his 'fiercely energetic, take-no-prisoners grandmother' who 'had
amazed her contemporaries by inventing silk stockings that wouldn't
run during World War II'.[108]

When Kay first arrived in Montreal, the committee handling the
pioneers held her there for several weeks because of the possibility that
she could open the difficult post of Anticosti Island, a privately-held
island. She also needed time to resolve her request for residency. In
the end, she found that she needed to have proof of her husband Raymond's approval before the residency could be given.[109]

Kay's first attempts at teaching sent alarm bells through the residents
of the remote island, who initially thought the Bahá'ís were Jehovah's
Witnesses. Kay was encouraged to teach by living a Bahá'í life. She
began to meet people by giving classes on painting, lectures and courses
on making hats, sewing and singing. During her first few months, she
visited Entry Island, Grand Entry Island, Gros Isle and Old Harry
Island, meeting several hundred people, but the trips required finding a
car or someone to drive her. By September, Mr and Mrs Larry Rowdon
had joined her on Grindstone.[110] Kay described the experience of living
on Grindstone Island in the winter of 1954–55:

The wind is whistling here these days, and we have had snow flur-
ries and ice. I am settled in my cottage with no water, no bath, but
electricity. The other pioneers here have a house, and as they have
no bed, they gathered grass and dried it, then sewed it into burlap
bags for their mattress on the floor. We are all learning how to get
along, aren't we? I am making friends, real ones, which is just what
our Guardian said to do.[111]

With the Anniversary of the Ascension of 'Abdu'l-Bahá I realized
some kind of climax was being reached, and with an overflowing
sense of gratitude I realized that a great many of my prayers were
being answered beautifully.[112]

In December, Kay noted that she had moved six times in her first six
months on the island, but that she was finally settled next door to the
biggest general store. This made it easy for people to drop by for a chat.

On 17 January, however, she wrote the New Territories Committee and broached the subject of leaving the island. She had been away from her husband for nine months, living in a house banked with eel grass in an attempt to ward off the chill. She had to carry all drinking and cooking water. On top of the basic hardships of life, being a single woman living alone was creating problems. Kay wrote:

> My position of being a married woman, seemingly happily married, they just can't understand. I can't teach young men who might be eager, or older men, they won't come near me partly for that reason I'd say. I've had several unpleasant experiences of men knocking on my door in the middle of the night and several making advancements.[113]

The New Territories Committee agreed that she had done her duty to open and hold a virgin territory, thus winning the goal, and allowed her to return to her home and Raymond in Colorado. She left about the beginning of March 1955, leaving the Rowdons to carry on.[114] Kay didn't think that she had done enough to deserve the title of Knight of Bahá'u'lláh, and wrote to the Guardian saying so. He responded, 'It's too late. Your name is already on the Scroll!'[115]

Returning to Colorado, Kay crossed the country on travel-teaching trips and served on the El Paso County West (Colorado) Spiritual Assembly. She also gave talks at summer schools and taught the Faith in Mexico and American Indian Reservations. In 1963, her research uncovered about 300 unknown Bahá'í Tablets. The next year, Kay went on pilgrimage and then travelled to Istanbul and Adrianople in Turkey, then Africa and Canada. She also compiled correspondence of Martha Root into the book *Martha Root: Herald of the Kingdom*.[116]

CAPE BRETON ISLAND, NOVA SCOTIA

Irving and Grace Geary

Irving (1887–1984) and Grace Geary (1888–1965) pioneered to Cape Breton Island, Nova Scotia, Canada on 11 October 1953. Irving was born in England and moved to Canada in 1906. He and Grace were married in 1912. The Gearys came into the Bahá'í Faith when Mabel

Rice-Wray Ives made a teaching trip to Moncton, New Brunswick, where the Gearys were living, in 1937. They were able to form the first Local Spiritual Assembly of Moncton the following year. In 1944, during the first Seven Year Plan, the Gearys pioneered to Charlottetown on Prince Edward Island. In 1951 the Canadian National Spiritual Assembly requested the Gearys to move to Halifax, Nova Scotia.[117]

After the 1953 Intercontinental Teaching Conference in Chicago, Grace volunteered them to open Cape Breton Island since Irving's work was taking him there. The couple arrived on 12 October and moved into the only house available in the town of Baddeck, a poorly insulated summer cottage, as Grace noted:

> The only place we could find to live in was a little cabin at the back of one of the hotels. It was not winterized and was very cold and drafty. Irving had to return to Canso, Nova Scotia, where his work was being held up. He did not expect to be in Baddeck before Christmas. I struggled on alone, but found it very difficult when the snow came, for I had to go halfway up a field to an old barn where the coal for the kitchen stove was kept. One day I decided I could not go on like this any more, and I said the Remover of Difficulties over and over again. Inside of 10 days, Irving's work had been transferred to Baddeck and by the beginning of February we had found a warm, comfortable apartment, where we remained during our stay in Baddeck. Irving joined the choir of one of the churches, but not the church. I became the librarian at a small public library.[118]

Irving had learned the art of old English script and put that to work to support them. In 1959, Irving and Grace moved to Sydney, another town on the island, and stayed there until 1961 when they were asked to return to Charlottetown on Prince Edward Island to preserve the Local Spiritual Assembly. They had the great bounty of attending the World Congress in London in 1963.[119]

Frederick and Jeanne Allen

Frederick and Jeanne Allen (1911–1969) also pioneered to Cape Breton Island, arriving a day after the Gearys and finding a place about 80 kilometres away from them.[120] Jeanne became a Bahá'í in British Columbia in 1940 and married Frederick a year later. During the Intercontinental Conference in Wilmette, they were inspired to volunteer as pioneers, selecting Cape Breton Island.

They opened a small grocery store and even though that required 'long hours and remaining open during the evenings . . . it provided an opportunity to meet many people and Jeanne was never too weary to invite them to her home to talk about the Bahá'í Faith. She had great tact and patience in explaining the principles of the Faith and in answering the questions of seekers.' Some of the high points of their time on the island were visits by Rúḥíyyih Khánum and Hand of the Cause John Robarts. They remained at their post until 1962, when economic conditions forced them to return to British Columbia where they spent their remaining years serving on various communities in the Okanagan Valley area.[121]

ST PIERRE AND MIQUELON ISLANDS (NEAR NEWFOUNDLAND)

Ola Pawlowska

Ola Pawlowska (1910–2004) pioneered to St Pierre Island in October 1953. She was originally from Poland, but escaped the German invasion with her daughter, Suzanne, in 1939 and ended up in Canada in August 1941. She first came into contact with the Bahá'í Faith in Winnipeg in 1944 and became a Bahá'í three years later. When the 1953 Intercontinental Conference was announced, Ola could not afford to go, but she bought the book *God Passes By* and became very inspired by it. In September 1953, Ola went to a Teaching Conference in Toronto and heard the call for pioneers and one place quickly caught her eye – St Pierre and Miquelon Islands, off the southern coasts of Newfoundland. Though just a few kilometres off the coast, the islands were the last remnant of France's New World colony and French was the dominant language.[122]

On 15 October 1953, Ola landed on St Pierre Island:

> How to describe the feeling I had, flying to this speck of rock on the grey Atlantic? In a way it was as if a mighty wind had broken my earthly moorings and was carrying me on the wings of 'be dependent on God alone'. It was a feeling at times described as a state of grace . . .

On the island it was cold and windy; the salty air and the presence of the ocean all conspired to give me a sense of unreality. After registering at Hotel Robert, an old wooden structure on the square, I prayed in the cold room. Here I was, an envoy from the Mighty King to this speck of land.[123]

Ola had 'friendly relations' with some of the local people, but others accused her to the Governor of being a spy, an accusation he laughed off, pointing out that there was nothing to spy on in St Pierre. For two years, Ola was given the 'outcast treatment'. All conversation stopped when she walked by or entered a store, gossip was spread about her and curtains were closed. To pass the time, she began to translate the *Bahá'í World* into Polish and took long, solitary walks in the hills. Ola rented a room over the kitchen at the Pension Lefèvre. This meant it was warm, but the noise made the Fast very difficult. To carry out the Fast, Ola was given permission to use a cabin about three kilometres out of town. After supper, she walked to the cabin carrying her prayer book, a thermos, some sandwiches and her alarm clock, which she had to put on her stomach at night to keep it from freezing. When she returned to town the next morning, there were many strange looks at this odd person.[124]

Her breakthrough came when she befriended a ten-year-old boy who liked to write poetry. His friendship opened up his parents and then others. His father being the Mayor of the town made her even more acceptable. But other than managing to make friends with a few of the islanders, Ola's attempts to teach the Faith were not overtly successful. After four years, Ola asked Shoghi Effendi if she might leave her post. His reply was that she could – if there was a replacement to fill such a hard-won goal. In April, a replacement was found and Ola left and went to England, and then continued on to Poland. In 1961, Ola pioneered to Africa, where she remained for over 30 years.[125] During Rúḥíyyih Khánum's 'Great African Safari', Ola travelled with her, for six weeks in Zambia during December and January of 1971–72 and five weeks in Zaire a year later.[126] In later life she returned to her native Poland, where she participated in the establishment of the Bahá'í community.

ANTICOSTI ISLAND, QUEBEC

Mary Zabolotny

In April 1956, one of the more difficult of Shoghi Effendi's Ten Year Crusade posts was finally filled: Anticosti Island, at the mouth of the St Lawrence River. Mary Zabolotny (1918–1996) was born in Manitoba, Canada, of Ukrainian immigrants, and attended the Winnipeg Art School. After school, she worked as a commercial artist and made several trips with a fellow artist to the Yukon and Alaska. In 1951, Mary received a pamphlet on the Bahá'í Faith from another artist she had known at school, Leonard Woods. She was immediately ready to learn more, but it was three months before he visited her and took her to a fireside. Mesmerised, she attended the firesides every Friday night until October 1951 when she declared her faith. Soon afterwards, she pioneered to Saskatoon, Saskatchewan and helped form the first Local Spiritual Assembly. Mary moved in succession to Verdun, St Lambert and Westmount, all in Quebec, and helped form assemblies in those communities.[127]

Then the New Territories Committee asked her to go to Anticosti Island. The Canadian National Spiritual Assembly had tried for three years to get a pioneer onto the island. The problem was that the island was privately owned and only people employed by the company were allowed on it. Until March 1956, no Bahá'í had been able to get a job with the company.[128] Shoghi Effendi counselled patience and perseverance:

> It is very unfortunate that Anticosti should prove such a hard nut to crack. He appreciates very much the determined efforts which your Body, and particularly Mr Rakovsky, made to get a pioneer into it before last Riḍván. No doubt eventually your efforts will be crowned with success; but you will have to be very tactful and careful in order not to arouse a permanently resistant attitude on the part of the Company that owns the Island.[129]

> The Guardian does not feel that it is possible or right to change Anticosti and to substitute another goal in its place. He fully realizes the difficulties involved; but feels convinced that sooner or later,

through perseverance and prayer, a way will open and a believer will be able to get into the Island on a more-or-less permanent basis.[130]

Canadian persistence paid off and in March 1956, Mary did the near impossible and managed to get a job on the company-owned island. Unfortunately, she was unable to keep it. Within a few months, she was forced to leave, but it was enough to garner her the title of Knight of Bahá'u'lláh. She did, however, return on three occasions to visit the island. Mary married Ken McCulloch, who was pioneering in Baker Lake in the Northwest Territories, in 1958. While there, they worked on translating Bahá'í literature into the Inuktitut language. In 1979, the couple moved to Churchill, Manitoba, and later settled in The Pas, Manitoba, where they helped form the first Local Spiritual Assembly in 1991. Mary also worked at translating the *Hidden Words* and the *Tablet of Aḥmad* into Ukrainian.[131]

THE CARIBBEAN, AND CENTRAL AND SOUTH AMERICA

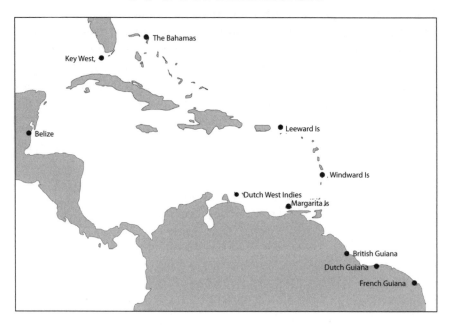

KEY WEST, FLORIDA

Arthur and Ethel Crane

The first pioneers to arise and go to Key West were Arthur (1889–1969) and Ethel Crane (1891–1968), both in their sixties. The Cranes were married in New York about 1917. Ethel heard of the Bahá'í Faith from her dentist in 1935 and became a Bahá'í in Teaneck, New Jersey, in January 1937.[1] She had held a responsible position in the Christian Science community, and upon accepting Bahá'u'lláh, wrote to her former church explaining the reasons behind her decision:

For the past year I have been studying the 'Bahá'í Revelation' which has helped me understand the Bible more clearly than I have before, to better appreciate the works of Christ Jesus as well as the other Manifestations of God, such as Abraham, Moses and Mohammed. Also it has given me a new understanding and realization that God never leaves us comfortless as he has sent us a Manifestation for this day and age: 'Bahá'u'lláh' . . .

All that I have ever said of Christian Science and the Church I have meant from the bottom of my heart and when I went in as First Reader I pledged myself to work for God and God alone and so he has prepared me to receive this higher and wider message that he has for man, for didn't Jesus say 'I have many things to tell you but ye cannot bear them now. Howbeit when he the Spirit of Truth is come, he will guide you unto all truth . . .' Therefore having received this revelation of the whole Truth it has become a responsibility to me to accept it and go forth and teach it . . .

This Faith having been revealed in the East . . . in 1844, it has the truths of C[hristian] S[cience] inculcated in it as well as a 'New World Administrative Order' for the establishment of the 'Kingdom of God on earth', as promised in the Lord's Prayer.

I shall ever be grateful to C.S. for preparing my thought to recognize this great Revelation as the Truth when I heard it.[2]

Shoghi Effendi was so impressed with her letter that he sent her a note expressing his 'profound appreciation' of the way it was written. The Guardian had the letter translated into Persian and published in a Persian newsletter.[3]

Arthur followed his wife into the Faith in about 1940 and the next year, the couple pioneered to Hackensack, New Jersey.[4] In 1946, the Cranes made a travel-teaching trip along the east coast, travelling as far as Prince Edward Island in the Gulf of St Lawrence in Canada.

In 1950, the Cranes moved to Orange County, Florida, to help the group become a Local Spiritual Assembly.[5] Three years later, they were asked by the Western Hemisphere Teaching Committee to pioneer to Key West,[6] which they did on 20 July 1953. By late 1955, Key West had ten Bahá'ís who were anticipating the formation of their first Local Spiritual Assembly at Riḍván. In November that year, the Cranes wrote to Shoghi Effendi asking if they could pioneer to Central or South America in order to help form the first Regional Spiritual Assembly there. The Guardian urged them to do so, as long as it did not prevent the formation of the Key West Local Spiritual Assembly.[7] The first Local Spiritual Assembly of Key West was elected at Riḍván 1956. Shoghi Effendi emphasized the importance of deepening the new believers, so the Cranes put aside their desire to pioneer elsewhere and stayed in Key West.

In 1959, Florence Kelley, Knight of Bahá'u'lláh for Monaco, and her husband were stationed in Key West by the Navy and served on the Local Assembly with the Cranes.[8] Arthur and Ethel remained at their post until the end of the Crusade in 1963, after which they moved to Pompano Beach, Florida, where they remained until they passed into the Abhá Kingdom, she in 1968 and he in 1969.

Howard Snider

Howard Snider (1884–1970) pioneered to Key West on 25 September 1953. Howard's parents were farmers and expected him to follow in their footsteps, but he had a strong desire for higher education. He went to the University of Illinois where he met two other young men who were interested in religion. The three visited every church they could, but remained unsatisfied until they encountered Albert Vail and the Bahá'í Faith. In 1915, Howard married Lucille Fischer, who was studying to become a missionary. 'It was he who brought the message home to her and it was she who delved into her Bible to sort and check each bit of news. He recognized Bahá'u'lláh with his heart and she convinced his intellect . . .'[9]

When the call for pioneers in the Ten Year Crusade was made, Howard, recently retired, arose and was sent to Key West. Lucille stayed behind to sell their house and settle their affairs. When Lucille joined him, her health failed in the hot climate and the doctor ordered her back to Illinois, where she passed away in 1960. After Lucille's death, Howard, at the age of 76, was asked to pioneer to Switzerland, which he did for four years. Howard refused to retire from pioneering and spent the last years of his life pioneering to Barbados, Switzerland again, Smyrna in Georgia, Bermuda and Mexico, passing away in 1970 at the age of 86.[10]

THE BAHAMAS

Ethel and Maurice Holmes

Ethel Holmes (1904–1972) was a Catholic when she married Maurice (1901–?). One day, he gave her a copy of *Gleanings from the Writings of Bahá'u'lláh* and asked for her opinion. For a solid week, she was absorbed in the book, but when she finally put it down she never questioned the Bahá'í Faith again. Arising for the Ten Year Crusade, Ethel and Maurice went from Florida to Hopetown, a village on the island of Great Abaco in the Bahamas, arriving in October 1953. The island had a church, a library, an elementary school and 100 inhabitants, but there was no electricity. The primary foods were conch meat, fish, turtles and lobster and there was no agriculture. For three years Ethel and Maurice stayed on the island observing Feasts and Bahá'í Holy Days, but with little response from the islanders. Late in 1956, Ethel's health began to fail rapidly and the couple returned to Florida. While they were gone, their house in Hopetown burned down, though the Bahá'í library was saved. The Holmes remained in Florida.[11]

Gail and Gerald Curwin

Gail (1921–2015) and Gerald Curwin (1910–2003) arrived in the Bahamas on 19 October 1953. They had become Bahá'ís in Detroit, Michigan, in 1949. A cousin who had become a Bahá'í came by in January of that year and invited them to a fireside. Gerald hadn't believed in God, but after just three months of firesides, they both accepted Bahá'u'lláh.[12]

When the Ten Year Crusade was announced, the Curwins thought that they could become home-front pioneers, but when they went to a summer school and saw the enthusiasm of others who were preparing to pioneer to the Guardian's goal areas, they decided that they would pioneer internationally. The Curwins offered their services to the Western Teaching Committee and Gail said that

> we had an 8-year-old daughter and first we were assigned to French Guiana and that was where Devil's Island is. That was off the coast. And when the Western Teaching Committee looked into it, they

decided that it was no place to send anybody with a child, so we finally ended up being assigned to the Bahamas.

When it came to the time when we knew where we were going, we had received word from Shoghi Effendi, that he wanted the Knights, as many as possible, to be at their posts by the anniversary of the birth of the Báb, it was October 20th. That gave us two weeks to get ourselves ready to go. We were just started when my husband strained his back and was in bed. Now, our family already thought that we were crazy and when this happened, they hovered over us saying 'Oh, it's a sign you shouldn't go.' And we thought it could have been a sign and we would have decided not to go, but it didn't enter our heads. It was like we had tunnel vision. We were going to be in that spot by the 20th of October. And so in two weeks, with him in bed, me getting rid of everything – I would have burned the whole thing in order to meet that deadline.

Our family didn't help us at all, but a friend who was not a Bahá'í found a doctor who would come in and give my husband a shot so on October 16th, we were on the bus with our daughter leaving Detroit for Miami. And we arrived in the Bahamas on the afternoon of the 20th of October.

When they first arrived, Gerald went out looking for information on how to get to Eleuthera, one of the islands. He

was introduced from one person to another until he met a newspaper man. 'I received my surprise when he led me into an inner office to show me a Bahá'í library.' . . . Through a non-Bahá'í friend of a Bahá'í, word of their going had preceded their arrival. 'Nassau in many respects is like a small town – they have a regular grapevine by which information flows and everyone knows what is happening. . . By now enough people knew about us that we were even getting phone calls from people who would say they had heard that we were Bahá'ís and that they had heard of the Faith at one time or another.[13]

Gail said:

Now, it wasn't easy going into another culture and country. We were told not to teach the European [and] not teach the tourists coming in, but to teach the native Bahamians. This is what we immediately began to do. My daughter and I would walk into the town. The first time in we met a woman who had a little building and she put up hems in dresses and things. She became the person that carried us around to meet all the people. She would say, 'These are my friends.' And when a lot of them heard that we were speaking of love and unity, they became Bahá'ís because their grandmothers had told them that this was the case.

Gail didn't initially receive her mother's blessing for international pioneering:

After we arrived, my mother wrote a letter and in this letter, she told me how foolish I was to have left the country and dragged my daughter to a place that nobody knew anything about. And she said in the letter, 'What the world really needs is people like the Disciples of Christ who will go out and bring people back to God.' I wrote my mother a long letter and explained that this is exactly what we think we are doing. Well, in 1963, my mother became a Bahá'í.

It took the next year and a half of slow, careful teaching for the results to begin to show. The second person to become a Bahá'í was a heavy drinker, but he was very attracted because his grandmother had told him if ever people came teaching love and unity, then he should listen. For a long while, every time there was a Bahá'í meeting, this man would stand outside watching and praying that he could become sober enough to attend. When he attended his first Bahá'í meeting, he 'he stood up under the single bulb that hung down from the ceiling, and he began to read from the Writings and he read about love and unity. He said, "My grandmother told me a long ago, that if people come here teaching love and unity, you should listen to them." He became a Bahá'í right away. He stopped drinking immediately.'

After a year and a half, Shoghi Effendi said that he hoped that the pioneers would be able to form Local Spiritual Assemblies by Riḍván 1955. So, the Curwins gathered all those who had expressed an interest in the Faith and asked them if they would meet every night for a week to find out what they needed to know for them to become Bahá'ís. By the afternoon of 19 April, enough had declared their faith in Bahá'u'lláh to form the first Local Spiritual Assembly of Nassau.

By the end of 1955, the Curwins' funds began to run out and the pioneering committee contacted the Guardian to see if the Curwins could leave Nassau. Permission was granted, but with the stipulation that they settle in the American South. Of their time in the Bahamas, Gail said:

> When we went there, we were a family, ordinary people with ordinary lifestyle, whatever, and we had our friends, and we had our social activities, all these things, and the Bahá'í Faith was a part of that . . .
>
> When we came back from the Bahamas, the Bahá'í Faith was our life and it was as though somebody had inoculated us with the idea that we were pioneers, so we spent most of our life moving . . .
>
> Going as a pioneer was something that changed our whole lives. We didn't know in the beginning that when we went that we had taken a step that was going to unfold and we would have experiences that we hadn't anticipated.

Gail and Gerald then moved to Charlotte, North Carolina in late 1955. After a year and a half, they were able to form the Local Assembly then, in 1960, they were asked to manage the Louhelen Bahá'í School. Gail was also asked to be a travel teacher so she spent the last three years of the Ten Year Crusade travelling the country teaching the Faith. In 1972, the Curwins retired and returned to Charlotte. The 1970s were a time when large numbers of African-Americans came into the Faith. In 1972, a group of twenty young people went out as part of what became known as the Army of Light. During a short time, thousands came into the Faith and the Curwins' house was a centre of the activity. The Curwins remained active in teaching the Faith until the end of their lives.

Andrew and Nina Matthisen

On 15 January 1954, Andrew (1885–1961) and Nina Matthisen (1895–1972) and their daughter, Mary Jane, arrived in Nassau, Bahamas to fill one of Shoghi Effendi's goals. Andrew's mother was an early American believer and Andrew had accepted the Bahá'í Faith as a young man. In

1922, he married Nina Benedict and the couple earned a reputation for their spiritual home. With the announcement of the Crusade, Andrew and Nina chose to go to the Bahamas.

They started up a fireside in their home in Nassau once or twice a week which usually had 16 or 17 people present. One of the first to declare was a 22-year-old member of the police force who initially learned of the Faith from Gerald Curwin and had become a Bahá'í by July. One day, the policeman came to the Matthisens' fireside and asked to be taught how to pray. A short time later, he phoned the Matthisens and urgently requested they come to the police barracks because he needed help telling a companion about the Faith. The man was visiting from Barbados and was captured by the spirit of the Faith. When he returned to his home, he took a copy of *Bahá'u'lláh and the New Era* to share with a co-worker.[14]

In March, the Matthisens began afternoon meetings in the small town of Adelaide, about 20 kilometres from Nassau. Of the many who attended their meetings, none realized what was being offered, so Andrew and Gail spent a week at Bluff and Current on the island of Eleuthera. No one was expecting them when they arrived in Current, so they rang the school bell and soon had a large audience. There was, however, no response to their message. Working with Gail and Gerald Curwin, a Local Assembly was elected at Riḍván 1955. When Nina's health deteriorated in 1959, they returned to Fort Myers, Florida, and raised up a Local Assembly.[15]

WINDWARD ISLANDS

Esther Evans and Lillian Middlemast

Esther Evans (1899–1989) learned of the Bahá'í Faith in 1952 from John and Valerie Woolson in Victor, New York, and said she was 'suddenly filled with tremendous joy and was enveloped in great, golden light. I felt as though there was no me and I was conscious of nothing about myself. I heard myself say "John, this is the truest thing that was ever said." And I believed. This was my answer.'

The next year Esther attended the dedication of the House of Worship in Wilmette and then the Teaching Conference afterwards. She initially had no desire to become a pioneer until Rúḥíyyih Khánum

THE KNIGHTS OF BAHÁ'U'LLÁH

got up and said, 'Now you old girls that have independent means and can do this, go to the far places of the world, stay there, live there, put your roots down, die there. Perchance, someone might come along and say, "Who is Bahá'u'lláh? What is a Bahá'í?" You'll be able to tell them . . .'[16]

That exhortation pushed Esther and her friend Lillian Middlemast to pack up and go to St Lucia in the Windward Islands, where they arrived on 13 October 1953. After ten months, Lillian's ill health forced her to return to the United States, leaving Esther alone.

Most of the people Esther and Lillian initially spoke to about the Faith were of the middle and upper classes and, though they all politely listened, none seemed to have more than a cursory interest in the Faith. Esther was slowly able to expand her efforts to the whole community. She took advantage of visitors from outside to try and generate interest. When Leroy Ioas's two sisters visited, Esther arranged for them to show their coloured movies of the Holy Land. One man who had been coming asked many questions about the Faith, along with several others:

> . . . he came with one of the 'powers-that-be' from the Catholic Church, I think he was a minister too. This man was like a guardian. He was standing over him. He came to see the pictures too. And all the time this man, he used to work where they sold men's suits and things, smelt like a saloon, he was reeking of alcohol, he wouldn't let this man who used to ask me questions. Poor fellow was so frightened that he kept quoting the Bible all the time the pictures were being shown. But everybody enjoyed them. After it was all over we discovered that there were a lot of people looking through the windows watching the pictures. They were people we hadn't invited and they were standing on the road watching the pictures. But when everyone left, those two sisters said to me, 'You know, I'd be frightened to death to have to invite them! That man acted vicious, the minister, you know, to have to put up with anything like that.'[17]

At a later time, Esther tried to put a few Bahá'í books into the local library. She gave them to the librarian who said that

> she couldn't give her permission, that there would have to be a

Board meeting, and they would have to make that decision. So I said, 'When will that be?' Well, she said she couldn't tell me, that there was no set time. They just met now and then. Well, each time I met her I would keep asking if there had been a meeting yet. About 4 months passed and so I said, 'Well, my goodness, they don't have meetings very often, do they?'

The next time I met her she said, 'Well we've had a meeting and the answer is NO. You know this thing isn't even Christian. And besides that, this island is 98% Christian, and this thing isn't even Christian.' So I said, 'Let me tell you something. If you would read the Bahá'í Faith, just go through the book you'd find, to your delight, that this Bahá'í Faith is more Christian than Christianity. And furthermore, what about the other 2%? Are they to be denied?' She didn't answer.[18]

In 1962 or 1963, Esther moved to Cap Estate, near the north end of the island. But after a number of years living alone and without any progress teaching the Faith, she wrote to the US National Spiritual Assembly: 'I think this place is a spiritual desert. I'd better go somewhere else.' Their response was, 'Stick to your post!' 'So I did', she wrote, 'It wasn't hurting me to stick to my post because I loved it here.'[19]

In 1964, Henrietta and Phil Trutza joined her. The new pioneers, the first since Esther had arrived 11 years before, opened new avenues for teaching the Faith and the first declarations occurred. Esther remembered that

> Phil was working down where the boats come in. He was building down there, and he had workers. He was talking about the Bahá'í Faith. Then we started to have meetings, getting the people who worked with him, to come up here. We used to have picnics and everyone would bring a little something. We would have games. I had shuffleboard and croquet, and we'd go to the beach and come back and have lunch. We'd have a jolly time and talk about the Bahá'í Faith.[20]

The first native person to become a Bahá'í in St Lucia was Patsy Vincent, a 16-year-old, who enrolled in May 1967.[21] Patsy remembered that Esther gave her courage:

She's very, very, very nice, and she gives you courage because most of the times I speak to her I tell her, just say what happened, and she say, 'Don't worry. Keep courage.' Even something we needed, something so we know about the Faith more, tell me so I can tell this. That's one thing. She used to tell me. She gives me courage.

. . . we used to go by Esther, keep our firesides, no problem, she prepare everything for us, tell us go by the beach; we go by the beach, and then she there first and prepare everything and we used to go to meeting – everything, she's there; always helping. If you don't know something, she explain it for you. I just love to visit for her. I don't know the meaning of something, I ask, then it gets written down for you; then I can teach somebody else in Patois, who is speaking Patois.[22]

In September of that year, Cecil Johannas became the first adult to join the Faith. By the end of the year, there were 26 Bahá'ís in the towns of St Lucia and Castries. The first Local Spiritual Assembly of Castries formed in 1969, followed the next year by the first Local Spiritual Assembly in St Lucia.[23]

In 1983, thirty years after Esther Evans' arrival, the National Spiritual Assembly of St Lucia was formed. By the time Esther died in 1990, still at her pioneering post, there were 1,800 Bahá'ís in the islands.[24]

LEEWARD ISLANDS

Earle Render

Earle Render (b.1920), a 33-year old accountant from Chicago, arrived on St Thomas Island on 20 September 1953. Earle was a new Bahá'í who joined the Bahá'í Faith on 6 April 1953 and excitedly arose to pioneer. On 7 September, he informed the US National Spiritual Assembly, for the first time, that he had quit his job and was pioneering to St Thomas in the Virgin Islands less than two weeks later. By December, Earle's initial enthusiasm had been tempered by reality:

I've been working since I arrived but have not earned a cent as all the employers either promise to pay or cannot pay, this, because of the economic status of the island. I've spent all of the monies I brought with me and the present play of employment is uncertain as my employer feels immune to a potential competitor . . .

In my opinion the chance to teach will be in the future as now the tests put to the natives here are not such as to look to God in plights which they do not acknowledge to exist. With the present advent of American continentals and their negative ways for which they are known the world over with [r]eference to racial, religious, and political and social bigotry, the natives here are just commencing to realize that their little island world is but a minification of the world at large.[25]

Shortly after his arrival, Earle cabled the Guardian, who confirmed him as a Knight of Bahá'u'lláh for the Leeward Islands.[26] Earle finally found work in a hotel and managed to stay for almost a year.[27]

Ben and Gladys Weeden

Ben (1892–1970) and Gladys Weeden (1906–1979) arrived on Antigua on 16 October 1953. Ben was first attracted to the Bahá'í Faith in Brattleboro, Vermont, in 1942. Quickly becoming engaged with the Guardian's writings, he bought a new Bible and a dictionary 'because he realized that the Guardian's beautiful translations into English of the Writings of the Faith required a full understanding of the exact meanings'. He accepted Bahá'u'lláh in 1943 and immediately began serving on the Local Spiritual Assembly of Brattleboro and on the New England Regional Teaching Committee. In 1948, he was invited to serve at the Bahá'í World Centre.[28]

Gladys had a tough childhood, her mother dying when Gladys was only five. In 1929, at the beginning of the Great Depression, she began her 'spiritual thinking'. On an outing one

sunny July day in 1932, Gladys and her husband. . . went on a day's excursion to the White Mountains in New Hampshire with another couple. [Mary Maxwell] and Rosemary Sala were motoring from Montreal to Green Acre in Eliot, Maine, and we all met at a sightseeing spot called Lost River. Years later Rosemary told Gladys that [Mary Maxwell] had said to her: 'that girl is going to become a Bahá'í'.[29]

Gladys became a Bahá'í in Massachusetts in 1937 and served on the

Local Spiritual Assembly and the Regional Teaching Committee. In 1942, in the closing years of the First Seven Year Plan, Gladys accepted the challenge of filling a home-front pioneering goal to Brattleboro, Vermont. A year later, she had raised up a Local Spiritual Assembly and met Ben, her future husband. In early 1947, she was invited to serve in Haifa, where she helped both Shoghi Effendi and Rúḥíyyih Khánum. Ben joined her in March 1948, and the couple were married in Jerusalem the day after he arrived.[30]

Ben's health forced the Weedens back to America in 1951. Shoghi Effendi asked the Weedens to visit as many Bahá'í centres as possible on their return and talk about their experiences in the Holy Land. Ben and Gladys obediently set out on what became a 34,000-mile tour that took them to all 48 states and 75 Bahá'í communities.[31]

By the time the goals for the Ten Year Crusade came out, Ben was better and Dorothy Baker suggested they pioneer to the Leeward Islands in the Caribbean, which include the Virgin Islands, Dominica, Guadeloupe, Montserrat, Antigua, Barbuda, St Kitts, St Thomas, Nevis and Anguilla. Dorothy assured them the islands were 'just ready to pop'. When they arrived, however, they found the islands in a terrible drought and prices very high. Their modest income was nowhere near sufficient for the 'astronomical' housing prices and they were quickly in debt. After two months they left 'to lick our spiritual wounds and straighten out our financial debts'.[32]

Moving to New Hampshire, the Weedens continued to serve. Ben died in 1973 and two years later, Rúḥíyyih Khánum asked Gladys to return to Haifa to help renovate the House of the Master. She stayed for five months and again in 1977. After returning from Haifa, Gladys spent her final two years on travel-teaching trips to Vancouver, Alaska, Ireland and New Mexico.[33]

David Schreiber

A fourth pioneer also gained the title of Knight of Bahá'u'lláh by moving to Antigua in the Leeward Islands. This was David Schreiber (b.1921), who arrived in February 1954. David had been confirmed as a Bahá'í by Dorothy Baker at the the Louhelen Bahá'í School when he was 15 years old.[34]

David chose the Leeward Islands because he couldn't afford to travel further since his non-Bahá'í wife was supporting his effort. His first challenge was housing for himself, his wife and their young daughter, Rosalie. There was none available so they were forced to stay in a hotel, which rapidly consumed their available resources. David did finally manage to rent a room from the widow of a missionary, but their finances were seriously depleted. He rode his bicycle around the island of Antigua to teach the Faith. Then Rosalie came down with dysentery and mother and daughter returned to the United States. David was not able to find any work and when his wife quit her job to return to America, he had no resources left. In August, after just six months, David was forced to leave.[35]

Though he had only been able to stay until August, he did find one receptive soul who accepted the Faith, McKensie Edwards. When Mrs Schreiber found a job in Honolulu, Hawaii, the family moved there.[36] David returned to the islands in 1965 and visited Montserrat, Nevis, Antigua and Barbuda with McKensie.[37]

After a divorce, and a marriage to Kimiko, David and his new wife lived in Hawaii for a while. Then Dr Muhájir suggested that he quit his job as a transmitter technician on top of Haleakala volcano and go to Palau.[38] So they pioneered to Palau and Papua New Guinea, where they had their greatest victories. From 1976 to 1978, David worked as a teacher at a trade school in Palau, and in 1982, David and Kimiko pioneered to Papua New Guinea. It was a very difficult place and they faced strong Lutheran opposition. At one time, they were teaching in the sugar region when a mob of 100 men appeared and began throwing stones at them, demanding that they leave. In spite of the difficulties, they were able to bring a man named Isamu into the Faith, who was later responsible for bringing in hundreds to recognize Bahá'u'lláh. In a letter to the Universal House of Justice in April 2013, David described how on one occasion he and the people in the village of Ngardmau made a float for the Palau Islands Fair parade. A summary made at the Bahá'í World Centre reads:

The float had the words 'Open the heart to all peoples' and 'Baha'i Faith' written on it. Likewise, invitations were made with the same wording, which were distributed to approximately 2,500 people, inviting them to attend a talk that was to be given by the Hand of the Cause Collis Featherstone.

At the same fair, David Schreiber persuaded the Superintendent of Public Instruction to have banners made, which David Schreiber paid for, that read 'Welcome-Palau Community Fair'. The banners also contained advertisements for the aforementioned talk. He communicates that once displayed, the banners provoked such an outcry from the local churches that the superintendent wanted to take them down. David Schreiber states that he spoke with the superintendent, and the banners not only remained up but, to his surprise, were also adorned with flashing "Christmas" lights, thus giving Collis Featherstone's talk even more public attention than before.

Finally, David Schreiber recalls how, when a new television station opened in Palau, he presented it with a series, created by Hand of the Cause William Sears, consisting of thirteen half-hour presentations on the Faith. The station took the series and aired it every Sunday morning.[39]

In 1986, after both David and Kimiko contracted malaria, they left to pioneer in other areas, including China, until David's blindness and health problems forced him to return to Hawaii about 1992.[40]

Charles and Mary Dayton

On 14 February 1954, Charles (1908–?) and Mary Dayton (1908–?), the first pioneers to go out from Miami, Florida, arrived in the Leeward Islands and settled on St Thomas Island. Charles was from Michigan and Mary from England, her father being Welsh and her mother from Pennsylvania.[41] Charles and Mary were married in about 1925.

The first thing the Daytons did was to give a few Bahá'í books to the library, but by August they still had not been put onto the shelves. They also started a fireside with a Catholic lady who was very interested until she told her priest about the Bahá'í Faith and 'that was the end of that'. Mary noted that 'the average person here is quite content with the easy going way of life most islands afford, they come here "to get away from it all", religion is their very last thought'. Charles opened a small cabinet shop but was initially hindered by a boat strike that kept his machinery from being delivered for six weeks.[42]

In February 1957, Mary suffered an eye injury and went to Puerto Rico for an operation. She was finally able to return home five months

Arthur and Ethel Crane (seated first and second left),
Knights of Bahá'u'lláh to Key West, Florida

*Howard Snider, Knight of Bahá'u'lláh to
Key West, Florida*

Esther Evans (right), *Knight of Bahá'u'lláh to St Lucia,* and above, *still at her pioneering post on St Lucia, meeting Amatu'l-Bahá Rúḥíyyih Khánum* (right) *in 1970, Martha Hocker in the background*

Ben and Gladys Weeden, Knights of Bahá'u'lláh to the Leeward Islands

*Mary and Charles Dayton, Knights of
Bahá'u'lláh to the Leeward Islands*

*David Schreiber, Knight of
Bahá'u'lláh to the Leeward Islands*

Andrew and Nina Matthisen, Knights of Bahá'u'lláh to the Bahamas

Gail and Gerald Curwin, Knights of Bahá'u'lláh to the Bahamas, in October 19
just before they left home to pioneer

Matthew Bullock, Knight of Bahá'u'lláh to the Dutch West Indies

Katharine Meyer, Knight of Bahá'u'lláh to Margarita Island

Shirley Warde, Knight of Bahá'u'lláh to British Honduras (Belize)

Cora Oliver, Knight of Bahá'u'lláh to British Honduras (Belize)

Elinor and Robert Wolff, Knights of Bahá'u'lláh to Dutch Guiana (Suriname)

Contributed by Jean and Scott Wolff

…e Wolff family in Suriname. Robert is holding their oldest son William Jan Wolff, who went pioneering
with them. Elinor is holding their second son, Thomas Randal Wolff, who was born in Suriname

Malcolm King (centre), *Knight of Bahá'u'lláh to British Guiana, with the Bahá'í community of Georgetown, 1955.* Back row from left: *Reginald Stone, Ivan Fraser, Allan Delph;* second row from left: *Richard and Vida Backwell, Radlene Fraser, Malcolm King, Adrianna Winter, Clarine Savory, Dr C. C. Nicholson;* front row: *Backwell and Fraser children*

Eberhart Friedland, Knight of Bahá'u'lláh to French Guiana

later with hope for a full recovery of her sight. By July she was home and Charles wrote that there had been severe trials but they had two strong contacts:

> These trials seem unbearable at the time but out of each one comes new Bahá'í contacts, a great bond of love with our old contacts, lessons learned, etc., that could not have been accomplished in any other way. Thru this last one, our first two Bahá'í contacts have been drawn close to us as never before . . .[43]

The Daytons were forced to leave their post for a while, but were back in early 1959. Both were then able to find work and, strangely, they were given their old post office box back. When they had requested a box, they were told that there were 200 people on the list and that it would be at least a year before they would get one. Suddenly, however, they were given the key to their old mail box.[44] In 1964, they were able to participate in the election of the first Local Spiritual Assembly of St Thomas. Three years later, in 1968, the first National Spiritual Assembly of the Bahá'ís of the Leeward, Windward and Virgin Islands was formed. The Daytons remained at their pioneering post until 1968.[45]

DUTCH WEST INDIES

Matthew Bullock

Matthew Bullock's (1881–1972) parents were not long from slavery when he was born, and that humble beginning showed no hint of his tremendous future. Matthew's father struggled to give him $50 for a start on his own, but he managed to attend Dartmouth and Harvard Universities and become a star athlete and 'the famous baritone singer of Dartmouth'. But a Harvard Law degree didn't open that many doors for a black man. He encountered the Bahá'í Faith when he attended a talk by Ludmila van Sombeck. The Faith sounded very good, but he watched to see if the nice words were matched by corresponding behaviour. Finally, in 1940, he decided that they did and became a Bahá'í. With his great capacity, he was soon serving on the Boston Local Spiritual Assembly and various national committees. In 1952 he was elected to the US National Spiritual Assembly. Then came the Ten Year Crusade.[46]

In 1953, Matthew went on pilgrimage and found his encounter with Shoghi Effendi to be transforming. After pilgrimage, he attended the Intercontinental Teaching Conference in Kampala and was inspired to travel teach in the Belgian Congo and Liberia afterwards. Returning to America, even at the age of 72 he could not resist the call to pioneer and, at the American Conference, he was on his feet to volunteer. He resigned his position as a member of the National Assembly and went to Curaçao in the Dutch West Indies on 20 November 1953 and helped raise up the first Local Spiritual Assembly. Because he could only get a tourist visa, Matthew always left the island in April and returned in December, arriving just before Christmas.[47]

At one point, Matthew was a delegate to the Convention held in Costa Rica to elect the Regional Spiritual Assembly. Matthew was the first delegate to arrive and when he went to check in at the hotel where the delegates were staying, the hotel owner refused to allow him, a black man, to stay there. When Matthew said that there would be delegates from many places, the owner, who was not a Costa Rican, became very aggressive, so the Bahá'ís quickly made other arrangements for all the delegates.[48]

Matthew continued his four-month stays in Curaçao until in 1960 old age and disabilities forced him back to the United States. He moved to Boston, but six years later, because of his poor health, he moved to Detroit to be close to his daughter. In 1970 and 1971, Harvard University and Dartmouth College bestowed honorary degrees on him. He passed away at the age of 92 in 1972.[49]

John and Marjorie Kellberg

John (b. 1926) and Marjorie Kellberg (b. 1927), from Oak Park, Illinois, arrived on the island of Curaçao in the Dutch West Indies, also called the Netherlands Antilles, on 21 April 1954, less than two months after they were married.[50]

Initially, the young couple stayed in a hotel belonging to a Dutch doctor. Finding a place to live proved difficult because rents were very high. During the first week in Curaçao, they looked for some sort of work, but found nothing. Because of the cost of living and their meagre savings, they worried that they would have to leave within three or four weeks. They received no help from the authorities, who were only interested in tourist dollars and not people looking for work. Marjorie noted:

> Curaçao is very interesting, although of course very different from what we are accustomed to. It is hot during the day, although the trade winds blow continually. The evenings are delightfully cool – a pleasant breeze blowing and sky clear. They say, however, this is the cool season and it will get much hotter . . . All of the natives have work and are very neat and clean, also Catholic. All of the Dutch employees of the oil company live in the oil company compound and have their own life – stores, movies, homes, etc.[51]

Matthew Bullock was also in Curaçao, but with only a tourist visa that required him to leave the island regularly. Matthew left Curaçao just as the Kellbergs were arriving. He returned in December and the Bahá'ís began having public meetings, the first one on World Religion Day, and firesides. In April 1955, Marjorie reported that there were 3 to 15 people coming to the firesides. Matthew left in mid-April, but returned the following autumn.[52] Slowly things worked out and they were able to stay.

In December 1957, Marjorie's parents Clarence and Margarite Ullrich came to Curaçao for several weeks in order to help with the teaching. Margarite wrote that John and Marjorie knew

> many, many people, both colored and white. 85% of the population here is colored and the rest Dutch, with some Americans, of course. They have had two public meetings at their home for the colored and one public meeting for whites, both American and Dutch. The last meeting there were 16 non-Bahá'ís present. At the other two meetings there were 13 non-Bahá'ís at one and 7 non-Bahá'ís at the other. As you know they have two native Bahá'ís and have another about ready to declare himself and several good prospects . . .
>
> After living in the environs of the Temple and the National office where one is close to everything that is going on, you surely feel isolated and cut off in a place like Curaçao and I imagine in all the places where the pioneers are. After being here and seeing how things are and hearing some of the things Marjorie and John went through before they finally got established, my heart goes out to

them and to all the pioneers. We who stay at home where everything is convenient and what we are used to don't realize what others are going through.[53]

The Kellbergs stayed in Curaçao through the rest of the Ten Year Crusade, though it took eight years to become financially stable.

MARGARITA ISLAND

Katharine Meyer

Katharine Meyer (1908–2006) was trained as a pianist, but also had a degree in business administration and economics. She worked as an economic analyst for the US government and became a Bahá'í in 1945. In 1947, when she learned that Shoghi Effendi wanted people to move to Latin America, she volunteered and pioneered to Caracas, Venezuela. When the first National Spiritual Assembly of the Leeward, Windward, and Virgin Islands was formed, Katharine served as its secretary.[54]

At the beginning of the Ten Year Crusade, Katharine saw a letter that said that the Margarita Islands, one of Shoghi Effendi's goals, were without a pioneer. She immediately volunteered to go, arriving on 7 October 1953. Katharine found work teaching English at two of the secondary schools during the day and in a commercial school in the evenings. She noted that everyone on the island was Catholic and that all of the priests came from Spain. During her 11 years in Margarita, three women, Elena Hernandez, Zenaida Mata and Cecilia de Pablo embraced Bahá'u'lláh. Cecilia moved with her family to the island of San Tomé, thus opening it up to the Faith. Several of her students also studied the book *Bahá'u'lláh and the New Era*.[55]

Katharine left Margarita on 1 October 1964 and moved to the Virgin Islands. In 1969, she pioneered first to the Mapuche Indian area in southern Chile, then to Iquique in the far north of that country, and finally returned to the south, serving in all areas as an Auxiliary Board member. While serving in the Mapuche area, Katharine would think nothing of walking 10 to 20 miles to visit her beloved Mapuche friends. Many years after she had moved away from that area, when she was in her 80s, she visited them and was received with joyous welcomes everywhere she went. In 1979, she published a book on the Faith's development in Latin America.[56] Katharine passed away, still in Chile, in 2006.[57]

BRITISH HONDURAS (NOW BELIZE)

Shirley Warde and Cora Oliver

Shirley Warde (1901–1991) was an actress and a writer who, with her mother, grandmother, aunt and daughter, investigated everything they 'could find or hear about in the way of esoteric and religious teachings'. In 1932, they fed a hungry man who told them about how he had painted a house for a man involved in 'some Eastern cult that believed in all religions'. That man was Roy Wilhelm and soon four generations of Wardes became Bahá'ís.

During the Depression, Shirley became the first writer-producer for the Columbia Broadcasting System, which allowed her to get a job with the Office of War Information when World War II started. In that position, she wrote radio programmes with Bill and Marguerite Sears, Marion Holley, the Ioas family, Marzieh Gail and others, and put many articles about the Bahá'í Faith into newspapers and on radio shows. In 1944, Shirley attended the Centenary of the Declaration of the Báb, where she volunteered to pioneer to South America.[58] Beginning in 1946, she spent three years spreading the Faith in Argentina, Brazil, Paraguay and Uruguay. Of those years, Shirley wrote:

> These were troubled times in Argentina and all Americans were sus-
> pected of being spies. Since publicity on my arrival had included the
> fact that I worked for the office of war information during the war, I
> had been followed since my arrival, my phone [was] tapped, all my
> mails [were] opened and the Bahá'ís [were] attacked in the radical
> newspaper because their summer school was near the airport. Now
> there followed a series of events which ended in nearly losing my life
> and bringing about my return to California in 1949 . . .[59]

Cora Oliver (1902–1997) had had a difficult life, losing her father when she was one month old, her mother when she was in high school and her husband after just a year and a half of marriage, so she was quite depressed when in 1930 she boarded with the Edgecomb family in Richmond, New York. The Edgecombs were Bahá'ís and joy soon returned to Cora's heart and she joined them in the Faith.[60] Cora moved to Washington DC where she served on the Local Spiritual Assembly. She pioneered to Panama in 1939 and her efforts there led to the election of the first Local Spiritual Assembly in 1945.[61] She was elected to the regional National Spiritual Assembly for Central America, Mexico and the Antilles in 1952.[62]

When the goals were announced for the Ten Year Crusade in 1953, Shirley and Cora, independently and unknown to each other, chose British Honduras (now Belize). Cora reached her goal on 16 September 1953 and Shirley followed in October. Shirley wrote:

> Belize in those days was truly a cultural shock, with its mostly wooden houses on stilts, its open sewerage canals, alleys and yard areas in the back of the better front houses jammed with little more than hovels, yet its charm evident in the pleasant, often large, homes of the wealthier populace living on the shores of the city while the narrow streets with no sidewalks swarmed with bicycles, and mule and carts, a few trucks, fewer taxis and a very few private cars . . .[63]

Initially Shirley joined Cora at a boarding house, but they were soon able to rent a nice house together for six months and pushed their teaching activities.

> When I arrived in Belize I, of course knew no one, but Mrs Oliver had once met a prominent Belizean lawyer in Jamaica and, on contacting him and his wife, who had just organized a Belize branch of the Federation of Women, she had met a good many people before I arrived. I think it was that very night that she took me to a Federation meeting where I met, among many others, Mrs Gwendolyn Lizarraga, the woman who was to become our first adult Bahá'í in Belize. Federation members were hoping to build a much-needed Day Nursery and I offered to produce a variety show for them to raise funds. This offered a chance to meet many people as I hoped . . . including two outstanding men who later became Bahá'i. One of the two cinema houses was given us free and I presented a musical fantasy variety program quite different from anything they had seen before and cleared a $400.00 profit, enough in those days to lay the

foundation for the nursery.[64]

Teaching was difficult and Shirley wrote:

> Cora and I were both trying to teach the Faith, of course, all the time
> but finding it difficult. We were meeting many people, were invited
> to the cocktail parties at Government House of the American Con-
> sulate (where we set a vogue for Coca-Colas), and talked with people
> everywhere, for the Belizeans are noted for their friendliness. But we
> met little response to our great message. The reason was obvious for
> the populace was then divided into various church groups, all schools
> being run by the churches, most social life revolving around them as
> well as all cultural activities. It took great courage, therefore, to step out
> of your whole life pattern. Moreover, being such a small population,
> then only some 30,000 in Belize City, social approval or disapproval
> became a great consideration. Everyone knew exactly what everyone
> else did, where they went and who they visited, for rumor spread like
> wildfire and the 'two American ladies' were tabbed as anything from
> CIA agents to Holy Rollers, with people warned to be very careful of
> them. While the rumor phase died out as more people got to know
> us, we still represented some strange religion – Eastern at that – and,
> because they learned we did not believe that Jesus was God incarnate,
> as the Catholics, Anglican and even the Wesleyans (Methodist) here
> taught, they now claimed we did not believe in God, a concept that
> has persisted in some quarters till now . . .[65]

In 1955, Cora and Shirley wrote that 'God works in mysterious ways'
and gave the story of a 15-year-old boy who had drowned. The boy's
grandparents went to the two pioneers for comfort and gained a new
perspective on death. Another member of the family began studying
Bahá'í books.[66] In early 1957, Cora and Shirley described an amazing
unity Feast:

> Mr Enos Peterkin . . . became a believer at our last Feast . . . We had
> planned to have a picture taken of the group . . . but there was some
> delay in getting the photographer . . . Then just as we had started,
> Mrs Rosita Stuart, a native lady who had been reading and attend-
> ing Firesides for some time, arrived . . . When we told her what was

going on she said, 'Then maybe I am just in time, for I am ready to become a Bahá'í.' We were really thrilled for we had been using the Tablet of Ahmad three times each evening for 19 days for the confirmation of those close and attracted souls . . . Once more we began the Feast, but had only completed the first prayer when Mr Nathaniel Neal arrived, saying he had felt impelled to come . . . He has read and studied . . . almost a year now . . . We told him of Mrs Stuart's declaration and invited him to stay, which he joyfully did and was deeply touched by the readings.[67]

After initially teaching among the more upper classes, the two women began to shift their focus:

The less sophisticated people began to attend, women who had stalls at the market, their friends and others we encountered in shops, offices in our daily activities. Perhaps many came for the refreshments served, but out of them came several fine Bahá'ís: Rosita Stuart, who later pioneered and lived in Guatemala where her two sons joined the Faith; Elena Blanford from Bluefields, Honduras, who later returned there for a time to teach, still later to serve as National Secretary in Costa Rica; and Florence Parks, an ardent Red Cross worker and ex-Anglican . . . We were often tested in those days to see if we believed the equality we taught. A fisherman or meat vendor would hold out a dirty hand to be shaken, I never hesitated, and a young Mayan man was attracted because we gave him water from a glass out of our own shelf rather than a tin from the kitchen . . .

Robert Reneau, known to all as 'Bob', used to come to these meetings. I had met him almost on my arrival, using him in that first show I produced for the Federation of Women, as he has a beautiful baritone voice. He was a Sunday school teacher and lay preacher for the Wesleyans but Bahá'u'lláh had His hand on Bob's shoulder and for all his struggles, would not let him go. He would come and talk with us and fire questions sometimes till one o'clock in the morning, and would go back to his Bible and return with new questions and barriers. It took him nine years to clear away all the veils, in spite of exposure to three Hands of the Cause, Counselors and visiting teachers. But he kept coming and one night at a meeting one simple statement by a Persian Pioneer, Rouhi Yeganyeh

[later Rouhi Huddleston], opened his vision. 'Where is that enroll-
ment card,' he asked. 'I want to sign it right now!' and he did . . .

There was a cabinet maker next to my wood shop and in doing
some work for me, told his young 19-year-old assistant about the
Faith. He had been reading Theosophy and the Rosa Crucian [sic]
teaching and being a seeker, was immediately interested and began
attending our meetings. His name was Luis Voyer with a transient
French father and a Creole mother. For two or three successive nights
a group of Jehovah Witnesses descended on us but finally, when
cornered with questions they could not answer, they gave up . . .
Luis became our first Bahá'í youth.[68]

By 1958, Shirley and Cora had managed to form their first Local Spiritual Assembly and had 11 Bahá'ís in the community. Cora had found a
job with the US Mission and Shirley was working in an airline office, as
well as her 'wood-turning'.[69]

With the Faith established, Cora and Shirley turned their attention
to the countryside. Shirley noted:

As a 'passport' to the villages I used a small tape recorder on which
I wanted to collect the Folk songs and stories of Belize as . . . the
old-timers who knew them were dying out and the new generation
did not know them. In seeking the old men and women who knew
the tales I met many villagers, made friends, and where I could, gave
the Message but it was purely proclamation effort. However, this
collection has proved most valuable in preserving.[70]

In 1963, both Cora and Shirley attended the World Congress in
London. When they returned, they extended their teaching outside
Belize City to the more rural Western District, but

the big problem was . . . transportation. One might get a bus or
truck to go west but there was no return trip that day, hotels only in
the one town of San Ignacio and miles between villages. But now,
Dr Ahmadiyeh had bought a car and in one weekend between Saturday afternoon and Sunday evening, he and I opened every village
on the Western Highway. In San Ignacio itself we drove along the
back street, saw a young woman sitting in her doorway and started

talking to her. Her heart was waiting for the message and in about half an hour she was ready to enroll. In the center of the town we met a man I knew from the Social Development Department, Noel McDougal . . . and he asked us to tell him about the Faith. He did a lot of subsequent reading before enrolling, while another man from the Forestry Department who joined us on the street that day, signed his card then and there after a short discussion. We began to be amazed at how ready and receptive the people outside Belize City were, where the churches had not such a hold on them.

We visited two largely Mayan and Spanish villages on the extreme border with Guatemala and opened both, then turned back towards Belize, stopping at every village on the highway where at any house we saw people on the verandas or in the yard. Bahá'u'lláh must have been guiding us because those we enrolled that day, although not visited for months afterwards, have remained the key people in each of those villages which today all have local Assemblies and many believers.

Radio has been a great instrument for proclamation, teaching and deepening. We began in 1972 with one free 15-minute program each . . . After a year we felt it was attracting considerable attention everywhere and decided to pay for the three remaining Wednesday mornings. Being the only Radio Station, government owned, the program is heard by everyone in the country, created much interest and received favorable comment among all classes of people. Then, for a reason never divulged . . . we were 'rested' with the excuse they had too many religious programs on the air and were going to 'rest' others in turn. This never happened, of course, only ours was taken off.[71]

Shirley later served on the National Spiritual Assembly of Belize when it was formed in 1967. By 1970, Belize had 25 Local Spiritual Assemblies and almost 1,250 believers. Shirley passed away still at her pioneer post in 1991.[72] Cora returned to the United States in 1973.

DUTCH GUIANA (NOW SURINAME)

Elinor and Robert Wolff

Robert (Bob) (1922–2015) and Elinor Wolff (b.1922) reached their pioneering post in Dutch Guiana on 14 October 1953. Bob's discovery of the Baháʼí Faith was amazing:

> Being a young Jewish boy in the Netherlands during the Nazi occupation, he was befriended by a Christian woman who hid him, as well as some others, in her home. Just like what Anne Frank described, they huddled together in close quarters with no chance to get away from one another. Over time, cooped up as they were, nerves got on edge. There came a time when the hostess told him to leave, knowing that capture and death were almost certain. Bob lived in the shadows, sleeping in the woods, eating out of garbage cans for two weeks. Fortunately, it was shortly before the allied liberation when he was freed of the Nazi threat. Some time later, the woman who had cast him out of her house met up with him. She apologized and said she had something important to tell him, but there was no time for it just then. She had found the Faith and was eager to share the message with Bob. She gave him a small Baháʼí prayer book and told him to read one each day and she would then see him in one month. By this time, Bob was a committed atheist, so a prayer book had little appeal. However, he was also a scientist at heart. He thought he would do as she asked to see if there was anything to it.
>
> Bob said that for the first few days he dutifully read the prayers. They seemed like so much gibberish. Then, slowly, they started to take on meaning. By the end of 30 days they produced deep feelings. When Bob and his benefactress met again, he was ready to become a Baháʼí.[73]

As a new Baháʼí, Robert served on a Local Spiritual Assembly with a man who had formerly been a Nazi.[74]

Elinor became a Baháʼí in America in the early 1940s in Illinois. While attending summer school at Geyserville in California, Elinor volunteered to fulfil one of the goals of the second Seven Year Plan in Europe. When the European Teaching Committee asked which country she was interested in, she replied that the only language she knew was French. The committee responded with 'We will give you Norway'. Elinor arrived at her post in May 1947 and joined American pioneer Johanna Schubarth (who had originally been from Norway) and they were soon joined by Mildred Clark. At Riḍván 1948, they were able to elect the first Local Spiritual Assembly in Norway in Oslo. At the European Teaching Conference in Brussels, Belgium the next year, Elinor met Robert Wolff. When she returned to America in 1950, he was there and they were married.[75]

In 1953, the couple attended the Intercontinental Teaching Conference in Chicago where they heard the goals of the Ten Year Crusade. Initially, they chose Indonesia as their goal because Robert had grown up there. Shoghi Effendi told them no because of political tensions between the Indonesians and the Dutch. They then tried to go either to Dutch Guiana or to Africa, before settling on Dutch Guiana, now called Suriname. Robert had been born in Dutch Guiana. It was a very difficult place to move to and it was only because Robert had been born there that he was able to enter. Elinor was only allowed in because she was married to Robert. They also had to pay a large bond before receiving permission.[76]

Shoghi Effendi had encouraged Robert to get his doctorate at the university, but as the end of the Holy Year drew near, they worried that finishing the degree would cause them to miss Shoghi Effendi's goal of being at their post before the Holy Year ended. Robert wrote to the committee in charge of assisting pioneers to reach their posts and said it would take him six months to finish his degree. The committee wrote back saying, 'We will give you six weeks.' They made it, but just barely. Robert finished his oral exams at 10 p.m. one night and they were on the plane for Dutch Guiana at 9 a.m. the next morning.[77]

Elinor and Robert and their young child, Jan, arrived on Dutch Guiana on 14 October 1953.

> Our first child was 19 months and I was expecting our second . . . It was very difficult. I probably suffered the most cultural shock. I had thought going abroad to Europe was something, but I had never lived in a country that was very undeveloped to begin with. And of course, with expecting a child and having a small child, you are very

sensitive to all the dangers of disease and dysentery and so on.

But it was a country that had such a background of people and had another kind of cultural standard there. There were the Hindus, the Pakistanis and the Javanese from Indonesia who had been brought in after slavery was abolished. The country had been colonized by the English and the Dutch. The Jews had come in from Europe . . . a very large Jewish colony of Portuguese Jews had been established . . . And the Negros were of course brought in for slavery for the plantations. There were some very primitive African type tribal groups in the jungle who escaped in the early days of slavery and . . . had sort of African kinds of tribal villages. There were Amer and Carib, the aboriginal Indians in the interior in the Amazon tropical rain forest . . . and the Chinese seemed to have stores on every corner. So you had a new mixture of various racial and cultural backgrounds that I had never encountered before.[78]

In April 1955, the Wolffs wrote:

I think how good pioneering is for us; it is a real test of world citizenry . . . After a year or so of resistance, we get a sort of crashing revelation that we are not just reading a book (to be laid down an hour later) about 'how the other half live'. We are experiencing it! And God's instrument – as imperfect as it is – must emanate that mystical but unifying oneness in our little geographical spots to bind up the golden chain that links all humanity together . . .[79]

We had our Feast on Thursday. It was wonderful to feel so in need of praying. There is a great power in feeling such a real dependence on God and His help . . . Jan, of course, is a wonderful drawing card. He is such a happy baby, our little boy. He is very blonde and blue eyed, and when we take him for a walk he greets everybody on the street, regardless of color, size, shape, costume, etc. in a mixture of English, Dutch and Ningre. Our pioneering is really a family project, and such a blessing. We need your continued prayers . . . We are truly pioneering. I in my job and Elinor in our home and social relations, as well as telling people about the Cause. How easy it is to teach the Baha'i Faith in a country like America which is open to new ideas and where people are free and reasonably responsible for their own acts!⁸⁰

Hand of the Cause Dr Muhájir loved to take Robert out on teaching trips. He would arrive and say:

> 'Okay, Bob, we are going to go out teaching today. So, they'd get in the car together and Bob would say, 'Which way are we going to go?' And Dr Muhájir would say, 'Let's go east.' So, they would drive east. And Bob would say, 'Where are we going to go?' and he goes, 'We are going east.' Then he would say, 'Take a left here!' and they would go out and the road would get really bad and Bob didn't know where they were going. But Dr Muhájir would say, 'This is the right way.'
>
> And finally after about an hour they came and there would be all these kids in the road and they'd say 'Oh, over here, we are waiting for you.' And they'd go into the village and they'd say to Dr Muhájir, 'We knew that you were coming,' and they would go in and teach.⁸¹

Robert and Elinor stayed in Dutch Guiana for two years. In the early 1960s, they moved to Oahu where Robert taught at the University of Hawaii.

BRITISH GUIANA (NOW GUYANA)

Malcolm King

Malcolm King (1985?–1966) became a Bahá'í in 1931 and was soon elected to the Local Spiritual Assembly of Milwaukee, Wisconsin. He answered the call for pioneers during the first Seven Year Plan (1937–1944) and remained a pioneer for the rest of his life, living in Nicaragua, Haiti, Dominican Republic, Antigua and Jamaica.⁸² On 16 October 1953, Malcolm arrived at Georgetown, British Guiana (now called Guyana) to fulfil one of the Guardian's goals and thus became a Knight of Bahá'u'lláh. The country was in political difficulties when he arrived, with British soldiers on the streets and a curfew imposed. To make his arrival more traumatic, he was robbed soon after his arrival. Even so, Malcolm set about teaching the Faith, visiting places where people were allowed to gather, such as libraries, post offices, public buildings and markets. When he met Allan Delph, he was able to organize his first meeting to present the Faith of Bahá'u'lláh. The meetings continued twice a week.[83]

With the meetings under way, Malcolm left Georgetown for a few months, returning in July 1954. Almost immediately, on 23 July, Allan Delph and Reginald Stone declared their belief in Bahá'u'lláh. Two months later, John Leacock and Alston Quow also became Bahá'ís. Alston had first heard of the Faith in French Guiana from Knight of Bahá'u'lláh Eberhard Friedland (next story). Alston soon thereafter moved to Mackenzie and opened up another area of British Guiana to the Faith. The four new Bahá'ís, with Malcolm's assistance, formed a Bahá'í group on 17 September. Malcolm then left Georgetown again, and visited other parts of the Caribbean to teach. The group continued to be active with the help of letters exchanged with Dorothy Campbell, who was the secretary of the National Spiritual Assembly of South America.[84]

When Malcolm returned to Georgetown in February 1955, he continued his meetings with the Bahá'ís and their contacts. Soon, Ivan Fraser, Clarine Savory, Adriana Winter, Radleen Fraser and Dr Charles Nicolson all joined the Faith. Shortly before Riḍván, Richard and Vida Backwell arrived as pioneers from the British Isles and, on 21 April, the first Local Spiritual Assembly was formed.[85]

Malcolm wrote to the *Crusader*, a newsletter for pioneers, that he had given the Message to 'Ministers in the Government and many of the legislators'.[86] With the formation of the Local Assembly supported by new pioneers, Malcolm left Georgetown to continue his teaching efforts throughout the Caribbean. In 1961, he pioneered to Jamaica where he died in 1966 at the age of 81, still a pioneer.[87]

FRENCH GUIANA

Eberhart Friedland

Eberhart Friedland (known as Hart) (1902–1991) was born in Germany and emigrated to America at the outbreak of the First World War. He became an American citizen and a Bahá'í. Attending the Conference in Wilmette in 1953, Hart chose to go to French Guiana. He travelled through Puerto Rico and Dutch Guiana (now Suriname), enjoying the company of other pioneers on the way.[88] In the crowded waiting room at the airport in Dutch Guiana, one couple caught his attention.

They turned out to be Elinor and Robert Wolff, Knights of Bahá'u'lláh for Dutch Guiana, who had arrived a few days before and were at the airport looking for some lost luggage.[89]

When Hart reached Cayenne, French Guiana, in the afternoon of 18 October 1953, he found that there were no rooms available anywhere, even though he had booked one at the only hotel in town, the Hotel del Palmistes. His driver from Pan American Airlines finally found him a place to stay – a classroom of a local school that had been converted to accommodate a dozen native football players. The next day he was able to move into the hotel. His first impression of the town was that it was orderly, but 'a good deal on the primitive side'.[90]

During 1955, Hart began visiting a leper hospital, which offered many opportunities for teaching:

> Twice a week I visit the hospital where some of the leper patients are kept, I read to them as well as to the others. One of the staff doctors always drives me home after these visits, and occasionally I show him certain passages in the Bahá'í Writings which are of interest to him. He has given me permission to leave Bahá'í literature in his reception room for the patients to read.[91]

By the summer of 1957, there were a number of Bahá'ís in Cayenne, but the number was diminishing for various reasons. He did have a twice-weekly class with two couples who were studying the book *Bahá'u'lláh and the New Era* in English, two French couples also studying the book and four members of the local police who had purchased the same book to read on their own. Hart remained in Cayenne for several years, then pioneered to Suriname until his death in 1991.[92]

EUROPE

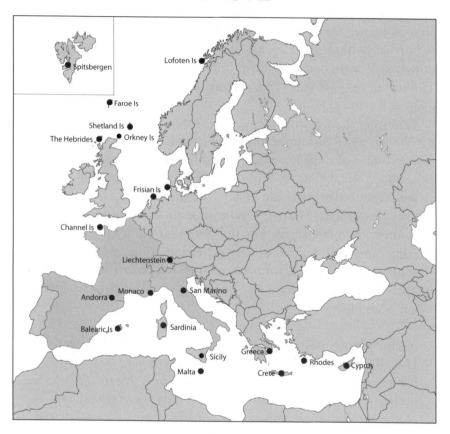

SPITSBERGEN

Paul Adams

On 27 June 1958, the next to the last of Shoghi Effendi's goals outside the Communist bloc was opened by Paul Adams (1937–2007). Paul grew up in difficult, post-war Britain and was taught the Bahá'í Faith while in his teens by Rose and John Wade. He became very active in the Bahá'í community and edited a Bahá'í youth journal. Jeanette and Owen Battrick expanded his knowledge of the Faith and Paul became very attached to the Guardian. When Shoghi Effendi passed away in London, Paul was doing his military service. He didn't ask for leave to attend the funeral, but simply told his commanding officer, 'My Guardian has died,' and left.[1]

Spitsbergen was an island group north of Norway at about 80° N latitude known for its isolation and extreme winters. While in England, Paul tried to find work on Spitsbergen, but was unsuccessful, so he moved to Tromsø in the far north of Norway, just to be closer. While in Tromsø, he learned that Hilmar Nois, a hunter from Spitsbergen, was looking for an apprentice.[2]

Paul took the job, the only one available, and became a Knight of Bahá'u'lláh when he landed at the town of Longyearbyen, a town that survived on coal mining, trapping and hunting. Spitsbergen's inhabitants tended to be 'few, far flung and for the most part alienated from society. They were hunters, miners, hard-drinkers . . .'[3] Soon after landing, Paul found Hilmar, a man three times his age who had lived 30 winters on Spitsbergen. For the next year, he lived in an isolated hunting camp with Hilmar usually as his only companion.[4] Paul wrote, 'The physical difficulties, immense as they sometimes are, are nothing compared with the spiritual struggle to be simply a Bahá'í'.[5] His time on the island was an

intensely lonely one. The winters were long, hard and bitterly dark. His only companion during his first years there was a man of strange habits and a closed mind, and the only alternative to cabin fever during six months of darkness in this person's company was to plunge into sub-zero temperatures outside, where a foot misplaced, a breath miscalculated, an aim misjudged could lead to a slow and icy end. But there were certain lessons he learned from the experience. One was never to throw bread away, even if it was mouldy, mildewed, leached of all nutritional value. Another was the rather laconic attitude he acquired to unchangeable circumstances it was not worth fighting against. He was fond of saying – 'Cold in the Arctic' – regarding the grim realities of life. A third was a phrase from one of the letters of Shoghi Effendi which he often quoted, calling for 'patience, persistence and perseverance' in taking up this difficult post. Although radiant acquiescence was not exactly his forte, a certain dogged stoicism became second nature to him.[6]

Kent Lansing, from Los Angeles, joined him for the summer of 1960. As the two passed through Norway on their way to the island, they were interviewed by a journalist who had learned of the Faith from Knights of Bahá'u'lláh Loyce Lawrence and Mildred Clark in Lofoten. The journalist was very impressed that the men were heading for Spitsbergen, not to make money as most youth did, but to share their faith. His article included a short summary of the history and principles of the Faith.[7]

The next year, Paul was joined by Arnold Zonneveld, a new Dutch Bahá'í who stayed there for the next three years working as a hunter and coal miner. Arnold later married Gisela von Brunn, daughter of Knight of Bahá'u'lláh Ursula von Brunn, in 1965. The couple pioneered to Bolivia in 1967.[8]

Paul stayed on Spitsbergen for five very difficult years. During his final year, he shot a polar bear whose skin he prepared and sent as a gift to the Bahá'í World Centre. It was placed in a room at Bahjí before the cabinet where the Guardian had displayed the facsimiles of the Hidden Words of Baha'u'llah.[9] Gunnar and Edel Lange-Nielsen, from Trondheim, Norway, pioneered to Spitsbergen in November 1970, to continue the work of Adams, Lansing and Zonneveld.[10]

Paul later moved to Queretaro, Mexico, 'from the cold of the Arctic to the heat of central America'.[11]

LOFOTEN ISLANDS

Loyce Lawrence

Loyce Lawrence (1905–1968) pioneered to the Lofoten Islands with Mildred Clark in August 1953. Loyce grew up in Massachusetts and trained as a nurse. She served as a nurse in the American South and had there encountered the Bahá'í Faith.[12] Harlan and Grace Ober helped her accept the station of Bahá'u'lláh in 1940.[13] In 1942, she married Gustavus Lawrence, a wealthy Californian, in Los Angeles. Nine years later, in 1951, after the couple moved to New York, Gustavus died. In 1953,

Loyce attended both the Asian Intercontinental Teaching Conference in New Delhi and the European Conference in Stockholm. Loyce was inspired to pioneer while in New Delhi, but went to Stockholm before deciding what to do. While in Stockholm, Shoghi Effendi's message stirred the great desire to answer his call and she offered to go to the Lofoten Islands with fellow American Mildred Clark.[14]

Loyce's plan had been to volunteer to go to a nice, warm, tropical island, and when she offered to go to Lofoten she did not realize that it was north of the Arctic Circle in Norway and known for being stormy and windy. But with the fulsome congratulations of her friends for filling the difficult goal, she stood by her commitment.

Immediately after the Conference, Loyce returned to America and collected the things she would need for her new post, including warm clothing. She also brought a new American car. Loyce and Mildred arrived in Svolvaer on 28 August 1953. Initially, Loyce had a tough time finding a place to live until the police built a new headquarters. She asked them for an apartment in the building and her request was granted. Most of the people in the town initially thought Loyce was just another American tourist, but when she didn't leave, they became suspicious, thinking she might be a CIA spy. One of Loyce's few luxuries during those years in Svolvaer was an annual trip back to Boston to have her hair done and take care of business.

After several years, she and Mildred were able to raise up the first Local Spiritual Assembly in the islands.[15] In 1966, Loyce was elected to the National Spiritual Assembly. On her way to the meetings in Oslo, she would commonly stop in Trondheim and visit Hooshang Rafat and his wife Polin, who were pioneering there. Loyce attracted the hearts of the people of the island through her magnetic personality and her sincere love for them. She associated with both the upper classes and the common people and people loved and respected her; she radiated love and spirituality in whatever gathering she entered. Loyce entertained hundreds of people with warm hospitality and love at her flat and taught the Faith with both words and example. Many souls embraced the Cause of God through the course of her pioneering there.

In 1968 Loyce went to Haifa for the second International Convention. She was good friends with Rúḥíyyih Khánum, but one day she rushed up to Hooshang and begged him to pray for her. Rúḥíyyih Khánum, knowing Loyce was a nurse, had asked her for a massage treatment. Nervous as she was initially, Loyce returned later very happy that her distinguished patient had enjoyed her massage.

Later in the same year, doctors found something wrong in Loyce's lungs and she was hospitalized in Trondheim. The pioneer families Rafat and Navidi visited her every day and had prayers with her. She was in great pain but endured it with great patience. When she passed away on 28 December 1968 the friends were with her. Her grave is in Trondheim and the Bahá'í community gathers there for prayers on special occasions. Loyce left a cabin to the Bahá'ís, who used it as a local centre for a number of years until the financial burden of keeping it up forced them to sell it.

Mildred Clark

Mildred Clark (1892–1967) had pioneered to Denver, Colorado during the first Seven Year Plan (1937–1944). In 1948, she arose to fill a goal of the second Seven Year Plan by pioneering to Norway, settling in Oslo and helping to form the first Local Spiritual Assembly there. In 1950, wishing to see other areas, she pioneered to the Netherlands and then, two years later, to Luxembourg. She was also a pioneer in Finland for a time. At the Stockholm Conference, she joined with Loyce and the two pioneered together to Svolvaer in the Lofoten Islands.[16]

Mildred remained in Svolvaer for over ten years, then pioneered to Trondheim. At one point in Trondheim, Mrs Meherangíz Munsiff visited her and gave a fireside attended by 87 people. Afterwards, a local newspaper carried a story about Mrs Munsiff, including a photograph with her in a sari. In 1965, Mrs and Mrs Hooshang Rafat pioneered to Trondheim and joined Mildred. At that time, Mildred was ill with a heart condition, but she still had firesides in her hotel room.[17] Shortly before her death, Mildred pioneered to Finland, where she passed away in 1967.[18]

FAROE ISLANDS

Eskil Ljungberg

Eskil Ljungberg (1886–1985) was born in Sweden, but went to London as a young man and worked for almost thirty years for various families of the British aristocracy. His first encounter with a Bahá'í happened one day when he was

> walking in a garden with the young lady to whom he was engaged to be married. They saw a distinguished-looking, grey-haired lady and he asked his fiancée who the lady was. He was told that she was an aunt who was probably 'a bit crazy', because she had 'fallen in love' with an old Persian gentleman who lived in the Holy Land. The young lady died before Eskil and she could be married; the aunt was Lady Blomfield.[19]

Eskil, however, did not become a Bahá'í until he returned to Sweden and encountered the Swedish pioneer Jennie Ottilia Anderson in 1947. When he accepted the Bahá'í Faith, Dorothy Baker was in Stockholm and she anointed his face and hands with attar of rose, for Eskil, an unforgettable event. He served on the Local Spiritual Assemblies of Stockholm and Gothenburg.[20]

Eskil wrote that he had wanted to pioneer to a warm place, going so far as to write to the Guardian in 1949 about pioneering to Casablanca in Morocco. Though he received approval, the move didn't happen. Then he considered the Canary Islands. Next he attended the Intercontinental Conference in Stockholm in 1953 and found himself agreeing to go to the subarctic Faroe Islands. He arrived from Sweden on 28 August 1953 at the age of 67 and remained there for the rest of his life. Eskil was a 'tall, dignified gentleman in his early retirement years' and patiently worked with the less than friendly local people. At first, the islanders treated him with suspicion and even considered him a spy.[21] He once wrote to Brigitte Hasselblatt on the Shetland Islands that even after several years on the Faroes, it was not unusual to be invited to someone's home only to arrive and find it deserted.[22]

Eskil was a prolific letter writer, corresponding with thousands of people around the world. In the summer of 1957, he travelled to Iceland and pioneered there briefly in 1961 to save a Spiritual Assembly at the request of the Canadian National Spiritual Assembly. He was greatly supported in his efforts by visits from Hand of the Cause Hermann Grossman and Auxiliary Board member Marion Hofman. The Faroe Islands were a lonely place and Marion had a copy of every book published by George Ronald sent to him. The books proved to be a great companion for Eskil as he slowly broke down the social barriers that surrounded him.[23]

Eskil was joined in May 1959 by Claire Copley (now Greenberg), then a young lady of 20. She had found a job taking care of the five boys of the Sivetsen family who were between the ages of 7½ months and 12 years. Initially, the Sivetsens lived in a very isolated house, but after just a week, Claire, the five boys and their parents, all moved into a flat that shared a hallway and toilet with Eskil's flat (the Sivetsens owned both flats). Eskil didn't particularly mind the additional traffic in the hallway, but loss of full-time access to the toilet was difficult for him. The chaos only lasted until the end of August when Claire left to pioneer to Newcastle.[24]

Teaching the Faith to the islanders was a slow process, but in 1965 Eskil met Emma Reinert who became the first native believer. In 1970, British pioneer Richard Bury joined Eskil and the first Local Spiritual Assembly in the Faroe Islands was formed in Tórshavn, the capital, in 1973. Eskil passed away in 1985 at the age of 98, still at his pioneering post.[25]

ORKNEY ISLANDS

Charles Dunning

Charles Dunning (1885–1967) arrived in the Orkney Islands on 9 September 1953. Charles was born in Leeds and could not walk until he was nine, but by the age of 13 he was driving a pony in a coal mine. Two years later, he went to sea as a galley boy on a merchant ship.[26]

Charles became a Bahá'í in 1948 and immediately arose and pioneered to Belfast. The year spent there prepared him for his next pioneering post, one of Shoghi Effendi's goals, the Orkney Islands off the northern tip of Scotland. He initially consulted with Brigitte Hasselblatt, who was about to pioneer to another goal, the Shetland Islands, and on 9 September, Charles landed in Kirkwall in the Orkney Islands. Charles spent his time exploring the town, visiting its churches and making friends where he could, saying, 'Our work is to tell the people and leave the rest to God.' Charles was physically odd and consequently was pursued and abused by gangs of boys and distrusted by adults. His primary support through this time was the memory of Ḥájí

Sulaymán Khán, who was martyred for his Faith in Tehran in the early days of the Faith.[27]

Marion Hofman visited Charles on a number of occasions. After having visited both Charles in Orkney and Brigitte Hasselblatt in Shetland, she noticed that the people of the Orkney Islands were 'different and less friendly' than on the Shetland Islands. She wrote:

> Then I knew the wisdom of Bahá'u'lláh sending Charles to the Orkney Islands. . . I came to appreciate why only a soldier and martyr-spirit, such as Charles, would be able to conquer a town like Kirkwall . . . I know too that his sufferings and endurance have brought him into intimacy of the spirit with the Dawnbreakers of the Heroic Age. Indeed, his comfort and support have been straight from them . . .[28]

As recounted in *Dayspring*, the children's magazine published by the UK National Spiritual Assembly, Charles was persecuted by everyone, even the children on the island. But some of those children were affected by this unusual visitor:

> One day, when a group of young children had been chasing him and he had run up the steps to the house where he was living, he paused outside the door and turned to look sadly at them. One of the children was a boy who was seven years old. He had not thrown stones at Charlie nor called any names, but he had run down the street with the other children.
>
> As Charles Dunning looked at him, the little boy felt ashamed and knew that what he and his friends were doing was wrong. And he never forgot that day. When he was a youth, he became friends with a travelling teacher who was living in Orkney for a year. His new friend told him about Bahá'u'lláh, and he and his sister went to firesides to hear more about the Faith. They were among the first four Orcadians to become Bahá'ís. Their names are Moira and Ian.[29]

When Brigitte Hasselblatt visited Charles he took her to meet Mrs and Mr Tait. He had originally met them when he noticed a large statue of Buddha in their garden, which they had brought back from a trip to India. Seeing the statue the first time, Charles walked up and rang the bell, then told them how much he liked the statue. He told them that he admired their courage in placing the Buddha there in a small town where everyone belonged to one church or another. They became good friends after that.[30]

To earn a living, Charles sold long-handled brushes and other household things door to door. He stayed in the Orkney Islands for several years until health issues forced him to move to Cardiff.[31] He was replaced by Daryoush Mehrabi, who continued his efforts. Jackie Mehrabi described meeting, in 1960, one woman who had been interested in the Faith. The lady plainly told Jackie that she was no longer interested and thought it would be best if she forgot about Bahá'u'lláh. The truth came out just before her husband came home. When she realized his arrival was imminent, she quickly rushed Jackie out through the back door so her husband wouldn't know she'd been talking with a Bahá'í.[32] But the seeds Charles planted grew into a Local Spiritual Assembly in 1969.

After leaving Orkney, Charles settled in Cardiff and spent the remainder of his life there.[33]

SHETLAND ISLANDS

Brigitte Hasselblatt

As Charles Dunning tried to settle onto the Orkney Islands, Brigitte Hasselblatt (1923–2008) arrived on the Shetland Islands, farther north in the North Sea. Brigitte was born in Estonia and by the age of 14 she was already interested in spiritual things. She organized a Bible study group to understand its teachings. She decided that 'something was wrong with religion as I knew it'. In 1939, the family moved to Germany and Brigitte studied nursing at the Martin Luther Hospital and lived at the school. After an air raid, a huge unexploded bomb was found behind the house that Brigitte lived in. After the war, she worked as a nurse in Germany until the English Ministry of Labour came looking for people to work in Britain. Once in England, she was trained as a midwife.

In 1950, Brigitte and a friend were invited to a Bahá'í summer school where they were met by Meherangiz Munsiff. During the first talk, Brigitte 'felt as if a beam of light had struck my heart and had torn away a veil'. She could barely sit through that first talk, so great was the desire to announce that she was a Bahá'í. Before leaving the school, she asked where she could pioneer to and was told Bournemouth, which she did in 1950. Two years later, she pioneered to Glasgow on the advice of the teaching committee.[34]

With the announcement of the Ten Year Crusade, Brigitte decided to fill one of the Guardian's goals and chose Estonia, but it was not available, being behind the 'Iron Curtain'. She then looked at the British goals and chose the Shetland Islands. She arrived at her pioneering post on 17 September 1953 not knowing anything about her new post or even where she would live. Her first look at her new home was on the hour-long drive from the airfield to the town of Lerwick, during which she saw 'no houses, no trees, no bushes or flowers, only brown peat-covered hills'. Not being British, Brigitte had to present her passport at the police station. The policeman asked all the questions she expected except what her religion was. She later found out that there were seven different churches in the little town, all competing for members.[35]

Pioneering was a much greater challenge than Brigitte had expected. In a letter to Marion Hofman a year after her arrival, she wrote, 'I had no conception of the nature of the tests and difficulties that are to assail every soul in his Service and without the spiritual forces released by the prayers of the friends, I cannot but fail in fulfilling the task before me.'[36]

Brigitte found work with the Public Health Office. She later worked for the wife of the island's veterinarian and finally as a midwife in the only hospital. It was there in July 1957 that she met Lilian McKay, who was having her second child. Lilian left the hospital with a new child and a new interest in Bahá'u'lláh. She soon became the first native believer. Her husband, Alex, became a Bahá'í a few years later. Brigitte had few women to care for and was thus able to spend time with each. Some were soothed by prayers, and soon the women in the maternity section were asking for Brigitte.[37]

Auxiliary Board member Marion Hofman visited Brigitte a number of times. On 17 March 1956, they had the island's first public Bahá'í meeting. Seventeen people attended and a newspaper reporting on the event carried a story that read: 'The highest stirring, the deepest longing and desire burning in the hearts of man, is the realization of the oneness of mankind. And the principles which will lead to it are mentioned in the Bahá'í teachings.'[38] Other newspapers were very much in opposition. Because of the positive response, Brigitte and Marion planned to have a weekend school in the autumn.

The next year, after another meeting, the paper took a very different view. Charles Dunning went on pilgrimage in January 1957 and when he returned he visited Brigitte. Charles was so excited about his pilgrimage that the two rented a room at the Town Hall for a public proclamation. On the night, no one came, but the event hadn't gone unnoticed. The next day, the *Shetland News* carried a headline, 'Heathen Faith preached in Town Hall!' While the two Bahá'ís had waited in the Town Hall room, a member of the local Presbyterian Church, who had just returned from the Holy Land as well, was warning the congregation about the 'dangerous, false religion that was spreading all over the world and had even come to the islands'. The story concluded: 'Surely there can be no comparison between this world-shaking event (the Return of Christ) and the unannounced coming into the world of a humble Persian.'[39]

Brigitte left Shetland in 1959 to pioneer to Finland at the suggestion of Rúḥíyyih Khánum. Initially supported by the Bahá'í Fund, she was eager to become self-supporting but could not find a job. In desperation, she said the Tablet of Aḥmad. The next morning, she felt that she should go to a nearby kiosk and buy a newspaper. There she saw an advertisement for a nursing position in the hospital and she was soon working. In early 1961, she married Milton Lundblade and the couple pioneered to Turku, Finland and, when more pioneers came, moved to Copenhagen, Denmark. By late 1961, Milton was unable to find work and the American pioneer committee suggested that the couple move to America, which they did, settling in California. Milton passed away in 1978 and in 1984, Brigitte was asked to pioneer to Finland.[40]

Brigitte soon found herself working with Bahá'ís from Estonia and began making trips there, the first in 1986. Two and a half years later, she was living in Estonia, fulfilling a long-held personal desire. In 1991, she was appointed as an Auxiliary Board member and two years later was elected to the Regional Spiritual Assembly of the Baltic States. When the first National Spiritual Assembly of Estonia was formed in 1999, Brigitte was a member of that as well.[41]

In 1993, Brigitte returned to the Shetland Islands for the 40th anniversary of the arrival of the Faith. She was amazed at the enthusiasm with which she was greeted by the local people. She also had the opportunity to meet with the Local Spiritual Assembly that had in part been raised through her efforts. She was again on the islands in 2003 for the Golden Jubilee. The local newspaper printed a full-page story with photos, and a celebration at the Town Hall attracted 100 guests. It was a huge metamorphosis from the less than friendly reception she had received a half-century earlier.[42]

Brigitte remained at her Estonian pioneering post until her passing in 2008.

THE HEBRIDES

Geraldine Craney

Geraldine Craney originally lived in Bray, Ireland, but moved to Nottingham in the United Kingdom, where she was a comptometer operator (key-driven calculator). She found the Bahá'í Faith in February 1953 and became a Bahá'í. Her acceptance of Bahá'u'lláh resulted, unfortunately, in her total rejection by her family. When Shoghi Effendi's goals for the Ten Year Crusade were announced, she chose to fulfil the one for the Hebrides Islands, off the coast of Scotland, landing there on 9 October 1953. Being isolated and called a 'Stranger' by native residents, as were all outsiders, she had few visitors. Geraldine lived in an isolated area from 1953 until 1959.[43]

FRISIAN ISLANDS

Elsa Maria Grossmann

Elsa Maria Grossmann (1896–1977) was the sister of Hand of the Cause Hermann Grossmann. She was born in Argentina, but the family moved to Germany in 1909. She first encountered the Bahá'í Faith in 1919 or 1920. Her brother, Hermann Grossmann, had found and accepted the Faith during a talk by Harlan and Grace Ober in Leipzig. When he returned to Hamburg, he was met by Elsa to whom he shared what he had learned. She immediately accepted the truth of the Faith. During the late 1930s, when the Faith was persecuted by the Nazi regime, Elsa was imprisoned for a short period because of her Bahá'í beliefs.[44]

At the Stockholm Intercontinental Teaching Conference in July

1953, Elsa Maria volunteered to pioneer to Westerland on the island of Sylt in the Frisians and on 24 September 1953, she reached her new post. The Frisian Islands are a long string of islands off the German and Dutch coasts. Shoghi Effendi called the Islands 'inhospitable and wind-swept' and though Elsa Maria's health was poor, she remained there for 11 years. In a letter Elsa Maria wrote to the US *Bahá'í News*, she described her life:

> The story of the opening of the Frisian Islands to the Cause of God is, as yet experienced, not a very crimson-coloured one when com-pared with many others from more radiant pioneer places. This was for a long time a heavy load on us here, but only the fact that our beloved Guardian was fully aware of the situation, and often transmitted to us his inspiration and loving comfort, lightened its weight. We think of the little white lighthouses everywhere on these islands, looking over the sea calmly and firmly, and fully indifferent to the storms and tempests around them, just showing the seeking sailor the right route. This exactly is our way: to be like lighthouses of His Cause for whomsoever seeks His Path. And this finally, God willing, may lead to His Spiritual victory.[45]

Elsa Maria taught English to the children and became known as 'Saint Johanna' in spite of the unfriendliness of the inhabitants. One woman, Martha Petersen, 'a fine and very cultured old lady of pure Frisian origin . . . with the swiftness of lightning, grasped the truth of the Cause, its authority and weight' and became a Bahá'í. In 1964, at the age of 68, Elsa Maria was forced back to the mainland by her deteriorating health. Elsa passed away in 1977. It took twenty more years before the first Local Spiritual Assembly of Westerland could be formed.[46]

Ursula von Brunn

Ursula von Brunn (1917–2002?) pioneered to the North Frisian Islands (Germany) in October 1953 with her nine-year-old daughter, Gisela. Ursula had attended the Stockholm Intercontinental Teaching Confer-ence and, though she had only been a Bahá'í for a little over a year, she dearly wished to fulfil one of the Guardian's goals. She faced many chal-lenges in responding to Shoghi Effendi's call: having lost her husband,

Eberhard, in the world war, her finances were tenuous, some in her family were extremely antagonistic toward her new Faith and 'bombarded her with reproaches and accusations', and the moving fund she was going to receive from the National Spiritual Assembly could not, at the last moment, be provided. To make things more difficult, she suffered a severe back problem shortly before leaving for her pioneering post and was constantly in pain.[47]

Arriving in the town of Wyk on the Island of Föhr on 7 October, she found that the islanders were very closed to outsiders. Her daughter Gisela remembers that

> In summer, everybody would move into garages etc., in order to rent every available space to the tourists; in winter, they would shut themselves up in their homes. There is a saying that one has to share the contents of a full bag of salt, before becoming friends with them – which hints to almost a lifetime of knowing each other!

The only people who were open to teaching were other outsiders. Ursula ordered a youth magazine subscription for Gisela and this gave her the opportunity to visit a local shop every two weeks and talk with the woman who owned it, a native of the island. Ursula repeatedly invited the lady and her sister over for afternoon tea. When they finally accepted, many months later, they greatly enjoyed the visit and looked forward to getting together more often. Unfortunately, a week later, in the spring of 1955, Ursula and Gisela were forced to leave because of very difficult financial straits.

Pioneering in the Frisian Islands had not been a pleasant experience for Ursula and she swore never to pioneer again. Then in 1967, she visited Gisela and her husband, Arnold Zonneveld, at their pioneering post in Bolivia. While there, Ursula received a letter from the Universal House of Justice welcoming her as a new pioneer in Bolivia. With that welcome, Gisela wrote, 'what could she do but stay and teach?'

> Whatever she might have missed out on her first pioneer post, she definitely made up for during her time in Bolivia. She often went, partly on foot, to distant villages and hamlets in the mountains, she belonged over the years to different institutions and committees, and her home was well-known for her hospitality.

Ursula's second pioneering post obviously delighted her heart. By staying near her family, she was also a great support to grandchildren and great-grandchildren, most of whom are very active Bahá'ís. She remained there until her passing in 2003.

Geertrui Ankersmit

Geertrui Ankersmit (b.1926), from Nijmegen, the Netherlands, became a Knight of Bahá'u'lláh on 6 October 1953 when she arrived in the town of Den Burg on Texel Island, the southern-most of the Dutch Frisian Islands. She became a Bahá'í in October in Brighton, England, in 1951.[48]

Geertrui's path to Texel started at the Intercontinental Teaching Conference in Stockholm. After listening to Hand of the Cause of God Ugo Giachery, she decided to pioneer to the Frisian Islands. She was a professional dress designer, but had no sewing machine. Rising to the aid of a future Knight of Bahá'u'lláh, Mr Sabet bought a sewing machine which could also be operated by hand. Geertrui initially thought about going to the island of Ameland because it was where her family had gone for holidays and she had contacts there. But it was suggested she go to Texel instead, which she did.

Initially, Geertrui boarded in Den Burg with Mrs Roos, 'an ardent Christian, whose son was a missionary in Africa'. She went with Mrs Roos to her meetings in order to get to know people, and that resulted in her getting sewing work. Geertrui rode all over the island with her sewing machine on the back of her bicycle. As she peddled along, she 'would sing out Yá Bahá'u'l-Abhá and Alláh-u-Abhá because Shoghi Effendi told us that it was very important that the Greatest Name should be sounded around the world'.

Since it was difficult to make a living out of sewing, Geertrui applied for a job in De Koog and went to live with Mrs Neeltje Epe-Kelderhuis, the widow of the forester on Texel. After telling Mrs Epe that Bahá'u'lláh was the return of Christ, the lady said that if Bahá'u'lláh was descended from Abraham then she could accept Him. Geertrui showed that Bahá'u'lláh was descended from Abraham through Ishmael, but though she was very close to the Faith, Mrs Epe never took the final step. While staying with Mrs Epe-Kelderhuis, she was asked by Mrs Kooper, who was preparing her house for paying guests, to sew furnishing items. Whilst Geertrui was sewing her curtains Mrs Kooper showed great interest in the Faith.

Next Geertrui found work in a children's home where she was the head of the household and cook. Working by day and caring for the children sleeping in the dormitory next to her room by night, she was infected by yellow jaundice and became quite ill. She then found another job at a home for the aged in Den Burg, where she helped the manager, nursed the elderly and cooked at weekends. With three roles, Geertrui overworked herself and fell ill again after of not getting enough sleep at night. The doctor said she needed rest, so Geertrui went to the National Bahá'í Centre in The Hague for a few weeks to care for an American pioneer, Eleanor Hollibaugh. Hand of the Cause Hermann Grossmann suggested that she go to Luxembourg because they needed enough Bahá'ís to reform the Local Spiritual Assembly of Luxembourg-Ville, with the goal of establishing the Benelux Regional Spiritual Assembly, and before the end of the World Crusade the election of the National Spiritual Assembly of the Grand Duchy of Luxembourg. To obtain a resident's permit in Luxembourg, she had to have a job and she found one with KLM Royal Dutch Airlines. Upon her arrival in January 1956, Geertrui became a member of the Local Spiritual Assembly of Luxembourg-Ville.

In 1960, Geertrui went on pilgrimage. She flew to Tel Aviv on a plane filled with South American Jews who were so excited to reach the Holy Land that they kissed the ground when they landed. Since it was one o'clock in the morning when she arrived, Geertrui went looking for a hotel, but the only place she could find was a bed on a stair landing of the floor the hotel employees lived on. Geertrui's train to Haifa was filled with German-speaking Jews. Once in Haifa, one of them helped her get a sherut to the Western Pilgrim House at 10 Haparsim where she was greeted by Jessie Revell. Geertrui was very impressed with the simplicity of the living conditions in the Pilgrim House. John and Dorothy Ferraby, Paul and Marjorie Haney, Leroy and Sylvia Ioas, and Horace and Doris Holley resided there and nearly all the friends and pilgrim guests shared a single shower room. There was only a solitary kerosene heater in the dining room to provide warmth, something very much needed in February. Doris Holley and a housekeeper took care of the Pilgrim House. Milly Collins lived in the House of the Master where she had to bathe herself with a bowl of warm water in her bed-sitting room.

Paul Adams, Knight of Bahá'u'lláh to Spitsbergen,
with Hilmar Nois, back from a trip in Advent Bay

Loyce Lawrence and Mildred Clarke, Knights of Bahá'u'lláh to the Lofoten Islands, 1953

Left to right: *Charles Dunning, Knight of Bahá'u'lláh to the Orkney Islands; Brigitte Hasselblatt, Knight of Baháu'lláh to Shetland; Philip Hainsworth; Hand of the Cause Hermann Grossmann; Ḍíá'u'lláh Asgharzádíh, Knight of Bahá'u'lláh to the Channel Islands; Dorothy Ferraby; Ruth Moffett*

Charles Dunning,
Knight of Bahá'u'lláh to the Orkney Islands

Brigitte Hasselblatt,
Knight of Bahá'u'lláh to Shetland

Elsa Maria Grossmann, Knight of Bahá'u'lláh to the Frisian Islands, with her brother Hand of the Cause Hermann Grossmann

Contributed by Gisela von Brunn

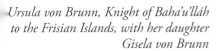

Ursula von Brunn, Knight of Bahá'u'lláh to the Frisian Islands, with her daughter Gisela von Brunn

...ertrui Ankersmit ...Bates), Knight of ...Bahá'u'lláh to the Frisian Islands

Geertrui Ankersmit (Bates) with Ray Humphrey and Hand of the Cause Jalal Khazeh, Haifa, 1960

Evelyn Baxter,
Knight of Bahá'u'lláh to the Channel Islands

Amír Húshmand Manúchehrí,
Knight of Bahá'u'lláh to Liechtenstein,
passport 1956

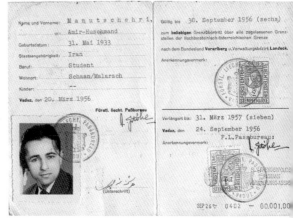

Diá'u'lláh
Asgharzádih,
Knight of
Bahá'u'lláh to the
Channel Islands

William Danjon,
Knight of Bahá'u'lláh for Andorra

Tabandeh and Sohrab Payman, Knights of Bahá'u'lláh to San Marino

Eskil Ljungberg,
Knight of Baha'u'lláh to the Faroe Islands

An early Spiritual Assembly of the Bahá'ís of Monaco
with Knights of Bahá'u'lláh Shamsí Navídi (standing second from left)*, Azízu'lláh Navídí*
(standing far right)*, Olivia Kelsey* (standing fourth from left)*, Florence Ullrich* (seated far left)*,

Olivia Kelsey,
Knight of Bahá'u'lláh to Monaco

Florence Ullrich (Kelley),
Knight of Bahá'u'lláh to Monaco

Nellie French,
Knight of Bahá'u'lláh to Monaco

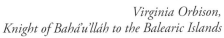

Virginia Orbison,
Knight of Bahá'u'lláh to the Balearic Islands

Knights of Bahá'u'lláh to the Balearic Islands:
Charles Ioas (left), with Jean and Tove Deleuran

Emma Rice,
Knight of Bahá'u'lláh to Sicily

Marie Ciocca,
Knight of Bahá'u'lláh to Sardinia

Left to right: *Carol, Stanley, Florence, Gerrold and Susan Bagley,*
Knights of Bahá'u'lláh to Sicily

Sylvia Ioas took Geertrui to the Shrine of the Báb for her first visit. In front of the then Eastern Pilgrim House, she had her first glimpse of the Shrine. Tears welled up in her eyes and she cried all the way to the Shrine as she felt so unworthy to be there when other long-serving pioneers had not yet had this privilege. While in the Shrine she noticed a curtain which had come loose from its rings and this unexpected reality brought her back to earth. Recomposing herself, she said her prayers, then went to the Shrine of 'Abdu'l-Bahá where she was surprised to find a completely different feeling. Hand of the Cause of God Mr Kházeh took her to Bahjí and she greatly enjoyed his company and sense of humour. Being the only pilgrim in the Shrine of Bahá'u'lláh, Geertrui was able to sing to her heart's content. She met the custodians, Dr Forsyth and Janet Ward. They were the parents of Alicia Cardell, wife of Knight of Bahá'u'lláh Ted Cardell, and had been on their way to visit them when they stopped to visit the Holy Places. They had been asked to stay and care for the Shrine.

An English meteorologist living in Libya, Ray Humphrey, arrived on pilgrimage and Mr Kházeh took them to 'Akká, the Temple land at the head of Mt Carmel and the new Archives building. The Archives building had been completed, but was not yet ready for pilgrim use. All the furniture inside was covered with sheets and the Archive materials were still being displayed in a back room of the Shrine of the Báb. Lotfullah Hakim showed Geertrui and Ray the historical artefacts and even let them hold the blood-stained clothing of Mírzá Mihdi and the sword of Mullá Ḥusayn.

One day, Mr Kházeh told Geertrui that, as a pioneer, she should be married. Geertrui answered: 'Yes, I will marry an Englishman when I am 35,' which was still a year and a half away. That comment usually ended that type of conversation. Six weeks later, when Mr Kházeh visited Geertrui in Luxembourg, he exclaimed, 'What, you are still not married? And I said prayers for you to be married.' But within a year, and before her 35th birthday, Geertrui met and married an Englishman, Ronald Bates, who had, interestingly, been on the pilgrimage immediately after Geertrui's. Ronald used to say that 'the angels above must have looked down and thought, "What was that prayer request we received last week for an Englishman? Send him to Luxembourg!"' After his pilgrimage, he offered to pioneer anywhere in the world. It was suggested to him to pioneer to Luxembourg, where he met Geertrui.

In 1960, Geertrui and Ronald travelled to Germany with a group of Bahá'ís for the laying of the foundation stone of the House of Worship. At the train station, Ronald said to Geertrui 'that I should give him an arm and we would get the Bahá'ís talking! So we walked along the platform together and from every window people watched us walking happily arm in arm.' In April 1961, Geertrui married her Englishman just as she had said she would. Theirs was the first Bahá'í wedding in Luxembourg.

In 1966, the couple moved to the United Kingdom with Ronald's job. Then in 1970, they were invited to come and serve at the Bahá'í World Centre. Initially, Ronald served as the Deputy Secretary General of the Bahá'í International Community. One of his biggest tasks, along with the Secretary General John Wade and his successor Donald Barrett, was the negotiation of a Status Agreement between the Bahá'í International Community and the State of Israel. The Israeli officials said such a precedent would not be possible and they had many objections. But John and Ronald knew that if the House of Justice said it had to be achieved, that it could be achieved. It took ten years, but in the end the Israeli Government: 1) recognized the Bahá'í Faith as an independent world religion with its spiritual and administrative centre in the Holy Land; 2) undertook to defend the Bahá'í Holy Places; and 3) gave the Bahá'í World Centre and the Holy Places tax-exempt status. While Ronald served as Deputy Secretary General of the Bahá'í International Community Geertrui served as a pilgrim guide. In 1988 Ronald became Secretary General of the Bahá'í International Community when Donald Barrett returned to the United States, and the Bates moved to Jerusalem, staying there until 1991, when they moved to New Zealand. Ronald passed away in 2006.

CHANNEL ISLANDS

Evelyn Baxter and Ḍiá'u'lláh Aṣgharzádih

Ḍiá'u'lláh Aṣgharzádih (1880–1956) and Evelyn Baxter (1883–1969) pioneered to Jersey, in the Channel Islands between England and France, on 1 and 5 September 1953, respectively.[49]

Ḍiá'u'lláh was born in Azerbaijan in 1880. When he was 15, the family moved to Russia to run Bahá'í schools. In 1903, he made the first of two pilgrimages during the time of 'Abdu'l-Bahá. On his second pilgrimage in 1920, he took a silk carpet woven specially for the Emir of Bokhara. Because of the Russian Revolution, it had not been possible to deliver the carpet, so he gave it to the Guardian, who placed it in the Inner Shrine of Bahá'u'lláh. In 1929, Shoghi Effendi gave that carpet for use in the American Mashriqu'l-Adhkár.[50]

After that second pilgrimage in 1920, Ḍíá'u'lláh moved to London where he was a companion to Shoghi Effendi. Ḍíá'u'lláh said that they went even boating on the Serpentine in Hyde Park and Shoghi Effendi had done the rowing.[51] On a pilgrimage in 1921, the Guardian gave him the task of making copies of 'Abdu'l-Bahá's original Will and Testament. He started a carpet business and married an Englishwoman, Winifred Pegrim, and had three daughters. He served on the National Spiritual Assembly at various times between 1925 and 1941 and pioneered several times.[52] Ḍíá'u'lláh was 73 when he pioneered to Jersey and spent the last three years of his life on the island, passing away in April 1956.[53]

Evelyn's parents were missionaries who, when they went overseas, left her with relatives at the age of nine. One day when she was at Sheffield University, she found a book about the Faith and, in 1923, before she met any Bahá'ís, accepted Bahá'u'lláh. She pioneered to Birmingham, Nottingham, Hove, Oxford and Cardiff and served on both the Local Spiritual Assembly of London and the National Spiritual Assembly.[54]

Evelyn pioneered at the age of 70 and remained at her post until she passed to the Abhá Kingdom in August 1969. She lived on her very small teacher's pension. In 1966, she claimed that it was the 'balmy Channel Islands' weather' that kept her alive.[55] The first Local Spiritual Assembly was elected at Riḍván 1972.[56]

LIECHTENSTEIN

Amír Húshmand Manúchehrí

Húshmand Manúchehrí (b.1933) was a 20-year old student in Stuttgart at the time of the Intercontinental Teaching Conference in Stockholm in July 1953. He was caught up in the enthusiasm of the Bahá'í community in Stuttgart and decided to attend. Unfortunately, being a student with very limited funds, he was not able to save enough money to be able to take a train or bus, so he decided to hitch-hike to the Conference. People were obliging and Húshmand was able to get rides in cars and trucks. He slept in youth hostels, on a wooden bench in a train station and, once, in the city of Odense, Denmark, in a brick factory. He arrived in Stockholm on the morning of registration and was happy to discover that the Bahá'í community there had prepared collective dormitories for youth without financial support.[57]

Húshmand greatly enjoyed the Conference and the talks given by Hands of the Cause Dr Giachery, Mr Khádem and Mr Furútan. When the goals for the Ten Year Crusade were presented, Húshmand offered to go to one of them and Dr Giachery and Mr Furútan suggested the German-speaking country of Liechtenstein. Returning to Stuttgart after the Conference, he proceeded to Zurich, where he spent a month. He then moved to Vaduz in Liechtenstein in August and rented a room from Mrs Kunz and Mrs Steinmetz.

Húshmand's two goals were to finish high school and to gain his permanent visa. But when he visited the Secretary of State, the official

> looked at me and asked me about my financial condition. I told him that I would receive money from my parents that lived in Iran and that I would like to finish my high school in Liechtenstein. He told me that I had two problems. The first one that they didn't have any high school in Liechtenstein so I had to go to Switzerland or Austria, and the second was that, the people coming to Liechtenstein are rich and bring a lot of money for the country and I as a student didn't have the same profile.

The official suggested that they could give him a three-month tourist visa that could be renewed once. After that six-month period, however, he would have to leave the country. Húshmand went to Feldkirch, an Austrian city on the border with Liechtenstein, where he registered himself in a Jesuit School, the Stela Matutina, and began his studies. He was, therefore, living in Liechtenstein and studying in Austria. He later moved from Vaduz to the city of Shaan, because it had a rail connection to Feldkirch. Every morning, he took the train to Feldkirch to go to school with many other youth doing the same thing. This allowed him to form many friendships.

After three months, the Secretary of State gave him another three-month visa. One week before the expiration of the second visa, the Government surprised both Húshmand and the Secretary of State by giving him a permanent visa, but one that had to be renewed every six months. The secretary said that he didn't know who had helped him but that it was the first time that somebody like a student had received a permanent visa.

Húshmand was the first Iranian to live in Liechtenstein and he made many friends because of his uniqueness. Because the country was strongly Catholic and closed, he had to be very careful in his teaching of the Faith. Many people thought that, being from Iran, he was a Muslim and Húshmand took advantage of those times to teach the Faith. The first person he spoke to about the Faith was a Swiss girl in Shaan named Rejane Imer. She was delighted to learn about the Bahá'í Faith. She didn't become a Bahá'í while Húshmand was in Liechtenstein, but did soon after he left, bringing in her whole family, her parents, Mr and Mrs Wohlwend, her two brothers and her sister.

Húshmand stayed in Liechtenstein for four years, then with the permission of the beloved Guardian he moved to Germany to continue his studies. He spent a year in Stuttgart, then, in 1958, pioneered to Aachen to help form the Local Spiritual Assembly. Ten years later, he finished his studies and moved back to Iran, where he married. After seven years in Iran, he and his wife decided to pioneer to Brazil. They arrived in February 1977. In 2014 Húshmand was still there, at the age of 80, still enjoying being a pioneer.

SAN MARINO

Tabandeh and Sohrab Payman

Tabandeh Payman (1923–2014) arrived in the tiny country of San Marino on 24 September 1953. She was joined a few months later by her husband, Sohrab (b.1921). San Marino is a tiny republic surrounded by Italy, near Italy's east coast and the cities of Rimini and Ravenna.

Tabandeh, originally from Soviet Turkmenistan, had moved to Tehran when she was ten years old. She was very active with the Bahá'í youth in Tehran and became the representative of a youth group whose chairman was Sohrab. The two were married in 1945 and their first child, Ghitty, was born three years later. Tabandeh and Sohrab attended the Intercontinental Teaching Conference in Stockholm in 1953 and were inspired to volunteer to pioneer to San Marino. Knowing 'that it was the wish of the beloved Guardian that the volunteers should go to their chosen places as soon as possible, she felt it would be inappropriate to hesitate', so Tabandeh went to her chosen goal as soon as the conference ended. She was accompanied by Maud Bosio, an American Bahá'í living in Florence, Italy, who was returning home.[58] Sohrab had to return to Iran to resolve difficulties with the company he was involved in.

San Marino was a country with 25,000 inhabitants and was dominated by Italy. The Italian Government handled all customs duties, municipal fees, licences for mass media and advertisements. The reality of this was that Tabandeh needed not one visa but two: one for San Marino and one for Italy. And to acquire each visa, she needed a residence in each country. Luckily, the owner of the hotel where she was staying in San Marino had a relative in Rimini who offered to declare that Tabandeh was a guest in her apartment there. Thus, both visas were acquired.

Her first months in San Marino were difficult:

Quite some time after the stay permit had been issued for Tabandeh, she remained under surveillance of the Italian police. More than once at lunch-time the hotelier made her aware that two guests having lunch in the hotel were Italian policemen who had come to observe her. Once in 19 days, when Tabandeh used to go to Florence or Rome to attend the Feast, she had to notify the police of the exact times of her departure from Rimini and also her return there. After three months these restrictions were removed without Tabandeh's intervention.

Sohrab, along with their daughter, Ghitty, joined Tabandeh in March 1954. For three years, they were unable to find any sort of work and began to contemplate returning to Iran. But then in November 1957, the Guardian passed away and the Paymans felt that 'Now, loyalty to our Beloved required that under any conditions we fulfil the obligation we had assumed as part of the spiritual Ten Year Crusade. So, we refrained from the plan to return to Iran, set our trust on His grace and decided that we will stay.'

This decision was followed on 27 December by the marriage according to Bahá'í law of two Iranian Bahá'ís, Paritschehreh Ataei and Jack Banani. Two days before the wedding, it looked as though it would not be possible, but after an evening of prayers, approval was given by the San Marino authorities. The marriage was performed by a member of the Italo-Swiss National Spiritual Assembly and witnessed by one of the heads of the San Marino Government.[59] In early January 1958, the marriage was officially recognized. The Assembly wrote, 'As far as we know, it is the first time on the European continent that a Bahá'í certificate of marriage has been recognized by the government of any nation.' When they received a copy of the marriage certificate, the Hands of the Cause of God resident in the Holy Land confirmed that 'This is an historic record to preserve and will be placed in the Mansion of Bahá'u'lláh for the friends to see, as was the custom of the beloved Guardian.'

Initially, the Paymans restricted themselves to making friends and distributing small brochures and books about the Faith, thinking that 'even if people didn't read themselves, the existence of books in their homes certainly wouldn't be effectless. One day either they themselves would consider reading or their children, intentionally or by chance, would come across the book, leaf through it and discover realities which concern them.'

The Paymans also began to invite their new friends to their home:

As time passed and our inhabitancy more and more stabilized, we started to invite friends for tea to our home. There they had the opportunity to talk about the Faith with a Bahá'í from outside San Marino, whom we asked to join. When invited for the next time, our friends often asked for permission to bring with them their friends. This way, our meetings grew ever larger and sometimes had forty to fifty participants. At one of these firesides with the attendance of Dr Giachery, a married couple – Vincenzo Giardi and Olga Carattoni – declared. The following year Vincenzo's younger brother, Marino . . . declared, and so three native inhabitants of San Marino joined the Faith.

In 1961, the Regional Spiritual Assembly of Italy and Switzerland was split into two National Spiritual Assemblies. To support the new Italian National Spiritual Assembly, the Paymans offered to organize a Bahá'í summer school in Rimini. Their offer was accepted and for the next ten years they were an important part of the Summer School Committee.

Also in 1961, Sohrab was finally able to start a business and expand the teaching possibilities. He wrote:

> I learnt for sure that two Iranians . . . had given up their shops and commercial activities in Rimini. So, I was freed from the commitment assumed that I would not enter into competition with them and began my own commercial activities. In 1962 I opened a presentable carpet shop in Rimini. This led to an enhancement of our relationship with the inhabitants of Rimini and even of San Marino. With everybody who entered the shop, a talk began about Iranian carpets and this led to the topics of Iran and the Bahá'í Faith. Regardless of whether the person was a customer who made a purchase or just curious, he or she would leave the shop with a brochure or a book about the Faith.

Two men often came to the shop, sometimes to buy, but usually to chat. One was the former Governor of the country and the other was the Secretary of Padua County. At the time, the National Spiritual Assembly of Italy had been given the task of organizing the International Youth Conference in Padua, held in 1971. Because of his contacts with the former Governor and the Secretary, Sohrab became involved with the conference. When the former Governor learned of the international scope of the planned conference, he told the new Governor to work closely with the conference committee.

The first Local Spiritual Assembly of San Marino was formed in 1972. In 1984 Maria Luisa Viccini, a native Bahá'í, donated a piece of land to the Bahá'í community. To register the land, the Spiritual Assembly had to be officially registered, as well, and this was done.[60]

In spite of some successes, teaching was difficult. In 1980, the Paymans distributed a booklet about the Faith to each of the 9,000 households in San Marino. Not one soul responded. A series of pioneers came to San Marino, but all left after a period of time. One family managed to stay for eight years, but finally was forced to leave due to a lack of work.

The Paymans actively engaged with various organizations in both San Marino and Rimini, and presented *The Proclamation of Bahá'u'lláh* and the Peace Message to the leaders of San Marino in 1968 and 1985, respectively. They also established a Bahá'í cemetery and, in 2003, were involved in the celebrations for the 50th anniversary of the arrival of the Faith into San Marino.

Tabandeh passed away in June 2014, but Sohrab still lives at his pioneering post.

MONACO

Nellie French

At the age of more than 85,[61] Nellie French (1868–1954), who had met 'Abdu'l-Bahá in 1921, filled a goal of the Italo-Swiss National Spiritual Assembly by pioneering from the United States to Monaco. Originally from Illinois, she went to Italy in 1888 to further her singing talent, learning Italian and French during her four-year stay. In about 1896, she and her mother learned of the Bahá'í Faith from Ibrahim Kheiralla. She lived as an isolated Bahá'í in Arizona from 1904 until 1918, when she moved to California. Her pilgrimage in 1921 and her meeting there with 'Abdu'l-Bahá focused her life. She served on the Local Spiritual Assembly of Pasadena from 1928 until 1938. Between 1930 and 1946, she was the chairman of the *Bahá'í World* Editorial Committee. She was also chairman of the InterAmerica Committee for four years from 1944. By 1946, Nellie had made travel-teaching trips to Spitsbergen, the Magallanes in South America, Iceland, Australia and other places. She made her second pilgrimage in 1952 and met Shoghi Effendi. Nellie arrived in Monaco on 12 September 1953, thus becoming the oldest Knight of Bahá'u'lláh. She died at her post in January 1954.[62]

Shamsí and 'Azízu'lláh Navídí

'Azízu'lláh (Aziz) Navídí (1913–1987) studied law at the University of Tehran, after which he went into private practice and tirelessly defended the rights of the innocent, be they Muslim or Bahá'í, rich or poor. He defended them with zeal and passion, free of charge:

> Every morning from 5 am there were queues of poor citizens who could not afford services of a lawyer and Dr Navidi made time to

see each one of them and help their cases. He was known for having acquitted a murderer but on the confession of the latter after his trial, he took him back to court and became the prosecutor of the trial and the man was put away! His knowledge and perspicacity in property law was a powerful tool to disenfranchised citizens, their right to property either unjustly confiscated or through family disputes corruptly appropriating land to themselves, was retrieved for them without any charge.[63]

The National Spiritual Assembly of Iran asked him to defend oppressed Bahá'ís in Shahrud and later in Shiraz, which he did with great eloquence and courage in the face of vicious opposition of the clergy. The Government later chose him as its legal advisor to the Ministry of Interior and the Ministry of Defence.

In 1940, Aziz married Shamsí (1925–2007), considered to be one of the most beautiful women in Tehran. Two daughters were born to the couple, Vida in 1942 and Guilda in 1949. They went on pilgrimage in 1953 and met the Guardian. During that life-changing pilgrimage, Shoghi Effendi spoke with Aziz about Iran for an hour, and said that his visitor would be the representative of the Guardian and 'had been chosen to safeguard the security' of Iran and that 'he would defend the Bahá'ís internationally'. Showing the pilgrims his map of the goals of the Ten Year Crusade, he asked them to 'spread to the four corners of the earth'. Shamsí, 'moved to the core of her being by the vision of Shoghi Effendi's Plan for the spread of the Bahá'í Faith throughout the globe, went to the Shrine of the Blessed Beauty and implored Him to grant her the unique bounty of participating in this divine Plan'. Shoghi Effendi told Aziz, however, that he had to stay in Iran and defend the Bahá'ís.

Aziz and Shamsí attended the Stockholm and Kampala Intercontinental Teaching Conferences. Of that time, Guilda wrote that Aziz 'was so successful in his practice and highly regarded by the "establishment" that when my Mother suggested pioneering', the people thought them insane. Their families thought that it was unthinkable for them to have it all, but want to leave it all behind. But they were determined to go, 'such was the effect of their meeting with the beloved Guardian in 1953 and the conferences of Stockholm and Kampala that they were ready to leave it all behind'. They wrote to Shoghi Effendi and he replied that they could pioneer after Aziz had finished defending the Bahá'ís of Yazd.

At first, the Guardian suggested that they go to the Marquesas Islands in the Pacific, so they booked passage and packed their cases. One week before departure a cable came from the Beloved Guardian, at the suggestion of Hand of the Cause Ugo Giachery, that said, 'Change of plans please proceed to Monaco as Mrs French has passed away.' Aziz had to stay in Iran to finish the Yazd defence, so Shamsí and their two daughters left in March 1954 to fill the post. Aziz joined them nine months later in November 1954.

For Shamsí, Vida and Guilda, it was quite a challenge: 'a courageous beautiful young woman of 28 arrived in a different continent without her husband leaving the entire tribal system of family, the enormous house with swimming pool and tennis court, friends, etc. to at first rent a single room and then an apartment, not knowing the language either.' The people in Monaco spoke French, but Shamsí's French was rudimentary when they arrived. Luckily, Vida had attended a French school in Tehran so the 12-year-old handled the initial language burden. Guilda wrote that 'we used to go to the different parks to meet other mothers and Mother would teach them the Faith and invite them for Tea in our small home'. Shamsí believed firmly in the role of women in the advancement of civilization.

When Aziz finally arrived in Monaco, at the suggestion of the Guardian he began to study international law at the University of Paris-Sorbonne, graduating with honours in 1955. That same year, the Guardian appointed him to the Commission that appealed to the United Nations in Geneva and New York about the Iranian attempt to exterminate the Bahá'í community. In 1962, Aziz became involved with the difficulties of the imprisoned Bahá'ís in Algeria and Morocco. For his efforts in defending the Bahá'ís, Shoghi Effendi gave him the title 'Shield of the Faith'.

Aziz travelled extensively throughout Europe as an Auxiliary Board member in addition to his legal practice. He also had to return to Iran regularly to keep up his income until he established his practice in Monaco. Their separation was difficult for Shamsí, alone in a foreign land. Aziz 'was so kind and utterly devoted to her, that she would be his inspiration and his soul mate'.

At some point, Aziz met Prince Rainier, the Head of the Principality of Monaco, and their meeting had an obvious impact on him: 'One of the most beautiful responses to the Peace message . . . was received by the House of Justice from Prince Rainier of Monaco.'

In 1968, Shamsí and Aziz pioneered to Mauritius at the suggestion of Rúḥíyyih Khánum, with whom they had a special relationship. They stayed in the islands for nine years and Aziz was involved with getting legal recognition for several Indian Ocean National Spiritual Assemblies. Aziz also travelled extensively throughout Africa for the Universal House of Justice, as the representative of the Baháʼí International Community, securing recognition for the Faith in several countries. In 1987, he passed away in London. At his passing, the Universal House of Justice sent a message praising his 'FEARLESS DEFENCE OF THE OPPRESSED BAHÁ'ÍS IN CRADLE OF THE FAITH . . . HIS CONTINUOUS SERVICE PIONEERING FIELD, CROWNED BY OUTSTANDING SUCCESS IN GAINING THE RECOGNITION OF THE FAITH BY MANY AFRICAN COUNTRIES . . . HIS INDEFATIGABLE RESOURCEFULNESS, SACRIFICIAL EFFORT . . . REQUESTING . . . MEMORIAL SERVICE IN THE MOTHER TEMPLE OF AFRICA IN RECOGNITION OF HIS UNIQUE SERVICES IN THAT CONTINENT'.

Shamsí, at the suggestion of Rúḥíyyih Khánum, went to London and started a 'diplomatic circle'. Her connections with the diplomatic world made her 'Salons' very successful and the diplomats of many European and African nations carried home a deep appreciation for the Baháʼí Faith. In 2008, the Universal House of Justice recognized her momentous efforts by giving her the title 'Ambassador of the Faith in the United Kingdom'.

Olivia Kelsey and Florence Ullrich

Olivia Kelsey (1889–1991) came from Ohio and after finishing her education moved to New York City, where she studied drama and music for 12 years and became very involved in Shakespearean theatre. Olivia's mother was Protestant and her father was Catholic, so religion was an unsettled question until she met Arthur Kelsey and he introduced her to Baháʼu'lláh. She married Arthur in 1929 and three years later became a Baháʼí. Olivia spent the next two decades writing articles, plays and books about the Baháʼí Faith. Her most notable book was *Baháʼí Answers*, a collection of 95 questions about the Faith with answers from the Writings, which was published in 1947.

When Arthur died, Olivia filled his loss with pioneering, first to

Louisville, Kentucky, then to Kansas. When the Ten Year Crusade was announced, Olivia was 'stunned, electrified'. She received a call from Edna True, asking her to settle in Monaco to replace Nellie French, who had died at her post, in order not to lose the momentum Nellie had begun.[64]

Florence Ullrich (1933–2016), a niece of Hand of the Cause Leroy Ioas, was fresh out of university in 1953 and, after attending the Intercontinental Teaching Conference in Chicago, spent several months trying to decide whether to continue her education in graduate school or fill one of the Guardian's Crusade goals. Finally, though, she sat down and said, 'Well, this is it. You've got to make up your mind right now.' And she decided that her duty was to God. Florence went to secretarial school to make it easier to find a job when she arrived in Monaco.[65]

Florence met Olivia in New York and they sailed to France together, reaching Monaco in March 1954. During the first three months, the women stayed at an inexpensive hotel. Shamsí Navídí and her two children were already living in Monaco at that time. Florence soon found a job with Aristotle Onassis's shipping company. She also found a room with a French family where she stayed for the next nine months.[66] To help in teaching the Bahá'í Faith, Florence began to take French lessons, but teaching was slow. In April 1955, however, Margaret Lantz, of Luxembourg, Mr Charbonnet, a French shopkeeper in Monaco, and Charlotte Campana, a Monaco native, all became Bahá'ís and they were able to form the first Local Spiritual Assembly of Monaco.[67] Following the election of the Local Assembly, Florence, Shamsí and Margaret all attended the Italo-Swiss National Convention in Lugano, Switzerland.[68]

After a year in Monaco, Florence decided she wanted to live on her own, and everyone said, 'Oh, no, no! French girls don't do this. It is not approved behaviour.' But when her French teacher found an apartment next to the Navídís, everyone was happy.

One day, a US Navy minesweeper came to Monaco and the Captain, Larry Kelley, held a party to which he invited some of the local people, including Florence. A relationship developed and Larry was posted to Rome, which allowed him to make frequent visits to see her. Finally, she told him that she wouldn't marry him unless he became a Bahá'í. Larry soon became a Bahá'í and spent the rest of his life as a very dedicated servant of Bahá'u'lláh.[69] Florence remained in Monaco until July 1957, when Shoghi Effendi gave her permission to leave in order to get married.

She moved to Rome and joined Larry, then spent the next two years there. They later served another goal in Key West, Florida. After Key West, the Kelleys moved to Long Beach, California, where they were able to help form an Assembly, then to Hawaii. Florence was elected to the National Spiritual Assembly of Hawaii in 1966. Two years later, the Navy sent them to Alexandria, Virginia.[70] Florence was elected to the US National Spiritual Assembly from 1972 to 1974. In 1975, she moved to Hawaii and still resides there.

Olivia stayed in Monaco until the first Local Spiritual Assembly was formed, as she had been instructed by the Guardian while on pilgrimage in 1954. In 1959, she moved to Toulouse to help the Bahá'í community. When Mason Remey proclaimed that he was the second Guardian, Olivia travelled throughout France, in response to a call from the Hands of the Cause, to fortify the French Bahá'ís when the crisis caused by the defection of Mason Remey struck. In 1964, with her health failing, she returned to America, settling in Columbus, Ohio, where she became involved with publicity work and extension teaching. During the Five Year Plan launched in 1974, at the age of 85, she made travel-teaching trips to South Carolina and West Virginia. She passed away in 1981.[71]

ANDORRA

William Danjon

William Danjon (1924–2014), was born in France to a French father and American mother. He studied journalism in Copenhagen, Denmark, and there encountered and accepted the Bahá'í Faith.[72]

William attended the Intercontinental Teaching Conference in Stockholm in 1953 and was inspired to arise and serve. When he heard Hand of the Cause Dorothy Baker call for a pioneer to go to Andorra, William volunteered. He arrived in the mountaintop country on 7 October 1953 and remained there for the rest of his life. William later said, 'To come to Andorra was the most important decision of my life. I liked the Andorra people from the very first and they liked me, I think.' Though initially, William had trouble finding a job, in July of the next year he was hired by Radio Andorra. Within a year, Andorrans Carmen Tost Xifre de Mingorance and her husband, Jose Mingorance

Fernandez, had joined the Bahá'í Faith.[73] In 1963, the Andorran Bahá'í community still numbered less than nine, but did have an official group.[74] Eleven years later, in 1974, they were able to form their first Local Spiritual Assembly.[75] By 2005, the estimated number of Bahá'ís had risen to ninety.[76]

William was known on the radio as Michel Avril, the combination of his middle name and his month of birth. In 1963, he became the Deputy Secretary of the Trade Union Initiative. In subsequent years, he worked as the representative of the Andorran Trust Board in Paris, as a journalist for South Radio and as a civil servant for the Ministry of Education and Culture. He was also a contributor to a weekly newspaper called the *Andorran People*. While serving on the Andorran Trust Board, he formally presented the *Tablets of Bahá'u'lláh* to two French presidents, who hold the title of co-prince of Andorra.[77] William passed away in Andorra at the age of 89 in February 2014.[78]

BALEARIC ISLANDS

Virginia Orbison

Virginia Orbison (1902–1985) arrived at Palma de Mallorca on the island of Mallorca in the Balearic Islands on 11 August 1953. She first heard of the Bahá'í Faith from Claudia Coles when she was just five years old in Philadelphia, but didn't pay much attention. Years later, in about 1932, she heard Helen Bishop speak about the Faith and said to herself: 'This is the Cause of God!' In 1942, she began what was to become over 40 years of pioneering, going to Chile, Argentina, Bolivia, Peru, Ecuador and Brazil between 1942 and 1946. After World War II, in 1947 she went to Madrid, Spain, where she helped raise up the first Local Spiritual Assembly in 1948, and then did the same in Barcelona the next year.[79] In July 1953, Virginia went to the Stockholm Intercontinental Teaching Conference where she offered to pioneer to the one of the Balearic Islands known as Mallorca. Upon arriving, she immediately joined a group called Amigos de Mallorca, which was where many Spaniards gathered to meet foreigners.[80]

Virginia was only able to stay in Mallorca for a year before returning to Barcelona in August 1954,[81] where she attended the Iberian Teaching Conference. At that time, the Faith was not officially known in

Spain. Sixty Bahá'ís attended. That night at 3 a.m., the police came knocking on her door. Apparently, a newly declared resident had been a police spy and had reported the meeting. Virginia and nine others were arrested and interrogated for 18 hours. It became apparent that the police thought the Bahá'ís were Communists. Virginia told them that one of the Bahá'ís named Lewis had been an atheist but now he was a Bahá'í and believed in God and said, 'That is an example of what the Bahá'í Faith can do.' All were soon released. Virginia later said, 'We thought at first that this was a calamity, but it was quite the opposite. It made the Faith known to the government in a favourable way.'[82]

In 1956, Virginia moved to Lisbon in Portugal. The next year, she was elected to the first Iberian Regional Spiritual Assembly. After three years in Portugal, she was forced to leave the country because of her 'Bahá'í activities, holding property and having a telephone!' Upon leaving Portugal, Virginia was asked to go to Luxembourg, where she spent nine years in 'this stubborn little country [which] wants to stay as it is'. After many pioneers and those nine years, there were only four native believers. Wishing to find greener pastures, she offered to pioneer where needed and was asked to go to Malaga, Spain. By 1972, Malaga had its Local Spiritual Assembly so she pioneered to Marbella in 1979. The National Assembly asked Virginia to write the history of the Faith in Spain, a task she completed in 1980. She passed into the Abhá Kingdom in 1985, still a pioneer.[83]

Tove and Jean Deleuran

Virginia Orbison was joined in the Balearic Islands by Tove (1927?–1996) and Jean Deleuran (1911–1998), from Denmark, on 30 December 1953. Jean (Larson) was partially paralyzed from polio and Tove's sight had deteriorated when she was 16 years old, but she still went on to become the first woman in Denmark to work in animation. She married Jean in 1944. Jean had suffered from polio and at 23 walked with crutches and was partially paralyzed. On the day they were married, Tove threw one of Jean's crutches into Tivoli Lake, saying, 'I will be your other crutch.' At one point, the young couple had to move to Jutland for work, so they rented out their flat. Two American women, Bahá'í pioneers Dagmar Dole and Eleanor Hollibaugh, became their tenants. Before leaving for Jutland, the Deleurans learned about the Bahá'í Faith and went with books to read. Eleanor visited the couple in Jutland and six months after returning to their home, they became Bahá'ís.[84]

At the Intercontinental Teaching Conference, Tove offered to pioneer anywhere, even though she had a handicapped husband and a daughter to teach. They left Denmark in a snowstorm and were met by Virginia Orbison in Mallorca and were able to assist in the formation of the first Local Spiritual Assembly in 1957. Tove was appointed to the first Auxiliary Board.[85] Later in 1957, the Deleurans moved to Dhaka, Bangladesh (then East Pakistan), where Tove became the first woman elected to the National Spiritual Assembly of Pakistan. Jean and Tove represented Pakistan at the election of the first Universal House of Justice and after attending the Jubilee in London, they returned to Denmark where they moved 18 times to serve the needs of the Danish Bahá'í community. Jean ultimately had to use a wheelchair so they pioneered yet again to the south of France, helping to form the first Local Spiritual Assembly of Alès. With failing health, they moved to Le Mousteiret. Tove was active in the Faith until the end in December 1996. Jean followed her two years later.[86]

Charles Ioas

Charles Ioas (b. 1927) arrived on Mallorca on 7 January 1954. Charles was a third-generation American Bahá'í. His grandparents, Charles and Maria Ioas, had emigrated from Germany to the United States and became Bahá'ís in 1898. All of their ten children were Bahá'ís, including Leroy Ioas, who became a Hand of the Cause and Shoghi Effendi's helper in the Holy Land. Charles, the grandfather, served on what functioned as the Local Spiritual Assembly of Chicago and, along with Albert Windust, drafted the letter to 'Abdu'l-Bahá that asked for permission to build an American House of Worship.[87]

From a young age, Charles was involved in teaching. In the children's classes he attended, the children prepared and gave short talks, so that by the time he was a youth, he was comfortable speaking to groups. When he entered Northwestern University, which is very close to the Bahá'í House of Worship in Wilmette, he served as a guide for tourists and also was the speaker or the chair of meetings held in the Temple.

During the second American Seven Year Plan, Charles served on the Inter-American Teaching Committee, one of whose goals was to prepare all the countries in South America to form their first National Spiritual Assemblies. To prepare himself for service to the Bahá'í Faith outside the United States, Charles studied Latin and Spanish at the university, so was ready when the Committee sent him to Colombia in late 1950 to help deepen the members of the Local Assemblies for the election:

> I intended to go pioneering. At that time, I was still a member of the Inter-American Teaching Committee. Our main goal that last year was to prepare all of the countries of Latin America to participate in the election of their first National Spiritual Assemblies . . . In this case, it was to be one national body for all of South America and one National Spiritual Assembly for all of Central America and the Caribbean. Our objective was to send somebody to visit every one of the existing Local Spiritual Assemblies in all of these countries because the members of the Local Assemblies would be the electors in voting for their national body.
>
> I graduated from law school in 1950. I was serving on this com- mittee and I left immediately for Colombia. There were some eight Local Assemblies there and I was to spend two to three weeks in each one of these communities deepening the Assembly members on Bahá'í administration.
>
> . . . wherever I went in Latin America, there was opposition. Bahá'ís could lose their jobs if their boss heard they were some- thing weird, they were not Catholics, they didn't go to Mass. So they could be ostracized by their friends, their neighbours . . . There was prejudice . . . and in Latin America we still had a great deal of dif- ficulty in having public meetings. There were a few places where we were able to rent a hall, but not many. To have any kind of outward propagation was always a little bit risky. I, being an outsider – I knew I would be going back home – just the fact that I visited some- body could draw attention to that individual that his neighbours wondered why are you seeing this American down here, and getting into difficulties. That was always in the background.

In early 1951, Charles was drafted into the army, where he served in Korea and Japan. He wanted to pioneer and just before he entered the service, he wrote to his uncle, Leroy Ioas:

the Guardian initiated a two-year teaching plan which he gave to the National Assembly of Great Britain with goals in Africa, all of the places which still had to be opened in Africa. By that time, my uncle, Leroy, was living and working with the Guardian in Haifa. Through him I wrote and offered to go, as I recall, I think it was Nairobi . . . but I made an offer through my uncle to the Guardian. Uncle Sam intervened, I couldn't go immediately . . . and while I was still in Japan, November of 1952, I had a letter from my uncle in which he said that the Guardian had been talking to him about my offer. It was no longer needed. They had filled all the goals in Africa . . . What I should do was to wait a little bit until I could look at the goals of a new plan that he would be announcing at the next year. That was in 1953. Ten Year Plan.

When the goals of the Ten Year Crusade were announced, Charles, recently released from the army, chose to go to the Balearic Islands, specifically to Palma on the island of Mallorca, where he joined the Deleurans and Virginia Orbison. Charles had his university degree in law, but was unable to practice in Mallorca, so he taught English to the Spaniards and Spanish to English-speakers. Since he had a car, he also acted as a tour guide for tourists.

In 1955, Charles met a young woman travelling with a group of students visiting tourist sites on Mallorca. One of the other members of the group had met Charles and invited him to his cousin's house, where he met Conchita. She wanted to be a journalist and thought it would be interesting to interview an American. Initially, Charles told her that he was on the island to write a book about his experiences in Japan. One thing led to another and soon Conchita became both the first person to accept the Faith on Mallorca and also Charles's wife. When asked what she saw in Charles, she replied: 'Being a Catholic, and I was going to Mass every day, my confessor had told me that if I saved a life, converted someone, my soul forever would be saved. So, when I saw Charles . . . My mother she complained. She met him, he was from America, that he was too thin. He was thin.'

It wasn't possible to get married on Mallorca because only Catholics could marry, so the couple went to Tangier and were married in Knight of Bahá'u'lláh Elsie Austin's apartment. Marrying a foreigner meant that Conchita lost her Spanish citizenship, so some time later they went to the United States and she became an American citizen.

Spain was not a very friendly country at that time under the dictator-ship of Franco and the mail of all 'suspicious' people and organizations was constantly checked. The Bahá'ís, some of whom had formerly belonged to the Socialist or Communist Parties, were also scrutinized, so the authorities knew about many Bahá'í activities. Charles attended summer schools in Spain and at one, the Spanish police arrested a dozen Bahá'ís on the first night and kept them in jail for 24 hours. Later, after the election of the National Spiritual Assembly of the Iberian Penin-sula, the police

> sent two or three big vans to our Bahá'í Centre, knocked on the door. They were prepared to walk in and see a mass of people. They were going to take us all . . . I think three of our members had a flu [so] . . . we weren't the full Assembly, there were only the six of us, and they were going to cart away dozens. But they took the six of us down to the headquarters then in the town. I was the chairman of the Assembly so I was taken in by the director of the unit for inter-rogation, and then our secretary was taken in by one of the others. The others just sat around in the other room.
>
> Our saving factor in every case . . . [was to] explain openly what the Bahá'í Faith is; that we are a religion, that we are law-abiding and among the Bahá'í principles is the requirement that we obey the laws of the land where we happen to live . . .
>
> The assurance that we are not propagandizing and that Bahá'í law is to obey the law of the country . . . was enough on that particular occasion . . . the chief said okay, go ahead and finish your meeting and see me on Tuesday. When I went back on Tuesday to see him, it was just a matter of him saying to be careful, to be careful.

The police chief recommended that the Bahá'ís acquire legal recogni-tion from the Government, so steps were taken. After delays, Matthew Bullock, Knight of Bahá'u'lláh for the Dutch West Indies and a lawyer, went to Madrid and met with Charles to move the process along. While there, Charles was offered a job. He explained the situation to the Guardian and Shoghi Effendi approved his moving to Madrid.

The move was beneficial to the Faith because the Bahá'ís were not able to publish or import books about the Faith into Spain. Charles's new job was officially as a civil servant of the US Government working on a military construction project and therefore his mail came through the Army Post Office, not the Spanish one. This allowed them to receive much Bahá'í literature.

By 1957, Charles was serving on the Regional Spiritual Assembly of the Iberian Peninsula, the Local Spiritual Assembly of Madrid and also serving as an Auxiliary Board member.

Charles served on the Regional Spiritual Assembly of the Iberian Peninsula from 1957 to 1961 and then on the National Spiritual Assembly of Spain from 1962 until 1965, where he served first as vice-chairman and then chairman.[88] In 1965, the Universal House of Justice said that Bahá'ís could not serve on administrative bodies and be an Auxiliary Board member at the same time. Charles resigned from the Assembly because he felt that it was functioning well and he could better serve on the Auxiliary Board.

Charles was asked to return to the United States in 1980, so moved to Alexandria, Virginia. He said that he thought that the time was right for him to leave because 'the members of the Assembly that existed were mature, developed, capable people and there was nothing much I could offer them beyond that'.

SARDINIA

Marie Ciocca

Marie Ciocca (1929–1968) learned about the Bahá'í Faith from the Revell sisters, Jessie and Ethel, in Philadelphia at the age of 19. She had taken a secretarial course and was sent to the office of Elwood Revell for on-the-job training. Elwood's sisters sensed her receptivity and brought her into the Faith in 1949. Four years later, when the goals for the Ten Year Crusade were announced, she quickly arose to pioneer to Italy, land of her ancestors, and opened the island of Sardinia to the Faith. Cagliari, where she settled on 28 October 1953, was the capital of the island and Marie knew little of the language, though she learned quickly. For the next nine years, she persisted virtually alone in her efforts to bring to that land Bahá'u'lláh's healing Message, teaching English to many and becoming known as 'Miss Mary' to both parents and children. Alone as she was, Hand of the Cause Ugo Giachery and his wife, Angeline, visited often to support her, as did others. Marie married James Holmlund in June 1962 and they had two children. Finally, in 1966, Livia Pargentino became the first to accept the Faith. She was followed by several others and Cagliari had a group. Unfortunately, in late 1967 Marie was diagnosed with cancer and passed away in her beloved Sardinia on the eve of the Oceanic Conference in Palermo in August 1968.[89]

SICILY

Emma Rice

Emma Rice (1898–1985) pioneered to Sicily in October 1953. Recovering from injuries in Boston in 1940, she became very attracted to the Bahá'í Writings, but didn't become a Bahá'í because of opposition from her husband. She didn't find the courage to declare her Faith until she had written to and received a letter from Shoghi Effendi in 1942. Her wealthy family did not understand her decision to follow a new Faith and scorned her, but Emma was dedicated to Bahá'u'lláh. She supported the Italian Bahá'í Fund to help with new publications, deputations and administration.[90]

In 1952, she went on pilgrimage and was privileged to carry with her some gold leaf that was used for gilding the balustrades of the octagon of the Shrine of the Báb. So, when the Guardian raised the call for pioneers in 1953, Emma arose and went to Sicily, arriving in Palermo on 20 October and continuing to Taormina the next day. Initially, she was horrified at the poverty, the unsanitary conditions and her inhospitable reception, but she soon learned to dance their dances and sing their songs, which helped bring her into the local community. She wrote that she

> was obliged to pray aloud . . . in Italian (a language entirely foreign to me); greet them as they came down their donkey trails from school and from work; eat what they had to offer, on their doorsteps and in their homes; admire their babies; visit the sick; sew with them; draw pictures for them; translate Bahá'í stories and share my hand-written excerpts copied from the only Italian Bahá'í book that could be had; show slides and photographs of our Temple and of our people; go to

their fiestas, churches, christenings, graduations, pageants, etc. . . .
The tourists and Bahá'í visitors . . . helped maintain my equilibrium
and release the solitude of a homesick heart.

Her initial success came quickly. An English-speaking chambermaid
saw her picture of 'Abdu'l-Bahá and asked who He was. Within two
months, both the chambermaid and the hotel laundress became Bahá'ís.
Within a short time, 25 others accepted the Faith. Unfortunately, these
new believers were never incorporated into the Sicilian Bahá'í community and were lost. Emma's overt teaching activities attracted the
ire of the authorities and her request for a visa renewal was denied,
forcing her to leave the island in October 1954. After spending a year
in Geneva, she was able to return to Sicily due to the intervention of the
American State Department. At the request of the Italo-Swiss National
Spiritual Assembly and Hand of the Cause Ugo Giachery, she settled
in Palermo and received a very different reception to the one she had
in Taormina. It was three and a half years before the first people there
realized the truth of Bahá'u'lláh.

Emma was a fearless teacher of the Faith and one of the seeds she
planted resulted in the declaration of the first Bahá'í in Lipari, one
of Sicily's offshore islands. In 1956, Emma was joined by Manucher
Majzub, his mother and his brother. Emma returned to America in
1958 because of her deteriorating health. She served for two years on
the Local Spiritual Assembly of Boston and spent her summers at the
Green Acre Bahá'í School. In 1961, she moved into Fellowship House
at Green Acre and stayed there until moving to a nursing home in
1984. She passed away the next year.

Florence, Stanley, Gerrold, Carol and Susan Bagley

Florence (1914–1990) and Stanley Bagley (1912–1993), along with
14-year-old Carol (b.1939), 16-year-old Gerrold (b.1937), and 17-year-
old Susan (b.1936), arrived in Sicily on 27 October 1953 and went to
Palermo. Florence had accepted the Bahá'í Faith in 1930, at the age of
16, when she attended a talk given by Elizabeth Greenleaf. Five years
later, Florence's soon-to-be husband, Stan, accepted the Faith. After
their marriage, they moved to Flint, Michigan where they were very
active. Florence, Gerrold and Susan attended the Intercontinental

Teaching Conference in Chicago in May 1953. Gerrold remembered that

> a call for pioneers was addressed to the 2,200 Bahá'ís gathered there. Amatu'l-Bahá encouraged the friends to arise and come up on the stage to announce their intention and where they wanted to go. She said the elderly should go and plant their bones for Bahá'u'lláh. She stated that all that was needed was the travel ticket and a passport. The believers were few in those days so encouragement was plentiful. The stage was overflowing with the friends awaiting their turn at the microphone. It was a moving moment. My sister Susan and I were sitting together and wondered why we didn't see Mom on the stage with the others. Later, Mom said that she couldn't make a commitment without consulting Dad and my sister Carol who were arriving the following day. We were amused to hear a number of times 'my husband/wife doesn't know this but . . .'[91]

Initially, Florence wrote to the Pioneering Committee for Africa, but never received a reply. When someone suggested they go to Sicily, the family turned to the Guardian, who approved the choice. On 17 October, Gerrold's 16th birthday, the Bagleys sailed for Sicily on board the *Conte Biancamano*. They arrived in Palermo ten days later and the whole family became Knights of Bahá'u'lláh. Carol, at just 14, and Gerrold, at 16, became the youngest Knights, along with Edward Tabe and Benedict Eballa from Cameroon, who were also 14 and 16, respectively.

During their first two weeks in Palermo, the family lived in a hotel while they searched for a place to settle. It was a strange new world and Gerrold wrote:

> The city seemed strange to us. There were horse-drawn carriages, donkey carts carved and painted, and unremitting noise as vehicles rolled over the cobblestone streets. Odor was ever-present due to the donkeys and horses in traffic. Swarms of people crowded the sidewalks and overflowed into the streets. Drivers seemed to use their horns rather than their brakes. At first it was daunting to venture out far from the hotel, but gradually we became more adventurous and extended the range of our investigations.

Finding an apartment in the modern section of town, the family set about making friends, with the three youngest members of the family opening the doors. They soon met Franco, a youth who lived in the same building, and he introduced the Bagley youth to many others:

> It was the custom in those days when women were still chaperoned, that young people would entertain afternoons with tea dances in their homes to celebrate birthdays, name-days, and family events. In each gathering we would receive invitations from others. Franco was our social guide, arranging at least two dance parties each week. A number of the parents were invited to tea in our home and learned that we were Bahá'ís. But Palermo was still tradition bound and practised the state religion . . .
>
> My sisters and I shared the same friends since girls had to be accompanied. Carol being youngest had to grow up fast. I learned Italian more quickly than my parents and was therefore doing much of the shopping and took on responsibilities beyond my age.

Franco didn't become a Bahá'í, but ten years later, his cousin, Fabio Tagliavia was studying in London and saw a poster advertising a Bahá'í public meeting at the Albert Hall during the World Congress. Thinking he might find his friend Gerrold there, Fabio attended the meeting. He didn't find Gerrold, but he and his Icelandic wife, Svava, began attending firesides and then declared.

During that first year in Sicily, the Bagleys had many illustrious visitors, including William Sears, Curtis and Harriet Kelsey, Cora and Clara Edge, Loulie Mathews and Marion Little. But Stanley was unable to find work and after a year, with their savings diminishing rapidly, they asked Shoghi Effendi if they could change posts. He agreed and Horace Holley suggested Chateauroux in France, where there was an American Air Force base. The family, except for Gerrold who stayed in Sicily at the suggestion of his mother, moved in 1954. Gerrold remained as the sole family representative on Sicily for the next ten years.

Emma Rice, who had also been pioneering in Sicily, was forced to leave in October 1954, so on the 10th of that month, Gerrold, still a week from turning 17, was the sole pioneer on the island, financially supported by his parents and sisters. Emma returned to Sicily in late 1955 and joined Gerrold in Palermo. Teaching the Faith was a slow and difficult task, but Gerrold kept at it. In the summer of 1956, his sister Carol came to Palermo for two months to help with the teaching and stayed with Emma. Emma invited Gerrold to stay with her as well and he remained in the household for a year. It was during that summer that the teaching efforts suddenly began to bear fruit. Gerrold became friends with Mario Piragino, whose father was a general in the Italian Air Force. The family invited Gerrold to join them at their beach cabin and Carol and Emma were soon invited too. The declaration of the first believers started with a party, as related by Gerrold: 'General Piragino, his wife and son, my friend Mario, invited me, Carol and Emma [Rice] to join them in their beach cabin each day. Here we met many VIPs and aristocrats.'

> While the other guests were being served cocktails, one of my friends, Carlo Alberto, rather loudly remarked that Gerry wasn't drinking. One of the guests, Carlo di Georgis, asked 'Why not?' I said, 'Because I'm a Bahá'í'. As he was curious to know what that was, Mrs Rice immediately invited him and his family to tea the next afternoon to learn more about the Faith.
>
> They came with three children. Magda Di Giorgis [Carlo's wife] believed immediately, but wisely waited for her husband to investigate . . . He came occasionally to firesides . . . but, as he was a busy businessman, we had to find subtle ways to involve him. Finally, during a visit of Dr Ugo Giachery, Hand of the Cause, he declared on 22 May, 1957 . . . Mrs Rice immediately insisted that they all stay to dinner to celebrate. I accepted the task of going outside to the public telephone to inform their children that their parents would be coming home late. I recall running and skipping up the street with great joy.
>
> Magda waited until the next day to add her declaration. What Joy! Two of the children also became believers later on. Within that year there were three more local Bahá'ís. The LSA was formed in 1958. I was too young to serve on that first LSA until the following October when I turned 21, and replaced a pioneer who had transferred to another city.

By 2014, Sicily had 13 Local Spiritual Assemblies and 500 Bahá'ís. The National Spiritual Assembly was first elected in 1995.

For the rest of the Bagley family, it was a different adventure. They stayed in France for nine years, except for a period in Belgium. They first helped form the Local Spiritual Assembly of Chateauroux, then Susan and Carol helped form the Local Spiritual Assembly of Orleans. Florence served on the National Spiritual Assembly of France from 1958 until 1963, except for a crucial period in 1960 when Stan lost his job and the family were forced to move to Belgium. It was during this absence that Mason Remey declared himself to be the second Guardian and seven of the nine members of the French National Spiritual Assembly initially followed him, though two later realized their mistake and returned to the Faith. Florence was protected by being in Belgium.[92] She quickly returned to France to help Hand of the Cause Mr Faizí in reassuring the French Bahá'ís.

The Bagley family, except for Gerrold, returned to America in 1963. Florence and Stan later pioneered to Guadeloupe and Martinique, where they both served on the National Spiritual Assembly. Susan joined her husband-to-be, David Barel, in Paraguay and later David managed the Bahá'í Publishing Trust in Argentina. Carol moved to southern Alabama and actively served the Faith there. Gerrold pioneered to Ecuador, Brazil, South Korea and Albania after leaving Sicily, serving on National Spiritual Assemblies in each country. He also pioneered to the Ivory Coast, then returned to Sicily between 2000 and 2011, where he was also a member of the National Spiritual Assembly.

MALTA

Una Townshend, Olga Mills and John Mitchell

Una Townshend (1921–2003), daughter of Hand of the Cause George Townshend, pioneered to Malta on 4 October 1953 to fulfil a goal of the Ten Year Crusade. Una had become a Bahá'í in 1940, to her father's delight, then became the first Bahá'í to live in Dublin, also becoming a member of the first Dublin Local Spiritual Assembly.[93] Initially, it was planned that her father would accompany her to Malta, where it was thought that the warm climate would improve his health. Unfortunately, George was not able to go, so Una went alone. Malta was described by David Hofman as having been 'savagely destroyed in the war and by 1953 it offered no savoury reputation to invite a young single woman of 33, delicately brought up and resident (nearly) all her life in Ireland.'[94] Unfortunately, when her father's illness advanced, Shoghi Effendi requested that she return home to help care for him and to help him with his 'crowning achievement' – the book *Christ and Bahá'u'lláh*. She left Malta at the end of 1954.[95] In 1957, after her father's passing, Una moved to Canada, where she married Richard Dean. She served on the Local Spiritual Assembly of Edmonton until 1987.[96]

In December 1953, Mary Olga Katherine Mills (1882–1975) arrived in Malta. Olga had travelled the world when she was young. By 1930, she was a Bahá'í and went on pilgrimage the next year. In 1947, she was pioneering in the British Isles at the request of the Guardian, short-term pioneering in Nottingham, Belfast, Edinburgh, St Ives, Brighton and Bournemouth. When the Ten Year Crusade arrived, Olga, at the age of 71, asked the Guardian to be allowed to pioneer to one of his goals. His reply said: 'Leave as promptly as possible for either Malta or Cyprus, preferably Malta, and there engage yourself with all your powers in teaching the Faith'. She chose Malta, joining Una in November 1953.[97]

Malta was a difficult place for the pioneers, but Shoghi Effendi's letters helped Olga find the strength to continue. In 1956, a letter written on his behalf read: 'He advises you, if the situation should become worse, to try your utmost to remain at your post, which he knows is the deep desire of your heart, also. He greatly appreciates your constancy and your spirit.' Another letter written in March 1957 said: 'He is happy to see that, although your local resources have been depleted . . . you nevertheless are remaining to "hold the fort", a service to which he attaches the greatest importance. . .'[98]

Olga remained steadfastly on Malta, because the Guardian had told her not to leave Malta until she was 'blown off the island'.[99] In 1963 she broke her wrist, which made it very difficult to write. Finally, after almost 20 years, the first Local Spiritual Assembly in Malta was elected at Riḍván 1973. Olga was 91 at that time and lived for another year before passing into the Abhá Kingdom in May 1974, still at her post.[100]

John Mitchell (1907–1957) moved to Malta in July 1954 to join Olga Mills. He became a Bahá'í in 1950 and was a member of the National Spiritual Assembly of the British Isles from 1952 to 1954. He went on pilgrimage in 1953 and meeting Shoghi Effendi changed his life. Immediately after returning to the United Kingdom, John pioneered to Blackpool, then to Malta. While on the island, John became ill and early in 1956 returned to London for treatment. Unfortunately, an operation left him paralyzed and he passed away in February 1957.[101]

GREECE

Sheila and Amin Banani

Sheila (b.1932) and Amin Banani (1926–2013) became Knights of Bahá'u'lláh for Greece. Amin was the son of Hand of the Cause Músá Banání and grew up in Tehran. In 1944, he went to the United States to attend Stanford and Columbia Universities.[102] Sheila, the daughter of Universal House of Justice member Charles Wolcott, met Amin at a Bahá'í youth conference in Los Angeles, California, the summer before entering the University of California Los Angeles. They were married in February 1951.[103]

Initially, the young couple considered joining Amin's parents who were already pioneering in Africa, and wrote to them about the idea. The elder Banánís were just about to leave for pilgrimage when the letter arrived, so they took it and showed it to the Guardian. Shoghi Effendi responded that Amin should first finish his graduate studies and then pioneer to a virgin goal in Europe, of which only Finland and Greece remained. In July 1953, Amin attended the Intercontinental Conference in Stockholm while Sheila and their new daughter, Susanne, waited in America. Amin was advised by the German National Spiritual Assembly that they should go to Greece. Obtaining his visa, he boarded the Tauren Express train in Stuttgart and travelled to Greece via Austria and Yugoslavia:

> The emotions of that journey are forever fresh and vivid in my life. The excitement of the opportunity to open a virgin country to the Faith masked all the heartache of being alone . . . and the anxiety of facing the unknown. There was a sense of electric vibrancy that became stronger as the train got nearer to Greece. I was standing in the corridor leaning out of the window into the dark and crying Yá Bahá al-Abhá at the top of my voice – filling the air of that country with the Greatest Name. Fortunately the sound of the tracks and the whistle of the engine were louder than my voice and my fellow passengers were spared any puzzlement.
> It was nearly noon-time on the 2nd of August 1953 when I

arrived at the railroad station in Athens. I had never been anywhere before where everything was incomprehensible. Here the unfamiliar script and the language, unrelated to any that I knew, were a new and isolating experience. I checked into the King George Hotel for the first two of three days. That same afternoon, I cabled my arrival to Haifa, and five days later I received a telegram reading: 'Assure prayers abiding appreciation. Shoghi.'

I had a letter of introduction from a dear Bahá'í friend to a former member of the UN Secretariat. I had some naïve hopes that he would be instrumental in aiding me in finding a job and getting me a residence permit. He was cordial and sympathetic; but . . . was politically out of favour with the regime in power.

I followed every possible lead for employment during the first month in Athens, with no success. By the end of the fourth week I was at a low ebb of hope. Then small things began to happen. In the next two weeks I was able to secure several odd jobs.

The first job was teaching English to Bulgarian refugees in a camp outside Athens, another was teaching English to Greek high school and university students, and the next was as night editor at the *Athens News*, the only English-language newspaper in Greece. He taught the students from 4 to 6 p.m., after which he had to take a 45-minute bus ride followed by a two-kilometre walk to the refugee camp. He taught there from 7:30 to 9:30 p.m., then reversed his travel to work at the newspaper from 10:30 p.m. until 3 or 4 in the morning. At that time, there were no buses, so he had to walk five kilometres to get home. In spite of this difficult schedule, Amin wrote that 'at no time in my life did I feel as vital and happy and thankful as in those days . . . I remember chanting prayers up and down the hill of the refugee camp, and drawing strength from the hidden sources that aid all pioneers.' The jobs paid a total of $52 a month, but that was enough for Amin to send for Sheila and baby Susanne. They arrived on 16 September and the family moved into a flat at the foot of the Acropolis.

To help teach the Faith, Amin had a Bahá'í pamphlet, *The Dawn of World Civilization*, translated into Greek by Manoli Papoutsakis, a man who worked with him. In September 1953, Sheila described their new life:

Last Saturday night (Sept. 26th) the four of us [the Bananis and Dwight and Carole Allen] held our first Feast . . . The last few days we've been entertaining Rolf Haug, the young (20) German Bahá'í on his way to Crete. He leaves tonight. He's a wonderful boy. It's thrilling to think of the maturity of the Bahá'í youth in this crucial period. They are certainly arising admirably to the call of the Guardian, and with such devotion and self-sacrifice . . .

We can see the Acropolis from our bedroom window. It's just up the top of the hill – ten minutes' walk...Night before last the Parthenon, on top of the Acropolis, was lighted to celebrate the anniversary of St Dionysius, the first Bishop of Athens. It was strikingly beautiful 'way up in the sky. Now I have an idea what the Bahá'í shrines must look like at night. It was breathtaking.

Everyone, absolutely everyone, loves the baby. She opens doors to new acquaintances with one smile. You've never seen such love for children as here . . . Already we are making contacts very quickly. We're going to hold a fireside next Sunday, 'a very momentous occasion in the history of Greece!' [104]

After only four months, the Bananis began to have problems with their residence permits. Amin's Persian passport proved to be a liability and the family was ordered to leave the country. They left for the United States in March 1954 and with the help of Sheila's father, Charles Wolcott, who was the head of the music department at MGM movie studios at the time, Amin was able to acquire US citizenship and a US passport. With the new passport, the family returned to Greece in September 1954 and Amin worked at the Anglo-American School in Athens. Sheila, and Knight of Bahá'u'lláh for Southern Rhodesia Roberta Christian, who had come with her husband Kenneth, put great effort into sharing the Bahá'í Faith, 'praying the needles off every pine tree' for the success of their teaching. But they noted that 'success, when measured against our anxious expectations, was dishearteningly slow'.

Shoghi Effendi told the Bananis to learn Greek in order to better teach the local population. He also said that if no one in Athens responded to their message, they should move elsewhere. Teaching was slow, but when Sheila went on pilgrimage in April 1956, she asked about how much deepening was needed before a contact could become a Bahá'í. One contact, Costas Kyriazis, was close to the Faith and the Guardian said he should be accepted as a Bahá'í and the deepening could come later. Costas declared his faith within three weeks of Sheila's return to Greece.[105] Two more men, George Kroustis and Nikos Mavromatis, declared their faith in Bahá'u'lláh in early 1957 and, with the addition of pioneers Ursula Kohler, Eric Blumenthal and Annie Langenhorst, they were able to form a Local Spiritual Assembly at Riḍván 1957.

Renewing their residence permits had been difficult from the beginning, but in late 1957 a new government closely associated with the Greek Orthodox Church was elected. Amin noted that 'they pursued a vigorous policy of proscribing what they termed as alien religious groups. Their main targets were evangelical Protestants, but apparently we were swept by the same broom.' By the spring of 1958, further extensions of their permits were formally denied and the Bananis were given a deadline to leave Greece. In July 1958, the family boarded the same train that had brought Amin to Greece in 1953, the Tauren Express, and left the country. But, Amin wrote, they left 'knowing that we were leaving behind an assembly and strong and deepened German pioneers'.

The Bananis returned to the United States, where Amin served on various national committees and on Local Assemblies in California, Oregon and Massachusetts. He presented sessions at the Bosch, Louhelen and Green Acre Bahá'í Schools in addition to those given in other countries. In 1980, he was appointed to the Board of Trustees of the Ḥuqúqu'lláh, a post he held until 2006. He passed away in 2013. Sheila, too, served on a number of national committees: including the US National Social and Economic Development Committee; the Administrative Committee for the Bahá'ís of Los Angeles, representing the National Spiritual Assembly; the Persian/American Affairs Committee; and the Association for Bahá'í Studies. She also served as an assistant to the Auxiliary Board and as a member of the Santa Monica Local Spiritual Assembly, a post she held for 50 years. Sheila has written a number of books of poetry, including the award-winning *Life's Rainbow*. She presently lives in Santa Monica, California.[106]

Dwight and Carole Allen

Dwight (b.1931) and Carole Allen (b.1933) became Knights of Bahá'u'lláh by pioneering from the United States to Greece. Dwight's parents, John and Valera Allen, also became Knights by pioneering to Swaziland.[107]

Una Townshend,
Knight of Bahá'u'lláh to Malta

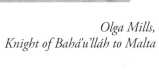

Olga Mills,
Knight of Bahá'u'lláh to Malta

John Mitchell,
Knight of Bahá'u'lláh to Malta

Sheila and Amin Banani with Dwight and Carole Allen,
Knights of Bahá'u'lláh to Greece

Elizabeth Bevan, Knight of Bahá'u'lláh to Rhodes, with her students

Elizabeth Bevan with Carole Allen

Rolf Haug, Knight of Bahá'u'lláh to Crete, with Waltraud Weber and Manolis, the first Cretan Bahá'í, c. 1954

Violet and Hugh McKinley,
Knights of Bahá'u'lláh to Cyprus

Abbas and Semire Vekil,
Knights of Bahá'u'lláh to
Cyprus

During his last year at Stanford University in 1952, Dwight wrote to the Guardian offering to pioneer. Shoghi Effendi's reply was that he should go to Thailand, but if that was not possible, Greece was an alternative. When Dwight and Carole were married and the Ten Year Crusade was announced, their goal was Thailand so they began taking lessons in the Thai language. Then one night, Carole had a dream: 'I saw clearly the globe centred on Thailand, but it slowly revolved and stopped around the world focusing on and highlighting Greece.' At first, they didn't understand the dream, but then they received a letter from Amin Banani, who had been a fellow student at Stanford and had pioneered to Greece, urging the Allens to come join him in Greece and that there were job possibilities.

Switching their goal to Greece, the next problem was that Dwight could not leave America without the permission of the American draft board (this was the time of the Korean war and American young men were subject to being drafted into the military). At first the board refused to allow Dwight to leave. Then Dwight suggested that, if they let him go, he would return after one year at his own expense and not seek any further deferments. Surprisingly, they agreed and the Allens were soon on their way.

On 15 September 1953, Dwight and Carole arrived in Athens – and found almost all the hotels booked solid. Finally, they found one hotel with an available room, but they had to be out by 8 a.m. the next morning. A taxi driver offered to take them to the hotel for the equivalent of $10. He then 'released the brake, rolled down the hill and around the corner to the hotel entrance without starting the engine'. A few days later, the Allens arranged to meet Amin at the Acropolis and walk up to the Parthenon in order to say prayers for their teaching work. Dwight wrote:

After climbing the Acropolis, we found the Parthenon to be closed. The whole top of the hill was locked up. After looking around we found a rock overlooking the city. There was a large bronze plaque written in Greek which we could not read. We went out to the edge of the rock and said our prayers. Later we found out that this was the Areopagus, the site where St Paul delivered the message of Jesus to the Athenians, nineteen hundred years before. How exciting that was.

Areopagus Hill is a short distance from the Acropolis and had been visited by Martha Root in 1934, along with Dionysios Devaris, the editor of an Athens newspaper who 'was beguiled by the Bahá'í teachings and had written a series of articles about them'. Devaris translated *Bahá'u'lláh and the New Era* into Greek for Martha.[108] It is interesting to note that though Martha Root had done travel-teaching in Athens, the Guardian still considered it a virgin territory.

Dwight was able to find part-time work teaching English at Athens College, as well tutoring students in English and mathematics for 67 cents an hour. Carole later found work as an editor for the *Athens News*, the only English-language newspaper in Greece. The big task was to find a place to live. Inflation was extreme at that time in Greece and when they did find an apartment to rent, Dwight wrote:

> We finally found a newly constructed apartment over the landlord's home. The rent was dr2,000,000 per month (US $67) [the Greek currency was the drachma]. Because of the hyper-inflation, the entire 9-month lease was payable in advance. Paying cash to the landlord took an entire afternoon as the largest bill was dr50,000. The dr20,000,000 rent filled an attaché case. Every bill was counted twice or three times.
>
> The coal heat cost over $50.00 US per month in the winter and still we froze, sleeping under four blankets and a goatskin rug.

Living in Greece was a new experience for the Allens, as Carole commented:

> Greece had just gone through terrible experiences during World War II which had ended in 1945. The Germans had occupied Greece during the war. The economy was in shambles. Greece was in slow recovery mode. Germans were not popular, so because we had lighter hair, the first question to us was 'Are you German?' Smiles appeared when we said 'American' as the United States was now helping Europe rebuild and the Marshall Plan and various aid grants had literally saved Greece from disastrous times. Greece was poor and there were many scarcities.
>
> The Greek Orthodox Church was the state religion. Everyone was expected to be a member of the official church. Other religions

were not allowed to teach or convert anyone. If a Greek wanted to become a member of another religion, he or she would have to leave Greece and come back after having changed faiths. We had to be cautious as to our teaching methods, honoring the rules of the state. For Americans who were used to unfettered publicity and freedom of speech, we had to constantly remind ourselves of these restrictions.

Teaching the Faith was very difficult because of the influence of the Greek Orthodox Church. They could not tell a Greek about the Faith unless he or she brought up religion first, so they spent their time making friends and inviting them to their home. The Allens showed multicultural slide shows and hoped that their Baháʼí pictures and books would elicit questions. They found that people commonly asked about their Baháʼí rings and that allowed them to mention the Faith.

One of their big problems was the lack of Baháʼí literature in Greek. They had a pamphlet produced by the European Teaching Committee so they consulted Shoghi Effendi about how to translate it. The Guardian suggested the Turkish Baháʼí Sami Doktoroglu. Mr Doktoroglu, however,

> was surprised when this request came, and flew to Athens to meet with us. It seems that he did not know Greek, but the process was worked out this way. We had the pamphlet translated from English to Greek by a trusted person who was studying the Faith. Mr Doktoroglu then had one of his secretaries translate the pamphlet from Greek to Turkish. Mr Doktoroglu now translated the pamphlet from English to Turkish. The two Turkish versions were compared and only one small detail had to be changed in the Greek version.

A few Greek friends began attending weekly Baháʼí study classes. A number were very attracted to the Baháʼí Faith, but none were able to make the last step and accept Baháʼuʼlláh. Shortly before their departure from Greece, one lady wrote them

> a long and thoughtful letter expressing her feelings. She said that she could observe the spirit of the Faith and live a Baháʼí life as a Christian. But she also expressed reservations about what she called

the 'dogma and ritual', meaning the administration and laws of the Faith. She was still quite attached to the unique position of Christ and had not yet accepted Bahá'u'lláh's station, though admiring many of the teachings and principles of the Faith. And, of course, the Greek Orthodox Church was an important part of life in Greece, always strongly present in the social, educational, and economic fabric of the life of the Greeks as well as being the spiritual center.

With a few people interested in the Faith, the Allens thought about organizing a Bahá'í summer school. The German National Spiritual Assembly, who oversaw their efforts, were enthusiastic about the idea, but Leroy Ioas wrote from Haifa saying that the Guardian thought it would be premature and a distraction.

Dwight and Carole had many visitors, including Dwight's parents, Valera and John Allen; Elizabeth Bevan, Knight of Bahá'u'lláh to Rhodes; Rolf Haug, Knight to Crete; Honor Kempton; Loyce Lawrence, Knight to the Lofoten Islands of Norway; Isobel Sabri; and William Sears. The Allens were also able to visit Adrianople and Istanbul in Turkey and went to Crete to spend time with Rolf.

Finally, their year was almost ended and the draft board refused to extend Dwight's deferment. Kenneth and Roberta Christian, Knights of Bahá'u'lláh for Southern Rhodesia, came to replace them. Initially, the travel plans of the Allens and the Christians would have meant that Carole and Dwight would have been gone before Kenneth and Roberta arrived. But Shoghi Effendi stressed the importance of continuity, so Dwight and Carol changed their departure and, when the Christians arrived on 7 August, the Allens met them at the dock and introduced them to some of their Greek friends, then, on 11 August, they boarded a ship and headed back to America. They arrived in New York on 23 August and Dwight was drafted into the army almost immediately.

The Allens, along with their five children, were able to visit Greece in 1970. In 1977, while Dwight and Carole were pioneering in Lesotho in Africa, they were invited to attend the formation of the first Greek National Spiritual Assembly. When they learned that, after all of those years, there were only 14 Greek Bahá'ís in spite of the efforts of many pioneers, and the more than 150 pioneers who were there at that time, they felt much better about their efforts to fulfil one of Shoghi Effendi's goals.

RHODES

Elizabeth Bevan

Elizabeth Bevan (1924–2013) chose Shoghi Effendi's goal of the island of Rhodes in the Aegean Sea for her pioneering post. When she was young, Elizabeth, known as Libby, had many questions about Christianity, so her parents took her to meetings of different religious groups to allow her to ask her questions. The answers always left her disappointed. It wasn't until they met Dorothy Baker, who sometimes stayed with them and held firesides in their home, that Libby found her answers. She became a Bahá'í at the age of 16, and her parents declared their belief at the same time. When the Ten Year Crusade began, Libby was in Los Angeles

> serving on a committee responsible to inform and encourage the community to arise and pioneer to the goal areas of the Crusade. Members of the committee had to present, at every Nineteen Day Feast, a list of countries and territories that needed to be filled and briefly mention what conditions were to be expected in those areas. She began to gradually feel awkward and self-conscious at these events, as she herself was not arising to serve in this capacity. Other members were having similar feelings, so after consulting they decided to all resign and follow the call of the Guardian. Consequently, at the following Nineteen Day Feast, after giving their usual presentation, they announced their decision to the community. The committee which replaced them would follow in their footsteps, as well as the one after that. Since the destinations were very varied, some seeming to offer greater hardship than others, the committee decided that each member would draw their country or territory from a hat so that it would be fair to all. Subsequently, Libby drew her slip of paper and the destination Rhodes (or Rodos), a small Greek Island very close to Turkey.[109]

Just a week before her departure, one of Libby's lungs suddenly collapsed, making her breathing laboured. In spite of this, she left on schedule and sailed to Italy in December. Luckily, her lung reinflated by itself.

Libby arrived in Rhodes on 8 January 1954. Soon after her arrival, she was asked by the American Coast Guard, which had a station on the island, if she could take charge of educating the children of the station personnel. Libby agreed, with the condition that the job would only be part time so that she would be able to meet and share the Bahá'í Faith with the island's residents. Libby created the Courier Community School, covering all ages from pre-school to high school, and was able to satisfy the standards of both the Greek Ministry of Education and the Coast Guard.

Shoghi Effendi had advised Libby to teach the Faith using the principles in a general way until she had developed closer friendships with her contacts. To help meet the island's inhabitants, she began visiting the surrounding villages, either by foot or by motorbike, as an experienced physical therapist and treating the children and adults who had been crippled by polio.

> She would show her patients exercises, bring them home-made equipment and accompany them to develop independence, whilst always radiating confidence and optimism. Her arrival would become a village event as people would run along the road to greet her at the sound of her approaching motor bike. She would later contract polio from one of her young patients which would leave her arms weak for the rest of her life, yet it would not stop her from continuing to offer her help. In more than one home a photograph of Libby was placed among the saints that decorated the walls. It greatly embarrassed her, but no amount of persuasion could remove the photo or stem the families' gratitude.

Because of her activities, Libby was able to make friends at many levels of society. Unfortunately, though she made many friends who were interested in the Bahá'í Faith, the power of the Orthodox Church was so strong that they would not take the final step of declaring their Faith in Bahá'u'lláh. One person finally did and became the first Bahá'í on Rhodes.

Because some of her friends had influence, Libby was able to keep renewing her residence permit until the middle of 1958, when she was forced to leave. Returning to the United States, she contacted the National Spiritual Assembly offering her services wherever needed. At first they asked her to fill a goal in Denmark, but then changed that to Sweden. Libby arrived in Stockholm in April 1960. She was taken from the airport to a Nineteen Day Feast where she met her future husband, Rouhollah Golmohammadi, whom she married a few years later. Libby then went to Uppsala where she was elected to the first Local Spiritual Assembly on 20 April. Two years later, she was elected to the National Spiritual Assembly. In 1994 the family, with their two children, pioneered to Hungary, where they spent most of their time in small villages and holding classes for Roma children. After the passing of her husband in 2005, Libby pioneered yet again, this time to China. She spent the last eight years of her life there. She was also able to return to Rhodes and visit the Bahá'í community in 2009, 51 years after leaving. Libby passed to the Abhá Kingdom at the age of 88, still in China.

CRETE

Rolf Haug

Rolf Haug (b.1933) was a German youth of 20 when he arrived in Iraklion on the island of Crete and was given the title of Knight of Bahá'u'lláh.[110] Rolf attended the Intercontinental Teaching Conference in Stockholm in July 1953, along with his brother, Guenther. Rolf wrote:

> The Conference itself was for me a deep spiritually moving experience, so that I spontaneously rose when the call was raised for pioneers to Greece. Greece was always a country which attracted me. The Culture, the Science and the Philosophy has been special for me. But in such a situation the actual motive is the wish to serve the holy Faith, and to put your whole trust in the Guidance of God. At such a moment one does not give one thought to the possible difficulties that may lie ahead or the problems that could arise for work or residence permission. One relies entirely on Bahá'u'lláh's promise in His Writings.[111]

While returning from the Conference by train to his home in Stuttgart, Hand of the Cause Adelbert Mühlschlegel told Rolf that the Hands wished that he would go to the Greek island of Crete instead of mainland Greece. Dr Mühlschlegel spread out a map and pointed to the town of Iraklion. Once home, Rolf, gave notice to the company he worked for and began looking for information about his new goal. He found a lady who had lived in Iraklion and she gave him a letter to a company in Crete and also informed her daughter, who was living in his goal city, of his intentions.

Rolf left Stuttgart on 2 October 1953 by train and arrived in Athens two days later. He spent two days visiting American pioneers Sheila and Amin Banani where he received much spiritual encouragement. Rolf arrived on 6 October in the harbour of Iraklion shortly after sunrise: 'The Sun had risen shortly before and shone on the island in its full splendour. The town was spread before me like a picture-book, framed in the background with high mountains, which seemed sizably near. Later I learned that it is the well-known Ida Mountain, nearly 2500 m[etres] high. The harbour was over crowded with people . . .'

Immediately after arriving, Rolf booked into a small hotel on Market Street, then contacted the daughter of the lady in Stuttgart, Sulka. Her husband collected him on his motorbike:

> I spent the first nice evening with this friendly family. I felt myself quickly at home. Sulka accompanied me the next day to find a place to live. In the evening, I already had rented a low-priced room with an elderly couple, who for four years gave me a real home. The next day I went with Sulka to look for work. I did not need the letter I had from Stuttgart at all, as she had selected another company. She took me to a firm exporting raisins, in which her father had worked . . . The same day my employment was fixed. I could hardly believe it. My arrival was on the 6th of October, I had found lodgings on the 7th and work on the 8th in a foreign Land, on an Island which during World War II had suffered a great deal under the German occupation. I soon realized that I had come to the right town and to the right company. Normally it was impossible for a German to receive a permission to stay or even a permission to work.

It was an exciting start to his pioneering, but soon the difficulties became apparent. Rolf spoke very little Greek, the language of the island, and his English was weak. He worked hard to learn Greek and within six months was able to hold basic conversations. He also prepared himself by deepening on the Writings of Bahá'u'lláh and the Bible.

In 1954, another German pioneer, Waltraud Weber, joined him and was a great support. Soon after Waltraud's arrival, Rolf had a surprise:

> A young man stopped me on the street. I was surprised. He knew a little German. He told me of a dream, in which he saw an exalted Person, who told him to request a book from me, and to read it. Overjoyed, I took him to my room. As he came into my room and saw the portrait of 'Abdu'l-Bahá on the wall: 'It is him who appeared to me in my dream. Who is it?', was his spontaneous question. I told him. 'And the book?', was his 2nd question. Yes, I had a Greek edition of *Bahá'u'lláh and the New Era* which the couple Banani had entrusted to me during my 4th of October, 1953 visit in Athens. It was an edition of the year 1934, which the unforgettable Martha Root, on one of her journeys to Greece, had given for translation.

The man's name was Manolis, and 'he took the book with great joy and very soon had read and studied it'. Rolf wrote, 'I have just passed through the great significance of this time spent in spirit and prayer when I dared to ask (a friend) the glorious question: "Do you wish to become Bahá'í?" One cannot measure the rapture that seized us, when, after an affirmative answer, we united in prayer and begged for steadfastness and guidance.'[112] That declaration on 26 August made Manolis the first Cretan Bahá'í.

Within two years of his arrival, Rolf was becoming well versed in Greek. In 1955, he met a young Cretan girl named Maro. She recounts:

> In 1955, I heard for the first time the word Bahá'í, as I got to know my brother's friend, Rolf . . . The Cause was so interesting, that also my parents asked several questions for their information. My parents were very open-minded people and their seven children were brought up in this spirit. We had a lot of contact and a close relationship developed. A year later we decided to get married.

Maro became a Bahá'í in 1966.

In 1963, Rolf was appointed as the German Honorary Consul of Iraklion and Eastern Crete, an unpaid but demanding position he held for 33 years. Because of his work, he received three Medals of Merit from the German Federal Republic. Rolf stayed on Crete for 60 years and is still there as of the writing of this book in 2016.

CYPRUS

Abbas and Semire Vekil

Abbas (1911–1984) and Semire Vekil (or Vakil) (b. 1934?) were married in 1952 and went to Istanbul for their honeymoon. During their stay there, they were in contact with the Bahá'í community and learned about the goals of the Ten Year Crusade. Semire wrote:

> It was an instant decision, as we did not have a lengthy discussion or prior planning. We wanted to respond to the Call by our Beloved Shoghi Effendi and we felt at a time this is what the Faith wanted from us . . . In one of my spiritual dreams Shoghi Effendi held my hands to raise me up, and made me move, I felt immediately the meaning of this dream was a confirmation for our decision. I was only 18 years old, but I knew that the pioneering decision we made with my husband was our joined and inevitable path together to show our love and gratitude to Bahá'u'lláh.[113]

With Semire eight months pregnant, Abbas went first and settled in Nicosia, Cyprus, on 19 August 1953. Semire joined him in November with their new son, Leroy.[114]

Initially, the Vekils rented a small house with Hugh and Violet McKinley, Knights of Bahá'u'lláh from Britain, in order to support each other, but they later found places of their own. The first few years were very difficult, but Shoghi Effendi's support helped them cope. After a year, Abbas had established good relations with the Turkish Cypriots and was given his first job offer in a bank in Nicosia. His ability to speak French, Arabic, Persian, Turkish and English helped expand their contacts among the Turkish and Greek Cypriots, who lived together in the same community at that time. Semire also spoke Arabic and English fluently and learned Turkish and some Greek.

For the first few years, the Vekils concentrated on making friends and gaining the trust of those around them through informal gatherings, friendship, family visits and personal contacts in their business, and they brought together people with different cultural, religious and ethnic backgrounds.

One of their contacts was an Armenian priest who was an important figure in the Greek Cypriot community. Shortly before he passed away, he declared his faith in Bahá'u'lláh to Abbas and Semire. Though he did not make his declaration public, he left his will with his son, requesting him to research the Bahá'í Faith. The son, Mr Garbis, later declared his faith and became part of the Bahá'í community in Cyprus. With the arrival of more pioneers and Semire reaching the age of 21, they were able to elect their first Local Spiritual Assembly in 1956.

A number of Hands of the Cause and other Bahá'ís visited Cyprus and gave support and encouragement to the pioneers there. Their second child, Suha, was born in Nicosia in 1959. By 1963, however, things became very difficult in Cyprus:

> On December 21, 1963 fighting erupted between the communities in Nicosia. In the days that followed it spread across the rest of the island between the population of Greek Cypriots and Turkish Cypriots. The community was under a curfew and the Vekils' house was under occupation. Abbas and Semire with their two children, four and ten years old, were forced to leave their home and lived in a hotel room in Nicosia for more than a month with no electricity and water. This is when Abbas, who had a very trustworthy reputation in the community and among business circles, was called to take the managerial position of the hotel. The couple prioritized the children's safety and decided to have Semire take them away from the conflict zone and move to Turkey temporarily. Needing the travel documents and essentials for the children, Semire courageously went back to their occupied home in the conflict zone in Nicosia, which was under army observation, requesting to enter her home.

Semire left Cyprus in 1964 for Ankara, Turkey. She initially hoped to return to Cyprus, but the conflict became worse and the island was divided into a Turkish northern part and a Greek southern part. Ultimately, after nine months of separation, Abbas left Cyprus and joined his family in Ankara. They moved to Istanbul, still hoping to return to Cyprus, but when the situation on Cyprus continued to deteriorate, they settled down in Istanbul.

A third child, Fulya, was born in 1965. Abbas served on the National Spiritual Assembly of Turkey and Semire was very active in Local Assemblies and committees and as a role model for travel teaching with children, visiting Bahá'í families and giving children's classes for Bahá'ís living in remote areas in Turkey. After Abbas's death in 1984, Semire continued to serve the Faith in Turkey before moving to Canada. Her greatest desire, however, was to return to Cyprus: 'I prayed for strength and health, because this was the second chance for me to return to Cyprus as a pioneer.'

In 2003, her dream was realized and she was able to return to Cyprus for two years, just at the time that the island's dividing border was opened for the first time in nearly 30 years, allowing the Bahá'í communities on both sides of the island to reunite. Suha pioneered to Cyprus with her family and two children in 2000, and served on the National Spiritual Assembly for 12 years. In 2014, Semire was living in Toronto, Canada, near to her children.

Hugh and Violet McKinley

Violet Watson (1882–1958) came from a Protestant and prosperous Irish Victorian family living in London. When she met and married Catholic David McKinley, her family disinherited her and her life changed from one of wealth to one of thrift. Initially, in the early 1920s, they lived in Oxford where, in 1924, a son, Hugh (1924–1999), was born. In Oxford, they attended meetings of the Theosophical Society and heard a talk on the Bahá'í Faith given by a Mr Wooller. At the meeting, they were given the book *Bahá'u'lláh and the New Era*, which they read in bed. When they finished, 'they looked at each other and declared'. Soon after accepting the Bahá'í Faith in 1928, David died.[115]

After David's death, Violet and Hugh lived in Cornwall and then Devon, where Violet was elected to the first Local Spiritual Assembly of the Torbay area, an Assembly that included Bernard Leach, the famous potter, Mark Tobey, the painter, Connie Langdon-Davies and the artist Reginald Turvey, father of the South African Bahá'í community. In September 1946, Hugh crashed on his motorbike, which resulted in severe skull damage and a severed mastoid. During his convalescence, he intensively studied the Bahá'í Writings, which served him well in the future.

During the British Six Year Plan (1944–1950), Hugh and his mother pioneered to Cardiff and served on its first Spiritual Assembly in 1948. While in Cardiff, Hugh discovered his musical talent which, he was advised, could result in him having a brilliant career in the operatic world. They moved to London in October of 1950 so that he could further this career.

In May 1953, a cablegram sent by the Guardian excited Hugh and he underlined the parts that caught his attention:

> The hour is ripe <u>to disencumber themselves of all worldly vanities</u>, to mount the steed of steadfastness, unfurl the banner of renunciation, don the armour of utter consecration to God's Cause, gird themselves with the girdle of a chaste and holy life, <u>unsheathe the sword of Bahá'u'lláh's utterance</u>, buckle on the shield of His love, carry as sole provision implicit trust in His promise, <u>flee their homeland, and scatter far and wide</u> to capture the unsurrendered territories of the entire planet.[116]

Then, in July, he attended the European Intercontinental Teaching Conference in Stockholm. Upon returning home, he consulted with his mother and they decided to go to Shoghi Effendi's goal of Cyprus because they thought that the dry, warm climate might suit Violet's delicate health. With this decision, Hugh had to abandon his budding music career just after he had given his first public performance at the Wigmore Hall in London. Hugh wrote to Shoghi Effendi about singing and pioneering. The Guardian replied: 'Do what you like! If you have a famous international career and become very well known, this is good for the Faith. If you go pioneering that also is very good for the Faith.' But it was Rúḥíyyih Khánum's postscript that turned Hugh onto the pioneering path: 'whatever we do for the Cause of God is eternal, of eternal value; the success of our struggles in life is uncertain, problematic.'[117]

Hugh left by train on 11 September 1953 and made a travel-teaching trip via Switzerland, Florence and Rome, where he was met by the Hands of the Cause Ugo Giachery and Mason Remey. Violet sailed from London on 14 November, teaching her fellow passengers on the week-long voyage. The ship docked in Haifa on 23 November and Violet wrote, 'A thick mist covered the port but the Golden Dome of the Shrine shone through it with an unearthly splendour. "The mystic Fane" – I could feel the power streaming forth and my whole being was abased in love and adoration of those to whom it was erected.'

Changing boats in Haifa, Violet arrived in Cyprus the next day and was met by Semire Vekil, because Hugh was away working – Hugh had managed to find a job as an accountant in an English business. That evening, Jessie Revell, who had come from Haifa for a rest, came to tea, supper and a devotional. Initially Hugh and Violet shared a 'charming bungalow with the Vekils'. The two families lived together until June of 1954, when the Vekils found a place of their own.[118]

Living on Cyprus proved to be very difficult. For the first two years, they lived in Nicosia and, with other pioneers, formed the first Local Spiritual Assembly in 1956. Hugh, who had a way with languages, quickly became proficient in Greek and translated *The Dawn-Breakers* into that language: 'This was no mean feat as he had had only minimal schooling, leaving at 15 years; he certainly didn't learn Greek in school! He was however a very good linguist and believed in looking up what he didn't know.' Hugh worked as an accountant with his own practice and later taught English. At one point, when money was really tight, he had to pawn his gramophone player, a big sacrifice since he loved music, which was his main relaxation.

In November 1954, mother and son were able to go on pilgrimage and meet the Guardian. Then, on 22 January 1955, Hugh married Shamsi Sedaghat from Britain. Hands of the Cause Jalál Kházeh and John Ferraby attended the wedding.

On 15 April 1958, Hugh, Shamsi and Violet moved to Famagusta, the city where Bahá'u'lláh's Covenant-breaking half-brother, Mírzá Yahyá, had been sent. This had left a 'pool of negativity' in Famagusta that the new pioneers had to overcome. 'Hugh often quoted the Guardian who said this would change when the first National Spiritual Assembly was formed.'

Just two weeks later, on 27 April, Violet developed a high fever and felt that she was dying. For the following ten days, she began to have a series of visions. She wrote that it was

> like looking at a curtain of rose petals, each perfect and flawless and with that lovely pearly iridescence that rose leaves have; the walls, floor, ceiling all vanished behind this lovely curtain . . . After

a short time the most lovely flowers began to appear, some like the flowers of earth, but others that I had never seen, but something like tulips, on long stalks, all colours . . . One flower was an enormous pure white one, something like a single poppy. . . Then also I saw horrible stuff, at first it seemed like balls of black crochet cotton, millions upon millions of them, covering all space, and as I looked they began to spin upon an invisible axis at an ever increasing speed until they finally fell in tatters and torn to pieces like enormous spiders' webs . . .

All the things I saw, flowers and afterwards faces, were perfectly silent . . . I was, I feel sure, [in] the valley of the shadow of death in which I was for a time, and the sense of peace and happiness (except for the black cotton balls) was marvellous. The faces and people were mostly of children and quite lifeless, like lovely dolls, just moving slowly across my vision all the time . . .

I was aware of a very wonderful being who looked after me and told me what to do. She had the outward appearance of a nurse and she told me that she was Irish but had passed on . . . as soon as I really began to improve, she ceased coming.

I felt the evil that Azal had left behind him; it was like a vast evil-smelling swamp of mud and slime and this had, I knew, to be removed, and how to do it I could not think at first, but then I realised that constant prayer was the only thing that could do it . . .

The visions lasted until late May when Violet became aware of the presence of Bahá'u'lláh. She asked why He had come and He replied: 'You are my servant.' He said that as there was work to be done, her life would be extended for a time. Her extended life lasted for 16 months, then on 11 August 1959, Violet fell ill again. Her condition declined and on the morning of 18 August she passed into the Abhá Realm. She was buried in the English Cemetery at Famagusta. On 15 September, the Hands of the Cause in the Holy Land wrote that 'it was our thought that a dignified and befitting tombstone should mark the resting place of this devoted pioneer in Famagusta, the very city where the arch-enemy of Bahá'u'lláh passed the end of his life and died'. They sent £300 for her grave marker. This marker consists of a plain slab of Carrara marble bearing the nine-pointed star and a quotation from the Writings of Bahá'u'lláh: 'They that have forsaken their country for the purpose of teaching Our Cause – these shall the Faithful Spirit strengthen through its power.'

Hugh remained in Famagusta working as an accountant and teaching English. His teaching efforts resulted in two of his best friends, Errol Olkar and Mustafa Salman, becoming Bahá'ís. Mustafa was elected to the National Spiritual Assembly when it was formed in 1978. Hugh also had to contend with the 'heated and militant political situation'. At one point, his name was on a Greek 'hit list' while the Turks thought highly of him because they 'saw in him all the qualities and attributes they didn't see in other Europeans'. The pioneers, however, were buoyed by the assurances of Shoghi Effendi that 'however great the tests that would assuredly confront those who arose to offset this baleful influence [of Mírzá Yaḥyá having lived there], the ultimate victory would be, in proportion, overwhelming'.[119]

When Mason Remey, a long-time correspondent and friend of Hugh, telephoned Hugh and declared that he was the second Guardian. Hugh immediately called the Hands in the Holy Land and proclaimed his loyalty to them, dropping his old friend.

Hugh stayed on Cyprus until 1963, when he left to attend the World Congress in London. After the Congress, Hugh stayed in London and established himself as a poet to earn his living. He lived in Sligo, Ireland for a time, where he married Olive. In 1965, they pioneered to the Greek island of Syros. A young bank clerk to whom Hugh taught English became the first native Bahá'í. Hugh wrote a literary column for the *Athens Daily Post* and wrote poetry. Olive left to finish her degree at Trinity College, but Hugh remained. He returned to the United Kingdom in 1977.[120]

Hugh returned to Cyprus in 1970 to visit his friends and then again in 1992 at the invitation of the Cyprus National Spiritual Assembly, when he opened the Turkish Bahá'í Centre in Nicosia. He also gave the National Assembly Violet's prayer beads, which had originally been 'Abdu'l-Bahá's. He married Deborah Waterfield in 1979 and they settled in Suffolk, where Hugh died on 9 February 1999. Upon his passing, his old friend Mustafa Salman wrote a tribute:

> Hugh McKinley really served during a time when Cyprus was in a turmoil. There were so many difficulties, political and terrorist activities, and he served during this time . . . He was one of the rare

people that I met, I had the privilege to know closely because he was the one who taught us.

He taught prayerfully, patiently, wisely, persistently and lovingly; that's why he was successful, and in him we saw all these virtues. And all this time he was in Cyprus during this very difficult, critical period, he was so humble, he was so loving and patient with the friends, and the enemies; I mean Turks and Greeks were not in good relations, and he could live under such conditions, and yet teach the Cause of God so wisely, lovingly and prayerfully.

He believed in the power of Bahá'u'lláh, he relied wholly on the power of Bahá'u'lláh because under those conditions . . . it is not an easy thing, but he managed what many of us say is the impossible in Cyprus. And the Knight of Bahá'u'lláh, as we remember him so lovingly, and also I have a special . . . love for Hugh McKinley for being my teacher, also, the first teacher in the family.

THE ATLANTIC OCEAN

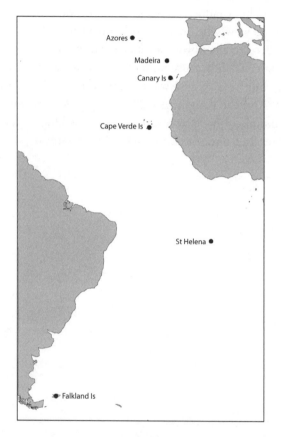

Azores

Richard and Lois Nolen

Richard Nolen (1914–1964) discovered the Bahá'í Faith through a newspaper advertisement in 1948. When he met his first Bahá'ís, Kenneth and Roberta Christian, in Michigan, he immediately accepted the Bahá'í Faith.

Richard had a defective heart, so when he and his wife, Lois (1917–1997), volunteered to pioneer during the Ten Year Crusade, the National Spiritual Assembly of the United States suggested the Azores Islands, off the coast of Portugal, with its mild climate. Richard, Lois and their children, Jean, Cynthia and John, set off from New York aboard a cargo ship called the *Ribiera Grande* and arrived at their pioneering post on 8 October 1953. Initially, the family stayed at the Hotel Atlantico near the docks while Richard tried to find work. Finding work and teaching the Faith was difficult because neither Richard or Lois knew Portuguese, but then Richard found work at an American Air Force base on Terceira Island.[1] Lois also found work at the base as a supply clerk.[2]

The Nolens then set themselves to learning Portuguese, and thus prepared, spread the Faith on all nine islands of the Azores. For three years, the Nolens shared the Faith without any notable results, but finally, in January 1957, their contacts at the Air Force base resulted in Nelson and Josie Wallace and Jack and Ethel Kerns becoming Bahá'ís. Several more American military personnel followed them into the Faith and by Riḍván 1958, the first Local Spiritual Assembly was formed on Terceira Island, composed solely of Americans. In December of that year, the first two islanders, Edmundo Cabral and Emberto Gonclaves, accepted the Faith.[3]

Though success was slow, by 1961 the Portuguese authorities had become worried about the growth of the Bahá'í community and the International Police told the Nolens that they had to stop teaching the Faith if they wanted to remain in the islands. They didn't stop teaching, but they did restrict their efforts to study classes held in Bahá'í homes.[4]

By 1962, there was a functioning Bahá'í community so, because of Richard's health, they returned to America in August. Richard passed away two years later.[5] In 1970, Lois pioneered to British Honduras, where she served on the National Spiritual Assembly.[6] Between 1981 and 1985, Lois served at the Bahá'í World Centre.[7]

MADEIRA

Elizabeth Hopper, Ada Schott, Ella Duffield and Sara Kenny

People of all sorts arose to fill Shoghi Effendi's goals. One of the older was Elizabeth Hopper (1883–1967), who earned her designation as a Knight of Bahá'u'lláh at the age of 70. After discovering the Bahá'í Faith, she served on the Local Spiritual Assembly of Washington DC for over 20 years. Upon hearing of the pioneering goals set by the Guardian, she packed and went. Ada Schott (1918–2006) joined her in order to have a Bahá'í team. On 20 September 1953, Elizabeth and Ada landed in Funchal, the chief port on the island of Madeira.[8] Ada had discovered the Faith in Washington DC and had become a Bahá'í in 1942. She first pioneered to Charleston, West Virginia in 1943 and helped form the first Local Spiritual Assembly. After that, she pioneered to other places in West Virginia, Michigan, Indiana and South Dakota.[9]

Ten days after Elizabeth and Ada arrived, they were joined by an even older pioneer, 80-year-old Ella Duffield (1873–1962) and her daughter, Sara Kenny (1900–1968).[10] Ella and Sara first learned about the Faith in 1933 in California and soon became Bahá'ís. While Sara was attending Stanford University, she met and married Robert Kenny, who later became a Senator and then a judge. Sara served the Faith on the National Teaching Committee, the Local Spiritual Assemblies of San Francisco and Los Angeles, and on the Area Teaching Committee for the Western States. When her husband began his rise in politics, it pushed Sara more deeply into the Faith, so that by 1953 she willingly left to fulfil the Guardian's goal.[11]

Their first months were very pleasant, but the teaching was slow. Ella and Sara were requested to move to France after nine months, where Sara was elected to the National Spiritual Assembly in 1958. She served on that body until 1963. When Mason Remey declared himself to be the second Guardian, Sara was one of the members of that National Assembly who remained constant. Ella served the Faith in France until her passing in 1962.[12] Sara left France in 1963 and returned to America. Six years later, she passed away while on vacation in London.[13]

Elizabeth and Ada continued their efforts and after three years of prayers and effort, three people joined the Faith. Ada returned to Indiana in 1958. She pioneered to Portugal between 1961 and 1963, then returned to Indiana. In 1984, Ada left for another foreign pioneer post, going to Denmark and then, in 1998, to South Africa. Her travel teaching took her to Malta and Albania.[14]

With Ada's departure, Elizabeth was the sole pioneer and lived on her own until 1961. Every time loneliness affected her, she would remind herself that 'Madeira is in the Divine Plan and the Guardian wanted an Assembly here'. Elizabeth was able to attend the Most Great Jubilee in

London in 1963 and, afterwards, go on pilgrimage. She was 80 by then, still living alone and having trouble with her hearing, but she rejected every suggestion that she return to America. In 1964, Isabel Horton came and stayed with her until she passed into the Abhá Kingdom on 3 May 1967, still at her pioneer post.[15]

CANARY ISLANDS

George and Marguerite (Peggy) True

George (1911–1984) and Marguerite True (1913–1998) arrived on the Canary Islands on 18 October 1953. George and Peggy met at Cornell University. For George, it was love at first sight, but Peggy took some convincing. After graduating, they moved to Grosse Pointe Farms, Michigan, and George went to work for an engineering company. They discovered the Bahá'í Faith when Peggy was on the board of a nursery school that was debating whether to enrol a child from a rare religion – a Bahá'í child. Peggy asked 'Why not?' Shortly afterwards, they attended a fireside at the home of George's boss in Detroit, Michigan. Peggy accepted the Bahá'í Faith first, but was followed the same day by George, in October 1935.[16]

When Shoghi Effendi called for pioneers, George and Peggy chose Nigeria, having previously been acquainted with Prince Orizu, who had visited them at their home in Grosse Pointe Farms. They left for Africa in September 1953, stopping over in England on the way to see whether their visa application had been approved. Arriving in England, they found a cable from the Guardian stating: 'Already one believer in Nigeria. More meritorious virgin territory. If not possible, continue to Nigeria.'[17] They sailed for Madeira, where George had been born, but learned that there were already four pioneers there. When they arrived in Tenerife in the Canary Islands on 18 October, they found no Nigerian visas. Then they realized that there were no Bahá'ís on the Islands and cabled Shoghi Effendi to ask whether they should set down roots there. The response was immediate: 'Settle Canaries'.[18]

George and Peggy settled in and began teaching. And initially, that proved to be almost impossible, so Peggy came up with a very innovative idea to spread the Faith internationally while they worked to open the Canaries. When they arrived it was practically impossible to teach the Faith here. Nothing was legalized, people were afraid to even listen to anything which wasn't directly from the Catholic church, and there was no way to put anything on the radio, television, or press, all of which had to have approval, and naturally, it wasn't permitted.

It was VERY frustrating.

Then one day, meditating on what I could do besides trying . . . I remembered hearing about messages in bottles. So I collected some bottles and got some corks and wrote short notes telling that Bahá'u'lláh had come, and inserted them in the bottles. It was just a simple note, but along with it I asked that whoever found the bottle please tell me where and when he found it.[19]

Peggy used other people's names and addresses on the notes in order to maintain their low profile in the Canaries. One bottle was quickly found on the Canary Island of Gomera. The finder, who spoke only Spanish, showed it to a Detroit newspaperman who took it home and called Peggy's sister, whose name was on the note. Her husband, who was not a Bahá'í, told the whole story of the Trues' pioneering to the Canaries. Peggy wrote that

there, splashed across the front page of the *Detroit News* was the story with a picture of the man who retrieved the bottle. I nearly collapsed when I saw it, because it was the last thing we wanted. I fully expected we would be ordered to leave the country again (we were still under observation, and not permitted any 'residence' papers. Incidentally, we lived in this sort of 'limbo' for nine years!) . . . Someone from the National Office in Wilmette . . . asked HOW we ever managed such publicity, front page, picture and all, because it was a space you couldn't possibly buy![20]

Fortunately, there were no repercussions. The bottles showed up in places like Cuba, Puerto Rico, Miami, Panama, Mexico, Venezuela and many of the islands in the Caribbean. In many places, their arrival led to some proclamation of the Faith as the finders would go around asking friends and neighbours what this 'Bahá'í' was. In other cases, people who found them knew Bahá'ís and would show them their discoveries. Quite a few ended up becoming Bahá'ís. The bottles kept showing up for years.

Teaching in the Canaries did begin to have an effect over time:

In spite of various handicaps of language, custom and political restrictions, much teaching has been done. God has been very kind to us and sent us three translators, and one knows both Spanish and English. For the first few months our new friends consisted mostly of Americans and Englishmen, because of the language barrier. Now, however, we have a large circle of native acquaintances.[21]

Though lacking skill with Spanish, George, an engineer, first set up a puzzolana factory (processed volcanic ash used to produce hydraulic cement) and, subsequently, a cement block factory, both of which were highly successful. By 1955, the Local Spiritual Assembly of Santa Cruz de Tenerife was formed.[22]

The Trues remained on Tenerife until 1979 when they retired to the Island of La Gomera, which they also opened to the Faith. George passed away in 1984 and Peggy, in 1998, both still at their pioneer post. There are currently over 700 believers on the Islands.[23]

Gertrude Eisenberg

On 13 November 1953, Californian Gertrude Eisenberg (1906–2001) landed on Grand Canary Island. Gertrude grew up in a Jewish family on Long Island, New York.[24] She became a Bahá'í after the Second World War and quickly caught the spirit of the Bahá'í Faith. She began learning Spanish in order to teach more widely and travelled through Guatemala, Paraguay and Brazil. Gertrude delighted in pioneering. After arriving in the Canaries, she wrote to the International Goals Committee saying, 'What a bounty for me and a privilege to assist in establishing the first Assembly on Grand Canary. I have to keep pinching myself.'[25] In 1954, Gertrude wrote that she had done much travelling and had been teaching an Arab Berber artist who was interested in the Faith.[26]

In the 1960s, Gertrude pioneered to Kauai in the Hawaiian Islands. Upon her arrival, she was asked to 'sit in at a local radio station and speak about philosophy and religion – but there wasn't even a person to interview her. They just sat her down, turned on the microphone and left her to her devices.' Later, she moved to the Los Angeles area.[27]

Shoghi-Riaz Rouhani

Shoghi-Riaz Rouhani (1922–2013) became a Knight of Bahá'u'lláh by pioneering to the Canary Islands. Better known as Riaz, he was born on 24 August 1922, in Alexandria, Egypt to Iranian parents who, from one side, were descended from the early Persian pioneers who settled in Egypt at the time of Bahá'u'lláh. On the other side, his grandmother had Moroccan roots. He had a passion for pioneering from his early youth. During Egypt's Seven Year Plan that ended in 1951, he chose home-front pioneering to Tanta, the capital of Egypt's Nile Delta, to strengthen its Bahá'í community.[28]

When the Ten Year Crusade was announced, Riaz was a few months away from graduation for a degree in philosophy and Islamic mysticism. Had he continued his education, the next year would have seen him studying at the famous Sorbonne University in France for his doctorate degree. Instead, he set his heart on fulfilling one of the goals set by the Guardian, one of the most difficult and elusive posts of the Plan, Rio de Oro (Spanish Sahara). Two Bahá'í pioneers from Egypt went there ahead of him (see earlier stories on Rio de Oro), only to be sent out of the country a few months later by the Spanish military, who were fighting a protracted war against local insurgents, a conflict that continues to this day. Riaz's mission may be likened to that of a caravan that lost its way in the desert – never to reach its set destination![29]

Riaz was heedless of his family's and friends' pleading to delay pioneering until his graduation. He even threatened to report a reluctant Bahá'í official at the Embassy of Iran in Cairo to the Guardian if he did not issue him a passport. On 8 October 1953, Riaz began a slow and protracted journey that was dictated by his virtual lack of financial resources.[30] On 12 October 1953, Rowshan Mustapha was in the Libyan village of El Marj, a hundred kilometres east of Benghazi, when he recognized a passenger in a truck headed west. The passenger was Riaz. Rowshan remembered that he stopped the truck and they embraced each other most warmly. Rowshan thought that Riaz 'must have been dressed up for what could be a sub-polar expedition':

> I asked him, further away from anyone to hear: 'Where are you going?'
> He answered: 'I am going to the Spanish Sahara!'

I exclaimed: 'Is that all? Do you know what this means? You are only 6,000 kilometres away, my dear Riaz.'

I gave him the phone number of Yusuf Jarrah in Benghazi, his next stop, and wished him all the best of protection, guidance, (and in my mind plenty of luck).[31]

After crossing the Libyan desert to Tripoli in such an uncomfortable means of transport, followed by an equally inconvenient sea voyage, Riaz made it to Spain and applied for a visa to the Spanish Sahara. He discovered, however, that the Government had closed the area and no visa was possible. Undeterred, Riaz decided to go to the Canary Islands with the thought of buying a small boat and sailing to the Spanish Sahara. He thought that a sailor would not be denied entry to the port of Cabo Juby. Arriving in the Canary Islands in April 1954, Riaz had no idea that he had just become a Knight of Bahá'u'lláh.[32] He joined the three other Knights already there, George and Peggy True and Gertrude Eisenberg.

The irony was that Riaz would not know of his knighthood until January 1970, when he looked over a copy of the *Bahá'í World* volume containing a list of the Knights – which included him.[33]

Even though he was now a pioneer in the Canary Islands, Riaz still had his heart set on Spanish Sahara. In 1955, he travelled to Morocco and, with two Moroccan pioneers, drove to Goulimine, the southernmost village in Morocco where the road ended. But even there, he found the border tightly closed. No one, not even the nomads who historically had crossed back and forth, was allowed to cross.[34] He later went back to the Canary Islands with Hormoz Zendeh[35] to help form the first Local Spiritual Assembly. Finding that the community only needed one pioneer to have the required nine, he returned to Morocco, but never achieved his heart's desire of pioneering to Spanish Sahara.[36] In 1956, Riaz was elected as a delegate to the first Convention to form the Regional Spiritual Assembly of North West Africa. There, he was elected to that Assembly and served on it for many years.[37]

During the following years, he settled in Rabat, Morocco and married his soul-mate, Soraya. He also brought his parents and uncle from Egypt to live with him. However, he was always ready to serve. From 1961 to 1963, he pioneered to The Gambia. From October 1969 to January 1970 he went to Liberia to help prepare for the Monrovia

Conference. After the conference he embarked on a travel-teaching tour that took him to Upper Volta (now Burkina Faso), Niger, Togo, Ghana, Dahomey (now Benin), Cameroon, Mauritania, Senegal and Mali, as well as revisits to the Canary Islands and Gambia. He was to make another four-month tour of the francophone countries of West Africa in 1992.[38]

After almost 30 years in Morocco, Riaz and his family moved to France at the request of the Universal House of Justice and settled in the town of Rouen in the north. However, in 2002, when he was 80, Riaz and his Soraya were asked by the French National Assembly to pioneer to Cyprus, where they managed to establish strong ties between the two (Greek and Turkish) Bahá'í communities of this divided island. Advancing age and poor health made it necessary for Riaz and Soraya to return to France in 2008, where they stayed until Riaz's passing in February 2013. His noble soul started the journey of eternity at the age of 91.[39]

CAPE VERDE ISLANDS

JoAnne and Howard Menking

JoAnne (1927–1988) and Howard Menking (b.1924) landed on the Cape Verde Islands in January 1954. Howard grew up in Indiana and served in the Navy during the second World War. He was one of the first Americans to reach Hiroshima, Japan, after it was destroyed by the first nuclear bomb.[40] Howard met JoAnne on a blind date during the war. After the war, they met again, by chance, in a drug store in Fort Wayne, Indiana and were married in 1948.[41]

Howard and JoAnne learned of the Bahá'í Faith at a fireside given by a Bahá'í pioneer to South America in 1949 on the unity of all religions and immediately accepted. They were so enthused with the idea of pioneering that they decided that very night to pioneer and a few months later they were in Brazil. But pioneering was more difficult than they had expected and after a few months of being unable to find work, they returned to the United States. At the Jubilee Convention for the dedication of the Mother Temple of the West in Chicago, the Menkings quietly watched all the excited volunteers ascending the stage to offer themselves as pioneers for the Ten Year Crusade. At least, they watched quietly until Dorothy Baker marched up to them and demanded, 'When are you two going to stand up?' Stand up they did and on 4 January 1954 they arrived at the former Portuguese penal colony of the Cape Verde Islands, 300 miles off the West African coast.

To JoAnne, the Cape Verde Islands were 'dry, miserable and tedious', but Howard loved it and the couple soon worked out a system whereby Howard found the contacts and JoAnne played hostess. But, as in Brazil, it was difficult. Howard had trouble finding work and nobody showed interest in their message. Finally, Howard asked Shoghi Effendi if they could go to Africa and work with Hand of the Cause Músá Banání. The Guardian, in reply, told of the Biblical prophecy in the book of Daniel where the 'angels of the Lord would spread to the four corners of the earth'. He said that the Knights of Bahá'u'lláh fulfilled that prophecy. The Menkings stayed.

JoAnne had been diagnosed as being medically unable to have children, but a Portuguese-trained Angolan doctor on the island thought he could change that. And to the surprise of everyone, she agreed. On 25 December 1955, Cristina Pauline was born and that changed everything. First, the Cape Verdeans adopted the little girl as 'our little *caboverdeana*', our little Cape Verdean. Second, they said, 'How could these people, with such a beautiful child – born on our soil on Christmas Day – be heathens as the church says?' Just a few months later, Frutuoso, whose name meant 'fruitful', became a Bahá'í. They were able to form the first Local Spiritual Assembly of Praia at Riḍván 1956. In 1957, the Menkings returned to America, JoAnne leaving first. After her departure, Howard received a letter from Shoghi Effendi giving his 'best wishes to your children'. At the time, Howard thought it was a mistake on the Guardian's part since they only had one child. In January 1958, however, there were children, with the birth of Clare Howard. Shoghi Effendi had known before JoAnne or the doctors.

The Menkings moved to Tennessee and then to Texas. JoAnne passed away in Dallas in 1988. After her passing, Howard joined a 'Bahá'í teaching group' and began travelling the country to train Bahá'í teachers.[42]

St Helena

Elizabeth Stamp

Elizabeth Stamp (1887–1970), Irish by birth but American by adoption, became a Bahá'í in New York in 1939 and did travel teaching in the American South and Midwest. Elizabeth was 67 when, inspired by the Ten Year Crusade, she wrote to the US National Spiritual Assembly offering to fulfil one of its goals, suggesting that she could join her sister in South Africa. After she had prayed and meditated about it, she wrote a second letter offering to go to St Helena Island in the middle of the South Atlantic. This offer was enthusiastically accepted.[43]

Elizabeth arrived on St Helena Island on 4 May 1954. The island was 2,000 kilometres off the coast of the Congo and consisted of a volcanic speck eight kilometres wide and 16 kilometres long with a population of less than 4,000. Since Elizabeth carried a British passport, her arrival was known to the Church of England Bishop before she arrived. A vicar serving the Bishop took a particular dislike to Elizabeth's presence and loudly warned his parishioners every chance he had to beware of this foreign cult. Elizabeth made him one of her first visits and, through patience and diplomacy, managed to at least gain his 'grudging' respect. She even gave him a few Bahá'í books.[44]

The Church of England was very strong on the island, forcing Elizabeth to be very cautious in her approach to the islanders. One couple did accept the Faith, but did not want their declaration to be known. The husband was a head teacher and, because of intense pressure from the Church, feared he would lose his job. They later withdrew from the Faith. In January 1960, Elizabeth was joined by Jagdish Saminaden, a Bahá'í from Mauritius. He helped Basil George, a policeman, Gay Corker, who sang in the church choir, and Eric Moyce to accept the Faith and remained on the island until 1962.[45]

Illness and a badly broken ankle forced Elizabeth to leave in early 1964, but instead of returning to America, she went to Durban, South Africa for two years. In 1966, she returned to America.[46]

Barbara George arrived on St Helena from Scotland in July 1964 and continued the teaching work.[47]

FALKLAND ISLANDS

John Leonard

John Leonard (1922–2006), from New York, pioneered to Port Stanley in the Falkland Islands on 10 February 1954.[48] According to fellow Knight Ben Guhrke, John was 'a bachelor on the move in south Chicago' until he wandered into a night club for a drink. There, he was quite taken with the singer, Julie Mitchum. She was the sister of actor Robert Mitchum and also a Bahá'í. John asked the waiter to invite her to join him for some conversation and she did. But the conversation changed his life. It led to his acceptance of Bahá'u'lláh and a journey to a remote, treeless island in the south Atlantic.[49]

He initially found work as a painter for the Public Works Department, but by August, John reported that he was working as an emergency night telephone operator and that the first resident of Port Stanley had declared her Faith in Bahá'u'lláh. As a newcomer, John was interviewed on the radio and later hosted an interview series called 'Peoples of the World'.[50] When John learned that children in the rural parts of the island had limited access to education, he found a job as a travelling teacher, which lasted four years.

The first islander to accept the Bahá'í Faith was Florence McKinnon. She was immediately pressured by the Church of England rector to return to the church. He sent her books to read and warned that she was abandoning Jesus. Her reply was that the Words of Bahá'u'lláh had filled her with spiritual happiness and that she was in no wise rejecting Jesus. She wrote, 'I take this opportunity of acquainting you with my decision, of remaining firm and steadfast in the Bahá'í Faith . . . These words I have penned come from a sincere heart, and not from one who is sadly delusioned . . .'[51]

In a letter in *Bahá'í News* in September 1955, John wrote that

Life continues to be wonderful. This job is so interesting and absorbing and I like the open life and the people so much, that sometimes I feel like bursting with gratitude. A short time ago one of the well-meaning friends wrote and said that any time I felt I was ready for a vacation, she would get together with a few other friends and raise funds for me to take a trip back. I wrote back that the real hardship would be to return to the States, and that it's more of a vacation for me to remain here. There is no feeling of homesickness. These people are very much a part of my family now.[52]

In 1964, a second pioneer, Margaret Mills, arrived at Port Stanley. Before very long, the two pioneers were married. In 1969, when the couple had to give up their rental house, John accepted a job with the Falkland Island Company which included the use of a house. John and Margaret helped to form the first Local Spiritual Assembly of Port Stanley in 1972. He retired in 1989, but continued to work as a photographer, tour guide, adult literacy tutor and a radio announcer. Margaret passed away in 1999 and John, after 52 years, followed her in 2006.[53]

AFTER THE TEN YEAR CRUSADE

1968–1990

Five of Shoghi Effendi's initial goals were not filled during the Ten Year Crusade because they were within the boundaries of the Soviet Union or its influence. These included Romania, Moldova, White Russia (now Belarus), Mongolia and Sakhalin Island.

ROMANIA

Fereydoun Khazrá'í

Fereydoun Khazrá'í (1914–1994) was the first Bahá'í to reach Romania in 32 years when he arrived in November 1968. Born into a Bahá'í family, Fereydoun didn't accept the Bahá'í Faith for many years. He moved to Rome in 1952 and set up a business. While there, he had a dream in which he asked a dervish whether the Faith was true. The dervish showed him two gems, one for the Báb and one for Bahá'u'lláh. Fereydoun immediately accepted the Faith as being true.[1]

In 1956, Fereydoun went on pilgrimage. While he was there, the Guardian spoke enthusiastically about the countries behind the Iron Curtain. During one such talk, Fereydoun suddenly interrupted him and asked if he could have the privilege of going there. Shoghi Effendi replied, 'Try and you will succeed!', repeating the phrase. On his last day of pilgrimage, the Guardian told him to 'return to Rome from where you will begin your pioneering career . . . It is in Rome that you will make your application to enter Romania as a pioneer. After, you will return here like Mr Banání, Mr Faizí, Dr Muhájir, a conquering victor.'[2]

It wasn't until 1968 that Fereydoun was able to go to Romania. Of the first few years, he wrote: 'I never found work in Romania, nor was

I able to conduct commercial transactions. I struggled for three years to secure a resident's visa, during which time I had to return to Rome each month to get temporary visas.' Shortly after arriving in Romania, Fereydoun met Arcela Spulber, who became the first Romanian Bahá'í. When they decided to get married, they found it wasn't particularly easy:

> To get the authorization of marriage, one had to apply to the President of the Republic, an easy enough thing, since Romania had excellent relations with the Embassy of Iran. But for the administrative formalities, I had to go to the secret police. They asked me to collaborate with them by making regular reports of all cocktail and reception discussions between visitors and members of the [Iranian] embassy. I refused on principle. They responded by threatening me. They said that one day I would return to them on bended knee asking for their help and then they would have their revenge.[3]

The couple were married in spite of the problems. Annemarie Krüger-Brauns, who was to become the Knight of Bahá'u'lláh to Moldova, visited Fereydoun in 1974 and again in 1977. During her second visit, she wrote that the spiritual conditions in Romania were becoming more and more difficult and that foreigners were under physical pressures, as well, in a closed and suspicious culture. Annamarie met two new pioneers, Mr and Mrs Yangandia, who came from Central Africa with their children.[4] Mr Yangandia was African and his wife was Romanian. Their difficulties reflected government policies and not the prejudices of the Romanian people.[5]

In 1972, Fereydoun was able to become accredited as a foreign journalist and a few years later was given a job at the Iranian Embassy. He lost his Embassy job when the Shah was overthrown in 1979. Two years later, in March 1981, he also lost his accreditation as a journalist. Then, Arcela was forced to renounce her citizenship because the secret police wanted her to be their informant. That act made them 'persona non grata' and two policemen came to their house and told them they had 24 hours to leave the country.[6]

They moved to Strasbourg, a home-front goal of the French National Spiritual Assembly. After a few months and a few declarations in Strasbourg, the Khazrá'ís moved to Lille and helped raise up its first Local

Lois (seated, left) a*nd Richard Nolen* (standing, right), *Knights of Bahá'u'lláh to the Azores*

JoAnne and Howard Menking (centre), *Knights of Bahá'u'lláh to the Cape Verde Islands, with their daughter Christina, c. 1956*

*Ella Duffield,
Knight of
Bahá'u'lláh to
Madeira*

*Ada Schott and Elizabeth Hopper,
Knights of Bahá'u'lláh to Madeira*

*George and Marguerite (Peggy)
True, and Gertrude Eisenberg,
Knights of Bahá'u'lláh to the
Canary Islands, with Barry
True (young boy)*

*Sara Kenny (standing,
second from right),
Knight of Bahá'u'lláh
Madeira*

Four Knights of Bahá'u'lláh, members of the first Spiritual Assembly of Santa Cruz de Tenerife, 1955. Standing, left to right: *George True, Hussein Ardekani (Knight to Morocco International Zone), Jose Perez, Issa Taheri.* Seated: *Nosrat Ardekani (Knight to Morocco International Zone), Batoul Taheri, Pilar Perez, Peggy True, Ernestina Clausell*

Three Knights of Bahá'u'lláh, members of the first Regional Spiritual Assembly of North West Africa, 1956. Standing, left to right: *William Foster, Shoghi-Riaz Rouhani (Knight to the Canary Islands), 'Abdu'l-Hamid El Khemiri, Valerie Wilson, Enoch Olinga (Knight to British Cameroon).* Seated: *Mustapha Bouchoucha, Elsie Austin (Knight to Morocco International Zone), Rowshan Mustapha, Shoghi Ghadimi*

Elizabeth Stamp,
Knight of Bahá'u'lláh to St Helena

John Leonard, Knight of
Bahá'u'lláh to the Falkland Islands,
travel teaching in one of the Camps

John with Margaret Mills (later
Leonard) before pioneering

Fereydoun Khazrá'í,
Knight of Bahá'u'lláh to Romania

Annemarie Krüger-Brauns, Knight of Bahá'u'lláh
to Moldova, with Antanas Kremenliev

Helmut Winkelbach, Knight of
Bahá'u'lláh to White Russia (Belarus)
with his wife Olga

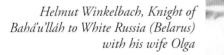

'Abbás and Rezvánieh Katirai,
Knights of Bahá'u'lláh to Sakhalin Island

Sean Hinton, Knight of Bahá'u'lláh to Mongolia,
with the first Mongolian Bahá'í Oyundelger, 1989

Knights of Bahá'u'lláh view the Roll of Honour bearing their names

Amatu'l-Bahá Rúḥíyyih Khánum places the Roll of Honour at the threshold of the Shrine of Bahá'u'lláh

Knights of Bahá'u'lláh gathered in the Holy Land, May 1992

Spiritual Assembly in 1983. With the fall of Communism in 1989, they tried to return to Romania, but were unsuccessful. In 1991, however, they were invited to attend the election of the first National Spiritual Assembly of the Bahá'is of Romania. Fereydoun died in 1994.[7]

MOLDOVA

Annemarie Krüger-Brauns

Annemarie Krüger-Brauns (1918–2006) was the granddaughter of Swiss Bahá'í Dr August Forel and the daughter of Bahá'í parents. During the Ten Year Crusade, Annemarie was deeply involved with the building of the European Mashriqu'l-Adhkár near Frankfurt. In 1970, she was elected secretary of the German National Spiritual Assembly. Three years later, Annemarie began to look for ways to teach the Bahá'í Faith in the Soviet Union.[8]

In 1974, Annemarie tried to visit Moldova. At first, the only possibility was to fly to Leningrad, Moscow and Kiev, spending just a single night in Chisinau (Kishinev), Moldova. Contacting the Russian Intourist travel agency, she learned that she could travel by plane or train to Bucharest and then on to Chisinau with the possibility of staying for up to 15 days. On 10 September, she left Germany for Bucharest, with hotel reservations for four days in Chisinau.

At the Russian border, 'Every written or printed paper was taken from me, each little slip with notes, numbers, addresses, and a number of pages of handwritten Bahá'í prayers (including "The Remover of Difficulties" in Russian). After 3 hours I received everything back without any remark.' Arriving at her hotel, she soon learned that a 'very nice lady' was to be her guide. In actuality, the lady was there to keep an eye on her foreign charge and went everywhere with her. After three days in Chisinau, however, her guide believed that Annemarie was 'harmless enough' and allowed her to go out unescorted. Using a Russian dictionary, French, some German and a little English, she was able to talk with many people.

After praying to be able to speak about the Faith, Annemarie began walking randomly around the city until she came upon a small garden where workers at a nearby factory were enjoying a break. Looking over those seated there, she was attracted to a 40-year-old woman with a 'warm-hearted smile'. The woman was a French teacher named

Larissa Malai. Since Annemarie also spoke French, she thought that her prayers had been answered. Larissa, however, proclaimed that she was a 'staunch atheist with no interest in religion'. But she also said that her husband, Vladimir Malai, might be interested. When Annemarie met him, Vladimir was interested enough to listen to her stories and remarked that the Bahá'í prayers were much like his Christian ones. With Vladimir's interest in prayers, Annemarie wrote down the prayers she had memorized in French and left them with him. As she departed Moldova at the end of her visa, a 'nice lady', who was actually a state security official, asked her many questions about how she liked Moldova and what had impressed her. Annemarie returned to Bucharest on 16 September, where she visited Fereydoun Khazrá'í, the Knight of Bahá'u'lláh for Romania.

In 1977, Annemarie again visited Fereydoun Khazrá'í in Romania, then returned to Chisinau and the Malai family. Again, the Customs officials took away all her written or printed papers, but, as before, returned them a few hours later. Because of the political suspicions of the time, Annemarie had not written to the Malais since her visit, but she contacted them as soon as she arrived. Visits between Moldovans and foreigners had to be circumspect. Initially, Larissa was only able to meet her for half an hour outside in a public restaurant (and only after Larissa gave her passport to a government official). Annemarie gave Larissa a copy of 'Abdu'l-Bahá's Tablet to August Forel, the only document from the Bahá'í Writings she had. A few days later, she was able to visit Larissa and Vladimir in their home. She had the taxi driver drop her some distance from the house so as not to bring them under suspicion. As she had before, Annemarie wrote down prayers in French to leave with the couple. They spent five hours together. Annemarie wrote that Vladimir 'asked and asked, all the fundamental principles of the Faith, special questions about laws . . . Late in the evening, Larissa's husband apologized for all his questions but his interest could not find an end. Very heartfelt were his thanks for all that was given to their "spirit and heart".' After six days, Annemarie returned to Germany.

Annemarie made her third trip to Chisinau in 1984, taking selected books on the Faith, including Bahá'u'lláh's *Hidden Words*. This time, probably because of her earlier trips, her luggage was checked only perfunctorily and she managed to keep her books. Again, she had not written to the Malais since her previous visit, but once she had arrived, they spent three full days together. Annemarie wrote down all of the Bahá'í laws and talked about getting the *Hidden Words* translated into Moldovan. On the night before her departure for Germany, Vladimir declared his acceptance of Bahá'u'lláh. He wrote down his declaration and Annemarie carefully concealed it in the belt of her dress, being worried that the authorities would confiscate it.

> The last evening Vladimir told me: 'I have decided to become a Bahá'í.' Within a couple of days he realized the importance of being a Bahá'í. We all knew that something of consequence had happened in Moldova. Larissa admitted that something had urged her to go to the place where we met for the first time ten years ago. I had never been there before, she said. We both tried to support the new Bahá'í. Vladimir could not talk about the Faith because it was dangerous. Therefore, I suggested to send them some Bahá'í literature. Larissa had a friend who lived in Moscow and she used to visit her twice a year. She was absolutely reliable and we decided to use her as an intermediary. Small parcels sent by post were usually opened and their contents checked . . .

After returning home, Annemarie forwarded Vladimir's declaration and a report of her activities to the Universal House of Justice. On 16 July, the House of Justice wrote that

> Your services to the Cause of God in the Balkans are truly historic, and must surely rejoice the hearts of your dear parents and your distinguished grandfather [August Forel] in the Abhá Kingdom. The acceptance of the Faith by Mr Vladimir Malaille [Malai], establishing the first Bahá'í centre in Moldavia, is a wonderful achievement, and you may be sure that the House of Justice will remember him and his dear wife, Larissa, in its prayers at the Sacred Threshold . . .[9]

Five months later, on 17 December 1984, Annemarie received another letter from the House of Justice which read: 'It also rejoices our hearts to be able to inform you that, as a result of your outstanding services, you have won for yourself the rank of Knight of Bahá'u'lláh for Moldova.'[10] At Riḍván 1996, the Moldova Bahá'í community invited Annemarie to attend the election of its first National Spiritual Assembly.

WHITE RUSSIA (NOW BELARUS)

Helmut Winkelbach

Helmut Winkelbach (b.1951) was a 27-year-old German youth when he arrived in Bobruisk, Belarus, previously called White Russia, on 23 December 1978. Helmut had become a Bahá'í four years earlier and quickly became a home-front pioneer. In April 1978, he also travelled through Hungary and Romania with just a backpack and a prayer book. This trip encouraged him to pioneer in the eastern part of Europe. Later in 1978, Helmut found a job as an electrical engineer in White Russia, an area closed to most foreigners, thus fulfilling one of the last of Shoghi Effendi's Ten Year Crusade goals. He and a group of Germans were building a factory, but he only had a visa for three months. In order to prolong his stay, he took on every job he was asked to do, relying completely on Bahá'u'lláh. Initially, the Universal House of Justice recommended that he should not speak openly about the Faith since the people were not receptive to spiritual ideas, but he remained in Belarus under the conditions present at that time.[11] Foreigners were not allowed to leave Bobruisk except for a once-a-month trip to Minsk.

> During one of those trips a young man, Anatoly [Kiryushkin] . . . approached Helmut in the middle of the street. The Belarusian people were curious and had interest in contact with foreigners. That day, Anatoly showed Helmut the city. Without exchanging any contact information or arranging to meet again Helmut left for Bobruisk.
>
> During his next trip to Minsk Anatoly and Helmut met again [by] coincidence and shared the wonderful time together. Again they separated without having arranged another meeting . . . During one of the following trips Anatoly and Helmut met by chance again. This time it was Anatoly's birthday and he invited Helmut to his place for the first time. Then it was not very safe to bring foreigners to one's home.
>
> During that visit Helmut met Olga, the four-year-old daughter of Anatoly. Ten years later, after being taught through continuous visits and conversations, and after a visit to Germany where she had the opportunity to meet other Bahá'í juniors and friends, Olga declared herself as a Bahá'í at the age of 14. She was the first Belarussian Bahá'í.

After a year, Helmut returned to Germany for a vacation and was able to go on pilgrimage. He had the idea that getting married to someone in Belarus would allow him to stay permanently in the country, so he prayed intensely while in the Shrines for God to help him find a wife. On the train back to Belarus, he had a dream in which he saw the face of a woman named Olga and heard her name. On his first day back in Bobruisk, he walked into the office and saw, behind a glass wall, the woman from his dream. And her name was Olga. In May 1981, after many problems, they were married. A month later, Helmut was forced to leave the country and Olga was not able to go with him to Germany. In an effort to try and stay, he asked the director of his Intourist hotel about the possibility of getting Soviet citizenship. A few days later, he 'was invited by the KGB to spy on German companies' in return for their support in acquiring citizenship. He declined and had to leave.

Seven weeks later, Helmut found another job in Chimkent, Kazakhstan, where he was joined by Olga. The couple stayed there for three years, after which they went back to Germany where their two children, Jana and Janis, were born. While in Germany, Olga declared her Faith in Bahá'u'lláh. In September 1986, the family was able to return to Belarus and worked in Mogiley for a year and a half. Then, in 1988, Helmut and Houshang Peseschkian, a Bahá'í from Germany, travelled to Ashkhabad in Turkmenistan, Dushanbe in Tajikistan, and Moscow at the request of the Universal House of Justice to meet with Bahá'ís who had been 'silent for over 60 years'.

In 1989, the Winkelbachs spent a year living in Moscow before they were able to move back to Belarus and settle in Minsk in 1990. Helmut and Olga's teaching efforts bore fruit nine months after their arrival. Agata Shpakovskaya was invited to a fireside and was struck by the concept of unity in the Faith as well as the 'love, calmness and spirituality' of the Winkelbachs. Other people also were attracted and in the first days of October 1991, the first Local Spiritual Assembly of Minsk was elected. Learning how to consult and work in unity was a 'difficult and painful' experience, but Helmut's 'diplomatic talent' pulled the group together. In 1992, the community acquired a Bahá'í Centre and the following year the community was privileged to host Amatu'l-Bahá Rúḥíyyih Khánum there. In 1991 the Soviet Union underwent dramatic changes and teaching the Faith became easier. Four years later, the Bahá'ís elected the first National Spiritual Assembly of Belarus.

The new National Assembly purchased two small 'blockhouses' in the village of Smolye, close to Minsk. These became the 'Bahá'í dacha' and the site of children's classes, seminars and Ruhi courses.[12]

Helmut, Olga and their children stayed in Minsk for the next 17 years. In 2006, Helmut was not able to find work and the family was forced to return to Germany. Later in the year, however, a friend learned of a company in the Czech Republic that needed a representative in Belarus. After his friend began saying the Tablet of Aḥmad, Helmut got the job and the family was able to move back to Belarus, where they lived and served until the end of 2013.

MONGOLIA

Sean Hinton

Sean Hinton (b.1966), born in England to Bahá'í parents, but raised in Australia, was the first Bahá'í to reside in Mongolia, arriving on 28 December 1988 at the age of 22. Sean had been inspired to serve in Mongolia by a brief conversation in Haifa the year before with Mr Ian Semple, then serving on the Universal House of Justice, who, seemingly in jest, challenged him by saying 'you should go and study music in Outer Mongolia'. Sean was then inspired by a passage from Shoghi Effendi:

> Under whatever conditions, the dearly loved . . . onward marching legions of the army of Bahá'u'lláh may be laboring, in whatever theatre they may operate, in whatever climes they may struggle, . . . to them all, as well as to those who, as the fortunes of this fate-laden Crusade prosper. . . will penetrate the jungles of the Amazon, scale the mountain-fastnesses of Tibet, establish direct contact with the teeming and hapless multitudes in the interior of China, Mongolia and Japan . . . traverse the steppes of Russia or scatter throughout the wastes of Siberia, I direct my impassioned appeal to obey, as befits His warriors, the summons of the Lord of Hosts, and prepare for that Day of Days when His victorious battalions will, to the accompaniment of hosannas from the invisible angels in the Abhá Kingdom, celebrate the hour of final victory.[13]

In order to enter Mongolia, Sean came as a British Council-funded research scholar in ethnomusicology from the University of Cambridge. He had permission to stay for nine months, but was able to live in Mongolia on and off for the next seven years until 1995. On that first visit in 1988, he was one of only a handful of westerners who were granted visas that year to live in Mongolia, as the country was among the most isolated in the Soviet Bloc. He lived in Ulaanbaatar for the first year he was there, as a student at the Mongolian National University taking Mongolian language classes as a necessary precursor to pursuing his musical research. Initially, Sean was unable to teach the Bahá'í Faith because of the political situation, but the entire political system was to be completely transformed within 18 months of his arrival by the ending of the Soviet era and the collapse of Communism.

In May 1989, Amatu'l-Bahá Rúḥíyyih Khánum, along with Counsellor Bijan Farid, Violette Nakhjavani and two other friends, visited Mongolia. Sean was told the news of her impending visit in a very roundabout way:

I had received a telegram from my parents in Australia that read: 'EXCITING NEWS. WILL CALL THURSDAY 17:00 BRITISH EMBASSY'. Telephoning Ulaanbaatar from Sydney was not easy in 1989. As a student living in the foreign students hostel along with the Vietnamese, Laotian, Cambodian, Chinese and Russian students, receiving a call wasn't easy either. My parents would send a telegram with a time and date, and I would sit at the British Embassy every night until they got through. The Australian operator would make the call to London where their operator would try to raise someone in Moscow. From there Moscow would try to patch through a call to Ulaanbaatar via Irkutsk. Once the Ulaanbaatar operator had the call, they would try to get a line across the town to the British Embassy which, if power cuts and blizzards had not cut the connection, would mean I could receive the call. Then, accompanied by 5 operators and a roar of static, we would try to share some news. On this occasion the message was deceptively simple: 'You are going to have some special visitors. Mrs Rabbani is coming to visit you, Sean, do you understand . . . Mrs Rabbani!' My father was avoiding using her formal title to deflect the interest of anyone listening on the line, but I was stunned by the news. I had no idea how I could adequately prepare and make all the arrangements for such a visit on my own.[14]

After dinner on Rúḥíyyih Khánum's first night in Ulaanbaatar, one of Sean's friends, who was with them that night, asked: 'Who is this woman and what is the Faith she talks about?' And for the first time since he had arrived, he was able to tell a Mongolian about Bahá'u'lláh. Over the course of her week-long visit, though not travelling in any official capacity, Rúḥíyyih Khánum met with the Deputy Chief Lama, addressed a group of 60 students at the Mongolian State University, was interviewed on Mongolian State Radio, where she made the first known mention of the Faith in public in Mongolia, and spoke with numerous Mongolians. On one occasion, the group was joined by an English-language student of Sean's, 22-year-old Ms Oyundelger. Four months later, just before Sean's return to Cambridge University, Ms Oyundelger became the first Mongolian to declare her faith as a Bahá'í. The next Mongolians to became Bahá'ís were husband and wife Ms O. Ina and Mr D. Ulambayar, who accepted the Faith in Ulaanbaatar in April 1990 as the result of the visit of the Bahá'í musical group 'El Viento Canta'. Some years later Ms O. Ina was appointed as one of Mongolia's first Auxiliary Board members.

Sean had lived mostly in Ulaanbaatar, but spent most of 1990–1991 living in Khovd Province in western Mongolia, including a nine-month stint living and travelling with nomadic herdsmen in the Altai Mountains. With the political changes in the country having opened it up, more and more Bahá'í visitors, travelling teachers and pioneers were able to come to Mongolia from Europe, Southeast Asia and North America. By Riḍván 1992, the first Local Spiritual Assembly of Ulaanbaatar was formed, and two years later, the National Spiritual Assembly of the Bahá'ís of Mongolia was elected in the presence of Rúḥíyyih Khánum, this time travelling in an official capacity as the representative of the Universal House of Justice. Sean served on the National Spiritual Assembly during its first year until he left Mongolia to return to Australia in 1995.

In the subsequent years the Bahá'í community in Mongolia has grown from strength to strength, now numbering more than 7,000 souls. Mongolia was blessed to be invited by the Universal House of Justice to host one of the 42 global conferences in 2009, and in 2013 to host one of the 114 youth conferences.

SAKHALIN ISLAND

'Abbás and Rezvánieh Katirai

'Abbás (1923–2001) and Rezvánieh Katirai pioneered from Japan to Sakhalin Island, off the eastern coast of what was then the Soviet Union. The Katirais had pioneered to Japan from Iran in 1953 and 'Abbás served on the National Spiritual Assembly for over 20 years. The couple arrived on Sakhalin Island in March 1990 and thus filled the final goal of Shoghi Effendi's Ten Year Crusade. By Riḍván 1991 there were six Local Spiritual Assemblies. The pioneers remained on the island until 1995, when they returned to Japan. In 1996, the Katirais went to the country of Georgia and helped raise up the National Spiritual Assembly there.[15] 'Abbás had been appointed a Counsellor. Rayyan Sabet-Parry remembers a travel-teaching trip to a distant city in Georgia: 'The Bahá'ís had rented a taxi van for the long journey. Mr Katirai sat in the front with another Russian-speaking Bahá'í. The journey was long and by the end of it we had found out that our taxi driver had embraced the Faith. Mr Katirai had taught him the Faith on the journey.'[16]

APPENDIX I

KNIGHTS OF BAHÁ'U'LLÁH BY GOAL AREA

Names in parentheses are the modern names or the nationality of the goal areas.

Admiralty Islands
(Papua New Guinea)
Violet Hoehnke

Aleutian Islands
(Alaska)
Elaine Caldwell
Jenabe Caldwell
Elinore Putney

Andaman Islands
(India)
Khodadad Fozdar

Andorra
William Danjon

Anticosti Island
(Quebec, Canada)
Mary Zabolotny

Ashanti Protectorate
(Ghana)
Benedict Eballa

Azores
Lois Nolen
Richard Nolen

Bahamas Islands
(The Bahamas)
Gail Curwin
Gerald Curwin
Ethel Holmes
Maurice Holmes
Andrew Matthisen
Nina Matthisen

Balearic Islands
Tove Deleuran
Jean Deleuran
Charles Ioas
Virginia Orbison

Baranof Island
(Alaska)
Gail Avery
Grace Bahovec
Helen Robinson

Basutoland
(Lesotho)
Elizabeth Laws
Frederick Laws

Bechuanaland
(Botswana)
Audrey Robarts
John Robarts
Patrick Robarts

Bhutan
Ardishir Furúdí
Shapoor Aspandiar
  Rowhani

British Cameroon
(Cameroon)
Enoch Olinga

British Guiana
(Guyana)
Malcolm King

British Honduras
(Belize)
Cora Oliver
Shirley Warde

British Togoland
(Ghana)
Albert Buapiah
Edward Tabe

Brunei
Harry Clark
Charles Duncan
John Fozdar

Canary Islands
Gertrude Eisenberg
Shoghi-Riaz Rouhani
George True
Marguerite (Peggy) True

Cape Breton Island
(Nova Scotia, Canada)
Jeanne Allen
Frederick Allen
Grace Geary
Irving Geary

Cape Verde Islands
Howard Menking
JoAnne Menking

Caroline Islands
(Papua New Guinea)
Virginia Breaks

Chagos Islands
Pouva Murday

Channel Islands
Ḍíá'u'lláh Aṣgharzádih
Evelyn Baxter

Chiloe Island
(Chile)
Zunilda de Palacios
Louise Groger

Cocos Islands
(Keeling Islands,
    Australia)
Frank Wyss

Comoros Islands
Mehraban Sohaili

Cook Islands
Edith Danielsen
Dulcie Dive

Crete
Rolf Haug

Cyprus
Hugh McKinley
Violet McKinley
Abbas Vekil
Semire Vekil

Daman
(India)
Ghulám-'Alí Karlawala

Diu Island
(India)
Gulnar Aftábí
Kaykhusraw Dahamobedi
Bahiyyih Rawhání

Dutch Guiana
(Suriname)
Elinor Wolff
Robert Wolff

Dutch New Guinea
(Indonesia)
Elly Becking
Lex Meerburg

Dutch West Indies
Matthew Bullock
John Kellberg
Marjorie Kellberg

Falkland Islands
John Leonard

Faroe Islands
Eskil Ljungberg

Franklin
(Canada)
Jameson Bond
Kathleen Bond

French Cameroon
(Cameroon)
Mererangiz Munsiff
Samuel Njiki Njenji

French Equatorial Africa
(Congo)
Max Kanyerezi

French Guiana
Eberhart Friedland

French Somaliland
(Djibouti)
Fahíma Elias
Sabrí Elias
Fred Schechter

French Togoland
(Togo)
Mavis Nymon
David Tanyi
Vivian Wesson

French West Africa
(Senegal)
Habíb Esfahani
Labíb Esfahani

Frisian Islands
(Germany)
Elsa Maria Grossmann
Ursula von Brunn

Frisian Islands
(Netherlands)
Geertrui Ankersmit

Galapagos Islands
Haik Kevorkian
Gayle Woolson

Gambia
(The Gambia)
Fariburz Rúzbihyán

Gilbert & Ellice Islands
(Kiribati)
Elena Fernie
Roy Fernie

Goa
(India)
Roshan Aftábí
Firoozeh Yeganegi

Grand Manan
(Canada)
Doris Richardson

Greece
Carole Allen
Dwight Allen
Amin Banani
Sheila Banani

Gulf Islands
(Canada)
Catherine Huxtable
Cliff Huxtable

Hadhramaut
(Yemen)
Adíb Radi Baghdádí
Vahídih Baghdádí
Husayn Halabi

Hainan Island
(China)
John Chang

The Hebrides
(United Kingdom)
Geraldine Craney

Italian Somaliland
(Somalia)
Mihdi Samandari
Suhayl Samandarí
Ursula Samandari

Juan Fernandez Islands
(Chile)
Adela Tormo
Salvador Tormo

Karikal
(India)
Salisa Kirmání
Shírín Núrání

Keewatin
(Canada)
Dick Stanton

Key West
(Florida, United States)
Arthur Crane
Ethel Crane
Howard Snider

Kodiak Island
(Alaska)
Ben Guhrke
Jack Huffman
Rose Perkal

Kuria Muria
(Oman)
Munír Vakíl

Labrador
(Canada)
Howard Gilliland
Bruce Matthew

Leeward Islands
Charles Dayton
Mary Dayton
Earle Render
David Schreiber
Ben Weeden
Gladys Weeden

Liechtenstein
Amír Húshmand
  Manúchehrí

Lofoten Islands
(Norway)
Mildred Clark
Loyce Lawrence

Loyalty Islands
(New Caledonia)
Daniel Haumont

Macao
(SAR China)
Frances Heller
Carl Scherer
Loretta Scherer

Madeira
Ella Duffield
Elizabeth Hopper
Sara Kenny
Ada Schott

Magdalen Islands
(Canada)
Kathleen Weston
Kay Zinky

Mahé
(India)
Khodarahm Mojgani
Lionel Peraji
Qudratullah Rowhani

Malta
Mary Olga Mills
John Mitchell
Una Townshend

Margarita Island
(Venezuela)
Katharine Meyer

Mariana Islands
Cynthia Olson
Robert Powers

Marquesas Islands
Gretta Jankko

Marshall Islands
Marcia Stewart

Mauritius
Ottilie Rhein

Mentawai Islands
(Indonesia)
Írán Muhájir
Raḥmatu'lláh Muhájir

St Pierre and Miquelon Islands
(Canada)
Ola Pawlowska

Moldova
Annemarie Krüger-
  Brauns

Monaco
Nellie French
Olivia Kelsey
'Azízu'lláh Navídí
Shamsi Navídí
Florence Ullrich

Mongolia
Sean Hinton

Morocco, International Zone
(Morocco)
Hussein Ardekani
Nosrat Ardekani
Elsie Austin
Manouchehr Hezari

Muhammad-Ali Jalali
Abbás Rafí'í
'Alí-Akbar Rafí'í
Sháyistih Rafí'í
Richard Suhm
Mary Suhm
Richard Walters
Evelyn Walters
Hormoz Zendeh

New Hebrides
(Vanuatu)
Bertha Dobbins

Nicobar Islands
(India)
Jeanne Frankel
Margaret Bates

Northern Territories Protectorate
(Ghana)
Julius Edwards
Martin Manga

Orkney Islands
(United Kingdom)
Charles Dunning

Pondicherry
(India)
Shyam Behrarilal Bhar-
  gava
Sa'íd Nahví
Shawkat Nahví

Portuguese Guinea
(Guinea-Bissau)
José Xavier Rodrigues
Hilda Summers

Portuguese Timor
(East Timor)
Harold Fitzner
Florence Fitzner
José Marques

Queen Charlotte Island
(Canada)
Edythe MacArthur

Reunion Island
(France)
Leland Jensen
Opal Jensen

Rhodes
(Greece)
Elizabeth Bevan

Río de Oro, Spanish Sahara
(Western Sahara)
Amin Battah

Ruanda Urundi
(Ruanda and Burundi)
Dunduzu Kaluli Chisiza
Mary Collison
Rex Collison

Romania
Fereydoun Khazrá'i

Sakhalin Island
(Russian Federation)
'Abbás Katirai
Rezvánieh Katirai

Samoa Islands
Lilian Wyss

San Marino
Sohrab Payman
Tabandeh Payman

Sardinia
Marie Ciocca

Seychelles
Kámil 'Abbás
'Abdu'l Rahmán Zarqani

Shetland Islands
(United Kingdom)
Brigitte Hasselblatt

Sicily
Carol Bagley
Florence Bagley
Gerrold Bagley
Stanley Bagley
Susan Bagley
Emma Rice

Sikkim
(India)
Udaya Narayan Singh

Society Islands
(Tahiti)
Gladys Parke
Gretta Lamprill

Socotra
(Yemen)
Kamálí Sarvistání

Solomon Islands
Alvin Blum
Gertrude Blum

Southern Rhodesia
(Zimbabwe)
'Aynu'd-Dín 'Alá'í
Tahireh 'Alá'í
Kenneth Christian
Roberta Christian
Claire Gung
Ezzatu'llah Zahra'i

South West Africa
(Namibia)
Edward (Ted) Cardell

Spanish Guinea
(Equatorial Guinea)
Elise Schreiber

Spanish Morocco
(Morocco)
Earleta Fleming
John Fleming
Alyce Barbara May Janssen
Luella McKay
Bahia Zein
Fawzi Zein

Spanish Sahara
(Western Sahara)
Muhammad Mustafa
  Soliman

St Thomas Island
(São Tomé and Príncipe)
Elise Schreiber

St Helena
(British Overseas Territory)
Elizabeth Stamp

Spitsbergen
(Norway)
Paul Adams

Swaziland
John Allen
Valera Allen
Bula Mott Stewart

Tibet
Udaya Narayan Singh

Tonga
Dudley Blakely
Elsa Blakely
Stanley Bolton

Tuamotu Archipelago
(France)
Jean Sevin

White Russia
(Belarus)
Helmut Winkelbach

Windward Islands
Esther Evans
Lillian Middlemast

Yukon
(Canada)
Ted Anderson
Joan Anderson

APPENDIX II

KNIGHTS OF BAHÁ'U'LLÁH BY NAME

Names in parentheses are the modern names of the goal areas.

'Alá'í, 'Aynu'd-Dín – Southern Rhodesia (Zimbabwe)
'Alá'í, Tahireh – Southern Rhodesia (Zimbabwe)
'Abbás, Kámil – Seychelles
Adams, Paul – Spitsbergen, Norway
Aftábí, Gulnar – Diu Island, India
Aftábí, Roshan – Goa, India
Allen, Carole– Greece
Allen, Dwight – Greece
Allen, Frederick – Cape Breton Island, Nova Scotia, Canada
Allen, Jeanne – Cape Breton Island, Nova Scotia, Canada
Allen, John – Swaziland
Allen, Valera – Swaziland
Anderson, Joan – Yukon, Canada
Anderson, Ted – Yukon, Canada
Ankersmit, Geertrui – Frisian Islands, Netherlands
Ardekani, Hussein – Morocco, International Zone
Ardekani, Nosrat – Morocco, International Zone
Asgharzádih, Ḍiá'u'lláh – Channel Islands
Austin, Elsie – Morocco, International Zone
Avery, Gail – Baranof Island, Alaska

Baghdádí, Adíb Radí – Hadhramaut, Yemen
Baghdádí, Vahídih – Hadhramaut, Yemen
Bagley, Carol – Sicily
Bagley, Florence – Sicily
Bagley, Gerrold – Sicily
Bagley, Stanley – Sicily
Bagley, Susan – Sicily

Bahovec, Grace – Baranof Island, Alaska

Banani, Amin – Greece

Banani, Sheila – Greece

Bates, Margaret – Nicobar Islands, India

Battah, Amin – Río de Oro, Spanish Sahara (Western Sahara)

Baxter, Evelyn – Channel Islands

Becking, Elly – Dutch New Guinea (Indonesia)

Beharilal Bhargava, Shyam – Pondicherry, India

Bevan, Elizabeth – Rhodes, Greece

Blakely, Dudley – Tonga

Blakely, Elsa – Tonga

Blum, Alvin – Solomon Islands

Blum, Gertrude – Solomon Islands

Bolton, Stanley – Tonga

Bond, Jameson – Franklin, Canada

Bond, Kathleen Gale – Franklin, Canada

Breaks, Virginia – Caroline Islands (Papua New Guinea)

Buapiah, Albert – British Togoland (Ghana)

Bullock, Matthew – Dutch West Indies (formerly Netherlands Antilles)

Caldwell, Elaine – Aleutian Islands, Alaska

Caldwell, Jenabe – Aleutian Islands, Alaska

Cardell, Edward (Ted) – South West Africa (Namibia)

Chang, John – Hainan Island, China

Chisiza, Dunduzu Kaluli– Rwanda Urundi (Rwanda and Burundi)

Christian, Kenneth – Southern Rhodesia (Zimbabwe)

Christian, Roberta – Southern Rhodesia (Zimbabwe)

Ciocca, Marie – Sardinia

Clark, Harry – Brunei

Clark, Mildred – Lofoten Islands, Norway

Collison, Mary – Ruanda Urundi (Rwanda and Burundi)

Collison, Rex – Ruanda Urundi (Rwanda and Burundi)

Crane, Arthur – Key West, Florida, United States

Crane, Ethel – Key West, Florida, United States

Craney, Geraldine – The Hebrides, United Kingdom

Curwin, Gail – The Bahamas

Curwin, Gerald – The Bahamas

Dahamobedi, Kaykhusraw – Diu Island, India
Danielsen, Edith – Cook Islands
Danjon, William – Andorra
Dayton, Charles – Leeward Islands
Dayton, Mary – Leeward Islands
de Palacios, Zunilda – Chiloe Island, Chile
Deleuran, Jean – Balearic Islands
Deleuran, Tove – Balearic Islands
Dive, Dulcie – Cook Islands
Dobbins, Bertha – New Hebrides (Vanuatu)
Duffield, Ella – Madeira
Duncan, Charles – Brunei
Dunning, Charles – Orkney Islands, United Kingdom

Eballa, Benedict – Ashanti Protectorate (Ghana)
Edwards, Julius – Northern Territories Protectorate (Ghana)
Eisenberg, Gertrude – Canary Islands
Elias, Fahíma – French Somaliland (Djibouti)
Elias, Sabrí – French Somaliland (Djibouti)
Esfahani, Habíb – French West Africa (Senegal)
Esfahani, Labíb – French West Africa (Senegal)
Evans, Esther – Windward Islands

Fernie, Elena – Gilbert & Ellice Islands (Kiribati)
Fernie, Roy – Gilbert & Ellice Islands (Kiribati)
Fitzner, Florence – Portuguese Timor (East Timor)
Fitzner, Harold – Portuguese Timor (East Timor)
Fleming, Earleta – Spanish Morocco (Morocco)
Fleming, John – Spanish Morocco (Morocco)
Fozdar, John – Brunei
Fozdar, Khodadad – Andaman Islands, India
Frankel, Jeanne – Nicobar Islands, India
French, Nellie – Monaco
Friedland, Eberhart – French Guiana
Furúdí, Ardishir – Bhutan
Geary, Grace – Cape Breton Island, Canada
Geary, Irving – Cape Breton Island, Canada

Gilliland, Howard – Labrador, Canada
Groger, Louise – Chiloe Island, Chile
Grossmann, Elsa Maria – Frisian Islands, Germany
Guhrke, Ben – Kodiak Island, Alaska
Gung, Claire – Southern Rhodesia (Zimbabwe)

Halabi, Husayn – Hadhramaut, Yemen
Hasselblatt, Brigitte – Shetland Islands, United Kingdom
Haug, Rolf – Crete, Greece
Haumont, Daniel – Loyalty Islands, New Caledonia
Hezari, Manouchehr – Morocco, International Zone
Heller, Frances – Macao (SAR China)
Hinton, Sean – Mongolia
Hoehnke, Violet – Admiralty Islands (Papua New Guinea)
Holmes, Ethel – The Bahamas
Holmes, Maurice – The Bahamas
Hopper, Elizabeth – Madeira
Huffman, Jack – Kodiak Island, Alaska
Huxtable, Catherine – Gulf Islands, Canada
Huxtable, Cliff – Gulf Islands, Canada

Ioas, Charles – Balearic Islands

Jalali, Muhammad-Ali – Morocco, Internaational Zone
Jankko, Gretta – Marquesas Islands
Janssen, Alyce Barbara May – Spanish Morocco (Morocco)
Jensen, Leland – Reunion Island, France
Jensen, Opal – Reunion Island, France

Kanyerezi, Max – French Equatorial Africa (Congo)
Karlawala, Ghulám-'Alí – Daman, India
Katirai, 'Abbás – Sakhalin Island, USSR (Russian Federation)
Katirai, Rezvánieh – Sakhalin Island, USSR (Russian Federation)
Kellberg, John – Dutch West Indies (formerly Netherlands Antilles)
Kellberg, Marjorie – Dutch West Indies (formerly Netherlands Antilles)
Kelsey, Olivia – Monaco
Kenny, Sara – Madeira

Kevorkian, Haik – Galapagos Islands

Khazrá'í, Fereydoun – Romania

King, Malcolm – British Guiana (Guyana)

Kirmání, Salisa – Karikal, India

Krüger-Brauns, Annemarie – Moldova

Lamprill, Gretta – Society Islands (Tahiti)

Lawrence, Loyce – Lofoten Islands, Norway

Laws, Elizabeth – Basutoland (Lesotho)

Laws, Frederick – Basutoland (Lesotho)

Leonard, John – Falkland Islands

Ljungberg, Eskil – Faroe Islands, Denmark

MacArthur, Edythe – Queen Charlotte Island, Canada

Manga, Martin – Northern Territories Protectorate (Ghana)

Manúchehrí, Amír Húshmand – Liechtenstein

Marques, José – Portuguese Timor (East Timor)

Matthew, Bruce – Labrador, Canada

Matthisen, Andrew – The Bahamas

Matthisen, Nina – The Bahamas

McKay, Luella – Spanish Morocco (Morocco)

McKinley, Hugh – Cyprus

McKinley, Violet – Cyprus

Meerburg, Lex – Dutch New Guinea (Indonesia)

Menking, Howard – Cape Verde Islands

Menking, JoAnne – Cape Verde Islands

Meyer, Katharine – Margarita Island, Venezuela

Middlemast, Lillian – Windward Islands

Mills, Mary Olga – Malta

Mitchell, John – Malta

Mojgani, Khodarahm– Mahé, India

Muhájir, Írán – Mentawai Islands, Indonesia

Muhájir, Raḥmatu'lláh – Mentawai Islands, Indonesia

Munsiff, Meherangiz – French Cameroon (Cameroon)

Murday, Pouva – Chagos Islands

Mustafa Soliman, Muhammad – Spanish Sahara (Western Sahara)

Nahví, Sa'íd – Pondicherry, India
Nahví, Shawkat – Pondicherry, India
Navídí, 'Azízu'lláh – Monaco
Navídí, Shamsí– Monaco
Njiki Njenji, Samuel – French Cameroon (Cameroon)
Nolen, Lois – Azores
Nolen, Richard – Azores
Núrání, Shírín – Karikal, India
Nymon, Mavis – French Togoland (Togo)

Olinga, Enoch – British Cameroon (Cameroon)
Oliver, Cora – British Honduras (Belize)
Olson, Cynthia – Mariana Islands
Orbison, Virginia – Balearic Islands, Spain

Parke, Gladys – Society Islands (Tahiti)
Pawlowska, Ola –St Pierre and Miquelon Islands, Canada
Payman, Sohrab – San Marino
Payman, Tabandeh – San Marino
Peraji, Lionel – Mahé, India
Perkal, Rose – Kodiak Island, Alaska
Powers, Robert – Mariana Islands
Putney, Elinore – Aleutian Islands, Alaska

Raffí'í, 'Abbás – Morocco, International Zone
Raffí'í, 'Alí-Akbar – Morocco, International Zone
Raffí'í, Sháyistih – Morocco International Zone
Rawhání, Bahíyyih – Diu Island, India
Render, Earle – Leeward Islands
Rhein, Ottilie – Mauritius
Rice, Emma – Sicily
Richardson, Doris – Grand Manan Island, Canada
Robarts, Audrey – Bechuanaland (Botswana)
Robarts, John – Bechuanaland (Botswana)
Robarts, Patrick – Bechuanaland (Botswana)
Robinson, Helen – Baranof Island, Alaska
Rodrigues, José Xavier – Portuguese Guinea (Guinea-Bissau)

Rouhani, Shoghi-Riaz – Canary Islands, Spain

Rowhani, Qudratullah –Mahé, India

Rowhani, Shapoor Aspandiar –Bhutan

Rúzbihyán, Fariburz – The Gambia

Samandari, Mihdi – Italian Somaliland (Somalia)

Samandarí, Suhayl – Italian Somaliland (Somalia)

Samandari, Ursula – Italian Somaliland (Somalia)

Sarvistání, Kamálí – Socotra (now part of Yemen)

Schechter, Fred – French Somaliland (Djibouti)

Scherer, Carl – Macao (SAR China)

Scherer, Loretta – Macao (SAR China)

Schott, Ada – Madeira

Schreiber, David – Leeward Islands

Schreiber, Elise– Spanish Guinea (Equatorial Guinea)

Schreiber, Elise– St Thomas Island (São Tomé and Príncipe)

Sevin, Jean – Tuamotu Archipelago, France

Singh, Udaya Narayan – Sikkim, India

Singh, Udaya Narayan – Tibet

Snider, Howard – Key West, Florida, United States

Sohaili, Mehraban– Comoros Islands (Comoros)

Stamp, Elizabeth – St Helena, British Overseas Territory

Stanton, Dick – Keewatin, Canada

Stewart, Marcia – Marshall Islands

Stewart, Bula Mott – Swaziland

Suhm, Mary – Morocco, International Zone

Suhm, Richard – Morocco, International Zone

Summers, Hilda – Portuguese Guinea (Guinea-Bissau)

Tabe, Edward – British Togoland (Ghana)

Tanyi, David – French Togoland (Togo)

Tormo, Adela – Juan Fernandez Islands, Chile

Tormo, Salvador – Juan Fernandez Islands, Chile

Townshend, Una – Malta

True, George – Canary Islands, Spain

True, Marguerite (Peggy) – Canary Islands, Spain

Ullrich, Florence – Monaco

Vakíl, Munír – Kuria Muria (Oman)
Vekil, Abbas – Cyprus
Vekil, Semire – Cyprus
von Brunn, Ursula – Frisian Islands, Germany

Walters, Evelyn – Morocco, International Zone
Walters, Richard – Morocco, International Zone
Warde, Shirley – British Honduras (Belize)
Weeden, Ben – Leeward Islands
Weeden, Gladys – Leeward Islands
Wesson, Vivian – French Togoland (Togo)
Weston, Kathleen – Magdalen Islands, Canada
Winkelbach, Helmut – White Russia (Belarus)
Wolff, Elinor – Dutch Guiana (Suriname)
Wolff, Robert – Dutch Guiana (Suriname)
Woolson, Gayle – Galapagos Islands
Wyss, Frank – Cocos Islands (Keeling Islands, Australia)
Wyss, Lilian (Ala'i)– Samoa

Yeganegi, Firoozeh – Goa, India

Zabolotny, Mary – Anticosti Island, Quebec, Canada
Zahra'i, Ezzatu'llah – Southern Rhodesia (Zimbabwe)
Zarqani, 'Abdu'l Rahman –Seychelles
Zein, Bahia (Bahíyyih Zaynu'l-Ábidin) – Spanish Morocco (Morocco)
Zein, Fawzi (Fawzi Zaynu'l-Ábidin) – Spanish Morocco (Morocco)
Zendeh, Hormoz –Morocco, International Zone
Zinky, Kay – Magdalen Islands, Canada

BIBLIOGRAPHY

Adams, Paul. *Arctic Island Hunter*. London: George Ronald, 1961.

Ala'i, Lilian. Talk given at the 50th Anniversary celebration of the Bahá'í Faith in Samoa, 2004.

Alaska Bahá'í News. Periodical. National Spiritual Assembly of Alaska.

Allen, Carole. *Pioneering in Greece during the First Year of the 10 Year Crusade*. Manuscript, January 2015.

Allen, Dwight. *Carole and Dwight Allen: Knights of Bahá'u'lláh in Greece, 1953–1954*. Manuscript, January 2015.

The American Bahá'í. Periodical. National Spiritual Assembly of the Bahá'ís of the United States.

Anderson, Ted; Anderson, Joan E. *Yukon Golden Hearts Discovered*. Manuscript, 1992.

Ardekani, Nosrat. Transcript of a phone conversation, 20 August 2013, and email to the author, 30 August 2013.

Austin, Elsie. 'Dr Elsie Austin Knight Morocco 23 Nov 1973 – Pilgrimage and after'. Audio recording, The Heritage Project of the National Spiritual Assembly of the United States.

Australian Bahá'í. Periodical. National Spiritual Assembly of the Bahá'ís of Australia.

Bagley, Gerrold. 'The Bagley family, Knights of Bahá'u'lláh', email to the author, 19 July 2014.

Bahá'í Canada. Periodical. National Spiritual Assembly of the Bahá'ís of Canada.

The Bahá'í Faith, Information Statistical and Comparative: Including the Achievements of the Ten Year International Bahá'í Teaching & Consolidation Plan 1953–1963. http://bahai-library.com/handscause_statistics_1953-63#56.

Bahá'í Journal UK. Periodical. National Spiritual Assembly of the Bahá'ís of the United Kingdom.

Bahá'í News. Periodical. National Spiritual Assembly of the Bahá'ís of the United States.

Bahá'í Newsletter. Periodical. National Spiritual Assembly of the Bahá'ís of the Seychelles.

The Bahá'í World: An International Record. Vol. X (1944-1946), Wilmette, IL: Bahá'í Publishing Trust, 1949; vol. XII (1950-1954), Wilmette, IL: Bahá'í Publishing Trust, 1956; vol. XIII (1954-1963), Haifa, The Universal House of Justice, 1970; vol. XIV (1963-1968), Haifa: The Universal House of Justice, 1974; vol. XV (1968-1973), Haifa: Bahá'í World Centre, 1976; vol. XVI (1973-1976), Haifa: Bahá'í World Centre, 1978; vol. XVII (1976-1979), Haifa: Bahá'í World Centre, 1981; vol. XVIII (1979-1983), Haifa: Bahá'í World Centre, 1986; vol. XIX (1983-1986), Haifa: Bahá'í World Centre, 1994; vol. XX (1986-1992), Haifa: Bahá'í World Centre, 1998.

New series: *The Bahá'í World, 1992–1993*, Haifa: Bahá'í World Centre, 1993; *The Bahá'í World, 1999–2000*, Haifa, Bahá'í World Centre, 2001; *The Bahá'í World, 2000–2001*, Haifa: Bahá'í World Centre, 2002; *The Bahá'í World, 2005–2006*, Haifa: Bahá'í World Centre, 2007.

The Bahá'í World: In Memoriam 1992-1997. Haifa: World Centre Publications, 2010.

Bahá'í World News Service. Online periodical. Haifa: Bahá'í World Centre.

Bahá'u'lláh. *Gleanings from the Writings of Bahá'u'lláh.* Wilmette, IL: Bahá'í Publishing Trust, 1983.

Bahovec, Fred. *The First 100 Years.* Frederick M. and Clothilde Bahovec, 1989.

Banani, Amin; Banani, Sheila. *Amin and Sheila Banani's Recollections of Pioneering in Greece, 1953–1958.* Report to the Universal House of Justice, 1986.
— *Pilgrim Notes of Sheila and Amin Banani.* 2 September 1975. The Heritage Project of the National Spiritual Assembly of the United States.

Bates, Geertrui Ankersmit. *Bahá'í Story: Geertrui (Ankersmit) Bates, Knight of Bahá'u'lláh.* Transcription of a video interview in New Zealand, 2005.

Baumgartner, Laurel. Interview by the author (recording), 15 October 2014.

Benatar, Sylvia. 'Kenneth and Roberta Christian, Knights of Bahá'u'lláh to Southern Rhodesia', email to the author, 31 July 2015.

Bhargava, Masroor. 'Shyam Beharilal Bhargava – The youthful pioneer', email to the author, 17 December 2015.

Brown, Don. *Sole Desire Serve Cause: An Odyssey of Bahá'í Service, Knights of Bahá'u'lláh Gale and Jameson Bond.* Oxford: George Ronald, 2017.
— 'Sole desire serve cause'. Talk given in 2013.

Caldwell, Jenabe. *From Night to Knight.* Wailuku, Hawaii: Best Publisher, 2008.

Caldwell, Elaine. Personal reminiscences, undated.

Cameron, Glenn. *A Basic Bahá'í Chronology.* Oxford: George Ronald, 1996.

Campuzano, Patricia (ed.) *Gayle Woolson, 1913–2011.* Manuscript,

Canadian Bahá'í Archives.

Cardell, Ted. *Experiences with the Guardian.* Audio recording, August 1988, ARC T-1199. With partial transcript. The Heritage Project of the National Spiritual Assembly of the United States.

Cardin, Heather. *The Bright Glass of the Heart.* Oxford: George Ronald, 2013.

Christianson, W. Kenneth. USBNA, Hattie Chamberlain Papers, 1955.

Crusader. Newsletter. Western Hemisphere Teaching Committee of the Bahá'ís of the United States, 1955–1961.

Curwin, Gail. Video interview. http://vimeo.com/11302838.

Dailey, Susan Maureen. *Elise Schreiber Lynelle: Double Knight of Bahá'u'lláh.* Manuscript, 2012.

Davis, Gail. *More Than a Touch of Madness.* Hell's Canyon Publishing: Halfway, Oregon, 1994.

Dayspring. Children's magazine. National Spiritual Assembly of the Bahá'ís of the United Kingdom, 2003.

De Vries, Jelles. *The Bábí Question you Mentioned: The Origins of the Bahá'í Community of the Netherlands, 1844–1962.* Leuven, Netherlands: Peeters, 2002.

Ebony. Magazine. 'Alaskan lady, jade hunter', in vol. IV, no. 2 (December 1948).

Ecclesia, Mariana. *Life for the Faith.* Sofia, Bulgaria: Sonm Publishers, 2004.

Edge, Clara. USBNA, Florence Reed Papers, 1954.

Etter-Lewis, Gwendolyn; Thomas, Richard. *Lights of the Spirit.* Wilmette, IL: Bahá'í Publishing, 2006.

Evans, Esther. Transcript of interviews with Pat Paccassi, various dates.

Fozdar, John. 'Brunei', email to the author, 5 February 2013.

Frankel de Corrales, Jeanne; Bates, Margaret. *Forget-me-not Nicobar.* Oxford: Oneworld, 1992.

Fraser, Ivan. Extract from a manuscript on the early history of the Faith in Guyana, undated.

Frye, Dorothy. Documents supplied to the author.

Gammage, Susan. 'Bruce Matthew – Knight of Bahá'u'lláh', 8 March 2013. http://susangammage.com/bruce-matthew-knight-of-bahaullah.

Garis, Mabel. *Martha Root: Lioness at the Threshold.* Wilmette, IL: Bahá'í Publishing Trust, 1983.

Golmohammadi, Haleh. Email to the author about Elizabeth Bevan, 22 October 2013.

Groger, Rosanne. *Knight of the Rose Garden: The Beginnings of an Early American Bahá'í Family.* Manuscript, May 2016.

Guhrke, Ben. *Ben's Story*. Manuscript, 2014.

Guhrke, Marvel. 'Ben Guhrke Addendum', email to the author, 23 June 2015.

Hainsworth, Philip. *Looking Back in Wonder*. Stroud: Skyset Ltd., 2004.

Hancock, Rodney. Eulogy delivered at Memorial Service for Frank Wyss in Brisbane, on June 10, 2007 at Brisbane Bahá'í Center of Learning.

Harper, Barron. *Lights of Fortitude*. Oxford: George Ronald, 1997.

Hassall, Graham. 'Bahá'í Faith in the Asia Pacific: Issues and prospects', in *Baha'i Studies Review*, vol. 6, pp. 1–10. Association for Baha'i Studies English-Speaking Europe, 1996.
— 'The Bahá'í Faith in the Pacific', in Phyllis Herda, Michel Reilly and David Hilliard (eds): *Vision and Reality in Pacific Religion: Essays in Honour of Niel Gunson*. Canberra/Christchurch: Pandanus Press with the Macmillan Brown Centre for Pacific Studies. 2005.
— 'The Fitzners of Portuguese Timor', in Claire Vreeland: *And the Trees Clapped Their Hands*, p. 321.
— 'Obituary: James Heggie', in *Bahá'í Studies Review*, vol. 9. Association for Bahá'í Studies, 1999.
— 'The origins of the Bahá'í Faith in the Pacific Islands: The case of the Gilbert and Ellice Islands', in *The Journal of Bahá'í Studies*, no. 16, 2006.
— 'Pacific Bahá'í Communities 1950–1964', in Donald H. Rubinstein (ed.): *Pacific History: Papers from the 8th Pacific History Association Conference*. Mangilao, Guam: University of Guam Press & Micronesian Area Research Centre, 1992.

Hassan, Gamal. *Moths Turned Eagles: The Spiritual Conquests of Sabrí and Raissa Elias*. Addis Ababa: National Spiritual Assembly of the Bahá'ís of Ethiopia, 2008.

Haug, Guenther, 'Rolf Haug: A still living story', email to the author, 26 April 2014.

Herald of the South. Periodical. National Spiritual Assembly of the Bahá'ís of Australia.

Hinton, Sean. 'A personal account of Amatu'l-Bahá Rúḥíyyih Khánum's first visit to Mongolia, 15–22 May 1989', 28 May 2001 (extracts from his diary at the time of the visit).
— 'Mongolia, 1992', email to the author.

Hofman, David. *George Townshend*. Oxford: George Ronald, 2002.

Hofman, Marion. Marion Hofman Papers, Private Collection.
— *The World Crusade*. Marion Hofman Papers, 1959.

Honnold, Annamarie. *Why They Became Bahá'ís*. New Delhi: Bahá'í Publishing Trust, 1993.

Ioas, Charles and Conchita. Video interview. Copyright held by the Bahá'í World Centre, undated.

Jackson, Lorol. *My Experiences as a Pioneer*. Undated report.

Johnson, Edith; Johnson, Lowell. *Heroes and Heroines of the Ten Year Crusade in Southern Africa*. Johannesburg: Bahá'í Publishing Trust, 2003.

Jónsson, Edvard; Philbrow, Roy. Report on the Faroe Islands, in Marion Hofman Papers, undated.

Kamálí, Rezvanieh, 'Mirza Áqá Kamálí Sarvistání', email to the author, 20 November 2013.

Katirai, Foad. Email to the author, 29 August 2013.

Kelley, Florence. Audio recording ARC T-1567, The Heritage Project of the National Spiritual Assembly of the United States, undated.

Khadem, Javidukht. *Zikrullah Khadem: The Itinerant Hand of the Cause of God*. Wilmette, IL: Bahá'í Publishing Trust, 1990.

Khan, Janet. *Heritage of Light*. Wilmette, IL: Bahá'í Publishing, 2009.

Kházeh, Jalál. 'After the passing of the Beloved Guardian'. Talk given at Monkstown, Ireland, 1969.

Kelsey, Olivia. *Bahá'í Answers*. Independence, MO: Lambert Moon, 1947; RP Wilmette, IL: National Spiritual Assembly of the Bahá'ís of the United States, 1974.
— USBNA, Olivia Kelsey Papers, 1956.

Khianra, Dipchand. *Immortals*. New Delhi: Bahá'í Publishing Trust, 1988.

Knox, Dermod. '50th anniversary of the establishment of the Faith in Goa', in *Bahá'í Journal UK*, July/August 2003.

Knox, Roshan. Audio recording by author, 3 September 2013.

Kolstoe, John. *Alaskan Bahá'í Community: Its Growth and Development*. Manuscript, 1999.
— *Crazy Lovers of Bahá'u'lláh: Inspirational Stories of Little Giants*. Ebook published by John Kolstoe, 2015.

Lamb, Artemus. *The Beginnings of the Bahá'í Faith in Latin America: Some Remembrances*. San Salvador: Van Orman Enterprises, 1995. http://bahai-library.com/lamb_bahai_latin_america.

Lee, Anthony. *The Establishment of the Bahá'í Faith in West Africa: The First Decade, 1952–1962*. Leiden: Brill, 2010.
— *The Bahá'í Faith in Africa: Establishing a New Religious Movement, 1952–62*. Leiden: Brill, 2011.

Lembke, Conrad. Eulogy at the Funeral Service of Frank Leonard Wyss, Canberra Bahá'í Centre, 18 May 2007.

Licata, Stephen. 'My memories of Trudy Eisenberg (Knight of Bahá'u'lláh)', email to the author, 19 June 2014.

Locke-Nyrenda, Suzanne. 'Knights of Bahá'u'lláh John William Allen and Valera 'Val' Fisher Allen', email to the author, 4 December 2014.

—; Dailey, Susan Maureen. *Dunduzu Kaluli Chisiza: Knight of Bahá'u'lláh for Ruanda-Urundi*. Manuscript, 2016.

Logsdon-Dubois, Judith Kaye. *Knight with a Briefcase*. Oxford: George Ronald, 2013.

Macke, Marlene. *Take My Love to the Friends: The Story of Laura R. Davis*. St Mary's, Ontario: Chestnut Park Press, 2011.

Manúchehrí, Húshmand. Email to the author, 14 April 2014.

McKay, Doris, with Paul Vreeland. *Fires in Many Hearts*. Nine Pines Publishers, 1993.

McKinley, Deborah. *Violet and Hugh McKinley: Knights of Bahá'u'lláh for Cyprus 1953–1963*. Manuscript, 2015.

McKinley, Olive. 'Life of Hugh McKinley, Knight of Bahá'u'lláh', in *Solas*, no. 4. Donegal, Ireland: Association for Baha'i Studies English-Speaking Europe, 2004.

McLaren, Edith. http://bahai-library.com/mclaren_pilgrims_notes, 1954.

McLean, J. A. *A Love That Could Not Wait: The Story of Knights of Bahá'u'lláh, Catherine Heward Huxtable and Clifford Stanley Huxtable*. Essex, Maryland: One Voice Press, 2016.

The Ministry of the Custodians, 1957–1963. Haifa: Bahá'í World Centre, 1992.

Misra, Zarangiz. Emails to the author, 25 and 26 October 2013.

Moffett, Ruth. USBNA, Charlotte Linfoot Papers, 1954; USBNA, Laurence & Ruth Laroque Papers, 1954.

Mojgani, Khodarahm. 'First pioneers in Mahé', in email from P. K. Premarajan to the author, 6 November 2013.

Morgan, Adrienne. *Claire Gung*. Johannesburg: National Spiritual Assembly of the Bahá'ís of South Africa, 1997.

Morgan, Dempsey. *Servants of the Glory*. Manuscript.

Muhájir, Írán. *Dr Muhájir*. London: Bahá'í Publishing Trust, 1992.

Munsiff, Jyoti. Obituary of Meherangiz Munsiff written for *The Bahá'í World*, 2009.

Mustapha, Rowshan. 'Amin Abu'l-Futuh Battah: Knight of Bahá'u'lláh to Rio de Oro', email to the author, 19 December 2013.

— 'In Memoriam, Labib Esfahani, Knight of Bahá'u'lláh to French West Africa', email to the author, 8 October 2013.

— 'Muhammad Mustafa Soliman: Knight of Bahá'u'lláh to The Spanish Sahara', email to the author, 28 December 2013.

Nakhjavání, 'Alí. *Glimpse of the life of Enoch Olinga as told by 'Ali Nakhjavani*, July 2012. Video interview published on Youtube, 27 Dec 2013: http://www.youtube.com/watch?v=zjPkoeglV1U.

Nakhjavani, Violette. *The Great African Safari.* Oxford: George Ronald, 2002.

Navidi-Walker, Guilda. Email to the author, 2 March 2015.

Nugent, Tom. 'The Sound Man', in *Chico*, a magazine from California State University (Spring 2008). http://www.csuchico.edu/pub/cs/spring_08/feature_04.html.

Olson, Cynthia. *Remembrances of Guam.* Privately bound manuscript held by the National Spiritual Assembly of the Baháʼís of the Mariana Islands, 1981.

Paccassi, Pat. *Baháʼí History of the Caribbean, 1920 to 1984.* http://www.bahaihistorycaribbean.info/.

Payman, Sohrab. *Payman Memoir,* 26 June 2015.

Peraji, Lionel. Email to the author, 16 December 2013.

Pfaff-Grossmann, Susanne. *The Life of a Pioneer.* San Diego, CA: Island Resort Publishing, 2008.
— *Hermann Grossmann, Hand of the Cause of God: A Life for the Faith.* Oxford: George Ronald, 2009.

Poostchi, Baháʼí. *Dawn of the Sun of Truth, Tamil Nadu, India.* New Delhi: Mirʼát Publications, 2015.

Power, Joey. *Political Culture and Nationalism in Malawi.* Suffolk, UK: University of Rochester Press, NY/Boydell & Brewer, 2010.

Quigley, Robert. Talk about Pouva Murday. Geyserville, CA, 1965.

Rabbani, Ruḥíyyih. *Enoch Olinga, Hand of the Cause of God: His Life and Work.* Lagos, Nigeria: Baháʼí Publishing Trust, 2002.

Rafíʼí, ʼAbbás. Email to the author, 21 September 2014.

Randel, Agata. Email to the author, 11 November 2013.

Redman, Earl. *Shoghi Effendi: Through the Pilgrim's Eye.* Vol. 2: *The Ten Year Crusade, 1953–1963.* Oxford: George Ronald, 2016.

Robert, Gilbert; Robert, Daisy. 'Report for the NSA of South Africa, 1999', in email from Violetta Zein to the author, 20 October 2015.

Robertson, Larry; Walker, Penny; Koirala, JoAnne Pach. 'Reminiscences of Mr. Udaya Narayan Singh, Knight of Bahaʼuʼllah', email to the author, 8 July 2016.

Rowhani, Mariam. *Two Doves of Love.* Manuscript, 2015.

Ruhe-Schoen, Janet. *An Enchantment of the Heart.* http://www.chilean-temple.org/images/stories/Early%20Baha/%27is/an_enchantment_of_the_heart.pdf, 1989.

Sarwal, Anil. http://www.religiousunity.org/BahArt/Bahaʼi%20Faith%20In%20Nepal.htm.

Saunders, Keithie. *Of Wars and Worship: The Extraordinary Story of Gertrude and Alvin Blum.* Oxford: George Ronald, 2012.

Schuurman, Suzanne. *Legacy of Courage: The Life of Ola Pawlowska, Knight of Bahá'u'lláh*. Oxford: George Ronald, 2008.

Sims, Barbara. *The Macau Bahá'í Community in the Early Years*, Tokyo, 1991. http://bahai-library.com/sims_macau_bahai_community.
— *Raising the Banner in Korea: An Early Bahá'í History*. Manuscript, 1998. http://bahai-library.com/sims_raising_banner_korea&chapter=all.

Shoghi Effendi. *Citadel of Faith: Messages to America, 1947–1957*. Wilmette, IL: Bahá'í Publishing Trust, 1965.
— *Dawn of a New Day: Messages to India, 1923-1957*. New Delhi: Bahá'í Publishing Trust, 1970.
— *God Passes By* (1944). Wilmette, IL: Bahá'í Publishing Trust, rev. ed. 1974.
— *Messages of Shoghi Effendi to the Indian Subcontinent 1923-1957*. Comp. Iran Furutan Muhajír. New Delhi: Bahá'í Publishing Trust, rev. ed. 1995.
— *Messages to the Antipodes*. Mona Vale: Bahá'í Publications Australia, 1997.
— *Messages to the Bahá'í World 1950–1957*. Wilmette, IL: Bahá'í Publishing Trust, 2nd ed. 1971.
— *Messages to Canada*. Thornhill, ON: National Spiritual Assembly of the Bahá'ís of Canada, 1965, rev. ed. 1999.
— *Unfolding Destiny: The Messages from the Guardian of the Bahá'í Faith to the Bahá'í Community of the British Isles*. London: Bahá'í Publishing Trust, 1981.

Sohaili, Mehraban. Letter report to the Universal House of Justice, 1988.

The Statesman. Newspaper. Austin, TX.

Tanyi, David. *The Story of My Pioneering*. Manuscript.

Tanyi Nyenti, Enoch. *The Story of David and Esther Tanyi: Adam and Eve of the Bahá'í Faith in Cameroon*. Oxford: George Ronald, 2016.
— 'Edward Tabe', email to the author, 18 December 2013.
— 'A short biography of Nyenti David Tanyi', email to the author, 4 October 2013.
— 'Knight of Bahá'u'lláh Dr Ben Eballa', email to the author, 4 October 2013.
— 'Martin Manga – A short biography', email to the author, 4 October 2013.

True, Bruce. Speech at the 50th Anniversary of the Faith in the Canary Islands (in Spanish), 2003.

True, Peggy. *In the Midmost Heart of the Ocean*, 21 November 1984, copy in Marion Hofman Papers.

Vekiloglu, Fulya. 'Knights of Bahá'u'lláh Semire and Abbas Vekil (Vekiloglu)', email to the author, 24 August 2014.

Van den Hoonaard, Will C. *The Origins of the Bahá'í Community of Canada, 1898–1948*. Waterloo, Ontario: Wilfrid Laurier University Press, 1996.

Vreeland, Claire. *And the Trees Clapped Their Hands*. Oxford: George Ronald, 1994.

Walters, Evelyn. *Memoirs of Knight of Bahá'u'lláh*. Manuscript, 1997. USBNA.

Warde, Shirley. *Pioneering Bounties and Tests*. Undated manuscript.

Washington, Bill. USBNA, Beatrice Ashton Papers, 1957.

Weinberg, Robert. 'Remembering the Knights of Bahá'u'lláh', in *Bahá'í Journal UK*, September/October 2003.

White, Roger, *Edythe MacArthur, Knight of Bahá'u'lláh*. 1986. Canadian Bahá'í Archives.

Winkelbach, Helmut. 'Helmut Winkelbach, Belarus', email to the author, 3 November 2013.

Winkelbach, Olga. Email to the author, 21 October 2013.

Wolff, Elinor. Audio recording ARC T-1657, The Heritage Project of the National Spiritual Assembly of the Untied States, undated.

Zein, Violetta. Unpublished interviews, 2000.

Zendeh, Hormoz. 'My life as a pioneer in Tangier, Morocco', email to the author, 8 April 2014.

NOTES AND REFERENCES

Introduction

1   Bahá'u'lláh, *Gleanings*, CIX, p. 215.

2   Shoghi Effendi, *Citadel of Faith*, p. 6.

3   Shoghi Effendi, *God Passes By*, p. 324.

4   Message from the Universal House of Justice to the Bahá'ís of the world acting under the Mandate of 'Abdu'l-Bahá, 26 March 2016, para. 2.

5   Shoghi Effendi, *Messages to the Bahá'í World 1950–1957*, p. 49.

6   Shoghi Effendi, *Dawn of a New Day*, pp. 164–5.

7   Amatu'l-Bahá Rúḥíyyih Khánum, in a speech to the Knights of Bahá'u'lláh, Haifa, 1992, quoted in Logsdon-Dubois, *Knight with a Briefcase*, p. 144.

8   Shoghi Effendi, *The World Order of Bahá'u'lláh*, p. 17.

9   Shoghi Effendi, *Messages to the Bahá'í World 1950–1957*, pp. 60–61.

10   Ben Guhrke, letter written to an unknown person in June 1954. Provided by Marvel Guhrke.

11   Shoghi Effendi, *Messages to the Bahá'í World 1950–1957*, p. 69.

12   *The Bahá'í World*, vol. XIII, p. 456.

13   Shoghi Effendi, *Messages to the Bahá'í World 1950–1957*, pp. 57, 68.

14   Letter from the Research Department, Bahá'í World Centre, to the author, 14 November 2013.

15   Shoghi Effendi, *Messages to the Bahá'í World 1950–1957*, p. 57.

16   Letter from the Research Department, Bahá'í World Centre, to Enoch Tanyi, 31 October 2004.

17   Letter on behalf of Shoghi Effendi, 13 January 1956, in Shoghi Effendi, *Messages to Canada*, p. 56.

18   Letter from Jameson Bond to John Leonard, 28 December 1992, in Marion Hofman Papers.

19   It might be noticed that South America is not included here. Shoghi Effendi designated four goal areas on the continent: the three Guianas, British, Dutch and French, which are included in the chapter on the Caribbean, and Chiloe Island, included with the Pacific Islands. South America had few goal areas because it had been opened to the Faith by North American pioneers and travel teachers during the first and second Seven Year Plans.

20   Letter from Leroy Ioas on behalf of the International Bahá'í Council, 7 December 1953.

21   Shoghi Effendi, *Messages to the Bahá'í World 1950–1957*, p. 113.

North Africa

1   Hormoz Zendeh, 'My life as a pioneer in Tangier, Morocco', email to the author, 8 April 2014. Mr Zendeh's story in these paragraphs is taken from this source unless otherwise indicated.

2   'Austinite helped introduce Baha'i faith to Morocco', in *The Statesman*, 25 June 2010; http://www.bahai.us/2010/09/13/manouchehr-hezari-helped-introduce-the-faith-to-morocco/.

3   ibid.

4   'Abbás Rafí'í, email to the author, 21 September 2014.

5   *The Bahá'í World*, 2005–2006, p. 239.

6   'Abbás Rafí'í, email to the author, 21 September 2014, pp. 11–12.

7   ibid. p. 13.

8   *The Bahá'í World*, 2005–2006, p. 239.

9   Nosrat Ardekani, transcript of phone conversation, 20 August 2013. The Ardekanis' story in these paragraphs is taken from this conversation and Mrs Ardekani's email to the author, 30 August 2013, unless otherwise indicated.

10   *The Bahá'í World*, vol. XIV, p. 319.

11   Nosrat Ardekani, email and phone conversation, and Rowshan Mustapha, email to the author, 5 September 2013.

12   Violette Nakhjavani, *The Great African Safari*, p. 189.

13   'Abbás Rafí'í, email to the author, 21 September 2014, p. 7.

14   Nosrat Ardekani, transcript of phone conversation, 20 August 2013.

15   'Abbás Rafí'í, email to the author, 21 September 2014, pp. 9–10.

16   ibid. pp. 10–11.

17   ibid. p. 12; and email of 2 April 2015.

18   ibid. p. 14.

19   ibid. p. 17.

20   *The Bahá'í World: In Memoriam, 1992–1997*, p. 319.

21   Nosrat Ardekani, email to the author, 6 November 2013.

22   'Abbás Rafí'í, email to the author, 21 September 2014, pp. 17–18.

23   *Bahá'í World News Service*, 'Standing up for the truth', 5 December 2004.

24   Elsie Austin, audio recording, 23 November 1973, The Heritage Project of the National Spiritual Assembly of the United States.

25   ibid.

26   Nosrat Ardekani, transcript of phone conversation, 20 August 2013.

27   Elsie Austin, audio recording, 23 November 1973, op cit.

28   Nosrat Ardekani, transcript of phone conversation, 20 August 2013.

29   Elsie Austin, audio recording, 23 November 1973, op cit.

30   Etter-Lewis and Thomas, Lights of the Spirit, pp. 135–6.

31   *Bahá'í News*, no. 281, July 1954, p. 8.

32   Elsie Austin, audio recording, 23 November 1973, op cit.

33 Etter-Lewis and Thomas, *Lights of the Spirit*, p. 137.
34 ibid.
35 Elsie Austin, audio recording, 23 November 1973, op cit.
36 *Bahá'í World News Service*, 'Standing up for the truth', 5 December 2004.
37 *The Washington Post*, 26 February 2004, p. B06.
38 *The Bahá'í World: In Memoriam, 1992–1997*, p. 352.
39 Nina Walters, personal communication, 14 May 2016.
40 Evelyn Walters, *Memoirs*, pp. 1–2, 4.
41 Nina Walters, personal communication, 14 May 2016.
42 Evelyn Walters, *Memoirs*, p. 5.
43 ibid. pp. 6–7.
44 'Abbás Rafí'í, email to the author, 21 September 2014, p. 12.
45 Evelyn Walters, *Memoirs*, p. 7.
46 Nosrat Ardekani, transcript of a phone conversation, 20 August 2013; and email to the author, 30 August 2013.
47 'Abbás Rafí'í, email to the author, 21 September 2014, p. 12.
48 Evelyn Walters, *Memoirs*, p. 8.
49 ibid.
50 *The American Bahá'í*, vol. 30, no. 6 (1 August 1999), p. 22.
51 Evelyn Walters, *Memoirs*, p. 9.
52 Nina Walters, personal communication, 14 May 2016.
53 Evelyn Walters, *Memoirs*, pp. 9–10.
54 ibid. pp. 10–11.
55 ibid. p. 11.
56 ibid. pp. 12–13.
57 ibid. p. 13.
58 Gamal Hassan, email to the author, 30 September 2015.
59 ibid.
60 ibid.; also *The Bahá'í World*, vol. XVI, p. 545; Rowshan Mustapha, email to the author, 28 March 2014.
61 *The Bahá'í World*, vol. XVI, p. 545.
62 Gamal Hassan, email to the author, 30 September 2015.
63 ibid.; see also Redman, *Shoghi Effendi: Through the Pilgrim's Eye*, vol. 2, pp. 374–81.
64 ibid.
65 ibid.
66 *The Bahá'í World*, vol. XVI, p. 545.
67 Cameron, *A Basic Bahá'í Chronology*, p. 306.
68 *The Bahá'í World: In Memoriam, 1992–1997*, pp. 216–17.
69 ibid. p. 217.
70 *Bahá'í News*, no. 281 (July 1954), p. 8.
71 *Bahá'í News*, no. 288 (Feb. 1955), p. 8.
72 *The Bahá'í World: In Memoriam, 1992–1997*, pp. 217–18.

73 *The American Bahá'í*, vol. 38, no. 3 (28 April 2007), p. 23.

74 USBNA, Letter from Earleta Fleming, 29 June 1956.

75 USBNA, 'Questionnaire for Prospective Pioneers in Africa', Africa Committee, and letter dated 3 September 1961.

76 *The Bahá'í World: In Memoriam, 1992–1997*, pp. 218-19.

77 *The Bahá'í World*, vol. XIV, p. 315.

78 Rowshan Mustapha, 'Muhammad Mustafa Soliman: Knight of Bahá'u'lláh to the Spanish Sahara', email to the author, 28 December 2013.

79 Rowshan Mustapha, 'Amin Abu'l-Futuh Battah: Knight of Bahá'u'lláh to Rio de Oro', email to the author, 19 December 2013.

80 ibid.

81 *The Bahá'í World*, vol. XVIII, pp. 769-70.

82 Rowshan Mustapha, 'Muhammad Mustafa Soliman: Knight of Bahá'u'lláh to the Spanish Sahara', email to the author, 28 December 2013.

83 ibid.

84 ibid.

85 ibid.

86 *The Bahá'í World*, vol. XVIII, pp. 769-70.

87 Rowshan Mustapha, 'Muhammad Mustafa Soliman: Knight of Bahá'u'lláh to the Spanish Sahara', email to the author, 28 December 2013.

88 Rowshan Mustapha, 'In Memoriam, Labib Esfahani, Knight of Bahá'u'lláh to French West Africa', email to the author, 9 October 2013.

89 Rowshan Mustapha, 'Taleb Kamal Adam, Memoirs', email to the author, 10 April 2015.

90 Cameron, *A Basic Bahá'í Chronology*, p. 320.

91 Rowshan Mustapha, 'In Memoriam, Labib Esfahani, Knight of Bahá'u'lláh to French West Africa', email to the author, 9 October 2013.

92 ibid.

93 ibid.

94 *The Bahá'í World, 2000–2001*, p. 270.

95 Khianra, *Immortals*, p. 141.

96 Lee, *The Establishment of the Bahá'í Faith in West Africa: The First Decade, 1952–1962*, p. 122.

97 Khianra, *Immortals*, p. 238.

98 Lee, *The Establishment of the Bahá'í Faith in West Africa*, p. 122.

99 ibid.

100 *Bahá'í News*, no. 298 (December 1955), pp. 3-4.

101 *Bahá'í News*, no. 296 (October 1955), p. 5.

102 *Bahá'í World News Service*, 'Two reasons for festivities', 25 January 2005; Lee, *The Establishment of the Bahá'í Faith in West Africa*, p. 123.

103 *The Bahá'í World*, vol. XIX, p. 686.

104 *The Bahá'í World, 2004–2005*, p. 290.

105 *The Bahá'í World*, vol. XIX, p. 686.

106 *The Bahá'í World, 2004–2005*, p. 290.

107 *The Bahá'í World*, vol. XIX, pp. 686–7.

108 *The Bahá'í World, 2004–2005*, p. 290.

109 USBNA, United States Office of Pioneering, Pioneer Files, Box 19.

110 *Bahá'í World News Service*, 'A love for all peoples', 20 June 2003. http://news.bahai.org/story/230.

111 Shoghi Effendi. *Unfolding Destiny*, p. 172.

112 *Bahá'í World News Service*, 'A love for all peoples', 20 June 2003.

113 ibid.

114 Rowhani, *Two Doves of Love*, pp. 14–15.

115 ibid. p. 15.

116 ibid. p. 17.

117 ibid. pp. 17–18.

118 Violette Nakhjavani, *The Great African Safari*, p. 27.

119 *Bahá'í Journal UK*, vol. 20, no. 3 (Sept/Oct 2003).

120 *The Bahá'í World*, vol X, p. 167.

121 Jim Schechter, email to the author, 11 January 2016, p. 2.

122 ibid.

123 ibid.

124 ibid. p. 3.

125 ibid. pp. 3–4.

126 USBNA, letters to Fred Schechter, 5 March, 14 July, 6 August and 9 October 1953; USBNA, letters from Fred Schechter, 7 August and 10 October 1953.

127 USBNA, letters to Fred Schechter, 5 and 13 February 1953; USBNA, letters from Fred Schechter, 23 February, 10 March and 9 April 1953.

128 USBNA, letter from Fred Schechter, 5 May 53.

129 USBNA, letter from Fred Schechter, 17 July 1953.

130 USBNA, letters from Fred Schechter, 4 August and 9 September 1953.

131 USBNA, letter from Fred Schechter, 26 September 53.

132 USBNA, letter from Fred Schechter, 2 November 1953.

133 USBNA, letters from Fred Schechter, 9 and 26 September 1953.

134 Jim Schechter, email to the author, 11 January 2016, p. 5.

135 USBNA, letters from Fred Schechter, 19 October and 11 November 1953.

136 Jim Schechter, email to the author, 11 January 2016, p. 6.

137 USBNA, letter from Fred Schechter, 8 December 1953.

138 USBNA, letter from Fred Schechter, 13 January 1954.

139 USBNA, letters from Fred Schechter, 14 February and 7 March 1954; USBNA, letters to Fred Schechter, 14 and 27 March 1954.

140 USBNA, letters from Fred Schechter, 27 April and 8 June 1954.

141 Jim Schechter, email to the author, 11 January 2016, p. 8.

142 ibid. p. 5.

143 ibid. p. 9.

144 ibid. p. 1.

145 Hassan, *Moths Turned Eagles*, pp. 37, 57, 66; *The Bahá'í World: In Memoriam, 1992-1997*, p. 256.

146 Isa. 18:7.

147 Hassan, *Moths Turned Eagles*, pp. 70, 80–81, 99–100.

148 ibid. pp. 110–12.

149 ibid. pp. 113–14.

150 ibid. pp. 114–15. See also Redman, *Shoghi Effendi Through the Pilgrim's Eye*, vol. 2, pp. 110–12 for a transcript.

151 Hassan, *Moths Turned Eagles*, pp. 118–19.

152 *Bahá'í News*, no. 300 (February 1956), p. 7; Gamal Hassan, email to the author, 27 February 2015.

153 Gamal Hassan, email to the author, 27 February 2015.

154 Hassan, *Moths Turned Eagles*, pp. 120, 131.

155 ibid. pp. 133-4, 137, 150.

156 *The Bahá'í World*, vol. XX, pp. 912–13.

157 Rezvanieh Kamálí, 'Mírzá Áqá Kamálí Sarvistání', email to the author, 20 November 2013.

Southern Africa

1 'Alí Nakhjavání, *Glimpse of the life of Enoch Olinga as told by 'Ali Nakhjavani, July 2012*.

2 ibid.

3 Harper, *Lights of Fortitude*, p. 412.

4 Shoghi Effendi, *Messages to The Bahá'í World*, pp. 133–4.

5 'Alí Nakhjavání, *Glimpse of the life of Enoch Olinga as told by 'Ali Nakhjavani, July 2012*.

6 Harper, *Lights of Fortitude*, pp. 412–13.

7 'Alí Nakhjavání, *Glimpse of the life of Enoch Olinga as told by 'Ali Nakhjavani, July 2012*.

8 *The Bahá'í World*, vol. XVIII, p. 622.

9 Tanyi Nyenti, *The Story of David and Esther Tanyi*, pp. 18–19.

10 Shoghi Effendi, cited ibid. p. 40; and in Vreeland, *And the Trees Clapped their Hands*, p. 273.

11 *The Bahá'í World*, vol. XVIII, pp. 22–4.

12 *Bahá'í News* (May 1984), p. 7.

13 *The Bahá'í World*, vol. XVIII, p. 626.

14 ibid. pp. 629–32.

15 *The Bahá'í World*, vol. XX, pp. 1013–14.

16 ibid. p. 1014.

17 ibid.

18 David Tanyi, *The Story of My Pioneering*, pp. 20–21, cited in Tanyi Nyenti, *The Story of David and Esther Tanyi*, pp. 20–21; see also Vreeland, *And the Trees Clapped their Hands*, pp. 272–3.

19   Shoghi Effendi, cited in Tanyi Nyenti, *The Story of David and Esther Tanyi*, p. 40; and in Vreeland, *And the Trees Clapped their Hands*, p. 273.

20   Vreeland, *And the Trees Clapped their Hands*, p. 273.

21   Enoch Tanyi, 'A Short Biography of Nyenti David Tanyi', email to the author, 4 October 2013, and in Tanyi Nyenti, *The Story of David and Esther Tanyi*, pp. 40–41.

22   David Tanyi, *The Story of My Pioneering*, p. 25; Enoch Tanyi, 'Edward Tabe', email to the author, 18 December 2013; and *The Story of David and Esther Tanyi*, p. 42.

23   Rabbani, *Enoch Olinga, Hand of the Cause of God: His Life and His Work*, p. 14.

24   David Tanyi, 'Notes, September 7, 1984', in Tanyi Nyenti, *The Story of David and Esther Tanyi,* p. 44.

25   *Bahá'í News*, no. 300 (February 1956), p. 6.

26   David Tanyi, *The Story of My Pioneering*, p. 33, in Tanyi Nyenti, *The Story of David and Esther Tanyi*, pp. 56–7.

27   For statistics on the growth of the Lomé Bahá'í community in these early years, see Tanyi Nyenti, *The Story of David and Esther Tanyi*, Appendix 4, pp. 201–17.

28   ibid. p. 68.

29   ibid. p. 119.

30   Unless otherwise indicated, the stories of Vivian Wesson and Mavis Nymon are based on *The Bahá'í World: In Memoriam 1992–1997*, pp. 109–13, and from *The American Bahá'í* (May–June 2013), http://www.american.bahai.us/9/news/2013/may-june/mavis-nymon-knight-of-bahaullah-served-in-africa-and-north-dakota/.

31   *Bahá'í News*, no. 300 (February 1956), p. 6.

32   Hanson-Runsvold Funeral Home, 2013. http://www.hansonrunsvold.com/obituaries/Mavis-Nymon/#!/Obituary.

33   *The Bahá'í World*, vol. XIX, pp. 615–16.

34   Jyoti Munsiff, obituary written for a *Bahá'í World* volume, 2009; and *The Bahá'í World: In Memoriam 1992–1997*, p. 251.

35   Gilbert and Daisy Robert, report for the NSA of South Africa, p. 3.

36   ibid. pp. 7–8.

37   ibid. p. 4.

38   ibid. pp. 4–5.

39   *The Bahá'í World*, vol. XIX, pp. 615–16.

40   See 'Samuel Njiki Njenji', in Appendix 1: 'The Cameroonian Knights of Bahá'u'lláh', in Tanyi Nyenti, *The Story of David and Esther Tanyi*, pp. 176–181.

41   Jyoti Munsiff, obituary written for a *Bahá'í World* volume, 2009.

42   ibid.

43   See 'Edward Tabe', in Appendix 1: 'The Cameroonian Knights of Bahá'u'lláh', in Tanyi Nyenti, *The Story of David and Esther Tanyi*, pp. 181–4; information also from Enoch Tanyi, 'Edward Tabe', email to the author, 18 December 2013. The story of Edward Tabe given here is from these sources unless otherwise indicated.

44   Violette Nakhjavani, *The Great African Safari*, pp. 237, 241, 244, 247.

45 Lee, *The Establishment of the Bahá'í Faith in West Africa: The First Decade, 1952-1962*, p. 138; Lee, *The Bahá'í Faith in Africa: Establishing a New Religious Movement, 1952-62*, p. 109.

46 See 'Dr Benedict (Yalla) Eballa', in Appendix 1: 'The Cameroonian Knights of Bahá'u'lláh', in Tanyi Nyenti, *The Story of David and Esther Tanyi*, pp. 160-65; information also from Enoch Tanyi, 'Ben Eballa', email to the author, 4 October 2013.

47 *Bahá'í News*, no. 277 (March 1954), p. 6.

48 *Bahá'í News*, no. 281 (July 1954), p. 5.

49 *The Bahá'í World*, vol. XIX, p. 665.

50 ibid.

51 *The Bahá'í World*, vol. XVIII, p. 778.

52 See 'Martin Manga', in Appendix 1: 'The Cameroonian Knights of Bahá'u'lláh', in Tanyi Nyenti, *The Story of David and Esther Tanyi*, pp. 165–76; information also from Enoch Tanyi, 'Martin Manga, A Short Biography', email to the author, 4 October 2013. The story of Martin Manga given here is from these sources.

53 The story of Elise Schreiber, including the quotations, is based on Dailey, *Elise Schreiber Lynelle: Double Knight of Bahá'u'lláh*, pp. 1–8.

54 McKay, *Fires in Many Hearts*, pp. 3–5.

55 *The Bahá'í World*, vol. XV, pp. 486–87.

56 *The Bahá'í World*, vol. XIX, p. 595.

57 *Bahá'í World News Service*, 'Spiritual solace in a recovering land', 2 January 2005.

58 See their 'In Memoriam' articles: 'Mary Collison', in *The Bahá'í World*, vol. XV, pp. 486–8; 'Reginald 'Rex' Collison', ibid. vol. XIX, pp. 595–6.

59 *The Bahá'í World*, vol. XIX, p. 596.

60 Locke-Nyrenda and Dailey, *Dunduzu Kaluli Chisiza*, pp. 2–3.

61 ibid. p. 4.

62 ibid. p. 5.

63 ibid.

64 *Bahá'í News*, no. 281 (July 1954), p. 6.

65 Locke-Nyrenda and Dailey, *Dunduzu Kaluli Chisiza*, p. 8.

66 ibid. p. 9.

67 ibid. p. 10.

68 ibid. p. 12.

69 Unless otherwise indicated, the story of Ezzat Zahra'i is based on Logsdon-Dubois, *Knight with a Briefcase*.

70 *The Bahá'í World*, vol. XVIII, pp. 803–4.

71 *The Bahá'í World: In Memoriam, 1992-1997*, p. 15.

72 Johnson and Johnson, *Heroes and Heroines of the Ten Year Crusade in Southern Africa*, p. 353.

73 *The Bahá'í World: In Memoriam, 1992-1997*, pp. 15-16.

74 Adrienne Morgan, *Claire Gung*, pp. 1-9.

75 ibid. pp. 10-11, 13.

76 Letter on behalf of Shoghi Effendi to Claire Gung, 11 January 1951, in her 'In Memoriam' article, *The Bahá'í World*, vol. XIX, p. 655.

77 Adrienne Morgan, *Claire Gung*, pp. 18–19.

78 Johnson and Johnson, *Heroes and Heroines of the Ten Year Crusade in Southern Africa*, pp. 372–4.

79 *The Bahá'í World*, vol. XIX, p. 655.

80 Johnson and Johnson, *Heroes and Heroines of the Ten Year Crusade in Southern Africa*, p. 380.

81 ibid. pp. 372–4.

82 Suzanne Locke-Nyrenda, email to the author, 12 November 2014.

83 Adrienne Morgan, *Claire Gung*, pp. 31–8.

84 ibid. pp. 39–51.

85 *The Bahá'í World*, vol. XIX, pp. 655–7.

86 ibid.

87 Adrienne Morgan, *Claire Gung*, p. 151.

88 Sylvia Benatar, 'Kenneth and Roberta Christian, Knights of Bahá'u'lláh to Southern Rhodesia', email to the author, 31 July 2015, p. 1.

89 ibid. p. 2.

90 ibid. p. 1.

91 ibid.

92 ibid. pp. 1–2.

93 *The Bahá'í World*, vol. XIII, p. 907.

94 ibid. pp. 906–7; *The Bahá'í World*, vol. XV, p. 497.

95 Ted Cardell, *Experiences with the Guardian*, audio recording and partial transcript (p. 1 of transcript).

96 ibid. p. 6 of transcript.

97 ibid. (audio).

98 ibid. p. 7 of transcript.

99 ibid. (audio).

100 Johnson and Johnson, *Heroes and Heroines of the Ten Year Crusade in Southern Africa*, pp. 410–11.

101 ibid. p. 408.

102 Suzy Cardell, email to the author, 9 October 2013.

103 *Bahá'í World News Service*, 'Secret rendezvous of faith', 20 December 2003.

104 *Bahá'í Canada*, Masá'il/Sharaf BE 147, p. 25.

105 *The Bahá'í World*, vol. XX, pp. 802–3.

106 Anderson, *Yukon Golden Hearts Discovered*, p. 218.

107 *The Bahá'í World*, vol. XX, p. 804.

108 Anderson, *Yukon Golden Hearts Discovered*, p. 218.

109 Tom Roberts, email to the author, 8 March 2014.

110 *The Bahá'í World*, vol. XX, pp. 804–5.

111 Tom Roberts, email to the author, 8 March 2014.

112 Harper, *Lights of Fortitude,* p. 432.

113 *The Bahá'í World*, vol. XX, pp. 805–7.

114 *Bahá'í Canada*, Masá'il/Sharaf BE 147, p. 26.

115 *The American Bahá'í*, vol. 38, no. 3 (28 April 2007), p. 24.

116 Suzanne Locke-Nyrenda, email to the author, 4 December 2014.

117 Khan, *Heritage of Light*, pp. 203–4; Johnson and Johnson, *Heroes and Heroines of the Ten Year Crusade in Southern Africa*, p. 430.

118 *The Bahá'í World*, vol. XVIII, p. 725; *Bahá'í World News Service*, 'Royal praise for development projects', 16 May 2004; *The Bahá'í World*, 2004–2005, p. 57.

119 *The Bahá'í World*, vol. XV, p. 726; *Bahá'í World News Service*, 'Royal praise for development projects', 16 May 2004.

120 Johnson and Johnson, *Heroes and Heroines of the Ten Year Crusade in Southern Africa*, pp. 417–18.

121 Suzanne Locke-Nyrenda, email to the author, 4 December 2014.

122 *The Bahá'í World*, vol. XV, p. 726; *Bahá'í World News Service*, 'Royal praise for development projects', 16 May 2004.

123 Suzanne Locke-Nyrenda, email to the author, 4 December 2014.

124 *The American Bahá'í*, vol. 24, no. 7 (17 May 1993), p. 35.

125 *The Bahá'í World*, vol. XX, p. 892.

126 ibid. vol. XVII, pp. 459–60.

127 ibid. vol. XVII, p. 449.

128 ibid. vol. XVII, p. 450.

129 ibid. vol. XX, p. 893.

130 ibid. vol. XVII, p. 460.

Indian Ocean

1   *The Bahá'í World*, vol. XVI, pp. 565–6.

2   Javidukht Khadem, *Zikrullah Khadem*, pp. 99–100.

3   National Spiritual Assembly of the Bahá'ís of Iraq, 'How Muria Muria Archipelago was opened to the Faith', Annual Report, 1957–1958, in Marion Hofman Papers.

4   Javidukht Khadem, *Zikrullah Khadem*, pp. 99–100.

5   ibid; *The Bahá'í World*, vol. XVI, p. 566.

6   National Spiritual Assembly of the Bahá'ís of Iraq, 'How Muria Muria Archipelago was opened to the Faith', Annual Report, 1957–1958, in Marion Hofman Papers.

7   *The Bahá'í World*, vol. XVI, p. 566.

8   Javidukht Khadem, *Zikrullah Khadem*, p. 101.

9   *The Bahá'í World*, vol. XVI, p. 566.

10   The story of Kamálí Sarvistání, including quotations, is based on the account by Rezvanieh Kamálí, 'Mirza Áqá Kamálí Sarvistání', email to the author, 20 November 2013.

11   The story of Kámil 'Abbás is based on the account by Rafí 'Abbas, email to the author, 11 September 2015.

12   *The Bahá'í World*, vol. XII, p. 607.

13 *Bahá'í World News Service*, 'Festivities exceed expectations at Seychelles celebration', 8 November 2003.

14 *The Bahá'í World: In Memoriam, 1992–1997*, pp. 174–5.

15 *Bahá'í Newsletter* (July 1975), p. 3.

16 ibid. p. 2.

17 *The Bahá'í World: In Memoriam, 1992–1997*, p. 175; *Bahá'í World News Service*, 'Festivities exceed expectations at Seychelles celebration', 8 November 2003.

18 *Bahá'í News*, no. 313 (March 1957), p. 7.

19 *The Bahá'í World: In Memoriam, 1992–1997*, pp. 175–6.

20 The story of Mehraban Soheili is taken from his report to the Universal House of Justice, 9 April 1988, unless otherwise indicated.

21 Violetta Zein, interview of Mrs Claire Andriambalo and daughter Harizo Andriambalo, Antananarivo, 11 December 2000.

22 Isfandiar Sohaili, email to the author, 14 October 2013.

23 *The Bahá'í World*, vol. XVIII, p. 703.

24 ibid. pp. 703–4; Johnson and Johnson, *Heroes and Heroines of the Ten Year Crusade in Southern Africa*, pp. 93–4.

25 Violetta Zein, interview of Mr Eddy Lutchmaya and Mr Roland Lutchmaya, Qutre-Bornes, Mauritius, 12–14 December 2000.

26 Johnson and Johnson, *Heroes and Heroines of the Ten Year Crusade in Southern Africa*, pp. 93–4.

27 *Bahá'í News*, no. 281 (July 1954), p. 5.

28 Johnson and Johnson, *Heroes and Heroines of the Ten Year Crusade in Southern Africa*, pp. 93–4.

29 *Bahá'í News*, no. 299 (January 1956), p. 4.

30 ibid. no. 338 (April 1959), pp. 9–10.

31 *The Bahá'í World*, vol. XVIII, p. 705.

32 Wikipedia, https://en.wikipedia.org/wiki/Leland_Jensen.

33 Johnson and Johnson, *Heroes and Heroines of the Ten Year Crusade in Southern Africa*, pp. 163–4.

34 Shoghi Effendi, *Messages of Shoghi Effendi to the Indian Subcontinent: 1923–1957*, p. 421.

35 Violetta Zein, interview of Mr Eddy Lutchmaya and Mr Roland Lutchmaya, Quatre-Bornes, Mauritius, 12–14 December 2000.

36 Wikipedia, https://en.wikipedia.org/wiki/Leland_Jensen.

37 Unless otherwise indicated, this story of Pouva Murday is based on a talk by Robert Quigley at the Geyserville Summer School, California, in 1965 (including quotations); and on Johnson and Johnson, *Heroes and Heroines of the Ten Year Crusade in Southern Africa*, pp. 83–6.

38 Story told by Pouva Murday to Shastri Rurushotma.

39 ibid.

40 Johnson and Johnson, *Heroes and Heroines of the Ten Year Crusade in Southern Africa*, pp. 84–6.

41 Violetta Zein, interview of Madame Loulou Rajaonarivo née Razaka, Antananarivo, 11 December 2000.

42 ibid.

43 Story told by Pouva Murday to Shastri Rurushotma.

44 *The Bahá'í World*, vol. XIII, pp. 892–3.

45 ibid. p. 893.

46 *The Bahá'í World*, vol. XIX, p. 62.

47 *The Bahá'í World*, vol. XIII, p. 893.

48 Unless otherwise indicated, this story of Jeanne Frankel and Margaret Bates is taken from their memoir: Frankel de Corrales and Bates, *Forget-me-not Nicobar*, various pages.

49 National Spiritual Assembly of India, Pakistan and Burma, Annual Bahá'í Reports, Marion Hofman Papers, p. 3.

50 *Bahá'í News*, no. 350 (April 1960), p. 2.

51 Bahá'í US, http://www.bahai.us/2012/06/13/jeanne-de-corrales-traveled-widely-to-support-faith-earned-honor-as-knight/

52 Conrad Lembke, Eulogy at the Funeral Service of Frank Leonard Wyss, Canberra Bahá'í Centre, 18 May 2007.

53 Shoghi Effendi, *Messages to the Antipodes*, p. 164.

54 *Herald of the South*, 'Pioneer move cut short', July–September 1992, p. 38.

55 Hassall, 'Obituary: James Heggie', in *Bahá'í Studies Review*, vol. 9.

56 Rodney Hancock, Eulogy delivered at Memorial Service for Frank Wyss, Brisbane Bahá'í Center of Learning, 10 June 2007.

57 ibid.

58 *Herald of the South*, 'Knights of Bahá'u'lláh', July–September 1992, p. 38.

59 Rodney Hancock, Eulogy delivered at Memorial Service for Frank Wyss, Brisbane Bahá'í Center of Learning, 10 June 2007.

India and the Himalayas

1 Roshan Knox, transcript of an audio recording, 3 September 2013.

2 *Bahá'í News*, no. 277 (March 1954), p. 7.

3 Zarangiz Misra, emails to the author, 25 and 26 October 2013.

4 Rob Weinberg, in *Bahá'í Journal UK* (September/October 2003), p. 17.

5 Zarangiz Misra, emails to the author, 25 and 26 October 2013.

6 ibid.

7 ibid.

8 Marion Hofman, *The World Crusade*, p. 414.

9 *The Bahá'í World, 2004–2005*, p. 286.

10 Zarangiz Misra, emails to the author, 25 and 26 October 2013.

11 ibid.

12 Khianra, *Immortals*, pp. 172–4.

13 *The Bahá'í World*, vol. XVII, p. 462.

14 Khianra, *Immortals*, p. 177.

15 ibid. p. 178.

16 ibid. pp. 177–9.

17 Roshan Knox, transcript of an audio recording, 3 September 2013.

18 Dermod Knox, '50th anniversary of the establishment of the Faith in Goa', in *Bahá'í Journal UK* (July/August 2003), p. 19.

19 Roshan Knox, transcript of an audio recording, 3 September 2013.

20 ibid.

21 ibid.

22 Roshan Knox, personal notes.

23 Roshan Knox, transcript of an audio recording, 3 September 2013.

24 Dermod Knox, '50th anniversary of the establishment of the Faith in Goa', in *Bahá'í Journal UK* (July/August 2003), p. 19.

25 See http://words-and-words.blogspot.ie/2008/07/funeral-of-mrs-firoozeh-yaga-negi.html.

26 Lionel Peraji, email to the author, 16 December 2013.

27 Cameron, *A Basic Bahá'í Chronology*, pp. 301, 312.

28 Lionel Peraji, email to the author, 16 December 2013.

29 ibid.

30 Khodarahm Mojgani, 'First pioneers in Mahé', email from P. K. Premarajan to the author, 6 November 2013.

31 ibid.

32 ibid.

33 ibid.

34 ibid.

35 Poostchi, *Dawn of the Sun of Truth, Tamil Nadu, India,* p. 23.

36 *The Bahá'í World*, vol. XX, pp. 871–2.

37 World Bahá'í Archives, summary of letter from Mrs Shokat Nahvi to the Universal House of Justice, 26 September 1990.

38 *The Bahá'í World*, vol. XX, p. 872.

39 ibid.

40 Shoghi Effendi, *Messages to the Bahá'í World 1950–1957,* p. 51.

41 Masroor Bhargava, 'Shyam Beharilal Bhargava – The youthful pioneer', email to the author, 17 December 2015.

42 ibid. pp. 1–2.

43 ibid. pp. 2–3.

44 ibid. p. 4.

45 ibid.

46 *The Bahá'í World*, vol. XIX, p. 637.

47 *Bahá'í News*, no. 567 (June 1978), p. 5.

48 *The Bahá'í World*, vol. XIX, p. 637.

49 Khianra, *Immortals*, pp. 156–9.

50 New Era High School, at Bahaikepedia, http://bahaikipedia.org/New_Era_High_School.

51 Poostchi, *Dawn of the Sun of Truth, Tamil Nadu, India,* p. 156.
52 ibid.
53 ibid. p. 157.
54 ibid. pp. 158–9.
55 *Bahá'í News,* no. 353 (August 1960), p. 9.
56 Poostchi, *Dawn of the Sun of Truth, Tamil Nadu, India,* p. 157.
57 *Bahá'í News,* no. 567 (June 1978), p. 5; no. 523 (October 1974), p. 7; no. 599 (February 1981), p. 3.
58 Poostchi, *Dawn of the Sun of Truth, Tamil Nadu, India,* pp. 158–60.
59 Penny Walker, in 'Reminiscences of Mr Udaya Narayan Singh, Knight of Bahá'u'lláh', email to the author, 8 July 2016.
60 Udaya Narayan Singh, interview recorded by Bharat Koirala, transcribed by Larry and Shyama Robertson.
61 ibid.
62 Bharat Koirala, email to the author, 22 September 2013.
63 Udaya Narayan Singh, interview recorded by Bharat Koirala.
64 ibid.
65 ibid.
66 ibid.
67 JoAnne Pach Koirala, in 'Reminiscences of Mr Udaya Narayan Singh, Knight of Bahá'u'lláh'.
68 Penny Walker, ibid.
69 Larry Robertson and Dirgha Shah, email to the author, 7 July 2016.
70 *The Bahá'í World,* vol. XIX, pp. 689.

China, Indonesia and Malaysia

1   *The Bahá'í World,* vol. XX, pp. 999.
2   Sims, *The Macau Bahá'í Community in the Early Years,* p. 3.
3   *Bahá'í News,* no. 279 (May 1954), p. 3.
4   Sims, *The Macau Bahá'í Community in the Early Years,* p. 4.
5   *Bahá'í News,* no. 279 (May 1954), p. 4.
6   ibid.
7   *The Bahá'í World,* vol. XX, p. 1000.
8   Sims, *The Macau Bahá'í Community in the Early Years,* p. 8.
9   *The Bahá'í World,* vol. XX, pp. 1000–01.
10 *Bahá'í News,* no. 279 (May 1954), p. 4.
11 Sims, *The Macau Bahá'í Community in the Early Years,* p. 19.
12 *The Bahá'í World,* vol. XVIII, p. 739.
13 Sims, *The Macau Bahá'í Community in the Early Years,* p. 14.
14 ibid. p. 26.
15 ibid. p. 30.
16 *The Bahá'í World,* vol. XVIII, p. 739.
17 Sims, *The Macau Bahá'í Community in the Early Years,* pp. 8, 26, 36.

18 *Bahá'í News*, no. 279 (May 1954), p. 2.

19 Charles Duncan, email to the author, 2 July 2016.

20 ibid.

21 *Bahá'í News*, no. 279 (May 1954), p. 3.

22 *Bahá'í News*, no. 288 (February 1955), p. 5.

23 *Bahá'í News*, no. 291 (May 1955), p. 9.

24 ibid.

25 *Bahá'í News*, no. 436 (July 1967), p. 11.

26 Sims, *Raising the Banner in Korea*, p. 62.

27 Charles Duncan, email to the author, 3 July 2016.

28 John Fozdar, personal communication, 5 February 2013.

29 ibid.

30 ibid.

31 ibid.

32 ibid.

33 *The Bahá'í World*, vol. XIII, p. 1150.

34 John Fozdar, personal communication, 5 February 2013.

35 http://en.wikipedia.org/wiki/Freedom_of_religion_in_Brunei.

36 *The Bahá'í World: In Memoriam, 1992–1997*, p. 328.

37 De Vries, *The Babi Question You Mentioned: The Origins of the Bahá'í Community of the Netherlands, 1844–1962*, p. 245.

38 ibid.

39 Muhájir, *Dr Muhájír*, p. 25.

40 ibid. pp. 25, 29–30.

41 ibid. pp. 34–40.

42 ibid. pp. 42–45.

43 ibid. pp. 47–48.

44 ibid. pp. 48–50.

45 Marion Hofman, *The World Crusade*, p. 475.

46 Muhájir, *Dr Muhájír*, pp. 64, 76.

47 Marion Hofman, *The World Crusade*, p. 475.

48 Muhájir, *Dr Muhájír*, pp. 52–53, 64, 76.

49 Marion Hofman, *The World Crusade*, pp. 476.

50 Dempsey Morgan, *Servants of the Glory*, pp. 46–47.

51 Muhájir, *Dr Muhájír*, pp. 76, 80.

52 *The Bahá'í World*, vol. XV, pp. 449–50.

53 Shoghi Effendi, *Messages to the Antipodes*, footnote p. 283.

54 *The Bahá'í World*, vol. XV, p. 450.

55 Hassall, 'The Fitzners of Portuguese Timor', in Vreeland: *And the Trees Clapped Their Hands*, pp. 320–21.

56 ibid. p. 322.

57 ibid. pp. 323–4.

58 *The Bahá'í World*, vol. XV, p. 450.

59 Hassall, 'The Fitzners of Portuguese Timor', in Vreeland: *And the Trees Clapped Their Hands*, pp. 328–29.

60 ibid. pp. 329–30.

61 ibid. p. 330.

62 Shoghi Effendi, *Messages to the Antipodes*, footnote 95, p. 283.

63 *The Bahá'í World, 1998–1999*, p. 310.

64 Shoghi Effendi, *Messages to the Antipodes*, footnote 131, p. 358.

The Pacific Islands

1 See Robert Powers at Wikipedia.org, https://en.wikipedia.org/wiki/Robert_B._Powers.

2 Honnold, *Why They Became Bahá'ís*, pp. 106–7.

3 *The Bahá'í World*, vol. XX, pp. 899–900.

4 Olson, *Reminiscences of Guam*. The story in these paragraphs is from this source unless otherwise indicated.

5 *Bahá'í World News Service*, 'Spiritual legacy now paying dividends', 2 May 2004; Marianas Bahá'í Community, at http://marianas.bahai.org/community.html.

6 ibid.

7 *The Bahá'í World*, vol XX, p. 901.

8 ibid. pp. 902–3.

9 ibid.

10 ibid.

11 ibid.

12 *Bahá'í News*, no. 277 (March 1954), p. 7.

13 *The Bahá'í World: In Memoriam, 1992–1997*, p. 102.

14 ibid.

15 Florence Kelley, personal communication, 3 December 2015.

16 *The Bahá'í World: In Memoriam, 1992–1997*, p. 102.

17 *Bahá'í News*, no. 278 (April 1954), p. 4.

18 *The Bahá'í World: In Memoriam, 1992–1997*, pp. 102–4.

19 *The American Bahá'í*, vol. 25, no. 1 (19 January 1994), p. 19.

20 Olson, *Reminiscences of Guam*, p. 20.

21 *The Bahá'í World: In Memoriam, 1992–1997*, pp. 102–4.

22 *The American Bahá'í*, vol. 25, no. 1 (19 January 1994), p. 19.

23 *The Bahá'í World: In Memoriam, 1992–1997*, pp. 102–4; Florence Kelley, personal communication, 3 December 2015.

24 Florence Kelley, personal communication, 3 December 2015.

25 *The Bahá'í World: In Memoriam, 1992–1997*, pp. 102–4; Florence Kelley, personal communication, 3 December 2015.

26 *Herald of the South*, ' "Sister Vi" conquers fear', July–September 1992, p. 30.

27 *The Bahá'í World, 2004–2005*, p. 288.

28 Hassall, 'Pacific Bahá'í Communities 1950–1964', p. 80; *Bahá'í World News Service*, 'A life in pursuit of noble endeavors', 29 June 2004.

29 Shoghi Effendi, *Messages to the Antipodes*, p. 369, footnote 136.

30 Hassall, 'Pacific Baháʼí Communities 1950–1964', p. 80; *Baháʼí World News Service*, 'A life in pursuit of noble endeavors', 29 June 2004.

31 Hassall, 'The Baháʼí Faith in the Pacific', p. 276.

32 *The Baháʼí World, 2004–2005*, p. 288.

33 Saunders, *Of Wars and Worship*. The story in these paragraphs is from this source unless otherwise indicated.

34 *Baháʼí World News Service*, 'Festivities honor community service', 1 March 2004, http://news.bahai.org/story/291.

35 *The Baháʼí World*, vol. XV, pp. 440–41; *Baháʼí World News Service*, 'Festivities honor community service', 1 March 2004, http://news.bahai.org/story/291.

36 *Baháʼí News*, no. 319 (September 1957), p. 8.

37 *Baháʼí World News Service*, 'Festivities honor community service', 1 March 2004, http://news.bahai.org/story/291.

38 *Herald of the South*, 'Life of sacrifice', July–September 1992, p. 32.

39 ibid.

40 *The Baháʼí World*, vol. XX, pp. 848–50.

41 ibid.

42 Bertha Dobbins, quoted in Marion Hofman, *The World Crusade*, p. 553.

43 Hassall, 'The Baháʼí Faith in the Pacific', pp. 274–5.

44 Saunders, *Of Wars and Worship*, p. 164.

45 *The Baháʼí World*, vol. XX, pp. 850–51.

46 *The Baháʼí World: In Memoriam, 1992–1997*, p. 80.

47 Hassall, 'Pacific Baháʼí Communities 1950–1964'.

48 *The Baháʼí World: In Memoriam, 1992–1997*, p. 80.

49 Richard Battrick, email to the author, 8 August 2015.

50 Ruhe-Schoen, *An Enchantment of the Heart*, pp. 6–8, 10.

51 ibid. pp. 33–5.

52 *Herald of the South*, July-September 1992, p. 38.

53 Ruhe-Schoen, *An Enchantment of the Heart*, pp. 35–6.

54 ibid. pp. 37–9.

55 http://en.wikipedia.org/wiki/Baháʼí%C3%AD_Faith_in_the_Marshall_Islands.

56 Honnold, *Why They Became Baháʼís*, pp. 62–3.

57 Hassall, 'The origins of the Baháʼí Faith in the Pacific Islands: The case of the Gilbert and Ellice Islands', p. 41.

58 Shoghi Effendi, *Messages to the Antipodes*, p. 347, footnote 121.

59 *The Baháʼí World*, vol. XIV, p. 308.

60 Hassall, 'The origins of the Baháʼí Faith in the Pacific Islands: The case of the Gilbert and Ellice Islands', p. 42. See also http://bahai-library.com/hassall_bahai_asia-pacific_issues.

61 Undated recorded interview with Elena Fernie, ibid. pp. 42–4.

62 ibid. p. 48.

63 *The Baháʼí World*, vol. XIV, pp. 309–10.

64 Hassall, 'The origins of the Bahá'í Faith in the Pacific Islands: The case of the Gilbert and Ellice Islands', p. 39.

65 http://bahaiblog.net/site/2014/06/heroic-stories-communities-celebrate-60th-anniversaries/#sthash.A70ETzC8.dpuf.

66 Bahá'í News, no. 345 (November 1959), p. 11.

67 Shoghi Effendi, Messages to the Antipodes, p. 347, footnote 121.

68 Hassall, 'The origins of the Bahá'í Faith in the Pacific Islands: The case of the Gilbert and Ellice Islands', p. 40.

69 Bahá'í News, no. 301 (March 1956), pp. 6–7.

70 Hassall, 'The origins of the Bahá'í Faith in the Pacific Islands: The case of the Gilbert and Ellice Islands', p. 40.

71 The Bahá'í World, vol. XIV, pp. 309–10.

72 Honnold, Why They Became Bahá'ís, p. 64.

73 Hassall, 'The origins of the Bahá'í Faith in the Pacific Islands: The case of the Gilbert and Ellice Islands', p. 40.

74 Elena Fernie, quoted in Marion Hofman, The World Crusade, p. 558.

75 http://bahai-library.com/hassall_bahai_asia-pacific_issues.

76 Bahá'í News, no. 345 (November 1959), p. 11.

77 Letter from Virginia Breaks to Marion Hofman, 11 October 1958, Marion Hofman Papers.

78 The Bahá'í World, 2001–2002, p. 308.

79 Sitarih Ala'i, email to the author, 17 September 2015.

80 Shoghi Effendi, Messages to the Antipodes, p. 280, footnote 93.

81 'Lilian Elizabeth Wyss-Ala'i: Knight of Bahá'u'lláh –Samoan Islands', Introduction for the 50th Anniversary celebration, Samoa, 2004.

82 Lilian Ala'i, talk given at the 50th Anniversary celebration, Samoa, 2004.

83 Sitarih and Suhayl Ala'i, talk given at the 50th Anniversary celebration, Samoa, p. 4.

84 'Lilian Elizabeth Wyss-Ala'i: Knight of Bahá'u'lláh –Samoan Islands', Introduction for the 50th Anniversary celebration, Samoa, 2004.

85 Lilian Ala'i, talk given at the 50th Anniversary celebration, Samoa, 2004.

86 Lilian Ala'i, quoted in Marion Hofman, The World Crusade, pp. 552–3.

87 Lilian Ala'i, talk given at the 50th Anniversary celebration, Samoa, 2004.

88 ibid.

89 Round Robin, Newsletter from the National Spiritual Assembly of the Bahá'ís of Canada, March 1955.

90 ibid.

91 Bahá'í News, no. 418 (January 1966), p. 3.

92 Lilian Ala'i, talk given at the 50th Anniversary celebration, Samoa, 2004.

93 Round Robin, Newsletter from the National Spiritual Assembly of the Bahá'ís of Canada, March 1955.

94 Canadian Bahá'í News, no. 111 (April 1959).

95 Sitarih Ala'i, email to the author, 17 September 2015.

96 ibid.

97 ibid.

98 *The Bahá'í World*, vol. XV, pp. 180–83.

99 Sitarih Ala'i, email to the author, 17 September 2015.

100 *Australian Bahá'í*, March 2016, pp. 14–15.

101 *Herald of the South*, 'A pioneer gives, but gains so much more!', July–September 1992, p. 27.

102 ibid.

103 ibid.

104 *Bahá'í News*, no. 284 (October 1954), p. 5.

105 *Herald of the South*, 'A pioneer gives, but gains so much more!', July–September 1992.

106 *Australian Bahá'í*, March 2016, pp. 14–15.

107 Shoghi Effendi, *Messages to the Antipodes*, p. 371, footnote 137.

108 *Herald of the South*, 'The happiest times of our lives', July–September 1992, p. 34.

109 ibid.

110 *Bahá'í News*, no. 294 (August 1955), p. 5.

111 *Herald of the South*, 'The happiest times of our lives', July–September 1992, p. 34.

112 Hassall, 'Pacific Bahá'í Communities 1950–1964', p. 81.

113 *The Bahá'í World*, vol. XX, pp. 929–30; see also *Bahá'í Faith in Tonga*, http://www.facebook.com/pages/Bahá%C3%AD-Faith-in-Tonga/124488667596606; *Nomoa*, http://www.nomoa.com/news/?sort=title&startnum=610.

114 Shoghi Effendi, *Messages to the Antipodes*, p. 371, footnote 137.

115 *The Bahá'í World*, vol. XIX, p. 625.

116 Edith M. Danielsen, quoted in Marion Hofman, *The World Crusade*, p. 552.

117 *Bahá'í News*, no. 278 (April 1954), p. 4.

118 *Bahá'í News*, no. 296 (October 1955), p. 6.

119 *Bahá'í World News Service*, 'Double blessing for Cook Islands', 15 October 2003; *The Bahá'í World*, vol. XIX, p. 625.

120 Shoghi Effendi, *Messages to the Antipodes*, p. 213, footnote 79.

121 ibid. p. 380, footnote 144; *The Bahá'í World*, vol. XIX, p. 626.

122 *Herald of the South*, 'The bicycling battler', July–September 1992, p. 24.

123 Shoghi Effendi, *Messages to the Antipodes*, p. 213, footnote 79.

124 *Herald of the South*, 'The bicycling battler', July–September 1992, p. 24.

125 *Bahá'í News*, no. 284 (October 1954), p. 6.

126 *Bahá'í News*, no. 301 (March 1956), p. 7.

127 *Herald of the South*, 'The bicycling battler', July–September 1992, p. 24.

128 Shoghi Effendi, *Messages to the Antipodes*, p. 213, footnote 79.

129 *The Bahá'í World*, vol. XV, pp. 534–5.

130 Shoghi Effendi, *Messages to the Antipodes*, p. 154, footnote 53.

131 *The Bahá'í World*, vol. XV, p. 535.

132 ibid. pp. 545–7.

133 ibid. p. 535.

134 Jean Sevin, letter to Marion Hofman, 1 December 1960, in Marion Hofman Papers.

135 *Herald of the South*, 'Islands in the sun . . . and rats!', July–September 1992, p. 25.

136 Jean Sevin, email to the author, 3 September 2015.

137 *Bahá'í News*, no. 341 (July 1959), pp. 21–2.

138 Jean Sevin, email to the author, 3 September 2015.

139 *Herald of the South*, 'Islands in the sun . . . and rats!', July–September 1992, p. 25.

140 Marion Hofman, *The World Crusade*, p. 564.

141 *Herald of the South*, 'Islands in the sun . . . and rats!', July–September 1992, p. 25.

142 *Bahá'í News*, no. 341 (July 1959), p. 22.

143 Shoghi Effendi, *Messages to the Antipodes*, p. 349, footnote 122.

144 *Herald of the South*, 'Flowers "for the prophet" . . . and rats!', July–September 1992, p. 29.

145 *The Bahá'í World*, vol. XV, pp. 543–44.

146 Gayle Woolson, 'Bahá'í service of Gayle Woolson', p. 4, in Campuzano (ed.), *Gayle Woolson, 1914–2011*.

147 http://www.bahai.us/2011/06/23/gayle-woolson-helped-establish-the-bahai-faith-in-latin-america/

148 ibid.

149 *The Bahá'í World*, vol. XV, pp. 483–5.

150 Cameron, *A Basic Bahá'í Chronology*, p. 413.

151 Bahá'í World Archives, letters from Salvador Tormo to Shoghi Effendi.

152 Lamb, *The Beginnings of the Bahá'í Faith in Latin America: Some Remembrances*, 1995.

153 Bahá'í World Archives, letter from Salvador and Adela Tormo to Shoghi Effendi, 15 June 1953.

154 *The Bahá'í World*, vol. XIII, pp. 908–9; *Bahá'í News*, no. 275 (January 1954), p. 4.

155 *Bahá'í News*, no. 294 (August 1955), p. 11.

156 *Bahá'í News*, no. 356 (November 1960), p. 3.

157 *Bahá'í World News Service*, 'Latin American nations elect assemblies for 50th time', http://news.bahai.org/story/ridvan2010/photographs.

158 *The American Bahá'í*, vol. 30, no. 4 (17 May 1999), p. 39.

159 ibid.

160 Extracts from Groger, *Knight of the Rose Garden: The Beginnings of an Early American Bahá'í Family*.

161 *The American Bahá'í*, vol. 30, no. 4 (17 May 1999), p. 39.

162 *Bahá'í News*, no. 336 (February 1959), p. 6.

Alaska and Canada

1   USBNA, Office of Pioneering, Pioneer Files, Box 11.
2   *The American Bahá'í*, vol. 32, no. 4 (28 April 2001), p. 33.
3   Kolstoe, *Alaskan Bahá'í Community: Its Growth and Development*, p. 164.
4   *Alaska Bahá'í News*, August 1953, p. 7.
5   *Crusader*, September 1955, p. 2.
6   Kolstoe, *Crazy Lovers of Bahá'u'lláh*, p. 30.
7   *The Bahá'í World, 2000–2001*, p. 270.
8   Ben Guhrke, *Ben's Story*. The story in these paragraphs is from this source unless otherwise indicated.
9   *Alaska Bahá'í News*, no. 60 (December 1963), p. 2; and no. 66 (August 1964), p. 3.
10 Marvel Guhrke, 'Ben Guhrke Addendum'.
11 ibid.
12 ibid., and email to the author, 19 December 2014.
13 Kolstoe, *Alaskan Bahá'í Community*.
14 Marvel Guhrke, 'Ben Guhrke Addendum'.
15 Jenabe Caldwell, personal reminiscence, 28 November 2015.
16 Kolstoe, *Crazy Lovers of Bahá'u'lláh*, p. 139.
17 Jenabe Caldwell, *From Night to Knight*, pp. 35–6.
18 Caldwell, Elaine, personal reminiscences from her son Mark Caldwell, p. 1.
19 Jenabe Caldwell, *From Night to Knight*, pp. 39–41.
20 Elaine Caldwell, personal reminiscences from Mark Caldwell, pp. 2–3.
21 Jenabe Caldwell, *From Night to Knight*, pp. 45–6.
22 *Alaska Bahá'í News*, March 1992, p. 10.
23 Elaine Caldwell, personal reminiscences from Mark Caldwell, p. 4.
24 ibid. pp. 4–5.
25 ibid. p. 5.
26 ibid. p. 6; Jenabe Caldwell, *From Night to Knight*, p. 52.
27 Jenabe Caldwell, *From Night to Knight*, pp. 46–50; *Alaska Bahá'í News*, March 1992, pp. 10–11.
28 Jenabe Caldwell, *From Night to Knight*, p. 51.
29 Elaine Caldwell, personal reminiscences from Mark Caldwell, p. 6.
30 ibid. p. 9.
31 ibid. pp. 10, 12–13.
32 Jenabe Caldwell, *From Night to Knight*, pp. 67–70.
33 Elaine Caldwell, personal reminiscences from Mark Caldwell, p. 13.
34 ibid. p. 14.
35 Kolstoe, *Crazy Lovers of Bahá'u'lláh*.
36 *Alaska Bahá'í News*, January 1969, p. 4; and April 1992, p. 11.
37 Laurel Baumgartner, interview with the author, 15 October 2014.
38 ibid.
39 ibid.

40 ibid.

41 *Alaska Bahá'í News*, April 1992, p. 11.

42 Elaine Caldwell, personal reminiscences from Mark Caldwell, p. 8.

43 Laurel Baumgartner, interview with the author, 15 October 2014.

44 Kolstoe, *Crazy Lovers of Bahá'u'lláh*.

45 *Alaska Bahá'í News*, April 1992, pp. 10–11.

46 Laurel Baumgartner, interview with the author, 15 October 2014.

47 *Alaska Bahá'í News*, no. 7 (March 1958), p. 4.

48 ibid. no. 496 (December 2009–March 2010), p. 18.

49 Lorol Jackson, *My Experiences as a Pioneer*, p. 6.

50 Letter from the Secretariat of the National Spiritual Assembly of Alaska to the author, 20 September 2013.

51 *Bahá'í News*, no. 278 (April 1954), p. 5.

52 *Alaska Bahá'í News*, no. 111 (January 1969), p. 4.

53 ibid.; also no. 56 (July 1963), pp. 3–4; no. 36 (January 1961), p. 4.

54 *Crisis* magazine, May 1943. p. 144.

55 'Alaskan lady, jade hunter', in *Ebony* magazine, vol. IV, no. 2 (December 1948), pp. 26–27, 29.

56 *The Bahá'í World*, vol. XI, pp. 775–6.

57 Bahovec, *The First 100 Years*, pp. 45–6.

58 *The Bahá'í World*, vol. XIII, p. 449.

59 *The Bahá'í World*, vol. XX.

60 Letter from the Research Department of the Bahá'í World Centre to the author, 27 July 2014.

61 The Sitka Bahá'í Community website at: http://www.akbahai.org/sitka/ – 1954 Gail Davis.

62 Davis, *More Than a Touch of Madness*, p. 190.

63 *Alaska Bahá'í News*, July 1990, pp. 18–19.

64 ibid.

65 Davis, *More Than a Touch of Madness*, p. 190.

66 See http://www.findagrave.com/cgi-bin/fg.cgi?page=gr&GRid=45084783.

67 Barbara Geno, personal communication to the author, 17 September 2014.

68 Davis, *More Than a Touch of Madness*, p. 191.

69 *Alaska Bahá'í News*, no. 8 (April 1958) pp. 1–2.

70 Macke, *Take My Love to the Friends: The Story of Laura R. Davis*, p. 40.

71 Ted and Joan E. Anderson, *Yukon Golden Hearts Discovered*, p. 11. The story in these paragraphs is taken from this source unless otherwise indicated.

72 *Bahá'í News*, no. 350 (April 1960), p. 9.

73 *Bahá'í News*, no. 276 (February 1954), p. 4; http://en.wikipedia.orgwiki/Baker_Lake,_Nunavut.

74 Email from Crispin Pemberton-Pigott to the author, 23 May 2014.

75 Brown, *Sole Desire Serve Cause: Knights of Bahá'u'lláh Gale and Jameson Bond*. The story in these paragraphs is taken from this source unless otherwise indicated.

76 Don Brown, 'Sole Desire Serve Cause', talk in 2013, p. 2.

77 Letter from Jameson Bond to John Leonard, 28 December 1992.

78 Bahá'í Archives Canada, Laura Davis Papers.

79 Lewis Walker, USBNA, email to the author.

80 Bahá'í Archives Canada, Laura Davis Papers.

81 *Bahá'í Canada*, BE 161 (September), p. 26.

82 Bahá'í Archives Canada, Laura Davis Papers.

83 USBNA, Office of Pioneering, Pioneering Files, Box 16.

84 *Crusader*, September 1955, p. 3.

85 USBNA, Kay Zinky Papers, Box 3.

86 Bahá'í Archives Canada, Laura Davis Papers.

87 Van den Hoonaard, *The Origins of the Bahá'í Community of Canada*, pp.183, 220.

88 *Canadian Bahá'í News*, August 1964, p. 4.

89 ibid.

90 *The Bahá'í World: In Memoriam, 1992–1997*, p. 144.

91 ibid.

92 ibid.

93 ibid. pp. 144–5, quoted from 'The story of Edythe MacArthur', in *Canadian Bahá'í News*, August 1964, p. 4.

94 White, *Edythe MacArthur*, Bahá'í Archives Canada, pp. 2–3.

95 Crispin Pemberton-Pigott, email to the author, 23 May 2014.

96 Letter on behalf of Shoghi Effendi to the National Spiritual Assembly of the Bahá'ís of Canada, 13 January 1956, in Shoghi Effendi, *Messages to Canada*, p. 56.

97 McLean, *A Love That Could Not Wait: The Story of Knights of Bahá'u'lláh Catherine Heward Huxtable and Clifford Stanley Huxtable*. The story in these paragraphs is taken from this source unless otherwise indicated.

98 *Bahá'í News*, no. 522 (September 1974), p. 16.

99 Bahá'í Archives Canada, Laura Davis Papers.

100 Van den Hoonaard, *The Origins of the Bahá'í Community of Canada*, pp. 190, 237.

101 Macke, *Take My Love to the Friends: The Story of Laura R. Davis*, p. 141.

102 *The Bahá'í World*, vol. XVII, pp. 410–11.

103 *Bahá'í News*, no. 321 (November 1957), p. 5.

104 *Bahá'í News*, no. 330 (August 1958), p. 20.

105 USBNA, Ruth Moffett Papers, Box 13.

106 ibid.

107 *The American Bahá'í*, vol. 31 (13 July 2000), p. 56.

108 Nugent, 'The Sound Man'.

109 Bahá'í Archives Canada, Laura Davis Papers.

110 USBNA, Kay Zinky Papers, Box 13.

111 *Crusader*, January 1955, p. 3.

112 Bahá'í Archives Canada, Laura Davis Papers.

113 USBNA, Kay Zinky Papers, Box 13.
114 ibid.
115 Will C. van den Hoonaard, email to the author, 15 April 2015.
116 *The American Bahá'í*, vol. 31 (13 July 2000), p. 56.
117 *The Bahá'í World*, vol. XIX, p. 652.
118 *Bahá'í Canada*, BE 159 (December), p. 27.
119 ibid.
120 *The Bahá'í World*, vol. XV, pp. 458–9.
121 ibid.
122 Schuurman, *Legacy of Courage*, pp. 78, 83, 92, 104–5.
123 ibid. p. 108.
124 ibid. pp. 108–11.
125 ibid. pp. 112–13, 117.
126 Violette Nakhjavani, *The Great African Safari*, pp. 272–308, 423–48.
127 *The Bahá'í World: In Memoriam, 1992–1997*, pp. 278–9.
128 *The Bahá'í World*, vol. XX, p. 104.
129 Letter on behalf of Shoghi Effendi to the National Spiritual Assembly of the Bahá'ís of Canada, 15 June 1954, in Shoghi Effendi, *Messages to Canada*, p. 45.
130 Letter on behalf of Shoghi Effendi to the National Spiritual Assembly of the Bahá'ís of Canada, 16 July 1954, in Shoghi Effendi, *Messages to Canada*, p. 53.
131 *The Bahá'í World: In Memoriam, 1992–1997*, pp. 279–80.

The Caribbean, and Central and South America

1 Dorothy Frye, 'Biographical facts for Arthur and Florence (Ethel) Crane', included in letter to the author, 13 July 2014.
2 Bahá'í World Archives, GAO19/059/00002.
3 Letter written on behalf of Shoghi Effendi to Ethel Crane, 20 December 1937.
4 Bahá'í World Archives, letter from Ethel Crane to Shoghi Effendi, 13 November 1941.
5 Joel Nizin, email to the author, 28 May 2014.
6 Letter from Ethel Crane, 31 December 1955, USBNA.
7 Letter written on behalf of Shoghi Effendi to Ethel Crane, 7 December 1955, USBNA.
8 Florence Kelley, email to the author, 23 May 2014.
9 *The Bahá'í World*, vol. XV, p. 481.
10 ibid. pp. 481–2.
11 *The Bahá'í World*, vol. XV, pp. 523–4.
12 Gail Curwin, transcript of video interview, 2008. The story in these paragraphs is from this source unless otherwise indicated.
13 *Bahá'í News*, no. 278 (April 1954), p. 6.
14 *Bahá'í News*, no. 282 (August 1954), p. 7.
15 *The Bahá'í World*, vol. XV, pp. 530–31.
16 *The Bahá'í World*, vol. XX, p. 942.

17 Paccassi, *Baháʼí History of the Caribbean, 1920 to 1984*.

18 ibid.

19 ibid.

20 ibid.

21 ibid., see http://www.bahaihistorycaribbean.info/photo_galleries_and_more/ island-history-articles/st-lucia-history/.

22 Paccassi, *Baháʼí History of the Caribbean, 1920 to 1984*.

23 ibid., see http://www.bahaihistorycaribbean.info/photo_galleries_and_more/ island-history-articles/st-lucia-history/

24 *The Baháʼí World*, vol. XX, pp. 942–3.

25 USBNA, O/S individual correspondence, Earle Render.

26 ibid.

27 Paccassi, *Baháʼí History of the Caribbean, 1920 to 1984*.

28 *The Baháʼí World*, vol. XV, p. 478.

29 *The Baháʼí World*, vol. XVIII, p. 692.

30 ibid. pp. 693–4.

31 *The Baháʼí World*, vol. XV, p. 479.

32 *The Baháʼí World*, vol. XVIII, p. 695.

33 ibid. pp. 695–96.

34 David Schreiber, talk at the Puna, Hawaii Baháʼí Centre, 6 December 2015.

35 Rosalie Schreiber, email to the author, 21 September 2014; David Schreiber, phone conversation with the author, 26 September 2014.

36 ibid.

37 Paccassi, *Baháʼí History of the Caribbean, 1920 to 1984*; see http://www. bahaihistorycaribbean.info/Complete_List_Pioneers_and_Travel_Teachers_to_ LWVI_Web_View.pdf;   http://bahaihistorycaribbean.info/EAST_LEEWARD_ ISLANDS.pdf.

38 David Schreiber, talk at the Puna, Hawaii Baháʼí Centre, 6 December 2015.

39 Baháʼí World Archives, summary of letter from David Schreiber to the Universal House of Justice, April 2013.

40 Rosalie Schreiber, email to the author, 21 September 2014; David Schreiber, phone conversation with the author, 26 September 2014.

41 1930 US Census report.

42 USBNA, Office of Pioneering, Pioneer Files, Box 16.

43 *Crusader*, May 1957, p. 5; *Crusader*, September 1957, p. 5.

44 *Crusader*, July-August 1959; USBNA, Office of Pioneering, Pioneer Files, Box 16.

45 Paccassi, *Baháʼí History of the Caribbean, 1920 to 1984*.

46 *The Baháʼí World*, vol. XV, pp. 535–9; see also Honnold, *Why They Became Baháʼís*, p. 302.

47 *The Baháʼí World*, vol. XV, p. 538.

48 Lamb, *The Beginnings of the Baháʼí Faith in Latin America: Some Remembrances*, p. 14, 1995.

49 *The Baháʼí World*, vol. XV, p. 539.

50 *Bahá'í News*, no. 277 (March 1954), p. 12.
51 USBNA, Office of Pioneering, Pioneer Files, Box 13.
52 ibid.
53 USBNA, Leroy Ioas Papers, Box 10.
54 http://bahaikipedia.org/Katharine_Meyer.
55 USBNA, Office of Pioneering, Pioneer Files, Box 38.
56 *The Bahá'í World*, vol. 2005–2006, p. 244; also personal note from Sharon O'Toole, 2017.
57 USBNA, Office of Pioneering, Pioneer Files, Box 38.
58 *The Bahá'í World*, vol. XX, pp. 1023–5.
59 Warde, *Pioneering Bounties and Tests*, p. 1.
60 *The American Bahá'í*, vol. 28 (31 December), p. 35.
61 Honnold, *Why They Became Bahá'ís*, p. 102.
62 See http://en.wikipedia.org/wiki/Bahá'%C3%AD_Faith_in_Mexico.
63 Warde, *Pioneering Bounties and Tests*, p. 2.
64 ibid.
65 ibid. p. 3.
66 *Crusader*, April 1955, p. 2.
67 *Crusader*, July and August 1957, pp. 3–4.
68 Warde, *Pioneering Bounties and Tests*, pp. 3–4.
69 Letter from Shirley Warde to Marion Hofman, 26 July 1958, in Marion Hofman Papers.
70 Warde, *Pioneering Bounties and Tests*, p. 5.
71 ibid. pp. 8–9.
72 ibid. p. 10.
73 Kolstoe, *Crazy Lovers of Bahá'u'lláh*.
74 Florence Kelley, conversation with the author in Hawaii, 3 December 2015.
75 *Bahá'í News*, no. 241 (March 1951), p. 7; Elinor Wolff, audio recording ARC T-1657, Heritage Project of the National Spiritual Assembly of the United States.
76 Elinor Wolff, audio recording, op. cit.
77 ibid.
78 ibid.
79 *Crusader*, April 1955, p. 4.
80 *Bahá'í News*, no. 278 (April 1954), p. 5.
81 Scott Wolff, talk at the Puna, Hawaii Bahá'í Centre, 6 December 2015.
82 *The Bahá'í World*, vol. XIV, p. 316.
83 Ivan Fraser, extract from a manuscript on the early history of the Faith in Guyana.
84 ibid.
85 ibid.
86 *Crusader*, 11 September 1955, p. 3.
87 *The Bahá'í World*, vol. XIV, p. 317.

88 *The Bahá'í World*, vol. XX, p. 1025.

89 USBNA, Office of Pioneering, Pioneer Files, Box 3.

90 ibid.

91 *Bahá'í News*, no. 298 (December 1955), p. 4.

92 USBNA, Office of Pioneering, Pioneer Files, Box 8; *Crusader*, June 1957.

Europe

1 Bahiyyih Nakhjavani, email to the author, 7 July 2015.

2 Ian Semple, 'Towards a spiritual civilization', talk available online at: http://www. bahai.az/lib/notables/0410_semple_towards_a_spiritual_civilization_en.doc.

3 Bahiyyih Nakhjavani, email to the author, 7 July 2015.

4 Adams, *Arctic Island Hunter*, p. 15.

5 Quoted in Marion Hofman, *The World Crusade*, p. 108.

6 Bahiyyih Nakhjavani, email to the author, 7 July 2015.

7 *Bahá'í News*, no. 357 (December 1960), p. 14.

8 *The Bahá'í World*, vol. XVIII, p. 824.

9 Bahiyyih Nakhjavani, email to the author, 7 July 2015.

10 *Bahá'í News*, no. 479 (February 1971), p. 13.

11 Mary Victoria, email to the author, 7 July 2015.

12 *The Bahá'í World*, vol. XV, p. 446.

13 Hooshang Rafat, phone conversation with the author, 15 July 2014. The story in these paragraphs is based on this source and on an email to the author from Gregory Dahl, 23 May 2014, unless otherwise indicated.

14 *The Bahá'í World*, vol. XV, p. 446.

15 ibid.

16 *The Bahá'í World*, vol. XIV, p. 303.

17 Hooshang Rafat, phone conversation with the author, 15 July 2014.

18 *The Bahá'í World*, vol. XIV, p. 303.

19 *The Bahá'í World*, vol. XIX, pp. 658–9.

20 ibid.

21 ibid.

22 Pfaff-Grossmann, *The Life of a Pioneer*, p. 43.

23 Edvard Jónsson and Roy Philbrow, report in Marion Hofman Papers.

24 Claire Greenberg, personal communication to the author, July 2012.

25 Edvard Jónsson and Roy Philbrow, report in Marion Hofman Papers; *The Bahá'í World*, vol. XIX, p. 660.

26 *Dayspring*, no. 56 (November 2003), p. 11.

27 *The Bahá'í World*, vol. XIV, pp. 307–8.

28 Pfaff-Grossmann, *The Life of a Pioneer*, p. 29.

29 *Dayspring*, no. 56 (November 2003), p. 12.

30 Pfaff-Grossmann, *The Life of a Pioneer*, p. 42.

31 ibid. p. 43.

32 Letter from Jacqueline Mehrabi to Marion Hofman, 7 July 1960, in Marion Hofman Papers.

33 *The Bahá'í World*, vol. XIV, p. 308.

34 Pfaff-Grossmann, *The Life of a Pioneer*, pp. 1–22.

35 ibid. pp. 24–5.

36 Letter from Brigitte Hasselblatt to Marion Hofman, 30 October 1954, in Marion Hofman Papers.

37 Pfaff-Grossmann, *The Life of a Pioneer*, pp. 25–31; letter from Lilian McKay to Marion Hofman, 13 July 1957, in Marion Hofman Papers.

38 Pfaff-Grossmann, *The Life of a Pioneer*, pp. 27, 38–40.

39 ibid.

40 Pfaff-Grossmann, *The Life of a Pioneer*, pp. 54–62, 64.

41 ibid. pp. 68, 94–95, 98.

42 ibid. pp. 110–12.

43 Emails and personal communications to the author from: Anneliese Haug, 5 August 2013; Eleanor Dawson, 30 January 2013; Adam Thorne, 10 August 2014. See also *Bahá'í News*, no. 277 (March 1954), p. 6.

44 *The Bahá'í World*, vol. XVII, pp. 440–41.

45 Pfaff-Grossmann, *Hermann Grossmann*, pp. 146–7.

46 ibid.

47 Gisela von Brunn, email to the author, 8 October 2013. The story in these paragraphs is from this source.

48 Bates, *Bahá'í Story: Geertrui (Ankersmit) Bates, Knight of Bahá'u'lláh*. The story in these paragraphs is from this source.

49 *Bahá'í News*, no. 277 (March 1954), p. 6.

50 *UK Bahá'í*, no. 20 (December 2015), p. 9.

51 Recollections of Marion Hofman, email from May Hofman, September 2013.

52 *UK Bahá'í*, no. 20 (December 2015), p. 9.

53 *The Bahá'í World*, vol. XIII, pp. 881–2.

54 *The Bahá'í World*, vol. XV, pp. 456–7.

55 *UK Bahá'í*, no. 20 (December 2015), , p. 9.

56 Weinberg, 'Remembering the Knights of Bahá'u'lláh', in *Bahá'í Journal UK*, September/October 2003; *The Bahá'í World*, vol. XV, p. 457.

57 Húshmand Manúchehri, email to the author, 14 April 2014. The story in these paragraphs is from this source.

58 Sohrab Payman, Payman Memoir, 26 June 2015. The story in these paragraphs is from this source unless otherwise indicated.

59 Marion Hofman, *The World Crusade*, p. 283.

60 See also Cameron, *A Basic Bahá'í Chronology*, p. 393.

61 *Bahá'í News*, no. 339 (May 1959), p. 10.

62 *The Bahá'í World*, vol. XII, pp. 699–701.

63 The story in these paragraphs is from emails to the author from Guilda Navidi-Walker, 2 March 2015, and Vidá Navidi, 20 October 2015; and from *The Bahá'í World*, vol. XX, pp. 886–8.

64 *The Bahá'í World*, vol. XVIII, pp. 774–5; *Bahá'í World News Service*, 'Celebrations

in a principality', 24 May 2004; USBNA, Olivia Kelsey papers;.

65   Florence Kelley, audio recording ARC T-1567, Heritage Project of the National Spiritual Assembly of the United States.

66   ibid.

67   *Bahá'í World News Service*, 'Celebrations in a principality', 24 May 2004.

68   Florence Kelley, audio recording ARC T-1567, Heritage Project of the National Spiritual Assembly of the United States.

69   Florence Kelley, personal communication to the author, 3 December 2015.

70   Florence Kelley, audio recording ARC T-1567, Heritage Project of the National Spiritual Assembly of the United States.

71   *The Bahá'í World*, vol. XVIII, pp. 774–5; *Bahá'í World News Service*, 'Celebrations in a principality', 24 May 2004.

72   Rochan Mavaddat, email to the author, 29 March 2016.

73   *Bahá'í World News Service*, 'Mountainous country marks anniversary', 18 November 2004.

74   *The Bahá'í Faith, 1844–1963: Information Statistical and Comparative*, p. 56.

75   Cameron, *A Basic Bahá'í Chronology*, p. 401.

76   WolframAlpha, http://www.wolframalpha.com/input/?i=Baha%27is+in+andorra.

77   *Bahá'í World News Service*, 'Mountainous country marks anniversary', 18 Nov 2004.

78   Reported in Diari d'Andorra, 8 February 2014. http://www.diariandorra.ad/index.php?option=com_k2&view=item&id=30935&Itemid=380.

79   *Bahá'í News*, January 1980, pp. 3–4.

80   *The Bahá'í World*, vol. XIX, pp. 693, 695.

81   ibid.; see also http://en.wikipedia.org/wiki/Bahá'%C3%AD_Faith_in_Spain.

82   *Bahá'í News*, January 1980, pp. 4–5.

83   *The Bahá'í World*, vol. XIX, pp. 696–7.

84   *The Bahá'í World: In Memoriam, 1992–1997*, pp. 368–9.

85   ibid.

86   ibid. pp. 369–70.

87   Charles Ioas, video interview. The story in these paragraphs is from this source unless otherwise indicated.

88   *Bahá'í News*, no. 316 (June 1957), p. 11; no. 329 (July 1958), pp. 21–2; no. 341 (July 1959), p. 15; no. 369 (December 1960), p. 18.

89   *The Bahá'í World*, vol. XV, pp. 438–9; James Holmlund, personal communication to the author, 2012.

90   The story of Emma Rice in these paragraphs is from *The Bahá'í World*, vol. XIX, p. 678–9; *Bahá'í News*, no. 326 (April 1958), p. 7; Gerrold Bagley, emails to the author, 11 July 2014 and 10 August 2014.

91   Gerrold Bagley, 'The Bagley Family, Knights of Bahá'u'lláh'; and letter to the author, 10 August 2014. The story in these paragraphs is from this source unless otherwise indicated.

92 *The Bahá'í World*, vol. XX, pp. 1003–4; *The Bahá'í World: In Memoriam, 1992–1997*, p. 64.
93 *Bahá'í World News Service*, 'Historic role in Ireland and Malta', 8 March 2003.
94 David Hofman, *George Townshend*, p. 287.
95 *Bahá'í World News Service*, 'Historic role in Ireland and Malta', 8 March 2003.
96 Townshend Family Records, http://www.astro.wisc.edu/~townsend/tree/record.php?ref=5C24.
97 *The Bahá'í World*, vol. XVI, pp. 532–3.
98 ibid. p. 533.
99 Phillip Hinton, *UK Bahá'í Histories*, 2014, at https://bahaihistoryuk.wordpress.com/2014/11/21/phillip-hinton-2/.
100 *The Bahá'í World*, vol. XVI, p. 534.
101 *The Bahá'í World*, vol. XIII, p. 902.
102 *The American Bahá'í*, September–October 2013, at http://www.american.bahai.us/news/2013/september-october/amin-banani-was-an-influential-scholar-and-a-knight-of-bahaullah/.
103 Amin and Sheila Banani, *Amin and Sheila Banani's Recollections of Pioneering in Greece, 1953–1958*. The story in these paragraphs is from this source unless otherwise indicated.
104 Sheila Banani, from a letter printed in the Los Angeles Bahá'í Journal, November 1953.
105 Amín and Sheila Banani, *Pilgrim Notes of Sheila and Amin Banani*.
106 Sheila Banani, personal resume, 2015.
107 The story in these paragraphs, unless otherwise indicated, is from Carole Allen, *Pioneering in Greece during the First Year of the 10 Year Crusade*; and from Dwight Allen, *Carole and Dwight Allen: Knights of Bahá'u'lláh in Greece, 1953–1954*.
108 Garis, *Martha Root: Lioness at the Threshold*, p. 401.
109 Haleh Golmohammadi, email to the author, 22 October 2013. The story in these paragraphs is from this source.
110 *Bahá'í News*, no. 277 (March 1954), p. 6.
111 Guenther Haug, email to the author, 26 April 2014. The story in these paragraphs is from this source unless otherwise indicated.
112 *Bahá'í News*, no. 289 (March 1955), p. 7.
113 Fulya Vekiloglu, 'Knights of Bahá'u'lláh Semire and Abbas Vekil (Vekiloglu)', email to the author, 24 August 2014. The story in these paragraphs is from this source unless otherwise indicated.
114 *The Bahá'í World*, vol. XIX, pp. 646–7.
115 Deborah McKinley, *Violet and Hugh McKinley: Knights of Bahá'u'lláh for Cyprus 1953–1963*. The story in these paragraphs is from this source unless otherwise indicated.
116 See also Shoghi Effendi, *Messages to the Bahá'í World*, p. 49.
117 Olive McKinley, 'Life of Hugh McKinley, Knight of Bahá'u'lláh', pp. 62–3.
118 ibid.

119 Olive McKinley, personal communication to the author, 2013.

120 Olive McKinley, 'Life of Hugh McKinley, Knight of Bahá'u'lláh', pp. 64–7.

The Atlantic Ocean

1   *The Bahá'í World*, vol. XIV, p. 317.

2   Tacoma Bahá'í Community, at http://www.tacomabahai.org/2009/05/31/early-tacoma-bahais-richard-lois-nolen-knights-of-bahaullah/, 2009.

3   ibid.

4   *The Bahá'í World*, vol. XIV, pp. 317–18.

5   ibid.

6   *The Bahá'í World*, 1997–1998, p. 276.

7   Tacoma Bahá'í Community, at http://www.tacomabahai.org/2009/05/31/early-tacoma-bahais-richard-lois-nolen-knights-of-bahaullah/, 2009.

8   *The Bahá'í World*, vol. XIV, p. 311.

9   *The American Bahá'í*, vol. 37, no. 8 (23 November 2006), p. 27.

10   *The Bahá'í World*, vol. XIV, p. 311; *The Bahá'í World*, vol. XIII, p. 922.

11   *The Bahá'í World*, vol. XV, p. 422.

12   ibid.

13   *Family Search*, 4 August 2013, at https://familysearch.org/photos/stories/2005072.

14   *The American Bahá'í*, vol. 37, no. 8 (23 November 2006,) p. 27.

15   *The Bahá'í World*, vol. XIV, pp. 312–13; *The Bahá'í World*, vol. XIII, pp. 922.

16   Bruce True, Speech at the 50th Anniversary of the Faith in the Canary Islands (in Spanish), pp. 2–3.

17   Honnold, *Why They Became Bahá'ís*, pp. 190–93.

18   ibid. pp. 193–94; Barry True, personal communication to the author, 8 January 2013; *The Bahá'í World*, vol. XIX, p. 635.

19   Peggy True, *In the Midmost Heart of the Ocean*, 21 November 1984.

20   ibid.

21   *Bahá'í News*, no. 281 (July 1954), p. 4.

22   Barry True, personal communication to the author, 8 January 2013; *The Bahá'í World*, vol. XIX, p. 635.

23   ibid.

24   Stephen Licata, *My Recollections of Trudy Eisenberg*, p. 1.

25   *The American Bahá'í*, vol. 32, no. 9, 4 November 2001, p. 29.

26   *Bahá'í News*, no. 281 (July 1954), pp. 6–7.

27   Stephen Licata, *My Recollections of Trudy Eisenberg*, pp. 1–3.

28   Chowghi Rouhani, recollections of his cousin Shoghi-Riaz Rouhani.

29   ibid.

30   ibid.

31   Rowshan Mustapha, email to the author, obituary of Shoghi-Riaz Rouhani, 14 April 2014.

32   ibid.

33   Chowghi Rouhani, recollections of his cousin Shoghi-Riaz Rouhani.

34 Rowshan Mustapha, email to the author, obituary of Shoghi-Riaz Rouhani, 14 April 2014.

35 Hormoz Zendeh, 'My life as a pioneer in Tangier, Morocco', email to the author, 8 April 2014.

36 Rowshan Mustapha, email to the author, obituary of Shoghi-Riaz Rouhani, 14 April 2014.

37 ibid.

38 Chowghi Rouhani, recollections of his cousin Shoghi-Riaz Rouhani.

39 ibid.

40 'Howard Menking, Knight of Bahá'u'lláh', in *Mindspring*, at http://home.mind-spring.com/~pilgrim1/livinglegends/id1.html.

41 *The Bahá'í World*, vol. XX, p. 907–9. The story in these paragraphs is from this source unless otherwise indicated.

42 'Howard Menking, Knight of Bahá'u'lláh', in *Mindspring*, at http://home.mind-spring.com/~pilgrim1/livinglegends/id1.html.

43 *The Bahá'í World*, vol. XV, pp. 491–2.

44 ibid.

45 Jagdish Saminaden and Barbara George, emails to the author, 26 July 2014, 1 August 2014 and 2 August 2014.

46 *The Bahá'í World*, vol. XV, pp. 491–92.

47 Barbara George, email to the author, 2 August 2014.

48 *Bahá'í News*, no. 277 (March 1954), p. 5.

49 Guhrke, *Ben's Story*, p. 8.

50 *The American Bahá'í*, vol. 37, no. 5 (13 July 2006), pp. 23, 29; *Bahá'í News*, no. 284 (October 1954), p. 4.

51 *Bahá'í News*, no. 292 (June 1955), p. 9.

52 *Bahá'í News*, no. 295 (September 1955), p. 4.

53 *The American Bahá'í*, vol. 37, no. 5 (13 July 2006), pp. 23, 29; *The Bahá'í World*, vol. XV, p. 650.

After the Ten Year Crusade

1 *The Bahá'í World: In Memoriam, 1992–1997*, p. 120.

2 ibid. p. 121.

3 ibid. pp. 121–2.

4 Annemarie Krüger-Brauns, copy of a report to the Universal House of Justice, 3 October 1977, from the National Spiritual Assembly of the Bahá'ís of Bulgaria.

5 Arcela Khazrá'í, email to the author, 8 November 2015.

6 *The Bahá'í World: In Memoriam, 1992–1997*, pp. 122–3; email from Arcela Khazrá'í to the author, 8 November 2015.

7 *The Bahá'í World: In Memoriam, 1992–1997*, pp. 122–3.

8 The story in these paragraphs, unless otherwise indicated, is from Ecclesia, *Life for the Faith*, pp. 67, 80–87; and from reports by Annemarie Krüger-Brauns to the Universal House of Justice, 20 December 1974 and 3 October 1977,

9   Letter from the Universal House of Justice to Annemarie Krüger-Brauns, 16 July 1984.

10 Letter from the Universal House of Justice to Annemarie Krüger-Brauns, 17 December 1984.

11 The story in these paragraphs, unless otherwise indicated, is from Helmut Winkelbach, 'Helmut Winkelbach, Belarus', email to the author, 3 November 2013; and Olga Winkelbach, email to the author, 21 October 2013.

12 Agata Randel, email to the author, 11 November 2013.

13 Shoghi Effendi, *Messages to the Bahá'í World*, pp. 37–8.

14 The story in these paragraphs is from Sean Hinton, *A personal account of Amatu'l-Bahá Rúhíyyih Khánum's first visit to Mongolia*, 15–22 May 1989; Sean Hinton, 'Mongolia', 26 May 1992; personal emails, 15 and 26 August 2013.

15 Foad Katirai, email to the author, 29 August 2013; see also http://bahai-studies.ca/journal/files/jbs/5.3%20Hassall.pdf; http://bahai-library.com/east-asia/traces/51-55.html; *The American Bahá'í*, vol. 21, no. 8 (August 1991), p. 11.

16 Rayyan Sabet-Parry, email to the author, 4 June 2014.

INDEX

Entries in the two alphabetical lists in Appendixes 1 and 2 have not been indexed.

ABOUT THE AUTHOR

Earl Redman worked for over 20 years as a geologist in Alaska, including for the Bureau of Mines and as a consultant. In 1999 he moved with his wife Sharon to Ireland, where he has researched and written five books, exploring the gold mines of the stories included in 'Abdu'l-Bahá in Their Midst, the two volumes of Shoghi Effendi Through the Pilgrim's Eye, and a forthcoming volume on pilgrims who visited 'Abdu'l-Bahá in the Holy Land. He now travels widely and for long periods of the year and is much in demand as a speaker and storyteller.

OTHER BOOKS BY EARL REDMAN

'Abdu'l-Bahá in Their Midst

The heartwarming story of 'Abdu'l-Bahá's journeys in the
West and their effect on those who met Him, told in
their own words.

ISBN: 978-0-85398-557-0, Soft Cover,

384 pages, 23.4 x 15.6 cm (9.75 x 6.25 in)

A Kindle version of this book is available through Amazon.com

Shoghi Effendi Through the Pilgrim's Eye
Volume 1: Building the Administrative Order, 1922-1952

The life and work of the Guardian of the Bahá'í Faith,
told through accounts by pilgrims and visitors as well as
those who worked to assist him.

ISBN: 978–0–85398–588–4, Soft Cover,

480 pages, 23.4 x 15.6 cm (9.75 x 6.25 in)

A Kindle version of this book is available through Amazon.com

Shoghi Effendi Through the Pilgrim's Eye
Volume 2: The Ten Year Crusade, 1953-1963

The story, through the eyes of those who were there, of
the Ten Year Crusade, including the tragic and untimely
death of Shoghi Effendi in 1957 and the decision by the
'Chief Stewards' of the Faith, the Hands of the Cause of
God, to carry forward the Guardian's Plan to its successful conclusion and the establishment of the final piece in
Bahá'u'lláh's Administrative Order, the Universal House of Justice.

ISBN: 978–0–85398–595-2, Soft Cover,

400 pages, 23.4 x 15.6 cm (9.75 x 6.25 in)

A Kindle version of this book is available through Amazon.com

BOOKS ABOUT KNIGHTS OF BAHÁ'U'LLÁH

Knight With A Briefcase, *The Life of Knight of Bahá'u'lláh Ezzat Zahrai*
by Judith Kaye Logsdon-Dubois
A glimpse into the life of a modern-day knight – a businessman who brought the teachings of Bahá'u'lláh to what is now Zimbabwe for the very first time.
ISBN: 978-0-85398-565-5

Sole Desire Serve Cause: An Odyssey of Bahá'í Service, *Knights of Bahá'u'lláh Gale and Jameson Bond*
by Don Brown
Jameson and Gale Bond's memoirs tell the story of their six decades of Bahá'í service, particularly as Knights of Bahá'u'lláh in the Canadian District of Franklin above the Arctic Circle.
ISBN: 978-0-85398-604-1

Legacy of Courage, *The Life of Ola Pawlowska, Knight of Bahá'u'lláh*
by Suzanne Schuurman
The story of a remarkable life that began in the Austro-Hungarian Empire of Franz Joseph, spanned two World Wars, and played out on three continents.
ISBN: 978-0-85398-524-2

The Story of David and Esther Tanyi, *Adam and Eve of the Bahá'í Faith in Cameroon*
by Enoch Tanyi Nyenti
At just 25 years old, David Tanyi was the oldest of the five young Cameroonian Knights of Bahá'u'lláh, whose stories are also told in this book. Newly married, he pioneered to French Togoland, where his young wife Esther was only able to join him several months later together with their first son, born in his absence. It was the start of 35 years of pioneering . . .
ISBN: 978-0-85398-597-6

Of Wars and Worship, *The extraordinary story of Gertrude and Alvin Blum*
by Keithie Saunders and Prue Rushton
From Kiev to New York to Little Rock to Guadalcanal – one couple's odyssey that led them through rejection, war and suspicion to the Solomon Islands and their final triumph of faith in humanity.
ISBN: 978-0-85398-563-1

More information about these books can be found on George Ronald's website
www.grbooks.com